LEGAL LIABILITY OF DOCTORS AND HOSPITALS IN CANADA

Second Edition
by
ELLEN I. PICARD

B.Ed., LL.B., LL.M.

Professor of Law, Honorary Professor of Medicine
University of Alberta

1984
CARSWELL LEGAL PUBLICATIONS
TORONTO   CALGARY   VANCOUVER

Canadian Cataloguing in Publication Data
  Picard, Ellen I., 1941 —
    Legal liability of doctors and hospitals
  in Canada

    Includes index.
    ISBN 0-459-35820-0 (bound). — ISBN
  0-459-36770-6 (pbk.)

    1. Physicians — Malpractice — Canada.
  2. Tort liability of hospitals — Canada.
  I. Title
  KE2710.M34P53 1984   346.7103′32   C84-091274-9

To Andrew

PREFACE

The writing of a law book is a labour of love. One must have a strong interest in the topic and a sincere concern about assisting others who have a need for the information. My goal in this second edition remains as it was for the first: to provide a resource and a summary of law on the liability of doctors and hospitals in Canada which will be helpful to both the legal profession and to health care professionals. My background as a professor of law and of medicine and as a practising lawyer made me aware of the need for a book readable by non-lawyers but with the analysis and references required by lawyers and judges. I have endeavoured to fulfil these requirements.

Every chapter in this second edition has been changed to reflect new law and to include comment on policy and emerging trends. In this work I have tried to follow a course that avoids the whirlpools of academic legal theory and also the safe harbour of mere case reporting.

The chapter on consent has been re-written to include discussion of the profound implications of the 1980 decisions of the Supreme Court of Canada and to include the topics of consent to research, sterilization and transplantation.

The Appendices have been expanded and re-organized to allow the reader to find cases using more varied criteria and to review a brief digest of each case referred to in the book. It became clear that it would not be possible to include a full discussion of criminal law in this book and I leave that for another time. The law is stated as it was April 1, 1984.

I am indebted to many colleagues who have written about health law: Wilbur F. Bowker, Bernard Dickens, Lorne and Fay Rozovsky, Gerald Robertson, Sanda Rodgers-Magnet, Margaret Somerville, Dr. G. Sawyer, Gilbert Sharpe, Marc Shiffer, Janet Storch and many others whose names appear in the footnotes.

The University of Alberta, by honouring me with a McCalla Professorship, allowed me the time to complete this work and I am most grateful. My Dean, Frank Jones and the administrative and secretarial staff at the Faculty of Law, especially Bob Graham, Diane Conlon, Liz Kobie and Lisa Bowes were very helpful. Marlene Welton did a splendid job of transcribing my notes into textform. I would also like to thank the law students who helped on various parts of the project, including Martin Kratz and Linda Wright, and especially Brent Windwick and Ursula Tauscher whose assistance was very important to me. Leslie McGuffin, my former student and a valued assistant on the first edition, continues to guide and assist me in her capacity as a senior legal editor with the Carswell Company.

But my primary motivation has come from the positive response to the first edition. It has been cited in Canadian and Commonwealth judgments. I have received letters from judges, lawyers and health care professionals who have been assisted by it. Students in law and the health care professions whom I have met have told me that it has been helpful to them.

My family has understood my commitment to this book and their love has sustained me. I have dedicated this edition to my son Andrew, my greatest joy, and a remarkable young man.

Ellen I. Picard
Professor
Faculty of Law
University of Alberta
April 28, 1984

CONTENTS

TABLE OF CASES

TABLE OF STATUTES

CANADA

ALBERTA

BRITISH COLUMBIA

MANITOBA

NEW BRUNSWICK

NEWFOUNDLAND

NORTHWEST TERRITORIES

NOVA SCOTIA

ONTARIO

PRINCE EDWARD ISLAND

QUEBEC

SASKATCHEWAN

YUKON TERRITORY

ENGLAND

1

The Doctor-Patient Relationship

1. NATURE OF THE RELATIONSHIP

(a) Historical Development

The legal relationship of doctor and patient has been described differently over the past six centuries.[1] Originally the medical profession, like that of apothecary, barbering and innkeeping, was a "common calling." This meant that when a doctor practised medicine a duty to his patient came into being. In order to protect the public, certain legal constraints were placed on the exercise of that duty. The doctor had to use proper care and skill[2] because *the law* required it.

Upon the development of the law of contract, this original *delictual*[3] basis for liability was superseded by a contractual one.[4] The offer could be

---

1 The first reported case against a doctor is dated 1374 and was an action against a surgeon: *Morton's case* (1374), 48 Edw. 11.
2 Holdsworth, 3 *History of English Law* 385-86; *Everard v. Hopkins* (1615), 2 Bulstrode 332, 80 E.R. 1164 (K.B.).
3 *See Black's Law Dictionary* 514 (4th ed. 1968). The term is "wider in both directions" than the term "tort" which is often used as a synonym.
4 Holdsworth, *supra* n. 2 at 448; Cheshire and Fifoot, *Law of Contract* (9th ed. 1976); for the American expression of this *see Leighton v. Sargent* (1853), 27 N.H. 460, 59 Am. Dec. 388 (N.H.S.C.). Note that in Quebec, "the relationship between physician and patient is contractual." Castel, *Nature and Effects of Consent With Respect To The Right To Life And The Right To Physical And Mental Integrity In The Medical Field: Criminal And Private Law Aspects* (1978), 16 A.L.R. 293 at 319.

found in the patient's request for treatment and the acceptance in the doctor's commencement of care. Consideration was not a problem unless the patient was unable to pay. In such circumstances the law of contract was strained somewhat and it was held that the patient's submission to treatment was sufficient consideration for the doctor's services.[5] Many terms of the contract were implied by law, as for example, that the doctor possessed and would use due care and skill[6] and thus the most common contractual relationship could be described as one of an implied contract between doctor and patient. There may have been some doctors and patients who left nothing to be implied but set out the exact terms of their agreement in an express contract.

The past century and a half has been dominated by the tort of negligence. It is therefore not surprising that the liability of the doctor came to be judged by its principles.[7] The "common calling" which gave birth to the concept of duty in the doctor-patient relationship contained within it the seed of the negligence action which sprang to life in the fertile environment of the Industrial Revolution.[8] Thus, for nearly a century most actions against doctors have been based on negligence.[9]

During the transition periods when the characterization of the relationship changed from common calling to implied contract and finally to negligence, there was confusion about the proper way to plead a case.[10] Some judges were prepared to allow the plaintiff to recover damages if it seemed fair. They would not "look with eagle's eyes [at] the evidence" and preclude recovery because the case had a technical defect.[11] This was not as onerous as it might seem because the duty of a doctor to his patient was essentially the same whether found in the practice of a common calling, in the term of an implied contract, or as the fulfillment of the appropriate standard of care in the modern negligence action.[12]

The duty of care that is born as soon as a doctor undertakes the medical treatment of a patient has been fostered by the medical profession for centuries[13] and is now held to exist independently of any contract between doctor

---

5 *Coggs v. Bernard* (1703), 2 Ld. Raym. 909, 92 E.R. 107 (K.B.); *Banbury v. Bank of Montreal,* [1918] A.C. 626 at 657 (H.L.).

6 *Slater v. Baker* (1767), 2 Wils. K.B. 359, 95 E.R. 860; note that the requirement of confidentiality would be another implied term. *See* Rogers-Magnet, *Common Law Remedies for Disclosure of Confidential Medical Information* in *Issues in Tort Law* 265 at 284 (1983, ed. Steel, Rodgers-Magnet).

7 *See infra* Chapter 4. Note that some patients may not have capacity to contract, *e.g.,* psychiatric patients.

8 Fleming, *The Law of Torts* 129 (6th ed. 1983).

9 *Edwards v. Mallan,* [1908] 1 K.B. 1002 (C.A.). For a discussion of a revival of the contract action *see* Chapter 2.

10 *Everard v. Hopkins supra* n. 2; *Edwards v. Mallan id.*

11 *Slater v. Baker supra* n. 6.

12 *Roe v. Min. of Health; Woolley v. Same,* [1954] 1 W.L.R. 128 at 131; affirmed [1954] 2 Q.B. 66 (C.A.); Nathan, *Medical Negligence* 7 (1956).

13 *Oath of Hippocrates infra.*

and patient. There is a duty to use reasonable care, skill and judgment when a doctor attends on an unconscious patient who cannot be held to have voluntarily submitted[14] or when a third party is paying for the service.[15] A doctor need not undertake the care of a patient, but once he has done so he must exercise proper care and skill.[16]

The ancient and honourable profession of medicine nurtured the development of the doctor-patient relationship into one of trust and confidence. The law raised its expectations accordingly but has not always given protection in the courts to this trust, since there is no privilege extended to the communications between doctor and patient.[17] The doctor, like the lawyer but unlike the architect or engineer,[18] is in a fiduciary or trust relationship with his patient.[19] This means the doctor has a duty to act with utmost good faith: he must never allow his professional duty to conflict with his personal interests;[20] he must not mislead his patient. This fiduciary duty is the foundation for the requirement that his patient's questions be honestly answered and that any consent obtained be an informed one.[21] It is also the reason that fee-splitting is illegal.[22]

In summary, the relationship of doctor and patient results in the creation of a duty owed by the doctor to the patient. The duty has both legal and equitable aspects. Historically it has been part of the law of common calling, implied contract and negligence. The doctor's duty in modern times is within the flexible framework of negligence and it is to use reasonable care, skill and judgment in the practice of his profession.

---

14 *Everett v. Griffiths*, [1920] 3 K.B. 163 (C.A.); *Matheson v. Smiley*, [1932] 2 D.L.R. 787 (Man. C.A.).

15 *Edgar v. Lamont*, [1914] S.C. 277 (Ct. Sess.); *but see infra*.

16 *Hurley v. Eddingfield* (1901), 59 N.E. 1058 (Ind. S.C.); note that in Quebec a doctor must give assistance in an emergency. *See* Rodgers-Magnet, *The Right to Emergency Medical Assistance in the Province of Quebec* (1980), 40 R. du B. 373 at 378, 407. Godfrey, *Emergency Care: Physicians should be placed under an affirmative duty to render essential medical aid in emergency circumstances* (1974), 7 U. Calif. Davis L. Rev. 246 at 249.

17 *See infra*.

18 *Bagot v. Stevens Scanlan & Co.*, [1966] 1 Q.B. 197 (Q.B.D.). *See also Bache* case referred to at [1973] L.S.U.C. Lec. 156.

19 *Kenny v. Lockwood*, [1932] 1 D.L.R. 507 (Ont. C.A.); *Halushka v. University of Sask.* (1965), 53 D.L.R. (2d) 436 (Sask. C.A.); *Smith v. Auckland Hosp. Bd.*, [1965] N.Z.L.R. 191 (N.Z.C.A.); Hopper, *The Medical Man's Fiduciary Duty* (1973), 7 Law Teacher 73. The relationship has been compared to that of parent and child, man and wife, confessor and penitent or guardian and ward. *Henderson v. Johnston*, [1956] O.R. 789.

20 *Ralston v. Tanner* (1918), 43 O.L.R. 77; Wasmuth, *Law for The Physician*, Lea and Febiger, Philadelphia, (1966).

21 *Kenny v. Lockwood supra* n. 19; *Reibl v. Hughes* (1977), 16 O.R. (2d) 306 at 312 (Ont. H.C.); trial judgment restored, (1980), 14 C.C.L.T. 1 (S.C.C.); Dickens, *Contractual Aspects of Human Medical Experimentation* (1975), 25 U. of T. L.J. 406 at 426. *See* Chapter 3.

22 *Henderson v. Johnston supra* n. 19.

(b) Characteristics

The doctor-patient relationship begins when the doctor agrees to treat the patient who has expressly or impliedly requested his services. This is true whether or not the doctor is paid.[23] Ethical considerations aside, the doctor is not required to accept any patient.[24] He may even refuse a patient though no other doctor is available.[25]

Once the relationship exists, however, the doctor is obliged to attend the patient for as long as good medical practice requires. Factors relevant to determine what length of time this might be include the patient's condition, the nature of the illness, and the availability and quality of other medical care.[26]

The patient may dismiss the doctor at any time[27] but the doctor must be very cautious should he decide to terminate the relationship.[28] The doctor should give a patient reasonable notice that he plans to discontinue his services. The best way to do this is to write a letter to the patient explaining the situation and allowing time for the patient to obtain other medical assistance. If possible, this document should be given to the patient or sent by double registered mail.

When a patient in need of treatment has severed the relationship with the doctor or discharged himself from hospital, the doctor is in a strong position to prove he did not abandon the case if he has a statement to this effect signed by the patient.[29] Whatever the action or reaction of the doctor to the termination of services, it must be reasonable in the circumstances, or he may be found liable for abandonment of the patient.[30]

---

23 Speller, *Law of Doctor and Patient* (1973); Haines, *Courts and Doctors* (1952), 30 Can. Bar. Rev. 483 at 487. *See Gragg v. Spenser* (1981), 284 S.E. (2d) 40 (Georgia C.A.) where a duty was found between a neuroradiologist and a patient although the only connection was that the doctor had briefly assisted a colleague in manipulating a catheter during a test on the patient.

24 Nathan, *supra* n. 12. Note that the *Code of Ethics* published by the Canadian Medical Association (1982), states: "An ethical physician shall, except in an emergency, have the right to refuse to accept a patient."

25 *See* authorities listed *supra* n. 16.

26 *Baltzan v. Fidelity Ins. Co.*, [1932] 3 W.W.R. 140, affirmed without reasons [1933] 3 W.W.R. 203 (Sask. C.A.); *Meyer v. Gordon* (1981), 17 C.C.L.T. 1 at 44 (B.C.S.C.); *Hajgato v. London Health Assn.* (1982), 36 O.R. (2d) 669 (Ont. H.C.); Stetler and Moritz, *Doctor and Patient and the Law* 123, 4th ed., C. V. Mosby, St. Louis, (1962).

27 In an early case, *Town v. Archer* (1902), 4 O.L.R. 383 at 386, it was said that consulting another doctor without the knowledge of it by the first is tantamount to a dismissal of him. It is doubtful whether this applies today.

28 *See Cook v. Abbott* (1980), 11 C.C.L.T. 217 at 222 (N.S.S.C.); reversed (1980), 13 C.C.L.T. 264 (N.S.C.A.).

29 Speller, *supra* n. 23; for suggestions as to proper statements *see* Stetler and Moritz, *supra* n. 26.

30 Waltz and Inbau, *Medical Jurisprudence* 147, MacMillan Co., New York (1971); *See also* Rosenthal, *Physician's Abandonment of Patient* (1975), 7 N. Carolina Cent. L.J. 149.

Whether an urban specialist with weekly office hours or a rural general practitioner who makes house calls,[31] the doctor is free, within the doctor-patient relationship and with the patient's consent, to determine time, place and type of medical treatment.[32]

The roles of the doctor and patient have received close scrutiny from social scientists who believe that the type of relationship may have a profound effect on the practice of medicine.[33] The traditional relationship is one in which the patient is passive and the doctor active, as in the emergency situation. Another common type of interaction is one in which the doctor, like the parent, gives guidance and direction and the patient, like the child, is expected to co-operate. It is assumed that both doctor and patient are actively working in the patient's best interests. For some patients with chronic diseases, the relationship of mutual participation may be more suitable: the doctor is helping the patient to help himself. Critics of the active-passive and guidance-co-operation relationships say the doctor is too much in control and the patient is vulnerable to exploitation. The doctor is told to stop playing the traditional "father image" role.[34] A more reasonable approach would seem to be for the modern doctor to remain in control of diagnosis and treatment but where possible to assist the patient to be an informed, active participant.

In whatever role the doctor is seen, he gives, and the patient expects to receive, certain reassurances. But the doctor is not an insurer of his patient's health. He does not normally warrant that his treatment will be beneficial nor does he guarantee a cure.[35] It may be otherwise if the doctor has entered into an express contract to produce a cure or certain results.[36] The distinction between a therapeutic assurance and a binding guarantee may not be clear to the ill or dissatisfied patient and could constitute a trap for the doctor.[37] The courts give some protection to the doctor by looking with suspicion on any

31 See *Cole v. Perrin* (1982), 52 N.S.R. (2d) 408 (N.S.T.D.) where a doctor broke his leg while making a house call; *Stark v. Council of College of Physicians & Surgeons of Sask.* (1965), 52 W.W.R. 157 (Sask. Q.B.); affirmed 55 W.W.R. 121 (Sask. C.A.).

32 Louisell and Williams, *Medical Malpractice* Matthew Bender, New York (1982), at 192-93; *See also* Waltz and Inbau, *id.* at 149.

33 Szasz and Hollender, *The Physician-Patient Relationship* in Gorovitz *et al., Moral Problems in Medicine*, Prentice-Hall, Englewood Cliffs, N.J., (1976). For an interesting, on-going Canadian study, *see* Christie, Hoffmaster, Bass, McCracken, *How Family Physicians Approach Ethical Problems* (1983), 16 Journal of Family Practice 1133.

34 Somers and Somers, *Doctors, Patients and Health Insurance* 476-82, Brookings Inst., Washington D.C.; *see also* Kouri, *The Patient's Duty to Co-operate* (1972), 3 Rev. de D. Univ. Sherbrooke 44.

35 *Johnston v. Wellesley Hosp.* (1970), 17 D.L.R. (3d) 139 (Ont.); Haines, *supra* n. 23; *Hughston v. Jost*, [1943] O.W.N. 3.

36 *Allard v. Boykowich*, [1948] 1 W.W.R. 860 (Sask.).

37 *Hawkings v. McGee* (1929), 84 N.H. 114, 146 A. 641 (S.C.); *Noel v. Proud* (1961), 189 Kan. 6, 367 P. (2d) 61 (S.C.); *Guilment v. Campbell* (1971), 188 N.W. (2d) 601 (Mich. S.C.).

claim that a doctor guaranteed a good result, unless he admits having done so, or a written agreement is produced to that effect.

Since 1968 and the enactment by the Canadian Parliament of the Medical Care Act,[38] most doctors are paid on a fee-for-service basis by a provincial medicare plan. Canadians are covered by the plan for all medically required services provided by doctors.[39] Most Canadian doctors have chosen to practise under the scheme.[40] Because the doctor's duty is founded on the doctor-patient relationship and not on contract, the patient's status to sue is not affected where the services, though requested by the patient, are gratuitous or paid for by a third party.[41]

There is some uncertainty about whether a doctor-patient relationship arises where the patient is being examined by a doctor at the request of a third party. This situation may arise when the patient requires a medical examination for employment, life insurance, or as a party to a law suit.[42] American authorities state there is no doctor-patient relationship in these circumstances.[43] The English courts have faced the problem in a few unusual cases and after some division of opinion, have concluded that there is a duty owed by the doctor to a patient being examined and certified[44] under mental treatment legislation. Thus, there was held to be a doctor-patient relationship although the patients whose mental health was in issue were not being examined at their own request. But these cases may be restricted by their facts.

A British Columbia case, *Leonard v. Knott*,[45] established that a doctor doing an annual check-up on a patient owes that patient a duty of care even though the examination was arranged and paid for by the patient's employer. It would seem to follow that a doctor-patient relationship would be found

---

38 R.S.C. 1970, c. M-8.

39 Andreopoulos, *National Health Insurance* 35, John Wiley & Sons, Toronto (1975).

40 *Id.* at 55.

41 Thomson, *Claims Arising Out of the Relationship Between Doctor and Patient,* [1963] L.S.U.C. Spec. Lec. 185 at 189. For a discussion of the situation where there is an express contract, *see infra.*

42 *Causton v. Mann Egerton (Johnsons),* [1974] 1 All E.R. 453 (C.A.).

43 Louisell and Williams, *supra* n. 32 at 191. *But see* [1982] Supplement citing *Beadling v. Sirotta* (1964), 197 A. (2d) 857 (N.J.S.C.), where the Appeal Court said at 860-61: "Whether or not a physician-patient relationship exists, within the full meaning of that term, we believe that a physician in the exercise of his profession examining a person at the request of an employer owes that person a duty of reasonable care . . . [However] the scope of the duty owed is clearly not co-extensive with the duty owed to a private patient who seeks from the doctor a report as to the status of his health."

44 Nathan, *supra* n. 12; *Hall v. Semple* (1862), 3 F. & F. 337, 176 E.R. 151 (Nisi Prius); *Everett v. Giffiths,* [1921] 1 A.C. 631 (H.L.); *Harnett v. Fisher,* [1927] 1 K.B. 402; *De Freville v. Dill* (1927), 96 L.J.K.B. 1056. *But see Urquhart v. Grigor* (1864), 3 Macph. 283 (Ct. Sess.) and *Pimm v. Roper* (1862), 2 F. & F. 783, 175 E.R. 1283.

45 [1980] 1 W.W.R. 673 (B.C.C.A.). The trial judge noted that the doctor refused to call the examinee a "patient" preferring "client." [1978] 5 W.W.R. 511 at 513 (B.C.S.C.).

between the doctor named by an insurance company to do a medical examination and an applicant for insurance who submits to the examination. If there is, what is the scope of the duty owed by the doctor? Surely it would only be to use reasonable care in the conduct of the examination. Yet it might be broad enough to subject the doctor to liability if he fails to diagnose an obvious disease in the applicant. Unfortunately, there is no Canadian authority on this point.[46]

The prudent doctor doing an examination at the request of a party other than the patient[47] ought to make clear to the patient that many incidents of the doctor-patient relationship, such as confidentiality, are absent and encourage the patient to seek advice, care and treatment from his own doctor. A Canadian court faced with the issue of whether, in the circumstances, the relationship of doctor and patient existed would have to consider the knowledge the patient had of the situation and the roles of the doctor and the third party.[48]

While both doctor and patient have a certain latitude within which to establish the terms of their relationship, this freedom is now circumscribed by ethical, legal and practical restrictions.

2.   COMMUNICATIONS BETWEEN DOCTOR AND PATIENT

(a) Basis for Confidentality

Communication between a doctor and patient is essential to the relationship. The doctor requires data from the patient in order to give proper advice and treatment and the patient has a responsibility to co-operate by providing it.[49] The patient may assume his confidences will not be revealed to third parties without his permission.

The Oath of Hippocrates sets out the moral obligations of the doctor. It reads:

---

46 See Wilcox v. Salt Lake City Corp. (1971), 26 Utah 78, 484 P. (2d) 1200 (S.C.). Waitresses sued city-employed doctors who had examined chest x-rays done pursuant to renewal of occupation permits. The doctors were negligent in their diagnoses but it was held that the waitresses had no action because there was no duty owed to them by the doctors. For a discussion of the current U.S. cases see Berg and Hirsh, Duty To Divulge — Update (Pre-employment Evaluations) (1984), 12 Leg. Aspects Med. Prac. 4.

47 Note the example of the team doctor and the athlete. See Robitaille v. Vancouver Hockey Club, [1981] 3 W.W.R. 481 (B.C.C.A.). See also Balbi, The Liability of Professional Team Sports Physicians (to be published 1984 A.L.R.).

48 Note that the Code of Ethics published by the Canadian Medical Association (1982), states: "An ethical physician when acting on behalf of a third party will assure himself that the patient understands the physician's legal responsibility to the third party before proceeding with the examination."

49 Kouri, The Patient's Duty to Co-operate supra n. 34.

Whatsoever I see or hear in the course of my practice, or outside my practice in social intercourse, that ought never to be published abroad, I will not divulge, but consider such things to be holy secrets.

The Canadian Medical Association, like most others in the world, embodies this principle in its Code of Ethics.[50] Rule six states:

An ethical physician will keep in confidence information derived from his patient, or from a colleague, regarding a patient and divulge it only with the permission of the patient *except where the law requires him to do so . . .* [emphasis supplied]

The requirement of confidentiality arises from the doctor-patient relationship and is older than the common law.[51] In a case[52] where the evidence was that on approximately 368 occasions Ontario doctors and hospital employees had provided medical information to the police without consent from the patient, Mr. Justice Dubin of the Ontario Court of Appeal set out the duty of confidentiality of doctors:[53]

Members of the medical profession have a duty of confidentiality with respect to their patients. They are under restraint not to volunteer information respecting the condition of their patients or any professional services performed by them without their patient's consent. In the absence of such consent, members of the medical profession breach their duty if they disclose such information unless required to do so by due process of law.

If there is no relationship, there is no obligation on the doctor to remain silent.[54] If, for example, a doctor riding as a passenger in a taxi cab observed the driver, not being a patient of his, to be ill and unfit to perform his duties, the doctor would be justified in reporting this to the proper authorities, and in some provinces would be protected by statute from liability for doing so.[55]

The communications protected by the ethical duty not to disclose may be in any form, oral or written.[56] The type of information which is protected is

---

50 Note that the nurse's duty of confidentiality is set out in the Code of Ethics of the International Council of Nurses. *See* Storch, *Patient's Rights* 75 (1982).

51 See authorities cited in *Damien v. O'Mulvenny* (1981), 34 O.R. (2d) 448 (Ont. H.C.). Note that the Charter of Rights and Freedoms s. 7 may protect the right to confidentiality. *See* generally Manning, *Rights, Freedoms and the Courts* (1983).

52 *Re: Inquiry into the Confidentiality of Health Records in Ontario* (1979), 98 D.L.R. (3d) 704 (Ont. C.A.).

53 *Id.* at 714. Note that an appeal was allowed but Mr. Justice Dubin's statement was not in dispute and was quoted with approval by Chief Justice Laskin. *Solicitor Gen. of Can. v. Royal Comm. Inquiry into Confidentiality of Health Records* (1981), 38 N.R. 588 at 608.

54 In the U.S. the relationship of doctor-patient does not exist unless treatment is contemplated. Thus examinations done for eligibility for insurance or employment are not within the relationship and the information obtained from the patient is not privileged. Stetler & Moritz, *supra* n. 26 at 261.

55 *For example,* Motor Vehicle Administration Act, R.S.A. 1980, c. M-22, s. 14(2). *See also* Canadian Medical Association, *Guide for Physicians in Determining Fitness to Drive a Motor Vehicle* 2 (1974).

56 Nokes, *Professional Privilege* (1950), 66 L.Q.R. 88 at 91.

broad and includes not only that concerning the patient and his illness, but also knowledge about the patient's family.[57]

Sometimes the doctor is required to divulge confidential information.[58] These situations can be best discussed as occurring inside or outside of a court of law.

(b) Disclosure inside a Court of Law

The search for truth, which is the goal of the judicial process, requires that all material facts be before the court. Occasionally courts are prepared to do without evidence that would be relevant and probative because its disclosure would harm a relationship important to society.[59] Evidence which is thus excluded is said to be "privileged."

Communications made within the doctor-patient relationship are not privileged. This means that if a doctor is asked a question and has the answer, though the question intrudes into the secrets told him by his patient, he must reply.

It is only the lawyer who can, within certain limitations, refuse to reveal confidences of his client. The justification for this unique treatment is that it is essential to the protection of basic human rights that an individual feel free to make a full disclosure to his legal advisor.[60]

The rule that communications between doctor and patient are not privileged in the courtroom has remained unchanged since the celebrated dictum of Lord Mansfield in the bigamy trial of the Duchess of Kingston in 1776.[61] Mr. Hawkins, the surgeon who had attended the lady, was called as a witness, and asked whether he knew "from the parties of any marriage between them." He replied that he did not know "how far anything that has come before me in a confidential trust in my profession should be disclosed, consistent with my professional honour."[62] Lord Mansfield thereupon stated the law as follows:[63]

> . . . a surgeon has no privilege where it is a material question, in a civil or criminal cause, to know whether parties were married or whether a child was born, to say that his introduction to the parties was in the course of his profession, and in that way he came to the knowledge of it. I take it for granted that if Mr. Hawkins understands that, it is a satisfaction to him and a clear justification to all the world. *If a surgeon was voluntarily to reveal these secrets, to be sure he would be guilty of a breach of honour, and a great*

---

57 Speller, *supra* n. 23 at 127; Jacob, *Speller's Law Relating to Hospitals and Kindred Institutions* 343 (1978).

58 For an interesting analysis of the component interests involved in medical confidentiality *see* London, *Privacy in the Medical Context* in *Aspects of Privacy Law* 281 (Gibson, ed. 1980).

59 Sopinka and Lederman, *The Law of Evidence in Civil Cases* 156 (1974).

60 *Id.* at 158. *See also Greenough v. Gaskell* (1833), 1 My. & K. 98 at 103, 39 E.R. 618 at 620 (Ch.).

61 *Kingston's (Duchess) Case* (1776), 20 State Tr. 619.

62 *Id.*

63 *Id., see also Wheeler v. LeMarchant* (1881), 17 Ch. D. 675 (C.A.).

indiscretion; but to give that information in a court of justice, which by the law of the land he is bound to do, will never be imputed to him as any indiscretion whatever. [emphasis supplied]

Courts in Canada have followed this rule and require a doctor to give evidence.[64] Any doctor who refuses could be held in contempt of court and fined or even jailed.[65]

In England there is some authority for the proposition that a judge has a discretion to refuse to require confidential information to be given in court. This dispensation by courtesy[66] was discussed in an obiter comment by Lord Denning in *A.G. v. Mulholland*:[67]

> The only profession that I know which is given a privilege from disclosing information to a court of law is the legal profession, and then it is not the privilege of the lawyer but of his client. Take the clergyman, the banker or the medical man. None of these is entitled to refuse to answer when directed to by a judge. Let me not be mistaken. The judge will respect the confidences which each member of these honourable professions receives in the course of it, and will not direct him to answer unless not only it is relevant but also it is a proper and, indeed, necessary question in the course of justice to be put and answered. A judge is the person entrusted, on behalf of the community, to weigh these conflicting interests — to weigh on the one hand the respect due to confidence in the profession and on the other hand the ultimate interest of the community in justice being done . . .

While it has been stated that Canadian courts do not have a general discretion to exclude evidence which is highly probative and relevant,[68] there is authority for the exercise of judicial discretion to protect the communications between patient and psychiatrist.[69]

Privilege has been given by statute in Quebec where the Medical Act states: "No physician may be compelled to declare what has been revealed to him in his professional character."[70] The Charter of Human Rights and Freedoms[71] states that everyone has a right to non-disclosure of confidential

---

64 *Halls v. Mitchell*, [1928] S.C.R. 125; *R. v. Potvin* (1971), 16 C.R.N.S. 233 (Que. C.A.); *R. v. Burgess*, [1974] 4 W.W.R. 310 (B.C. Co. Ct.); *Children's Aid Soc. v. M.* (1982), 137 D.L.R. (3d) 767 (Ont. Prov. Ct.).

65 Note that many doctors may be unaware of this. *See* Sharpe and Sawyer, *Doctors and the Law* 102-103 (1978).

66 Freedman, *Medical Privilege* (1954), 32 Can. Bar Rev. 1 at 10.

67 [1963] 2 Q.B. 477 at 489-90 (C.A.). For discussions of the English position *see* Jacob, *Speller's Law Relating to Hospitals and Kindred Institutions* 348-49 (1978); Mason and McCall Smith, *Law and Medical Ethics* 95-110 (1983); Finch, *Health Services Law* 225-40 (1981).

68 *R. v. Wray*, [1971] S.C.R. 272; Sopinka and Lederman, *supra* n. 59 at 205 and 217. *But see R. v. St-Jean* (1976), 34 C.R.N.S. 378 (Que. C.A.) and *R. v. Hawke* (1974), 3 O.R. (2d) 210 (H.C.).

69 *See infra.*

70 R.S.Q. 1977, c. M-9, s. 42; *See Scarlat v. Deschamps* (1981), 131 D.L.R. (3d) 203 (Que. C.A.). For an excellent analysis of the law in Quebec *see* Knoppers, *Confidentiality and Accessibility of Medical Information: A Comparative Analysis* (1982), 12 R.D.U.S. 395.

71 Charter of Human Rights and Freedoms, R.S.Q. 1977, c. C-12, s. 9.

information.[72] These extensions of privilege might be limited by the legislative jurisdiction of the provinces.[73]

More than two-thirds of the United States have statutes granting privilege to doctors, the first enacted in New York in 1828.[74] The result has been confusion and controversy about the doctor-patient relationship.[75] Critics of the granting of privilege note that it is more often used by plaintiffs to exclude evidence that would defeat or limit their claim for money and not to protect them from humiliation or embarrassment at all[76] and therefore truth which ought to be disclosed is suppressed.[77] Exceptions to the legislation have proliferated and recent draft law reform does not provide for privilege at all. One American authority says the death knell has sounded for doctor-patient privilege in his country.[78]

In Europe, most countries provide for doctor-patient privilege. Indeed many continental codes set out civil and even criminal remedies for the patient whose confidences have been revealed by a doctor.[79]

Should the law in Canada be changed to give a doctor professional privilege? What criteria should be used in making this decision?

Wigmore,[80] an American authority on the law of evidence, has set out four requirements for the establishment of privilege. These have been approved as conditions precedent for the extension of privilege by the Supreme Court of Canada in *Slavutych v. Baker*:[81]

   (1) The communications must originate in a confidence that they will not be disclosed;

   (2) This element of confidentiality must be essential to the full and satisfactory maintenance of the relationship between the parties;

---

72 Newfoundland also grants privilege to religious advisors: Newfoundland Evidence Act, R.S.N. 1970, c. 115, s. 6.

73 *R. v. Potvin supra* n. 64; *but see R. v. Sauve*, [1965] Que. S.C. 129 where it was held that the civil law and not the common law applied with respect to privilege in criminal cases; *Comment* at (1965), 15 R. du B. 562; *See also R. v. Hawke supra* n. 68

74 Waltz & Inbau, *supra* n. 30 at 236. For a succinct analysis of the U.S. position, *see* Rodgers-Magnet, *Common Law Remedies for Disclosure of Confidential Medical Information* in *Issues in Tort Law* 276 (Steel, Rodgers-Magnet ed., 1983).

75 Stetler & Moritz, *supra* n. 26 at 253.

76 DeWitt, *Privileged Communications Between Physician and Patient 33*, Chas. C. Thomas, Springfield, 1958.

77 8 *Wigmore on Evidence*, 828-32 (3d ed. 1961).

78 Waltz & Inbau, *supra* n. 30 at 253.

79 Hammelmann, *Professional Privilege: A Comparative Study* (1950), 28 Can. Bar Rev. 750. *See also* Sharpe and Sawyer *supra* n. 65 at 107.

80 *Wigmore, supra* n. 77 at 531.

81 [1975] 4 W.W.R. 620 (S.C.C.); *see also Strass v. Goldsack* (1975), 58 D.L.R. (3d) 397 (Alta. C.A.). Note that Wigmore's conditions were applied and the deliberations of a credentials committee of a hospital were held to be privileged. *Smith v. Royal Columbian Hospital*, [1981] B.C.D. Civ. 3612-05, 123 D.L.R. (3d) 723 (B.C.S.C.). For a comment *see* McLachlin, *Confidential Communications and the Law of Privilege* (1977), 2 U.B.C. L. Rev. 266.

(3) The relationship must be one which in the opinion of the community ought to be sedulously fostered; and

(4) The injury that would inure to the relation by the disclosure of a communication must be greater than the benefit thereby gained for the correct disposal of litigation.

Does the communication between doctor and patient meet the four tests?[82]

(1) Do communications by patients originate in a confidence that they will not be disclosed? The fairest answer would seem to be, not always. It has been pointed out that many patients speak freely to friends, neighbours and relatives about their ailments.[83]

(2) Is confidentiality essential to the doctor-patient relationship? An obvious but rather weak answer is it cannot be because the medical profession has carried on without it for centuries. The McRuer Commission's findings[84] were that patient care had not been affected by the absence of privilege. There is some force in the argument that the traditional general practitioner-patient relationship was more dependent on confidentiality than the modern super-specialist-patient relationship. There is also the problem of which medical professionals would qualify. Privilege exists by statute in Quebec,[85] yet there is no evidence to show that the doctor-patient relationship is treated any differently there than in the common law provinces.

(3) Should the relationship be fostered by the community? Yes. There is no disagreement on this point.

(4) Would the injury to the relation from disclosure be greater than the social benefit? There would be no injury to many relationships. It might be otherwise if the subject matter is venereal disease or abortion, but to completely seal the lips of the doctor is to invite injustice.[86] The proper administration of justice is fettered where relevant probative evidence is kept from the court. For example, if there was privilege the patient could exclude all unfavourable medical evidence in a personal injury claim. Clearly, there are some situations where the social benefit is greater.[87]

---

82 Freedman, *supra* n. 66 at 5; Hawkeye, *Recent Developments in the Law of Privilege: R. v. Littlechild* (1981), 19 A.L.R. 493.

83 *See* Law Reform Commission of Canada, Law of Evidence Project, Report, *Professional Privileges Before the Courts* 12 (1975), where it has also been suggested that Canadians are less reluctant to a limited public disclosure than Europeans!

84 Royal Commission into Civil Rights, 2 *Report No. 1* 822 (1968).

85 Medical Act, R.S.Q. 1977, c. M-9, s. 42.

86 Bok, *The Limits of Confidentiality* Hastings Center Report Feb. 1983, 24. *R. v. Stewart* Alta., McDonald J., 1977 (unreported); Freedman, *supra* n. 66 at 6.

87 *See, for example, Bergwitz v. Fast* (1980), 108 D.L.R. (3d) 732 (B.C.C.A.); *R. v. Waterford Hosp.* (1981), 32 Nfld. & P.E.I.R. 400 (Nfld. T.D.).

However, the relationship between psychiatrist and patient may often fulfill Wigmore's tests.[88] Perhaps it is for this reason that some Canadian courts have refused to compel a psychiatrist to give evidence. In *Dembie v. Dembie*,[89] the wife's psychiatrist was called by the husband and asked to reveal information affecting the wife's right to alimony. The psychiatrist refused to answer, saying the information was highly confidential and to reveal it would be a breach of professional secrecy and the Hippocratic Oath.

Stewart J., refusing to force the psychiatrist to testify, said:[90]

> . . . I think it is inimical to a fair trial to force a psychiatrist to disclose the things he has heard from a patient, and, in addition to that, I think it rather shocking that one profession should attempt to dictate the ethics of another, which the courts are doing when they see fit to state what a doctor will say and what he will not. They are forcing a breach of [the Hippocratic] oath, and the legal concept that the doctor is not breaching it, that he shall not disclose anything a patient shall tell him unless mete to do so, the idea that it is mete when he gets in the witness box is nonsense . . .

Landreville J. in *G. v. G.*,[91] a custody action in which a husband on examination for discovery refused to reveal communications made to a marriage counsellor, commented in dicta that full disclosure between psychiatrist and patient was "fundamental to the practice of psychiatry" and "can only be obtained if the patient knows that what he is to say and hear will be of strict confidential nature."[92]

Haines J. in *R. v. Hawke*[93] commented that not only might Wigmore's four tests be met in the appropriate case of psychiatric evidence but that there was an additional ground for protecting a witness from disclosure of his psychiatric history.[94]

> What of the right of privacy of a witness, or the right to privilege from disclosure of communication in circumstances an ordinary citizen would consider confidential? Our

---

88 *See* Sharpe, *Legislative Recognition of A Physician-Patient Privilege* (1975), 23 Chitty's L.J. 64 at 66 wherein it is suggested psychiatrists may be "a special breed of physician who require the certainty of confidentiality even if their brethren can exist without it." For an excellent discussion of the unique difficulties of the psychiatrist, *see* generally Schiffer, *Psychiatry Behind Bars* (1982), and especially 90-93. *See also* various articles in (1981), 2 H.L. in C.

89 (1963), 21 R.F.L. 46 (Ont. H.C.). *See also Re: S.A.S.* (1977), 1 L. Med. Q. 139 (Ont. Prov. Ct.).

90 *Id.* at 50.

91 [1964] 1 O.R. 361 (Ont. H.C.).

92 *Id.* at 365-66. In the U.S. similar arguments have been advanced on behalf of psychologists and social workers. In some states privilege has been extended to clinical psychologists, Curran & Shapiro, *Law, Medicine and Forensic Science* 381, Little, Brown & Co., Boston (1970). In Canada *see* Kirkpatrick, *Privileged Communications in the Correctional Services* (1964-65), 7 Cr. L.Q. 305.

93 *Supra* n. 68. The Ontario Court of Appeal chose not to deal with the trial judge's comments on this point but to remark somewhat tersely that *obiter* comments on the rights of the witnesses were inappropriate. *See R. v. Hawke* (1975), 29 C.R.N.S. 1 (Ont. C.A.).

94 *Supra* n. 68 at 226. *Quaere* what protection the Charter of Rights and Freedoms might provide. *See* Manning *supra* n. 51.

federal Government may be said to have expressed a Government policy in the recent wiretap legislation. If private telephone conversations are to be protected from electronic eavesdropping, how much more important is it to protect the confidential communications between doctor and patient, whether that patient seeks assistance voluntarily or has the relationship thrust upon him by involuntary admission procedures when he is placed in hospital? The doctor to whom he speaks has taken an oath of secrecy based on concepts older than our common law. He is responsible in damages if he violates that relationship. Everyone recognizes that confidentiality is essential to diagnosis and therapy. Indeed, one may go further and say public health is involved if those requiring assistance refrain from seeking it for fear that it will be disclosed. No better illustration of the disaster that could befall a man is needed than the disclosure that a political candidate or an incumbent of office has received psychiatric treatment.

It has been suggested the communication of a patient to a psychiatrist may be protected from disclosure on other bases too.[95] The psychiatrist might be acting in the capacity of conciliator where spouses are honestly attempting to reconcile their differences.[96] If the psychiatrist was appointed by the court he would be prohibited by the Divorce Act[97] from revealing conversations with the parties.

There are courts refusing to follow this trend. In *R. v. Potvin*,[98] a criminal case to which the provincial legislation allowing privilege in civil cases was held inapplicable, the Quebec Court of Appeal allowed an appeal on the ground that the trial judge had erred in ruling a psychiatrist had professional privilege. *Dembie v. Dembie*[99] was distinguished in *R. v. Burgess*[100] and the statements made by an accused to a psychiatrist were held admissible. The court was sympathetic to the psychiatrist for the patient relationship being accorded special consideration but ruled that once the evidence was given by the psychiatrist, it could not be held inadmissible.

It appears that the law of evidence requires modification to allow privilege to cover some doctor-patient relationships. This could be brought about by Canadian judges following the example of their English brethren and assuming greater discretion to exclude evidence.[101] Wigmore's four tests

---

95 *See R. v. Pettipiece,* [1972] 5 W.W.R. 129 (B.C.C.A.) and *Perras v. R.,* [1973] 5 W.W.R. 275 (S.C.C.). *Re: S.A.S.* (1977), 1 L. Med. Q. 139 (Ont. Prov. Ct.).

96 Sopinka and Lederman, *supra,* n. 59 at 202 and 207.

97 R.S.C. 1970, c. D-8, s. 21 states that:

"(1) A person nominated by a court under this Act to endeavour to assist the parties to a marriage with a view to their possible reconciliation is not competent or compellable in any legal proceedings to disclose any admission or communication made to him in his capacity as the nominee of the court for that purpose.

"(2) Evidence of anything said or of any admission or communication made in the course of an endeavour to assist the parties to a marriage with a view to their possible reconciliation is not admissible in any legal proceedings."

98 *Supra* n. 64.

99 *Supra* n. 89.

100 *Supra* n. 64. *See also Children's Aid Soc. v. M. supra* n. 64.

101 *See supra.*

could be used as the criteria for determining whether a particular doctor-patient relationship merited privilege. Indeed this approach has recently received strong judicial approval.[102] The Law Reform Commission of Canada is studying the possibility of legislation.[103] Should such a statute recognize privilege and set out specific limitations to its application or should the courts be given a discretion to grant privilege in the appropriate cases?[104]

The Law Reform Commission of Canada in its Report on Evidence[105] recommends that the courts be granted a discretionary power. Section 41 of the proposed Evidence Code states:

> 41. A person who has consulted a person exercising a profession for the purpose of obtaining professional services, or who has been rendered such services by a professional person, has a privilege against disclosure of any confidential communication reasonably made in the course of the relationship, if, in the circumstances, the public interest in the privacy of the relationship outweighs the public interest in the administration of justice.

The English Law Reform Commission agrees that the trial judge should be given a discretion.[106]

The Federal/Provincial Task Force on Uniform Rules of Evidence[107] favours the expansion of privileges at common law and by statute "as the need emerges in specific situations." With respect to psychiatrists it recommends:[108]

> . . . that a privilege be enacted for communications made between an accused and an assessing physician during a remand for observation: such communications would be inadmissible against the accused in any criminal proceeding other than a fitness hearing except where the accused waives privilege by putting his or her mental state in issue.

In summary, the doctor-patient relationship is not privileged in a court of law. Exceptions exist by statute in Quebec for a doctor in a non-criminal case and from time to time by judicial courtesy for communications between a psychiatrist and patient. There is a need to provide for privilege in some doctor-patient relationships. Reform could be brought about by judicial or legislative action.

---

102 *Slavutych v. Baker; Strass v. Goldsack;* McLachlin; all *supra*, n. 81. *See also* Manitoba Law Reform Commission, *Report on Medical Privilege* (1983), where there is support for this position.

103 Law Reform Commission of Canada *supra* n. 83. For support for legislation as the answer *see* Haines J. in *R. v. Hawke supra* n. 68 at 227. *See also* Hammelmann, *supra* n. 79 at 758.

104 Ludwig, *The Doctor's Dilemma* (1975), 6 Man. L.J. 313 at 315; Rodgers-Magnet *supra* n. 74 at 274-5.

105 Law Reform Commission of Canada *Report on Evidence* 80 (1975).

106 Law Reform Committee, 16th Report, *Privilege in Civil Proceedings*, Cmnd. No. 3472 at 21-22 (1967); Meredith made the strong recommendation that the North Carolina statute providing for judicial discretion be enacted across Canada. In this he was following the 1937-38 report of the American Bar Association's Committee on the Improvement of the Law of Evidence. Representations made by the medical profession to this Committee indicated that doctors were satisfied with the exercise of judicial discretion. *See* Meredith, *Malpractice Liability of Doctors and Hospitals* 23 (1956).

107 *Report on Evidence* 417 (1982).

108 *Id.* at 423.

(c) Disclosure outside a Court of Law

(i) Under statute

Just as the search for truth by the judicial system results in an intrusion into confidentiality between doctor and patient, so does the public interest in safety and health care. In all of the provinces of Canada there are statutes requiring the doctor to divulge information obtained from a patient.[109]

The earliest provisions were found in acts dealing with communicable and venereal diseases[110] and vital statistics[111] and involving reporting to public officials. The expansion of medical care and the need for its assessment as well as the proliferation of health and social services has greatly expanded the legislation and increased the bodies entitled to have access to the confidential data of patients.

Certain statutes provide for the transmission of confidential information for reasons that include the protection of public health, the assessment of standards of health care, the improvement of procedures, the fostering of research and teaching, the obtaining of vital data such as deaths and births, the protection of children and the compensation of workers.[112]

There is an attempt in some of the legislation to protect the identity of the patient or to require the recipient of the information to keep it confidential.[113]

The patient who is unfit to drive a motor vehicle is specifically dealt with by many provinces. For example, in Quebec,[114] British Columbia[115] and Ontario[116] a doctor is required to report to a public official the name of a

---

109 In the U.S. a statutory requirement of disclosure has been compared to qualified privilege in defamation. *See Smith v. Driscoll* (1917), 94 Wash. 441, 162 P. 572 (Wash. S.C.).

110 *E.g.:* Public Health Act, R.S.A. 1980, c. P-27; Venereal Diseases Prevention Act, R.S.A. 1980, c. V-2.

111 *E.g.,* Vital Statistics Act, R.S.A. 1980, c. V-4.

112 *See, for example,* these Alberta statutes: Tuberculosis Act, R.S.A. 1980, c. T-11; Naturopathy Act, R.S.A. 1980, c. N-6; Venereal Diseases Prevention Act, R.S.A. 1980, c. V-2; Hospitals Act, R.S.A. 1980, c. H-11; Mental Health Act, R.S.A. 1980, c. M-13; Cancer Treatment and Prevention Act, R.S.A. 1980, c. C-12 [title am. 1982, c. 10, s. 2] now Cancer Programs Act; Fatality Inquiries Act, R.S.A. 1980, c. F-6; Vital Statistics Act, R.S.A. 1980, c. V-4; Child Welfare Act, R.S.A. 1980, c. C-8; Workers' Compensation Act, R.S.A. 1980, c. W-16.

113 For example, in regard to venereal disease, cancer treatment, mental health care, hospital patients and child battery. *See also Carter v. Carter* (1974), 53 D.L.R. (3d) 491 (Ont. S.C.) where evidence from records of a health officer that a party to an action may have had venereal disease was held inadmissible on grounds that it was in the public interest to encourage persons to be treated in the knowledge that their affliction will be kept confidential. *See* the issues raised in *Damien v. O'Mulvenny* (1981), 34 O.R. (2d) 448 (Ont. H.C.).

114 Transport Act, R.S.Q. 1977, c. T-12.

115 Motor Vehicle Act, R.S.B.C. 1979, c. 288, s. 221.

116 Highway Traffic Act, R.S.O. 1980, c. 198, ss. 176-78. *See Gordon v. Wallace* (1973), 2 O.R. (2d) 202 at 206 (Ont. H.C.).

patient whom he considers unfit to drive.[117] In Alberta a doctor is encouraged to report such a patient[118] and the statute purports to protect the doctor from liability for doing so.[119]

If the public is to be protected and if medical science and care are to advance, access to information, albeit confidential, is essential. This need must, however, be balanced with protection of the confidentiality of the doctor-patient relationship.

(ii) By consent of the patient

A. Express

If the patient consents, the doctor is free to disclose confidential information to whomever the patient designates. However, for his own protection the doctor should get the consent in writing. An example would be a patient requesting that his doctor send a summary of his medical history to an employer, lawyer, insurer or another doctor.

In an Ontario case,[120] a doctor attended on a patient on two occasions: in an emergency department and to do an employment physical examination. He incorporated a warning about the patient's health in his report to her employer based on his earlier diagnosis in the emergency department. The patient sued when she lost her job. While the judge recognized a cause of action for breach of an implied term of the contract between doctor and patient, the patient lost. The court held that the patient had impliedly consented because she did not restrict the doctor to information based on the annual examination and she had signed a form, which although loosely drawn and ambiguous, was an express authorization.

The right to confidentiality is the patient's. Thus, if the patient requests that the doctor divulge information, the doctor cannot refuse. In an English case[121] a doctor refused to respond to the request of his patient to provide a medical report which would have shown the patient had venereal disease. The doctor said he would only give his evidence in court, but the judge ruled that the doctor had to provide the information as requested by the patient.

The Quebec Medical Act[122] states that "[n]o physician may be compelled to declare what has been revealed to him in his professional character,"

---

117 In England, a doctor was convicted of failing to give the police information about one of his patients as required by the Road Traffic Act 1972 (Eng.), c. 20; *R. v. Hunter*, The Times, 9 February 1974.

118 Motor Vehicle Administration Act, R.S.A. 1980, c. M-22, s. 14.

119 *Id. See* discussion, *infra*.

120 *Miron v. Pohran* (1981), 8 A.C.W.S. (2d) 509 (Ont. Co. Ct.). Note that the case is discussed in more depth in Canadian Medical Protective Association, *Annual Report* 18-20 (1982).

121 *C. v. C.*, [1946] 1 All E.R. 562 (P.D.A.).

122 Medical Act, R.S.Q. 1977, c. M-9, s. 40.

and would seem to give the doctor the right to make the decision.[123] But Quebec courts have interpreted this provision as giving the patient the right to compel the doctor to give evidence about his medical care,[124] although the doctor can decide what he should or should not say.[125]

Those jurisdictions which have enacted statutes granting privilege[126] have provided that the patient shall be the one who decides whether the privilege will be invoked or waived.

Compelling the doctor to speak puts him in a difficult position. He may be forced to give information which he believes harmful to the patient or to others. There may be judgments and conclusions he has not previously revealed to the patient[127] because he believes to do so would be deleterious. Some judges have taken the view that there is a public interest in safeguarding professional secrets.[128] This opinion is shared by authorities in France and other European countries where even the consent of the patient does not free a doctor from his duty of secrecy.[129]

Nevertheless, the interest of the public or the medical profession in safeguarding medical information should not outweigh the interest of the patient in having access to his own medical information, for himself or for those to whom he wishes to make it available.[130]

B. Implied

There are situations where the patient's consent may be reasonably implied, for example, to allow the doctor to consult with colleagues, or arrange for nursing care or therapy.[131] However, some discretion should be exercised in responding to questions about a patient even if they be from a colleague.[132]

---

123 *Hebert v. La Cie d'Assurance Sur La Vie de la Sauvegarde* (1927), 66 Que. S.C. 32 at 36.
124 *Mut. Life Ins. Co. v. Jeannotte-Lamarche* (1935), 59 Que. K.B. 510 at 529; *Rheault v. Metro. Life Ins. Co.* (1939), 45 R.L.N.S. 446 (Que. S.C.); *Gagne v. Alliance Nationale* (1946), 13 I.L.R. 13 (Que S.C.).
125 *Mut. Life Ins. Co. v. Jeannotte-Lamarche, id.*
126 Some U.S. states, the State of Victoria in Australia, and New Zealand.
127 Hammelmann, *supra* n. 79 at 756; *Gordon v. Wallace* (1973), 2 O.R. (2d) 202 (Ont. H.C.).
128 *Hebert v. La Cie d'Assurance Sur La Vie de la Sauvegarde supra* n. 123.
129 Hammelmann, *supra* n. 79 at 757.
130 *See also* Medical Records, Chapter 10.
131 *See* Mason and McCall Smith, *supra* n. 67 at 97 where the authors state: "What patient at a teaching hospital out-patient department is likely to refuse when the consultant asks 'You don't mind these young doctors being present, do you?' — the pressures are virtually irresistible and truly autonomous consent is impossible, yet the confidential doctor/patient relationship which began with his general practitioner has, effectively, been broken."
132 The Medical Defence Union, *Annual Report 1975* 21 reports a case where a doctor responded to questions asked by another doctor about a patient on the belief that the patient would be attending at the latter doctor's hospital. In fact the inquiring doctor was a relative of the patient and on the other side of a family dispute. *See also Re: Lavasseur and College of Nurses of Ontario* (1983), 18 A.C.W.S. (2d) 126 (Ont. H.C.), for a successful appeal by a

Is there implied consent to release information about the patient to a spouse or other members of the family? Canadian authorities 20 years ago answered yes to this question.[133] Today the answer has to be qualified.[134] On the one hand good medical public relations and common sense say there are family members who must be told, for example, that a patient has had a miscarriage. On the other hand, the patient may not want anyone to know of this fact and she has the right to have the information kept confidential. Likewise, a child who has the capacity to consent to medical treatment is in a doctor-patient relationship requiring confidentiality.[135]

Ideally, the patient should be asked to appoint a person to whom the doctor can speak freely. This has the added advantage of sparing the doctor numerous explanations. If this has been done or is not possible, it is probably reasonable for the doctor to speak to a spouse or near relative such as a parent, brother or sister. It may be otherwise if he is aware of family strife. If a doctor took a very rigid approach and refused to speak to anyone about the patient, his practice would likely suffer.[136]

Making information available to those beyond the family, such as to an employer, is fraught with risk.[137] In any case, the doctor should avoid giving information over the telephone except to someone the patient has named and whose voice he recognizes.

Whether consent to release information can be implied or not is a question of fact. Should a patient object to the release of information, the doctor has the onus of providing that there was consent.

(iii) In the public interest

Concern for the protection of the public may cause the doctor as a responsible citizen to breach the duty of confidentiality to his patient. When does a doctor's duty to society so outweigh his duty to maintain secrecy that he is justified in revealing information about his patient of his own accord?

The authorities now agree that if a doctor learns that a serious crime such as murder, rape, robbery or kidnapping is about to be committed or has been committed, he should contact the police.[138] Some go so far as to question

---

nurse from a disciplinary body's finding of professional misconduct in that she failed to exercise discretion in giving out confidential information about a patient.

133 Freedman, *supra* n. 66 at 19, Meredith, *supra* n. 106 at 24.
134 *See* Mason and McCall Smith *supra* n. 67 at 100-104.
135 *See Re: D and Council of the College of Physicians & Surgeons of B.C.* (1970), 11 D.L.R. (3d) 570 (B.C.S.C.); *see also* Mason and McCall Smith *supra* n. 67 at 103; Finch *supra* n. 67 at 238-39.
136 *A.B. v. C.D.* (1904), 7 Fraser's S.C. 72 (Scot. C.S.); *Furniss v. Fitchett*, [1958] N.Z.L.R. 396 (N.Z.S.C.).
137 Medical Defence Union, *Law and the Doctor* 52 (1975); Hopper, *The Medical Man's Fiduciary Duty supra* n. 19.
138 Speller, *supra* n. 23 at 132; Meredith, *supra* n. 106 at 26; Rozovsky, *Canadian Hospital Law* 105 (1979); Freedman, *supra* n. 66 at 14; Jacob, *supra* n. 67 at 346; Sharpe and Sawyer

whether a doctor-patient relationship should even exist where the patient is such an extreme threat to society.[139] The attitude of the medical profession on this question has changed dramatically in the last 30 years, due in part, no doubt, to the grave threat posed to society by the increase in violent crime.[140]

But the doctor who decides to put society's interests first is doing so as a matter of conscience because there is no legal duty to assist the police. For while it is a criminal offence to obstruct the police in their investigations,[141] it is not an offence to refuse to assist them.[142]

The protection of children who have been mistreated by adults justifies a doctor breaching his duty of confidentiality.[143] Indeed, in many jurisdictions there is legislation requiring the reporting of an abandoned, deserted or physically ill-treated child.[144]

A patient who is unfit to drive by reason of illness or alcohol or drug abuse is a great risk to society. While some provinces have enacted statutes requiring a doctor to report such a patient, others say the doctor *may* do so or are silent on the point.[145] None of the Acts set out a penalty for the failure to report. Thus, the doctor is thrown back to weighing the duty to society against the duty not to disclose information about a patient. Modern authorities would support the doctor who reports.[146] The victim of a patient-driver whom a doctor failed to report could sue the doctor, relying on the legislation as the source of duty of care.[147] It is arguable that such accidents are those which the

---

supra n. 65 at 98-105. Note that a doctor need not fear that his name will be disclosed. *Sol. Gen. of Can. v. Royal Comm. of Inquiry into the Confidentiality of Health Records* (1981), 38 N.R. 588 (S.C.C.).

139 Speller, *id.;* Freedman, *id.* at 17. As to the duty to warn *see* Schiffer *supra* n. 88 at 67.

140 *See* Chafee, *Privileged Communications: Is Justice Served or Obstructed by Closing the Doctor's Mouth on the Witness Stand?* (1942-43), 52 Yale L.J. 607, wherein it is reported that an American doctor who went to prison for two years rather than report to the police that he had treated the fugitive Dillinger for gunshot wounds was commended by Lancet, a well-known British medical journal. *Compare with* Medical Defence Union, *Annual Report 1968* 20-21 where it is stated that in certain circumstances a doctor might be under a duty to report an unfit driver or give information to protect a battered child. *But see* Finch *supra* n. 67 at 233-35 for a case where a doctor was fined under a Road Traffic Act for refusing to reveal information about patients.

141 Criminal Code, R.S.C. 1970, c. C-34, s. 127 (1) [re-en. 1972, c. 13, s. 8].

142 *R. v. Semeniuk* (1955), 111 C.C.C. 370 (Alta. D.C.). For the perspective of a policeman *see* Stewart, *The Role of the Police in the Confidentiality of Health Records* (1981), 2 H.L. in C. 31.

143 Medical Defence Union, *supra* n. 137, n. 121.

144 *E.g.,* Child Welfare Act, R.S.A. 1980, c. C-8, ss. 35-37. Note that Alberta provides for a penalty for the failure to do so.

145 *Supra.*

146 Medical Defence Union, *supra* n. 137 at 52; Sharpe, *Driving, Disease and the Physician's Responsibility* (1975), 23 Chitty's L.J. 99. *But see* Meredith *supra* n. 106 at 30. In a panel discussion of the Canadian Bar Association in 1953 opinions were expressed that a doctor would be unwise to tell the Department of Highways that a patient was an epileptic. *See Problems in Litigation* (1953), 31 Can. Bar Rev. 503 at 535.

147 Sharpe, *id.,* at 102; *New Horizons in Medical Ethics: Confidentiality,* [1973] 2 British Med. J. 700 at 701; *Doctors, Drivers and Confidentiality,* [1974] 1 British Med. J. 399. *See also Boomer v. Penn* (1965), 52 D.L.R. (2d) 673 (Ont.).

legislation is intended to prevent, and that such victims are those it is intended to protect, and therefore, the criteria for reliance on a statutory duty of care would be satisfied. But such a claim might be rejected on the principle of remoteness as to both liability and damages.[148] There is no doubt that a doctor should warn a patient of the dangers of continuing to drive when disease or treatment affects his ability to do so.[149]

A doctor is required, by statute, to report communicable and venereal disease to the proper authorities.[150] It may be unwise for a doctor to do more.[151] If he knows a third party is at risk, as the wife of a patient who has venereal disease, he should certainly bring this to the attention of the medical officer of health.[152] The information is thereby kept within the medical profession and, presumably, held confidential but the third party will be properly protected. In an American case, *Simonsen v. Swenson,*[153] a doctor advised a hotel manager that a patient staying at the hotel had syphilis. The court found this to be a breach of confidence but held that there was an overriding duty to society to prevent the spread of this disease. Likewise an English authority[154] has concluded that if disclosure was made by the doctor to the third party to protect her against the risk of infection to which a patient was exposing her, a court would be unlikely to award damages against the doctor. But an Ontario case seems to require strict confidentiality when venereal disease is diagnosed. In *Carter v. Carter,*[155] evidence that a party to the action may have had venereal disease was ruled inadmissible. The judge stated that since venereal disease statutes encourage persons to seek treatment on the basis that it will be held confidential, it is not in the public interest to reveal the information. The best advice for the Canadian doctor is to avoid divulging information about the patient's venereal disease to those who might be infected unless there is no other way to protect them.

Society must be protected against violent criminals, dangerous drivers, child batterers and persons with serious diseases. In such situations, a doctor should act to protect the public even when so doing requires him to breach his duty of confidentiality to his patient.

---

148 *Gootson v. R.,* [1947] 4 D.L.R. 568 at 579; affirmed [1948] 4 D.L.R. 33 (S.C.C.).

149 Canadian Medical Association *supra* n. 55 at 2.

150 *See R. v. Gordon* (1923), 54 O.L.R. 355 where a doctor was prosecuted for failing to report a case of diphtheria. He was not convicted as it was found that he did not have the necessary *mens rea,* or mental intent required by law, to commit the offence.

151 For facts that raise this issue *see Damien v. O'Mulvenny* (1981), 34 O.R. (2d) 448 (Ont. H.C.). Note that in Ontario a doctor can give information to the patient's family for the protection of health: Veneral Diseases Prevention Act, R.S.O 1980, c. 521.

152 Gray, *Law and the Practice of Medicine* 39, Ryerson Press, Toronto, (1947).

153 (1920), 104 Neb. 224, 177 N.W. 831 (S.C.). *See* Hirsch, *Physician's Legal Liability to Third Parties Who Are Not Patients* (1977), 23 Med. Tr. Tech. Oly. 388.

154 Speller, *supra* n. 23 at 234. *See also* London *supra* n. 58 at 290.

155 *Supra* n. 113.

(d) Action for Breach of Confidence

Four situations in which a doctor may be justified in disclosing information about a patient have been discussed:

1. when giving testimony in a court of law;
2. where the patient has expressly or impliedly given his consent;
3. where there exists a statutory duty;
4. where it is demanded by the public interest.

In situations other than these, a disclosure of information is wrongful, and certain legal consequences follow for the doctor.[156]

A wrongful disclosure of information is a breach of a doctor's ethical duty[157] for which he could be subjected to disciplinary proceedings by his profession[158] for conduct unbecoming a physician and be reprimanded, suspended or even struck off the register.[159]

However, as punitive to the doctor as these administrative proceedings may be, they do not compensate the patient. For this, the patient must sue the doctor in civil action.

Over 200 years ago Lord Mansfield emphasized that a doctor who voluntarily revealed secrets would be "guilty of a breach of honour, and of great indiscretion,"[160] but there have been few occasions where this statement of a legal duty has been tested in the courts.[161] One of these rare cases was *A.B. v. C.D.*,[162] where a doctor who had examined the wife of an elder of the Presbyterian Church revealed in a report put before the Kirk Session that "the pregnancy had commenced before marriage." The doctor, who was sued for a breach of professional confidence argued that secrecy was not part of the contract[163] between patient and doctor, but merely an "honourable

---

156 For this discussion it is assumed that the disclosures are true, for if they are not the appropriate action might be defamation. For a discussion *see* Rodgers-Magnet, *supra* n. 74 at 279. For a discussion of defamation *see infra*.

157 *See supra*. Note that in *Furniss v. Fitchett supra* n. 136 this ethical duty was said to be far broader than any common law duty. Note also that it is a breach of ethical duty to reveal information about a dead patient: Medical Defence Union, *supra* n. 137 at 52. Winston Churchill's physician was criticized for revelations he made concerning his famous patient. *See* (1965), 2 Lancet 785-86. *See also* Robitscher, *Doctors' Privileged Communications, Public Life , and History's Rights* (1968), 17 Clev. Marsh L. Rev. 199.

158 In Alberta, Medical Profession Act, R.S.A. 1980, c. M-12, ss. 34, 56. In Ontario, Health Disciplines Act, R.S.O. 1980, c. 196, s. 60(3), (6).

159 In 1969 in England, a doctor who discussed a patient with a third party was held to have committed "infamous conduct in a professional respect" and was erased from the register: Medical Defence Union, *supra* n. 137 at 51.

160 *Supra* n. 61 at 573.

161 Note that most of the continental codes create a strict duty of professional secrecy a breach of which makes the doctor liable for damages: Hammelmann, *supra* n. 79.

162 (1851), 14 Dunlop's S.C. 177 (Scot. C.S.).

163 *See infra* Chapter 2.

understanding,''[164] the breach of which could not be the basis for the law suit. The Scottish court was unanimous in finding otherwise and for the patient's husband who had sued. Lord Fullerton said:[165]

> The question here is . . . whether the relation between such an adviser and the person who consults him, is or is not one which may imply an obligation to secrecy, forming a proper ground of action if it be violated. It appears to me that it is . . . that a medical man, consulted in a matter of delicacy, of which the disclosure may be most injurious to the feelings, and possibly, the pecuniary interests of the party consulting, can gratuitously and unnecessarily make it the subject of public communication, without incurring any imputation beyond what is called a breach of honour, and without the liability to a claim of redress in a court of law, is a proposition to which, when thus broadly laid down, I think the Court will hardly give their countenance.

A paucity of judicial authority notwithstanding, the New Zealand Supreme Court made a cautious extension of the law in the 1958 case of *Furniss v. Fitchett*.[166] Reviewing our modern concept of the duty of care as expressed in the famous case of *Donoghue v. Stevenson*,[167] the learned Chief Justice found to be included in the doctor's duty of care to his patient the obligation of confidentiality. However, he restricted the case to those situations in which the doctor can reasonably foresee the information coming into the patient's knowledge and causing physical harm, and where the public interest does not require disclosure.

The case has been soundly criticized[168] but remains important because it found a duty, albeit narrow, against wrongful disclosure upon which the award of damages was based.

Canadian courts have paid lip service to the right to have medical information kept confidential, but no Canadian patient has obtained an injunction or recovered damages in an action.[169]

In spite of a dearth of strong authority, a well known English text states that in the proper case a court would find there was a legal duty not to disclose anything about a patient and grant the remedy of damages or an injunction to a

---

164 *Supra* n. 162 at 179.
165 *Supra* n. 162 at 180. This reasoning was accepted in a later Scottish case, but with the caution that "it must depend on circumstances whether any disclosure made to others is a wrong, for which compensation may be sought by an action of damages in a court of law." *A.B. v. C.D. supra* n. 136 at 81.
166 *Supra* n. 136.
167 [1932] A.C. 562 (H.L.).
168 Fleming, *English Law of Medical Liability* (1959), 12 Vand. L. Rev. 633 at 643. *But see* Rodgers-Magnet *supra* n. 74 at 294 who says the judgment "is a correct one and the duty recognized by Mr. Justice Barrowcough is one which ought to be recognized by law."
169 *Re: Inquiry into the Confidentiality of Health Records in Ontario* (1979), 98 D.L.R. (3d) 704 at 714; affirmed 38 N.R. 588 (*sub nom. Solicitor Gen. of Can. v. Royal Comm. of Inquiry into the Confidentiality of Health Records in Ontario*) (S.C.C.); *Re: Lavasseur and College of Nurses of Ont.* (1983), 18 A.C.W.S. (2d) 126 (Ont. H.C.); *Wooding v. Little* (1982), 24 C.C.L.T. 37 (B.C.S.C.); *Miron v. Pohran* (1981), 8 A.C.W.S. (2d) 509 (Ont. Co. Ct.); *Damien v. O'Mulvenny* (1981), 34 O.R. (2d) 448 (Ont. H.C.).

patient who has suffered loss or damage to his reputation or perhaps only embarrassment as a result of the doctor's breach of his duty of confidentiality.[170]

American authorities hold that a doctor is liable to his patient for damages arising out of a truthful, but wrongful, disclosure of medical confidences.[171]

A patient has a natural right to control the promulgation of information about himself. It is now clear that a patient should be compensated where his doctor, whose duty it is to respect that right, wrongfully discloses information.

On what basis should such actions be brought: contract, tort or fiduciary relationship?[172]

Each cause of action has its advantages and limitations, with the negligence action being the most flexible framework within which to resolve these claims.[173]

However, the recommendation of Mr. Justice Krever[174] is clearly the direction the law must go if there is a sincere concern about the unwarranted disclosure of medical information and a commitment to take action soon. The Commission said:[175]

> That a statutory right be created permitting a patient whose health information has been disclosed without his or her authorization, to maintain a civil action for the greater of his or her actual damages or $10,000.00 against:
>
> (a)   any health care provider or other person under an obligation to keep health information about the patient confidential, who unjustifiably discloses his or her health information to a third person; and
>
> (b)   any person who induced anyone under an obligation to keep health information about a patient confidential, unjustifiably to disclose his or her health information.

---

170 Speller, *supra* n. 23 at 128. Jacob, *Speller's Law Relating to Hospitals and Kindred Institutions supra* n. 67 at 344. *See also* Samuels, *The Duty of the Doctor to Respect the Confidence of the Patient* (1980), 20 Med. Sci. Law 58 at 59.

171 Stetler and Moritz, *supra* n. 26 at 271-72; *see, for example, Simonsen v. Swenson supra* n. 153. The Americans too have had few of these kind of cases; *see* Hanning and Brady, *Extrajudicial Truthful Disclosure of Medical Confidences: A Physicians Civil Liability* (1967), 44 Denver L.J. 463, wherein it is stated that from the Simonsen case to 1967 there were only seven cases in the entire U.S.

172 For an excellent discussion of all alternatives, *see* Rodgers-Magnet, *supra* n. 74 at 278-98; *see also* Boyle, *Medical Confidence — Civil Liability for Breach* (1973), 24 North Ireland L.Q. 19 and Hopper *supra* n. 19. Glasbeek *Limitations on the Action of Breach of Confidence* in *Aspects of Privacy Law* 217 (Gibson ed., 1980).

173 It is unclear whether a cause of action under any of these heads would survive the death of the patient. *See* Mason and McCall Smith *supra* n. 67 at 109.

174 Report of the Commission of Inquiry into the Confidentiality of Health Information (1980).

175 *Id.* at 15 (Vol. I). Note that there is support for this recommendation. *See* Rodgers-Magnet *supra* n. 74 at 298. *See also* Samuels *supra* n. 170 at 59 referring to the English Law Commission Working Paper No. 58 (1974), and its recommendation of a statutory legal duty.

2

Civil Actions

This chapter outlines the nature of the various civil actions which might be brought by a patient against a doctor. The actions which are most commonly used will be discussed in depth in later chapters.

It is important to note at the outset that a plaintiff may have more than one cause of action available out of one set of facts. For example, a patient who suffers burns as a result of treatment for acne might bring actions against his dermatologist based on negligence, battery or even breach of contract.

1.   ASSAULT AND BATTERY[1]

A patient who has been touched without his consent has suffered a trespass to his person and can sue for the torts of assault and battery. An important feature of these torts is that the patient need not have suffered any damage to bring the action.[2]

Battery is committed by intentionally bringing about harmful or offensive contact with another. The essence of the action is the touching of another without his consent, so the individual is protected not only against bodily harm but also against any interference with his person which is offensive to

---

1 For a general discussion, *see* Fleming, *The Law of Torts* 23-26 (6th ed. 1983).
2 *McNamara v. Smith*, [1934] 2 D.L.R. 417 (Ont. C.A.).

honour and dignity.[3] Accordingly a person may be battered although he is asleep or unconscious at the time of the touching.[4]

An assault is the apprehension of a battery.[5] Normally, a person is apprehensive if unauthorized physical contact is imminent, and so it has been said that assault and battery go together like ham and eggs.[6] But the actions can occur separately: when one is unconscious or otherwise unaware of an impending battery, or when one is threatened but no actual contact takes place. The term "assault" is often used today to cover assault and battery together or even battery itself.[7] "Surgical assault" is sometimes used to refer to a battery which has been committed by a doctor on a patient. Assault and battery involving force are crimes as well as torts and are dealt with by the Criminal Code.[8]

The validity of both of these actions depends on the absence of the victim's consent, which is a complete defence to the assault and battery actions. So, while the treatment and care of patients necessitates touching, many potential assault and battery actions against doctors are precluded on this basis.

The consent may be implied from the patient's conduct. For example, when he presents himself and complains of certain symptoms he is impliedly consenting to such examination as is reasonable for diagnosis and treatment.[9] Written consent is not a requirement in most jurisdictions[10] but should be obtained if possible when surgery or dangerous tests are involved, as it protects the doctor by providing him with solid proof that consent has been given.

In an emergency, the doctor needs no consent from the patient; he can touch the patient as necessary to treat him and no liability will follow for

---

3 Note that a battery may be alleged by a patient in a psychiatric institution. In *Brennan v. The Dir. of Mental Health,* Alta. D., March, 1977 (Alta. S.C.) the patient's unsuccessful claim was than an orderly knelt on his throat causing permanent paralysis of his vocal chords. For an excellent analysis of the difficulties and restrictions in such an action *see* Schiffer, *Psychiatry Behind Bars* 201-203 (1982).

4 *See, for example, Hankai v. York County Hosp.* (1981), 9 A.C.W.S. (2d) 354 (Ont. C.A.) where a doctor who performed "extra" surgery (a meatotomy) on an anaesthetized patient was held liable for battery. Note that battery must be specifically pleaded; *see Allan v. New Mount Sinai* (1981), 19 C.C.L.T. 76 (Ont. C.A.).

5 *Supra* n. 1 at 26.

6 Prosser, *Law of Torts* 41 (4th ed. 1971).

7 *See Gambriell v. Caparelli* (1974), 7 O.R. (2d) 205 (Co. Ct.) where it has been suggested that the nomenclature be changed to reflect modern usage.

8 R.S.C. 1970, c. C-34, ss. 244-46 [re-en. 1980-81-82-83, c. 125, s. 19]. *See R. v. Ogg-Moss* (1981), 5 L. Med. Q. 146 (Ont. C.A.), where an employee of a hospital for mentally retarded persons was found guilty of common assault (ss. 244-45) for punishing a voluntary patient by hitting him on the head with a spoon.

9 *O'Brien v. Cunard S. S. Co.* (1891), 154 Mass. 272, 28 N.E. 266 (S.C.)

10 *But see, for example,* R. Regs. M. 1970, Reg. P130-R1, s. 6; N.B. Reg. 66/47 as amended, s. 40; R.R.O 1980, Reg. 862, s. 50; R.R.Q., c. S-5, s. 58; Sask. Reg. 331/79, s. 55.

assault and battery.[11] However, the importance of obtaining consent in a non-emergency situation cannot be overstressed.[12] A patient who has not consented will have a good cause of action whether or not he has suffered harm and even if he has benefitted from the unauthorized treatment.[13]

2. FALSE IMPRISONMENT

Of the same family as trespass to the person, false imprisonment protects the liberty of the individual as well as his reputation and dignity.[14] While no damage need be proven, the plaintiff must show that he was restrained and that no reasonable avenue of escape was available. He need not be conscious of his confinement.[15]

The tort is committed by failing to release a person so entitled or by confining an individual against his will without lawful authority. Therefore, since a patient is free to refuse medical treatment, confining him or forcing treatment upon him without statutory[16] authority could render the doctor liable for false imprisonment. There have been a number of actions brought by patients against psychiatrists and psychiatric institutions.[17]

In a 1973 case, *Coulombe v. Watier,*[18] the patient sued the psychiatrist who had arranged for his admission to a mental institution. The certificate leading to the patient's confinement was not signed by the defendant but by another doctor who was not sued. The patient was released the day after his admission to the hospital. The Supreme Court of Canada held that the doctor sued was not liable for false imprisonment, but the doctor who had signed the certificate might have been, had he been sued.[19]

---

11 *Marshall v. Curry,* [1933] 3 D.L.R. 260 (N.S.S.C.). For an unusual case *see A.G. B.C. v. Astaforoff,* [1983] 6 W.W.R. 322 (B.C.S.C.) which involved the force-feeding of a woman prisoner. *See also Leigh v. Gladstone* (1909), 26 T.L.R. 139 (K.B.).

12 For a full discussion of cases *see infra* Chapter 3.

13 *Mulloy v. Hop Sang,* [1935] 1 W.W.R. 714 (Alta. C.A.).

14 *See* Fleming, *supra* n. 1 at 26.

15 Linden, *Canadian Tort Law* 46 (1982).

16 *See, for example,* the following statutory provisions authorizing medical care or examinations without consent in certain circumstances: Child Welfare Act, R.S.A. 1980, c. C-8, s. 9; Corrections Act, R.S.A. 1980, c. C-26, s. 33; Mental Health Act, R.S.A. 1980, c. M-13, s. 15; Occupational Health and Safety Act, R.S.A. 1980, c. O-2, s. 15 [am. 1983, c. 39, ss. 19, 20]; Tuberculosis Act, R.S.A. 1980, c. T-11, s. 7; Venereal Diseases Prevention Act, R.S.A. 1980, c. V-2, ss. 2 and 8. *See also* Draper, Due Process and Confinement for Mental Disorders (1976), 14 A.L.R. 266.

17 For a discussion *see* Schiffer *supra* n. 3 at 143-46. For an excellent review of Canadian cases see Milliken, *Medical Certification of the Mentally Ill: A Protection for the Individual's Rights* (1983), 28 Can. J. Psychiatry 137; See also Menuck, Littman and Kelly, *Habeas Corpus and the Ontario Mental Health Act* (1981), 2 H.L. in C. 91.

18 [1973] S.C.R. 673. *See also McIntosh v. Homewood Sanitarium,* [1940] O.W.N. 118 (H.C.); Swadron, *The Legal Aspects of Compulsory Confinement of the Mentally Disordered* (1962), 5 Cr. L.Q. 175.

19 Although in the U.S. the certifying doctor is not usually held liable, for various policy reasons. *See* Sauer, *Psychiatric Malpractice: A Survey* (1971-72), 11 Washburn L.J. 461 at 464.

In a 1980 case from Alberta, *Tanner v. Norys,*[20] a patient sued the psychiatrist who had signed the documents committing him. While he was successful at trial and was awarded aggravated and exemplary damages for the loss of dignity and deprivation of liberty, the Court of Appeal reversed the decision holding that the requirements of the Mental Health Act had been complied with.

An authority[21] on the Charter of Rights and Freedoms[22] opines that this new legislation will have a very great effect on patients, doctors and institutions. He states:[23]

> Proceedings leading to deprivation of liberty in both civil and criminal proceedings will now be tested against the legal rights found in the charter and governments will have to justify any limits on those legal rights by demonstrating that they are reasonable limits prescribed by law as can be demonstrably justified in a free and democratic society.

There are patients who because of their very poor mental or physical condition may require some restraint. For example, the epileptic with a propensity to wander or leap from windows may require close supervision;[24] the elderly patient who tends to fall out of bed may need securing; the patient with an infectious disease may call for isolation. Although none of these measures would generally lead to liability for false imprisonment, it ought to be remembered that, in general, a patient must be allowed to leave a hospital if he demands to do so and he must not be given medication to make this impossible for him, nor be deprived of the means of leaving by such tactics as refusing to return his clothes, money or personal effects. However, should a patient choose to reject the advice of his doctor and leave a hospital, he ought to be required to sign a document setting out the facts and containing a statement that he is leaving against medical advice.

3.   NEGLIGENCE

(a)   General

Negligence is the most common basis for a lawsuit against a doctor or hospital. Malpractice[25] is a term that is often applied, sometimes even in

---

20 [1980] 4 W.W.R. 33 (Alta. C.A.), leave to appeal denied (1980), 25 A.R. 274 (sub nom. *Tanner v. Morys*) (S.C.C.). *See also Attar v. Frank* (1983), 18 A.C.W.S. (2d) 52 (Ont. H.C.).
21 Manning, *Rights, Freedoms and the Courts* 550-85 (1983).
22 Constitution Act, 1982, Part I: Canadian Charter of Rights and Freedoms, ss. 7, 8, 9, 10 and 12 protect the security of the person and the right not to be arbitrarily detained or imprisoned or to be subjected to cruel and unusual treatment.
23 *Supra* n. 21 at 550. For a recent case where the Charter was applied and a patient ordered released from a psychiatric ward, *see Lyssa v. Health Sciences Centre*, unreported, Nov. 17, 1983, No. 3234/83 (Man. Q.B.)
24 *University Hosp. Bd. v. Lepine; Monckton v. Lepine,* [1966] S.C.R. 561. *Worth v. Royal Jubilee Hosp.* (1980), 4 L. Med. Q. 59 (B.C.C.A.).
25 Meredith, *Malpractice Liability of Doctors and Hospitals* at xii (1956); *McQuay v. Eastwood* (1886), 12 O.R. 402 (C.A.).

statutes,[26] to negligent practice, but the scope of its meaning is not clear.[27] Until the term is adequately defined by the legislature or the courts, its use is best avoided. The classical definition of "negligence" is:[28]

> . . . the omission to do something which a reasonable man, guided upon those considerations which ordinarily regulate the conduct of human affairs, would do, or doing something which a prudent and reasonable man would not do.

Liability for negligence will not be found unless the following factors are present:

(a) the defendant must owe a duty to the plaintiff to exercise care;

(b) the defendant must breach the standard of care established by law for his conduct;

(c) the plaintiff must suffer loss or injury as a result of this breach;

(d) the conduct of the defendant must be the "proximate cause" of the plaintiff's loss or injury.

It is clear that a doctor or hospital has a duty to a patient to exercise reasonable care toward him and not to expose him to unreasonable risk or harm.

A person holding himself out as having a special knowledge or skill will have his conduct judged by the standard of a reasonable member of his profession, and so a doctor must meet the standard of the average reasonable doctor. This "standard of care" as it is called will be discussed in more detail later on.[29]

The doctor will only be held liable for negligence if it results in loss or injury to the plaintiff; liability may still be escaped if the damage suffered is held to be too "remote" from the negligent act; that is, although the negligence may be the "factual" cause of the plaintiff's injury, it may not be the legal or "proximate" cause.[30]

(b) Negligence and Other Actions

Of the many differences between negligence and the other actions such as assault and battery and false imprisonment, the most important is that negligence is not an "intentional" tort. A doctor will be held liable for battery only if he *intended* to touch the patient, but he may be held liable for negligence in the absence of any intention to perform in a negligent or substandard way.

---

26 *See, for example*, Dental Association Act, R.S.A. 1980, c. D-7, s. 36; Dental Auxiliaries Act, R.S.A. 1980, c. D-8, s. 8; Limitation of Actions Act, R.S.A. 1980, c. L-15, s. 55.

27 For example, it has some times included assault and battery. *See Davy v. Morrison*, [1931] 4 D.L.R. 619 at 623 (Ont. C.A.); *Boase v. Paul*, [1931] 4 D.L.R. 435 at 438 (Ont. C.A.); *Schweizer v. Central Hosp.* (1974), 6 O.R. (2d) 606 at 607 (H.C.).

28 *Blyth v. Birmington Waterworks Co.* (1856), 11 Exch. 781, 156 E.R. 1047 at 1049.

29 *See infra* Chapter 4.

30 *See infra* Chapter 4.

Another difference between the two types of action is that in the negligence action, as noted above, damage must be proven, whereas in assault and battery such proof is not necessary to establish *liability*.[31]

The patient's case is complete once he proves the doctor intentionally interfered with his person. The onus of establishing the defence of the patient's sufficient and effective consent is on the doctor.[32]

A unique quality of the negligence suit is that it is possible in some cases to find some negligent conduct on the part of *both* parties. For example, a court might hold that the doctor was negligent by prescribing a certain drug, but that the patient was also negligent by not reporting suspicious side effects. In such cases, the patient's conduct is referred to as contributory negligence and his recovery is reduced by the degree, expressed in terms of a percentage, to which he has been found negligent. Therefore, if it were found that 30 per cent of the negligence which caused the patient's injuries was his own, and his damages were assessed at $15,000, he would be entitled to recover from the doctor only the remaining 70 per cent or $10,500.

The confusion in Canadian jurisprudence as to whether battery or negligence is the proper action to bring in cases where consent to medical treatment is in issue has been dealt with by the Supreme Court of Canada in *Hopp v. Lepp*[33] and *Reibl v. Hughes*.[34] These cases and their implications are discussed in some depth in Chapter Three.

4.   CONTRACT

It was recognized over 300 years ago that a contract existed between a doctor and his patient, the breach of which afforded the patient a cause of action.[35] But the tort of negligence better covered most situations where a patient was given substandard medical care and very few suits were brought for breach of contract alone.[36]

---

31 Failure to prove damage will result, however, in the plaintiff receiving nominal damages.

32 *Schweizer v. Central Hosp. supra* n. 27. *Allan v. New Mount Sinai* (1980), 11 C.C.L.T. 299 at 306 (Ont. H.C.); reversed on pleadings issue 19 C.C.L.T. 76 (Ont. C.A.).

33 (1980), 112 D.L.R. (3d) 67 (S.C.C.).

34 (1980), 14 C.C.L.T. 1 (S.C.C.).

35 *Everard v. Hopkins* (1615), 2 Bulstrode 332, 80 E.R. 1164 (K.B.); *Slater v. Baker* (1767), 2 Wils. K.B. 359, 95 E.R. 860. Jackson and Powell, *Professional Negligence* 205 (1982). *See also supra* Chapter 1.

36 *See supra* Chapter 1. Note that in Quebec the situation is different. *See* Sommerville, *Structuring the Issues in Informed Consent* (1981), 26 McGill L.J. 740 at 742 (Note 5) where the author states:

   "However, a claim based on a breach of duty in the physician-patient relationship is more likely to sound in contract in the civil law than it would at common law, and contrary to the civilian doctrine of *cumul*, which would allow a plaintiff to claim in both delict or quasi-delict and contract in relation to the same facts which it is alleged give rise to liability, there is a trend to exclude delictual or quasi-delictual liability to the extent that the obligation in issue has a contractual basis. Support for this trend depends on also

A most common yet confusing approach of some courts is to discuss both the contract action and the tort action and their attributes without making clear which is the more appropriate.[37] One explanation for these failures to distinguish the actions is that the standard of care and skill required in a contract action is the same as that required in the tort action.[38] An example of the uncertainty of the bar and bench over the two actions is the Saskatchewan case, *Allard v. Boykowich*,[39] where counsel for the plaintiff, who sued the defendant dentist in tort, amended to contract, assuring the court that it was not a tort action,[40] and yet at the close of the trial applied for leave to set up the claim in tort.[41] The patient claimed that extractions and dentures had not corrected her speech defect as promised by the dentist. She lost on the contractual ground, and the late application to amend being disallowed, the issue of negligence was never decided.[42]

A contract is a legally enforceable agreement between two or more persons.[43] The basic requirements for the existence of a contract are that:

(1) there be an intention to create legal relations;

(2) the parties be known and competent;

(3) the terms be certain or ascertainable;

(4) there be consideration.

Are these requirements present in the doctor-patient relationship? There is no doubt that the relationship itself involves the intention to create legal relations.[44]

---

excluding a doctrine of *option*, as argued by Professor P. A. Crépeau (*Le responsabilitié médicale et hospitalière dans la jurisprudence québécoise recente* (1960), R. du B. 434, 470-2), but the doctrine of *option* was recently endorsed by a unanimous bench of the Supreme Court of Canada in *Wabasso Ltd. v. The National Drying Co.* (dated 22 June 1981)."

In general *see* Bernardot and Kouri, *La Responsabilité Civile Médicale* 103-237 (1980).

37 *See, for example, Hughston v. Jost,* [1943] O.W.N. 3 (H.C.); *G. v. C,* [1960] Que. Q.B. 161. *Dunn v. Young* (1977), 86 D.L.R. (3d) 411 (Ont. Co. Ct.); *Dunsmore v. Deshield* (1977), 80 D.L.R. (3d) 386 (Sask. Q.B.); *Doiron v. Orr* (1978), 86 D.L.R. (3d) 719 (Ont. H.C.). *See also Gibson v. Bagnall* (No. 2) (1979), 24 O.R. (2d) 567 (Ont. H.C.), where the court ordered that issues of contract, battery and negligence should be tried together.

38 *Worth v. Royal Jubilee Hosp.* (1980), 4 L. Med. Q. 59 at 67 (B.C.C.A.); *Dunn v. Young supra* n. 37 at 420. Louisell and Williams, *Medical Malpractice* Matthew Bender, New York (1982), at 197.

39 [1948] 1 W.W.R. 860 (Sask K.B.).

40 *id.* at 866.

41 *Id.* at 868.

42 Even if the amendment had been allowed, the defendant might have pleaded *res judicata* (that the matter had been adjudicated upon). This possibility has been raised in U.S. courts. *See* Miller, *The Contractual Liability of Physicians and Surgeons,* [1953] Wash L.Q. 413 at 431.

43 Fridman, *Law of Contract* 3 (1976).

44 *See supra* Chapter 1.

It involves the purchase of professional services where the parties, patient and doctor are known. The parties must be competent to contract and under no undue influence. However, the doctor in providing required professional services would be delivering necessaries of life for which even a minor, or in the case of an insane person, his estate, would be liable to pay.[45]

The terms of the contract for professional services will rarely be written or expressly discussed by the doctor and patient. Most often they are ascertainable by looking at the terms in the usual doctor-patient relationship,[46] and at the term usually implied by law to such contracts, for example, the obligation of the doctor to exercise due care and skill,[47] and to keep confidential the information he obtains.[48]

To be enforceable, a contract must be supported by consideration, that is, there must be a balance of benefits and detriments on both sides.[49] In the contract between doctor and patient, the doctor renders professional service and receives payment; the patient renders payment and receives services.[50] Thus, there is a balance of benefit and detriment on both sides as well as between the parties. Today doctors are paid through universal medical schemes for which the head of the household or another individual pays a premium. Indeed premiums may be waived in the case of the elderly or those on social assistance. The consideration must come from the person who receives the benefit, and therefore, it is arguable that since the patient himself may not be paying, there is a no consideration supporting the contract. However, the law requires only that a person receiving a benefit be required to do something in exchange for the benefit. The fact that what he is required to do may in fact be beneficial is irrelevant; the legal detriment lies in the requirement that it be done. Therefore, there is some support for the proposition that the patient, by submitting to treatment, is suffering an adequate detriment which could serve as consideration.[51]

---

45 *Supra* n. 43 at 136-7 and 152. *See Dunn v. Young supra* n. 37 where the plaintiff was three years old.

46 Wasmuth, *Law for the Physician* 19, Lea and Febiger, Philadelphia, 1966. *See Dendaas (Tylor) v. Yackel* (1980), 12 C.C.L.T. 147 (B.C.S.C.), where it was held that there was no agreement or meeting of minds on an important term of the contract, namely, whether a sterilization procedure would be permanent.

47 *Davy v. Morrison*, [1932] O.R. 1 at 6 (C.A.). *Gibson v. Bagnall supra* n. 37 at 570. This term implied in the contract is identical to the standard of care expected of the doctor by law, in a negligence action.

48 *Furniss v. Fitchett*, [1958] N.Z.L.R. 396 at 397 (S.C.); Rodgers-Magnet, *Common Law Remedies For Disclosure of Confidential Medical Information* in *Issues in Tort Law* 265 at 284 (Steel and Rodgers-Magnet ed. 1983); *see also supra* Chapter 1.

49 Fridman, *supra* n. 43.

50 *See Matheson v. Smiley*, [1932] 2 D.L.R. 787 (Man. C.A.), which held this to be true even where it is not the patient who engages the doctor. *But see Allen v. Froh*, [1932] 1 W.W.R. 593 (Sask. C.A.).

51 *Supra* Chapter 1.

The conclusion, it would appear, is that the necessary contractual relationships can be found in most doctor-patient relationships.

The law suit based on an allegation of breach of contract presents advantages and disadvantages to both doctor and patient in terms of limitation periods, the expense of bringing the action, the damages recoverable, and the acceptability of such an action by Canadian lawyers and judges.

The limitation period, or time period within which a person must sue, differs for tort and contract actions.[52] As a general rule, the patient must sue in tort within one or two years from the termination of professional services, whereas he has six years from the date of breach to sue in contract.[53] So the patient who may have discovered his damage at too late a date to commence a negligence action may still be in time to sue in contract. However, the precise wording of the relevant limitation statute must be examined closely because all actions against doctors may be covered by a broad definition or interpretation of the words which appear in many statutes: ". . . negligence or malpractice by reason of professional services requested or rendered . . ."[54] This would mean that in any case where the defendant is a doctor, even a contract case, the shorter limitation time applicable to doctors would apply. But barring such an interpretation of the statute, a contract action gives the patient a longer time within which to begin an action and exposes the doctor to the risk of being found liable for a greater period.

The second factor relevant to the patient contemplating a contract action is that it will usually be less expensive to prove a case in contract than in tort against a doctor, for to succeed in a contract action the patient would have to prove only a contract existed and that it had been breached. Put another way, all the patient has to do is prove that the doctor made a promise and failed to perform it.[55] By contrast, in a negligence action, the patient must, by calling doctors who qualify as experts, prove the standard at which the doctor ought to have performed, and perhaps call additional experts to prove the doctor did not do so. The patient must also prove injury or damage and the causal

---

52 *See infra* Chapter 5.

53 Dickens, *Contractual Aspects of Human Experimentation* (1975), 25 U. of T. L.J. 406 at 434; *see also* McLaren, *Of Doctors, Hospitals and Limitations: "The Patient's Dilemma"* (1973), 11 O.H.L.J. 85; *Boase v. Paul supra* n. 27. Note that some U.S jurisdictions have legislation making the time the same for both contract and tort actions against doctors. *See* Miller, *the Contractual Liability of Physicians and Surgeons*, [1953] Wash. Univ. L.Q. 413 at 429.

54 Limitation of Actions Act, R.S.A. 1980, c. L-15, s. 55; *See Johnson v. Vancouver Gen. Hosp.*, [1974] 1 W.W.R. 239 at 244 (B.C.C.A.); *Philippon v. Legate*, [1970] 1 O.R. 392 (C.A.). *See also Goff v. Barker* (1978), 92 D.L.R. (3d) 125 (Ont. H.C.), where a corporate defendant, a dispensary-laboratory had the benefit of the shorter limitation period (six months). *See also Letiec v. Rowe* (1981), 130 D.L.R. (3d) 379 (Nfld. C.A.), where with regard to a hospital the limitation was one year for a tort or a contract action. *See also Fishman v. Waters* (1983), 22 A.C.W.S. (2d) 382 (Man. C.A.). *See* Chapter 5.

55 Fridman, *supra* n. 43 at 547.

connection linking it to the doctor's treatment. Assuming that the doctors who qualify as experts are prepared to testify against a colleague, it can, for various reasons, be difficult and expensive for the patient to arrange their appearance in court.

While the contract action may be open longer and be less expensive to the patient, it also has some disadvantages for him.

The purpose of damages in a contract case is to place the plaintiff in the position in which he would have been had the contract been performed; in a tort case, to restore the plaintiff to the condition in which he would have been had the tort not been committed.[56] A number of consequences flow from this distinction.

For a breach of contract, the doctor would be liable to pay only for the loss that reasonable persons in the positions of the doctor and patient at the time of the making of the contract would have considered *likely* to occur in the event of a breach by the doctor, whereas in tort the scope of liability is much broader: the doctor would be liable for all damage foreseeable to a reasonable person. This is a more flexible test and can include losses *unlikely* to occur;[57] for example, injuries of greater extent than would be expected, due to the patient having, unknown to anyone, an abnormal weakness.[58] It could also include sums for such items as pain and suffering and mental anguish.[59]

There is a modern trend to expand the kinds of injuries compensable in a breach of contract action and the differences in the scope of damages recoverable in tort compared to contract may become negligible.[60]

Although the extent of damages the doctor would have to pay could be less in a contract action, he may risk having to pay them from his own pocket if he has standard insurance coverage, which is usually for tort claims only.[61] To date, the Canadian Medical Protective Association has not denied the request of a member to be assisted simply because he has been sued in contract.

---

56 *Id.* at 559.

57 Linden, *Canadian Tort Law* 339-96 (1982).

58 This is sometimes called the "thin-skull" situation. *See* Linden, *id.* at 359-68.

59 Miller, *supra* n. 42 at 424; Bonebrake, *Contractual Liability in Medical Malpractice — Sullivan v. O'Connor* (1974), 24 De Paul L.R. 212 at 221.

60 *LaFleur v. Cornelis* (1979), 28 N.B.R. (2d) 569 at 579 (N.B.Q.B.); Rafferty, *The Tortious Liability of Professionals to Their Contractual Clients* in *Issues In Tort Law* 243-44 (Steel and Rodgers-Magnet ed. 1983); Cooper-Stephenson and Saunders, *Personal Injury Damages in Canada* 584-86 (1981); Swinton, *Foreseeability: Where Should The Award of Contract Damages Cease?* in *Studies in Contract Law* 61 (Reiter and Swan ed. 1980). Note that in the U.S. damages normally awarded only in tort cases have been granted in contract cases: *see* Miller, *supra* n. 42 at 425.

61 *See* Dickens, *supra* n. 53 at 437. *See also* Birnbaum, *Express Contracts to Care: The Nature of Contractual Malpractice* (1974-75), 50 Indiana L.J. 361.

The contract action would seem to be more advantageous to patients than the tort action in the short run, but some authors believe it would have a detrimental effect on the practice of medicine as doctors would have to be extremely cautious about what they said to patients.[62] There is a thin line between a statement of mere opinion or a therapeutic reassurance which would not be a term of a contract and a representation of fact which might be.

In an early American case, a doctor said to a badly burned patient, ''I will guarantee to make the hand a hundred percent perfect hand.'' He was held to have made an express promise in spite of the fact that he was unskilled at skin grafting and argued that he had expressed an opinion which no reasonable person could interpret as a guarantee.[63]

There is a very little Canadian law or comment on the contract action and the doctor.[64] One of the few discussions can be found in *Hughston v. Jost*[65] where Hope J., while finding against a doctor for negligence, indicated that an express contract is possible between a doctor and patient within which the doctor might agree to special terms or even to warrant or insure a certain result. Those comments were prophetic of the judgment in *LaFleur v. Cornelis.*[66] Mr. Justice Barry found that the patient and a plastic surgeon entered into a contract whereby for a fee of $600 the surgeon agreed to reduce the size of the patient's nose according to certain sketches he provided. Furthermore, the surgeon gave an express warranty of success by saying ''no problem, you will be very happy.''[67] When the result of the surgery was unsatisfactory with scarring and some deformity, Barry J. held that the contract was breached and awarded damages to include ''emotional stress and upset.'' While the learned justice also found liability in negligence he acknowledged the uniqueness of his decision:[68]

> I appreciate that I am embarking on a relatively new course in law in finding a contractual relationship of a specific kind between the doctor and the patient. Such has been done in the United States for many years. I also realize that I am adopting a relatively new method of assessing damages for some items not allowed even ten years ago, but I have never been able to find any logical reason why an injured party should not be compensated for foreseeable results of a breach of contract, just as in negligence.

---

62 Miller, *supra* n. 42 at 419; Maynard, *Establishing the Contractual Liability of Physicians* (1974), 7 U. Calif. Davis L. Rev. 84 at 91-92; Bonebrake, *supra* n. 59 at 226.

63 *Hawkins v. McGee* (1929), 84 N.H. 114, 146 A. 641 (S.C.); also *Noel v. Proud* (1961), 189 Kan. 6, 367 P. (2d) 61 (S.C.); *Guilment v. Campbell* (1971), 385 Mich. 57, 188 N.W. (2d) 601 (S.C.).

64 As to Quebec *see supra* n. 36. *See also* Bernadot, *De l'obligation de soigner dans le contract medical* (1977), 37 R. du B. 204.

65 *Supra* n. 37 at 4.

66 *Supra* n. 60. For a case comment *see* Berquist, *Legal Liability of Cosmetic Surgeons,* [1983] 21 A.L.R. 533.

67 *Supra* n. 60 at 577

68 *Supra* n. 60 at 579.

It is not yet possible to predict whether other Canadian judges will follow the "bold spirit" of Mr. Justice Barry. The great potential for the action is shown by the large number of cases in the United States[69] and the growing comment on them.[70]

Lord Nathan[71] recognized the contract action as a companion to the tort action. He saw in it a potential for liability which had not yet been realized: a doctor could be absolutely liable if the substances or materials he uses in his care or treatment cause damage or injury to the patient. This would be founded on the principle that there is implied in a contract to do work and supply materials an absolute warranty that the materials are reasonably fit for the purpose for which they are supplied.[72] This principle was applied in a case where veterinary surgeons inoculated the plaintiff's cattle with a defective toxoid.[73] The trial judge found there was an implied term in the contract between the owner and the veterinarian that the substance used for the inoculations would be reasonably fit for the purpose for which it was requested and that the term had been breached. The owners were awarded damages for loss of the cattle. It was not necessary for the owners to prove that the veterinarians were negligent in failing to discover the defect in the substance. In commenting on this case Lord Nathan says:[74]

> It is not easy to see why the same principle should not be applied, for example, to the case of a patient who employs his doctor to give him a course of injections against colds or an anaesthetist who is employed for the purposes of an operation. It would seem unreasonable if a less stringent contractual obligation were to be implied in the case of a contract to give an injection to a human being than in a contract for the inoculation of a cow.

A Canadian authority in the field of products liability[75] believes there may be policy considerations to justify exempting doctors from such strict liability,[76] but because no case has yet come before a Canadian court the question whether the contract between a doctor and patient contains an implied undertaking that all products supplied will be fit for the purposes intended is a matter of conjecture.

---

69 See, for example, Sullivan v. O'Connor (1973), 296 N.E. (2d) 183 (Mass. S.C.). See also authorities listed supra n. 63.

70 See, for example, Epstein, Medical Malpractice: The Case for Contract (1976), 35 Am. Bar Research J. 87; Maynard, supra n. 62; Bonebrake, supra n. 59; Birnbaum, supra n. 61. Kvochak, Salem Orthopedic Surgeons, Inc. v. Quinn: Express Contract Actions (1980), 16 New Eng. L.R. 93. In general see Louisell and Williams, supra n. 38 at 225-27.

71 Nathan, Medical Negligence 16 (1957).

72 Myers v. Brent Cross Service Co., [1934] 1 K.B. 46.

73 Dodd v. Wilson, [1946] 2 All E.R. 691 (K.B.D.).

74 Nathan, supra n. 71 at 17-18. Note that in an English case, Samuels v. Davis, [1943] 1 K.B. 526 (C.A.), it was suggested that a doctor could be liable for supplying defective equipment.

75 Waddams, Products Liability 92-93 (1974).

76 U.S. courts have dealt with this by holding that there can be no strict liability unless there is a sale of product rather than a service or supply of it. So the supply of tainted blood by hospitals has been held to be a service, not a sale, resulting in no liability. See Waddams, id. at 40.

Thus, the contract action remains the silent, but perhaps potentially stronger companion of the negligence action; whether it would be acceptable in Canadian courts remains to be seen.[77]

5.   DEFAMATION[78]

Although there have been very few cases of defamation[79] brought against doctors, the action seems to be of concern to many and is a potential basis of liability.

A defamatory statement is any communication, oral or written, which would cause a person to be "shunned, avoided or discredited."[80]

In the words of Salmond:[81]

> The typical form of defamation is an attack upon the moral character of the plaintiff, attributing to him any form of disgraceful conduct, such as crime, dishonesty, untruthfulness, ingratitude or cruelty. But a statement may be defamatory if it tends to bring the plaintiff into ridicule or contempt even though there is no suggestion of any form of misconduct.

The statement must be "published,"[82] or communicated, to a third party and must refer to the person defamed.[83] The person to whom publication is made must understand what is said but whether he believes it or not is irrelevant.[84]

In some jurisdictions in Canada, special legislation with respect to defamation has been enacted, and such statutes provide that a plaintiff need not prove his damage in such actions.[85]

However, in the other jurisdictions the plaintiff must prove his damage unless the defamatory material constitutes libel, that is, it takes a permanent

---

77 Note that it seems the most likely cases to succeed will involve elective procedures such as plastic surgery (see *LaFleur v. Cornelis supra* n. 60) or sterilization (*see Doiron v. Orr* (1978), 86 D.L.R. (3d) 719 (Ont. H.C.); *Dendaas (Tylor) v. Yackel* (1980), 12 C.C.L.T. 147 (B.C.S.C.); Dickens, *Medico-Legal Aspects of Family Law* 21 (1979). For an excellent discussion of the U.S. cases *see* Robertson, *Civil Liability Arising From "Wrongful Birth" Following an Unsuccessful Sterilization Operation* (1977), 4 Am. J. Law & Med. 131 at 145).

78 For a discussion of this area of tort law *see* Williams, *The Law of Defamation in Canada* (1976). *See also* Grange, *The Silent Doctor v. The Duty To Speak* (1973), 11 Osgoode Hall L.J. 81.

79 This is true even in the U.S. *See* Waltz and Inbau, *Medical Jurisprudence* 263, MacMillan Co., New York (1971), for the report of a very early Canadian case where one doctor was held liable for defaming another by calling him a "butcher". *See also* Riddell, *A Medical Slander Case in Upper Canada 85 Years Ago* (1912-13), 46 Lancet 330.

80 Williams, *supra* n. 78 at 6. Note that a College of Pysicians and Surgeons has been held to be entitled to sue for defamation: *College of Physicians & Surgeons of Sask. v. Co-Op Commonwealth Federation Publishing Etc. Co.* (1965), 52 W.W.R. 65 at 77 (Sask. Q.B.).

81 *Salmond on Torts* 133 (18th ed. Heuston 1981).

82 *See* Williams, *supra* n. 78 at 58-68.

83 *Id.* at 11-13.

84 Fleming, *supra* n. 1 at 508.

85 Williams, *supra* n. 78 at 50.

written form,[86] or unless the case involves an imputation:[87]

(1) which adversely reflects upon the plaintiff's business, trade, profession or calling;[88]

(2) that the plaintiff committed a serious crime;[89]

(3) that the plaintiff, if a woman, is unchaste;[90]

(4) that the plaintiff has or had a contagious or infectious disease.[91]

Of the defences to the action available we will discuss only the two most likely to avail a doctor: justification and privilege.

It is important to remember that a defamatory statement is by definition *false*. Therefore, the most obvious defence is to prove that the statement is true. This, the defence of justification, does, however, constitute the most dangerous defence to adopt for two reasons. First, in order to prove that what he said was true, in both substance and fact,[92] the defendant must prove some elements of defamation which will work to his disadvantage if he is unable ultimately to prove truth.[93] Second, should the truth defence fail, the damages awarded to the plaintiff may be increased, as the defendant's insistence on the truth of what he said will have tended to exacerbate the situation.

The defence of privilege[94] is of two kinds, absolute and qualified. A statement which is absolutely privileged cannot be used by anyone as the basis for a defamation action. Such statements are, among others, those made in preparation for and during the course of a judicial proceeding such as a hearing or a trial.[95]

---

86 The historical importance of libel and slander and the modern differences are discussed in Williams, *supra* n. 78 at 53-55.

87 Williams, *supra* n. 78 at 50-53.

88 *See, for example, Warren v. Green* (1958), 25 W.W.R. 563 (Alta. S.C.), where the defendant, at a meeting of the hospital district ratepayers, referred to the plaintiff doctor as a "quack". The court found the doctor to have been defamed.

89 *See, for example, Willows v. Williams*, [1950] 2 W.W.R. 657 (Alta. S.C.), where it was held that a nurse was defamed by the Chairman of a hospital board who alleged that she trafficked in narcotics.

90 *See C. v. D.* (1924), 56 O.L.R. 209 (H.C.), where the defendant doctor told the plaintiff patient, her father, and her employer that she had a venereal disease. However, qualified privilege was accepted as a defence.

91 *See R. v. Z.*, [1947] Que. K.B. 457 (C.A.), where the plaintiff succeeded in a defamation action against the government because the manner in which its doctor employee arranged to examine him led to rumours that he had a venereal disease, which he did not.

92 *See, for example, Sabapathi v. Huntley*, [1938] 1 W.W.R. 817 at 827 (P.C.).

93 Williams, *supra* n. 78 at 117.

94 The meaning of "privilege" as it is used here ought to be distinguished from that which it carried in Chapter 1. In that context, "privileged" describes a relationship such that at least one of the parties to it will not be required by court to divulge communications made within it. In this context, "privileged" describes circumstances in which a person uttering defamatory words will not be held liable in defamation for the utterance.

95 *See Foran v. Richman* (1975), 64 D.L.R. (3d) 230 (Ont. C.A.), where letters written by a doctor to a patient's lawyer to assist in preparing for trial were held to be occasions of absolute privilege.

Of greater interest to the doctor is the defence of qualified privilege. A statement made or written on certain occasions is not actionable provided it is made without malice, that is, spite or ill-will.[96] Such statements include those made:

(1) in performing a duty;

(2) in protecting an interest (such as property or reputation);

(3) in a fair and accurate report of proceedings in a court or other tribunal (for example, a General Medical Council);

(4) in a confidential communication arising out of a professional relationship.

Many doctor-patient communications fall into the first and last categories. To be covered by the first, the speaker or writer must have a legal, moral or social duty to make the comment and the recipient must have a corresponding interest in receiving it. Some examples exist in the few Canadian cases. In *Arnott v. College of Physicians & Surgeons of Sask.,*[97] a statement in a provincial medical journal that certain treatment was quackery was held to be privileged because the defendant College had a duty to make it and the doctors had a corresponding interest in receiving it. In *C. v. D.,*[98] the defendant was the family doctor to the plaintiff, her father and her employer. A man the doctor was treating for venereal disease named the plaintiff as the source of his infection whereupon the doctor told the employer that the plaintiff had an "infectious disease" and told her father that she had venereal disease. She did not, and sued. The doctor raised the defence of qualified privilege, and the court held that the doctor had a moral duty to warn those parties that he did of this dangerous disease and that they had a corresponding interest in receiving the information. It was further held that failure to examine the patient before making the statements did not show malice. Thus, the doctor was not liable for defamation because the statements were made in a privileged situation. In *Foran v. Richman,*[99] although the patient's action was barred by the limitation legislation, the Ontario Court of Appeal outlined that entries by a doctor on a hospital record referring to an earlier whiplash injury which had brought the patient "a high compensation" and erroneous statements in an insurance claim that she had been disagnosed by two psychiatrists as a hypochondriac were made on occasions of qualified privilege. The patient could not discharge the onus on her to establish malice.

---

96 *McLoughlin v. Kutasy* (1979), 97 D.L.R. (3d) 620 (S.C.C.). See also *Sabapathi v. Huntley supra* n. 92 where malice was found when a defendant sent a letter to his business association condemning his medical treatment by the plaintiff doctor. Note, also, it is the nature of the occasion, rather than the statement, which is privileged: Williams, *supra* n. 78 at 71.

97 [1954] S.C.R. 538.

98 *Supra* n. 90.

99 *Supra* n. 95. Leave to appeal to Supreme Court of Canada dismissed May 3, 1976.

This applied also in *McLoughlin v. Kutasy.*[99A] Although the trial jury found malice and a minority of the Supreme Court of Canada agreed, the majority held there was no malice shown by the "project" doctor's medical report rejecting the plaintiff for employment. It was found that statements that the plaintiff was a "psychopathic personality," "would be dangerous" and "had no comprehension of the responsibilities involved" in the job were made on an occasion of qualified privilege.

An important Canadian case, *Halls v. Mitchell,*[100] besides discussing the reciprocal duty and interest which was the basis for the decision in *C. v. D.*, went on to deal with the effect of the confidential communication made in the course of a professional relationship.[101] At the time the issue of defamation arose, the defendant doctor was the medical officer for the plaintiff's employer, but at an earlier time he had been the plaintiff's personal physician. While investigating the plaintiff's claim for workers' compensation, the doctor communicated to others that the plaintiff had stated to him during this earlier time that he had suffered from a venereal disease. In fact, none of this was true. The court warned that secrets acquired from a patient should not be divulged.[102] These statements of the Supreme Court of Canada are sufficiently broad that one author has concluded that a qualified privilege extends to confidential communications made in the course of a doctor-patient relationship.[103]

From a doctor's perspective, it should be borne in mind that defamatory communciations about a patient to a colleague, to a public health agency, to a member of the patient's family, or even to a member of the public will likely be covered by qualified privilege, in the absence of malice, so long as there is a duty to reveal and a reciprocal interest in obtaining the information. Similarly, criticism of colleagues will be privileged in these circumstances.[104]

However, from a patient's point of view, it is wiser to express dissatisfaction with professional services to the College of Physicians and Surgeons, since the law is extremely protective of the reputation of professionals.[105]

99A *McLoughlin v. Kutasy* (1979), 97 D.L.R. (3d) 620 (S.C.C.).
100 [1928] S.C.R. 125.
101 *Supra* Chapter 1.
102 *See supra* Chapter 1.
103 Williams, *supra* n. 78 at 94.
104 Note that a doctor may be protected by legislation in relation to communications made in good faith as a member of a hospital medical staff review committee. *See* Hospitals Act, R.S.A. 1980, c. H-11, s. 31.
105 Note that the British Medical Defence Union has advised against doctors' rushing into defamation actions. *See* Medical Defence Union, *Law and the Doctor* 41 (1975).

3

Consent

1. INTRODUCTION

For centuries the law has protected the right to be free from offensive bodily contact,[1] but since touching is a necessary and often enjoyable incident of living in society, it is also recognized that an individual may waive his strict right to bodily security. So a person who consents to being kissed in a movie, body-checked in a sporting event, or jostled in a crowded bus cannot collect damages for the torts of assault and battery.[2]

---

1 *Salmond on Torts* 113 (18th ed. Heuston 1981); *See* Garant, *Fundamental Freedom and Natural Justice* (Sec. 7) in *The Canadian Charter of Rights and Freedoms* 257-75 (ed. Tarnopolsky & Beaudoin 1982) for a discussion of the possible implications of the Canadian Charter of Rights and Freedoms.

2 For a discussion of assault and battery, *see supra* Chapter 2.

Physical contact with the patient is essential in virtually all medical treatment.[3] The doctor may need to palpate the abdomen, use a tongue depressor, or attach the electrodes of an electrocardiograph. In these examples, the patient may have given more than mere passive consent and actually have requested the examination or procedure. "Every human being of adult years and sound mind has a right to determine what shall be done with his own body"[4] so it might seem that bodily contact in medical situations differs little from that in social or sports situations. But there is an important difference in that the parties are not in an equal position because the doctor is far more knowledgeable about the condition of the body involved than the patient himself.[5] In the past, when the doctor occupied a paternal role, there were fewer problems with consent because most patients expected and accepted his direction. While some modern patients continue to accept this traditional model of the doctor-patient relationship, many do not, and want to know more about the medical treatment or procedure involved. Furthermore, recent pronouncements by the Supreme Court of Canada[6] give a patient the right to a thorough disclosure of information.

On one side is the patient who has the right to examination, diagnosis, advice and consultation[7] and, specifically, the right to a full explanation of any treatment or procedure.[8] He is presently being told that he is a consumer of medical services and that his rights are not being respected by health care professionals.[9]

On the other side is the doctor who is highly trained to carry out complicated treatment with sophisticated tools. The nature of the explanation given to a patient about to undergo a dangerous or complicated procedure may be part of the treatment of therapy because his response to it might affect the results.[10] There are those who believe the doctor is in the best position "to balance the patient's interest in his own body with the responsibility for the

---

3 For a discussion of the situation where there is no touching, as where the medical treatment involves the patient taking drugs, *see* Gilborn, *Legal Problems Involved in the Prescription of Contraceptives to Unmarried Minors in Alberta* (1974), 12 A.L.R. 359 at 370 where the author concludes that it is not settled "[w]hether or not the giving of a pill could amount to such an 'application of force' as to constitute the tort of battery . . . " *See also* Rozovsky, *Informed Consent and Investigational Drugs* (1977), 1 L. Med. Q. 162 at 163.

4 *Schloendorf v. New York Hosp.* (1914), 211 N.Y. 125 at 129, 105 N.E. 92 at 93 (N.Y.C.A.).

5 *Kenny v. Lockwood*, [1932] 1 D.L.R. 507 at 520 (Ont. C.A.).

6 *Reibl v. Hughes* (1980), 14 C.C.L.T. 1 (S.C.C.); *Hopp v. Lepp* (1980), 112 D.L.R. (3d) 67 (S.C.C.); discussed *infra*.

7 *Parmley v. Parmley*, [1945] 4 D.L.R. 81 (S.C.C.).

8 *Reibl v. Hughes supra* n. 6.

9 *See* Rozovsky, *The Canadian Patient's Book of Rights* (1980); Storch, *Patient's Rights* (1982); Coy, *Informed Consent — the Patient's Perspective* (1981), 2 H.L. in C. 55; *see also Medical Malpractice* (1977), 43 Consumer Reports 544, 598 and 674; Annas, *Patient's Rights* (1976), Harvard L.S. Bull. 31.

10 *McLean v. Weir* (1977), 3 C.C.L.T. 87 (B.C.S.C.); affirmed [1980] 4 W.W.R. 330 (B.C.C.A.).

exercise of judgment by the doctor,''[11] and that the patient is not assisted, but rather the doctor is "cribbed and confined" by "participatory democracy and egalitarianism''[12] which is the basis for requiring a full, informed consent by a patient.

This variance between the expectations and attitudes of doctors and patients with respect to consent to medical care has precipitated a change in the law which will be discussed.

2.   FORMS OF CONSENT

(a)   Express Consent

Consent may be express in an oral or written form, but to say it is express does not necessarily mean it is explicit. This is especially true of oral consent. Rarely would a patient say, "I consent to a subclavian angiogram being carried out on my person by D. at the B. Hospital on C. date." His reply is likely to be a word or phrase indicating agreement or acquiescence.

Consent need not be written but this form may be more precise and provides some evidence that the patient's permission has been obtained.[13] It is the practice of most hospitals to obtain consent in writing, especially for major treatment such as surgery,[14] and in some jurisdictions, it is a requirement.[15] Many prototypes are available,[16] but even the most carefully worded, thorough form is worthless if the patient's consent lacks one of the prerequisites for validity.[17] Many forms presently in use are "blanket consents" authorizing unspecified additional or alternative procedures. Such a broadly worded consent might be so indefinite that a court would give it little weight.[18] A

---

11 Scott, *Report of General Counsel for the Year 1976* in Canadian Medical Protective Association, *Annual Report* 25 at 26 (1977).

12 *Id.* at 35.

13 *See Doiron v. Orr* (1978), 86 D.L.R. (3d) 719 (Ont. H.C.).

14 Rozovsky, *Canadian Hospital Law* 51 (1979).

15 *See, for example,* R. Regs. Man. 1970, Reg. P130-R1, s. 6; N.B. Reg. 66/47 as amended, s. 40; R.R.O. 1980, Reg. 862, s. 50; R.R.Q., c. S-5, s. 58; Sask. Reg. 331/79, s. 55. *See also Schweizer v. Central Hosp.* (1974), 6 O.R. (2d) 606 (H.C.).

16 *Supra* n. 14 at 54. *Canadian Health Facilities Law Guide* 1180 (1983). See also, Medical Defence Union, *Consent to Treatment* 13-23 (1974), for a complete set of forms. *See* Dickens, *The Modern Law of Informed Consent* (1982), 37 Modern Medicine of Canada 706 where a suggestion is made for an "information form" with a tear-off portion so the patient may retain the body of the form. Note that normally a witness to the signature of a patient is only attesting to that fact. *See* Somerville, *Structuring the Issues in Informed Consent* (1981), 26 McGill L.J. 740 at 788.

17 Discussed *infra; see also* Somerville, *Consent to Medical Care* 45 (L.R.C. 1979).

18 *Hajgato v. London Health Assn.* (1982), 36 O.R. (2d) 669 at 679 (H.C.); *Bickford v. Stiles* (1981), 128 D.L.R. (3d) 516 at 520 (N.B.Q.B.); *Kelly v. Hazlett* (1976), 1 C.C.L.T. 1 (Ont. H.C.); *Rogers v. Lumberman's Mutual* (1960), 119 So. (2d) 649 (La. C.A.); *Valdez v. Percy* (1939), 35 Cal. App. (2d) 485, 96 P. (2d) 142 (Cal. D.C.A.). Note that a written consent,

piece of paper is not a substitute for the rapport of doctor and patient which should precede the obtaining of consent. However, in practice, consent is more often implied than express.

(b) Implied Consent

Most consent to medical treatment is implied from the words or conduct of the patient.[19]

It is not hard to imply consent in the case of the patient who presents his arm for an injection,[20] or opens his mouth for an examination.[21] But it is sometimes difficult, especially in retrospect, for the doctor and patient to agree on the extent of the implied consent.[22]

For example, in *Reynen v. Antonenko*,[23] the plaintiff was taken to hospital by police to submit to a rectal search for drugs. At the hospital he removed his clothes and assumed the requested position. The defendant doctor performed the examination both by finger and sigmoidoscope and found drugs. The plaintiff sued the doctor for battery but the trial judge found that there had been an implied consent on the basis of the plaintiff's conduct and his words, "Let's go to the hospital," uttered when he was given the choice by the police either to remove the drugs himself or be taken to hospital. There was also testimony by the doctor that such an examination would have been impossible without the patient's cooperation.

There is no legal or medical test to determine how much can be implied from what a patient says or does.[24] It is not quite clear whether a subjective or objective[25] standard is to be applied to the patient.

A subjective test would require that all the characteristics of the particular patient be considered. This requires a doctor to know his patient fairly well. However, an objective test would only consider what a "reasonable person" would be consenting to by words or conduct, and would be consistent with the test propounded by the Supreme Court of Canada for determining whether consent is informed.[26] But the final choice of an appropriate test or an enunciation of clear guidelines awaits judicial determination.

---

even if ineffective as proof of consent, may be evidence of a waiver of an explanation of the risks. *See* Somerville, *Structuring The Issues in Informed Consent* (1981), McGill L.J. 740 at 790.

19 *Marshall v. Curry*, [1933] 3 D.L.R. 260 at 274 (N.S.S.C.).

20 *O'Brien v. Cunard S.S. Co.* (1891), 154 Mass. 272, 28 N.E. 266 (Mass. S.C.).

21 *See* Medical Defence Union, *Law and the Dental Practitioner* 7 (1974).

22 *See, for example, Allan v. New Mount Sinai* (1980), 11 C.C.L.T. 299 (Ont. H.C.) and Picard, *Annotation* (1980), 12 C.C.L.T. 1.

23 (1975), 30 C.R.N.S. 135 (Alta. S.C.).

24 *See* Rozovsky, *supra* n. 14 at 36. He suggests an objective test as a "useful guide".

25 *See* Nathan, *Medical Negligence* 160 (1957).

26 *See infra.*

Because most conflicts over implied consent are reduced to contests over who has the best evidence, and in view of the fact that trials may occur years after the event, a prudent doctor after obtaining the patient's consent ought to get it in writing from the patient, or note the words or actions from which consent is implied. The presence of a reliable witness can also be valuable.[27]

3.   SPECIAL SITUATIONS

(a) Emergencies

A person may be unable to give consent due to unconsciousness or extreme illness. In such circumstances a doctor is justified in proceeding without the patient's consent, subject to a number of restrictions.[28]

While the legal basis for substituting the doctor's decision for that of the patient has been debated by academics,[29] Canadian judges have taken a realistic approach. Refusing to strain the law to find consent, the courts have recognized that sometimes a doctor may proceed without consent.[30]

A few important Canadian cases illustrate the limits of this emergency doctrine.

In *Marshall v. Curry*,[31] the doctor discovered a grossly diseased testicle in the course of a hernia repair operation. He removed the testicle, firstly because it was necessary for the hernia repair, and secondly because he judged it potentially gangrenous and therefore a menace to the patient's life and health. Because the patient was under general anaesthetic, the doctor proceeded without consent, and subsequently was sued for battery.[32] Prior to this case it had been held that in emergencies, the doctor became the patient's representative with authority to give his consent on the patient's behalf. Here the court refused to employ this reasoning and instead justified the doctor's action in emergency circumstances on "the higher ground of duty."[33] The

---

27 *See* Medical Defence Union, *supra* n. 21 at 7.

28 See *Reibl v. Hughes* (1980), 14 C.C.L.T. 1 at 13 (S.C.C.) where Laskin C.J. said that "actions of battery in respect of surgical or other medical treatment should be confined to cases where surgery or treatment has been performed or given to which there has been no consent at all or where, *emergency situations aside*, surgery or treatment has been performed or given beyond that to which there is consent." [emphasis supplied.]

29 For an excellent discussion, *See* Skegg, *A Justification for Medical Procedures Performed Without Consent*, [1974] 90 L.Q. Rev. 512; *see also* Rodgers-Magnet, *The Right to Emergency Medical Assistance in the Province of Quebec* (1980), 40 R. du B. 373 at 411.

30 *Marshall v. Curry supra* n. 19; Note that in some provinces the nurse or doctor who renders emergency care without expecting compensation where facilities are inadequate must be grossly negligent before she or he would be liable. *See* Emergency Medical Aid Act, R.S.A. 1980, c. E-9; Emergency Medical Aid Act, S.N. 1971, No. 15, s. 3; Emergency Medical Aid Act, R.S.S. 1978, c. E-8 , s. 3; Medical Act, S.N.S. 1969, c. 15, s. 38.

31 *Id.*

32 Note that negligence was alleged in the pleadings but not proceeded with at trial. *Id.* at 263.

33 *Id.* at 275.

Chief Justice of Nova Scotia said that "where a great emergency which could not be anticipated arises" a doctor can act without consent "in order to save the life or preserve the health of the patient."[34] The action against the doctor was dismissed.

However, in *Murray v. McMurchy*,[35] a doctor who tied a patient's fallopian tubes because he had discovered fibroid tumours in the uterine wall during a Caesarian section, and was concerned about the hazards of a second pregnancy, was held liable. The trial judge found that while it was convenient to carry out the procedure at that time, there was no evidence that the tumours were an immediate danger to the patient's life or health.

Similarly, in *Parmley v. Parmley*,[36] in which a patient requested the removal of two teeth and the defendant dentist extracted all of her upper teeth because he found advanced tooth decay and pyorrhea in the gums, the court held the dentist liable. Again there was no evidence of emergency and thus no basis for proceeding without consent. However, an important *obiter* comment was made in the case:[37]

> There are times under circumstances of emergency when both doctors and dentists must exercise their professional skill and ability without the consent which is required in the ordinary case. Upon such occasions *great latitude may be given to the doctor or dentist.* [emphasis supplied]

A reconciliation of these cases leads to the principle that consent is unnecessary only where the procedure or treatment is required in order to save life or preserve health. Consent is required on all other occasions and it is no answer for the doctor to say that it was more convenient to perform the unauthorized procedure at that time or that he believed it was then that the patient would have wanted it done.[38]

In short, our Canadian courts differentiate between a procedure that is "necessary" and one that is "convenient".

(b) Refusal to Consent

A patient has the right to refuse medical treatment.[39]

---

34 *Id.* at 275. *But see Boase v. Paul*, [1931] 1 D.L.R. 562; affirmed [1931] 4 D.L.R. 435 (Ont. C.A.).

35 [1949] 2 D.L.R. 442 (B.C.S.C.).

36 [1945] 4 D.L.R. 81 (S.C.C.).

37 *Id.* at 89. *See also* Skegg, *supra* n. 29.

38 In *Murray v. McMurchy supra* n. 35, a witness testified that 97 per cent of patients would be annoyed if the additional procedure of removing the tumours had not been taken.

39 *Mulloy v. Hop Sang*, [1935] 1 W.W.R. 714 (Alta. C.A.); *Masny v. Carter-Halls Aldinger Co. Ltd.*, [1929] 3 W.W.R. 741 (Sask. K.B.); *Allan v. New Mount Sinai* (1980), 11 C.C.L.T. 299 (Ont. H.C.); time for amended pleadings granted (1980), 19 C.C.L.T. 76 (Ont. C.A.); *Laporte v. Langanier J.S.P et al*, [1972] 18 C.R.N.S. 357 (Que. Q.B.); Dickens, *The Right to a Natural Death* (1981), 26 McGill L.J. 847 at 876; Magnet, *Withholding Treatment from Defective Newborns: Legal Aspects* (1982), 42 R. du B. 187 at 216; Kouri, *Blood Transfusions, Jehovah's Witnesses and the Rule of Inviolability of the*

This right is circumscribed by legislation where society is in need of protection as in the case of certain communicable diseases.[40] There is also legislation precluding the refusal of beneficial medical treatment by certain members of society.[41] In some provinces, mental health legislation dispenses with the need for consent to treatment by a person brought within its scope.[42]

The Criminal Code[43] requires that necessaries of life be provided by parent or guardian for a child under 16 years of age, and by anyone for a person under his charge who is by reason of age, illness, or insanity, unable to provide for himself. Necessaries of life have been held to include medical care.[44] Thus, parents of minors under 16 and guardians of adults not competent to consent who fail to provide or refuse to provide medical treatment for those under their care could face criminal charges. Moreover, provincial child welfare legislation[45] allows a child who is not receiving required medical treatment to be made a ward of the government so that consent may be given on his behalf.

The right of a mature or emancipated minor to refuse beneficial or life-saving medical treatment is unclear.[46] In those provinces with statutes

---

Human Body (1974), 5 R.D.U.S. 157 at 158; *Medical Treatment and Criminal Law* 70-73 (L.R.C. 1980). For a discussion of dissention in the province of Quebec, *see* Rodgers-Magnet, *The Right to Emergency Medical Assistance in the Province of Quebec* (1980), 40 R. du B. 413 at 447 (FN 154); *see also* Somerville, *Consent to Medical Care* 39 (L.R.C. 1979); as to the right of the police to seize blood *see Capostinsky v. Olsen* (1981), 27 B.C.L.R. 97 (S.C.); *R. v. Carter* (1982), 144 D.L.R. (3d) 301 (Ont. C.A.); *R. v. Santa*, [1983] Sask. D. 6075-01 (Sask. Prov. Ct.). Note that legislation for the mandatory taking of blood samples has been put before Parliament. *See Report on Investigative Tests: Alcohol, drugs and driving offences* (L.R.C. 1983). B.C. and Saskatchewan, meanwhile, have enacted legislation.

40 *See* Venereal Diseases Prevention Act, R.S.A. 1980, c. V-2, ss. 2, 8; Tuberculosis Act, R.S.A. 1980, c. T-11, s. 7.

41 *See, for example,* the following statutes authorizing medical care or examinations without consent in certain circumstances: Corrections Act, R.S.A. 1980, c. C-26, s. 33; Occupational Health and Safety Act, R.S.A. 1980, c. O-2, s. 15 [am. 1983, c. 39, ss. 19, 20]; Dependent Adults Act, R.S.A. 1980, c. D-32, s. 10.1 [en. 1980 (Supp.), c. 6, s. 10].

42 For a list of such legislation and critical comment, *see* Schiffer, *Psychiatry Behind Bars, A Legal Perspective* 180-81 (1982). *See also Re Osinchuk* (1983), 45 A.R. 132 (Surr. Ct.).

43 R.S.C. 1970, c. C-34, s. 197 [am. 1974-75-76, c. 66, s. 8].

44 *See Medical Treatment and Criminal Law* 23 (L.R.C. 1980) for a list of cases. Family and Child Services Act, 1981 (P.E.I.) c. 12, s. 1(2)(*f*). But note that s. 197 *id.* does not require an institution to force feed a conscious patient. *A.G.B.C. v. Astaforoff*, [1983] 6 W.W.R. 322 (B.C.S.C.).

45 *See, for example,* Child Welfare Act, R.S.A. 1980, c. C-8; Note that in Ontario and P.E.I. a court proceeding is necessary before treatment may be authorized and this slows down the process.

46 By Lord Nathan's test it would seem impossible, *see infra* 4(b)(i) Minors. However, it is arguable that true capacity to consent includes the right not to consent. Minors can consent to risks in other activities; *see* Bowker, *Legal Liability to Volunteers in Testing New Drugs* (1963), C.M.A.J. 745 at 748; *see* Dickens, *Medico-Legal Aspects of Family Law* 110-11 (1979). Note that to force unwanted treatment may offend s. 12 of the Charter of Rights and Freedoms and be "cruel and unusual treatment." For the situation in Quebec, *see* Kouri,

setting an age for consent, only beneficial treatment seems anticipated.[47]

A refusal of treatment by a minor or mentally disabled adult with capacity may well put that capacity in question[48] especially where the consequences are health or life threatening. Consultation with a parent, child welfare authorities, or a public trustee, should be considered until the limits of consent in these cases are clarified.[49]

Some Canadian cases have dealt with refusal to consent. In an Alberta case, *Mulloy v. Hop Sang,*[50] a doctor found an amputation to be necessary and performed it despite the patient's objections to an amputation on two occasions. The court agreed that the surgery was necessary and satisfactorily performed but held the doctor liable in battery for performing an unauthorized operation. In a 1929 Saskatchewan case,[51] an employee injured on the job and suing his employer refused surgery that would save his life. The judge expressed regret that there was no legislation to prevent the 29-year-old "self-made martyr [from] going to a self-inflicted death."[52]

The strength of the right to refuse medical treatment is illustrated in a criminal case, *Laporte v. Langaniere J.S.P.,*[53] where a Quebec judge quashed a search warrant which would have allowed a surgical search of an adult accused's body for a bullet without his consent. The judge said to hold otherwise would be "a grotesque perversion of the machinery of justice and an unwarranted invasion upon the basic inviolability of the human person."[54]

Blood Transfusion, Jehovah's Witnesses and the Rule of Inviolability of the Human Body (1974), 5 R.D.U.S. 157 at 169. He states that a minor of 14 or over would likely not be able to refuse an essential blood transfusion although a minor "emancipated by marriage" or judicial order is a possible exception.

47 *See* Medical Consent of Minors Act, S.N.B. 1976, c. M-6.1; Infants Act, R.S.B.C. 1979, c. 196, s. 16; note that in Ontario written consent of a 16-year-old in hospital to a surgical operation is accepted. R.R.O, 1980, Reg. 862, s. 50.

48 *See* Dickens, *The Right to Natural Death* (1981), 26 McGill L.J. 847 at 850; note that under the Dependent Adults Act, R.S.A. 1980, c. D-32, s. 20.1(1) [en. 1980 (Supp.), c. 6, s. 16], where a dependent adult has previously withheld consent, a provision for surrogate consent fails.

49 *See* Dickens, *Medico-Legal Aspects of Family Law* 111 (1979); in Alberta an application might be made under the Dependent Adults Act, R.S.A. 1980, c. D-32, s. 6(1). *See also* *Pentland v. Pentland* (1978), 86 D.L.R. (3d) 585 where evidence that a 17-year-old refused to consent to a blood transfusion seems to have been ignored and the custody order affecting him changed so that his grandmother could consent on his behalf. In a very old case, *Ash v. Ash* (1696), 90 E.R. 526 a daughter of unspecified age successfully sued her mother when she had medical treatment forced upon her by the mother.

50 [1935] 1 W.W.R. 714 (Alta. C.A.).

51 *Masny v. Carter-Malls-Aldinger Co. Ltd.,* [1929] 3 W.W.R. 741 (Sask. K.B.).

52 *Id.* at 745. The judge assessed damages as if the surgery had taken place: $2,500 general damages.

53 [1972] 18 C.R.N.S. 357 (Que. Q.B.). The judge noted that although the surgery would have been without consent, and although there was no urgency, a doctor would be protected from civil and criminal proceedings by the Criminal Code, R.S.C. 1970, c. C-34, s. 25(1)(c).

54 *Id.* at 369.

In a recent case, *Allan v. New Mount Sinai Hosp.*,[55] Mr. Justice Linden found a battery had occurred when a doctor ignored a patient's warning, "Please don't touch my left arm. You'll have nothing but trouble there."[56] The case illustrates the pitfalls of a retrospective interpretation of a patient's words. The doctor may feel he heard merely a concern or extraneous advice while the patient may feel he prohibited or refused a procedure.

There are a number of cases dealing with the right or lack thereof of a parent to refuse medical treatment required by his child.[57] In the majority of cases, parents were members of the Jehovah's Witness faith and believed blood transfusions to be forbidden by the Bible. In *Forsyth v. Children's Aid Soc. of Kingston*,[58] an order declaring a baby a neglected child was granted at a hearing at the hospital and a blood transfusion was given. Later, the order granting temporary wardship to the Children's Aid Society was quashed because of the failure to give the parents reasonable notice and opportunity to call or cross-examine witnesses. In a Saskatchewan case, *Re Wintersgill and Min. of Social Services*,[59] the parents argued that they could provide alternative treatment to blood transfusions. Judge Carter, in granting a temporary wardship order to the Minister, said that while parents are not obliged to provide the best and most modern medical care for a child, they must provide a recognized treatment that is available.

In an Alberta case, *Re D.*,[60] section 2(*a*) of the Canadian Charter of Rights and Freedoms[61] was raised by the parents in support of the argument that the provincial Child Welfare Act was *ultra vires* as offending the guarantee of religious freedom. Judge Catonio ruled that the provincial Act in pith and substance dealt with child welfare and public health, not religion. He said:[62]

55 (1980), 11 C.C.L.T. 299 (Ont. H.C.); Picard, *Annotation* (1980), 12 C.C.L.T. 1. On appeal it was held that as battery had not been pleaded the trial judge erred in placing liability on that ground. The parties were given time to amend their pleadings; (1980), 19 C.C.L.T. 76 (Ont. C.A.).

56 *Id.* at 301.

57 There are also numerous articles, *see* Dickens, *The Medico-Function and Limits of Parental Rights* (1981), L.Q.R. 462; Crepeau, *Le Consentement Du Mineur Mon Matiere De Soins Et Traitements Medicaeux Ou Chirurgicaux Selon Le Droit Civil Canadien* (1974), 52 C.B.R. 247.

58 (1962), 35 D.L.R. (2d) 690 (Ont. H.C.); note that it is quite clear that an adult Jehovah's Witness may refuse a transfusion for himself. *See Re Brook's Estate* (1965), 205 N.E. (2d) 435 (Ill. S.C.); For an excellent discussion, *see* Kouri, *Blood Transfusions, Jehovah's Witnesses and the Rule of Inviolability of the Human Body* (1974), 5 R.D.U.S. 157; note than an American court has ordered that a pregnant Jehovah's Witness accept a blood transfusion *see Raleigh Fitkin - Paul Morgan Memorial Hosp. v. Anderson* (1964), 201 A (2d) 537 (N.J.S.C.). For a comment *see* Kouri, *id.* at 170.

59 (1981), 131 D.L.R. (3d) 184 (Sask. U.F.C.).

60 (1982), 22 Alta. L.R. (2d) 228 (Alta. Prov. Ct.).

61 Constitution Act 1982, Part I.

62 *Supra* n. 60 at 231-32.

As between the state's right to safeguard the health and welfare of children and the rights of parents to freely practise their religion, the former must prevail. If a responsible adult refuses to accept a blood transfusion for himself or herself on religious grounds, the state should not and will not intervene, but when medical treatment, that is, a blood transfusion, is withheld from the offspring of the adult, the state must and has valid legislation to intervene.

In *R. v. Cyrenne*,[63] the legislation in issue was not a provincial child welfare act but the Criminal Code. Parents of a 12-year-old girl and their minister were charged with criminal negligence causing death when they removed the child from hospital and she died. While Judge FitzGerald held that they acted in reckless disregard for the child's life and safety, he said the evidence failed to prove beyond a reasonable doubt that this reckless conduct caused her death. There was not proof beyond a reasonable doubt that a transfusion would have saved her.

In another case, *Pentland v. Pentland*,[64] the minor was 17 and thus beyond the protection of Ontario child welfare legislation. The parents were divorced and the mother was granted custody of the son. She then became a Jehovah's Witness and when the boy required blood, an application was brought to vary the custody order. Although the natural father was willing to consent, custody was granted to the grandmother who assured the court she would consent.

There are also cases where a parent refuses to consent to medical treatment, usually of a newborn, on the basis that his quality of life will be so poor because of his deformities that death is the preferable alternative.[65]

The criteria to be used in deciding such cases is in definition deceptively simple. If the treatment in issue is by medical standards ordinary treatment, consent cannot be withheld.[66] If it is extraordinary, however, neither parent nor doctor can be held liable for not providing it. The decisions of the two courts hearing the *Dawson* case illustrate the dichotomy.[67]

---

63 (1981), 62 C.C.C. (2d) 238 (Ont. D.C.). The mother appears to have testified that the child told her she did not want a transfusion and said "if I die we'll blame the hospital;" *see id* at 255. *Quaere* whether this might have been a mature minor.

64 (1978), 86 D.L.R. (3d) 585 (Ont. Co. Ct.). Judge Winter stated at p. 590: "I hold that every child has the right to life and to the continuation of life so long as is humanly possible." Note that the 17-year-old had refused to consent. This fact seemed to be ignored yet his refusal might have been effective.

65 Parents must be given the opportunity to consent or refuse. For a sad case of medical usurping of parental rights, *see* Stinson, *On the Death of a Baby* (1981), 7 J. of Med. Ethics 5. For a discussion of these issues in the U.S. see Magnet, *Withholding Treatment from Defective Newborns: Legal Aspects* (1982), 42 R. du B. 187 at 244-49. *See also* Annas, *Disconnecting the Baby Doe Hotline* (1983), Hastings Centre Report 14.

66 Note that "ordinary treatment" can be ascertained by reference to custom or approved practice in the medical profession and would fulfill the "best interests of the child" standard or appropriate treatment as required by s. 197 [am. 1974-75-76, c. 66, s. 8] Criminal Code, R.S.C. 1970, c. C-32; *see supra* n. 65 at 208-209 and 221.

67 *See Euthanasia, Aiding Suicide and Cessation of Treatment* 34-36 (L.R.C. 1982) where the dichotomy, used by Pope Pius XII in 1957, is disfavoured by the Law Reform Commission.

In Family Court,[68] the judge held that on the basis of medical evidence, the replacement of a blocked shunt to drain fluid from the brain of seven-year-old Stephen Dawson, who was hydrocephalic and severely handicapped, was extraordinary treatment. Therefore the parents could refuse to consent without breaching thereby either section 197 of the Criminal Code or the Family and Child Service Act. Indeed, the judge found that the surgery suggested would be cruel and unusual treatment as defined in section 12 of the Canadian Charter of Rights and Freedoms.

In the British Columbia Supreme Court,[69] McKenzie J. relied on the *parens patriae*[70] power of the court to hold a new trial. The medical evidence was different and, not surprisingly, so was the legal conclusion. New evidence was adduced that Stephen could survive without the shunt operation in pain and with progressive deterioration. On this basis the court ordered that the surgery be carried out. Although different in result, the decision of each court was consistent with the evidence presented and gives some guidance. The importance of medical evidence in such cases is obvious.

The distinction between ordinary and extraordinary treatment is irrelevant in the case of the competent adult because he can refuse either. When an adult is not competent, his guardian or committee must make the decision and the same principles relied on in the *Dawson* case would apply. Ordinary treatment[71] cannot be refused.

The spectre of a death, which could be delayed or avoided and is not, causes the medical profession great ethical and legal concern. Yet it need not. Civil and criminal law so strongly support the right of the competent adult to refuse treatment even if the consequence is death that the Law Reform Commission has recommended that the right be specifically recognized by the Criminal Code.[72]

Note however that the definition of death proposed by the Commission in another document depends on "ordinary standards of current medical practice," when artificial means of life support have been used. *See Criteria for the Determination of Death* 25 (L.R.C. 1981).

68 *Re S.D.* (1983), 42 B.C.L.R. 153 (Prov. Ct.).

69 *Supt. of Family & Child Service v. R.D. and S.D.* (1983), 42 B.C.L.R. 173 (S.C.). Note that the court found a number of U.S. cases of assistance but especially the case *In the Matter of Karen Quinlan* (1976), 335 A (2d) 647 (N.J.S.C.). Note that this court relied heavily on the English decision, *Re B. (A Minor)*, [1981] 1 W.L.R. 1421 (C.A.) where the court held that surgery on a Down's syndrome child to remove an intestinal blockage was in the child's best interests and must be done.

70 For a discussion *see* Magnet *supra* n. 65 at 215.

71 *See In the Matter of Karen Quinlan supra* n. 69. The categorization of a treatment as ordinary or extraordinary flows, not only from its inherent characteristics but also from its effect on the patient; *see* Dickens, *Right to Natural Death* (1981), 26 McGill L.J. 847 at 856-62. For the applicability of this case to Canadian jurisprudence, *see* Magnet, *supra* n. 65 at 249.

72 *Medical Treatment and Criminal Law* 70-73 (L.R.C. 1980). Note that it is no longer a crime to commit suicide (*see* Criminal Code, R.S.C. 1970, c. C-34, s. 225 [repealed 1972 (Can), c. 13, s. 16]) but it is still an offence to counsel, aid or abet a person to do so. (Criminal

Ethical concerns are alleviated by the Code of Ethics of the Canadian Medical Association which states that the ethical physician "will recognize that the patient has the right to accept or reject any physician and any medical care recommended to him;"[73] "will allow death to occur with dignity and comfort when death of the body appears to be inevitable" and "need not prolong life by unusual or heroic means."[74]

If a patient is given medical treatment in spite of his refusal he has an action in battery. Battery is also the appropriate action where treatment is given beyond that to which there was consent.[75] However, a Canadian court would have some difficulty assessing damages where a doctor by such a battery improved the health or prolonged the life of the patient.[76]

As Professor Dickens has said:[77]

> The basis of compensatory damages is to put the plaintiff into the position in which he would have been had the wrong not occurred. Thus, a plaintiff claiming that a physician's battery or negligence resulted in his wrongful survival and resultant pain and suffering, would have the court measure the difference between his life as it endured and the void of death he was denied. Even if the court would recognize in principle that there may be conditions of life to which death is preferable, it is not easy to see how substantive damages might be calculated in this circumstance. Further, the patient's survival in a vegetative or unconscious state may appear to reduce or eliminate compensation for suffering.

However, a court has the power to award punitive or exemplary damages for a battery "as a means of punishing the defendant for reprehensible conduct in invading the plaintiff's personal rights without justification."[78] Such damages are a means of highlighting unacceptable conduct. It would appear that to

---

Code, s. 224). *See* Evans, *'No Resuscitation' Orders — An Emergency Consensus* (1981), 125 C.M.A.J. 882.

73 C.M.A. (Sept. 1982) s. 5. *See* Magnet *supra* n. 65 at 218 where the point is made that the C.M.A. Code of Ethics is incorporated into the Health Disciplines Act, S.O. 1974, c. 47 [now R.S.O. 1980, c. 196].

74 *Id.* ss. 18 and 19.

75 *Reibl v. Hughes* (1980), 14 C.C.L.T. 1 at 13 (S.C.C.); *Hankai v. York County Hosp.* (1981), 9 A.C.W.S. (2d) 354 (Ont. C.A.). *See* Chapter 3 and *infra*. Note that if a patient has clearly refused treatment the emergency doctrine should not be used to justify treatment. For a view *contra see* Rozovsky, *Canadian Hospital Law* 49 (1979), where the point is made that the patient may have changed his mind; *see also* Dickens, *supra* n. 71 who suggests that there may be a "right of rescue" argument pursuant to s. 45 and s. 7(3) of the Criminal Code.

76 *But see Mulloy v. Hop Sang supra* n. 50 where damages of $50 were awarded in 1932 and said to be "substantial." *See also Cataford v. Moreau*, [1978] 7 C.C.L.T. 241 (Que. S.C.) where damages for a wrongful birth were awarded; For an excellent comment *see* Robertson, *Civil Liability Arising From "Wrongful Birth" Following an Unsuccessful Sterilization Operation* (1977), 4 Am. J. Law Med. 131.

77 Dickens, *The Right to Natural Death* (1981), 26 McGill L.J. 847 at 854. *See also Doiron v. Orr* (1978), 20 O.R. (2d) 71 at 74-75 (Ont. H.C.); *Cataford v. Moreau*, [1978] 7 C.C.L.T. 241 (Que. S.C.).

78 *Hankai v. York County Hosp. supra* n. 75. Nathan, *Medical Negligence* 156 (1957); *See also* Fridman, *Punitive Damages in Tort* (1970), 48 C.B.R. 373; Linden, *Canadian Tort Law* 51-55 (1982). *See Lepp v. Hopp* (1979), 8 C.C.L.T. 260 at 291 where Morrow J.A. notes the possibility of exemplary damages.

force medical treatment on a patient may offend his rights under section 12 of the Canadian Charter of Rights and Freedoms, and is cruel and unusual treatment.[79]

In summary, the medical profession must not usurp the right of a patient to consent[80] nor ignore his refusal to do so.

4.   REQUIREMENTS

Consent must meet certain requirements before it will be an effective defence to an action for battery or negligence.[81] These requirements are that it must be:

(a) given voluntarily;

(b) given by a patient who has capacity;

(c) referable both to the treatment and the person who is to administer that treatment; and

(d) given by a patient who is informed.

A consent which is defective with respect to any one of these requirements will be null: therefore each will be examined in detail.

(a)   Consent Must be Given Voluntarily

While it is true that consent must be the result of freedom of choice, an anxious, ill person, often with a concerned family hovering and advising, will be unable to make a decision without some degree of fear, constraint or duress. However, it is usually easy to identify the extreme cases.[82] A consent is invalid if there was coercion or deceit involved, or a fraudulent misrepresentation as to the nature of the treatment.[83] If a doctor has reason to believe that

---

79 Constitution Act 1982, Part I.

80 Note that in the U.S. a patient's right to autonomy has been protected through the constitutional right to privacy, see Dicksen, supra n. 77 at 855-6.

81 For a discussion of the appropriate cause of action see infra.

82 See Latter v. Braddell (1881), 50 L.J.Q.B. 448 (C.A.) where it was held that a housemaid who submitted most reluctantly to a physical examination order by her employer, had consented to it. This case would be decided differently today.

83 See Re D. and Council of College of Physicians & Surgeons of B.C. (1970), 11 D.L.R. (3d) 570 (B.C.S.C.). See also the American case of Hobbs v. Kizer (1916), 263 F. 681 (U.S.C.A. 8th Ct.). The doctor told the patient he operated for an abscess when, in fact, he performed an abortion. The patient's consent was not valid because of the fraud. Note also that a criminal prosecution may be justified; see R. v. Maurantonio (1967), 65 D.L.R. (2d) 674 (Ont. C.A.) where a conviction for indecent assault was upheld when a man posing as a doctor examined six women; see also Bolduc v. R. (1967), 63 D.L.R. (2d) 82 (S.C.C.) where a doctor examined a woman with a friend present who posed as a doctor. The two were acquitted of indecent assault because the doctor's examination was proper and the friend did not touch the patient.

the consent was given because the patient felt fear or compulsion from others, then he has a duty to discuss the matter with the patient alone.[84]

A difficult situation arises in cases where consent is obtained after the patient has received pre-operative sedation. A number of Canadian cases have dealt with this issue.

In *Beausoleil v. Sisters of Charity*,[85] a patient requiring a disc operation advised the anaesthetist that she wanted a general anaesthetic, not a spinal. This doctor called in the chief anaesthetist who had never examined the patient, but 30 minutes before the operation convinced her over her objections to submit to a spinal. When the patient later sued the chief anaesthetist for paralysis suffered as a result of the spinal, it was held that the consent was not voluntarily given because the patient was sedated and it was clear from her language that the spinal anaesthetic was the doctor's wish, not hers.

It does appear, however, that a patient may give an adequate voluntary consent in spite of having received pre-operative sedation.

In *Kelly v. Hazlett*,[86] the patient had received pre-operative sedation in preparation for surgery involving an ulnar nerve transplant and a cleaning out of the elbow joint when she demanded of the orthopaedic surgeon that he perform an osteotomy as well to straighten her elbow. Against his better judgment, he agreed. Partially as a consequence of the osteotomy, the patient suffered permanent stiffness and sued the surgeon. The court held that in these circumstances it is incumbent on the doctor "to prove affirmatively that the effect of the sedation probably did not adversely affect the patient's understanding of the basic nature of the contemplated operation."[87] It was found that this consent had been *voluntary,* but the doctor was nevertheless held liable because the consent had not been *informed.*

In *MacKinnon v. Ignacio, Lamond and MacKeough*,[88] an anaesthetist first saw his patient in the operating room after she had received a mild tranquilizer, yet Jones J. held her consent to thyroid surgery was "free."[89] Likewise in *Allan v. New Mount Sinai Hosp.*,[90] a patient who had been mildly sedated was held to have had capacity to prohibit the use of her left arm for anaesthetic purposes. In *Ferguson v. Hamilton Civic Hosp.*,[91] Krever J. held

---

84 For an excellent discussion, *see* Somerville, *Consent to Medical Care* 46-58 (L.R.C. 1979). The author states that a subjective test should be used to assess the patient's state of mind and that the burden of proof of the voluntariness of consent is on the doctor.

85 (1964), 53 D.L.R. (2d) 65 (Que. C.A.); *see also Browne v. Lerner* (1940), 48 Man. R. 126 (K.B.).

86 (1976), 1 C.C.L.T. 1 (Ont. H.C.).

87 *Id.* at 32.

88 (1978), 29 N.S.R. (2d) 656 (S.C.).

89 *Id.* at 689.

90 (1980), 11 C.C.L.T. 299 (Ont. H.C.); amendment of pleadings allowed 19 C.C.L.T. 76 (Ont. C.A.).

91 (1983), 23 C.C.L.T. 254 (Ont. H.C.).

that a patient under the effects of "anxiety allaying" medication had voluntarily consented but he endorsed expert medical evidence to the effect that obtaining consent from a sedated person who is "on the table" should be avoided.

In each of these cases, the trial judge based his conclusion on the patient's apparent comprehension of information. But there is an inherent weakness in the evidence used because it usually comes from the defendants or their employees, and even if the patient testifies, his evidence may be suspect because of the medication. Furthermore, the setting and the immediacy of the medical procedure militate against a patient being able to make a free or voluntary decision.

Every effort must be made by doctors to obtain consent in a non-coercive environment from a patient whose judgment is not affected by medication.[92] In cases such as those discussed, there ought to be a rebuttable presumption that the consent was not voluntarily given.[93]

(b) Patient Must have Capacity

A consent will be valid only if given by a patient who has the legal capacity to give it. Thus the consent of a minor or a person not mentally competent by reason of disease or the influence of alcohol or drugs may not be valid.

(i) Minors

A person under the age of majority[94] can consent to medical or dental treatment for his benefit provided that he is capable of appreciating fully the nature and consequences of the particular treatment.[95]

Although this right was recognized in England hundreds of years ago,[96] there is still a reluctance to treat minors without parental consent.[97]

---

92 For a doctor's perspective *see* Stokes, *Consent in Captive Circumstances* (1981), 2 H.L. in C. 83.

93 *See Kelly v. Hazlett supra* n. 86.

94 Note that the common law age of majority of 21 years has been reduced by legislation to 18 years in Alberta, Manitoba, Ontario and Quebec and to 19 years in British Columbia, Saskatchewan and Nova Scotia.

95 Nathan, *supra* n. 78 at 176. Note that Lord Nathan stated that the treatment must be *"bona fide* in the interests of the infant's own health." Bowker, *Minors and Mental Incompetents: Consent to Experimentation, Gifts of Tissue and Sterilization* (1981), 26 McGill L.J. 951; Dickens, *Medico-Legal Aspects of Family Law* 94 (1979); *see also* Bowker, *Legal Liability to Volunteers Testing New Drugs* (1963), 88 C.M.A.J. 745; Gilborn, *Legal Problems Involved In the Prescription of Contraceptives to Unmarried Minors in Alberta* (1974), 12 A.L.R. 359 at 376.

96 Blackstone, *Commentaries on the Laws of England* 454 (1765), quoted in Dickens, *supra* n. 95 at 94; *Gladwell v. Steggall* (1839), 5 Bing N.C. 733; *Ash v. Ash* (1696), 90 E.R. 526; *See also* Somerville, *Consent to Medical Care* 73 L.R.C. (1979).

97 *See* Boldt, *The Provision of Birth Control Services to Unwed Minors: A National Survey of Physician Attitudes and Practices* (1982), 73 Can. J. Pub. Health, where a survey showed

This hesitancy to accept the competency of minors may be the reason for the existence of two tests used to measure the minor's capacity.[98] The "mature minor" is one who meets the requirement of fully appreciating the nature and consequences of beneficial treatment and this requirement is traditionally referred to as the "mature minor rule."[99] An example of a mature minor would be a teenager, living with parents, attending school, with the intelligence and experience to fulfill the "mature minor rule." The "emancipated minor test" is met by the minor who by his lifestyle is assuming the responsibility for his own life. Features of his independence may include: residing away from home, being employed, perhaps being married and a parent, and in general, making his own decisions about important matters.[100] Mature and emancipated minors have the capacity to consent to medical treatment.[101]

Two Canadian cases illustrate the tests. In *Booth v. Toronto Gen. Hosp.*,[102] the consent of a 19-year-old plaintiff to throat surgery was at issue. Chief Justice Falconbridge assessed the plaintiff in these terms:[103]

> He is not of the highest intelligence, but it appears that he was nineteen years of age and capable of taking care of himself.

On the issue of whether this minor was capable of consenting to the treatment he said:[104]

> The only question of law involved was whether the boy's parents should have been consulted, but that was effectively answered, and it has been shewn that he is capable of doing a man's work. Indeed, he is at present doing hard work for 10 hours a day.

The plaintiff's battery action was dismissed[105] on the basis that he was an emancipated minor.[106]

---

physicians were reluctant to provide birth control services or information to minors without parental consent although the demand was great, particularly in Quebec and B.C. *See also* Landau, *Barriers to Consent to Treatment: The Rights of Minors in the Provision of Mental Health Services* (1979), 2 C.J.F.L. 245 where at p. 260 the author, a psychiatrist-lawyer, says "the vague threat of potential liability has acted as a powerful deterrent to [physicians and other health care professionals] offering treatment to adolescents." Note that s. 7 of the Canadian Charter of Rights and Freedoms — "Everyone has the right to life, liberty and security of the person" — might be relevant. *See also* Tarnopolsky and Beaudoin, *The Canadian Charter of Rights and Freedoms* 261 (1982).

98 Dickens, *supra* n. 95 at 96-97; *see also* Rozovsky, *Consent to Treatment* (1973), 11 Osgoode Hall L.J. 103; Wadlington, *Minors and Health Care: The Age of Consent* (1973), 11 Osgoode Hall L.J. 115; Somerville, *Consent to Medical Care* 71-75 (L.R.C. 1979).

99 Wadlington, *supra* n. 98 at 117.

100 McLeod, *Birth Control: The Minor and the Physician* (1980), 16 Q.L.J. 269.

101 A situation of some concern to doctors and nurses is the capacity of the minor mother to consent on behalf of her baby. She may meet either or both tests.

102 (1910), 17 O.W.R. 118 (K.B.).

103 *Id.* at 120. Note that the age of majority was 21 at that time.

104 *Id.* at 120.

105 Falconbridge C.J. said *id.*, that he might have entered a nonsuit against the plaintiff but he felt, in view of the attack on the defendant hospital, that the true story should be brought out.

106 Dickens, *supra* n. 95 at 97. Note that in Quebec emancipation may occur through marriage (Art. 314 C.C.) or by judicial pronouncement (Art. 315 C.C.). For an interesting analysis of the status of a minor *see Blair v. Fundytus* (1978), 11 A.R. 243 (Alta. S.C.).

The plaintiff was 20 years of age in the second case, *Johnston v. Wellesley Hosp.*[107] He consented to treatment for acne by a duly qualified specialist in dermatology. Addy J., looking at whether the consent of the plaintiff's parents or guardian was required, said:[108]

> Although the common law imposes very strict limitations on the capacity of persons under 21 years of age to hold, or rather to divest themselves of, property or to enter into contracts concerning matters other than necessities, it would be ridiculous in this day and age, where the voting age is being reduced generally to 18 years, to state that a person of 20 years of age, who is obviously intelligent and as fully capable of understanding the possible consequences of a medical or surgical procedure as an adult, would, at law, be incapable of consenting thereto. But, regardless of modern trend, I can find nothing in any of the old reported cases, except where infants of tender age or young children were involved, where the Courts have found that a person under 21 years of age was legally incapable of consenting to medical treatment. If a person under 21 years were unable to consent to medical treatment, he would also be incapable of consenting to other types of bodily interference. A proposition purporting to establish that any bodily interference acquiesced in by a youth of 20 years would nevertheless constitute an assault would be absurd.

The plaintiff fit within the mature minor rule. Of interest is the fact that the treatment for acne could be classified as cosmetic and elective. Thus, if there is some benefit to the minor in the treatment it is within his capacity to consent to it.[109]

Although most medical treatment will fulfill the requirement of some benefit to the minor,[110] the prevention and termination of pregnancy is an area where the interests of third parties may complicate the determination of benefit.[111]

Since all legal abortions are therapeutic by virtue of section 251 of the Criminal Code, the benefit for a minor from a therapeutic abortion would seem to be determined by the doctors involved and by the therapeutic abortion committee. Indeed, a parent who refuses to consent or attempts to block a legal abortion may be committing an offence under provincial child welfare laws[112] and section 197 of the Criminal Code. In an English case a pregnant 15-year-old with a baby was held to be competent to consent to a therapeutic abortion and the objection of her parents was overridden by the court.[113] Likewise a doctor or hospital may be in breach of duties to the minor by failing to act on the minor's consent and the abortion committee's decision.[114]

---

107 (1970), 17 D.L.R. (3d) 139 (Ont. H.C.). Note that this case was applied in *Gillick v. West Norfolk and Wisbech Area Health Authority*, The Times 27 July 1983 (Q.B.).

108 *Id.* at 144. Note that the age of majority was 21.

109 Dickens, *supra* n. 95 at 96.

110 For an excellent discussion of the problems associated with minors and mental health care *see* Landau, *Barriers to Consent to Treatment: The Rights of Minors in the Provision of Mental Health Services* (1979), 2 C.J.F.L. 245. Research, transplantation and sterilization are discussed later in this chapter. Note that philanthropic donation of blood may be permissible as giving a psychological benefit. Dickens, *supra* n. 95 at 96.

111 For an excellent discussion, *see* Dickens, *supra* n. 95 at 47-54.

112 *See, for example*, Child Welfare Act, R.S.A. 1980, c. C-8.

113 *Re P. (A Minor)* (1981), 80 Loc. Gov. R. 301 (F.D.).

114 Dickens, *supra* n. 95 at 54.

An assessment of the extent of birth control advice or treatment required by a minor flows from the exchange of information between patient and doctor, and perhaps through examinations and tests.[115] It is from and within this doctor-patient relationship that the decision that there is a benefit to the minor must be made. In a recent English case, it was held that a doctor was not liable for providing contraceptive advice and treatment to a child under 16 (the statutory age of consent). However, the court warned that a doctor must not encourage an under-age child to have intercourse. The doctor must be very careful not to put himself in a position where his own values or those of the parents preclude him from meeting his professional duties to the minor.[116]

Consent by a minor must be informed and a doctor must meet the requirements set out by the Supreme Court of Canada in this regard. The age, situation and maturity of the patient are relevant to the standard and scope of the disclosure.[117]

In summary, a minor who because of maturity could be said to appreciate fully the nature and consequences of treatment or who is emancipated and to whom the requisite disclosure of information has been made can give a valid consent to beneficial medical treatment.[118]

In order to provide some certainty, legislation has been passed in some jurisdictions and proposed in others.[119] In 1972, Quebec passed the Public Health Protection Act[120] which states that care may be provided by a hospital

---

115 For an excellent discussion *see* McLeod, *Birth Control: The Minor and the Physician* (1980), 16 Q.L.J. 269; Gilborn, *Legal Problems Involved in the Prescription of Contraceptives to Unmarried Minors in Alberta* (1974), 12 A.L.R. 359. *See* Sklar, *Teenagers, Birth Control and the Nurse,* Canadian Nurse, Nov. 1978, 14. *See also* the case of *Re Dr. D. and College of Physicians & Surgeons of B.C.* (1970), 11 D.L.R. (3d) 570 (B.C.S.C.) where a 15-year-old without parental consent had an I.U.D. inserted. The issue was the conduct of the doctor in fondling and kissing her. *See also* Dickens, *Medico-Legal Aspects of Family Law* 34 (1979), for a discussion of a similar English case.

116 *Gillick v. West Norfolk & Wisbech Area Health Authority,* The Times, 27 July 1983. For a comment *see* Brahams, *Under-age Girls and Contraception: the Parent's Right to Be Informed,* The Lancet, 6 Aug. 1983 at 350. The minor in such a case has a right to confidentiality; *see* Brahams, *Confidentiality and Under-age Girls Who Seek Contraceptive Advice,* The Lancet, 6 July 1983 at 177.

117 For a discussion of the duties, *see infra.*

118 It is not clear whether a minor has the capacity to refuse life-saving treatment. *See* Dickens, *supra* n. 95 at 110-11.

119 For a more detailed discussion *see* Picard, *Recent Developments in Medical Law* (1977), 3 L. Med. Q. 201; *see also* Wadlington *supra* n. 98; Family Law Reform Act 1969, c. 46, s. 8. *See* Skegg, *Consent to Medical Procedures on Minors* (1973), 36 Mod. L. Rev. 370. *See also Hewer v. Bryant,* [1969] 3 All E.R. 578 (C.A.). In England age 16 has been set: Family Law Reform Act, 1969 (17 Eliz. II), c. 46).

120 Public Health Protection Act, L.R.Q. 1977, c. P-35, s. 42. *See* Joyal-Poupart, *La notion de danger et al protection des mineurs* (1976), 36 R. du B. 495; Crepeau, *Le Consentement Du Mineur au Matiere De Soin et Traitements Medicaux ou Chirurgicaux Selon Le Droit Civil Canadien* (1974), 52 Can. Bar Rev. 247; Castel, *Nature and Effect of Consent With Respect to the Right to Life and the Right to Physical and Mental Integrity in the Medical Field: Criminal and Private Aspects* (1978), 16 A.L.R. 293 at 319.

or physician to a minor 14 years of age or older. But if the minor is sheltered for more than 12 hours or if there is extended treatment, the person having parental authority must be informed.

In 1973, British Columbia added a new section to the Infants Act[121] which provides that the age of consent to medical or dental treatment be 16 years. During debate, an amendment added a subsection making the minor's consent effective only if "a reasonable effort" has been made to get parental consent, or in lieu thereof, if a written opinion is obtained from another practitioner that the treatment is in the best interests of the minor. The physician is empowered to inform the parent that the minor has been treated.

In 1976, New Brunswick accepted the act proposed by the Conference of Commissioners on Uniformity of Legislation in Canada,[122] but excluded procedures for preventing pregnancy from the definition of "medical treatment" (including dental treatment). Thus, the age of consent in New Brunswick is set at 16. Under that age, a minor may consent if there is a second medical opinion to the effect that the minor is "capable of understanding the nature and consequences of the treatment," and it is in his best interests.[123]

Ontario sought a partial solution by regulations under the Public Hospitals Act permitting surgical operations and other treatment in hospitals with the consent of a person of 16 years, or one who is married.[124] Saskatchewan has a similar provision except that the age is set at 18.[125]

Other provinces are looking at the problem and recommendations have been made by the Commissioners on Uniformity,[126] the Law Reform Commission of Saskatchewan,[127] and the Institute of Law Research and Reform in Alberta.[128]

The arbitrary designation of an age at which consent is valid is common to all of the proposed legislative reforms.[129] What then is the status of a minor under the statutory age? The common law is preserved in England by statute,[130] while the effect of the Alberta recommendation is to defeat it.[131] Some

---

121 R.S.B.C. 1979, c. 196, s. 16. For a criticism *see* Gosse, *Consent to Medical Treatment: A Minor Digression* (1974), 9 U.B.C.L. Rev. 56.
122 Proceedings of the Fifty-Seventh Annual Meeting of the Uniform Law Conference of Canada 162 (1975).
123 Medical Consent of Minors Act, S.N.B. 1976, c. M-6.1.
124 R.R.O. 1980, Reg. 862, s. 50
125 R.S.S. 1978, Reg. 331/79, s. 55.
126 *Supra* n. 122.
127 Law Reform Commission of Saskatchewan, *Consent of Minors to Health Care* (1978).
128 Alberta Institute of Law Research and Reform, *Report No. 19, Consent of Minors to Health Care* (1975); note that a discussion paper on consent issued by the Ontario Interministerial Committee on Medical Consent covered consent of minors. *See Options on Medical Consent* 17 (1979).
129 For a criticism of this approach *see* Landau, *Barriers to Consent to Treatment: The Rights of Minors in The Provision of Mental Health Services* (1979), 2 C.J.F.L. 245 at 264.
130 *Supra* n. 119.
131 Bowker, *Minors and Mental Incompetents* (1981), 26 McGill L.J. 951 at 959.

statutes purport to deal with the minor below the age of statutory consent by requiring a second medical opinion.[132] To alleviate the concerns of the health care professions and of hospitals, specific provisions for this group must be made clear in any future legislation.

Although the Alberta Institute of Law Research and Reform report was issued in 1975, no action has been taken on it, and a private members bill on the topic put before the Saskatchewan Legislature in 1973 was defeated.[133] There seems to be great reluctance on the part of government to legislate in the area of consent of minors to health care, and yet the medical profession is extremely insecure about the common law. Unfortunately for minors in most Canadian provinces, the problem remains unresolved.

If a patient does not satisfy the mature or emancipated minor criteria, and is not covered by statute, the doctor ought to obtain the consent of a parent or guardian before treating the minor.[134] Where the parents are divorced, it is the parent with custody of the child whose consent must be sought.[135]

Some concern has been expressed about the situation where the person purporting to consent is neither parent nor guardian, but merely has the child in his care or is *in loco parentis,* for example, the school teacher who brings an injured child to a doctor for treatment. In many of these cases, the doctor will be justified in proceeding because there is an emergency, or because he has a *bona fide* belief that the adult has been vested with authority by the parent or guardian,[136] but in some cases resort to the courts might be necessary with the assistance of provincial social service departments.

Where the minor has capacity to consent, it is valid and ought not to be overridden by an adult's decision to the contrary.[137]

(ii) Adults with a disability

An adult who is not of sound mind cannot give a valid consent.[138] However, a patient under psychiatric care, or a voluntary or involuntary patient in a mental institution may have capacity to consent.[139] A doctor

132 New Brunswick, *supra* n. 123. Saskatchewan Law Reform Commission, *supra* n. 127. Uniform act, *supra* n. 122.
133 Somerville, *supra* n. 98 at 20.
134 Somerville, *supra* n. 98 at 71-75; Skegg, *Consent to Medical Procedures on Minors* (1973), 36 M.L.R. 370. For a case where parental consent was not and should have been obtained *see* Stinson, *On the Death of a Baby* (1981), J. of Med. Ethics 5.
135 *Pentland v. Pentland* (1978), 86 D.L.R. (3d) 585 (Ont. S.C.); *see Kruger v. Kruger* (1979), 11 R.F.L. (2d) 52 at 71-73 (Ont. C.A.).
136 See Tompkins, *Health Care for Minors: The Right to Consent* (1974-75), 40 Sask. L. Rev. 41.
137 Dickens, *supra* n. 95 at 100 and 114. *See also,* Dickens, *The Modern Function and Limit of Parental Rights* (1981), L.Q.R. 462.
138 Frenkel, *Consent of Incompetents (Minors and Mentally Ill) to Medical Treatment* (1977), 3 L.M.Q. 187.
139 Rozovsky, *Canadian Hospital Law* 43 (1979); Marshall *The Physician and Canadian Law*

should be alert to the possibility that a patient may not be competent to consent to medical treatment.[140] There are no statutory or judicial tests to measure such competency, but a test suggested by Sharpe and Sawyer is:[141] "Can the patient appreciate the nature and consequences of the proposed treatment so as to be capable of rendering an informed judgement?" Relevant considerations might include the patient's history and present state of health, interest in and appreciation of alternatives or options, willingness and apparent reliability to assume responsibility, and understanding of benefits and risks.[142]

Because patients about whom there may be a question of competency may be institutionalized, duress and coercion are of special concern and so far as possible should be assessed.[143]

If the doctor is in doubt, he should not depend solely upon an apparent subjective understanding by the patient, but should consult with a psychiatrist. While relatives or friends of the patient may have information to offer, it cannot always be assumed that they are acting in the patient's best interests.[144]

If a patient is not of sound mind or is not competent to consent to medical or dental treatment which is necessary or beneficial,[145] the consent of a substitute is required. There may be provision in provincial legislation for a court-appointed guardian,[146] or for substituted consent by doctors,[147] or a relative,[148] or hospital official.[149] Surrogates of any type must make decisions in the best interests of the patient.

---

33 (1979); Sharpe and Sawyer, *Doctors and the Law* 29 (1978). *See also,* Rozovsky, *New Developments in N.S. Psychiatric Legislation* (1980), Dal. L.J. 505 at 514. For an excellent discussion *see* Schiffer, *Psychiatry Behind Bars* 178-228 (1982). For a discussion of the implications of the Canadian Charter of Rights and Freedoms, *see id.* at 200-201. For legislation protecting this right, *see* Hospitals Act, R.S.N.S. 1967, c. 249 s. 46(1) [en. 1977, c. 45, s. 8].

140 With regard to competence to make a will, *see* Dickson, *Legal Aspects of Competence* (1982), 3 H.L. in C. 69.

141 *Supra* n. 139 at 29. *See also* Rioux, *Sterilization* 116 (L.R.C. 1979). Note that even the President's Commission On Informed Consent, a study requested by the U.S. Congress, did not deal with the position of the institutionalized mentally ill. *See* Lasagna, *The Professional-Patient Dialogue* (1983), Hastings Centre Report 9.

142 Somerville, *Consent to Medical Care* 94 (L.R.C. 1979).

143 For an interesting discussion of the divergence between psychiatrists and lawyers in evaluating the capacity of patients to consent, *see* Kaufmann, Roth, Lidz and Meisel, *Informed Consent and Patient Decisionmaking* (1981), 4 Int. J. Law & Psych. 345.

144 *See* Sharpe & Sawyer *supra* n. 139 at 29. See also *Clark v. Clark* (1982), 3 C.R.R. 342 (Ont. Co. Ct.).

145 In an emergency no consent is required. Experimentation and sterilization are discussed later in this Chapter.

146 *See, for example,* Dependent Adults Act, R.S.A. 1980, c. D-32.

147 *See, for example, id* s. 20.1 [en. 1980 (Supp.), c. 6, s. 16].

148 *See, for example,* Hospitals Act, R.S.N.S. 1967, c. 249, s. 46(2) [en. 1977, c. 45, s. 8]; *Re Boudreau* (1980), 43 N.S.R. (2d) 212 (S.C.)

149 Mental Health Act, R.S.B.C. 1979, c. 256, s. 8(1) [am. 1981, c. 21, s. 44]; *Re Osinchuk* (1983), 45 A.R. 132 (Surr. Ct.). For a thorough review of mental health legislation in various provinces *see* Schiffer, *supra,* n. 139 at 180; *See also* Rozovsky, *supra* n. 139 at 43-44.

In 1978, the Dependent Adults Act was proclaimed in Alberta.[150] This innovative and effective legislation provides for the appointment by a court of a guardian charged with making certain personal decisions on behalf of an adult who is unable to care for himself and make reasonable judgments in respect of his person.[151] One of the powers granted to a guardian is the right to consent to any health care in the best interests of the dependent adult.[152]

In slightly more than three years, there were 2,412 orders granted and a number of applications to the courts.[153] Under the Act, health care is broadly defined[154] and includes any procedure taken for the purpose of preventing pregnancy. The guardian is accountable to the court and the Public Guardian monitors guardianship, may intervene and may, if necessary, assume the role of guardian.[155]

There is also provision in the act for consent when there is no guardian. Where medical or dental treatment is necessary and an adult is unable because of mental or physical incapacity to consent to it, but has never prohibited it, a written consensus of two doctors (or dentists if it is dental care) is adequate.[156]

In 1981, the Act was amended[157] to include a procedure for confining the dependent adult where he is a danger to himself or others, and requires confinement as a proper means of treating his condition. A judge must review the evidence supporting the need for confinement before making the order, and the dependent adult's status is reviewed quarterly by the "place of care" and annually by an appeal panel.[158]

It is not necessary to obtain the consent of one spouse for treatment of the

---

150 R.S.A. 1980, c. D-32.
151 Note, however, Rozovsky's concern about the cost and time involved in guardianship proceedings; *see* Rozovsky, *Consent to Treatment* (1973), 11 O.H.L.J. 103 at 111.
152 s. 9(1)(*h*); *see* Christie, *Guardianship: The Alberta Experience: A Model for Change* (1982), 3 H.L. in C. 58 at 60 where the Public Guardian for the Province of Alberta, Mr. Joel Christie, explains the guardian should consider the following:
    "(1) What are the alternatives to this treatment?
    "(2) What are the risks involved in this treatment?
    "(3) What are the risks if the advised treatment is not carried out?
    "(4) Is this treatment in the best interests of the dependent adult?
    "(5) Is this treatment the least restrictive treatment possible?
    "(6) How does the dependent adult feel about the procedure or treatment?
    "If the guardian feels that a second medical opinion is necessary before he/she makes a decision in this area then, on behalf of the dependent adult, the guardian should obtain one. For more serious operations or medical procedures, the guardian may ask the Court for advice and direction."
153 *Id.* at 64. Unfortunately none of the decisions of which the author is aware have been reported.
154 s. 1(*h*).
155 Christie, *supra* n. 152 at 63. *See Re Osinchuk supra* n. 149 where the powers of the Public Guardian were restricted.
156 s. 20.1 [en. 1980 (Supp.), c. 6, s. 16].
157 s. 10.1 [en. 1980 (Supp.), c. 6, s. 10]. *See* Christie, *supra* n. 152 at 62.
158 *Id.* "Place of care" s. 1(*k*.1) [en. 1980 (Supp.), c. 6, s. 2] is designated by regulation.

other.[159] There is legislation to protect this right in two provinces. The Family Law Reform Act in Ontario states:[160]

A married person has and shall be accorded legal capacity for all purposes and in all respects as if such person were an unmarried person.

Quebec has passed legislation dispensing with the need for consent of "the consort" for the furnishing of services in a health establishment.[161] This is true even where the procedure involved is sterilization or therapeutic abortion.[162] As Professor Dickens stated:[163]

The concept that a father's legal interests are injured by termination of his partner's pregnancy is without foundation in modern times.

While the desirability of shared decision-making by a couple cannot be disputed, each person has the legal right to autonomy over his body.[164]

Unfortunately, doctors and hospitals sometimes hold out to patients that the consent of a spouse is required for treatment. Such representations may be based on a desire to encourage consensus between spouses, or on perceived concerns about legal liability.

However, the fears of doctors and hospitals that successful legal action will result from a failure to obtain spousal or paternal consent are unfounded.[165] Moreover, a representation that spousal consent is required may in fact constitute a misrepresentation or breach of a legal duty owed to the patient.[166]

Prisoners have the same right to accept or refuse medical treatment as any other person.[167] However, Professor Somerville has suggested that compulsory examinations for contagious diseases may be justified as the loss of a right essentially connected with the fact of imprisonment.[168] Hunger strikes

---

159 Jacob, *Speller's Law Relating to Hospitals And Kindred Institutions* 202-204 (1978).

160 R.S.O. 1980, c. 152, s. 65(2). There are similar provisions in three other provinces.

161 Health Services and Social Services Act, R.S.Q. 1977, c. S-5, art. 156.

162 Dickens, *supra* n. 115 at 31, 49; *Medhurst v. Medhurst*, Ont. S.C., 22nd March 1984 (not yet reported); *Whalley v. Whalley* (1981), 122 D.L.R. (3d) 717 (B.C.S.C.); Rozovsky L. and F., *Legal Sex* 20, 25 (1982); Sharpe and Sawyer, *Doctors and the Law* 48 (1978); Bowker, *Minors and Mental Incompetents: Consent to Experimentation, Gifts of Tissue and Sterilization* (1981), 26 McGill L.J. 951 at 973. *See* sterilization *infra*.

163 *Id*. at 49.

164 *Id*. "What cannot be accommodated in law, however, is [the father's] right to prevail over the woman's claim to legal abortion, since this is incompatible with an individual's bodily autonomy and entitlement to health care and protection".

165 Sharpe and Sawyer, *supra* n. 139 at 47-48; Dickens, *supra* n. 115 at 49; *see also* Medical Defence Union *Consent to Treatment* 9 (1974); Jacob, *supra* n. 159.

166 *See* discussion on informed consent. *See also* Constitution Act, 1982, Part I: Canadian Charter of Rights and Freedoms, s. 7.

167 Vandervort, *Medical Treatment of Penitentiary Inmates* (1977), 3 Q.L.J. 368; Somerville, *Consent to Treatment* 95 (L.R.C. 1979); Bowker *Experimentation on Humans and Gifts of Tissue: Articles 20-23 of the Civil Code* (1973), 19 McGill L.J. 166 at 177. *See A.G.B.C. v. Astaforoff*, [1983] 6 W.W.R. 322 (B.C.S.C.); *Freeman v. Home Office*, The Times, 20 May 1983.

168 Somerville, *id*. at 96, 103. *See Maltby v. A.G.Sask.* (1982), 143 D.L.R. (3d) 649 (Sask. Q.B.) which confirms this view.

by prisoners raise ethical dilemmas for the medical profession, but where competence to make that choice and consent to the risks entailed are established, and there is a clear prohibition of medical treatment, the medical profession has no right to intervene and override the patient's decision.[169]

(c) Consent Must be Referable to Both the Treatment and the Person Who is to Administer it

(i) The treatment

It is in the best interests of both the doctor and the patient that they each understand the limits of the consent. The essence of consent is an agreement by the patient to accept the specific risks involved, so it is important that he receive only the treatment to which he has consented. Should more extensive or difficult treatment be rendered, then apart from circumstances of emergency, the patient might be successful in bringing suit against the doctor, even if the unauthorized treatment was beneficial.[170]

The Supreme Court of Canada[171] has held that a doctor has a duty to disclose the nature of a proposed procedure and its gravity. An important element of the nature of the procedure is whether it is elective; this should be disclosed.[172] Although it would seem that sub-procedures or reasonable variations of the procedure would be covered,[173] the onus is on the doctor to establish this by reference to custom or common practice, and to common knowledge on the part of lay persons.[174]

A Manitoba case, *Gorback v. Ting*,[175] indicates that a patient has the right to choose procedures where more than one is medically feasible. In that case, an anaesthetist was held liable for injuries to a patient's teeth and bridge

---

169 *A.G.B.C. v. Astaforoff supra* n. 167; affirmed 47 B.C.L.R. 217 (B.C.C.A.). Dooley-Clarke, *Medical Ethics and Political Protest* (1981), Hastings Center Report 5; Horton, *Forceable Feedings in W. Germany: Medical/Legal Problems* (1982), 22 Med. Sci. Law 235; *see Leigh v. Gladstone* (1909), 26 T.L.R. 139 (K.B.) where women prisoners were force-fed. For a comment *see* Zellick, *The Forcible Feeding of Prisoners: An Examination of the Legality of Enforced Therapy*, [1976] P.L. 153.
170 *See* discussion *infra*.
171 *Hopp v. Lepp* (1980), 112 D.L.R. (3d) 67 (S.C.C.).
172 *Reibl v. Hughes* (1980), 14 C.C.L.T. 1 (S.C.C.). Note that an argument that the "nature" of a test included the likely consequences of alternate responses to the test was rejected. *See Ferguson v. Hamilton Civic Hosp.* (1983), 23 C.C.L.T. 254 (Ont. H.C.).
173 *See, for example, Male v. Hopmans* (1967), 64 D.L.R. (2d) 105 (Ont. C.A.); *Johnston v. Wellesley Hosp.* (1970), 17 D.L.R. (3d) 139 (Ont. H.C.); *Caron v. Gagnon* (1930), 68 Que. S.C. 155; *LaFrenier v. Hôpital Maisonneuve*, [1963] Que. S.C. 467.
174 For example, a dentist could establish that a sub-procedure in an extraction is the fixing of a rubber dam in the mouth.
175 [1974] 5 W.W.R. 606 (Man. Q.B.). *See also Kangas v. Parker*, [1976] 5 W.W.R 25 (Sask. Q.B.), where it was held that a dental patient should have been given the choice of a hospital or the dentist's office and a general or local anaesthetic; *Sunne v. Shaw*, [1981] C.S. 609 (Que. S.C.). *But see Leadbetter v. Brand and MacLellan* (1980), 37 N.S.R. (2d) 581 at 602 (S.C.).

work following an attempted administration of general anaesthetic. The decision was based in part on the finding that although there was no evidence that medical considerations required a general anaesthetic, the patient was not given the option of choosing a local anaesthetic.

Most problems of this nature have arisen from inadequate or ambiguous communication between doctor and patient prior to treatment, resulting in the doctor's belief that consent has been obtained for something when in fact it has not.[176]

The most extreme case is *Schweizer v. Central Hosp.*,[177] in which a patient entered a hospital expecting an operation on his great toe but instead received a spinal fusion. While the doctor had received approval for both procedures from the Workman's Compensation Board, the consent form signed by the patient made no reference to a spinal fusion. The patient was adamant that back surgery was never discussed, and the trial judge found the doctor's recollection of the facts wholly unsatisfactory. This, combined with conflicting evidence in the hospital records, contributed to the finding of liability against the doctor.

Two further cases of extending treatment beyond that for which consent was given are *Parmley v. Parmley*[178] and *Boase v. Paul.*[179] In both cases, the defendant dentist removed all of the patient's upper teeth under general anaesthetic. In the former case consent was given only for the removal of two teeth, and in the latter case, for one tooth. The dentist in *Parmley* was held liable, and in the *Boase* case, there was no liability only because the limitation period had expired.

If the communication of consent is faulty because the patient has given unclear instructions, the medical practitioner might not be held liable.[180] Two examples, again involving dentists, are *Nykiforuk v. Lockwood*,[181] where the patient wanted two upper molars extracted but appeared to the dentist to have indicated the two lower ones, and *Guimond v. Laberge*,[182] where the patient replied "Oui" to the dentist's query "Toutes les dents, Madame Guimond?" even though she meant only the upper teeth. The actions were dismissed in both cases, on the basis that the patient consented to the treatment given.

---

176 *See* Pickering, *Policing the Health Professions — Consent to Health Care* (1981), 2 H.L. in C. 52.

177 (1974), 6 O.R. (2d) 606 (H.C.). *See also McBain v. Laurentian Hosp.* (1982), 19 A.C.W.S. (2d) 70 (Ont. H.C.), where surgery was performed on the wrong foot.

178 [1945] 4 D.L.R. 81 (S.C.C.).

179 [1931] 1 D.L.R. 562; affirmed [1931] 4 D.L.R. 435 (Ont. C.A.).

180 *See, for example, McBain v. Laurentian Hosp.* (1982), 19 A.C.W.S. (2d) 70, where the patient who had deformed feet gave written consent to surgery on the *left* foot but before the operation discussed and requested surgery on the right foot. Surgery was done on the right foot. The court held that there was adequate consent. In any case, the one year limitation period had passed.

181 [1941] 1 W.W.R. 327 (Sask. D.C.).

182 (1956), 4 D.L.R. (2d) 559 (Ont. C.A.).

The cases discussed above all emphasize the importance for the protection of both the doctor's and the patient's interests, of an unequivocal consent from the patient to the treatment to be administered.

(ii) Consent to the person administering treatment

Consent is personal and normally authorizes a specific person to carry out a specific treatment. A patient has the right to treatment by the doctor with whom he has a doctor-patient relationship and a contract, but can agree to the delegation of responsibilities by the doctor to others. For example, the patient is assumed to know that the doctor engaged to perform the surgery will not also be administering the anaesthetic. In fact, there is support[183] for the proposition that the doctor has implied authority to engage another to administer the anaesthetic. In a hospital setting, it is common knowledge that care will be given by many employees whom the patient may never know by name.

Consent should be obtained by the person who will touch the patient, i.e., carry out the care or treatment. The doctor who delegates his responsibility to a hospital employee such as a nurse takes the risk that the consent so obtained may be inadequate.[184] Where the doctor or hospital employee to whom consent is given immediately proceeds with the procedure or treatment on a conscious patient, it is not difficult to find an implied consent to the individual.

However, where a patient is to be anaesthetized for a procedure, a consent form is often used by hospitals to cover the many persons who will participate in the care. One form recommended for use in Canada states:[185]

"I, (Name of Patient) of (City, town) hereby consent to submit to the following procedure, operation or treatment . . . *to be performed by such members of the (Name of Hospital) medical staff or employees as required and with the assistance of such employees* of the (Name of Hospital) as required for the procedure, operation or treatment." [emphasis added]

---

183 *Villeneuve v. Sisters of St. Joseph*, [1971] 2 O.R. 593 (H.C.); *Burk v. S.* (1951), 4 W.W.R. 520 (B.C.S.C.).

184 *Considine v. Camp Hill Hosp.* (1982), 133 D.L.R. (3d) 11 (N.S.S.C.); note that the requirements for an adequate consent set out by the Supreme Court of Canada clearly anticipate the doctor explaining risks; *see infra; see also* Pickering, *Policing the Health Professions — Consent to Health Care* (1981), 2 H.L. in C. 52 at 53.
"In the view of the [Ontario Health Disciplines Board], responsibility for obtaining consent rests primarily with the surgeon performing the operation. If more doctors took personal responsibility for this important part of the surgical experience, there would be less apprehension and concern on the part of patients, and fewer complaints for physicians to contend with."

185 Rozovsky, *supra* n. 139 at 54. Note that this form is signed by both the patient and the doctor. A similar form is used in England. *See* Farndale, *Law On Hospital Forms* (Ravenswood Pub. 1979). For other variations *see* Meredith, *Malpractice Liability of Doctors and Hospitals* 149 (1956); Medical Defence Union, *supra* n. 165 at 15: *Canadian Health Facilities Law Guide* (1983).

Teaching hospitals have a special problem because it may not be reasonable to assume there is patient awareness that house staff or students may be involved in care or treatment.[186] The position of the medical or nursing student is particularly anomalous because they are not employees of the hospital, yet may by their manner and dress seem to be "doctors" and "nurses."[187] The presence and role of house staff and students should be made clear to patients, and consideration should be given to including such information in any consent form.[188]

A practical solution for a hospital may be to use an appropriately drawn "group consent" to cover admission, processing and day-to-day care, and to provide a more precise "named doctor or doctors" form for surgery or high-risk tests. However, it must be remembered that consent is a process, not a document.[189]

(d) Patient Must be Informed

The patient requires information before he can make a decision whether or not to consent. However, the process is a bilateral one in which both the patient and the doctor have the right to knowledge of critical facts and the duty to respond in a way appropriate to their roles. So while the patient has the right to be told of the risks of treatment,[190] he has a corresponding duty to apprise the doctor of the specifics of his complaint and to co-operate in establishing essential acts.[191] The doctor has the right to be told everything, including that which might be irrelevant; he must decide what information may be eliminated and then must elicit such further information as he thinks necessary. He should then be in a position to exercise his duty to inform the patient of the risks involved in the treatment.

After the patient has received the required explanation of the risks, it is up to the patient to unequivocally communicate to the doctor his decision to accept or reject the proposed treatment.[192]

---

186 Storch, *Patient's Rights* 84 (1982). *See also* Mason and McCall Smith, *Law and Medical Ethics* 97 (1983), where the authors query whether a consent obtained at bedside to be seen by a "teaching group" is valid.

187 *See* Basson et al., *The "Student Doctor" and a Wary Patient* (1982), Hastings Centre Report 27.

188 Annas, *The Extravagant, Wasteful, and Superfluous Debate About Unnecessary Surgery* (1979), Hastings Centre Report 13.

189 Jacob, *Speller's Law Relating to Hospitals and Kindred Institutions* 178-92 (1978).

190 *Reibl v. Hughes* (1980), 14 C.C.L.T. 1 at 6. *See* Somerville, *Structuring the Issues in Informed Consent* (1981), 26 McGill L.J. 740 at 753. As to the importance of time and place *see Ferguson v. Hamilton Civic Hosp.* (1983), 23 C.C.L.T. 254 (Ont. H.C.). Note that consent in the research situation is discussed *infra*.

191 Note that this might include the patient asking questions: *Hopp v. Lepp* (1980), 112 D.L.R. (3d) 67 (S.C.C.). *See also Smith v. Auckland Hosp. Bd.*, [1965] N.Z.L.R. 191 (C.A.).

192 For cases where the patient fell short *see Nykiforuk v. Lockwood*, [1941] 1 W.W.R. 327 (Sask. D.C.); *Boase v. Paul*, [1931] 4 D.L.R. 435 (Ont. C.A.).

The scope of a doctor's duty which determines which risks must be revealed to a patient in order for that patient to be adequately informed is a matter of law.[193] Canadian law on this issue of "informed consent" was radically changed in 1980 by two Supreme Court of Canada decisions in the cases of *Hopp v. Lepp*[194] and *Reibl v. Hughes*.[195]

In order to understand this change in the law and the previous case law, it is necessary to review the situation in Canada and also to have a rudimentary understanding of American case law.[196]

(i) Before Hopp and Reibl

Prior to the Supreme Court of Canada decision in *Hopp v. Lepp*[197] in May 1980, a doctor had to disclose to a patient those risks that his colleagues would normally disclose about the proposed treatment.[198] But the doctor had to take into account the particular patient's intellectual and emotional characteristics, as well as the relationship between himself and the patient. The standard of disclosure for the doctor was described as "the professional disclosure" standard. The patient was measured subjectively rather than by an objective "reasonable patient" test.[199] A subjective test also was used to resolve the causation issue, that is, whether *that* patient, informed of the risks, would have chosen the treatment.[200]

The classical statement of these standards of disclosure is found in a New Zealand case, *Smith v. Auckland Hosp. Bd.*,[201] which was brought into Canadian law by *Male v. Hopmans*.[202] Certain factors were to be borne in mind by a doctor when deciding what to tell his patient: the gravity of the condition, the probability and nature of any risks, the benefits of treatment, the intellectual and emotional characteristics of the patient and the degree of dependency in the doctor-patient relationship. In addition, the doctor had a duty to answer his patient's questions fully and honestly.

However, the *Smith v. Auckland Hosp. Bd.*[203] case itself, and other

---

193 *Hopp v. Lepp* (1980), 112 D.L.R. (3d) 67 at 71 and 81 (S.C.C.); *Hajgato v. London Health Assn.* (1982), 36 O.R. 669 at 679 (Ont. H.C.); For the U.S. *see Truman v. Thomas* (1980), 27 Cal. (3d) 285 at 292-93.
194 [1980] 4 W.W.R. 645, 22 A.R. 361, 13 C.C.L.T. 66, 112 D.L.R. (3d) 67 (S.C.C.).
195 (1980), 14 C.C.L.T. 1 (S.C.C.).
196 For a more thorough review *see* Picard, *The Tempest of Informed Consent,* in *Studies in Canadian Tort Law* 129 at 142 (2d ed. Klar, 1977).
197 *Supra* n. 194.
198 This standard was applied at trial and in the Court of Appeal in *Reibl v. Hughes* (1977), 16 O.R. (2d) 306 at 313 (H.C.); (1978), 6 C.C.L.T. 227 at 239 (Ont. C.A.).
199 *Reibl v. Hughes* (1978), 6 C.C.L.T. 227 at 233 and 234 (Ont. C.A.).
200 *See, for example, Strachan v. Simpson,* [1979] 5 W.W.R. 315 at 344 (B.C.S.C.).
201 [1964] N.Z.L.R. 241; reversed on another point [1965] N.Z.L.R. 191 (C.A.).
202 (1966), 54 D.L.R. (2d) 592 (Ont. H.C.); *see Hopp v. Lepp* (1980), 112 D.L.R. (3d) 67 at 79 (S.C.C.) where Laskin C.J. comments on the *Auckland* and *Male* cases.
203 *Supra* n. 201

Canadian cases which followed, recognized limitations on the disclosure of risks. A patient was expected to realize that medical science is not infallible and that hindsight is clearer than foresight. It was held not to be necessary to explain risks "inseparable from any operation, such as failure or death under an anaesthetic, the danger of infection, of tetanus, of gas gangrene or gangrene,"[204] to tell of details "calculated to frighten or distress the patient,"[205] nor to tell of risks that are extremely remote, for example, one in a thousand.[206] The actual medical techniques did not have to be explained in detail "as long as the nature of the treatment is fully understood."[207]

The law in Canada prior to May 1980 was succinctly stated in *Halushka v. University of Sask.*[208] and specifically accepted by the trial judge in *Hopp v. Lepp.*[209]

> In ordinary medical practice the consent given by a patient to a physician or surgeon, to be effective, must be an "informed" consent freely given. It is the duty of the physician to give a fair and reasonable explanation of the proposed treatment including the *probable effect* and any *special or unusual* risks.

(ii) The United States

By contrast, in the United States two possible standards exist for the scope of disclosure.[210] One is the "professional disclosure" standard discussed earlier and the other is a "full disclosure" standard which requires that all material risks be revealed. A majority of American jurisdictions enforce the "professional" disclosure standard.[211]

The "full disclosure" standard is founded upon the right of the individual to self-determination with full knowledge. In the oft-quoted words of a famous American judge, Cardozo J., "every human being of adult years and sound mind has a right to determine what shall be done with his own body."[212] The two leading American cases of *Canterbury v. Spence*[213] and *Cobbs v. Grant*[214] made it clear that the measure of adequate disclosure of

---

204 *Kenny v. Lockwood*, [1932] 1 D.L.R. 507 at 523 (Ont. C.A.); *see also McLean v. Weir* (1977), 3 C.C.L.T. 87 (B.C.S.C.).
205 *Id.* at 525.
206 *McLean v. Weir supra* n. 204.
207 *Johnston v. Wellesley Hosp.* (1970), 17 D.L.R. (3d) 139 at 146 (Ont. H.C.).
208 (1965), 52 W.W.R. 608 at 615 (Sask. C.A.).
209 *Hopp v. Lepp* (1977), 2 C.C.L.T. 183 at 194 (Alta. S.C.). Note that the Court of Appeal also accepted the *Halushka* case. *Lepp v. Hopp* (1979), 8 C.C.L.T. 261 at 276 and 297. *See also* Picard, *Annotation*, 8 C.C.L.T. 261.
210 Seidelson, *Medical Malpractice: Informed Consent Cases in "Full-Disclosure" Jurisdictions* (1976), Duquesne L. Rev. 309.
211 Kapp, *Placebo Therapy and the Law: Prescribe With Care* (1983), 8 Am. J. Law Med. 371 at 393.
212 *Schloendorf v. Soc. of New York* (1914), N.E. 92 (N.Y.C.A.).
213 (1972), 464 F. (2d) 772 (U.S.C.A.).
214 (1972), 502 P. (2d) 1 (Cal. C.A.).

risks comes from the patient's need for information rather than from medical practice. The patient is characterized as a reasonable person.[215]

Two observations must be made about the American "full disclosure" standard.[216] First, the words must be analyzed carefully as they may not mean what they seem to mean. The adjective "full" must be given meaning by reference to the reasonable patient, but after the exercise of professional judgment by the doctor.[217] There may be some risks which need not be explained to the reasonable patient such as "the relatively minor risks inherent in common procedures, when it is common knowledge that such risks inherent in the procedure are of very low incidence."[218] In summary, "full" disclosure *may* not mean that every possible risk must be disclosed. It depends on what the reasonable patient would need to know in order to make an informed choice.[219]

The second alternative is that while more state courts are accepting the full disclosure standard,[220] there has been a movement to counter this by enacting legislation to establish the "professional standard" of disclosure.[221] Legislation on informed consent was seen to be the cure for the malpractice crisis by some American states, but it has not been.[222]

(iii) The metamorphosis

The interest of both doctor and patient seemed well-balanced in Canadian law prior to the *Hopp* and *Reibl* cases, for whereas the professional disclosure standard was less onerous to the doctor, it was he who had to prove

---

215 In describing this standard, Professor Bowker said:
   "The standard is objective: would the reasonable person be likely to attach significance to the risk or cluster of risks in deciding whether or not to forego the proposed therapy."
   See Bowker, *Minors and Mental Incompetents: Consent to Experimentation, Gifts of Tissue and Sterilization* (1981), 26 McGill L.J. 951 at 952.
216 *Salgo v. Leland Stanford Jr. Univ. Bd. Trustees* (1957), 317 P. (2d) 170 at 181.
217 Picard, *The Tempest of Informed Consent* in *Studies in Canadian Tort Law*, 129 (2d ed. Klar, 1977).
218 *Cobbs v. Grant* (1972), 502 P. (2d) 1 at 10 (Cal. C.A.) For an extension to "more" full disclosure, *see Truman v. Thomas* (1980), 27 Cal. (3d) 285 (Cal. S.C.) where it was held that a doctor had a duty to inform his patient of the risk of not having a pap smear. *See also* Shank, *Informed Refusal: An Unnecessary Burden on Physicians?* (1981), 49 U.M.K.C. L.R. 365.
219 Rodgers-Magnet, *Recent Developments in the Doctrine of Informed Consent to Medical Treatment* (1971), 14 C.C.L.T. 61 at 67; *see also* Somerville, *The Issues in Informed Consent* (1981), 26 McGill L.J. 740 at 754.
220 Seidelson, *Medical Malpractice: Informed Consent Cases in "Full Disclosure"* (1976), Duquesne L. Rev. 309.
221 For an excellent discussion *see* Rodgers-Magnet, *Legislating for an Informed Consent to Medical Treatment by Competent Adults* (1981), 26 McGill L.J. 1056.
222 *Id.* For excellent analyses of the current U.S. situation *see Making Health Care Decisions* (1982). This is a report of the President's Commission for the Study of Ethical Problems in Medicine and Biomedical and Behavioral Research. Meisel and Roth, *Toward An Informed Discussion of Informed Consent: A Review And Critique Of The Empirical Studies* (1983), Arizona L.R. 265.

this standard. The patient, meanwhile, had an advantage in being measured subjectively rather than objectively. He could expect to have the risks material to *him* brought to his attention and it was a question of whether *he* then would have consented. Furthermore, until July 1976, actions where a doctor failed to inform a patient of a risk were tried in battery or negligence without the confusion being experienced by American courts over the appropriate cause of action.[223]

The critical analysis of the state of Canadian law on informed consent that culminated in the Supreme Court of Canada in the *Hopp* and *Reibl* cases began in the Ontario Supreme Court in July of 1976. In an innovative judgment in the case of *Kelly v. Hazlett*,[224] Mr. Justice Morden set up a dichotomy that raised many questions. He held that the lack of informed consent could give rise to both battery and negligence, but that the breadth of information to be given differed for each action. The learned justice said that to avoid liability in battery, there must be informed consent as to the basic nature and character of the medical treatment, whereas liability in negligence could only flow from a failure to inform the patient of the collateral risks of the treatment. The problem of the appropriate cause of action will be discussed later in this chapter.[225]

By differentiating between risks going to the "basic nature and character," and those characterized as "collateral," Mr. Justice Morden implicitly raised the issue of the scope of disclosure of risks and the alternatives of the professional or full disclosure standard for the doctor and the objective or subjective standards for the patient.

In finding that the collateral risk of stiffness of an arm after an osteotomy operation had not been explained to the patient, and thus that the doctor was liable in negligence, Mr. Justice Morden did not need to resolve the theoretical issues set up by his approach; but the re-examination of the law on informed consent had begun.

Within six months, another justice of the Ontario High Court, Mr. Justice Haines, was grappling with the issue of informed consent in *Reibl v. Hughes*,[226] one of the cases destined to go to the Supreme Court of Canada. The patient in this case was an intelligent, 44-year-old man whose command of English was limited. His complaint was of severe headaches. Tests showed an arterial occlusion reducing blood flow to the brain. This condition made Mr. Reibl vulnerable to a stroke or even death; the same risks were attendant upon any elective surgery to correct the problem. According to Dr. Hughes,

---

223 *See* Picard, *The Tempest of Informed Consent* in *Studies in Canadian Tort Law* 129 (2d ed. Klar, 1977).

224 (1976), 1 C.C.L.T. 1 (Ont. H.C.); note that Mr. Justice Morden now sits on the Court of Appeal of Ontario.

225 *Infra.*

226 (1977), 16 O.R. 306, 78 D.L.R. (3d) 35 (Ont. H.C.).

the neurosurgeon who ultimately performed an internal carotid endarterectomy on Mr. Reibl, the cumulative risk factor was 14 per cent: a 4 per cent risk of death and a 10 per cent risk of stroke. Dr. Hughes had previously done 60 to 70 operations of the type he performed on Mr. Reibl. During surgery, or immediately following it, Mr. Reibl suffered a massive stroke that left him paralyzed on the right side of his body and impotent. In the three courts that heard the case, the issue was whether Dr. Hughes had properly explained the risks of the surgery to Mr. Reibl.

The facts, as found by the learned trial judge, indicate that there was very poor communication between doctor and patient. Mr. Reibl was told only that he would be better off having the operation. Furthermore, he was left under the erroneous impression that the surgery would relieve his complaint, the headaches.

The trial judge, Haines J.,[227] held that although Dr. Hughes imparted an understanding of the mechanics of the operation, he did not take sufficient care to communicate its purpose or the gravity, nature and extent of risks involved. Indeed, he found that the patient was left with the impression that the operation carried no risks beyond those incidental to any surgical procedure.

Mr. Justice Haines[228] applied a professional disclosure standard and evaluated the patient subjectively both as regards the scope of disclosure and causation. He concluded that there was negligence and battery in failing to inform the patient of the risks. In doing so, he acknowledged the judgment of his brother Morden J. in *Kelly v. Hazlett*,[229] and seemed to characterize the risk of stroke as being both basic and collateral.[230]

A majority of the Ontario Court of Appeal[231] (Justices Brooke and Blair) directed a new trial as to both liability and damages. While Mr. Justice Jessup was prepared to follow the reasons of Haines J. and find liability, he felt that there ought to be a new trial on the issue of damages.

Mr. Justice Brooke, who wrote the majority opinion, clearly felt that the trial judge had misapprehended the evidence and consequently had set too high a standard for the scope of disclosure. Specifically, Brooke J.A. said that he did not agree with Haines J., that the doctor did not sufficiently explain the purpose of the operation, and also disagreed that there was a duty on the doctor to discuss the degree or statistical incidence of the risks. But the learned justice went beyond the scope of this disagreement to suggest, *obiter*, modified approaches to the proper cause of action and the test for causation.

---

227 *Id*. at 44.

228 *Id*. at 42. *See also* Picard, *Tempest of Informed Consent in Studies in Canadian Tort Law* 129 at 144 (2d ed. Klar, 1977).

229 (1976), 1 C.C.L.T. 1 (Ont. C.A.).

230 *Id*. at 44. Note, however that earlier Haines J. stated that such risks ''are in no meaningful sense collateral, they are definitive.'' *Id*. at 42. *See Rodgers-Magnet, Recent Developments in the Doctrine of Informed Consent to Medical Treatment* (1981), 14 C.C.L.T. 61 at 64.

231 (1978), 6 C.C.L.T. 227 (Ont. C.A.).

Mr. Justice Brooke held that battery was not an appropriate cause of action in the case because the patient had consented to the basic nature and character of the operation. He concluded that previous cases decided in battery "are cases where there was an intentional deviation from the consent given, or fraud, or a serious misrepresentation as to the procedure and/or risks" and he cited the American case of *Cobbs v. Grant*[232] in support of his position. Such a negative characterization of battery was new in Canadian jurisprudence and will be discussed later in this chapter.[233]

The learned justice of appeal, like the trial judge, seems to have applied a professional disclosure standard[234] to the doctor and assessed the patient in subjective terms.[235] However, his suggested test for the causation issue indicated his agreement with advocates of the American objective test that it was time to move from the subjective test which had been adopted by Canadian courts. He recommended a marriage of the two so that the patient's position would be tested objectively and then subjectively. The learned justice described how the test would be used where a patient had not been informed of a risk:[236] ". . . would the plaintiff or a reasonably prudent patient have rejected the recommendation and declined treatment?"[237]

The effect of the judgments of Haines J. and Brooke J.A. in *Reibl v. Hughes* was to reinforce Canadian jurisprudence on some aspects of informed consent but also to reflect a discontent and a desire for change.

The judgments at trial and in the Alberta Court of Appeal in the companion case, *Hopp v. Lepp*,[238] reinforced the need for a definitive statement of the law on informed consent. In this case, the patient was a 66-year-old retired farmer suffering from a "slipped disc" and after the appropriate tests (myelograms) the defendant orthopaedic surgeon performed a hemilaminectomy operation in Lethbridge, Alberta. Dr. Hopp had performed or assisted in 60 to 75 similar operations as a resident, but this was his first such operation since becoming qualified as an orthopaedic surgeon. When the patient did not recover as expected, he was referred to a neurosurgeon in Calgary. This doctor found a "large chunk of extruded disc material" but the trial judge,

---

232 (1972), 8 Cal. (3d) 229, 502 P. (2d) 1 (Cal. C.A.).
233 For an excellent discussion *see* Gochnauer and Fleming, *Informed Consent — New Directions for Medical Disclosure — Hopp v. Lepp and Reibl v. Hughes* (1981), 15 U.B.C. L. Rev. 475.
234 (1978), 6 C.C.L.T. 227 at 238-39.
235 *Id.* at 234-35.
236 Note that the test is described as proceeding objectively and then subjectively but the example is set up in reverse order. *Quaere* whether there is any difference.
237 *Id.* at 244. Note that shortly afterwards Anderson J. called Brooke J.A.'s test "confusing" and stated a preference for the objective test. *Petty v. MacKay* (1979), 10 C.C.L.T. 85 (B.C.S.C.). As to whether he did, in fact, apply a purely objective test, *see* Picard, *Case Comment: Petty v. MacKay* (1979), 10 C.C.L.T. 98.
238 (1977), 2 C.C.L.T. 183 (Alta. S.C.). For an excellent critique of this case, *see* Klar, *Developments in Tort Law: The 1979-80 Term* (1981), 2 S.C.R. 325.

Brennan J., held that it was impossible to determine whether this condition was present prior to or during the operation by Dr. Hopp, or whether it occurred later.[239] It is important to note that the learned trial judge found no damages and that the alleged risk, the "extra" extrusion of disc material, was not proven to have resulted from an act or omission of the doctor, nor even to be a probable or possible risk of the surgery.[240]

The patient alleged battery[241] on the grounds that his consent was not informed: because he was not told that this was Dr. Hopp's first hemilaminectomy as a qualified orthopaedic surgeon, and because Dr. Hopp had indicated that the operation could be performed as well in Lethbridge as in Calgary.

The trial judge held the patient's consent was valid because a doctor did not have to advise a patient about his experience, and because the statement that the operation could be performed equally well in Lethbridge was correct.[242] Of interest is the *obiter* comment by Brennan J. that had he found otherwise, damages would have been token.[243]

Although *Kelly v. Hazlett*[244] was cited, there was no discussion in the judgment of negligence in explaining risks and, therefore, no need to discuss causation or injury.[245] In any case, Brennan J. said the patient had not established that he suffered any damages.[246]

The judgments in the Alberta Court of Appeal[247] are very difficult to analyze because different facts were found and different law was held to be appropriate. The majority opinion, written by Mr. Justice Morrow and concurred with by Mr. Justice Haddad, indicates an acceptance of the "professional disclosure" standard but a requirement of "full disclosure" in responding to patient's questions.[248] The Court of Appeal agreed with the trial judge in his conclusion that there was no need for the doctor to volunteer information about his experience, but they found that there was a "query respecting Calgary" and the seriousness of the procedure, and that, applying a "full disclosure" standard, the doctor's answer was inadequate. Liability was found in negligence and battery on the basis that the same reasoning was appropriate for both.[249] The causation issue was never discussed. The injury

---

239 *Id.* at 194.

240 *Id.* at 189.

241 Note that the allegation was of an "assault", a term which by common usage has come to mean "battery" or "assault" and "battery"; see Chapter 2.

242 *Supra* n. 238 at 191.

243 *Supra* n. 238 at 195.

244 (1976), 1 C.C.L.T. 1 (Ont. H.C.).

245 For a discussion of the allegations of negligence in carrying out the surgery *see* Chapter 4.

246 It is perhaps worth noting that *Hopp v. Lepp* was not a case in which any risk was realized.

247 (1979), 8 C.C.L.T. 260 (Ont. C.A.); for an attempt, *see* Picard, *Annotation* (1979), 8 C.C.L.T. 261.

248 *Id.* at 271-72. Note the authority cited was *Smith v. Auckland Hosp. Bd. supra* n. 201.

249 *Id.* at 289.

was stated to be "impairment and mental distress"[250] but was not examined.

The dissenting justice, Prowse J.A.,[251] would have dismissed the appeal, but unlike the trial judge who treated the action as battery, characterized the action as negligence. He found the only question asked to be with regard to the doctor's experience, and applying a "full disclosure" standard, found Dr. Hopp's answer to be sufficient.[252] The learned justice found that there was no specific question about risks attendant on an operation in Lethbridge as compared with Calgary, concluding that the standard of professional disclosure was met on this issue.[253]

As can be seen, there was a mosaic of judgments in *Hopp v. Lepp*. Some might be rationalized on the basis of different findings of fact, but this would not hide the confused state of the law. It was appropriate that the highest court in Canada agreed to hear the two cases.

(iv) The Supreme Court of Canada

The Supreme Court of Canada judgments in *Hopp v. Lepp*[254] and *Reibl v. Hughes*[255] were delivered by the Chief Justice of Canada and pronounced on May 20, 1980 and October 7, 1980 respectively.[256]

The judgment in *Hopp v. Lepp* was precursor to that in *Reibl v. Hughes*. Together they provide the authoritative statement on the law of informed consent in Canada. Each will be analyzed and then their components reviewed, along with cases subsequently decided in order to provide some guidance.

In *Hopp v. Lepp*,[257] Chief Justice Laskin restored the trial decision dismissing the action against Dr. Hopp. The Chief Justice accepted the findings of the trial judge, but had great difficulty with the majority judgment of Mr. Justice Morrow, especially insofar as it seemed to hold that the patient had raised a specific question about risks.

Anticipating a more appropriate case,[258] Chief Justice Laskin made it clear that he would not deal with the relationship between or the availability of the alternative actions of battery and negligence. He did begin his adjudication in the critical area of the duty of disclosure and its extent, but left many issues to be resolved in *Reibl v. Hughes*. Chief Justice Laskin stated that the

---

250 *Id.* at 291.
251 *Id.* at 291.
252 *Id.* at 297-98.
253 *Id.* at 298.
254 (1980), 112 D.L.R. (3d) 67 (S.C.C.).
255 (1980), 14 C.C.L.T. 1 (S.C.C.).
256 Each court was composed of seven justices, six of whom were on each case: Laskin C.J.C., Martland, Beetz, Estey, McIntyre and Chouinard JJ. with Dickson J. sitting for *Hopp v. Lepp* and Ritchie J. for *Reibl v. Hughes*.
257 *Supra* n. 254 at 74-75.
258 *Reibl v. Hughes* was heard on June 5, 1980. For a criticism of the case, *see* Klar, *supra* n. 238 at 338.

issue of informed consent was before the Supreme Court of Canada for the first time.[259]

The Chief Justice acknowledged the right of a patient to decide what should be done with his body and to be informed prior to giving consent.[260]

> The term "informed consent", frequently used in American cases, reflects the fact that although there is, generally, prior consent by a patient to proposed surgery or therapy, this does not immunize a surgeon or physician from liability for battery or for negligence if he has failed in a duty to disclose risks of the surgery or treatment, known or which should be known to him, and which are unknown to the patient. The underlying principle is the right of a patient to decide what, if anything, should be done with his body: see *Parmley v. Parmley and Yule*, [1945] 4 D.L.R. 81 at p. 89, [1945] S.C.R. 635 at pp. 645-6 . . . It follows, therefore, that a patient's consent, whether to surgery or to therapy, will give protection to his surgeon or physician only if the patient has been sufficiently informed to enable him to make a choice whether or not to submit to the surgery or therapy.

He described the concept of a duty of disclosure and its relationship to informed consent. [261]

> The issue of informed consent is at bottom a question whether there is a duty of disclosure, a duty by the surgeon or physician to provide information and, if so, the extent or scope of the duty.

Assisted by the Ontario Court of Appeal case of *Kenny v. Lockwood* and the American literature and case law, the Chief Justice established his parameters for the scope of disclosure.[262]

> In summary, the decided cases appear to indicate that, in obtaining the consent of a patient for the performance upon him of a surgical operation, a surgeon, generally, should answer any specific questions posed by the patient as to the risks involved and should, without being questioned, disclose to him the nature of the proposed operation, its gravity, any material risks and any special or unusual risks attendant upon the performance of the operation. However, having said that, it should be added that the scope of the duty of disclosure and whether or not it has been breached are matters which must be decided in relation to the circumstances of each particular case.

The Chief Justice expressed strong reservations about the professional disclosure standard described in *Smith v. Auckland,* and cited with favour *Canterbury v. Spence* and the "full disclosure" standard. He noted that "evidence of medical experts of custom or general practice as to the scope of disclosure cannot be decisive, but at most a factor to be considered."[263]

---

259 *Supra* n. 254 at 70. Note that Laskin C.J.C. referred to five Canadian cases: *Parmley v. Parmley*, [1945] S.C.R. 635 at 645-46 (S.C.C.); *Halushka v. Univ. of Sask.* (1965), 53 D.L.R. (2d) 436 (Sask. C.A.); *Kenny v. Lockwood*, [1932] 1 D.L.R. 507 (Ont. C.A.); *Male v. Hopmans* (1967), 64 D.L.R. (2d) 105 (Ont. C.A.); *Kelly v. Hazlett* (1976), 1 C.C.L.T. (Ont. H.C.); and through them to *Smith v. Auckland Hosp. Bd.,* [1964] N.Z.L.R. 241; reversed [1965] N.Z.L.R. 191 (N.Z.C.A.); *Hedley Byrne & Co. v. Heller & Partners,* [1964] A.C. 465; *Nocton v. Lord Ashburton,* [1914] A.C. 932 and to the U.S. case, *Canterbury v. Spence* (1972), 464 F. (2d) 772 (U.S.C.A.). In addition he referred to one British and three U.S. journal articles.
260 *Supra* n. 254 at 70-71.
261 *Supra* n. 254 at 71.
262 *Supra* n. 254 at 81.
263 *Supra* n. 254 at 80.

The Chief Justice reviewed a variety of classifications of risks: probable and possible, material and immaterial, special or unusual and inherent, but expressed no preferences. In passing, he commented that specific questions would introduce another element, but withdrew from further discussion saying only that "the specific character of the question will first have to be assessed."[264]

The Chief Justice alludes to other factors that will be relevant to the scope of disclosure such as common knowledge (i.e., larger centres more easily able to deal with complications), conditions that would allow the withholding of information (emotions, apprehension of patient), and whether treatment is necessary or elective.

In summary, the Chief Justice of Canada in *Hopp v. Lepp* began the restructuring of the law on informed consent.[265] The basic right to control one's body and be informed was accepted and the parameters for the scope of the disclosure were roughly outlined. Many alternates were canvassed without approval being given to any. The case of *Reibl v. Hughes*[266] allowed him the opportunity to complete the task.

Dr. Hughes was held liable in negligence to Mr. Reibl for $225,000 because he did not obtain Mr. Reibl's informed consent to surgery and one of the risks of that surgery, a stroke, occurred causing paralysis and impotence. This was the result because the Supreme Court of Canada restored the decision of the trial judge, Mr. Justice Haines.

As in the *Hopp v. Lepp* case, the Chief Justice accepted the findings of the trial judge, but he had some difficulty with the Court of Appeal's treatment of the evidence. Briefly, the Chief Justice agreed that Dr. Hughes had failed to meet the standard of disclosure expected of him by failing to disclose the risks of stroke and death even though Mr. Reibl had raised the question. Although Laskin C.J. in conclusion agreed with Haines J., he did so by creating "new" law on informed consent.

The most dramatic change in the law brought about by *Reibl v. Hughes* was the restriction of the battery action to "cases where surgery or treatment has been performed or given to which there has been no consent at all or where, emergency situations aside, surgery or treatment has been performed or given beyond that to which there was consent."[267] In doing this the Chief Justice acknowledged the advantages of a battery action to a plaintiff.[268] He also reviewed and rejected the dichotomy for battery and negligence suggested by Morden J. in *Kelly v. Hazlett*.[269]

---

264 *Supra* n. 254 at 81.
265 Professor Klar notes that this was by *obiter dicta;* Klar, *supra* n. 238.
266 (1980), 14 C.C.L.T. 1 (S.C.C.).
267 *Id.* at 13.
268 *Id.* at 12.
269 *Id.* at 14.

But the Chief Justice seems to have concurred with the Court of Appeal on one point, namely Mr. Justice Brooke's contention that misrepresentation or fraud may sometimes underscore the battery action.[270] The now diminished battery action will be discussed in more detail later in this chapter.

Prior to setting down the remainder of the new law, Chief Justice Laskin reiterated the principles enunciated in *Hopp v. Lepp*.[271]

> It is now undoubted that the relationship between surgeon and patient gives rise to a duty of the surgeon to make disclosure to the patient of what I would call all material risks attending the surgery which is recommended. The scope of the duty of disclosure was considered in *Hopp v. Lepp* . . .

Although in *Hopp v. Lepp*[272] the Chief Justice seemed merely to review possible classifications without making a commitment to any, in *Reibl v. Hughes* he interpreted those words to give further guidance.[273]

> The Court in *Hopp v. Lepp* also pointed out that even if a risk is a mere possibility which ordinarily need not be disclosed, yet if its occurrence carries serious consequences, as for example, paralysis or even death, it should be regarded as a material risk requiring disclosure.

The Chief Justice used these criteria to characterize the risks of stroke or death in the *Reibl* case as material and noted that the surgery was elective.

In order to determine the scope of voluntary disclosure described by the Chief Justice, a doctor must have reference to a standard. As is evident from the review done above, all lower court justices on both cases had applied the accepted "professional disclosure" standard for this purpose.

In *Reibl v. Hughes*, Chief Justice Laskin soundly rejected the professional disclosure standard in these words:[274]

> To allow expert medical evidence to determine what risks are material and, hence, should be disclosed and, correlatively, what risks are not material is to hand over to the medical profession the entire question of the scope of the duty of disclosure, including the question whether there has been a breach of that duty . . .

He was not deterred by the realization that this meant a rejection of a standard similar to that used to measure a doctor's professional activities.[275]

> The issue under consideration is a different issue from that involved where the question is whether the doctor carried out his professional activities by applicable professional standards. What is under consideration here is the patient's right to know what risks are involved in undergoing or foregoing certain surgery or other treatment.

The Chief Justice replaced the "professional disclosure" standard with one very similar to the American "full disclosure" standard, given content by reference to two sources:

---

270 *Id*. at 14.
271 *Id*. at 6.
272 (1980), 112 D.L.R. (3d) 67 at 80 (S.C.C.).
273 *Supra* n. 266 at 6.
274 *Supra* n. 266 at 16-17.
275 *Supra* n. 266 at 17.

a)   the patient and what he deems relevant to his decision; and

b)   medical knowledge and material risks recognized thereby. As Chief Justice Laskin stated:[276]

> What the doctor knows or should know that the particular patient deems relevant to a decision whether to undergo prescribed treatment goes equally to his duty of disclosure as do the material risks recognized as a matter of required medical knowledge.

On the matter of what medical evidence would be relevant he concluded what he had begun in *Hopp v. Lepp* when he said:[277]

> Expert medical evidence is, of course, relevant to findings as to the risks that reside in or are a result of recommended surgery or other treatment. It will also have a bearing on their materiality but this is not a question that is to be concluded on the basis of the expert medical evidence alone.

As mentioned earlier, in the lower courts in both *Hopp v. Lepp* and *Reibl v. Hughes,* the patient was assessed subjectively with regard to the scope of disclosure, i.e., what risks would *this* patient wish to know? This was consistent with Canadian law.[278]

Chief Justice Laskin appears to advocate a subjective assessment of the patient in order to derive the ''patient portion'' of the scope of disclosure standard for he said:[279]

> The materiality of non-disclosure of certain risks to an informed decision is a matter for the trier of fact, a matter on which there would, in all likelihood, be medical evidence but also other evidence, *including evidence from the patient or from members of his family.* It is, of course, possible that *a particular patient* may waive aside any question of risks and be quite prepared to submit to the surgery or treatment, whatever they be. Such a situation presents no difficulty. Again, it may be the case that *a particular patient* may, because of emotional factors, be unable to cope with facts relevant to recommended surgery or treatment and the doctor may, in such a case, be justified in withholding or generalizing information as to which he would otherwise be required to be more specific. [emphasis supplied]

Such words do not seem to support the objective reasonable patient approach. But the most convincing evidence that Chief Justice Laskin is prepared to allow some subjectivity here is the manner in which he deals with a particular attribute of the particular patient, Mr. Reibl. Mr. Reibl had a misapprehension, for he believed that the surgery would relieve his complaint, the headaches. The Chief Justice accepted this as a ground of judgment against Dr. Hughes. Yet if all a doctor must do to meet the standard of disclosure is to disclose those risks relevant to a reasonable patient, would not a particular patient's misapprehension be irrelevant? It must be noted, however, that an assessment of the patient for purposes of setting the scope of disclosure is a different issue than the causation issue. While the Chief Justice was

---

276 *Supra* n. 266 at 16.
277 *Supra* n. 266 at 17.
278 Picard, *supra* n. 228.
279 *Supra* n. 266 at 17.

expressly against a subjective test for causation, he said nothing about the alternatives with respect to the issue of scope of disclosure to the patient.[279a]

Although Chief Justice Laskin cited the two American "full disclosure" standard cases, *Canterbury v. Spence* and *Cobbs v. Grant*, his new Canadian standard of disclosure is unique for two reasons. First, while the Chief Justice requires some reference to the medical profession, in the United States lay testimony may now in itself be enough.[280] Second, the United States full disclosure standard refers to the patient as a reasonable person, an objective test. Chief Justice Laskin seems to favour a far more subjective evaluation of the patient and even of his family.[281]

On the appropriate test for causation, the Chief Justice was emphatic that it be objective. Thus, a patient would have to prove that, had a reasonable person in his position known of the risk, *that* reasonable person would *not* have consented to the treatment. Chief Justice Laskin adopted this approach although the jurisprudence to that date indicated a subjective approach was used by courts.[282] He stated:[283] "If Canadian case law has so far proceeded on a subjective test of causation, it is in Courts other than this one . . . The matter is *res integra* here." The Chief Justice cited an American article to illustrate the "case" for the objective standard. The comment said:[284]

> The objective standard is preferable, since the subjective standard has a gross defect: it depends on the plaintiff's testimony as to his state of mind, thereby exposing the physician to the patient's hindsight and bitterness.

In addition, Chief Justice Laskin expressed his own grave reservations about a patient's evidence:[285]

> It could hardly be expected that the patient who is suing would admit that he would have agreed to have the surgery, even knowing all the accompanying risks.

Ironically, another concern was based on negligence now being the only action:[286]

> Since liability rests only in negligence, in a failure to disclose material risks, the issue of causation would be in the patient's hands on a subjective test, and would, if his evidence was accepted, result inevitably in liability unless, of course, there was a finding that there was no breach of the duty of disclosure.

It is worth noting that the Chief Justice did examine the combined objective-subjective test proposed by Mr. Justice Brooke in the Court of

---

279a For further discussion of the scope of disclosure and causation see 4(d)(v) C. *infra* pp. 000-000 and 4(d)(v) D. *infra* pp. 000-000.

280 Bamberg, *Informed Consent After Cobbs — Has the Patient Been Forgotten* (1973), 10 San Diego L. Rev. 913.

281 *Supra* n. 266 at 17.

282 *See for example, Strachan v. Simpson*, [1979] 5 W.W.R. 315 at 344, 10 C.C.L.T. 145 at 182 (B.C.S.C.); *see also* Picard, *Annotation*, 10 C.C.L.T. 145 at 148.

283 *Supra* n. 266 at 19-20.

284 Comment, *Informed Consent — A Proposed Standard for Medical Disclosure* (1973), 48 N.Y.U.L. Rev. 548 at 550.

285 *Supra* n. 266 at 21.

286 *Supra* n. 266 at 22.

Appeal on a question which, obviously, concerned him: would a reasonable patient ever refuse recommended surgery? But the Chief Justice said he doubted whether the objective-subjective test would solve the problem:[287]

> Merely because medical evidence establishes the reasonableness of a recommended operation does not mean that a reasonable person in the patient's position would necessarily agree to it, if proper disclosure had been made of the risks attendant upon it, balanced by those against it. *The patient's particular situation* and the degree to which the risks of surgery or no surgery are balanced would reduce the force, on an objective appraisal, of the surgeon's recommendation. [emphasis supplied]

A careful reading of that statement and of the Chief Justice's judgment on the causation issue leads one to the conclusion that in fact the Chief Justice's objective test has a subjective component. For example, the Chief Justice said:[288]

> I think it is the safer course on the issue of causation to consider objectively how far the balance in the risks of surgery or no surgery is in favour of undergoing surgery. The failure of proper disclosure pro and con becomes therefore very material. And so too are any special considerations affecting the particular patient. For example, the patient may have asked specific questions which were either brushed aside or were not fully answered or were answered wrongly. In the present case, the anticipation of a full pension would be a special consideration, and, while it would have to be viewed objectively, it emerges from the patient's particular circumstances. So too, other aspects of the objective standard would have to be geared to what the average prudent person, the reasonable person in the patient's particular position, would agree to or not agree to, if all material and special risks of going ahead with the surgery or foregoing it were made known to him. Far from making the patient's own testimony irrelevant, it is essential to his case that he put his own position forward.

But he carefully sets the limits to this subjective aspect:[289]

> In saying that the test is based on the decision that a reasonable person in the patient's position would have made, I should make it clear that the patient's particular concerns must also be reasonably based; *otherwise, there would be more subjectivity than would be warranted under an objective test*. Thus, for example, fears which are not related to the material risks which should have been but were not disclosed would not be causative factors. However, economic considerations could reasonably go to causation where, for example, the loss of an eye as a result of non-disclosure of a material risk brings about the loss of a job for which good eyesight is required. *In short, although account must be taken of a patient's particular position, a position which will vary with the patient, it must be objectively assessed in terms of reasonableness.* [emphasis supplied]

In summary, the Chief Justice's test seems to be an objective one modified to some extent by a subjective assessment of the particular patient.

There can be no better reference for an understanding of how the test should be used than to peruse its application by Chief Justice Laskin himself:[290]

---

287 *Supra* n. 266 at 21.
288 *Supra* n. 266 at 21.
289 *Supra* n. 266 at 22.
290 *Supra* n. 266 at 60.

Relevant in this case to the issue whether a reasonable person in the plaintiff's position would have declined surgery at the particular time is the fact that he was within about one and one-half years of earning pension benefits if he continued at his job; that there was no neurological deficit then apparent; that there was no immediate emergency making the surgery imperative; that there was a grave risk of a stroke or worse during or as a result of the operation, while the risk of a stroke without it was in the future, with no precise time fixed or which could be fixed except as a guess of three or more years ahead. Since, on the trial Judge's finding, the plaintiff was under the mistaken impression, as a result of the defendant's breach of the duty of disclosure, that the surgery would relieve his continuing headaches, this would in the opinion of a reasonable person in the plaintiff's position, also weigh against submitting to the surgery at the particular time.

In my opinion, a reasonable person in the plaintiff's position would, on a balance of probabilities, have opted against the surgery rather than undergoing it at the particular time.

As later cases will illustrate, Mr. Reibl became one of the very few patients to satisfy a court on the causation issue.

In conclusion, although Chief Justice Laskin was able in *Reibl v. Hughes* to add some flesh to the skeleton he created in *Hopp v. Lepp,* it will fall, of necessity, to the provincial courts to breathe life into this new body of law.

The issues of scope of disclosure, description of risks, causation, proper cause of action, and some evidentiary problems such as onus of proof, and the role of the court, will be discussed in light of the judgments in cases decided since *Hopp v. Lepp* and *Reibl v. Hughes,* and with reference to the spate of Canadian articles on the issues.

(v) Applying the Supreme Court tests

A. The duty

An acknowledged attribute of the doctor-patient relationship is the responsibility of the doctor to tell his patient of the risks of any treatment.[291] This commitment, though cast many years ago and flowing from the trust or fiduciary nature of the relationship,[292] has been remoulded by very recent judicial decisions.[293]

Perhaps a more modern description would be that in a relationship marked by an imbalance of power, the person in the position of authority, the doctor, has a positive duty to accord respect to the patient's right to autonomy and inviolability.[294]

Stated succinctly, a doctor has a duty to provide information to his patient. The depth and breadth of this duty will be discussed by reference to

---

291 *Reibl v. Hughes* (1980), 14 C.C.L.T. 1 at 6 (S.C.C.).
292 *Slater v. Baker* (1767), 2 Wils. 359, 95 E.R. 80. *See* Chapter 1. But note that the Chief Justice of B.C. has said that the doctor-patient relationship is not a fiduciary one. *See Diack v. Bardsley,* unreported 14 June 1983, No. C822253 (B.C.S.C.).
293 *Hopp v. Lepp supra* n. 272; *Reibl v. Hughes supra* n. 291.
294 Somerville, *Structuring the Issues in Informed Consent* (1981), 26 McGill L.J. 740 at 753.

judicial pronouncements on the requisite standard and scope of disclosure.

B. The standard of the duty of disclosure

It is the function of the judge to set the standard of disclosure.[295] Because the action is based on negligence, the onus rests on the plaintiff, the patient, to adduce the evidence from which the judge construes the standard.[296]

The Supreme Court of Canada has determined that there must be two sources of such evidence: the medical profession and the patient and that these are of equal importance.[297]

The evidence from the profession would be provided by expert witnesses and likely, the defendant himself, and would focus upon the risks that are recognized,[298] their nature and the likelihood of their occurrence, and whether or not they are customarily explained to patients.[299]

The evidence from the patient (and perhaps from the defendant doctor) would be directed to what the doctor knew or ought to have known about him and about what he, the patient, deemed relevant.[300] It should be noted that the patient must use the reasonable patient, rather than himself alone, as the reference point for the standard. While some commentators,[301] including the Chief Justice,[302] have noted that the test cannot be purely objective, there is a strong statement from Chief Justice Howland of the Ontario Court of Appeal that the test must be objective.[303]

There is no doubt that the plaintiff patient's onus of proof is a heavy one. Much of what he must prove is within the knowledge of the medical profession:

---

295 *Reibl v. Hughes* (1980), 14 C.C.L.T. 1 at 14 (S.C.C.) where Laskin C.J.C. accepted the words of Brooke J.A. of the Court of Appeal (1978), 6 C.C.L.T. 227 at 238. Note at p. 58 Laskin C.J.C. stated that in the case the trial judge was in a better position to do this.

296 *Videto v. Kennedy* (1981), 17 C.C.L.T. 307 at 317-18 (Ont. C.A.); *Mang v. Moscovitz* (1982), 37 A.R. 221 at 266 (Alta. S.C.); *Hankins v. Papillon* (1980), 14 C.C.L.T. 199 at 205 (Que. S.C.).

297 *Reibl v. Hughes, supra* n. 295 at 16.

298 *See, for example, Mang v. Moscovitz* (1982), 37 A.R. 221 at 268 (Alta. S.C.) where it was held that no obstetrician-gynaecologist could be expected to know of the risk of air embolism. *See also McLean v. Weir,* [1980] 4 W.W.R. 330 at 337 (B.C.C.A.).

299 *See, for example, Ferguson v. Hamilton Civic Hosp.* (1983), 23 C.C.L.T. 254 (Ont. H.C.) where there was such evidence from highly qualified experts. *Note* that there may be some question of an ascertainable practice. *See Canterbury v. Spence* (1972), 464 F. (2d) 772 at 783; "... the reality of any discernible custom reflecting a professional consensus or communication of option and risk information to patients is open to serious doubt."

300 *See, for example, Videto v. Kennedy* (1981), 17 C.C.L.T. 307 (Ont. C.A.) at 317 where it was held there was no evidence that the doctor knew or ought to have known that the size of a scar was of "prime" importance to the patient.

301 Picard, *Consent to Medical Treatment in Canada* (1981), Osgoode Hall L.J. 140 at 146-47; Gochnauer and Fleming, *Tort Law — Informed Consent — New Directions for Medical Disclosure — Hopp v. Lepp and Reibl v. Hughes* (1981), 15 U.B.C. L. Rev. 475 at 480-81.

302 *Reibl v. Hughes supra* n. 295 at 17.

303 *Videto v. Kennedy supra* n. 300 at 319. *See also Bickford v. Stiles* (1981), 128 D.L.R. (3d) 516 at 523 (N.B.Q.B.).

that the risk exists, is known, and is customarily explained (because the doctor ought to have known that the reasonable patient would want to know of the risk). It is perhaps worth noting that this burden is a new one for the patient. Under the professional disclosure test, it was the doctor who established which risks his colleagues would normally explain.[304]

Some courts are experiencing difficulty in balancing the professional and patient components required to set the standard of disclosure and it is perhaps to be expected that it is the new patient element that has been neglected. In order for there to be evidence of what the doctor knew or ought to have known about the patient there must have been communication between them. Thus, it is not surprising that in those cases where there was little or no communication, the courts have had little or no evidence of the doctor's knowledge of the patient to use in setting the standard of disclosure.

In the Alberta case of *Mang v. Moscovitz*,[305] the patient was to have a therapeutic abortion and tubal ligation. As the patient spoke little English, all conversations were between the doctor and the patient's husband. The doctor testified only that he "would be surprised if he did not give it [a form explaining abortion] to them"[306] and he admitted that the form did not cover the risks of tubal ligation. The husband testified that the doctor never did give him the form. Mr. Justice Dixon held that the standard of disclosure had been met.[307]

Another example of a case where the medical aspect of the standard of disclosure seems to have attracted all the attention is a New Brunswick case.[308] The patient was tentatively diagnosed as having sarcoidosis, a disease with effects ranging from mild to debilitating. Although the doctor doing the surgical test to confirm the diagnosis spoke to the patient in the hospital, no one told her that this test was diagnostic nor that there were any risks,[309] including the risk of vocal chord paralysis which the court found to be material.[310] There is no indication in the reported case of any evidence of what the doctor knew or ought to have known about the patient, although the tests of the Supreme Court of Canada for the standard of disclosure were cited. It appears that the 29-year-old Mrs. Bickford's condition was improving and that she was reluctant to undergo surgery. Did Dr. Stiles know or ought he to have known of her concerns about the surgery, and specifically, about the

---

304 Picard, *The Tempest of Informed Consent* in *Studies in Canadian Tort Law* (2d ed. Klar 1977), 129 at 138, 144. Note that this might be construed as the doctor establishing the defence of custom or approved practice.
305 (1982), 37 A.R. 221 (Alta. Q.B.).
306 *Id*. at 258.
307 *Id*. at 17.
308 *Bickford v. Stiles* (1981), 128 D.L.R. (3d) 516 (N.B.Q.B.).
309 *Id*. at 517.
310 *Id*. at 523.

effect voice paralysis would have on her or on a reasonable person in her position?

If there is an apparent failure to give "equal importance" to what the doctor knew or ought to have known about the patient, it may well be because the patient has not brought the necessary evidence to the court. The patient's lawyer must attend to this new aspect of informed consent. Having brought forward evidence of the patient and what the doctor knew or ought to have known, it then rests with the court to construe the standard from it.

An example of two different conclusions can be seen in *Videto v. Kennedy*.[311] The trial judge, Grange J.,[312] found that the doctor and patient did discuss the size of the scar that would result from an incision and the trial judge found two attributes of the patient to be very important: that she was a Catholic who thus faced religious objections to the proposed sterilization, and that she chose the laparoscopic technique because it would leave only a small scar.

By contrast, on appeal and in reversing the trial judge's finding of liability, Mr. Justice Brooke[313] held that the patient failed to satisfy the onus of proving that the size of the scar was something the doctor knew or ought to have known was significant to her. The learned justice said that the trial judge had erred in applying a subjective rather than an objective standard, and that there was no evidence that the doctor knew or ought to have known the patient was a Catholic, and did not want anyone but her husband to be aware that she had been sterilized. Mrs. Videto "deemed relevant" these facts, but Mr. Justice Brooke did not accept them as part of the standard of disclosure required to be met by Dr. Kennedy.

The patient in *Guertin v. Kester*[314] did not tell the doctor, a plastic surgeon planning to operate on her eyelids, that she had very little vision in her right eye, and he did not examine her vision. Dr. Kester did not remember his conversations with Mrs. Guertin but testified he would have asked her about trouble with her eyes, or any surgery or major problem. Unfortunately, during the surgery to remove excess skin from her eyelids, Dr. Kester inadvertently removed too much skin from the lid of her left eye resulting in irritation and sensitivity, cysts, and failure of the eyelid to close. By his holding that the defendant need not have examined the patient's vision nor learned of the limited vision in her right eye, Mr. Justice Dryer seems to have concluded that a surgeon about to operate on a patient's eyelids need not know about the condition of the patient's eyes.

No doubt it will require time and experience for counsel and the courts to properly construe the standard of disclosure in accordance with pattern set by

---

311 (1981), 17 C.C.L.T. 307 (Ont. C.A.); reversing 107 D.L.R. (3d) 612 (Ont. H.C.).
312 *Id*. (H.C.) at 613, 621.
313 *Id*. (C.A.) at 317.
314 (1981), 20 C.C.L.T. 225 (B.C.S.C.).

the Supreme Court of Canada. Courts in the future may have to consider a more express acceptance of the subjective features of the patient component, perhaps following the model used by Chief Justice Laskin in determining the causation issue: taking account of what the doctor knew or ought to have known about the particular patient and then assessing that objectively in terms of reasonableness.[315]

It has been suggested[316] that a doctor ought to know that a patient will be concerned about a "normal range of interests and values," and this will provide a core of information which may be expanded in two ways. Medical knowledge may indicate the existence of special or unusual risks for a particular patient, or the patient may ask a specific question. If either or both of these situations occur, it will increase what the doctor ought to know.

It may be, as has been observed,[317] that Chief Justice Laskin was unaware of the difficulty presented by giving equal weight to information deemed relevant to a decision by the patient and to medical knowledge. At one extreme, it could require the doctor "to do an extensive analysis of the patient's values, interest and personal situation;"[318] on the other, it could lead the doctor to endeavour to know as little about the patient as possible.

Surely, neither extreme was encouraged by the Supreme Court of Canada when it said that the standard of disclosure must be established by reference not only to the doctor and his profession, but equally to the patient and his right to information. Courts must strike a balance in setting the standard of disclosure so as to assure that the main intention of the standard is met: namely, that the patient is provided with the information that he requires in order to make an informed decision.

C. The scope of the duty of disclosure

As with the standard of disclosure, it is the judge who sets the scope of the disclosure and decides whether it has been met[319] and, as Chief Justice Laskin made clear, these are matters which must be decided in relation to the circumstances of each particular case.

---

315 *Reibl v. Hughes supra* n. 295 at 22.
316 Gochnauer and Fleming, *Tort Law — Informed Consent — New Directions for Medical Disclosure — Hopp v. Lepp and Reibl v. Hughes* (1981), 15 U.B.C.L. Rev. 475 at 481. (This approach was accepted by the dissenting justice Zuber J.A. in *Zamparo v. Brisson* (1981), 16 C.C.L.T. 66 at 77 (Ont. C.A.)).
317 *Id.*
318 Note that the advice given by C. Scott, Q.C., counsel to the Canadian Medical Protective Assoc., was: "Treat the patient as though he were your best friend and you are telling him all about it." *see CMPA Annual Report* 46 (1980).
319 *Reibl v. Hughes supra* n. 295 at 59. Note that the Chief Justice refers to this as "the scope of the duty."

The Supreme Court of Canada set out the basic requirements for an adequate disclosure in *Hopp v. Lepp*[320] and reiterated them in *Reibl v. Hughes*.[321] The Chief Justice said:[322]

> In summary, the decided cases appear to indicate that, in obtaining the consent of a patient for the performance upon him of a surgical operation, a surgeon, generally, should answer any specific questions posed by the patient as to the risks involved and should, without being questioned, disclose to him the nature of the proposed operation, its gravity, any material risks and any special or unusual risks attendant upon the performance of the operation.
>
> . . . even if a certain risk is a mere possibility which ordinarily need not be disclosed, yet if its occurrence carries serious consequences, as for example, paralysis or even death, it should be regarded as a material risk requiring disclosure.

For purposes of analysis and comment, the constituent elements of this model of disclosure must be dealt with separately.

The doctor should answer any specific questions about risks.

The source for this directive for Mr. Justice Laskin was the judgment of *Kenny v. Lockwood*.[323] The Court of Appeal of Ontario in that case founded its judgment on the English case of *Nocton v. Lord Ashburton*[324] and construed the doctor-patient relationship as a fiduciary one requiring honesty from the doctor.[325] Chief Justice Laskin noted that the *Nocton* case was one of the underpinnings of the *Hedley Byrne & Co. Ltd. v. Heller & Partners Ltd.*[326] decision. It is interesting that the Court of Appeal of New Zealand employed the *Hedley Byrne* doctrine of negligent misstatement in *Smith v. Auckland Hosp. Bd.*[327]

Although that doctrine would seem to add little to Chief Justice Laskin's requirement, there are some limiting aspects of the doctrine, such as the requirement of reasonable reliance, the possibility of no proof of reliance, or the denial of assumption of obligation[328] that could be invoked by a doctor to restrict his duty and might arise where the patient has more than one doctor.

Chief Justice Laskin extrapolated from *Kenny v. Lockwood*[329] certain features of the question and answer situation for doctor and patient. After describing risks which might voluntarily be disclosed, he said:[330]

---

320 *Supra* n. 272.
321 *Supra* n. 295.
322 *Reibl v. Hughes supra* n. 295 at 6.
323 [1932] 1 D.L.R. 507 (Ont. C.A.).
324 [1914] A.C. 932.
325 *Quaere* whether the answers to patients in *Koehler v. Cook* [1975], 65 D.L.R. (3d) 766 (B.C.S.C.), and *Calder v. Gilmour*, [1978] 3 A.C.W.S. 57 (Sask. Q.B.), would meet this test.
326 [1964] A.C. 465.
327 [1965] N.Z.L.R. 191 (C.A.). Note, however, that this court concluded that a doctor is under no obligation to answer a patient's questions. For a discussion, *see* Sharpe, *Informed Consent* 54 (1979).
328 For an excellent explanation of the doctrine, *see* Linden, *Canadian Tort Law* 431-63 (1981).
329 *Supra* n. 323.
330 *Supra* n. 272 at 77.

Apart from situations of this kind, a surgeon need not go into every conceivable detail of a proposed operation so long as he describes its nature, *unless the patient asks specific questions not by way of merely general inquiry,* and, if so, *those questions must be answered, although they invite answers to merely possible risks.* If no specific questions are put as to possible risks, the surgeon is under no obligation (although he may do so) to tell the patient that there are possible risks since there are such risks in any operation. *It becomes a question of fact of how specific are any questions that are put . . .* [emphasis supplied]

Thus it appears that the questions must be specific, must be answered and the answers must include a discussion of the risks and "details" not otherwise requiring disclosure. Further on in his judgment and after surveying the various adjectives to describe risks, Laskin C.J. said:[331]

Of course, if specific questions are asked, this introduces another element but here the evidence touching the specific character of the question will first have to be assessed.

In other words, a court must look at the question in context.

There is a hint that some imprecision in the question might be acceptable in the Chief Justice's statement referring to the dissenting judgment of Mr. Justice Prowse in the Court of Appeal:[332]

Had there been a specific question of the kind alleged (and, I assume, it would be sufficient if the question or questions asked could reasonably be construed as inviting a response to possible risks), it would have been the duty of the appellant to answer it.

A number of problems exist with regard to patients asking questions. For example, unless a patient is secure in the relationship, he is unlikely to ask questions.[333] Or he may not know enough to be able to frame specific or even general questions.[334] This imbalance has led two commentators to suggest that the burden of initiating discussion be put on the doctor.[335] A major problem is that both doctor and patient frequently either do not recall their conversations or recollect them differently.[336]

In view of these problems, it is perhaps not surprising that few of the reported cases indicate that questions were asked by the patient.[337] The

---

331 *Supra* n. 272 at 81.

332 *Supra* n. 272 at 72. *See* Sharpe *supra* n. 327 at 80.

333 Somerville, *Legal Investigation of a Medical Investigation* (1981), A.L.R. 171 at 180; *See* Rozovsky, *The Canadian Patient's Book of Rights* (1980); Storch, *Patient's Rights* (1982). Note that in *Reibl v. Hughes supra* n. 295 the patient's complaint was debilitating headaches yet he failed to ask whether the proposed surgery would alleviate them.

334 Note that this was the patient's problem in *Hopp v. Lepp supra* n. 272; *see also Videto v. Kennedy* (1981), 17 C.C.L.T. 307 (Ont. C.A.); *Mang v. Moscovitz* (1982), 37 A.R. 221 (Alta. Q.B.).

335 Sharpe, *Informed Consent* 66 (1979); Castel, *Nature and Effects of Consent With Respect to the Right to Life and The Right to Physicial and Mental Integrity in the Medical Field: Criminal and Private Law Aspects* (1978), 16 A.L.R. 1 at 9. *See also* Strong, *Informed Consent: Theory and Policy* (1979), 5 J. of Med. Ethics 196.

336 *See Rawlings v. Lindsay* (1982), 20 C.C.L.T. 301 at 304 (B.C.S.C.); *Guertin v. Kester* (1982), 20 C.C.L.T. 225 at 235-36 (B.C.S.C.); *Ferguson v. Hamilton Civic Hosp.* (1983), 23 C.C.L.T. at 254 (Ont. H.C.); *Hankins v. Papillon* (1980), 14 C.C.L.T. 198 at 201 (Que. S.C.).

337 In 26 cases decided *since Reibl v. Hughes* only two report questions.

notable exceptions include *Smith v. Auckland Hosp. Bd.*,[338] where the patient asked, "is there any risk attached to this?;" *Koehler v. Cook*,[339] where the question was about the risks in an operation; *Calder v. Gilmour*,[340] where a patient specifically asked about "the danger of diplopia;" *Videto v. Kennedy*,[341] where the patient testified that she asked "how big the scar would be;" and *Rawlings v. Lindsay*,[342] where a dental patient asked the dentist "if he foresaw any difficulty in removing wisdom teeth . . ."

The borderline between specific questions and only general questions or concerns may give the courts some pause. Chief Justice Laskin says the question must be specific and that its specificity is a question of fact. Yet it seems likely that a general question about *all* risks of a procedure[343] should be answered and could be described as specific when compared with a question such as: "Doctor, tell me all about a hysterectomy."

Patients frequently couch their questions in terms of concerns. When might an expressed concern be interpreted as a specific question? Could a concern about death on the operating table ever be interpreted as a query about the risk of death during the proposed procedure? Chief Justice Laskin seems to countenance a less thorough response to concerns than to questions:[344]

> The patient may have expressed certain concerns to the doctor and the latter is obliged to meet them in a *reasonable* way. [emphasis supplied]

Obviously questions must be taken more seriously than ever not only by those who are questioned but also by patients, lawyers and judges. It is appropriate to remember that a question does far more than supply the questioner with an answer, since it should alert the doctor to an attribute or concern of the patient and thereby may affect the scope of disclosure and the determination of the causation issue.[345] Although in most cases the doctor's grasp of what he knows or ought to know about the patient would be increased by such questioning, the doctor might also be led to assuming from the question that the patient already had certain relevant information.[346]

As important as the quality of the question is, the scope of the response or answer is of even greater consequence.[347] There seems little doubt that the

---

338 *Supra* n. 327.
339 *Supra* n. 325.
340 *Supra* n. 325.
341 *Supra* n. 311.
342 *Supra* n. 336.
343 Note in the *Smith v. Auckland* case *supra* n. 327 a question about "any risk" was adequate.
344 *Reibl v. Hughes supra* n. 295 at 16.
345 *See* Bowker, *Minors and Mental Incompetents: Consent to Experimentation, Gifts of Tissue and Sterilization* (1981), 26 McGill L.J. 951 at 957; Gochnauer and Fleming, *Tort Law Informed Consent — New Directions for Medical Disclosure — Hopp v. Lepp and Reibl v. Hughes* (1981), 15 U.B.C.L. Rev. 475 at 482. Somerville, *Structuring the Issues in Informed Consent* (1981), 26 McGill L.J. 740 at 798.
346 *Reibl v. Hughes* (1978), 6 C.C.L.T. 227 at 236 (Ont. C.A.).
347 For the view that an objective test must be used to measure the response, *see* Rodgers-Magnet, *Recent Developments in the Doctrine of Informed Consent to Medical Treatment* (1980), 14 C.C.L.T. 61 at 72.

Chief Justice felt that the patient should be given all information, even about "merely possible" risks, in response to a specific question. Such a reply goes beyond what the doctor is expected to give in any voluntary disclosure. It seems the term "full disclosure" in its true sense can be used to describe the quality of the answer required in law.[348]

But the reality for the doctor may be that even a full disclosure answer is not appreciated by the patient who is certainly nervous, may have a language problem, is usually ill and perhaps in pain. In an Ontario case, *Hajgato v. London Health Assn.,*[349] a patient whose English was poor was complaining that the risk of infection associated with a Chiari osteotomy had not been explained to her. Mr. Justice Callaghan found that three doctors independently on three occasions had, in fact, done so, but that because of her state of anxiety the patient did not recall it.

Modern medical practice inside or outside of the hospital frequently puts a patient in the care of more than one doctor or health care professional. Furthermore, the common practice of doctors in hospitals has been to have a nurse or member of the house staff provide information about proposed treatment to the patient. The Supreme Court of Canada requirement that the doctor (referred to by Laskin C.J.C. as "the surgeon") answer specific questions raises the issue of whether this duty is delegable. The cases support the proposition that the doctor can satisfy his duty of disclosure in a voluntary disclosure situation if he can provide evidence that the patient was informed about the risks by someone.[350] Although it may be a rare case where a doctor wishes to defer answering a specific question, it would seem the importance attached by Chief Justice Laskin to questions requires the doctor who is asked to assume full responsibility for the patient receiving an answer.

Perhaps questions will become a more common feature of the doctor-patient relationship. The Supreme Court of Canada has established that the doctor and the patient should now have high expectations of receiving respectively specific questions and full answers. This will no doubt support better doctor-patient relationships but adequate evidence of the communciations will be necessary to support litigation.

The doctor should, without being questioned, disclose the nature of the proposed procedure and its gravity.

---

348 *See Hopp v. Lepp* (1979), 8 C.C.L.T. 260 at 298 (Alta. C.A.), where Mr. Justice Prowse, dissenting, drew a distinction between the scope of disclosure required generally and that required when a patient asked a specific question. He said the doctor in the latter situation has "to make a *reasonably* frank and full disclosure . . . [emphasis supplied].

   See also Sharpe *Informed Consent* 54 (1979), who points out the court in *Smith v. Auckland Hosp. Bd.* required an answer that met only the professional standard of disclosure.

349 (1982), 36 O.R. (2d) 669 at 679 (Ont. H.C.). *See also Bucknam v. Kostiuk* (1983), 20 A.C.W.S. (2d) 542 (Ont. H.C.).

350 *Ferguson v. Hamilton Civic Hosp.* (1983), 23 C.C.L.T. 254 (Ont. H.C.). For further discussion see *infra* E. Foreseeable Problems.

The Supreme Court of Canada requires that the "essential qualities" of the treatment or procedure be disclosed voluntarily. Canadian doctors seem to be more successful at this than at any other aspect of disclosure, likely because this has always been the "heart" of conversations between doctor and patient. Indeed, innovative measures are taken by some doctors including sketching a mammoplasty procedure,[351] reviewing x-rays and drawing diagrams of a Chiari osteotomy,[352] and handing out an information sheet on abortion which even stated the time of day that the therapeutic abortion committee met.[353]

In *Ferguson v. Hamilton Civic Hosp.*,[354] Mr. Justice Krever considered and rejected an argument that a doctor describing the nature of a diagnostic test must discuss the nature and risks of follow-up surgery. But there seems to be some force in the argument that included in the "nature" of a test is the likely consequence of alternative responses to the results of the tests. A person making an informed choice about consenting to a test may well wish to know more about the follow-up alternatives and their risks.

The need to disclose information about the gravity or seriousness of a treatment or procedure raises the issue of elective procedures.[355] Procedures categorized as elective by Canadian courts include plastic or cosmetic surgery,[356] sterilization,[357] and even abortion.[358] But such procedures may have therapeutic benefits too, for example, the reduction of pendulous breasts,[359] the removal of excess skin from eyelids,[360] the removal of wisdom teeth to reduce discomfort and improve mouth opening,[361] the replacement of the middle ear with a prosthesis to improve partial hearing,[362] and a sterilization to avoid an unwanted pregnancy and adverse health problems.[363]

---

351 *White v. Turner* (1981), 15 C.C.L.T. 81 at 86 (Ont. H.C.).

352 *Hajgato v. London Health Assn.* (1982), 36 O.R. (2d) 669 at 672 (Ont. H.C.).

353 *Mang v. Moscovitz* (1982), 37 A.R. 221 at 256 (Alta. Q.B.). Note the comments of Bouck J. in *Falez v. Boothroyd* (1980), 22 B.C.L.R. 41 (B.C.S.C.), to the effect that doctors can explain medical issues in lay terms.

354 (1983), 23 C.C.L.T. 254 (Ont. H.C.).

355 Note the term is used in the sense that any therapeutic benefits are secondary and not to differentiate emergency from non-emergency as was the case in *Hajgato v. London Health Assn.* (1982), 36 O.R. (2d) 669 at 680 (Ont. H.C.).

356 *LaFleur v. Cornelius* (1979), 28 N.B.R. (2d) 569 (N.B.Q.B.); *White v. Turner* (1981), 15 C.C.L.T. 81; affirmed (1982), 20 C.C.L.T. xii (Ont. C.A.); *MacDonald v. Ross* (1983), 24 C.C.L.T. 242 (N.S.S.C.); *Guertin v. Kester* (1981), 20 C.C.L.T. 225 (B.C.S.C.); *Hankins v. Papillon* (1980), 14 C.C.L.T. 198 (Que. S.C.).

357 *Videto v. Kennedy* (1981), 17 C.C.L.T. 307 at 310 (Ont. C.A.), and at trial 107 D.L.R. (3d) 613 at 622.

358 *Mang v. Moscovitz* (1982), 37 A.R. 221 at 270 (Alta. Q.B.).

359 *White v. Turner supra* n. 356; *MacDonald v. Ross supra* n. 356.

360 *Guertin v. Kester supra* n. 356.

361 *Rawlings v. Lindsay* (1982), 20 C.C.L.T. 301 (B.C.S.C.).

362 *Zamparo v. Brisson* (1981), 16 C.C.L.T. 66 (Ont. C.A.).

363 *Zimmer v. Ringrose* (1981), 16 C.C.L.T. 51 at 59 (Alta. C.A.). Note that even a nude dancer with a prominent abdomen argued that she *required* an abdominoplasty, *Petty v. MacKay* (1979), 10 C.C.L.T. 85 (B.C.S.C.).

The fact that a procedure is not required but is elective must be brought to the attention of the patient, for the patient may wish to delay or even forego the treatment.[364]

What is the effect on the scope of disclosure when treatment is elective? The surgery performed on Mr. Reibl was said by Chief Justice Laskin to be elective and this fact must have affected his decision on disclosure and causation, but he said nothing explicit about the issue of elective surgery and disclosure.[365] Thus it has been left to the provincial courts to develop some jurisprudence in the area.

With regard to the scope of disclosure required when a procedure is elective, Mr. Justice Linden said:[366]

> Where an operation is elective, as this one was, *even minimal* risks must be disclosed to patients . . . *A fortiori,* in a case where the predominant aim is a cosmetic one, *possible risks* affecting the appearance of the breasts . . . must be classified as material. [emphasis supplied]

The learned justice referred to the trial judgment in *Videto v. Kennedy,* a case of sterilization, where Mr. Justice Grange said:[367]

> The important thing to me is that this was a totally elective operation; it need not have been performed then or ever. While it may well not be necessary to warn a patient — it may even be a disservice — of *minimal risks* where an operation is essential or advisable for his continued good health, *the frequency of the risk becomes much less material* when the operation is unnecessary for his medical welfare. [emphasis supplied]

In applying his criteria, Mr. Justice Grange found the risk of perforating the bowel during a laparoscopic sterilization significant enough to require its disclosure. He said the danger was "not great but it is real and it is outside the danger inherent in any operation."[368] He found that as a result of almost non-existent post-operative care the patient nearly died from peritonitis resulting from the perforation.

On appeal,[369] Mr. Justice Howland acknowledged that the procedure was elective, and although he did not disagree with the scope of disclosure set by the lower court, he noted that the appeal was argued on the basis of the risk of a large scar rather than the risk of perforation of the bowel. However, he did go on to say, *obiter,* that a perforation dealt with expeditiously is not serious and commented that the situation was a very different one from *Reibl* where

---

364 This can be implied from the judgment in *Reibl v. Hughes supra* n. 295; *see also* Somerville, *Structuring the Issues in Informed Consent* (1981), 26 McGill L.J. 740 at 756; Ferguson, *Informed Consent: What the Law Requires* (1980), 1 H.L. in C. 56 at 57.

365 *Supra* n. 295 at 7.

366 *White v. Turner* (1981), 15 C.C.L.T. 81 at 103 (Ont. H.C.); affirmed (1982), 20 C.C.L.T. xxii (Ont. C.A.).

367 (1980), 107 D.L.R. (3d) 612 at 622 (Ont. H.C.).

368 *Id.* at 623.

369 (1981), 17 C.C.L.T. 307 at 310 (Ont. C.A.).

the operation itself could result in death or paralysis.[370] He reversed the trial decision and found for the doctor.

This Court of Appeal decision seems to accept the principle that in elective procedures even minimal or possible risks must be disclosed, but the Chief Justice of Ontario would have characterized a perforation of the bowel as less than a minimal risk.[371]

There is authority for requiring a doctor effecting a sterilization to explain other methods or techniques.[372] It would seem that this can be generalized to cover any elective procedure.[373]

But as well as being told about alternatives, comparative risks, and minimal or possible risks, some patients would like a doctor to advise them to have or not to have the elective treatment. The Ontario Court of Appeal has drawn the line at this point. In *Zamparo v. Brisson*,[374] Madame Justice Wilson speaking for the Ontario Court of Appeal, said:[375]

> While it may be that a surgeon is under a duty to give his patient his assessment of how the benefits of surgery measure up against the risks of having it, it seems to me that in the case of elective surgery only the patient can truly evaluate the benefits for him or her. There is a substantial subjective element to the evaluation of those benefits which are more than merely physical. There are sociological and psychological aspects, the importance of which will vary from patient to patient. Should the surgeon step outside his area of medical and surgical expertise and tell the patient what is "best" for him or her?

In interpreting the Supreme Court of Canada's decision in *Reibl v. Hughes*,[376] the provincial courts have said that for an elective procedure, minimal or possible risks and alternative procedures and their comparative risks must be explained voluntarily. The critical determination in many cases will be whether risk of the elective procedure in issue was even less than minimal. As will be seen, this characterization of risks is the most challenging part of any case in which informed consent is in issue.

The doctor should, without being questioned, disclose any material risks and any special or unusual risks or procedure.

---

370 *Id.* at 318.

371 *See also McBride v. Langton*, [1982] A.W.L.D. Sept. 24, 1982 (Alta. Q.B.) (liability in negligence for after care); *Gouin-Perreault v. Villeneuve* (1982), 23 C.C.L.T. 72 (Que. S.C.) (no liability).

372 *Zimmer v. Ringrose* (1981), 16 C.C.L.T. 51 at 60 (Alta. C.A.); motion for leave to appeal to S.C.C. dismissed (1981), 28 A.R. 92. In the U.S. *see Thornton v. Annest* (1978), 574 P. (2d) 1199 (Wash. App.); *Steele v. St. Paul Fire & Marine Ins. Co.* (1979), 371 So. (2d) 843 (L.C.A.). *See also* Thompson, Sanbar, *Wrongful Conception or Wrongful Pregnancy* (1983), 11 Legal Aspects Med. Prac.

373 *Sunne v. Shaw*, [1981] C.S. 609 (Que. S.C.). Bowker, *Minors and Mental Incompetents: Consent to Experimentation, Gifts of Tissue and Sterilization* (1981), 26 McGill L.J. 951 at 955.

374 (1981), 16 C.C.L.T. 66 (Ont. C.A.). Mr. Justice Zuber dissented; note also that Wilson J. is now a member of the Supreme Court of Canada.

375 *Id.* at 80.

376 *Supra* n. 295.

A risk that is a mere possibility should be regarded as material and disclosed if its occurrence carries serious consequences, as for example, paralysis or even death.

The Supreme Court of Canada has used the following words to describe risks: material, probable, special or unusual, mere possibilities. In regard to elective procedures, the terms used are minimal or possible. Do these terms have meanings that allow for differentiation amongst them? Is it possible to assign precise meanings?[377] The quandary presented by the vagueness of these terms[378] may be dealt with perfunctorily by saying that a risk is whatever the trier of fact says it is. But while there is no doubt that it is a question of fact,[379] the doctor and the lawyer still require some guidance.

The Supreme Court of Canada cases seem to say, in essence, let the *serious*[380] risks be disclosed by a doctor after a judgmental process by him involving a review of the risks known to medicine, a consideration of the reasonable patient and also of the specific patient from a physical, psychological and social perspective.[381] The process requires using those qualities the law has always required of the doctor; skill, knowledge and judgment.[382] If in subsequent litigation it appears this judgment by the doctor has been arrived at in a proper manner, he will have met the standard of care set by the legal concept of informed consent and the standard of care required by the law of negligence.

Chief Justice Laskin reviewed the possible classifications and the deficiencies thereof before setting out his own description of risks.[383] He stated that "materiality" must be determined with reference to the standard required for adequate disclosure, i.e., reference to medical knowledge, but equally to the patient. In the words "special or unusual," there is a sense of the very patient being the critical factor, and perhaps, a unique feature of the patient's physical or psychological make-up rendering an otherwise rare risk "special" to this procedure on this patient.[384]

The possibility of grave consequences is the determinant which transforms the very small risk called a "mere possibility" into one requiring disclosure. The Chief Justice gave the examples of death and paralysis as contrasted with residual stiffness. In a New Brunswick court, Mr. Justice

---

377 For an excellent discussion, *see* Somerville, *Structuring the Issues in Informed Consent* (1981), 26 McGill L.J. 740 at 753-62.
378 For a helpful discussion, *see* Gochnauer and Fleming *supra* n. 345.
379 *Reibl v. Hughes supra* n. 295 at 17.
380 *See* Bowker *supra* n. 373 at 965; One author has suggested that a risk with greater than one percent probability of causing irreversible morbidity be disclosed. Somerville, *Structuring the Issues in Informed Consent* (1981), 26 McGill L.J. 740 at 756.
381 *See Reibl v. Hughes supra* n. 295 at 7, 17.
382 *See supra* Ch. 4.
383 *Hopp v. Lepp supra* n. 272 at 80-81.
384 *See* Gochnauer and Fleming *supra* n. 345 at 479.

Stevenson held the risk of loss or impairment of voice to be such a grave consequence that it required revelation.[385]

Each court will of necessity have to grapple with the categorization of risks. Two judgments of provincial courts are helpful.

In *White v. Turner*, Mr. Justice Linden described "material" and "unusual or special" risks in these terms:[386]

> The meaning of "material risks" and "unusual or special risks" should now be considered. In my view, *material* risks are significant risks that pose a real threat to the patients' life, health or comfort. In considering whether a risk is material or immaterial, one must balance the severity of the potential result and the likelihood of its occurring. Even if there is only a small chance of serious injury or death, the risk may be considered material. On the other hand, if there is a significant chance of slight injury this too may be held to be material. As always in negligence law, what is a material risk will have to depend on the specific facts of each case.
>
> As for "unusual or special risks", these are those that are not ordinary, common, everyday matters. These are risks that are somewhat extraordinary, uncommon and not encountered every day, but they are known to occur occasionally. Though rare occurrences, because of their unusual or special character, the Supreme Court has declared that they should be described to a reasonable patient, even though they may not be "material". There may, of course, be an overlap between "material risks" and "unusual or special risks". If a special or unusual risk is quite dangerous and fairly frequently encountered, it could be classified as a material risk. But even if it is not very dangerous or common, an unusual or special risk must be disclosed.

In the result, Linden J. held that the risk of scars opening up and requiring further corrective surgery and the risk of a certain type of scarring were "special or unusual" and had not been disclosed. He also found certain "material" risks, such as the likelihood of an imperfect breast shape, an asymmetrical appearance and stretch and tissue scars, had not been disclosed.

Another thoughtful and useful judgment is that of Madame Justice McLachlin in *Rawlings v. Lindsay*.[387] Once again a learned justice has set out an interpretation of the types of risks that must be explained and analyzed the facts accordingly.

Of the terminology of risks she said:[388]

> The terminology of "material", "special", and "unusual" risks has in the past given rise to confusion. However, a fair summary of the effect of those decisions, in my view, is that a medical person must disclose those risks to which a reasonable patient would be likely to attach significance in deciding whether or not to undergo the proposed treatment. In

---

385 *Bickford v. Stiles* (1981), 128 D.L.R. (3d) 516 at 523 (N.B.S.C.). The learned justice opined that a list of losses in terms of seriousness might be: sight, hearing, voice, taste, smell. Note that Laskin C.J. mentions the risk of hearing impairment in *Hopp v. Lepp supra* n. 272 at 79-80. *See also Reynard v. Carr* (1983), 50 B.C.L.R. 166 (B.C.S.C.), where "bone failure" was found to be a serious consequence of drug treatment with prednisone and required disclosure.

386 (1981), 15 C.C.L.T. 81 at 99 (Ont. H.C.); affirmed (1982), 20 C.C.L.T. xxii (Ont. C.A.).

387 (1982), 20 C.C.L.T. 301 (B.C.S.C.).

388 *Id.* at 306.

making this determination, the degree of probability of the risk and its seriousness are relevant factors. Thus an "unusual" or improbable risk should be disclosed if its effects are serious. Conversely, a minor result should be disclosed if it is inherent in or a probable result of the process.

McLachlin J. held a five to ten per cent risk of nerve impairment to be an unusual risk that should have been disclosed.

A very likely variation of the terminology discussed will be for the courts to use the term "material" in the broad sense to cover all risks which, after the determination by the trier of fact, are held necessary of disclosure.

All that can be said for certain about the attempt to describe risks precisely is that there will be uncertainty.[389] Doctors and patients can only hope that the lawyers and the courts will not weave a web of words to further complicate doctor-patient communications but instead will try to apply, case by case, the general principles fashioned by the Supreme Court of Canada.

One trend already apparent is an attempt to give a precision, even a scientific quality to the description of risks[390] by assessing them in terms of percentages or statistics. This was seen in *Reibl v. Hughes*[391] where the Court of Appeal was very critical of the use of statistics by the trial judge,[392] prompting Chief Justice Laskin to say that the failure to mention statistics should not affect "the duty to inform nor be a factor in deciding whether the duty has been breached."[393] Evidence of risks assessed on a statistical basis must be carefully researched and proven by counsel and subjected to cautious scrutiny by courts because it may be misleading or misunderstood.

The doctor can under some circumstances withhold or generalize information.

The scope of disclosure outlined above can, according to the Supreme Court of Canada cases, sometimes be narrowed. This discretion is not new but is, indeed, a recognition of the unique nature of the doctor-patient relationship wherein the doctor has a fiduciary relationship with the patient and has a duty to act with the utmost good faith and honesty. The duty is a moral as distinguished from a legal one.[394]

The relevant words of the Supreme Court of Canada in *Reibl v. Hughes* describing the circumstances when the normal scope of disclosure may be reduced are:[395]

---

389 For a critique of the risk description in *Hopp v. Lepp, supra* n. 272 *see* Somerville *supra* n. 380 at 761.

390 *See, for example, Considine v. Camp Hill Hosp.* (1982), 133 D.L.R. (3d) 11 (N.S.S.C.); *Rawlings v. Lindsay* (1982), 20 C.C.L.T. 301 (B.C.S.C.); *Hajgato v. London Health Assn.* (1982), 36 O.R. (2d) 669 (Ont. H.C.); *McBride v. Langton,* [1982] A.W.L.D. Sept. 24, 1982 (Alta. Q.B.).

391 *Supra* n. 295.

392 (1978), 6 C.C.L.T. 227 at 239 (Ont. C.A.).

393 *Supra* n. 295 at 16.

394 *Kenny v. Lockwood,* [1932] 1 D.L.R. 507 at 521 (Ont. C.A.). *Reibl v. Hughes supra* n. 295 at 76. *See also* Chapter 1. *See also Considine v. Camp Hill Hosp.* (1982), 133 D.L.R. (3d) 11 at 39 (N.S.T.D.).

395 *Reibl v. Hughes supra* n. 295 at 17.

It is, of course, possible that a particular patient may waive aside any question of risks and be quite prepared to submit to surgery or treatment, whatever they be. Such a situation presents no difficulty. Again, it may be the case that a particular patient may, because of emotional factors, be unable to cope with facts relevant to recommended surgery or treatment and the doctor may, in such a case, be justified in withholding or generalizing information as to which he would otherwise be required to be more specific.

And there is this further pertinent observation [quoting from *Kenny v. Lockwood*, [1932] 1 D.L.R. 507 at 523]:[396]

"Nor do I for a moment think that the dangers inseparable from any operation, such as failure or death under an anaesthetic, the danger of infection, of tetanus, of gas gangrene or gangrene, were proper or necessary to be disclosed to a patient before an operation."

I would add, taking the trial Judge's finding on the point in the present case, that the risk or possibility of complications as being more easily dealt with in larger centres is also common to all operations and does not ordinarily call for particular disclosure . . .

No doubt, a surgeon has some leeway in assessing the emotional condition of the patient and how the prospect of an operation weighs upon him; the apprehension, if any, of the patient, which may require placating; his reluctance, if any, to submit to an operation, which, if the surgeon honestly believes that the operation is necessary for the preservation of the patient's life or health, may demand detailed explanation of why it is necessary . . .

These circumstances where information may be withheld or generalized will now be discussed.

Waiver

Waiver must be initiated by the patient. It is of course the patient's ultimate right to self-determination, but should be acceptable only when a patient is truly declining an explanation.[397]

There must be evidence of an express waiver in circumstances where from the patient's perspective, the doctor was willing to provide an explanation. It is only with these qualifications that waiver should prove to be "no difficulty". To date, there have been no cases where waiver has been raised by the doctor.[398]

Common Risks

Chief Justice Laskin has said that common, everyday risks need not be disclosed. This admonition must be based on the premise that common risks can be ascertained and are accepted by our society. Although this seems eminently practical, it may not be easy to realize a consensus amongst doctors and patients on a list of such risks.

The Chief Justice seems to have accepted the list given by Hodgins J.A. in *Kenny v. Lockwood*:[399] failure or death under anaesthetic, infection, tetanus,

---

396 *Hopp v. Lepp supra* n. 272 at 76-7.
397 *See* Jazvac, *Informed Consent: Risk Disclosure and the Canadian Approach* (1979), 36 U.T.L.R. 191 at 195.
398 Note that a prudent doctor should document such a waiver and perhaps even have a witness.
399 *Supra* n. 394 at 521 quoted in *Hopp v. Lepp supra* n. 272 at 76.

gas gangrene, gangrene, and added the fact of the capacity of large centres to better deal with complications. Yet such consequences vary a great deal in degree and import.[400] While it is true that even a healthy adult might have an unforeseen cardiac arrest during the surgery[401] or contract a staphylococcus infection, there are individuals at greater risk of these unfortunate events, such as the person already ill with other health problems for whom perhaps these commonplace risks are "special or unusual" risks requiring disclosure.

A point made by Mr. Justice Linden is well taken. He expresses doubt that all of the risks listed in *Kenny v. Lockwood* would now be accepted as common, everyday risks.[402] Indeed one of the goals of medical science is to reduce and keep all risks to a minimum, and although incredible advances have been made, new risks may arise.[403] Mr. Justice Linden's list of common, everyday risks would include: bleeding, pain and a scar from an incision, a chance of infection, minor discomforts from surgery.[404]

No doubt a list of the common risks the patient must accept will evolve from the cases and be shaped by the rule of judicial notice[405] and expert evidence. But it is important to distinguish at the outset those common risks which materialize without negligence and those which are a consequence of negligence because a patient cannot be said to accept negligence as a common, everyday risk.

In view of its use in other areas of informed consent, the courts and the doctor might be expected to use as a test what the reasonable person in these circumstances would understand to be the common, ordinary risks involved.[406]

Emotional Factors (Therapeutic Privilege)

In both *Reibl v. Hughes*[407] and *Hopp v. Lepp*,[408] the court anticipated a doctor having the discretion to vary the information he gives a patient to reflect emotional "conditions" or "factors" affecting the patient.

If a patient is apprehensive about an operation the doctor honestly believes is necessary, a detailed explanation of why it is necessary may be required. On the other hand, emotional factors may be the justification for

---

400 *Hajgato v. London Health Assn.* (1982), 36 O.R. (2d) 669 (Ont. H.C.).

401 *See Considine v. Camp Hill Hosp. supra* n. 394 at 39.

402 *White v. Turner* (1981), 15 C.C.L.T. 81 at 99 (Ont. H.C.); Note that in *Reibl v. Hughes* (1977), 78 D.L.R. (3d) 35 (Ont. H.C.), Haines J. listed only risks of anaesthesia and of infection.

403 *See* Ilich, *Medical Nemesis: The Experimentation of Health* (1976).

404 *Supra* n. 402.

405 For an explanation of this doctrine, *see* Sopinka & Lederman, *The Law of Evidence in Civil Cases* 357 (1974).

406 *Note* the comment in Ferguson, *Informed Consent: What the Law Requires* (1980), 1 H.L. in C. 56 at 57, that a doctor would be foolish to omit to mention these risks.

407 *Supra* n. 295.

408 *Supra* n. 272.

withholding or generalizing information. This discretion has been given the name "therapeutic privilege" by the American courts.[409]

This concept has led courts to assess the emotional status of patients. In *Reibl v. Hughes*,[410] Chief Justice Laskin found that there was "no evidence that the plaintiff was emotionally taut or unable to accept disclosure of the grave risk to which he would be exposed." In *Rawlings v. Lindsay*,[411] McLachlin J. said the patient's "attitude toward her dental health was . . . mature and intelligent . . . " In *Hajgato v. London Health Assn.*,[412] the doctor described the patient as "labile," and as a consequence did not tell her that a massive infection could destroy her hip. Clearly the courts must take a restrictive approach to the exercise of discretion because interpreted broadly, it could destroy the patient's right to be informed. There would seem, for example, to be many medical situations where it could be alleged that explaining the risk would "scare" the patient,[413] the argument being that the procedure could only be done safely on a patient who is not apprehensive.

Thus the courts must set limits to the concept of therapeutic privilege. Professor Somerville has submitted that:[414]

> . . . the physician may rely on therapeutic privilege to justify a non-disclosure of risks where the reasonable physician in the same circumstances would have believed that the disclosure, *in itself, [emphasis Somerville's] would physically or mentally harm the patient to some significant degree.* The doctrine should not apply if the only reason for the non-disclosure is that it may cause the patient to refuse treatment that the physician regards as necessary. [emphasis supplied]

The only logical test by which to measure the patient is a subjective one. Thus, the question the doctor should consider is whether the disclosure would in itself cause physical or mental harm to *this* patient.[415]

Waiver, knowledge and acceptance of common risks, and therapeutic privilege all have the effect of requiring the doctor to disclose less and, ultimately, to shield the doctor from liability. Thus, the burden of proving each should rest with the doctor.[416]

---

409 For a list of references *see* Somerville *Consent to Medical Care* 13 (1979 L.R.C.).
410 *Supra* n. 295 at 59.
411 (1982), 20 C.C.L.T. 301 at 307 (B.C.S.C.).
412 (1982), 36 O.R. (2d) 669 at 678 (Ont. H.C.); *see also White v. Turner* (1981), 15 C.C.L.T. 81 at 103 (Ont. H.C.).
413 *See, for example, McBride v. Langton*, [1982] A.W.L.D. Sept. 24, 1982 (Alta. Q.B.); *Gouin-Perrault v. Villeneuve* (1982), 23 C.C.L.T. 72 (Que. S.C.); *McLean v. Weir*, [1980] 4 W.W.R. 330 (B.C.C.A.).
414 Somerville, *Structuring the Issues in Informed Consent* (1981), 26 McGill L.J. 740 at 767.
415 Note, however, that Professor Somerville advocates an objective-subjective test. *Id.* at 769-70.
416 Somerville, *Structuring the Issues in Informed Consent* (1981), 26 McGill L.J. 740 at 773.

D. Causation

Because the appropriate action where a patient alleges he has not given an informed consent is negligence, the patient has the onus of proving that the doctor's substandard disclosure was the cause-in-fact and the proximate cause of his injury. To put it in another way, the patient may prove that the risk was of the sort that required disclosure and thus that the doctor breached his duty to disclose by not doing so, but will lose the lawsuit unless he also proves that the reasonable person in his position would *not* have proceeded after being informed of the said risks. Thus the patient must prove a negative.

The Supreme Court of Canada in its judgments in *Hopp v. Lepp*[417] and *Reibl v. Hughes*[418] substituted an objective test for the previously established subjective one. Thus, the patient must now prove on a balance of probabilities that a *reasonable* person would *not* have consented to the treatment had the disclosure been adequate, not just that he, the patient, would not have done so.[419] However, the case law and the literature since the Supreme Court of Canada decisions indicate that the test actually applied by Chief Justice Laskin is a blend of objectivity and subjectivity.[420]

There has been some variation in the manner of application of the new test. The judgment in the Court of Appeal in *Videto v. Kennedy* seems to be the strongest statement for pure objectivity.[421] Chief Justice Howland said that the trial judge had not the benefit of the Supreme Court of Canada decision, but had followed the test of Brooke J.A. in the Ontario Court of Appeal in *Reibl v. Hughes*,[422] and had therefore tested the plaintiff's case objectively and then considered it subjectively. He held that the trial judge "erred in not applying the objective test of the reasonable man"[423] to Mrs. Videto. The trial judge said "it would have taken very little to dissuade her from the operation [sterilization]"[424] and the fact that she was a Catholic, and had agreed to the operation because of the small scar which would result, were weighty considerations. The Court of Appeal reversed the finding of liability, having found no breach in the duty of disclosure in any case.

---

417 *Supra* n. 272.
418 *Supra* n. 295.
419 See Robertson, *Overcoming The Causation Hurdle In Informed Consent Cases: The Principle In McGhee v. N.C.B.* (1983), 21 U. W. Ont. L. Rev. (forthcoming), where the point is made that this objective test does not, of itself, establish a causal link between the particular plaintiff's injury and the defendant's negligence.
420 Somerville, *Structuring the Issues in Informed Consent* (1981), 26 McGill L.J. 740; Gochnauer and Fleming, *Tort Law — Informed Consent — New Directions for Medical Disclosure — Hopp v. Lepp and Reibl v. Hughes* (1981), 15 U.B.C.L. Rev. 475; Picard, *Consent to Medical Treatment in Canada* (1981), 19 Osgoode Hall L.J. 140; *but see* Rodgers-Magnet, *Recent Developments in the Doctrine of Informed Consent* (1981), 14 C.C.L.T. 61.
421 (1981), 17 C.C.L.T. 307 (Ont. C.A.).
422 (1978), 6 C.C.L.T. 227 (Ont. C.A.).
423 *Supra* n. 421 at 317.
424 (1980), 107 D.L.R. (3d) 612 at 621 (Ont. H.C.).

Mr. Justice Linden seems to have anticipated a subjective assessment of the patient when he said of the objective test:[425]

> It is not enough, therefore, for the Court to be convinced that the plaintiff would have refused the treatment if he had been fully informed; the Court must *also [emphasis Justice Linden's] be satisfied* that a reasonable patient, *in the same situation* would have done so. That is the meaning of the objective test adopted in *Reibl v. Hughes.* [emphasis supplied]

In the case of *Zimmer v. Ringrose*,[426] the Alberta Court of Appeal used an analysis which does not seem to violate the principles enunciated by the Supreme Court of Canada. Mr. Justice Prowse, after recognizing that *Reibl v. Hughes* had advocated an objective test, stated:[427]

> In his judgment, Laskin emphasized two corollaries of the concept of the "patient's particular situation". Firstly, arising from the patient's particular circumstances may be "special considerations" which the trier of fact should take into account when determining whether the patient would have withheld his consent. In *Reibl v. Hughes,* the fact that the patient would have been entitled to a full pension if he had postponed the surgery for two years represented such a special consideration.

> Secondly, the patient's particular situation must be "objectively assessed in terms of reasonableness". In other words, the specific concerns which a patient may have with regard to the proposed therapy must be viewed objectively.

Applying the two corollaries of "special considerations" and the "assessment of reasonableness" of the patient's particular situation, Prowse J.A. held that a special consideration was Mrs. Zimmer's desire to avoid being hospitalized, an obstacle surmounted by submitting to the office sterilization by silver nitrate. He also held that her allegation that she would not have consented to Dr. Ringrose's suggested procedure was not reasonable in view of the confidence she showed in him by returning to him for a tubal ligation after the unsuccessful sterilization and subsequent abortion.

The Supreme Court of Canada in *Reibl v. Hughes*[428] was concerned about subjective assessments favouring the patient. In *Zimmer v. Ringrose*,[429] the reverse situation occurred. The court held that while the doctor had not met the duty of disclosure because he had not informed the patient of the novelty of the procedure and had not told her of alternate sterilization procedures, the patient had not established her case on the causation issue.

There are boundaries to the application of the Supreme Court of Canada test for causation.[430] At the one extreme is a total commitment to a "pure" objective test with a total disregard of subjective factors [431] and at the other a full recognition given to the subjective aspect.[432]

425 *White v. Turner* (1981), 15 C.C.L.T. 81 at 100-101 (Ont. H.C.).
426 (1981), 16 C.C.L.T. 51 (Alta. C.A.); motion for leave to appeal dismissed 28 A.R. 92.
427 *Id.* at 61-62.
428 *Supra* n. 295.
429 *Supra* n. 426.
430 *See* Somerville *supra* n. 420 at 800 where it has been observed that the approach of the Supreme Court of Canada is unitary rather than dual and is limited as to which subjective factors may be introduced.
431 *Videto v. Kennedy* (1981), 17 C.C.L.T. 307 (Ont. C.A.); *see* Rodgers-Magnet *supra* n. 420.
432 *See* Gochnauer and Fleming *supra* n. 420.

Between the two extremes there is a scope for recognition of the merit of both objective and subjective assessments. As has been shown, Brooke J.A.[433] suggested a dual approach, Linden J.[434] a concurrent assessment of the objective and the subjective and Prowse J.A.[435] a precise delineation of a corollary to the main objective test. Professor Robertson[436] has argued that the subjective test is the true test of causation and that the objective test with its evidentiary function complements it and affords a means of testing the patient's testimony and decision, and disposes of unreasonable claims. Clearly, balancing the two aspects of the so-called objective test is a critical part of deciding the causation issue. Each aspect gives rise to complex questions.

Professors Gochnauer and Fleming[437] point out a defect in the objective approach, namely that there may not be a "uniquely determinable decision" which a reasonable person would make. Professor Robertson[438] argues that either decision (to accept or to decline) could be reasonable. Yet in all cases the court must arbitrarily establish which decision the reasonable person would have made.

Another enigma arises from the fact that the "reasonable patient" in a negligent disclosure action is a more nebulous concept than the reasonable person in an ordinary negligence suit.[439] What, in fact, are the appropriate criteria? Are they the same or similar to those used in the ordinary negligence suit? Is a reasonable patient "the man on the Clapham omnibus" or "on the Yonge Street subway"? The reasonable person test of negligence is varied for each kind of professional, for children and for those with certain disabilities. What effect, if any, should the status of the patient, the trauma of his or her decision-making situation and the spectre of illness or death have on the standard? Will a court in Canada one day construe the standard of a reasonable patient as the person on the examining room table full of self-confidence, *sans* fear, and as concerned for the consequences of his/her diagnosis on the health care system as on him/herself?

Certain decisions, for example, to undergo cosmetic surgery or sterilization or to refuse blood transfusions or life-saving procedures are difficult to equate to those normal to the world of the reasonable man. There are examples of cases where a factor relevant to a reasonable man may not affect

---

433 *Reibl v. Hughes* (1978), 6 C.C.L.T. 227 (Ont. C.A.).
434 *White v. Turner supra* n. 425.
435 *Zimmer v. Ringrose supra* n. 426.
436 *Supra* n. 419 at (10).
437 *Supra* n. 420 at 493; *see also* Sharpe, *Five Recent Canadian Decisions on Informed Consent* (1981), 1 H.L. in C. 79 at 81.
438 *Supra* n. 419.
439 For a thorough discussion *see* Linden, *Canadian Tort law*, 111 (1982). Note the interesting approach of the Chief Justice of B.C. who constructed a hypothetical dialogue between the patient and his dentist in order to decide the causation issue. *See Diack v. Bardsley*, unreported 14 June 1983, No. C822253 (B.C.S.C.).

the reasonable patient. For example, a reasonable man might forego stomach reduction surgery[440] or sterilization[441] by silver nitrate once apprised of the risks, but apparently, a reasonable patient would not.

Another difficulty is raised by the patient who has fears which may be unreasonable, because the Supreme Court of Canada has said that the patient's particular concerns must be reasonably based. Chief Justice Laskin said:[442]

> . . . fears which are not related to the material risks which should have been but were not disclosed would not be causative factors.

It has been noted that this passage may imply exclusion of fears related to risks which did not require disclosure, or fears related to disclosed material risks, or both.[443] Yet surely fears are relevant even to a reasonable patient. Professor Somerville has submitted:[444]

> . . . no matter how unreasonable a particular patient's concerns, if the physician knows of them and if there is a risk relating to these concerns, then if that risk is not disclosed and the patient undergoes treatment which he would have refused had that particular risk been disclosed, non-disclosure of that risk will be the cause-in-fact of its realization.

An example may serve to demonstrate how the problem may arise. Suppose a patient has a fear of needing a blood transfusion. If prior to treatment he is informed of the risk of blood loss that may require transfusion, he can certainly refuse treatment. Thus if the doctor does not inform the patient of this arguably non-material risk knowing he fears a transfusion, non-disclosure of the risk should constitute inadequate disclosure and satisfy the causation criteria.[445]

There have been questions raised about whether the Supreme Court of Canada test is any more efficient or just than its predecessor.[446] Chief Justice Laskin expressed concern about leaving the issue of causation in the hands of patients given the effect of hindsight, their bitterness and the likelihood of their admitting that they would have agreed to the procedure even knowing the risks.[447] In response it has[448] been argued that the adversary system is the accepted method of testing the credibility of witnesses, and that judges can and do reject the evidence of patients.[449]

---

440 *Petty v. McKay* (1979), 10 C.C.L.T. 85 (B.C.S.C.).

441 *Zimmer v. Ringrose* (1981), 16 C.C.L.T. 51 (Alta. C.A.).

442 *Reibl v. Hughes supra* n. 295 at 22.

443 Somerville *supra* n. 420 at 800-1.

444 *Supra* n. 420 at 801.

445 *See* Bamberg, *Informed Consent After Cobbs — Has the Patient Been Forgotten* (1973), 10 San Diego L. Rev. 913 at 922 quoted in Picard, *Consent to Medical Treatment in Canada* (1981), 19 Osgoode Hall L.J. 140 at 149.

446 *See* Somerville, Gochnauer and Fleming, Picard, Rodgers-Magnet *supra* n. 420; *see* Sharpe *supra* n. 437. *See* also McIntosh, *Liability and Compensation Aspects of Immunization Injury: A Call For Reform* (1980), O.H.L.J. 585 at 597.

447 *Reibl v. Hughes supra* n. 295.

448 Picard *supra* n. 420 at 148.

449 *See Hankins v. Papillon* (1980), 14 C.C.L.T. 198 (Que. S.C.); *Konkolus v. Royal Alexandra Hosp.* (1982), 21 Alta. L.R. (2d) 359 (Q.B.); *Ferguson v. Hamilton Civic Hosp.* (1983), 23 C.C.L.T. 254 (Ont. H.C.).

Professors Gochnauer and Fleming have summarized their opposing concerns as follows:[450]

> It is difficult to see why the Supreme Court of Canada would have chosen a policy which results in a finding that the plaintiff has failed to prove causation in these cases of clear "subjective" evidence of what the patient would have done. The subjective test will yield results in every case in which the objective test will succeed, and will then go on the handle situations beyond the capability of the objective test.
>
> With hindsight and bitterness a problem for both tests, it is unclear how justice is advanced by wilfully closing our eyes to evidence of what the patient actually would have done in those cases where the reasonable patient test fails. In the end, the objective test as it is developed by the Supreme Court not only fails to solve the major difficulties of application which the Court saw for the subjective test, but may even fail to produce determinate results in as many cases as would the subjective test. It appears that little or no improvement in efficiency or justice can result from the new test of causation.

Bickford v. Stiles[451] illustrates the consequences of the new test. In that case it was held that the failure to disclose the risk of vocal chord paralysis was a breach of the duty to disclose. However, it was held that the reasonable patient would have proceeded with the diagnostic surgery in any case because it could not only confirm or negate sarcoidosis but also cancer and tuberculosis, termed by the court "the more serious diagnosis." But Mrs. Bickford, whose condition was improving on medication when the biopsy was suggested, was never told of the more serious diagnosis, probably because there was no evidence of these symptoms in her. On a subjective analysis, it seems likely that a patient, knowing of a risk of vocal chord paralysis from diagnostic surgery testing for sarcoidosis (a condition which may have very mild symptoms), in a steadily improving state of health with a reluctance to undergo surgery, would *not* have chosen the diagnostic surgery. From it she suffered a paralyzed vocal chord for which she then required remedial surgery (although she no longer had sarcoidosis). The patient was not successful. Her case floundered on the causation issue.

In any negligence action, the patient must prove that the negligent conduct was the cause-in-fact and the proximate cause of his injury. Yet there is not a great deal of guidance to be gleaned from the cases on this issue for several reasons. It is only when the patient has been successful in proving a breach of the duty of disclosure that the causation issue is relevant.[452] Furthermore, the patient's case often develops such that proof of the cause-in-fact fulfills the criteria for proof of proximate cause.[453] However, proof of the cause-in-fact is often very difficult, a situation exemplified by the case of

---

450 *Supra* n. 420 at 495.
451 (1981), 128 D.L.R. (3d) 516 (N.B.Q.B.).
452 Thus, any comments on causation are made in passing, as *obiter dicta*, or the point is not dealt with. *See, for example, Videto v. Kennedy* (1981), 17 C.C.L.T. 307 at 319 (Ont. C.A.). In Quebec *see Schierz v. Dodds*, [1981] C.S. (Que. S.C.) and *Sunne v. Shaw*, [1981] C.S. 609 (Que. S.C.).
453 Sommerville *supra* n. 420 at 796.

Hankins v. Papillon,[454] where the brown spots the patient complained of could have been caused either by the dermabrasion surgery performed by the defendant or by her birth control pills. Also, there are no judgments where the law on causation has been thoroughly reviewed and a choice made of tests or rules.[455] Thus, some speculation on the development of the law is in order.

With regard to proving cause-in-fact in negligence, the "but-for" test has been accepted[456] and seems likely to be used in negligent disclosure. The patient must prove that but for the doctor's negligent disclosure, he would not have been injured.

However, a new test for cause-in-fact has been applied in a number of Canadian medical negligence cases and could be utilized in negligent disclosure cases. The principle originated in the House of Lords case of *McGhee v. Nat. Coal Bd.*[457] Professor Robertson explains its possible application:[458]

> The *McGhee* principle operates if it can be established that the defendant's negligence materially increased the risk of injury to the plaintiff. Thus, if it can be shown that the doctor's negligence in failing to inform his patient of a particular risk materially increased the likelihood of a patient consenting to the proposed treatment, and therefore exposing himself to the risk of injury, it follows that the doctor's negligence has materially increased the risk of injury to the patient.

While there are a wide range of possible injuries that might be alleged by the patient in a negligent disclosure action including the acceleration or exacerbation of ill health, economic loss, wrongful life and wrongful birth, in most cases the injury complained of is the undisclosed risk which has materialized.

But, as with negligence in general, the doctor should not be liable for all injuries suffered. A rule or test to limit liability is required.

The principles most likely to be used on the issue of causation in negligent disclosure are those used in negligence in general where the foreseeability test is employed. According to these criteria, the injury must be foreseeable in a general sort of way to a reasonable person in the position of the defendant. As discussed earlier, this is the rule used in the determining of the scope of disclosure. It is also the test advocated by the Supreme Court of Canada in *Cardin v. Montreal*[459] for determining proximate cause in medical negligence. Thus, it is not surprising that foreseeability has emerged as the most likely test to limit liability for negligent disclosure.

Because the Supreme Court of Canada did not establish any new rules in this area, it would be open to a court to adopt a novel approach, although the

---

454 (1980), 14 C.C.L.T. 198 (Que. S.C.); *see also Ferguson v. Hamilton Civic Hosp.* (1983), 23 C.C.L.T. 254. (Ont. H.C.).
455 For the alternatives *see* Linden *supra* n. 439 at 354.
456 *Id.* at 86.
457 [1972] 3 All E.R. 1008 (H.L.). For a discussion *see* Chapter 4.
458 *Supra* n. 419 at (15). Note that the consequence of applying the *McGhee* principle is a shift of the onus of proof to the defendant.
459 (1961), 29 D.L.R. (2d) 492 at 494 (S.C.C.).

effect would be a broadening of liability. Some possible steps might include construing the breach of duty to disclose as the reason for a patient consenting to surgery, thereby exposing him "to the risk of injury flowing from misadventure in the course of surgery;"[460] or, an acceptance that misadventure in the course of surgery is foreseeable.[461]

A court might take heed of the statement in *Hopp v. Lepp*[462] in which the Supreme Court of Canada, referring to *Halushka v. Univ. of Sask.*[463] said:[464]

> In the view of the Court of Appeal, there were undisclosed or misrepresented facts and . . . it added "[they] need not concern matters which directly cause the ultimate damage if they are of a nature which might influence the judgment upon which the consent is based".

In other words, the failure to disclose a fact or risk may make a defendant accountable even when it is not that risk but another that materializes.[465] The critical question is whether the substandard disclosure influenced the consent.

A court might return to the use of the directness test of *Polemis*,[466] whereby the negligent doctor would be liable for all direct consequences of the negligent act, which could be the negligent disclosure, or a court might fix the defendant with the burden of proof. Madame Justice McLachlin has raised an interesting difference between the rules applied to doctors and lawyers with respect to the onus of proof. She said *obiter:*[467]

> It will be seen that I have treated the burden of proof on the issue of causation as lying on the plaintiff. This approach seems to be implicit in the reasons of the Supreme Court in *Reibl v. Hughes* (although it was not specifically discussed at the Supreme Court level), as well as in accord with the general principle of negligence that the burden is on the plaintiff to establish both breach of duty and damages proximately flowing from that breach. However, there are comments indicating the situation may be otherwise in the case of a solicitor's negligence in *Howard v. Cunliffe* (1973), 36 D.L.R. (3d) 212 (B.C.C.A.), per McFarlane J.A. at pp. 220-1. It is unnecessary for me to determine the question of onus in this case . . .

Of course, if the principle in the *McGhee*[468] case, discussed earlier, were applied to negligent disclosure, there would be an onus shift from the patient to the doctor. But such measures seem unrealistic and unlikely unless the present criteria for establishing the causation issue are rendered incapable of producing just results.

---

460 *Per* Zuber J.A. in *Zamparo v. Brisson* (1981), 16 C.C.L.T. 66 at 78 (Ont. C.A.).
461 *Id.; see Kolesar v. Jeffries (sub. nom Joseph Brant Memorial Hosp. v. Koziol)* (1974), 9 O.R. (2d) 41 (Ont. H.C.); affirmed 2 C.C.L.T. 170 (S.C.C.). Note that another possibility is to compensate a patient for the "loss of a chance," *see* Robertson *supra* n. 419 at 33-47.
462 *Supra* n. 272.
463 (1965), 53 D.L.R. (2d) 436 at 445 (Sask. C.A.).
464 *Supra* n. 272 at 78.
465 *See Sunne v. Shaw*, [1981] C.S. 609 (Que. S.C.).
466 [1921] 3 K.B. 560.
467 *Rawlings v. Lindsay* (1982), 20 C.C.L.T. 301 at 309 (B.C.S.C.). *But see Diack v. Bardsley,* unreported June 14, 1983, No. C822253 (B.C.S.C.).
468 *Supra* n. 457.

In eight of the twenty-seven cases since *Reibl v. Hughes*[469] in which the plaintiff was unsuccessful, the patient proved a breach of disclosure but was not able to prove causation.[470] However, in six cases decided on other grounds, causation would have been an alternative basis for denying recovery.[471] Thus, causation was a determinative issue in half the cases.[472] It rests with higher courts and future courts to assess the fairness of these decisions.

It is crucial that the issues of the standard and scope of the duty of care and causation be seen as parts of a whole. It remains to be seen whether the new law created for these parts by the Supreme Court of Canada has effected a "new" balance[473] of the interests of doctors and patients, allowing freedom for the courts to come to a just decision in each case.

E. Foreseeable problems

Because the Supreme Court of Canada cases are fairly recent, there is no large body of case law for analysis. However, some problems have appeared or can be predicted.

---

469 *Supra* n. 295.

470 *Petty v. MacKay* (1979), 10 C.C.L.T. 85 (B.C.S.C.); *Zimmer v. Ringrose* (1981), 16 C.C.L.T. 51 (Alta. C.A.); *Bickford v. Stiles* (1981), 128 D.L.R. (3d) 516 (N.B.Q.B.); *Considine v. Camp Hill Hosp.* (1982), 133 D.L.R. (3d) 11 (N.S.S.C.); *Ferguson v. Hamilton Civic Hosp.* (1983), 23 C.C.L.T. 254 (Ont. H.C.); *Diack v. Bardsley* unreported 14 June 1983, No. C822253 (B.C.S.C.); *Moore v. Shaughnessy Hosp.* (1982), 15 A.C.W.S. (2d) 390 (B.C.S.C.); *O'Connell v. Munro* unreported November 7, 1983 No. (unavailable) (Ont. S.C.).

471 *Zamparo v. Brisson* (1981), 16 C.C.L.T. 66 (Ont. C.A.); *Videto v. Kennedy* (1981), 17 C.C.L.T. 307 (Ont. C.A.); *Hajgato v. London Health Assn.* (1982), 36 O.R. (2d) 669 (Ont. H.C.); *Gonda v. Kerbel* (1982), 24 C.C.L.T. 222 (Ont. S.C.); *Bucknam v. Kostiuk* (1983), 20 A.C.W.S. (2d) 543 (Ont. H.C.); *Sanderson v. Lamont* (1983), 21 A.C.W.S. (2d) 157 (B.C.S.C.).

472 The other cases are: cases where the patient succeeded in proving negligent disclosure: *White v. Turner* (1981), 15 C.C.L.T. 81 (Ont. H.C.); *Rawlings v. Lindsay* (1982), 20 C.C.L.T. 301 (B.C.S.C.); *Schierz v. Dodds*, [1981] C.S. 589 (Que. S.C.); *Sunne v. Shaw*, [1981] C.S. 609 (Que. S.C.). Cases where the patient's case was dismissed as disclosure adequate: *Hankins v. Papillon* (1980), 14 C.C.L.T. 198 (Que. S.C.); *Guertin v. Kester* (1982), 20 C.C.L.T. 225 (B.C.S.C.); *Govin v. Villeneuve* (1982), 23 C.C.L.T. 72 (Que. S.C.); *Poulin v. Health Science Centre* (1982), 18 Man. R. (2d) 274 (Man. Q.B.); *Reynard v. Carr* (1983), 50 B.C.L.R. 166 (B.C.S.C.).
Cases where risks did not require disclosure:
McBride v. Langton, [1982] A.W.L.D. Sept 24, 1982 (Alta. Q.B.) (sterilization — bowel perforation); *Mang v. Moscovitz* (1982), 37 A.R. 221 (Alta. Q.B.), (sterilization — air embolism); *Konkolus v. Royal Alexander Hosp.* (1982), 21 Alta. L.R. (2d) 359 (Alta. Q.B.) (ulnar nerve release — numbness); *MacDonald v. Ross* (1983), 24 C.C.L.T. 242 (N.S.S.C.) (breast reduction — gross distortion); *Schinz v. Dickinson* (1983), 20 A.C.W.S. (2d) 456 (B.C.S.C.) (dental extraction — nerve damage).

473 *See* Edwards, Hopkins, White, *Annual Survey of Tort Law* (1982), 14 Ottawa L.R. at 183; Paterson, *Responsibilité-Civile* (1980), 40 R. du B. 816. Note that counsel for the Canadian Medical Protective Assoc. has stated that "the first year [since the Supreme Court of Canada decisions] has been a satisfactory one in the courts." Scott, *CMPA Annual Report* 32 (1982).

The Standard of Knowledge

The doctor may argue that the unexplained risk was unknown to him and not reasonably foreseeable. In an Alberta case, *Konkolus v. Royal Alexandra Hosp.*,[474] McNaughton J. found that the risks of numbness and pain in the forearm of the patient were not "reasonably foreseeable" to the surgeon who performed an ulnar nerve release on the patient. This conclusion was possible because the medical evidence was divided on whether there might have been a severance of the medial cutaneous nerve which could have caused the condition.

Where the actual result of a breast reduction operation was beyond anything even the doctor could have reasonably anticipated, it was held that there was no negligence in failing to advise the patient of the way she might be affected by the operation.[475]

In *Mang v. Moscovitz*,[476] the patient who had undergone a therapeutic abortion and a tubal ligation suffered severe brain damage as a result of an air embolism. The expert evidence was that this risk during the procedure was extremely rare, indeed one witness assessed it as less than one in a hundred thousand. Mr. Justice Dixon said the question was whether Dr. Moscovitz knew or ought to have known prior to the day of the operation that there was a risk of an air embolism as a special, unusual or inherent risk of a therapeutic abortion by suction curettage. He referred to two American authorities which stated that "the extent of disclosure must be evaluated in terms of what the physician knew or ought to know"[477] and "the physician must . . . describe material risks peculiar to the procedure which may be reasonably foreseeable . . ."[478]

Applying these criteria Dixon J. said:[479]

> The question whether Dr. Moscovitz should then have known of the hazard of air embolism as a special, unusual or inherent risk to this procedure, is uniquely a question of medical competence to be answered with assistance from the strength of expert medical evidence as to the standards of knowledge which existed in Calgary at the time of the operations in question.
>
> The plaintiffs did not call evidence directed to the question of the standard of knowlege to which Dr. Moscovitz should be held . . . The evidence of all the medical witnesses who addressed the question of air embolism is consistent with the conclusion that no obstetrician-gynecologist practicing in Calgary in 1976 could be expected to have present in his mind in May of 1976 the hazard of air embolism as a special, unusual or inherent risk of a suction [curettage] abortion.

474 (1982), 21 Alta. L.R. (2d) 359 (Alta. Q.B.).
475 *MacDonald v. Ross* (1983), 24 C.C.L.T. 242 (N.S.S.C.). Note that this extreme result followed from the doctor's negligence.
476 (1982), 37 A.R. 221 (Alta. Q.B.). *See also McLean v. Weir*, [1980] 4 W.W.R. 330 (B.C.C.A.).
477 *Holton v. Pfingst* (1975), 534 S.W. (2d) 786 at 789 (K.C.A.).
478 *Mason v. Ellsworth* (1970), 474 P. (2d) 905 at 918.
479 *Supra* n. 476 at 268. Note the reference which could be interpreted as an application of the locality rule. *See* Chapter 4.

Thus, it would appear that a doctor must know those risks that are reasonably foreseeable to the medical community. Evidence of the standard of knowledge required of the defendant will be required at trial. A doctor who does not know of a risk which he ought, as a reasonable doctor, to know, cannot raise that in defence if the risk is one that ought to have been disclosed.[480]

Sources of Information

Although the Supreme Court of Canada criteria for the disclosure of information was laid out in terms of the doctor providing the information, it is true that information about the nature and gravity of a procedure, and indeed about its attendant risks, and perhaps even answers to specific questions, might come from other sources.

There is judicial opinion that so long as it can be proven that the patient had the critical information, the source is irrelevant. Mr. Justice Krever said:[481]

> What is important is that before the patient is subjected to the procedure he or she has been properly informed *by or from some person or source*. [emphasis supplied]

In that case, the patient underwent a diagnostic angiography following which he became a quadraplegic. The possibility of a stroke was not mentioned to the patient by either the neurosurgeon or the resident in radiology who did the test. Mr. Justice Krever noted that although in some cases, a referring doctor may depend on the doctor actually performing the test to explain risks, this is not the case where the referring doctor knows that the other, here a resident, is not qualified to do so. Thus, in this case neither doctor explained the risk of a stroke and there was no evidence that the patient had this information from any other source. Disclosure was held to be inadequate.

In an earlier Ontario case[482] cited by Krever J. in support of his own decision, Linden J. held that a patient who suffered paralysis from a rare allergic reaction to the administration of anti-rabies vaccine knew of the risk of paralysis or death. He said that even if the doctors treating the patient had failed in their duty of disclosure, the patient had been fully informed by a virologist employed by the British Columbia Department of Health who was consulted by the vacationing patient.

In British Columbia in 1982,[483] an issue was directed to Mr. Justice Trainor as to whether a patient under cross-examination could be asked about

---

480 *See White v. Turner* (1981), 15 C.C.L.T. 81 at 103 (Ont. H.C.); *Reynard v. Carr supra*, n. 472.
481 *Ferguson v. Hamilton Civic Hosp.* (1983), 23 C.C.L.T. 254 at 297 (Ont. H.C.).
482 *Davidson v. Connaught Laboratories* (1980), 14 C.C.L.T. 251 (Ont. H.C.).
483 *MacDuff v. Vrabec* (1982), 24 C.C.L.T. 239 (B.C.S.C.).

information regarding risks which she may have received from others. He held such information was relevant and said:[484]

> This is not a question of the defendant discharging his duty by turning over that responsibility to someone else. The duty to disclose continues when a surgeon undertakes to perform an operation. The extent of the duty and whether or not that duty is discharged must be met on information that was made available to the patient either directly by the surgeon himself or through other sources.

In a recent Ontario case,[485] arising from a bowel perforation during a sigmoidoscopic examination Hollingsworth J., in deciding whether there had been an adequate disclosure of risks, noted that the patient had testified that he had discussed the procedure with "a close friend in the United States who was a doctor and it is to be *presumed* that all of the ramifications of the sigmoidoscopy were discussed including the possibility of perforation." [emphasis supplied][486]

It is far better to have a patient informed more than once than not at all. Indeed, a second or third disclosure might facilitate the patient's better understanding, yet can be declined if the patient does not require it.

Chief Justice Laskin was clear in his direction that the duty to provide information is the doctor's. To make it less than a positive duty would denigrate the doctor-patient relationship and could result in doctors assuming that other sources have brought the required information to the attention of their patients,[487] and that such information was reliable. Furthermore, the scope of commonly known and accepted risks could be unreasonably expanded by unreliable sources such as popular magazines and unqualified persons.

It is not consistent with the philosophy of the doctor-patient relationship that a defendant doctor be allowed to assume that a patient has received or will receive information from other sources. The patient is thereby forced to take the chance that he will not receive the necessary information, or at best, is given the responsibility of finding it out for himself.

Patient Comprehension

To obtain an adequate, informed consent, a doctor has a duty to provide information including an explanation of certain risks. Does the doctor have a responsibility to assess the patient's comprehension of the disclosure?

There is a statement by the Supreme Court of Canada in *Reibl v. Hughes* that would give credence to the existence of such a duty.[488]

---

484 *Id*. at 241.
485 *Gonda v. Kerbel* (1982), 24 C.C.L.T. 222 (Ont. H.C.).
486 *Id*. at 233.
487 *See also Strachan v. Simpson* (1979), 10 C.C.L.T. 145 (B.C.S.C.); Picard, *Annotation* at 147; *McLean v. Weir*, [1980] 4 W.W.R. 330 (B.C.C.A.); Picard, *Annotation*, 3 C.C.L.T. 88.
488 *Supra* n. 295 at 59.

. . . it must have been obvious to the defendant that the plaintiff had some difficulty with the English language and that he should, therefore, *have made certain that he was understood.* [emphasis supplied]

The trial judge, whose judgment was upheld by the Supreme Court of Canada, said:[489]

. . . the defendant did not take sufficient care to convey to the plaintiff *and assure that the plaintiff understood* the gravity, nature and extent of risks . . . [emphasis supplied]

A requirement that a doctor somehow "test" his patient's comprehension of the information is impractical for there is simply no reasonable technique for doing so.[490] Thus the above statements must be rationalized on the basis that Mr. Reibl did have a language problem, and in cases where this is true, the scope of disclosure is increased.[491] Thus, it may be necessary for a doctor under such circumstances to do more; to repeat statements, look for signs of misunderstanding, or enlist the assistance of a translator.

It has been suggested that a doctor should be able to rely on a patient's consent if it is given pursuant to an "apparent subjective understanding" of the information.[492] The test would be "that the doctor must take reasonable steps in relation to the particular patient to ensure that he understood and that objectively, or apparently, he did."[493] This seems a sensible compromise between requiring the doctor to "get inside the patient's head" and allowing him to relate to the patient as a mere mannikin.

New Directions

Two recent cases from California are worthy of comment. In *Truman v. Thomas*,[494] a 30-year-old mother died of cervical cancer. For six years prior, her family doctor had recommended that she submit to a pap smear test, but she continually postponed doing so. The doctor did not explain the risks of ignoring his recommendation. The California Supreme Court held that the doctor had a duty to do so and reiterated its commitment to the full disclosure test set out in *Cobbs v. Grant*.[495] The court said the doctor must provide all

---

489 (1977), 78 D.L.R. (3d) 35 at 44.

490 Professor Somerville makes the point that the patient may not wish to be so tested. Somerville, *Structuring the Issues in Informed Consent* (1981), 26 McGill L.J. 740 at 778. *But see* Pickering, *Policing the Health Professions — Consent to Health Care* (1981), 2 H.L. in C. 52 at 54, where the author states that asking patients to repeat information is recommended by the Ontario Health Disciplines Board. For a thorough review of U.S. studies on patient comprehension *see* Meisel and Roth, *Toward An Informed Discussion of Informed Consent: A Review And Critique Of The Empirical Studies* (1983), 25 Arizona L.R. 265.

491 See *Hajgato v. London Health Assn.* (1982), 36 O.R. (2d) 669 at 678 (Ont. H.C.), where a doctor, aware of a patient's poor English, was satisfied she understood him.

492 *Id.* at 778.

493 Somerville, *Consent to Medical Care* 25 (L.R.C. 1979).

494 (1980), 27 Cal. (3d) 285, 165 Cal. Rptr., 308 P. (2d) 902 (Cal. S.C.). For a comment *see* Shank, *Informed Refusal: An Unnecessary Burden on Physicians* (1981), 49 U.M.K.C.L.R. 365.

495 (1972), 104 Cal. Rptr. 505, 502 P. (2d) 1, 8 Cal. (3d) 229 (Cal. S.C.).

material information not commonly known but regarded as significant by the reasonable person in that patient's position. Moreover, the doctor was also held to a duty to supply information on all material risks to the patient if she refused the test.

The Supreme Court of Canada has already espoused much of the jurisprudence underlying this decision. It remains to be seen how far Canadian lower courts will be prepared to go.

In another California case, *Tresemer v. Barke*,[496] a doctor was held liable for failing to recall a former patient to advise her of newly discovered dangers associated with the use of the intrauterine device which he had inserted for her. Subsequently, a New York court found for a patient in a very similar fact situation.[497] The duty found in these cases has been labelled the "duty to recall" and is actually a *continuing* duty to disclose risks.

As one commentator has noted,[498] such a duty has widespread implications in these times of innovative medicine where there is an increasing use of prostheses such as artificial heart valves, joints, auditory laryngeal devices and implanted lenses. The practical implications of a responsibility to recall are very great, yet manufacturers of motor vehicles and appliances do so for dangers of less consequence.

Once again we must wait to see whether the persuasiveness of American authorities continues with our Canadian courts.[499]

(vi) Conclusion

The change in Canadian law on consent to health care has been discussed.[500] The implications of the Supreme Court of Canada decisions in *Hopp v. Lepp*[501] and *Reibl v. Hughes*[502] are profound.

---

496 (1978), 86 Cal. App. (3d) 656, 150 Cal. Rptr. 384. For a comment *see* Berg and Hirsch, *Physicians Duty to Recall Revisited* (1983), Legal Aspects of Medical Practice 6.

497 *Reyes v. Anka Research Ltd. et al* (1981), 443 N.Y.S. (2d) 595.

498 *Berg and Hirsch supra* n. 496; *see also, Medical Products Liability* (Gingerich ed. 1981).

499 Note that English courts have refused to follow U.S. and Canadian decisions such as *Hopp v. Lepp* and *Reibl v. Hughes* because they reflect "a clear divergence in principle" from English law. *Sidaway v. Bethlem Royal Hosp.* (1982), The Lancet (April 3) 808 (Q.B.); *Hills v. Potter* The Times 23 May 1983 (Q.B.).

500 Note that the English courts continue to apply the professional disclosure standard and a subjective test for causation. *Chatterton v. Gerson*, [1981] 1 All E.R. 257. The changes reflected in *Hopp v. Lepp* and *Reibl v. Hughes* have been expressly rejected. *Sidaway v. Bethlem Royal Hosp.* (1982), The Lancet (April 3) 808 affirmed, The Times February 24, 1984 at 24; *Hills v. Potter*, The Times 23 May 1983 (Q.B.). For the English law *see* Mason and McCall, *Law And Medical Ethics* (1983); Jackson and Powell, *Professional Negligence* 221 (1982); Finch, *Health Services Law* 245 (1981); Robertson, *Informed Consent to Medical Treatment* (1981), 97 L.Q.R. 102; Samuels, *What the Doctor Must Tell the Patient* (1982), 22 Med. Sci. Law 41.

501 *Supra* n. 272.

502 *Supra* n. 295.

There has been concern expressed that no policy reasons were given to indicate the need being served or the injustices being remedied by such a shift in the direction of the law.[503] But the most exacting criticism of these precedent-setting cases is that the highest court in Canada failed to structure adequately the doctrine of negligent disclosure[504] which it had created.[505]

Furthermore the problem is compounded by the fact that the *milieu* which must absorb and follow the restructured law is itself in a state of change. There is a new emphasis on the granting and enforcing, through the courts, of individual rights. This is to be contrasted with the traditional paternalistic doctor-patient relationship many still believe in and prefer. Yet as has been said: "Consent links physical welfare and legal rights."[506]

Some doctors explaining risks to patients today qualified in the 1980's, while other may have done so in the 1930's. Most judges remember a time when it was a crime to dispense birth control information or to choose death over a life of pain.[507] Many lawyers and doctors know more about informed consent in the United States than in Canada. Some patients hold that their beliefs should guide health care decision-making while others believe that the health care system has a responsibility to fulfill their every need.

The uniqueness of the concept of consent in medical negligence law is its concern, not with the usual negligence criteria of reasonable skill, knowledge, and judgment, but with communication, rapport and sensitivity. A common feature of the cases examined is no communication[508] or poor communication[509] between doctor and patient. Thus it would seem that the Supreme Court of Canada decisions were aimed at improving doctor-patient relationships. Mr. Justice Linden, a torts scholar and now a judge put it in this way:[510]

> This does not mean that Canadian doctors must now give complicated seminars on medicine to all of their patients. It does mean, though, that more time may have to be spent explaining things to their patients than in the past. The law as espoused by the Supreme Court of Canada requires that patients should be treated as intelligent, mature, and rational individuals. The ultimate effect of this new approach should be medical practitioners who are even more senstitive, concerned and humane than they now are. Moreover, the

---

503 Gochnauer and Fleming, *Tort Law — Informed Consent — New Directions For Medical Disclosure — Hopp v. Lepp and Reibl v. Hughes* (1981), 15 U.B.C.L. Rev. 475 at 495.
504 This term seems more appropriate for the future than the doctrine of informed consent and reflects the fact that there is always in the doctor-patient relationship a *duty* to disclose.
505 Somerville, *Structuring the Issues in Informed Consent* (1981), 26 McGill L.J. 740.
506 Gochnauer and Fleming *supra* n. 503 at 475.
507 Re: birth control, S.C. 1968-69, c. 41, s. 13; It is no longer a crime to commit suicide, S.C. 1972, c. 13, s. 16.
508 For a case where the surgeon chose to not speak to the patient prior to surgery, *see Considine v. Camp Hill Hosp.* (1982), 133 D.L.R. (3d) 11 at 39 (N.S.S.C.).
509 For a case where a gynaecologist was described by a judge as "perhaps" not callous but casual, *see Videto v. Kennedy* (1980), 107 D.L.R. (3d) 614 at 617 (Ont. H.C.). The finding of liability was reversed on appeal 17 C.C.L.T. 307 (Ont. C.A.).
510 *White v. Turner* (1981), 15 C.C.L.T. 81 at 104-105 (Ont. H.C.).

doctor-patient relationship should be improved greatly by the better communication between doctors and their patients.

General Counsel to the Canadian Medical Protective Association commenting of the effect of *Reibl v. Hughes* said:[511]

> Unless and until the Supreme Court of Canada restricts its language or there is legislation — except in emergencies or where the patient waives all discussion or where the patient is emotionally unable to cope with unpleasant information — the best advice is to make full and frank disclosure of all facts and risks relative to the patient's illnesses, the treatment recommended and all alternatives, including the risks of non-treatment. All patient's questions must be answered on the same basis. *Treat the patient as though he were your best friend and you are telling him all about it.* [emphasis supplied]

At a practical level there is reflection and action required as a consequence of the decisions of the Supreme Court of Canada.[512] Doctors must keep better records of conversations with patients[513] and should consider enlisting help with communication. This could be done by groups of specialists preparing checklists or information sheets to guide them and perhaps to be given to patients[514] or by training nurses or paramedics to assist. Although the duty is the doctor's he can have assistance in carrying it out. A doctor practising today must accept the fact that the patient has the right to decide what, *if anything*, should be done with his body and that the Supreme Court of Canada had the right to make this a requirement of the practice of medicine in Canada.[515] He must organize his time so that communication can take place.

Patients who decide to seek shelter within the paternalistic doctor-patient relationship should communicate a waiver of their right to information to the doctor. Otherwise they must accept the responsibility of making a decision using the information the doctor must now give them. A patient should be as concerned about the reason he requires surgery as he would be about the reason his car needs an engine job. He should ask questions in expectation of receiving the fullest disclosure.[516] He must provide the doctor with informa-

---

511 *C.M.P.A. Annual Report* 46 (1980). Note that Professor Robertson concluded in his study, *infra* n. 512, 515 that this communication to Canadian doctors ''appears to have gone unnoticed.''

512 For a reflection on the decisions in England, *see* Robertson, *Informed Consent to Medical Treatment* (1981), 97 L.Q.R. 102. Note that Professor Robertson has done an empirical study of English and Canadian doctors. Robertson, *Informed Consent In Canada: An Empirical Study* (1984), O.H.L.J. (to be set).

513 There are many cases where poor memories and worse records were a weakness in the doctor's defence and also in the patient's case. *See, for example, Guertin v. Kester* (1981), 20 C.C.L.T. 225 at 235 (B.C.S.C.).

514 Linden J., *The Patient, the Doctor, and their Duty to Communicate With One Another* (1981), 2 H.L. in C. 57; Heller, *The Question of Informed Consent: A Progress Report*, M.D. Sept. 1982 at 165.

515 *Reibl v. Hughes* (1980), 14 C.C.L.T. 1 at 70 (S.C.C.); *see also Parmley v. Parmley*, [1945] S.C.R. 635. Note that Professor Robertson concluded after his study of 620 Canadian surgeons *supra* n. 512 that the Supreme Court of Canada decisions had had little impact on them.

516 *See infra*.

tion about himself because such information is required to construe the standard of disclosure the doctor must meet. Patients must be prepared to lose lawsuits or have compensation reduced if they maintain a low profile and the doctor knows nothing of their concerns and motivations. Doctors cannot be expected to be clairvoyant.

The legal system must take note of the need for pleadings to be drafted more carefully[517] and be prepared for the greater role the patient's evidence will have in a negligent disclosure lawsuit.[518] Lawyers will have to assist the judges in the continuing task of structuring the doctrine of negligent disclosure. Because of the diverse sources of the new law and the gaps within it, it may be necessary to refer to traditional negligence principles and also to other areas of law such as that of negligent misstatement and even manufacturers' liability.[519]

The provincial courts must resolve the conundrum of deciding each case on its own circumstances, and of clarifying and supplementing the law handed down by the Supreme Court of Canada. This will only be achieved by thoughtful reasoned judgments that allow doctors and patients to better understand and accept their duties. However, as Professor Somerville has said, "it *is not* the function of the court to ensure progress in medicine." Moreover, the courts must be careful not to make patients "the necessary materials for such progress rather than the purpose of medical progress being to benefit them."[520]

It is to be hoped that the courts can shape just decisions and jurisprudence that is respected because the only alternative, legislation, is not a solution but another quest.[521]

5.   SPECIAL TREATMENT

(a) Research

The words "human experimentation" produce antithetical images. The dark scenes of prison camps like Dachau and Ravensbruch along with the horrifying revelations about the Tuskegee syphilis study, the Jewish Chronic

---

517 *See, for example, Allan v. New Mt. Sinai Hosp.* (1980), 11 C.C.L.T. 299 (Ont. H.C.) where battery was not pleaded; reversed on appeal; *see also Guertin v. Kester* (1982), 20 C.C.L.T. 225 at 235 (B.C.S.C.) and discussion *infra* to the effect that risks may have to be set out.

518 This arises because of the reference to the patient in determining the standard and scope of disclosure as well as the causation issue.

519 *See White v. Turner* (1981), 15 C.C.L.T. 81 at 97 (Ont. H.C.).

520 Somerville, *Legal Investigation of a Medical Investigation* (1981), 19 A.L.R. 171 at 186-87.

521 See Rodgers-Magnet, *Legislating for an Informed Consent to Medical Treatment by Competent Adults* (1981), 27 McGill L.J. 1056. *See also Making Health Care Decisions* (1982), A report of The President's Commission for the Study of Ethical Problems in Medicine and Biomedical and Behavioral Research.

522 *See* Storch, *Patients' Rights* 78-81 (1982).

Hospital cancer study, and the Willowbrook State School hepatitis study[522] contrast dramatically with bright hospital waiting rooms and wards where patients and their loved ones wait to be briefed by cheerful nurses and serious doctors who use audio-visual aids and encourage questions.[523]

One might conclude from the very few cases brought by patients and the absence of legislation that there is little monitoring of or concern about the adequacy of consent to human experimentation. This is not the case, however.[524] Although modern medical research tends to be associated with cures and benefits rather than with perversity and suffering, we dare not forget the past, for as the Medical Research Council of Canada said in its report *Ethical Considerations in Research Involving Human Subjects,*[525] "Good science is not necessarily good ethics."[526] The torts scholar Fleming, in describing the purpose of the tort of battery (a form of trespass to the person, and a possible action against a medical researcher), stated:[527]

> [Battery] serves the dual purpose of affording protection to the individual not only against bodily harm but also against any interference with his person which is offensive to a reasonable sense of honour and dignity.

Thus, the rights of the patient as the subject of research must be protected.

Three cases, two federal government studies, and academic writing form the body of discussion on the major legal issues arising in this area: the definition of research, the standard and scope of disclosure required for an informed consent, the requirement of extra protection for special classes of persons, and whether or not the law is satisfactory.

(i) Definition of research

The Medical Research Council of Canada, through a working committee of medical and legal experts, undertook a major study on the topic of human experimentation. The Medical Research Council is a source of funding for this purpose and sees itself "at the interface between the scientist and the public."[528] The Report defines research on human subjects as being "research carried out according to scientifically valid protocol in which human beings are submitted to procedures, the purposes of which may go beyond the

---

523 This is certainly the procedure at the Renal Care Unit, University Hospital, Edmonton.
524 For the concerns of a doctor-lawyer, *see* Marshall, *The Physician and Canadian Law* (1979).
525 Report No. 6 (1978).
526 *See* Brahams, *The Need for Consent in Medical Trials* (1982), New Law J. 687 for an unsettling report. In 1981 in Birmingham General Hospital (Eng.) no consent was sought nor obtained from subjects in an experiment although the randomized controlled trial was reviewed by *eleven* ethics committees! A patient-subject died as a consequence of treatment involving the induction of anti-cancer drugs via the portal vein into her liver.
527 Fleming, *The Law of Torts* 23 (1983).
528 *Supra* n. 525 Foreword to Report No. 6.

subject's need for prophylaxis, diagnosis or therapy or may invade the subject's privacy."[529]

Professor Bowker[530] states that the terms "research" and "experimentation" can be given the same definition. Both he and Professor Somerville[531] see the term "innovative therapy" as ambiguous and thus not of assistance in defining terms. The dichotomy of elective and non-elective treatment can be eliminated from a discussion of research on the basis that all research is necessarily elective for the patient. This leaves then the alternatives used by most commentators: therapeutic research and non-therapeutic research.

The Medical Research Council of Canada and an American body, the National Commission for the Protection of Human Subjects of Biomedical and Behavioral Research,[532] reject the distinct concept of therapeutic research for good reasons given in their mandate. Their approach is cautious, protective and reflects a concern that benefits may be merely potential and that the distinction between research and therapy is blurred because they are often concomitant.[533] For purposes of setting up safeguards perhaps a litmus-test approach could be used and, so long as there is any element of research present, this categorization should be made.

In fact, many ethical codes such as the Declaration of Helsinki[534] use the terms "therapeutic" and "non-therapeutic" research, as does the British Medical Research Council. As the Medical Research Council of Canada acknowledges, such an approach does allow a risk-benefit analysis.[535]

In the end, the research subject may not be affected significantly by whether the category of therapeutic research is recognized, except that if he is in a non-therapeutic research program, the fact that there is no benefit (except perhaps a monetary one) must be made patently clear. This is especially important if the research subject is in a doctor-patient relationship with any member of the research team because the research subject might make assumptions that are invalid.[536] However, the distinction between therapeutic research and "pure" therapy may be very important for the patient as is illustrated by Alberta cases in which Dr. Ringrose was the defendant.[537]

---

529 *Supra* n. 525 at 6-7.
530 Bowker, *Minors and Mental Incompetents: Consent to Experimentation, Gifts of Tissue and Sterilization* (1981), 26 McGill L.J. 951 at 961; *see also* Bowker, *Experimentation on Humans and Gifts of Tissue: Articles 20-23 of the Civil Code* (1973), 19 McGill L.J. 161.
531 Somerville, *Therapeutic and Non-Therapeutic Medical Procedures — What are the Distinctions* (1981), 2 H.L. in C. 85 at 86.
532 *The Belmont Report* (1978), cited in Bowker *supra* n. 530 at 962 and in M.R.C. *supra* n. 525 at 7. For a discussion *see* Somerville, *Clarifying the Concepts of Research Ethics: A Second Filtration* (1981), 29 Clinical Research 101.
533 *Supra* n. 525 at 6.
534 Adopted by 18th World Medical Assembly, Helsinki Finland 1964; Revised 29th Medical Assembly, Tokyo, Japan 1975.
535 *Supra* n. 525 at 16.
536 Somerville *supra* n. 531 at 87.
537 *See infra* n. 542.

(ii) Standard and scope of disclosure

One reason for identifying the research content is that a higher level of disclosure of information and risks has been held to be necessary.[538] Not only must the research subject consent but his or her consent must be explicit and based on what might well be called a "perfect" disclosure.

In Quebec, by article 20[539] of the Civil Code, an adult may consent in writing to an experiment provided that "the risk assumed is not disproportionate to the benefit anticipated." The standard and scope of disclosure for experimentation was first set out in Canada in a judgment of Hall J.A. in *Halushka v. University of Sask.*,[540] where the research subject, a student, was paid $50 to participate in the test of a new anaesthetic. He was told that the test was safe "and there was nothing to worry about," but was not told that the experiment involved a new drug, that there were risks, and that a catheter would be advanced toward his heart. He signed a consent form which purported to release the doctors from liability for accidents. During the test he suffered a cardiac arrest, and later succeeded in an action against the doctors. Holding the consent to be ineffective, the court awarded damages of $22,500 and said:[541]

> There can be no exceptions to the ordinary requirements of disclosure in the case of research as there may well be in ordinary medical practice. The researcher does not have to balance the probable effect of lack of treatment against the risk involved in the treatment itself. The example of risks being properly hidden from a patient when it is important that he should not worry can have no application in the field of research. *The subject of medical experimentation is entitled to a full and frank disclosure of all the facts, probabilities and opinions* which a reasonable man might be expected to consider before giving his consent. [emphasis supplied]

It is worth noting that this judgment predated by 15 years the Supreme Court of Canada's statements on informed consent to therapeutic treatment. Thus, when Mr. Justice Hall described the standard, it was the professional standard that was being used to measure the adequacy of consent to "ordinary" or therapeutic medical treatment. A point of concern about the test he used is its use of the objective reasonable patient test when the more pro-patient subjective test would be more appropriate to the research setting and in fact was used at that time when therapeutic treatment was in issue.

Sterilization by a silver nitrate procedure was characterized as experimental by two Alberta courts[542] and the *Halushka v. University of Sask.*[543] test was

---

538 For an excellent discussion *see Cryderman v. Ringrose*, [1977] 3 W.W.R. 109 (Alta. D.C.); affirmed [1978] 3 W.W.R. 481.

539 S.Q. 1971, c. 84.

540 (1965), 52 W.W.R. 608 (Sask. C.A.).

541 *Id.* at 616-17. Note this case was brought in battery but could have been sued in contract.

542 In *Cryderman v. Ringrose*, [1977] 3 W.W.R. 109 (Alta. S.C.); affirmed [1978] 3 W.W.R. 481 (Alta. C.A.), the patient succeeded in negligence; in *Zimmer v. Ringrose* (1978), 89 D.L.R. (3d) 647 (Alta. S.C.), the patient succeeded in battery; on appeal,

applied. Both cases were appealed and in *Zimmer v. Ringrose*,[544] the court found the procedure to be therapeutic. Mr. Justice Prowse said:[545]

> In the case of a truly "experimental" procedure, like the one conducted in *Halushka v. University of Sask., supra,* no therapeutic benefit is intended to accrue to the participant. The subject is simply part of a scientific investigation designed to enhance human knowledge. By contrast, the sterilization procedure performed by the appellant in this case was directed towards achieving a *therapeutic end.* By means of a successful sterilization, the respondent could avoid the occurrence of an unwanted pregnancy and the adverse health problems associated with it. *In my opinion, the silver nitrate method was experimental only in the sense that it represented an innovation* in sterilization techniques which were relatively untried. According to the testimony of the respondent's expert witness, the procedure itself could not be dismissed out of hand as being medically untenable. Indeed, his primary criticism of the method appears to have been the absence of adequate clinical evaluation. To hold that every new development in medical methodology was "experimental" in the sense outlined in *Halushka v. University of Sask.* would be to discourage advances in the field of medicine. In view of these considerations, the application of the standard of disclosure stated in the *Halushka* case would be inappropriate in this instance. [emphasis supplied]

Thus, the Alberta Court of Appeal felt that the procedure was therapeutic and innovative. This case and the *Cryderman*[546] case reinforced the appropriateness of the *Halushka*[547] test to the experimentation context. At the same time these decisions illustrate how different evidence can lead to the designation of the same procedure as being experimental, or therapeutic and innovative.

The enunciation by the Supreme Court of Canada of a full disclosure standard for therapeutic treatment has narrowed the gap between the *Halushka*[548] standard and scope of disclosure and that required for therapeutic treatment, but there are still some differences.

Authorities agree that neither therapeutic privilege nor waiver apply to the research subject.[549] There must be an increased recognition of the potential for duress, coercion and misrepresentation, and steps must be taken to cope with them.[550] Furthermore, and notwithstanding obvious deleterious effects on the research, a research subject must be free to withdraw at any

---

reversed on this point 16 C.C.L.T. 51 (Alta. C.A.). Note that in an earlier case the procedure was characterized as therapeutic; see *Colp v. Ringrose,* unreported 6 Oct. 1976, No. 84474 (Alta. S.C.).

543 *Supra* n. 540.

544 *Supra* n. 542.

545 *Supra* n. 542 at 59-60.

546 *Supra* n. 542.

547 *Supra* n. 540.

548 *Id.*

549 Dickens, *Contractual Aspects of Human Medical Experimentation* (1975), 25 U.T.L.J. 406 at 426; Somerville, *Consent to Medical Care* 23 (L.R.C. 1979). *See* discussion *supra* on informed consent.

550 Somerville *id.* at 48-58. Somerville, *Randomized Controlled Trials and Randomized Control of Consent* (1980), 1 H.L. in C. 58; Kapp, *Placebo Therapy and the Law: Prescribe With Care* (1983), 8 Am J.L.M. 371.

time.[551] If and when a Canadian court is asked to set the standard and scope for the disclosure of information in a research setting, no doubt there will be references to the numerous ethical codes and guidelines promulgated for researchers.[552] Professor Bowker[553] has noted that in the United States there has been a re-examination of the ethical requirements for research. He and Professor Somerville[554] identify the United States Food, Drug and Cosmetic Act[555] and Regulations[556] and the Department of Health and Human Services, as models of detailed disclosure for therapeutic and non-therapeutic research. The definition of consent and the requirements for an adequate consent are described in the Food and Drug Regulations as follows:[557]

> "Consent" means that the person involved has legal capacity to give consent, is so situated as to be able to exercise free power of choice, and is provided with a fair explanation of pertinent information concerning the investigational drug, and/or his possible use as a control, as to enable him to make a decision on his willingness to receive said investigational drug. This latter element means that before the acceptance of an affirmative decision by such person the investigator should carefully consider and make known to him (taking into consideration such person's well being and his ability to understand) *the nature, expected duration, and purpose of the administration of said investigational drug; the method and means by which it is to be administered; the hazards involved; the existence of alternative forms of therapy, if any; and the beneficial effects upon his health or person that may possibly come* from the administration of the investigational drug. [emphasis supplied]

The Department of Health and Human Sciences definition is more expansive:[558]

> (c) "informed consent" means the knowing consent of an individual or his legally authorized representative, so situated as to be able to exercise free power of choice without undue inducement of any element of force, fraud, deceit, duress, or other form of constraint or coercion. *The basic elements of information necessary to such consent include:*
> (1) A fair explanation of the procedures to be followed, and their purposes, including indentification of any procedures which are experimental;
> (2) A description of any attendant discomforts and risks reasonably to be expected;
> (3) A description of any benefits reasonably to be expected;
> (4) A disclosure of any appropriate alternative procedures that might be advantageous for the subject;
> (5) An offer to answer any inquiries concerning the procedure; and
> (6) An instruction that the person is free to withdraw his consent and to discontinue participation in the project or activity at any time without prejudice to the subject. [emphasis supplied].

---

551 Somerville *supra* n. 531 at 87; Dickens *supra* n. 549 at 483.
552 For example, Declaration of Helsinki *supra* n. 534; Nuremberg Code (1949); C.M.A. Code of Ethics (1982); For an excellent analysis of the various codes, *see* Somerville, *Does the Aim of Human Experimentation Affect Its Legal or Ethical Validity?* (1979), 3 L. Med. Q. 83.
553 *Supra* n. 530 at 964.
554 Somerville *supra* n. 531 at 87.
555 21 U.S.C.A., para. 355.
556 Para. 130.37, Fed. Reg., June 20, 1967, p. 8753.
557 *Id.* at 8754.
558 45 C.F.R., s. 46.107 (1975).

A recently added requirement is: the subject must be told whether the institution provides compensation in the case of injury.[559]

Clearly, when research is involved the disclosure must be fuller than "full."[560]

(iii) Special persons

Another reason for differentiating research from ordinary treatment or therapy is that the capacity of certain persons to consent is restricted. Minors and adults with a mental disability may not have the capacity to consent and even if they do, it is arguable that their status should preclude them from doing so.

The most controversial group is minors. Although children require and are given special consideration and protection by the law, research on diseases unique to children must sometimes involve children as subjects. A mature or emancipated minor can consent to therapeutic treatment but does he or she have the capacity to consent to non-therapeutic or therapeutic research?[561]

In Quebec the answer is yes, subject to certain qualifications. Article 20 of the Civil Code of Quebec says:[562]

> A minor capable of discernment may [submit to an experiment] with the authorization of a judge of the Superior Court and with the consent of the person having parental authority, provided that no serious risk to his health results therefrom.

In the other provinces of Canada there is no clear answer, although it has been argued that a mature or emancipated minor who would appreciate fully the nature and consequences of an experiment would have the capacity to consent.[563] However, the legislation in seven provinces and the Northwest Territories prohibits minors from donating non-regenerative tissue.[564] It is worth noting, too, that the capacity to consent acquired by the minor as a consequence of maturity or emancipation relates only to treatment *"bona fide*

---

559 Bowker *supra* n. 530 at 964 citing Fed. Reg. Nov. 3 1978.

560 *See* Bowker *supra* n. 530 at 169.

561 For a thorough canvas of the authorities, *see* Somerville, *Consent to Medical Care* (L.R.C. 1979) 71-85; *see also* Waddams, *Medical Experiments on Human Subjects* (1967), 25 U.T.F.L. Rev. 25; Dickens *The Use of Children in Medical Experimentation* (1973), 43 Med. Leg. J. 166.

562 1971, c. 84 s. 3 [am. 1977, c. 72, s. 1]; *see* Baudouin, *L'experimentation sur Les Humains: Un Conflit de Valeurs* (1981), 26 McGill L.J. 809; Bowker, *Experimentation on Humans and Gifts of Tissue: Articles 20-23 of the Civil Code* (1973), 19 McGill L.J. 161.

563 Bowker, *Legal Liability to Volunteers in Testing New Drugs* (1963), C.M.A.J. 745 at 748 and *supra* n. 562 at 173; Castel, *Nature and Effects of Consent With Respect To The Right To Life and The Right To Physical And Mental Aspects* (1978), 16 A.L.R. 293 at 350. For a contrary opinion *see* Sharpe, *The Minor Transplant Donor* (1975), 7 Ottawa L.R. 85 at 89 and 91.

564 *See* Sharpe, *The Minor Transplant Donor* (1975), 7 Ottawa L.R. 85; See *infra* 5(b) Transplantation.

in the interests of the infant's own health.''[565] Although this would seem to cover therapeutic research it would not cover non-therapeutic research. It may be argued that the mature or emancipated minor still lacks one important prerequisite for capacity to consent to research; namely experience.

In view of this uncertainty, most cases of research on minors will entail seeking the consent of a surrogate, parent or guardian. But the controversy continues with some authorities arguing that such a person has no power to consent to any procedure with risks and no benefit to the minor,[566] and others arguing that there is a moral obligation to do so.[567]

The Medical Research Council of Canada[568] has made a proposal which should be given serious consideration. Consent would be required from a parent or guardian and also from an ombudsman or advocate on behalf of the child. Risks and benefits would be weighed as is done for adults. The door would be left open for the research subject to be involved in the decision-making process, and in the case of an older child, this would seem an important step.[569]

Obviously the second level of proxy consent,[570] that of the advocate or ombudsman, is critical. The Medical Research Council proposal would require the advocate to be well informed about the subject and the research and be in touch with the subject on a daily basis. The ombudsman would be found:[571]

> . . . attached to or be an integral part of the hospital or institution in which the research is to be performed. He may be a person salaried by the hospital or institution, a volunteer, or a patient or a group representative, such as a person designated by a parent group.

Such a plan may seem unwieldly to some but it could provide the answer for those medical scientists who are fearful of the legal consequences of research on children.

The situation of the adult with a mental disability is analogous to that of the child.[572] Indeed the Medical Research Council suggests the same model for obtaining consent.[573] One difference between the two groups is that an

---

565 Nathan, *Medical Negligence* 177 (1957).

566 Bowker *supra* n. 530 at 967-68; Somerville *supra* n. 561 at 113; *Quaere* where the circumcision and ear piercing of infants fits in. *See* Dickens, *Contractual Aspects of Human Medical Experimentation* (1975), 25 U.T.L.J. 406 at 418. For cases of botched circumcisions *see* Gray v. *LaFleche*, [1950] 1 D.L.R. 337 (Man. K.B.); *Gilbert v. Campbell*, [1976] B.C.D. 369 (B.C.S.C.).

567 *See* Somerville *supra* n. 561 at 76 quoting McCormick.

568 *Supra* n. 525 at 30-32.

569 For the U.S. guidelines see Bowker *supra* n. 530 at 967.

570 Note that Somerville *supra* n. 561 at 81 suggests the term "proxy" does not reflect what is done. *See also* Freedman, *A Moral Theory of Informed Consent* (1975), 32 Hastings Centre Report 52.

571 *Supra* n. 525 at 31.

572 Bowker *supra* n. 530 at 968; Somerville *supra* n. 561 at 113-14. *See also* Frenkel, *Consent of Incompetents (Minors and Mentally Ill) to Medical Treatment* (1977), 3 L. Med. Q. 187.

573 Note that the proposed administrative structure set up to review the research protocol and the consent is discussed in the M.R.C. Report *supra* n. 525 at 35-47 and covers responsibilities of the institution, department heads and ethics review committees.

adult, albeit with a mental disability, may have the experience and maturity that a child lacks and therefore should not be assumed incapable of meeting the criteria necessary to give an informed consent.[574]

The Alberta Dependent Adults Act[575] does not grant a guardian the power to consent to experimentation on the dependant adult.

The adult with a mental disability and the incarcerated adult are, after all, adults, and research on adults should be carried out only on those who are as free and able as possible to give an adequate consent.

There are two points of view on whether prisoners should be used in human experimentation. One is that the use of prisoners should be "strongly disapproved if not actually prohibited"[576] because their liberty, freedom of choice and capacity to give a truly voluntary consent is restricted. The other is that prisoners have "no less right to contrition than other men and . . . more need of outlets through which to make amends" and therefore "a blanket prohibition of their opportunity genuinely to consent denies freedom of choice to prisoners, and to society . . ."[577] In fact, the controversy and absence of case law or legislation makes the likelihood of research on prisoners very small.

For another class of research subjects, the capacity to give an informed consent may be affected by "undue motivation". Nurses, laboratory technicans, students, and even the researchers themselves may volunteer to participate in research.[578] Professor Castel suggests that it should be against public policy to engage in auto-experimentation where unwarranted risks are taken.[579] Certainly the consent of a person involved in the research program or employed by the institution in which the research takes place must be carefully scrutinized by a research or ethics committee in the institution.

(iv) The state of the law

In summary, the state of the law with regard to human experimentation is unsatisfactory and there is controversy amongst the academic authorities so

---

574 Note that Somerville reports that the civil law commentators are unanimous that a surrogate may not consent to non-therapeutic research on mentally incompetent persons *supra* n. 561 at 91.

575 R.S.A. 1980, c. D-32. *See* Bowker *supra* n. 530 at 968-69; *But see* Kouri and Somerville, *Comments on the Sterilization of Mental Incompetents in Canadian Civil and Common Law* (1980), 10 R.D. U.S. 599 at 621 where the opposite view is expressed.

576 Castel, *Nature and Effects of Consent With Respect to the Right to Life and Right to Physical and Mental Integrity in the Medical Field: Criminal and Private Law Aspects* (1978), 16 A.L.R. 293 at 352.

577 Dickens, *Contractual Aspects of Human Medical Experimentation* (1975), 25 U.T.L.J. 406 at 425. *See also*, Bowker *supra* n. 530 at 177.

578 Dickens *id.* at 426.

579 *Supra* n. 576 at 336. Note, however, that it is no longer a crime to commit suicide, Criminal Code, R.S.C. 1970, c. C-34, s. 225 [repealed 1972, c. 13, s. 16].

that even speculation is not helpful.[580] It is not clear how the Supreme Court of Canada decisions on informed consent[581] will affect the test set out in the *Haluska*[582] case. The causation issue would seem to be even more onerous for the research subject than it is for the ordinary patient, in part because an inherent feature of research is that not all risks are foreseeable.

The battery action and the negligent disclosure action would seem far more feasible than an action for negligence *per se* where it would be necessary to establish a standard of care and prove a breach thereof causing injury. Experts knowledgeable enough about the research to testify might be very difficult to find.[583]

From the perspective of the medical profession, the requirements for adequate consent and the concerns about capacity to consent to research are so diverse that the cautious, concerned researcher may be reluctant to proceed. While the lawyer may understand the anomaly of the same procedure being characterized in the courts as therapeutic and as experimental, the doctor-researcher finds it incredible. Even to simpler questions such as whether consent is needed to use blood or urine samples or data for research purposes where these were originally taken for therapeutic reasons, one can find contradictory answers in the authorities.[584] Certain types of research, for example, where minors are involved, may be curtailed because of concern about legal liability. The impact, if any, of the Canadian Charter of Rights and Freedoms is as yet an unknown.[585]

There is, in fact, no standardization of procedures for ensuring that consent is adequate. Each institution, usually each department, in a hospital or faculty or school sets up a research or ethics committee to scrutinize research proposals but there is wide variation in criteria, procedure and follow-up monitoring.[586]

While there is no doubt that codes, ethical guidelines and the commitment of compassionate researchers are helpful, they are not sufficient to give

---

580 This has been the situation for some time. *See* Rozovsky, *Informed Consent and Investigational Drugs* (1977), 3 L. Med. Q. 162.

581 See *supra.*

582 *Supra* n. 540.

583 Note that the English *Report of the Royal Commission on Civil Liability and Compensation for Personal Injury* Cmnd. 7054 (1978), Chapter 24 recommended that a volunteer for research or a clinical trial who suffers severe damage should have a cause of action based on strict liability.

584 "No" by M.R.C. Report, *supra* n. 525 at 24; "Yes" by Somerville *supra* n. 561 at 40.

585 *See* Tarnopolsky and Beaudoin, *The Canadian Charter of Rights and Freedoms* 389 (1982); MacDonald, *Legal Rights in the Canadian Charter of Rights and Freedoms* 115 (1982).

586 *See* M.R.C. *supra* n. 525 at 36-39. For an interesting U.S. publication to assist committees *see* I.R.B., a monthly publication of the Hastings Centre, Hastings-on-Hudson, N.Y. *See supra* n. 526 for a discussion of a study which was approved by *eleven* ethics committees in England but involved experimentation without consent.

the researcher and the subject confidence about their rights and responsibilities. Clarification is unlikely to come from the courts and proposals from government departments or hospitals are not enforceable. There must be legislation in Canada to describe the legal requirements for human experimentation.

(b) Transplantation

Balancing the conflicting demands of members of society and providing solutions that are as just as possible is a continuing responsibility of the legal system. The unique feature of decisions about *inter vivos* transplantations is the potential for great injustice both to the donor and to the recipient. To take a kidney or bone marrow from a child incapable even of testifying in a court of law seems macabre, yet to allow a sibling to die prematurely for want of it seems cruel.[587] And even an optimal balance, whether legislative or judicial, is susceptible to distortion by changes in medical knowledge or resources. In fact, advances in medical science have made the transplantation of kidneys and corneas highly successful. Unfortunately, demand for these non-regenerative organs continues to outstrip the supply.[588] Resolution of the issues involved in transplantation is made more complex by the fact that "the donation of tissue for transplantation falls between the two extremes of the therapeutic and the experimental."[589]

There are no Canadian cases in which a transplant from one human being to another has been in issue,[590] but nine provinces[591] and the Northwest Territories and Yukon[592] have enacted legislation based on the Uniform

---

587 *See* Fost, *Children as Renal Donors* (1977), 296 New Eng. J.M. 363.

588 Sells, *Live Organs From Dead People* (1979), 72 J. Royal Soc. Med. 109; Pessimier et al, *Willingness to Supply Human Body Parts: Some Empirical Results* (1977), 4 J. Consumer Research 131. Farfor, *Organs for Transplant: Courageous Legislation* (1977), Br. Med. J. 497. Transplant surgeon Dr. Calvin Stiller stated 1,200 Canadians a year need a kidney transplant but only 400 cadaver kidneys are available: Edmonton Journal, Sept. 9, 1983. Newsweek, 29 August 1983 38 at 40 reports 23,076 kidney transplants done in the U.S. in the last 5 years.

589 Sugiyama, *Inter Vivos Transplantation and the Human Tissue Gift Act, S.O. 1971 c. 83* (1976), 34 U.T. Fac. L. Rev. 124.

590 Note however the case of *Urbanski v. Patel* (1978), 84 D.L.R. (3d) 650 (Man. Q.B.) in which a surgeon negligently removed a patient's only kidney believing it to be a cyst. Damages of $8,650 were awarded to the father who donated a kidney to the patient. For a comment *see* Robertson, *A New Application of the Rescue Principle* (1980), 96 L.Q.R. 19. There are a number of U.S. cases; for a discussion of them *see* Bowker, *Minors and Mental Incompetents: Consent to Experimentation, Gifts of Tissue and Sterilization* (1981), 26 McGill L.J. 951.

591 The Human Tissue Gift Act, R.S.A. 1980, c. H-12; The Human Tissue Gift Act, R.S.B.C. 1979, c. 187; The Human Tissue Act, R.S.M. 1970, c. H-180; The Human Tissue Act, S.N. 1971, No. 66; The Human Tissue Act, R.S.N.B. 1973, c.H-12; The Human Tissue Gift Act, S.N.S. 1973, c. 9; The Human Tissue Gift Act, R.S.O. 1980, c. 210; The Human Tissue Gift Act, R.S. P.E.I. 1974, c. H-14; The Human Tissue Gift Act, R.S.S. 1978, c. H-15.

592 The Human Tissue Ordinance, R.O.N.W.T. 1974, c. H-4; The Human Tissue Gift Ordinance, (1st) (Y.T.) 1980, c. 14

Tissue Gift Act.[593] Quebec has accommodated the area in sections 20 and 21 of the Civil Code.[594]

While to the health care professional the Uniform Tissue Gift Act[595] may seem straightforward, it has been sharply criticized by legal writers for being too protective of doctors, vague, filled with internal conflicts, and out of touch with the law in general and with reality.[596] A dissection of the Act and a look at the Quebec solution is necessary before discussing possible improvements to the legislation.

It is important to note that the Act[597] deals with non-regenerative tissue from a living donor and any body parts or parts from a cadaver.[598] The non-regenerative organ most frequently transplanted is the kidney. The more common regenerative tissues for transplant are blood, bone marrow and skin.[599]

Any adult who has the capacity to consent and is making a free and informed decision[600] may, in writing,[601] consent to the removal and implantation of tissue specified by him. Minors and mentally incompetent persons are precluded from doing so. If a donor does not meet these criteria, a doctor is legally protected if he had no reason to believe the donor did not qualify.[602]

Different rules apply to gifts of the body or parts thereof made just before death or after death. An adult in writing or orally, in the presence of *at least* two witnesses "during his last illness," may donate.[603] Under these circumstances,

---

593 *Proceedings Conference of Commissioners on Uniformity of Legislation in Canada* 151 (1970).
594 1971, c. 84.
595 *Supra* n. 593.
596 Starkman, *Consent and the Human Tissue Gift Acts: A Rationale for Change* (1980), 1 H.L. in C. 5; Sugiyama, *Inter Vivos Transplantation and the Human Tissue Gift Act, S.Q. 1971 c. 83* (1976), 34 U.T. Fac. L. Rev. 124; Clements, *The Human Tissue Gift Act* (1979), 3 L. Med. Q. 39.
597 The Human Tissue Gift Act, R.S.A. (1980), c. H-12 will be used for reference.
598 *Id*. 1(b). Note that "tissue" is used in Part I (Inter Vivos Gifts) to refer to non-regenerative tissue. In Part II (Post Mortem Gifts) "body" or "body parts" is used and could cover regenerative and non-regenerative although as death has occurred or is imminent tissue regeneration is unlikely.
599 *See* Dickens, *The Control of Living Body Materials* (1977), 27 U.T.L.J. 142 at 154; *see also* Dickens, *The Ectogenetic Human Being: A Problem Child of Our Time* (1980), 17 U.W. Ont. L. Rev. 240.
600 *Supra* n. 597 ss. 2, 3. This raises the question of whether a donor is "free" where the recipient is a member of his family. It could raise the allegation that an imprisoned person should be prohibited from donating.
601 In Alberta there is a form set out on the driver's licence. It, however, requires two witnesses, preferably next-of-kin. This seems an unnecessary but cautious measure. For a criticism of the practice of the medical profession in seeking further consents, *see* Freedman, *"By Good Appliance Recovered": New Reflections On Organ Transplantation and the Definition of Death in Canada* (1982), 3 H.L. in C. 3.
602 *Supra* n. 597 s. 3(2).
603 *Supra* n. 597 s. 4(1). Note that in Alberta approximately 90 bodies per year are donated to "medical education or scientific research." *Alberta Report*, June 27, 1981, 37.

the doctor is also protected by law.[604] However, if a person acting on the consent knows the donor changed his mind, then the consent is not valid.[605]

Body parts can be taken from children as well as incompetent adults and normal adults without personal consent where the person has died, or, "in the opinion of a physician, is incapable of giving a consent by reason of injury or disease and death is imminent."[606] There must be consent, of course, but the statutory mechanism for obtaining the consent which must come from certain relatives is very practical, providing a next-of-kin list beginning with the spouse and ending with "any other of his adult next of kin." Again there is the directive that any objection of the patient must be heeded.[607] Certain persons such as a medical examiner or a funeral director who might be subject to a conflict of interest are excluded from the consent process.[608] The body or body parts taken pursuant to these sections are only taken after death.

The death of the donor must be established by "at least 2 physicians in accordance with accepted medical practice."[609] Doctors who are associated with the donor or recipient must not participate in this process but there is an exemption for doctors removing eyes for cornea transplants.

The sale of tissue or body parts is prohibited as being against public policy.[610] Blood or blood constituents are specifically exempted and thus can be sold.[611]

There is a provision to prohibit disclosure or identification of the donor or recipient except by the person affected.[612] A fine of up to $1,000 and/or a prison term of no more than six months can be levied against a person contravening the Act.[613] Civil liability is precluded where a person has acted in good faith and without negligence.[614]

In Quebec, article 20 of the Civil Code says:[615]

---

604 *Supra* n. 597 s. 4(2).
605 *Supra* n. 597 s. 4(3).
606 *Supra* n. 597 s. 5(1).
607 *Supra* n. 597 s. 5(2).
608 *Supra* n. 597 s. 5(4).
609 *Supra* n. 597 s. 7. For an excellent discussion of the difficulties associated with defining death *see Criteria For The Determination of Death — Report 15* (L.R.C. 1981); *Euthanasia, Aiding Suicide And Cessation of Treatment — Report 20* (L.R.C. 1983).
610 *Supra* n. 597 s. 8. Tissue or a body or body parts which are for any reason not used as specified by the gift must be, along with the body, "dealt with and disposed of as if no consent had been given."
611 *Supra* n. 597 s. 10; *see* Brams, *Transplantable Human Organs: Should Their Sale Be Authorized by State Statutes* (1977), 3 Am. J. Law Med. 183, where the case is made for allowing the sale of organs.
612 *Supra* n. 597 s. 11.
613 *Supra* n. 597 s. 13.
614 *Supra* n. 597 s. 9. It would not be possible in a provincial statute to deal with the criminal law.
615 1971, c. 84 s. 3 [am. 1977, c. 72, s. 1] Note that this section has also been discussed *supra* 5(a) Research.

A person of full age may consent in writing to disposal *inter vivos* of a part of his body or submit to an experiment provided that the risk assumed is not disproportionate to the benefit anticipated.

A minor capable of discernment may do likewise with the authorization of a judge of the Superior Court and with the consent of the person having the paternal authority, provided that no serious risk to his health results therefrom.

   The alienation must be gratuitous unless its object is a part of the body susceptible of regeneration.

The consent must be in writing; it may be revoked in the same way.

The Code differs from the Uniform Act in a number of respects. It covers *inter vivos* gifts of both regenerative and non-regenerative tissue and permits the sale of regenerative tissue.[616] It specifically provides for the mature minor to donate or sell tissue if a parent and a judge agree. The adult who lacks capacity to consent is not mentioned but an authority has stated that by inference such a person is excluded.[617]

   While it is not clear[618] why minors and mental incompetents were excluded from the Uniform Act, it would seem appropriate over a decade later to re-examine their position. The need for kidneys for transplantation into minors is impossible to overlook.[619] But the rationale behind allowing minors to consent to a medical procedure of any type is that it is "bona fide in the interests of the infant's [minor's] own health."[620] With respect to mentally incompetent adults or minors who are not mature or emancipated, a guardian or committee or parent can only consent to treatment in the charge's best interests.[621] If minors and mental incompetents are to be permitted to donate non-regenerative tissue, some method must be developed to obtain the best substitute for a "free and informed decision."[622] There seem to be two alternatives. The first, favoured in the United States, is to put each case before the courts for a decision, allowing the scope of "benefit" to be contracted and expanded on a case by case basis.[623] The second is to require a unanimous positive decision from a committee composed of a parent or guardian, an

---

616 For a discussion of discord between the law reform body and the legislature *see* Bowker, *Experiments on Human and Gifts of Tissue: Articles 20-23 of the Civil Code* (1978), 19 McGill L.J. 161 at 162.

617 Bowker, *id.* at 177-78. He notes that there is no provision for consent by a guardian.

618 *See, for example,* Starkman *supra* n. 596 at 6 who says the question was likely not considered; *see* Sugiyama, *supra* n. 596 at 137.

619 Fost, *Children As Renal Donors* (1977), 296 New Eng. J. of Med. 363; Sharpe, *The Minor Transplant Donor* (1975), 7 Ottawa L.R. 85 at 91.

620 Nathan, *Medical Negligence* 176-77 (1957).

621 *See* Magnet, *Withholding Treatment From Defective Newborns: Legal Aspects* (1982), 42 R. du B. 187 at 207-211 for a discussion of the possible scope of "best interests." The author states that customary practices in the community and in the medical profession provide guidelines.

622 Note that this is the requirement with respect to adults under the Uniform Act.

623 *See* Sugiyama, *supra* n. 596 at 131; *see also* Bowker *supra* n. 590 at 971; *see also* Sharpe *supra* n. 619 at 98.

objective third party such as a judge or a Public Guardian, and the donor.[624] In some cases the donor will not have the legal capacity to consent but must be consulted in any case.

Shared decision-making is appealing as it provides an apparent means of measuring the benefits and risks to the donor of a transplantation. However, the grave problem of fairly doing so in fact and in appearance might prove as difficult for a committee as it has for the United States courts. If such a committee approach were implemented, it would be appropriate to use it for all minors (including the mature or emancipated minor) and mentally incompetent persons. Some minors and mentally incompetent adults could no doubt appreciate fully the nature and consequences of the procedure while others because of age or disability could not. The Medical Research Council of Canada has suggested a very similar process for obtaining the consent of these same types of persons to research. The only difference is that the objective perspective on consent in the research setting would be that of an ombudsman or special advocate, whereas for transplantation, that person would be a judge or a Public Guardian.[625] The committee approach is, of course, the *modus operandi* of the Civil Code but it provides only for the consent of mature or emancipated minors.[626]

The Uniform Act covers non-regenerative tissue to be taken while the donor is alive. Therefore, the common law is left to govern the *inter vivos* donation of regenerative tissue, such as bone marrow, bone, blood and skin. Under the common law, an adult, if fully informed, can consent to having regenerative tissue removed from his body.[627] Indeed, the Red Cross Blood Transfusion Service is wholly dependent on such donations. Under the Act, a competent adult may even sell blood or a blood constituent.[628]

Should the Uniform Act and article 20 be amended to forbid the sale of blood or blood constituents?[629] In the United States, blood is a medium of commerce and litigation.[630] Two reasons have been given for prohibiting the sale of blood. One is scientific; donated blood is of better quality than

---

624 *See* Bowker, *supra* n. 590 at 970; *see also* Australian Law Reform Commission on Human Tissues Transplant referred to in Bowker, *supra* n. 590 at 970-71; *see also* Kirby, Mr. Justice, *Human Tissue Transplants: Legal Possibilities* (1977), L. Med. Q. 107.

625 The difference is practical, assuming transplants to be more rare.

626 *Supra* n. 615.

627 Bowker, *supra* n. 590 at 969. But note that by s. 14 of the Criminal Code, "No person is entitled to have death inflicted upon him." *See* Dickens, *The Control of Living Body Materials* (1977), 27 U.T.L.J. 142 at 164.

628 *Supra* n. 597 s. 10.

629 *See* Bowker, *supra* n. 616 at 184. Professor Bowker says "yes" but would exempt the Red Cross program of plasmapheresis.

630 For a discussion of whether a blood-letting is a sale or a service and the U.S cases thereon, *see* Dickens, *Medico-Legal Aspects of Family Law* 17 (1979); *see also* Brams, *Transplantable Human Organs: Should Their Sale Be Authorized* (1977), 3 Am. J. of Law Med. 138 at 187.

purchased blood. The other is humanitarian; a donation procedure encourages altruism.[631]

Concerns have been expressed about the problem of obtaining blood should a great demand arise; and also about the commercial clinics operating in Canada called plasmaspheresis centres, where donors are injected with a chemical to promote antibody production and after blood is taken the red cells are re-injected, allowing two donations per person per week.[632]

With regard to the first concern, it might be expected that if the sale of blood were prohibited, Canadians would voluntarily respond to an appeal for blood by the Red Cross as they have since the end of World War II. As to the second, indeed it would seem that a commercial enterprise in blood could eventually threaten the operation of the Red Cross Transfusion Service.[633]

Obviously there are many good reasons for a review of the Human Tissue Gift Act provision relevant to the sale of human tissue in Canada. Complex questions arise from modern medical technology: semen is being sold,[634] wombs are being rented and tissue is being banked.[635] The Human Tissue Gift Act[636] has been criticized as being "legislation by reaction . . . flawed by overreaction."[637] Any amendments or changes in it should correct those flaws and not add to them.

As mentioned, the Act does not cover *inter vivos* gifts of regenerative tissue. Professor Bowker has stated that the Act does by inference allow gifts of regenerative tissue by minors or mental incompetents and does not circumscribe such gifts with the safeguards surrounding non-regenerative tissue gifts.[638] Therefore, as in the case of adults and *inter vivos* regenerative tissue gifts, one must turn to the common law. However, there are no Canadian cases and thus little guidance. The Canadian Red Cross does accept blood donations from minors,[639] and article 20 of the Civil Code does permit a mature or emancipated minor to donate and even sell regenerative tissue if a parent and the court also consent.[640] Unless a psychological benefit is found

---

631 Titmuss, *The Gift Relationship* (1970), quoted in Bowker *supra* n. 616 at 183.

632 *See* Dickens, *supra* n. 627 at 167. He states that male university students are paid $15 per 500 c.c. of blood.

633 *Id.* It has been stated that the open market in blood "extends to a massive and international scale" involving the sale to overseas blood brokers of serum albumen, a blood derivative.

634 There has been the suggestion that providing semen for artificial insemination is a service, not a sale, and thus not covered by the Human Tissue Gift Act. *See* Dickens, *Medico-Legal Aspects of Family Law* 81 (1979).

635 *See* Dickens, *supra* n. 627 at 161-72 and also *supra* n. 634 at 15-20, 80-88.

636 *Supra* n. 597.

637 Starkman, *supra* n. 596 at 5.

638 *Supra* n. 616 at 182.

639 Information obtained from Red Cross — May 1983 — when 17-year-olds were accepted as donors with the consent of a parent.

640 *See Model Act* (1981), H.L. in C. 67 which suggests consent for regenerative tissue gifts by those not mentally competent must come from the nearest relative or the Public Trustee or a

and considered adequate,[641] it is difficult to see how a parent or guardian could consent to the giving of regenerative tissue, especially since the process of taking the tissue carries some risk.[642]

The committee approach suggested for donations of non-regenerative tissue by minors and mental incompetents could work equally well where the gift is of regenerative tissue. An interesting issue is whether standard criteria should be established to measure risks and benefits (for example, designating an intra-familial donation a benefit),[643] or be worked out by the committee on a case by case basis. Two requirements of the consent of the informed adult should be heeded by such a committee: the decision must be free and informed.[644]

An examination of the Human Tissue Gift Act in the context of other provincial legislation reveals potential conflict. Which statute would take precedence when one allows minors to consent to medical treatment at age 16 while the other prohibits the *inter vivos* donation of tissue by minors? This dilemma exists in British Columbia and Ontario at the present time. The better opinion is that the Human Tissue Gift Act, dealing as it does quite precisely with tissue, would limit the broader capacity of minors to consent given by another statute.[645]

In some provinces,[646] legislation allows a medical examiner or coroner to remove the pituitary gland of a deceased person so long as no objection was or is raised by the deceased or his family. The purpose of this intervention is to produce a hormone used to treat dwarfism. The conflicting demands of society and individuals are exemplified in this procedure. There is no doubt that this hormone is of great value to society, yet by these statutory provisions an organ can be legally removed without the consent of the individual or his next of kin or family.[647] A logical extension of this premise might be the

---

designated person and be approved by a Committee. Criteria are provided for the Committee; there must be significant benefit to the recipient and minimal risk to the donor.

641 *See* Freebury, *Psychological Implications of Organ Transplantation — A Selective Review* (1974), 6 Can. Psych. Assoc. J. 593-97.

642 *See* Dickens, *supra* n. 627 at 154 where the risks to the donor of bone marrow being taken include: bone fracture, infection, rupture of an artery with loss of a limb, skin scarring.

643 *See* Bowker, *supra* n. 590 at 973; *see also Model Act supra* n. 640 at 71; Note that in a resolution adopted in 1978 by the Committee of Ministers of the Council of Europe non-regenerative tissue donations were confined to genetically related persons. *See On Harmonization of Legislation of Member States Relating to Removal, Grafting and Transplantation of Human Substances* (1979), 2 Med. Sci. Law 141 at 142. *But see* Sharpe, *supra* n. 619 at 104 who would prohibit transplants between live, related persons.

644 *Supra* n. 597 s. 3(1); *see* Clements, *The Human Tissue Gift Act* (1979), 3 L. Med. Q. 39.

645 *See* Clements, *supra* n. 644 at 40; Sharpe, *supra* n. 619 at 94.

646 Fatality Inquiries Act, R.S.A. 1980, c. F-6, s. 27; An Act to Amend the Human Tissue Act, S.M. 1979, c. 20; Human Tissue Act, S.N. 1971, No. 66; Coroners Act, R.S.O. 1980, c. 93, s. 29.

647 It will be the rare case where a person would know of the practice of taking pituitary glands and, thus, object.

inclusion of kidneys and corneas in such provisions, since many persons critically require them.[648] But it is arguable that a person should be assured that his organs will never be removed without a valid consent from the proper person.[649] Indeed the Human Tissue Gift Act seems to be constructed upon that principle. Clearly, the public as well as medical and legal professions must be canvassed to ensure that the topic of transplantation of human tissue is regulated by legislation that reflects a fair balance of all interests.

(c) Sterilization

The dead hand of history affects this area of medical law more than any other. There is a vague feeling of unease about a procedure that cuts off the power to procreate. This anxiety has its historical roots in Europe in ancient times when castration was the ultimate indignity inflicted upon the loser.[650] In more modern times in North America, there are disquieting words of the great jurist Chief Justice Oliver Wendall Holmes who in upholding involuntary sterilization of "mental defectives" said: "Three generation of imbeciles are enough."[651]

Eugenic sterilization of over 56,000 persons was done in the first year of operation of the 1933 Nazi sterilization statute.[652] In our own country, there was a statute allowing involuntary sterilization of an inmate of a British Columbia mental institution who, if discharged, might parent a mentally defective child.[653] In Alberta, a similar act was amended over the years, and at the time of its repeal, authorized sterilization for psychosis, mental retardation, syphilis, epilepsy and Huntington's chorea. Consent of the patient was required except for mental defectives and if the patient was psychotic, a parent or guardian could consent on his behalf.[654]

Contraceptive sterilization of adults has been seen by some to be hedonistic. In 1954 the great English judge Lord Denning, who is usually associated with

---

648 Note that in France there is a law allowing for the harvesting of organs for transplantation. *See* Farfar, *Organs for Transplant: Courageous Legislation* (1977), Br. Med. J. 497.

649 *Quaere* whether s. 7 of the Canadian Charter of Rights and Freedoms covers a cadaver and if so whether taking an organ without consent violates "security of the person." *See also* s. 12 re: "cruel and unusual treatment."

650 Castration was a mayhem (maim). For an excellent discussion *see* Dickens, *Retardation and Sterilization* (1982), 5 Int. J. Law & Psych. 295; *Medico-Legal Aspects of Family Law* 28 (1979); *see also* Somerville, *Medical Interventions And the Criminal Law* (1980), 26 McGill L.J. 82.

651 *Buck v. Bell* (1927), 274 U.S. 200. Applied in *In re Sterilization of Moore* (1976), 221 S.E. (2d) 307 (N.C.S.C.).

652 Green, *Law, Sex and the Population Explosion* (1977), 1 L. Med. Q. 82 at 87.

653 *Sexual Sterilization Act*, S.B.C. 1933, c. 59 [repealed S.B.C. 1973, c. 79, s. 1].

654 *Sexual Sterilization Act*, S.A. 1928, c. 37 [repealed S.A. 1972, c. 87, s. 1]. For a criticism, *see* McWhirter and Weijer, *The Alberta Sterilization Act, a Genetic Critique* (1969), U.T.L.J. 424; Christian, *The Mentally Ill and Human Rights in Alberta: A Study of the Alberta Sexual Sterilization Act* (1974). Unpublished paper.

modern views, stated that it was injurious to the public interest and spouses, degrading, and conducive to licentiousness.[655]

The taint of sterilization has left doctors and hospitals very insecure about the procedure and although in Canada it is now an extremely popular and common contraceptive measure,[656] its availability is restricted. In Alberta a consultation is required by regulation to the Alberta Hospitals Act.[657] Consent forms used by some hospitals require spousal consent for sterilization and certain hospital law manuals support this position.[658]

To be critical of the failure to throw off the weight of history is not to say that every person in our society has or should have the right to be sterilized. What is necessary is to recognize and respect the right of those who do. An adult, male or female, who is of sound mind, can consent to a sterilization procedure.[659] There is no legal requirement for spousal consent or concurrence[660] and no need to support the decision by seeking a benefit for the patient in the procedure.[661] This right is supported by statute in Ontario,[662] Prince Edward Island[663] and Quebec.[664] In the United States there is a constitutionally protected right to sterilization.[665]

---

655 *Bravery v. Bravery*, [1954] 3 All E.R. 59 (C.A.) at 67-68. Note that the majority disassociated themselves from this opinion.

656 Dickens, *Medico-Legal Aspects of Family Law* 27 (1979); *see* Robertson, *Civil Liability Arising From "Wrongful Birth" Following an Unsuccessful Sterilization Operation* (1977), 4 Am. J.L. & M. 131 at 135. Sterilization is second in use only to oral contraceptives amongst white married couples in the U.S. and the most popular method for couples married 10 years or more; *see* Kouri, *Non-therapeutic Sterilization (Cataford v. Moreau)*, [1979] 57 C.B.R. 89. In Quebec sterilizations are increasing. *See* Wilson, *Voluntary Sterilization: Legal and Ethical Aspects* (1979), 3 L. Med. Q. 13 at 19.

657 Alta. Reg. 146/71. An interesting question is whether this is required as a check on a doctor's judgment or a patient's decision. This applied only to sterilization done in a hospital. It is only sterilizations on females that must be done in a hospital.

658 *See* Sharpe and Sawyer, *Doctors and the Law* 48 (1978); *see also* Wright, *The Right to Parenthood* (1979), 2 Fam. L. Rev. 173 at 175.

659 Bowker, *Minors and Mental Incompetents: Consent to Experimentation, Gifts of Tissue and Sterilization* (1981), 26 McGill L.J. 951 at 973; Dickens, *Medico-Legal Aspects of Family Law* 31 (1979); Sharpe and Sawyer, *Doctors and the Law* 43-48 (1978); Kouri and Somerville, *Comments on the Sterilization of Mental Incompetents in Canadian Civil and Common Law* (1980), 10 R.D.U.S. 599 at 607; Jacob, *Speller's Law Relating To Hospitals And Kindred Institutions* 203 (1978). Note that in a Quebec case, *Cataford v. Moreau* (1978), 7 C.C.L.T. 241 (Que. S.C.), Chief Justice Deschênes reviewed the legality of contraceptive sterilization in Quebec. In a comment Kouri says the effect of this decision is that there is no longer any doubt about the legality, criminal and civil, of contraceptive sterilization *see* Kouri, *Non-therapeutic Sterilization (Cataford v. Moreau)*, [1979] 57 C.B.R. 89 at 104.

660 Sharpe and Sawyer, *supra* n. 658 at 47; Rozovsky L.E. & F.A., *Legal Sex* 20 (1982); Wilson, *Voluntary Sterilization: Legal and Ethical Aspects* (1979), 3 L. Med. Q. 13.

661 Starkman, *Sterilization of the Mentally Retarded Adult: The Eve Case* (1981), 26 McGill L.J. 931 at 936. Kouri and Somerville, *supra* n. 659 at 605; Kouri, *Non-therapeutic Sterilization (Cataford v. Moreau)*, [1979] 57 C.B.R. 89 at 92.

662 Family Law Reform Act, R.S.O. 1980, c. 152, s. 65(2).

663 Family Law Reform Act, S.P.E.I. 1978, c. 6, s. 60.

664 Health Services and Social Services Act, L.R.Q. 1977, c. S-5, art. 156.

665 This right flows from the constitutional right to privacy in matters of reproduction; *see* Griswold v. Connecticut (1965), 381 U.A. 479; Thompson & Sanbar, *Wrongful Conception*

There are now a number of cases in which the sterilization procedure was an issue.[666] In each case, liability of the doctor was not based on a lack of competence of the woman to consent, but rather on an inadequacy of the information disclosed to her,[667] or on negligence in carrying out the procedure, or after care.[668]

A patient must give an informed consent to sterilization as to any procedure and since sterilization is normally an elective procedure a more complete disclosure is required.[669] As with any treatment or procedure, the doctor must meet the standard of care required in carrying it out.[670]

Sterilization may be a natural consequence of treatment or surgery required by and beneficial to the patient. An example of this is a hysterectomy performed because of disease. A doctor must disclose the loss of procreative capacity to the patient before surgery because it is an aspect of the nature of the surgery and goes to its gravity. A sterilization carried out in these circumstances presents no special consent problem for the informed adult of sound mind. Thus, in Canada, sterilization is not illegal[671] and, provided that an adult of sound mind gives an informed consent[672] and the doctor meets the standard of care required of him in carrying out the sterilization and follow-up care, no liability will be imposed on the doctor. Hopefully doctors and hospitals will come to realize that in the aforementioned circumstances, the sterilization procedure presents no greater risk to them than any other procedure.

But when the sterilization of a minor or an adult without capacity to consent is proposed, the lessons of history must be heeded. There is in Canada no legal justification for involuntary eugenic sterilization and the contraceptive sterilization of minors or mentally incompetent adults must be approached

---

or Wrongful Pregnancy (1983), 11 Leg. Aspects Med. Practice 1. *Quaere* whether sterilization is encompassed in the Constitution Act 1982, Part I: Canadian Charter of Rights and Freedoms, s. 7 as a right by way of "security of the person."

666 *Colp v. Ringrose,* unreported October 1976 No. 84474 (Alta. S.C.); *Cryderman v. Ringrose,* [1978] 3 W.W.R. 481 (Alta. C.A.); *Zimmer v. Ringrose* (1981), 124 D.L.R. (3d) 215 (Alta. C.A.); leave to appeal to S.C.C. dismissed (1981), 37 N.R. 289 (S.C.C.); *Doiron v. Orr* (1978), 86 D.L.R. (3d) 718 (Ont. H.C.); *Cataford v. Moreau* (1978), 7 C.C.L.T. 241 (Que. S.C.); *Videto v. Kennedy* (1981), 125 D.L.R. (3d) 127 (Alta. Q.B.); *Gouin-Perrault v. Villeneuve* (1982), 23 C.C.L.T. 72 (Que. S.C.); *Mang v. Moscovitz* (1982), 37 A.R. 221 (Alta. S.C.).

667 *Id. Cryderman v. Ringrose.*

668 *Id. Zimmer v. Ringrose; Cataford v. Moreau; Videto v. Kennedy; McBride v. Langton.*

669 *See supra* discussion on informed consent.

670 *See* Chapter 4. Damages for a failed sterilization may be for "wrongful birth" or "wrongful life" and are discussed in Chapter 4.

671 For an excellent discussion of criminal law and consent, *see* Starkman, *A Defence to Criminal Responsibility for Performing Surgical Operations: Section 45 of the Criminal Code* (1981), 26 McGill L.J. 1048; *see also* Somerville, *Medical Interventions and the Criminal Law* (1980), 26 McGill L.J. 82; *see also* Starkman, *Sterilization of the Mentally Retarded Adult: The Eve Case* (1981), 26 McGill L.J. 931.

672 For a case where a doctor performed a sterilization (tubal ligation) after a Caesarian without the patient's consent *see Murray v. McMurchy,* [1949] 2 D.L.R. 442 (B.C.S.C.).

with great caution. However, a therapeutic sterilization may be justified as being for the benefit and in the best interests of the patient.

The two concerns about the sterilization of a person who has no capacity to consent are that the medical judgment may be inaccurate and that the law may be unfair. As to the first concern, it may be said that the criteria used to designate a person as of unsound mind or of a certain level of retardation, or as unable to appreciate the nature and consequences of treatment, are arbitrary,[673] and a minor or adult could be wrongly categorized. Moreover, a medical judgment that sterilization is required for reasons of physical or even mental health may put the procedure into the category of therapeutic sterilization, a very different designation than that of non-therapeutic sterilization.[674]

As to the second concern, the legal requirements that a decision made for such a person be in his best interests,[675] and there be no conflict of interest are very difficult to establish. Consequently, out of an abundance of caution, a decision not to allow a sterilization would likely be made, perhaps representing an abrogation of the rights of the individual.[676] Unfortunately, the state of the art in sterilization is still at the stage where there may be no second chance — sterilization is generally irreversible.

The issue of sterilization and the minor requires the consideration of four categories of persons: the mature or emancipated minor, the minor over the age of consent in those provinces with a statutory minimum age for consent, the retarded or mentally incompetent minor and the minor falling in none of these categories.

Looking at the last group, mentally competent minors, there is a consensus that parents lack the power to consent to a non-therapeutic sterilization of their child even with the minor's concurrence. By contract, parents can consent if by reason of illness or disease it is necessary for the minor to undergo a procedure which results in sterilization. Such a procedure would be characterized as therapeutic.[677]

---

673 *See Re D.*, [1976] 1 All E.R. 326 for an example.

674 Note that a hysterectomy performed on a retarded girl because of her inability to handle menstruation is categorized as therapeutic by some doctors but the Ontario Association for the Mentally Retarded says it is non-therapeutic. Also the Law Reform Commission of Canada in its report on *Sterilization* 155 (1979), would call it non-therapeutic. *See* Bowker, *supra* n. 659 at 975.

675 *See* Magnet, *Withholding Treatment From Defective Newborns: Legal Aspects* (1982), 42 R. du B. 187 at 207-211 where the author points out that customary practices in the community and in the medical profession are important considerations in ascertaining "best interests."

676 *See* Rioux, *Sterilization* 31-35 (L.R.C. 1979), where certain benefits of sterilization are discussed. *See also* Kouri and Somerville, *supra* n. 659 at 615.

677 Dickens, *Medico-Legal Aspects of Family Law* 33 (1979). Note that parental consent to contraception may not be improper although it could make the child neglected or in need of care under provincial child welfare legislation; Kouri and Somerville, *Comments on the Sterilization of Mental Incompetents in Canadian Civil and Common Law* (1980), 10 R.D.U.S. 599.

Since there is no Canadian case with respect to the sterilization of a retarded minor, reference to an English case is helpful. In *Re: D.*,[678] a mother, on a pediatrician's advice, consented to the sterilization of her 11-year-old retarded daughter who had reached puberty. The medical advice was that any offspring of the child could be abnormal and that the daughter could never cope with a baby. A psychologist who had worked with D. had the case brought before a court.[679] Madam Justice Heilbron ruled that the right of a woman to reproduce was a basic one and a non-therapeutic sterilization done without her consent violated that right.[680] Decisions in the United States support this position.[681]

Statistics relating to the sterilization of minors in Alberta and Ontario illustrate that there are cases where sterilization is categorized as therapeutic. In Alberta in 1976-78, there were 78 hysterectomies, 11 other sterilizations on girls, and 8 on boys. In Ontario in 1976, there were 109 hysterectomies, 149 other sterilizations on girls, and 50 on boys.[682]

The Law Reform Commission of Canada published a working paper on sterilization in 1979 proposing that non-therapeutic sterilizations on minors under 16 years of age be permitted only with legal authorization from a multi-disciplinary board.[683] The criteria set out for such a deliberation would seem to be exactly what a court of law might consider in resolving such a case.[684]

Thus, a parent has the power, and indeed the responsibility, to provide therapeutic treatment for a child and sterilization may constitute part of that therapeutic treatment. However, there is no parental power to consent to a non-therapeutic procedure and although the courts may have the power to do

---

678 [1976] 2 W.L.R. 279 (Fam. D.).
679 In Canada, child welfare authorities might intervene; *see* Sharpe and Sawyer, *supra* n. 658 at 45.
680 Professor Green asks whether a similar decision would have been rendered by a male judge. *See* Green, *Law, Sex and the Population Explosion* (1977), 1 L. Med. Q. 82 at 88.
681 *Wade v. Bethseda Hosp.* (1973), 356 F. Supp. 380 (D.C. Ohio); *In the Interest of M.K.R.* (1974), 515 S.W. (2d) 467 (Mo. S.C.); *A.L. v. G.R.H.* (1975), 325 N.E. (2d) 501 (Ind. C.A.); referred to in Dickens, *supra* n. 677 at 32.
682 Cited in Rioux, *Sterilization* 100 (L.R.C. 1979), referring to a study of Zarfas.
683 *Id.* at 117. Note that the recommendations address changes to criminal law because it is the only relevant area of federal jurisdiction.
684 Rioux, *Sterilization* 118-19 (L.R.C. 1979), the minimum criteria are:
   (i) the individual is probably fertile, and there is some evidence to that effect;
   (ii) the individual is both of child-bearing age and sexually active and other forms of contraception have proved unworkable . . . or are inapplicable . . .
   (iii) there is more compelling evidence than age or mental handicap alone that childbirth itself or childrearing itself will probably have a psychologically damaging effect on the individual;
   (iv) the sterilization will not in itself cause physical or psychological damage . . . greater than the beneficial effects . . .
   (v) the views of the individual have been taken into account . . .

so it seems unlikely that such a power would be exercised for a non-therapeutic sterilization.[685]

In four Canadian provinces, Quebec,[686] British Columbia,[687] New Brunswick,[688] and Ontario,[689] legislation establishes a minimum age of consent for mentally competent minors. In Quebec, the minimum age is 14; in the other three provinces it is 16. The Conference of Commissioners on Uniformity of Legislation in Canada has proposed an Act,[690] as have provincial law reform bodies in Alberta[691] and Saskatchewan.[692] The latter two provinces specifically exclude sterilization. By contrast, the Uniform Act implicitly includes even non-therapeutic sterilization by including as medical treatment "any procedure for preventing pregnancy."[693]

Legislators in New Brunswick passed a statute modelled on the Uniform Act, but dropped the section covering sterilization. Since the statutory provision in Quebec relates to "care and treatment required by the state of health of the minor," non-therapeutic sterilization would be excluded.[694] The British Columbia statute requires a reasonable effort to contact the parent, or a second opinion that the treatment is in the best interests of the patient, as a preliminary to the minor's consent. These prerequisites would negate the capacity of a minor of 16 or over to consent to non-therapeutic sterilization.

Ironically, it has been through the Ontario regulation that parents have succeeded in having retarded minors under 16 years of age sterilized in that province.[695] It must be noted that the provision deals only with surgical operations in public hospitals. By further regulation and because of the number being sterilized, contraceptive sterilization of those under 16 was prohibited in Ontario.[696]

---

685 Kouri and Somerville *supra* n. 677 at 625. *But see* Starkman, *Sterilization of the Mentally Retarded Adult: The Eve Case* (1981), 26 McGill L.J. 931 at 950. *See Re Eve infra.* For a discussion of a U.S. case where the court did ratify the parents' consent to the sterilization of their mentally retarded child *see* Lachance, *In re Grady: The Mentally Retarded Individual's Right to Choose Sterilization* (1981), 6 Am. J. L. & M. 559.

686 Public Health Protection Act, L.R.Q. 1977, c. P-35.

687 Infants Act, R.S.B.C. 1979, c. 196.

688 Medical Consent of Minors Act, S.N.B. 1976, c. M-6.1.

689 Public Hospitals Act, R.S.O. 1980, c. 410; R.R.O. 1980, Reg. 862, s. 50.

690 Proceedings Conference of Commissioners on Uniformity of Legislation in Canada 162 (1975).

691 Alberta Institute of Law Research and Reform, *Consent of Minors to Health Care* (1975).

692 Law Reform Commission of Saskatchewan, *Tentative Proposals for Consent Minors to Health Care Act* (1978).

693 *Supra* n. 690 1(d). Note, however, under 16 years consent is valid with two medical opinions only as to treatment in his best interests, etc.

694 *See* Kouri and Somerville, *supra* n. 677 at 614.

695 Note that Krever J. expressed concerns about this legislation *see* Krever, *Minors and Consent for Medical Treatment*, lecture delivered at the U. of T. March 18, 1974 cited in Sask. L.R.C. *supra* n. 692 at 1. *See also* L.R.C. *supra* n. 684 at 79 which quotes the official Guardian of Ontario as having stated that "sterilizations being performed on hundreds of Ontario children are illegal."

696 R.S.O. 1970, c. 378, Ont. Reg. 968/78, continued by Ont. Reg. 241/80.

In summary, in all provinces but Ontario, minimum age of consent legislation does not endow minors with the capacity to consent to non-therapeutic sterilization. Therapeutic sterilization is justifiable as necessary or beneficial treatment.[697]

Governments have avoided the issue of sterilization and consent in enacting minimum age of consent legislation. This can be explained as prudent politics, or it simply may reflect a reluctance to allow a "normal" minor to make such a profound and irreversible decision. Such reasoning is equally applicable to the mature or emancipated minor. The policy behind allowing a minor who is mature or emancipated to consent to medical treatment is to allow him access to services necessary to attain and maintain good health. It would be a very rare case indeed where a non-therapeutic sterilization would fit within this goal. As has been noted, some minors have the capacity to consent to advice and treatment for birth control and the availability of these alternatives militates against the need to allow consent to an irreversible procedure such as sterilization.

An adult who has some mental disability may nevertheless be competent to consent to sterilization.[698] The Law Reform Commission of Canada in its working paper on sterilization has suggested that:[699]

> Mentally handicapped persons who understand the nature and consequences of the sterilization procedure and are under no coercion or duress should have the same options to consent to, or to refuse, sterilization as other persons.

Here, as is the case with competent adults, the patient must be given enough information to allow for an informed consent.[700]

When the mental disability of the adult is serious enough that he is not competent to consent to sterilization, the question becomes: can anyone else consent on his behalf? A substitute or guardian or committee may be given this power by court appointment pursuant to legislation.[701] But a substituted consent can only be for treatment which is in the best interests of the patient, and thus, once again the critical assessment is a medical one: is this sterilization therapeutic or non-therapeutic?

The Dependent Adults Act[702] in Alberta provides for the appointment of a legal guardian to whom the court may give the authority to consent to health care in the best interests of the dependent adult.[703] Health care is defined to include among other things "any procedure taken for the purpose of prevent-

---

697 Note that the Alberta Institute of Law Research and Reform Report, *supra* n. 691 states: "Nothing in the proposed Act permits a minor to consent to surgical sterilization."

698 Kouri and Somerville, *supra* n. 677 at 616.

699 *Supra* n. 684 at 116.

700 Kouri and Somerville, *supra* n. 677. at 618.

701 *See, for example*, Dependent Adults Act, R.S.A. 1980, c. D-32; Mental Incompetency Act, R.S.O. 1980, c. 264; Hospitals Act, R.S.N.S. 1967, c. 249.

702 R.S.A. 1980, c. D-32.

703 *Id*. s. 9(1)(h).

ing pregnancy."[704] A further provision allows a guardian to apply for "the opinion, advice or direction"[705] of a judge on any question. These provisions would allow a guardian to be granted the power to consent even to a contraceptive sterilization if in the best interests of the dependent adult.[706] Could contraceptive sterilization ever be in the best interests of the mentally disabled adult? Are those guardians and committees who consent to it and arrange for it acting in their own interests only? It depends on whether one sees contraceptive sterilization as being a "threat or an opportunity"[707] for the mentally incompetent adult. The words of Mr. Justice Campbell in the Court of Appeal in the case of *Re Eve* reflect the unenviable situation of a typical incompetent adult.[708]

> Eve has the potential to live a happy life within a protected environment. However, the prospect of her pregnancy has, and will continue to place restrictions upon her freedom of action. Her social contacts, her privileges in a group home, even the modest privileges of attending a movie, taking a stroll or making use of public transit are in prospect of limitations, controls and restrictions for the very reason that she is [more] vulnerable to sexual abuse and pregnancy. I am of the opinion that without the protection of a permanent sterilization the protected environment will become a guarded environment and the loss to Eve in terms of her social options and her relative freedoms would cause substantial injury . . .

There is considerable pressure on all institutions to treat disabled adults, so far as possible, as normal. Indeed, the Canadian Charter of Rights and Freedoms guarantees equality before and under the law without discrimination based on mental disability.[709] Moreover, some mentally handicapped persons have the capacity to consent to sterilization, and as a contraceptive measure for normal adults sterilization is accepted and popular. Provided that the judgment of a guardian is open to review by a court, as is the case in the Dependent Adults Act,[710] contraceptive sterilization should not be denied to the mentally disabled or dependent adult.

---

704 *Id*. s. 1(*h*)(ii).
705 *Id*. s. 45(1).
706 *In Re T*. unreported August 24, 1981. No. 594 (Alta. Surr Ct.); an order provided for "birth control or sterilization." *Re A* unreported 2nd June 1981, No. 1542 (Alta Surr. Ct.) authority granted to a partial guardian to consent to a therapeutic abortion. *Re Durdle* unreported 27 Sept 1983, No. D.A. 2503 (Alta. Surr. Ct.) authority granted to consent to a hysterectomy. *See* Bowker, *supra* n. 659 at 975 who notes that at the time the Act was introduced it was said it was not intended to cover sterilization. He says " . . . it would be odd to find that a legislature which repealed *the Sexual Sterilization Act* out of solicitude for the fundamental right to procreate had by a side-wind conferred on the guardian of a dependent adult the power to authorize sterilization in the name of contraception." *See also* Kouri and Somerville, *supra* n. 677 at 621.
707 Dickens, *Retardation and Sterilization* (1982), 5 Int. J. Law & Psych. 295.
708 *Re Eve* (1980), 115 D.L.R. (3d) 283 at 319-20 (P.E.I.S.C. *in banco*).
709 Constitution Act 1982, Part I: Canadian Charter of Rights and Freedoms, s. 15(1); *see also* s. 12. Everyone has the right not to be subjected to cruel and unusual treatment or punishment.
710 *Supra* n. 701. For a discussion of the Dependent Adults Act, *see* Christie. *Guardianship: The Alberta Experience: A Model for Change* (1982). 3 H.L. in C. 58.

The Supreme Court of Canada in *Re Eve* will examine the jurisdiction of a court over the contraceptive sterilization of a mentally incompetent adult in the absence of legislation. "Eve" is in her mid-twenties, is mildly to moderately retarded, physically mature and likely to be sexually active. Her mother, a woman nearly 60, applied to the court to be appointed Eve's committee (guardian) and to be authorized to consent to a contraceptive sterilization for her daughter. The trial judge[711] believed her mother was sincerely concerned about Eve, but held that the court had no jurisdiction to authorize the solely contraceptive procedure. On appeal[712] this decision was reversed by a divided court. Mr. Justice Campbell held that the court had jurisdiction to authorize the contraceptive (non-therapeutic) sterilization of Eve because of the equitable doctrine of *parens patriae*.[713] He found that it would be in her best interest, that she would suffer substantial injury to her freedom if she were not sterilized and that her committee could consent on her behalf. The type of procedure was to be left to the committee (her mother). Mr. Justice Lange agreed and felt that the trial judge had not placed enough weight on the medical witnesses who all believed sterilization was advised. Mr. Justice MacDonald dissented. He said the court had a *parens patriae* jurisdiction and listed 14 points to be considered in each case.[714] While he felt that in exceptional circumstances a court can order a non-therapeutic sterilization of a mentally incompetent person, he felt that this should not be done for "Eve" as it would deprive her of a basic human right and was nothing more than a social convenience.

Thus, the court was unanimous in holding that it had the jurisdiction to authorize the non-therapeutic sterilization of a mentally incompetent person because of its *parens patriae* power over individuals who are unable to look after themselves.[715] The Supreme Court of Canada has the opportunity to bring some certainty and order into a most confusing and emotional set of relationships: the mentally incompetent adult, the guardian or committee, and the courts.

---

711 *Re E.* (1979), 10 R.F.L. (2d) 317 (P.E.I.S.C.).

712 (1980, 1981), 115 D.L.R. (3d) 283 (P.E.I.S.C. *in banco*) on appeal to the S.C.C. Note, that, pursuant to Rule 60 of the Supreme Court of Canada leave to intervene has been granted to the Consumer Advisory Committee of the Canadian Association for the Mentally Retarded, and to the Public Trustee for the Province of Manitoba.

713 Literally, "parent of his country." Originates from English common law where the King had a prerogative to act as guardian to infants, idiots and lunatics. *Blacks Law Dictionary* (1979). For an excellent discussion *see* Magnet, *Withholding Treatment From Defective Newborns: Legal Aspects* (1982), 42 R. du B. 187 at 211-16. For an example of the use of *parens patriae* in Quebec, *see Institut Philippe Pinel v. Dion* (1983), 2 D.L.R. (4th) 234 (Que. S.C.).

714 *Supra* n. 712 at 307-309. Note that these cover topics as diverse as the "method and manner of sterilization" and the assurance of "no overriding public interest."

715 For a critique of the case, *see* Starkman, *Sterilization of the Mentally Retarded Adult: The Eve Case* (1981), 26 McGill L.J. 931.

Hopefully, sterilization can now be viewed in a modern progressive manner. Legislation may be a partial answer for the problems of defining types of sterilization, capacity to consent, the decision making process, and adequate safeguards for the rights of all parties.[716] But a message from the past must not be ignored: grouping people without heed to individual needs is inappropriate with regard to sterilization. Judicial decisions reflecting modern mores are required.

6. REMEDIES — BATTERY OR NEGLIGENCE

Prior to the decision of the Supreme Court of Canada in *Reibl v. Hughes*,[717] a patient could sue in battery or negligence or both where the allegation was that his consent was deficient. The majority of reported cases were brought in battery.[718] However, the action for battery has now been dramatically restricted by the Supreme Court of Canada.

The battery action has definite advantages for the patient over the negligence action. The patient does not have to prove causation or damage, nor does he have to find medical experts to testify.[719] Also, the doctor bears the onus of providing that consent was given to the treatment. The battery action protected the patient against unauthorized touching, whereas the negligence action was the means by which a patient could seek compensation when a duty required of a doctor was carried out in a substandard way and the patient was injured. However, the battery action covering as it also does harmful and offensive bodily contact has a record of being associated with aggressive anti-social behavior and came to be seen in the United States as an inappropriate means of dealing with the problems of consent in the medical context. Thus, the battery action was abandoned for negligence as the proper action where a doctor was the defendant.[720] The Supreme Court of Canada has by its ruling in *Reibl v. Hughes*[721] followed the same route.

---

716 *For example*, the Dependent Adults Act, *supra* n. 701 and the New Zealand Contraception, Sterilization and Abortion Act set out in Rioux, *Sterilization* 149 (LRC 1979); *See also* Rioux *id*. for possible federal legislation.

717 (1980), 14 C.C.L.T. 1 (S.C.C.).

718 Picard, *The Tempest of Informed Consent in Studies* in *Canadian Tort Law* 129 (2d ed. Klar. 1977).

719 Note, too, that there may be an argument that limitation periods differ. *See* McLaren. *Of Doctors, Hospitals and Limitations — The Patient's Dilemma* (1973), 11 O.H.L.J. 85 at 97: *See also* Dickens, *Contractual Aspects of Human Medical Experimentation* (1975). 25 U.T.L.J. 406 at 534. *Cf. Boase v. Paul*, [1931] O.R. 625 (C.A.) and *Marshall v. Curry*. [1933] 3 D.L.R. 260 (N.S.S.C.).

720 Picard, *supra* n. 718 at 130-31. For an excellent discussion of the situation in England *see* Robertson, *Informed Consent to Medical Treatment* (1981). 97 L.Q.R. 102 at 123.

721 *Supra* n. 717.

However, the first step toward narrowing the scope of the battery action was taken by an Ontario judge who was aware of the change in direction in American jurisprudence. In 1976 in *Kelly v. Hazlett,*[722] Mr. Justice Morden said the battery action should be resorted to where there was no informed consent as to the basic nature and character of the medical treatment, but that negligence was the proper action if it was a collateral risk that was not explained. Because of the differences between the two actions, the characterization of the risk was critical, yet doing so was a very difficult task given the variables in medical practice and in patients.

The complexity of the *Kelly v. Hazlett*[723] dichotomy was evident in the *Reibl v. Hughes*[724] case where, at trial, Haines J.[725] said the failure to inform of the risk of a stroke sounded both in battery and in negligence. On appeal Mr. Justice Brooke, affected by the American trend, said:[726]

> In cases such as this, the notion of battery seems quite inappropriate. In the circumstances when the evidence is consistent only with the fact that the doctor has acted in *good faith and in the interests of the patient,* but in so doing was negligent in failing to make disclosure of a risk inherent in treatment which he recommends and as a result has caused his patient loss or damage, the action should properly be in negligence and not in battery. The finding then of battery cannot stand. [emphasis supplied]

Noting Mr. Justice Morden's comment that most Canadian cases had proceeded in battery, Brooke J.A. concluded:[727]

> They are cases where there was an intentional deviation from the consent given, or fraud, or a serious misrepresentation as to procedure and/or risks.

Thus the Ontario Court of Appeal associated the battery action with intentional deviation, fraud, serious misrepresentation and perhaps even with bad faith and selfish interests.

It is interesting to compare this picture of battery with that suggested by an authoritative legal text. Fleming says in speaking of battery:[728]

> The action, therefore, serves the dual purpose of affording protection to the individual not only against bodily harm but also against any interference with his person which is offensive to a reasonable sense of honour and dignity. The insult in being touched without consent has been traditionally regarded as sufficient even though the interference is trivial and not attended with actual physical harm.

Chief Justice Laskin deferred discussion of the battery versus negligence issue in *Hopp v. Lepp*[729] because he agreed with the trial judge's conclusion of no liability. However, the trial judge had done so on the basis of battery and

---

722 (1976), 1 C.C.L.T. 1 (Ont. H.C.).
723 *Id.*
724 (1977), 78 D.L.R. (3d) 35 (Ont. H.C.).
725 *Id.*
726 (1978), 6 C.C.L.T. 227 at 246-47 (Ont. C.A.). *See* Picard, *Annotation,* 6 C.C.L.T. 226.
727 *Id.* at 245. For a listing of cases under each heading *see* Picard *supra* n. 718.
728 Fleming, *The Law of Torts* 23 (6th ed. 1983).
729 (1980), 112 D.L.R. (3d) 67 (S.C.C.).

Chief Justice Laskin's terse statement that he thought the doctor had discharged any duty of disclosure foretold that his analysis in *Reibl v. Hughes*[730] would be in negligence.

In the Alberta Court of Appeal in *Hopp v. Lepp,*[731] the majority found the doctor liable in both battery and negligence. Morrow J.A. said:[732]

> . . . the same reasoning as is appropriate for battery is on my understanding of the authorities equally appropriate for negligence.

In summary, the situation at the time of the hearing of *Reibl v. Hughes*[733] in the Supreme Court of Canada was that battery was the more common action and one more advantageous to patients. But the American courts and the Court of Appeal of Ontario were in favour of restricting its application to situations associated with negative practice where the defendant was a doctor.[734] Although a suggestion had been made by Morden J. to circumscribe battery and negligence, the courts were certainly having difficulties.

Chief Justice Laskin brought battery to its present narrow focus. He said battery should be restricted to situations where:[735]

> . . . there has been no consent at all or where, emergency situations aside, surgery or treatment has been performed or given beyond that to which there was consent.
>
> This standard would comprehend cases where there was misrepresentation of the surgery or treatment for which consent was elicited and a different surgical procedure or treatment was carried out . . .
>
> . . . I can appreciate the temptation to say that the genuineness of consent to medical treatment depends on proper disclosure of the risks which it entails, but in my view, *unless there has been misrepresentation or fraud to secure consent to the treatment*, a failure to disclose the attendant risks, however, serious, should go to negligence rather than to battery. Although such a failure relates to an informed choice of submitting to or refusing recommended and appropriate treatment, it arises as the breach of an anterior duty of due care, comparable in legal obligation to the duty of due care in carrying out the particular treatment to which the patient has consented. It is not a test of the validity of the consent. [emphasis supplied]

Chief Justice Laskin indicated that he was aware of the dichotomy suggested by *Kelly v. Hazlett*[736] and said he found it "very difficult of

---

730 *Supra* n. 717.

731 (1979), 8 C.C.L.T. 260.

732 *Id*. at 289.

733 *Supra* n. 717.

734 *See supra* n. 726. An American advocate of so doing suggested that appropriate cases for battery included: making sexual advances to a patient; *Bryan v. Grace* (1940), 63 Ga. App. 373; or inserting an instrument into the womb to dismember a foetus; *Keen v. Coleman* (1942), 67 Ga. App. 331, *see* McCoid, *A Reappraisal of Liability for Unauthorized Medical Treatment* (1957), 41 Minn. L. Rev. 381.

735 *Reibl v. Hughes supra* n. 717 at 13-14. *See also Allan v. New Mount Sinai Hosp.* (1980), 11 C.C.L.T. 299 (Ont. H.C.); reversed on appeal. 19 C.C.L.T. 78 (Ont. C.A.); Picard. *Annotation* (1980), 12 C.C.L.T. 1.

736 *Supra* n. 722.

application, but also incompatible with the elements of the cause of action in battery."[737] About the advantages of battery to the patient he said:[738]

> True enough, it has some advantages for a plaintiff over an action of negligence since it does not require proof of causation and it casts upon the defendant the burden of proving consent to what was done. Again, it does not require the adducing of medical evidence, although it seems to me that if battery is to be available for certain kinds of failure to meet the duty of disclosure there would necessarily have to be some such evidence brought before the Court as an element in determining whether there has been such a failure.

An important cause of action was abrogated by the Supreme Court of Canada.[739] It seems battery is now available where there was "no consent at all," or treatment "beyond" consent, or "misrepresentation of the surgery or treatment," or "misrepresentation or fraud to secure consent." Reaction to this dramatic change in the law has been mixed. The provincial courts are, of course, bound to follow this Supreme Court of Canada precedent. In *Zimmer v. Ringrose,*[740] the court recognized the discrimination now required with respect to battery. Prowse J.A. said:[741]

> Unlike the conduct traditionally associated with battery, the physician's conduct in performing surgery or providing treatment is not of an intentionally harmful or offensive nature. Indeed, his actions are generally motivated by a sincere desire to promote the best interests of his patient. Furthermore, the essence of a plaintiff's complaint is not the "touching" but the ramifications of the course of treatment of which he was not informed. (See *Trogun v. Fruchtman* (1973), 207 N.W. 2d 297 and *Downer v. Veilleux* (1974), 322 A. 2d 82.)

While a trial judge in 1978[742] had found a battery in respect of a silver nitrate sterilization and awarded $1 in damages, he also found negligence in the after care and awarded $5,000 damages. The Court of Appeal[743] hearing the case after the judgment of the Supreme Court of Canada, concurred on the latter basis for liability and found battery inappropriate, and no negligence because causation was not proven although there had been inadequate disclosure. In another Alberta case, *Mang v. Moscovitz,*[744] battery was raised in argument but Mr. Justice Dixon said he did not propose to deal with it except to say that "battery has virtually been eliminated as a cause of action in medical malpractice cases."[745] In *White v. Turner,*[746] Mr. Justice Linden commented on the Supreme Court of Canada judgment:[747]

---

737 *Supra* n. 717 at 12.
738 *Id.*
739 Note that the English courts are in accord on this narrow scope for the battery action. *See Chatterton v. Gerson,* [1981] 1 All E.R. 257; Robertson, *Informed Consent to Medical Treatment* (1981), 97 L.Q.R. 102 at 123; Picard, *Patients, Doctors and the Supreme Court of Canada* (1981), 1 Oxford L.J. Leg. Studies 441.
740 (1981), 16 C.C.L.T. 51 (Alta. C.A.).
741 *Id.* at 56.
742 *Zimmer v. Ringrose* (1978), 89 D.L.R. (3d) 646 (Alta. Q.B.).
743 *Supra* n. 740.
744 (1982), 37 A.R. 221 (Alta. Q.B.).
745 *Id.* at 262.

Where there has been a basic consent to the treatment, there is no place left for discussions of battery. The problems associated with inadequacy of information about risks are to be handled with negligence theory.

The first reported case to deal with the "new battery" in any depth was *Ferguson v. Hamilton Civic Hosp.*[748] The patient underwent a bilateral carotid arteriography (dye-injection x-ray). Neither of his two doctors told him of the risk of a stroke. Shortly after the tests were completed (and showed the provisional diagnosis of carotid stenosis to be unfounded), the patient lost sensation in his limbs and became a quadraplegic. He sued in both battery and negligence. Mr. Justice Krever said:[749]

Because the law relating to the connection between informed consent and battery, on the one hand, and negligence, on the other, has recently been *clarified by the Supreme Court of Canada* it is not necessary to analyze all the cases on the subject. It is no longer possible baldly to say that a patient who does not give a fully informed consent to a medical procedure will be treated by the law as having had his bodily integrity interfered with without his or her consent and is therefore entitled to a cause of action in battery. *Although it may not solve all the problems in this branch of law, the decision of the Supreme Court of Canada in Reibl v. Hughes, [1980] 2 S.C.R. 880, . . . 114 D.L.R. (3d) 1 . . . has limited liability in battery for non-disclosure of risks in medical cases . . .* [emphasis supplied]

After quoting from *Reibl v. Hughes,* Krever J. continues:

In going on to declare that a failure to disclose risks is relevant to negligence and not battery, Chief Justice Laskin does not foreclose the availability to the plaintiff of battery in a case in which there has been misrepresentation or fraud involved in the securing of consent to treatment . . .

The patient argued that there was a misrepresentation as to the nature of the procedure because he was not told that the purpose of the diagnostic test was to ascertain if surgery was necessary. His position was based on the premise that if he refused the surgery, which was his right, the purely diagnostic test he underwent should not have been used. Krever J. held that while a discussion of the surgery might have been commendable he was:[750]

. . . unable to conclude that there was any misrepresentation within the meaning of that word in the portion of the reasons of Chief Justice Laskin . . .

In the result, Krever J. held there was no battery and no negligence because although the disclosure of risks was inadequate, the patient could not prove that a reasonable person in his position would not have consented. It was another case of a patient being unable to prove causation. This case raises in a

---

746 (1981), 15 C.C.L.T. 81 (Ont. H.C.).

747 *Id.* at 97.

748 (1983), 23 C.C.L.T. 254 (Ont. H.C.). Note that the Ontario Court of Appeal in an earlier (but only summarily reported) case held there was a battery when a doctor while performing a dilation and curettage also performed a "meatotomy" but without the patient's consent. *Hankai v. York County Hosp.* (1981), 9 A.C.W.S. (2d) 354 (Ont. C.A.). A new trial was directed for the assessment of damages as a jury had awarded general damages of $35,000 and exemplary damages of $25,000.

749 *Id.* at 290.

750 *Id.* at 293.

tragic fashion the question of whether the law on informed consent as it is now structured gives adequate scope for the courts to come to just decisions.[751]

The restructuring of battery has sparked a good deal of comment.[752] While, in general, there seems to be an acknowledgment that the two causes of action needed to be analyzed and guidelines provided, a concern remains about the grey areas and the implications of some of the words of the court, as well as about the adequacy of this "new battery."[753] There seems to be some consensus that the Supreme Court of Canada test is no simpler than that of Morden J. in *Kelly v. Hazlett*.[754] Indeed, there is the suggestion that it would be helpful to refer to that case for the interpretation of the Supreme Court of Canada test.[755]

One area of great concern springs from the comments of the Supreme Court of Canada on misrepresentation and fraud. Professor Klar has said that the Chief Justice "was not clear as to what the misrepresentation or fraud must relate or how it will operate."[756] Professors Gochnauer and Fleming[757] find an internal inconsistency in the Chief Justice's words and ask whether by them he meant to give an illustration of or an exception to the test for battery. Professor Somerville raises a number of concerns about the step taken by the Supreme Court of Canada and says a basic question is: "Why does 'misrepresentation or fraud to secure consent to the treatment' cause non-disclosure of a risk to give rise to a cause of action in battery, where it would not do so if the elements of misrepresentation or fraud were not present?"[758]

---

751 *Id.* at 313. Mr. Justice Krever in a postscript to his judgment states he has "a feeling of discomfort" where a person such as the patient is not entitled by present law to be compensated.

752 Bowker, *Minors and Mental Incompetents: Consent to Experimentation, Gifts of Tissue and Sterilization* (1981), McGill L.J. 951; Edwards, Hopkins, White, *Annual Survey of Canadian Law — Torts I* (1982), O.L.R. 175. Gochnauer and Fleming, *Tort Law — Informed Consent — New Directions for Medical Disclosure — Hopp v. Lepp and Reibl v. Hughes* (1981), 15 U.B.C.L. Rev. 475; Klar, *Developments in Tort Law: The 1979-80 Term* (1981), 2 S.C.L.R. 325 and *The 1980-81 Term* (1982), 3 S.C.L.R. 385 at 413; Picard, *Consent to Medical Treatment in Canada* (1981), 10 O.H.L.J. 140; Rodgers-Magnet, *Recent Developments in the Doctrine of Informed Consent to Medical Treatment* (1981), 14 C.C.L.T. 61; Scaletta, *Informed Consent and Medical Malpractice: Where Do We Go From Here?* (1980), 10 Man. L.J. 289; Sharpe, *Five Recent Canadian Decisions on Informed Consent* (1981), 1 H.L. in C. 79; Somerville, *Structuring the Issues in Informed Consent* (1981), 26 McGill L.J. 740.

753 *But see* Bowker *Id.* at 956 who says the decision "put an end to confusion" and "placed the battery action on its proper basis."

754 *Supra* n. 722; *see* Rodgers-Magnet *supra* n. 752 at 66; Gochauer and Fleming *supra* n. 752 at 489; Sharpe *supra* n. 752 at 86.

755 *See* Rodgers-Magnet *supra* n. 752.

756 Klar, *Developments in Tort Law: The 1980-81 Term* (1982), 3 S.C.L.R. 385 at 415.

757 *Supra* n. 752 at 486.

758 *Supra* n. 752 at 749. Note also that Somerville points out that the problem of proper cause of action does not present itself in the same way in Quebec. *See id.* at 742, n. 5.

She suggests an analysis that minimizes the Supreme Court ruling and its consequence of making a battery unavailable where it would in the past have been available.

At the bottom of the reservations expressed by a number of commentators is the apparent attempt by the Supreme Court of Canada to separate risks and consent. The criticism is strong. As Professor Somerville has summarized it:[759]

> . . . it is submitted that to the extent that the Supreme Court has limited the availability of an action in battery by stating the law to be that *risks do not relate to the basic nature and character of an act and, consequently, their non-disclosure cannot vitiate battery-avoiding consent,* the ruling may not be desirable. [emphasis supplied]

Professors Gochnauer and Fleming say:[760]

> The Court's position separating risk and consent is a distortion of our ordinary understanding of the concepts and in a number of cases will defeat our normal, reasonable expectations.

They are critical of the failure of the Supreme Court of Canada to give any policy considerations to justify its position and say:[761]

> By cutting us off from our ordinary intuitions in these matters without setting up signposts of policy the decision fails to clarify wholly the applicability of battery and negligence when there has been a breach of the duty to disclose risks of medical treatment.

The parameters of the new battery action have not yet been fully tested by litigation.[762] Although the number of cases where fraud or "serious" misrepresentation (such as negligent or fraudulent misrepresentation as contrasted with innocent misrepresentation) will be alleged and proven will likely be few, there may be some confusion in the "grey" areas. For example, in a case where a person is told he will be given an anaesthetic but is not told this will be done by moving a needle into his heart would there be a misrepresentation?[763] Would there be misrepresentation if a tonsillectomy was described as a minor, routine and safe procedure when for that patient it was not?[764] What about the prescription of tranquilizers for emotional complaints given without a description of the risks of addiction and misuse? Hopefully future judicial review of battery will provide answers if not an assuagement of the critics.

Communication between the health care professional and the patient is the means by which a valid consent to treatment is given. It is also part of the therapy of good medicine. The absence of good communication is the reason for most lawsuits against health care professionals and hospitals.

---

759 *Supra* n. 752 at 751.

760 *Supra* n. 752 at 488.

761 *Supra* n. 752 at 489.

762 *See Hankai v. York County Hosp.* (1981), 9 A.C.W.S. (2d) 354 (Ont. C.A.) where a doctor who did a meatotomy without the patient's consent admitted liability.

763 Klar, *Developments in Tort Law: The 1980-81 Term* (1982), 3 S.C.L.R. 385 at 415-16 based on *Halushka v. Univ. of Sask.* (1965), 52 W.W.R. 608 (Sask. C.A.).

764 *See* Gochnauer and Fleming, *supra* n. 752 at 487-88.

4

Negligence

1. INTRODUCTION

The law of negligence is emphasized in this book because it governs the majority of actions brought against hospitals and doctors and other health care professionals. While the general principles are easily stated, an understanding of their application is more difficult to acquire. This is especially so in the typical medical negligence case because it involves members of an honourable calling, the exercise of professional judgment and technical skills, and a body of complex scientific knowledge. Each case requires a decision on its unique facts and, therefore, close attention to precedents and adherence to the doctrine of *stare decisis* is often of less value to a judge that it is in some other kinds of cases.[1] However, as certain a statement of the law as is possible will

---

1 *See Crits v. Sylvester* (1956), 1 D.L.R. (2d) 502 at 508; affirmed [1956] S.C.R. 991. *See also* Samuels, *Medical Negligence Today — An Appraisal* (1983), 23 Med. Sci. Law 31 at 33. This article contains a helpful analysis of the English cases. In this regard *see also* Jackson and Powell, *Professional Negligence* 204-48 (1982). As to Australia *see* Fricke, *Medical Negligence* (1982), 56 Aust. L.J. 61.

be of value both to lawyers who require a basis on which to advise clients and prepare cases, and to doctors and hospitals who need to understand the legal standards against which their conduct is to be measured. This chapter and the two following attempt to satisfy this need.

2.   BASICS OF NEGLIGENCE

To be successful a negligence action must meet four requirements:[2]

(a) the defendant must owe the plaintiff a duty of care,

(b) the defendant must breach the standard of care established by law;

(c) the plaintiff must suffer an injury or loss;

(d) the defendant's conduct must have been the actual and legal cause of the plaintiff's injury.

If the case fails to meet any of these requirements, then the action will be dismissed; therefore, each of the above will now be considered in more detail.

(a) Duty

A pre-condition to any discussion of standard of care, or any of the other elements of the negligence action, is the finding that the defendant owed a duty of care to the plaintiff. If it cannot be shown that there was a duty upon this particular defendant to exercise care with respect to this particular plaintiff, there can be no finding of liability, regardless of how ''negligent'' the defendant's conduct may appear.[3]

The duty of a doctor to exercise care with respect to a particular patient springs into being upon the formation of the doctor-patient relationship[4] and therefore the issue in medical negligence cases tends to be concerned less with the existence of the duty than with its scope. The scope of a duty is closely related to the standard of care, and Part 3 of this chapter analyzes the standard of care involved in the exercise of the doctor's most important duties.

The duty placed on the doctor is to exercise care in all that he does to and for the patient, which includes attendance, diagnosis, referral, treatment and instruction.[5] The nature of each of these facets of duty, together with its attendant standard of care are also discussed in detail in Part 3.

In many cases, for example, where a patient is hospitalized, the doctor is not the only professional who owes a duty to the patient, and in certain

---

2 *See supra* Chapter 2.

3 For a detailed discussion of the use and abuse of the duty concept in negligence law *see* Smith, *The Mystery of Duty* in *Studies in Canadian Tort Law* 1 (2nd ed. Klar 1977).

4 *See supra* Chapter 1.

5 In the U.S. the duty has been extended to include a duty to warn third parties of a serious danger from a patient under treatment: *Tarasoff v. Regents of University of California* (1976), 131 Cal. Rptr 14, 529 P. (2d) 553 (Cal. S.C.). For a comment *see* Stone, *The Tarasoff Decision: Suing Psychotherapists to Safeguard Society* (1976), 90 Harv. L. Rev. 358.

circumstances the doctor can, as the courts say, "rely"[6] on the duty owed by the other professional. That is, the doctor's duty is suspended with respect to matters falling within the scope of the other professional's duty to the patient. Thus it has been held that in the operating room a surgeon can rely on the anaesthetist to perform his tasks properly,[7] the resident to assist in performing the surgery[8] and to close the incision[9] and the nurse to count the sponges.[10] (The doctor in charge at the time of closing has a duty to perform a final search for sponges, but the extent of the search required varies with the nature of the operation.)[11] Hospital personnel may be relied upon to properly secure the patient for surgery[12] and in the recovery room the nurses' duty to the patient is paramount.[13] On the ward, the work of the nurses, doctors and others is established by hospital rules and practice and generally the doctor is entitled to assume competence on the part of these other participants in the patient's care. This is so even where dangerous drugs are involved. Where a patient died from an injection of adrenalin provided by a nurse in response to the doctor's request for Novocaine, it was held that the doctor had no duty to check the label notwithstanding that his doing so would have prevented the death.[14] In a recent Alberta case[15] liability was apportioned 40 per cent against the doctor and 60 per cent against a hospital where during cataract surgery an ophthalmologist requested that he be shown the bottle of solution he proposed to use, but failed to notice that the hospital pharmacy and a nurse had negligently delivered the wrong drug.

However, there are limitations on the extent to which a doctor may rely on the duty of others. When he relinquishes the care of his patient to others it is incumbent upon him to take steps for the patient's continued care.[16] In *Foote v. Royal Columbian Hosp.*[17] a doctor who had varied the drug therapy

---

6 For a discussion of when he will be liable for the acts of others *see* Chapter 8.

7 *MacKinnon v. Ignacio, Lamond and MacKinnon* (1978), 29 N.S.R. (2d) 656 (N.S.S.C.). *See Leadbetter v. Brand* (1980), 37 N.S.R. (2d) 581 (N.S.S.C.), where a dentist relied on an anaesthetist.

8 *Considine v. Camp Hill Hosp.* (1982), 133 D.L.R. (3d) 11 (N.S.S.C.); *Hajgato v. London Health Assn.* (1982), 36 O.R. 669 (Ont. H.C.); *see also infra* (House Staff and Students).

9 *Karderas v. Clow* (1973), 32 D.L.R. (3d) 303 (Ont. H.C.).

10 *Jewison v. Hassard* (1916), 10 W.W.R. 1088 (Man. C.A.); Meredith, *Malpractice Liability of Doctors and Hospitals* 80 (1957).

11 *Cosgrove v. Gaudreau* (1981), 33 N.B.R. (2d) 523 (N.B.Q.B.). *See also Van Wyck v. Lewis,* [1924] App. D. 438 (S. Africa C.A.).

12 *Knight v. Sisters of St. Ann* (1967), 64 D.L.R. (2d) 657 (B.C.S.C.). *See also Armstrong v. Bruce* (1904), 4 O.W.R. 327 (Ont. H.C.) where a patient was burned with a hot water pad placed by a nurse during an operation.

13 *Laidlaw v. Lions Gate Hosp.* (1969), 70 W.W.R. 727 (B.C.S.C.); *Kolesar v. Jeffries* (1976), 59 D.L.R. (3d) 367 at 377 (Ont. H.C.).

14 *Bugden v. Harbour View Hosp.,* [1947] 2 D.L.R. 338 (N.S.S.C.).

15 *Misericordia Hosp. v. Bustillo,* [1983] Alta. D. 2632-01 (Alta. C.A.).

16 *Hajgato v. London Health Assn.* (1982), 36 O.R. (2d) 669 at 684 (Ont. H.C.); *Considine v. Camp Hill Hosp.* (1982), 133 D.L.R. (3d) 11 at 39 (N.S.S.C.).

17 [1982] B.C. D. Civ. 2632-05 (B.C.S.C.).

of an epileptic patient, thereby putting her in a high risk position of having *grand mal* seizures, did not advise the hospital staff of this, nor of the fact that she had already had such a seizure at home in a bath and thus required observation. The doctor was held liable for the serious brain damage suffered by the patient when she had a *grand mal* seizure while taking an unsupervised bath in hospital. In a case where a patient was discharged from hospital with a supply of anticoagulent drugs[18] it was held that the doctor could not rely on the resident to inform the patient of dangerous side effects, and that the doctor ought to have foreseen the action and had a duty to adequately instruct his patient.

The modern move to specialization sometimes creates a problem in this area. Whether the situation be a referral from a general practitioner to a specialist or from one specialist to another, a patient may have a number of doctors all believing erroneously that another is carrying out his duty to the patient. Each doctor then assumes that the other has discharged a duty such as explaining the risks of a dangerous test,[19] or informing himself of "factual data pertinent and necessary to diagnosis" and taking appropriate action,[20] when in fact neither has done so, with disastrous consequences for the patient.[21] In this situation too much care is preferable to too little, and if the medical profession fails to develop a practice for the protection of the patient, the courts will be forced to do so.[22] One alternative would be to apportion liability between the two doctors as was done in *Leonard v. Knott* [23] where a patient was referred by an internist to a radiologist for an intravenous pyelogram test as part of an "executive health programme." Neither doctor ascertained whether there were any clinical indications for the invasive test and each took the position that it was the other's duty to do so. The patient died as a result of an allergic reaction to the contrast medium used for the test. The internist was held to be 75 per cent liable and the radiologist 25 per cent liable.

Therefore, where parts of medical care or treatment are normally the responsibility of others, those persons are alone accountable to the patient for any negligence with respect to those aspects of the treatment. But the funda-

---

18 *Crichton v. Hastings,* [1972] 3 O.R. 859 (C.A.).
19 *McLean v. Weir* (1977), 3 C.C.L.T. 87 (B.C.S.C.) and Picard, *Annotation;* affirmed [1980] 4 W.W.R. 330 (Ont. C.A.).
20 *Holmes v. Bd. of Hosp. Trustees of London* (1978), 5 C.C.L.T. 1 (Ont. H.C.) and Picard, *Annotation.*
21 *Id.,* where there was a failure of both doctors to read or consult or obtain a report on cervical x-rays for five days while the patient's condition, an infection described as "retropharyngeal abscess" went undiagnosed. As a result the patient was rendered a quadriplegic.
22 *See Anderson v. Chasney,* [1949] 4 D.L.R. 71 (Man. C.A.); affirmed [1950] 4 D.L.R. 223 (S.C.C.).
23 [1980] 1 W.W.R. 673 (B.C.C.A.). *See also Osburn v. Mohindra* (1980), 29 N.B.R. (2d) 340 (N.B.Q.B.). *See* Jackson and Powell, *Professional Negligence* 223-24 (1982).

mental and residual duty to the patient lies with the doctor.[24] Another factor which promises to become more critical if consumerism in health care continues to grow, is the duty a patient owes to himself: to provide information,[25] to follow instructions,[26] and generally to act in his own best interests.[27]

A doctor who refuses to treat a patient commits no breach of legal duty[28] (although he may be in breach of his professional ethics), but upon the formation of the doctor-patient relationship, his duty exists until the clear severance of the relationship[29] and includes the duty to take affirmative action, for example, where it is evident that a hip dislocation has not been reduced by the treatment given and resetting is required.[30]

(b) Standard of Care

Under our legal system every person is required to conduct himself in such a way as not to cause harm to others. The standard against which individuals are measured is that of the "reasonable man"[31] and conduct which fails to meet this standard and causes injury to another will render the wrongdoer liable to the person injured.

Persons who hold themselves out as possessing special skills or abilities must practise their art, profession, or business[32] so as to meet a standard of conduct equivalent to that of a reasonably competent member of their group. Accordingly, the standard of care required of a doctor is "that of a reasonable medical man considering all the circumstances . . ."[33] The standard was formulated during the Roman era[34] and remains largely unchanged in modern times.[35]

---

24 *See* Nathan, *Medical Negligence* 36-40 (1957); Rozovsky, *Canadian Hospital Law* 63 (1979).
25 *See Leadbetter v. Brand* (1980), 37 N.S.R. (2d) 581 (N.S.S.C.); *see also* Chapter 3 (Consent).
26 *See Crossman v. Stewart* (1977), 5 C.C.L.T. 45 (B.C.S.C.).
27 *Moore v. Large* (1932), 46 B.C.R. 179 at 183 (B.C.C.A.); *see also Bergstrom v. G.*, [1967] C.S. 513 (Que. S.C.).
28 Nathan, *supra* n. 24 at 37.
29 *Pellerin v. Stevenson* (1945), 18 M.P.R. 345 at 357 (N.B.C.A.); *see also Hunter v. Ogden* (1871), 31 U.C.R. 132 (Ont. H.C.) and *supra* Chapter 1.
30 *Dangerfield v. David* (1910), 17 W.L.R. 249 at 257 (Sask. S.C.).
31 *Blyth v. Birmingham Waterworks* (1856), 11 Exch. 781 (Ct. of Exch.); *Donoghue v. Stevenson*, [1932] A.C. 562 (H.L.).
32 *Lanphier v. Phipos* (1838), 8 C. & P. 475, 173 E.R. 581 (*Nisi Prius*); *R. v. Bateman* (1925), 19 Cr. App. R. 8 (Ct. of Crim. App.)
33 *Cryderman v. Ringrose*, [1977] 3 W.W.R. 109 at 118 *per* Stevenson J.; affirmed [1978] 3 W.W.R. 481 (Alta. C.A.). *See also McCormick v. Marcotte*, [1972] S.C.R. 18 at 21. Note that this is the same standard as would apply in a contract action; *see Worth v. Royal Jubilee Hosp.* (1980), 4 L. Med. Q. 59 at 67 (B.C.C.A.); *see also* Jackson and Powell, *Professional Negligence* 207 (1982).
34 *Lex Aquilia* 287 B.C. Digest 9.2.1.
35 Glose, *Torts — Doctrine of Professional Negligence — Standard of Professional Care* (1963), 41 Can. Bar Rev. 140. *For example, Slater v. Baker* (1767), 2 Wils. K.B. 359, 95

The law's expectations of the doctor have been described in more detail as follows:[36]

> The legal principles involved are plain enough but it is not always easy to apply them to particular circumstances. Every medical practitioner must bring to his task a reasonable degree of skill and knowledge and must exercise a reasonable degree of care. He is bound to exercise that degree of care and skill which could reasonably be expected of a normal, prudent practitioner of the same experience and standing, and if he holds himself out as a specialist, a higher degree of skill is required of him than of one who does not profess to be so qualified by special training and ability.

Whether a defendant has met the requisite standard of care is a question of fact for the jury or if there is no jury the trial judge,[37] and one which lies at the heart of every negligence suit. As one Canadian authority has said:[38]

> No court in a negligence suit can escape a decision about whether or not the defendant's conduct breached the standard of care fixed by law . . . The bulk of legal talent and judicial resources is expended on this matter.

(i) Proof of the standard

A judge or jury is in no position to compare the conduct of the doctor to that required of the "reasonable medical man"[39] without expert evidence. The court needs such information in order to decide whether the defendant acted according to "approved practice," failed to meet the standard of care, or only made an "error of judgment."[40] The experts are usuall;y doctors who practise the same specialty as the defendant or who are specialized in the medical area in issue.[41]

The difficulties and peculiarities of proof in the medical negligence action are discussed in detail in Chapter Six.

E.R. 860; *Pippin v. Sheppard* (1822), 11 Price 400, 147 E.R. 512 (Ct. of Exch.); *Lanphier v. Phipos supra* n. 32; *Leighton v. Sargant* (1853), 27 N.H. 460, 59 Am. Dec. 388 (N.H.S.C.); *Rich v. Pierpont* (1862), 3 F. & F. 34, 176 E.R. 16 (*Nisi Prius*).

36 *Crits v. Sylvester supra* n. 1 at D.L.R. 508 *per* Schroeder J.A. *See also Cardin v. Montreal* (1961), 29 D.L.R. (2d) 492 at 494 (S.C.C.) wherein it is made clear that the same standard applies in Quebec. *See also* Crépeau, *La Responsabilité Civile du Medicin Et De L'Etablissement Hospitalier* 69 Wilson et La Fleur, Montreal, 1956. Crépeau, *La Responsabilité Médicale et Hospitalière Dans La Jurisprudence Québécoise Récent* (1960), 20 R. du B. 433.

37 *Czuy v. Mitchell*, [1976] 6 W.W.R. 676 at 678 (Alta. C.A.).

38 Linden, *Canadian Tort Law* 101 (1982). *See, for example,* the decision of Linden J. in *White v. Turner* (1981), 15 C.C.L.T. 81 (Ont. H.C.); appeal dismissed 20 C.C.L.T. xxii (Ont. C.A.). *See also* Haines, *The Medical Profession and the Adversary Process* (1973), 11 Osgoode Hall L.J. 41 at 44; McCoid, *The Care Required of Medical Practitioners* (1959), 12 Vand. L. Rev. 549 at 614.

39 *Hajgato v. London Health Assn.* (1982), 36 O.R. (2d) 669 at 683 (Ont. H.C.). Sherman, *The Standard of Care in Malpractice Cases* (1966), 4 Osgood Hall L.J. 222.

40 For a detailed discussion of these defences *see infra* Chapter 5.

41 *See Leadbetter v. Brand* (1980), 37 N.S.R. (2d) 581 (N.S.S.C.); *Wipfli v. Britten* (1982), 22 C.C.L.T. 104 (B.C.S.C.). *See also Wilson v. Swanson* (1956), 5 D.L.R. (2d) 113 at 126 (S.C.C.) where the evidence of a doctor who fitted neither category was held to be inadequate.

(ii) The nature and character of the standard of care

The test of whether an individual's conduct meets the standard of the "reasonable person" is an objective test;[42] that is, no account is taken of the individual's own physical characteristics, intelligence or personality. In the context of medical negligence, the test of whether the doctor meets the standard of the "normal, prudent practitioner" is also said to be objective,[43] but most authorities[44] acknowledge that a subjective element is involved in the application of the test:[45]

> Thus in order to decide whether negligence is established in any particular case the act or omission or course of conduct complained of must be judged, not by ideal standards nor in the abstract but against the background of circumstances in which the treatment in question was given.

Thus the medical practitioner is measured objectively against a reasonable medical person who possesses and exercises the skill, knowledge and judgment of the normal, prudent practitioner of his special group. The comparison is made, however, with reference to the particular circumstances at the material time.[46] The inquiry into the doctor's milieu will fall into three broad categories:

(a) the education, experience and other qualifications of the doctor;

(b) the degree of risk involved in the procedure or treatment; and

(c) the equipment, facilities and other resources available to the doctor.

Each of the above will now be considered in turn.

A. Qualifications of the doctor

General practitioner and specialist. The standard of care expected of a doctor is directly related to his qualifications and therefore a specialist is expected to possess and exercise a higher degree of skill in his particular field than would be expected of a general practitioner in that field.[47]

> If [a doctor] holds himself out as a specialist, a higher degree of skill is required of him than of one who does not profess to be so qualified by special training and ability.

The point is illustrated by a number of cases. While there was evidence that a specialist might in the circumstances have diagnosed gas gangrene, a general practitioner in a small town was held not liable for failing to do so.[48]

---

42 Linden, *supra* n. 38 at 111.

43 *Hajgato v. London Health Assn.* (1982), 36 O.R. (2d) 669 at 683 (Ont. H.C.).

44 Louisell and Williams, *Medical Malpractice*, Matthew Bender, New York (1982), at 200-206; McCoid, *supra* n. 38 at 614.

45 Nathan, *supra* n. 24 at 22-23.

46 Meredith, *supra* n. 10 at 62. For an excellent judicial treatment of these *see* Lieberman J. in *Tiesmaki v. Wilson*, [1974] 4 W.W.R. 19; affirmed [1975] 6 W.W.R. 639 (Alta. C.A.).

47 *Crits v. Sylvester supra* n. 1; *Wilson v. Swanson supra* n. 41 at 119 *per* Rank J. and at 124 *per* Abbott J. Meredith, *supra* n. 10 at 62-63.

48 *Challand v. Bell* (1959), 18 D.L.R. (2d) 150 at 154 (Alta. S.C.); *see also Ehler v. Smith* (1978), 29 N.S.R. (2d) 309 (N.S.T.D.).

Similarly, in a case where specialists called at trial were critical of a small town general practitioner's failure to diagnose carbon monoxide poisoning, the court held that the general practitioner was not negligent in the circumstances.[49] In a case where it was shown that a pediatrician would have diagnosed epiglottitis in a child, another small town practitioner was held not negligent by failing to do so.[50]

The difference in the standard of care required of general practitioners and specialists extends to treatment as well as diagnosis, of course. In *Wilson v. Stark*,[51] two general practitioners in a small Saskatchewan centre who worked for over three hours in an unsuccessful attempt to locate and remove the patient's retrocecal appendix were held not liable although it was shown that a specialist would have had little difficulty.

There are areas where the standards of care for general practitioners and specialists are equivalent. One example is treatment of circulatory complications in fracture cases; it has been held that "there is a usual and normal practice in the profession, regardless of specialty, namely to split or bi-valve the cast."[52] It is probably no coincidence that this area has been the subject of many lawsuits involving patients who have suffered serious losses.[53]

Once the court has determined the doctor's specialty it can, with the help of expert evidence, determine the appropriate standard of care.[54] Courts will soon have to grapple with setting a standard of care in evolving areas of practice such as sports medicine,[55] genetic counselling[56] and the prenatal diagnosis of genetic defects.[57]

Evidence of education (degrees, certificates and memberships, publications and privileges) and training (internship, residency, research and special study) provides formal and relatively objective criteria for establishing special-

---

49 *Ostash v. Sonnenberg* (1968), 63 W.W.R. 257 (Alta. C.A.).

50 *Tiesmaki v. Wilson supra* n. 46.

51 (1967), 61 W.W.R. 705 (Sask. Q.B.); *see also Gonda v. Kerbel* (1983), 24 C.C.L.T. 222 (Ont. H.C.).

52 *Ares v. Venner*, [1970] S.C.R. 608 at 614-15 *per* Hall J. quoting the trial judge, approved in *Vail v. MacDonald* (1976), 66 D.L.R. (3d) 530 at 534 (S.C.C.).

53 *See infra* (casts).

54 *Demoura v. Mississauga Hospital* (1979), 3 L. Med. Q. 215 (Ont. H.C.).

55 *Robitaille v. Vancouver Hockey Club* (1979), 19 B.C.L.R. 158 (B.C.S.C.); Balbi, *The Liability of Professional Team Sports Physicians* (to be published); Ferguson, *Physicians' Legal Responsibilities in Managing Ski Trauma* (1982), 10 Am. J. of Sports Med. 206; Pitt, *Malpractice on the Sidelines: Developing a Standard of Care for Team Sports Physicians* (1982), 2 J. Comm, & Ent. L. 579; King, *The Duty and Standard of Care for Team Physicians* (1981), 18 Houston L.R. 657; Weistart & Lowell, *The Law of Sports* (1979), at p. 982. For a comment on the state of sports medicine *see* Smith, *Sports Medicine Doctors Find New Ways to Treat The Breaks of the Game* (1982), 7 Alberta Western Living, 8.

56 Dickens, *Legal Approaches to Genetic Diagnosis and Counselling* (1980), 1 H.L. in C. 25; Capron, *Tort Liability in Genetic Counselling* (1980), 4 Spec. L. Digest: Health Care 3.

57 Knoppers, *Physician Liability and Prenatal Diagnosis* (1981), 18 C.C.L.T. 169.

ization status.[58] In general, the greater the education and training, the higher the standard expected. Evidence of extensive experience in a specialty will certainly raise the standard[59] and may even be a substitute for some of the formal criteria just mentioned.[60] But while the acquisition of experience by the doctor may raise the standard expected by him, a lack of experience will not lower it. A doctor may hold himself out as a specialist either by formal certification or by the more subtle means of gradually restricting his practice to a particular type of medical problem, patient, or treatment,[61] and once he does so he will be expected to practise his profession at the standard of care required of the specialist. As one authority on tort law has explained, the problem is one of balancing the protection of society against the encouragement of beginners:[62]

> The skill demanded from beginners presents an increasingly difficult problem in modern society. While it is necessary to encourage them, it is equally evident that they cause more than their proportionate share of accidents. The paramount social need for compensating accident victims, however, clearly outweighs all competing considerations and *the beginner is, therefore, held to the standard of those who are reasonably skilled* and proficient in that particular calling or activity. [emphasis supplied]

Thus a doctor described as a "relatively novice surgeon" who had never before performed the particular operation was nonetheless held liable when he cut a nerve[63] as was an anaesthetist performing a trans-tracheal ventilation for the first time.[64] A classical statement of the standard of care is that a doctor is to meet the standard of the "normal, prudent practitioner of the same experience and standing."[65] However, there is no authority for the use of this comment to support a lower standard for the inexperienced.[66]

---

58 *MacDonald v. York County Hosp.* (1973), 41 D.L.R. (3d) 321 (Ont. C.A.) *per* Brooke J.A.; *affirmed sub nom. Vail v. MacDonald supra* n. 52; *Eady v. Tenderenda,* [1975] 2 S.C.R. 599.

59 *Johnston v. Wellesley Hosp.* (1970), 17 D.L.R. (3d) 139 at 141 (Ont. H.C.).

60 *MacKinnon v. Ignacio, Lamond and MacKeough* (1978), 29 N.S.R. (2d) 656 (N.S.T.D.). In *Fluevog v. Pottinger* (1977), unreported (B.C.S.C.) one of the issues was whether the defendant dentist was to be judged as a specialist in prosthodontics. On the basis of his experience he was held to have to meet that standard, albeit that he had no formal certification as a specialist.

61 *Id.* Ferguson, *Physicians' Legal Responsibilities in Managing Ski Trauma* (1982), 10 Am. J. Sports Med. 206 at 207.

62 Fleming, *The Law of Torts* 105 (6th ed. 1983). This passage in other editions was quoted with approval in *Challand v. Bell supra* n. 48 at 152 and in *McKeachie v. Alvarez* (1970), 17 D.L.R. (3d) 87 at 100 (B.C.S.C.). Note that the skill of the older physician may be another "increasingly difficult problem," *see MacKinnon v. Ignacio, Lamond and MacKeough* (1978), 29 N.S.R. (2d) 656 (N.S.T.D.).

63 *McKeachie v. Alvarez id.*

64 *Holmes v. Bd. of Hosp. Trustees of London supra* n. 20. Note that there is no requirement that the patient be informed that the doctor is performing a procedure for the first time, *Lepp v. Hopp* (1980), 13 C.C.L.T. 66 (S.C.C.).

65 *Crits v. Sylvester supra* n. 1.

66 *Dale v. Munthali* (1977), 16 O.R. (2d) 532 (Ont. H.C.); affirmed 21 O.R. (2d) 554 (Ont. C.A.).

The recognition of such informal criteria as experience, association with specialists, and hospital appointments to raise the standard, as well as the overlap of certain specialties has led to some difficulties for the courts. *Vail v. McDonald*[70] is an illustrative case. The doctor had formal qualifications as a general surgeon, a fellowship, and 15 years experience in general surgery. His practice was approximately 60 per cent with traumatic injuries including "orthopedic work." He had hospital privileges in "emergency vascular problems." At issue was his treatment of a fractured ankle by performing a closed reduction which resulted in impaired circulation and the patient's loss of his foot. The trial judge held[71] that there had been no evidence that the defendant was qualified "to a . . . higher degree than a general practitioner on the staff of a city general hospital" and applied the standard of a general practitioner.

In the Court of Appeal[72] one justice thought the relevant standard to be that of general surgeon with "extensive training, experience and responsibility in orthopedic surgery" while the two others held the standard to be "greater than that of a general practitioner but less than a cardiovascular specialist." The Supreme Court of Canada held that the standard of care, whether that of a general practitioner, general practitioner with cardiovascular expertise, or general surgeon with orthopaedic expertise, would be the same in regard to a circulatory problem.

In any event, each of the judges involved, after applying the standard he thought appropriate, found that the defendant failed to meet it.

In another case[73] a doctor who, it seemed, had no special education, training or experience in surgery but who had joined the surgical department

There is some suggestion that a higher standard might be expected from a doctor or dentist who holds a university teaching appointment[67] or from one who holds an administrative post such as a medical superintendent.[68] It would seem unreasonable to take this suggestion beyond its relevance to tasks within the normal competence of these positions. For example, to hold a general practitioner who is a medical superintendent of a hospital to a higher standard by virtue only of his position does not seem reasonable.[69]

---

67 *Kangas v. Parker*, [1976] 5 W.W.R. 25 at 47 (Sask. Q.B.); affirmed [1978] 5 W.W.R. 667 (Sask. C.A.); *Neufeld v. McQuitty* (1979), 18 A.R. 271 at 274, 276 (Alta. T.D.). *See Leonard v. Knott*, [1978] 5 W.W.R. 511 (B.C.S.C.); varied [1980] 1 W.W.R. 673 (B.C.C.A.) *per* Kirke Smith J. at 515: " . . . divergence being patent as between those who work mainly, as Milton put it, in 'the olive grove of Academe' in a teaching role on a salaried basis, and their fellow specialists in private practice."
68 *Jarvis v. Int. Nickel Co.*, [1929] 2 D.L.R. 842 at 847 (Ont. S.C.).
69 *Id.*
70 *Vail v. MacDonald supra* n. 52. *See also* Sherman *supra* n. 39 at 230.
71 *MacDonald v. York County Hosp. supra* n. 58 at 332.
72 *Id.* at 321.
73 *McKeachie v. Alvarez supra* n. 62 at 87.

of a small clinic and said he had "minor surgical privileges and some major surgical privileges, but none very major"[74] was held to the standard of a surgeon.[75]

In *Chipps v. Peters*[76] a general surgeon by education, training and experience removed the uterus of a patient and did "repair work to improve her bladder and to stop the protrusion of her vagina." Difficulties ensued and the patient brought action alleging that the doctor was negligent in undertaking gynaecological surgery. Both the trial judge and the Court of Appeal accepted expert evidence that general surgeons have a role in performing this type of surgery, and there was also evidence that the defendant had done 48 hysterectomies and vaginal repairs. The defendant was held to have met the required standard of care, which was that of a general surgeon.

House staff and students. A member of the hospital's house staff (interns and residents) may be found negligent if he fails to meet the standard of care required, which is the average level of competence of the group to which he belongs. Hospitals and other institutions which take on house staff have basic educational requirements. The period of training and experience available varies in intensity and quality both from hospital to hospital and according to the motivation of the individual student, and therefore the courts consider the education, stage of training and experience of these defendants.[77] The courts' consideration of these factors may result in the raising of the standard of care, but inadequacies in these factors will not shield house staff from the necessity of meeting the basic standard of the average level of competence.

The public interest in the proper training of future doctors must be balanced by the protection of the hospital patient who may not always be sure of the status of the "doctor" who is treating him,[78] and house staff have been successfully sued on a number of occasions.[79] In an early case[80] an intern performing a tonsillectomy accidently removed the uvula. While both the trial judge and the appeal court were prepared to hold that this surgery did not meet

---

74 *Id.* at 89.

75 *Id.* at 101.

76 (unreported) Ont. C.A. 1976 Brooke J.A.

77 *Murphy v. St. Catharines Gen. Hosp.* (1964), 41 D.L.R. (2d) 697 at 703 (Ont. H.C.); *Rietze v. Bruser*, [1979] 1 W.W.R. 31 at 45 (Man. Q.B.).

78 For discussion of the difficulties of protecting the patient, see Storch, *Patient's Rights* (1982); *see also* Simpson, *Misrepresentation of Medical Students in Teaching Hospitals* (1977), 23 Med. Tr. Tech. Qtly. 233; Basson, *The 'Student Doctor' and a Wary Patient* (1982), Hastings Center Report 27.

79 House staff have been sued and found *not* liable in a number of recent cases: *Rietze v. Bruser*, [1979] 1 W.W.R. 31 (Man. Q.B.); *Lloy v. Milner* (1981), 15 Man. R. (2d) 187 (Man. Q.B.); *Considine v. Camp Hill Hosp.* (1982), 133 D.L.R. (3d) 11 (N.S.T.D.); *Hajgato v. London Health Assn.* (1982), 36 O.R. (2d) 669 (Ont. H.C.); *Mang v. Moscovitz* (1982), 37 A.R. 221 (Alta. Q.B.); *Ferguson v. Hamilton Civic Hosp.* (1983), 23 C.C.L.T. 254 (Ont. H.C.).

80 *McNamara v. Smith*, [1934] 2 D.L.R. 417 (Ont. C.A.).

the appropriate standard, the medical evidence was that there was no injury suffered by a child deprived of this part of her body, thus the requirement of injury was not satisfied and no liability followed. In another case[81] an intern performing an intravenous injection severed the tubing which then remained in the patient's vein. His failure to correctly position the patient's arm and to follow the written instructions accompanying the Intracath device was found to be negligence. A senior resident in anaesthesiology assisting an anaesthetist was held not to have met the high standard of care expected of a well-qualified resident who had assisted in 12 to 15 "heart-lung pump operations." The hospital was held liable for his negligence[82] as was another hospital when a resident closing an incision did not explain how a sponge came to be left behind.[83]

Fraser v. Vancouver Gen. Hosp.[84] is the leading decision on the standard of care expected of house staff. Following an accident the patient was examined in the emergency ward by two interns who took x-rays and interpreted them. They decided that there was nothing abnormal and so advised a general practitioner by telephone, although the patient continued to complain of a stiff neck. The patient was discharged and eventually died with what was later diagnosed as a dislocated fracture of the neck. All three courts held that the interns had failed to meet the requisite standard of care by reading the x-rays incorrectly and by not calling the radiologist who was available. The case pointed out some expectations unique to the standard of care as it applies to house staff. Rand J. of the Supreme Court of Canada said that the intern[85]

> . . . must use the undertaken degree of skill, and that cannot be less than the ordinary skill of a junior doctor in appreciation of the indications and symptoms of injury before him, as well as an appreciation of his own limitations and of the necessity for caution in anything he does.

Interns and residents are normally employees of the hospital and therefore it is the institution which may pay any judgment arising out of the negligence of the house staff.[86] However, the responsibilities and discretion an intern or resident has are set not only by the hospital, but also by the doctor whom the house staff person is assisting. The cases illustrate a wide range of

---

81 *Murphy v. St. Catharines Gen. Hosp. supra* n. 77 at 697. Note that the hospital was also held liable for failing to supervise or instruct him. In addition, the hospital was liable for the negligence of the intern. *See* Chapter 9.

82 *Aynsley v. Toronto Gen. Hosp.* (1969), 7 D.L.R. (3d) 193 (Ont. C.A.); [1972] S.C.R. 435 upholding the Court of Appeal as to the resident only, since the anaesthetist did not appeal.

83 *Karderas v. Clow supra* n. 9.

84 [1952] 2 S.C.R. 36.

85 *Id.* at 46.

86 *Id.* at 36; *Karderas v. Clow supra* n. 9. *See also* the *obiter* comments of Krever J. in *Ferguson v. Hamilton Civic Hosp.* (1983), 23 C.C.L.T. 254 at 307 (Ont. H.C.) and of Clarke J. in *Considine v. Camp Hill Hosp.* (1982), 133 D.L.R. (3d) 11 at 29 and 30 (N.S.T.D.). Note *Lloy v. Milner* (1981), 15 Man R. (2d) 187 at 188 (Man. Q.B.), where an anaesthetist was prepared to "accept responsibility" for the actions of a resident.

supervision by these clinicians. In an Alberta case[87] the anaesthetist took over when an intern made "an abortive attempt to intubate" the patient and the surgeon repaired the bladder immediately after the same intern pierced it at the commencement of a tubal ligation. By contrast in two cases involving after care, residents in radiology[88] and orthopaedic surgery[89] were left to make critical diagnostic and treatment decisions and in one case an angiogram was performed by a resident without supervision. In both cases it was found that systems set up by the hospital or instructions given by clinicians had been adequately followed. In an extreme case[90] where the patient saw the surgeon for the first time 13 days after the transurethral resection operation the judge remarked that the situation was an "incredible" one. He said that the urologist chose to delegate so much of his responsibility to the resident that had the resident been responsible in law for the patient's loss he would have held the urologist "equally responsible." The shared responsibility of hospitals and clinicians for the education of house staff receives close scrutiny when the negligence of house staff is alleged. Judicial comment in these cases indicates that the division of liability could be varied to include the liability of the clinician as well as the hospital for negligence of house staff.

No cases against the medical undergraduate student involved in clinical medical school programs have been reported.[91] These so-called "student-interns" are now found in many Canadian hospitals and it is likely that a standard of care analogous to that for doctors and house staff will be developed for this group.

It is clear that the courts expect students of the profession at all stages to exercise caution against their own inexperience.

Non-doctors. The layman who undertakes a task requiring the professional services of a doctor will be expected to meet the standard of care appropriate to a doctor.[92] So where a chiropractor represented that he possessed special skill and knowledge with regard to human ailments generally, it was held that he had to meet the standard of a general practitioner. He did not, because he made no diagnosis and his treatment injured the patient, and he was held liable.[93]

---

87 *Mang v. Moscovitz* (1982), 37 A.R. 221 (Alta. Q.B.); *see also Lloy v. Milner* (1981), 15 Man. R. (2d) 187 (Man. Q.B.) and *Rietze v. Bruser,* [1979] 1 W.W.R. 31 (Man. Q.B.) where residents were closely supervised.

88 *Ferguson v. Hamilton Civic Hosp.* (1983), 23 C.C.L.T. 254 (Ont. H.C.).

89 *Hajgato v. London Health Assn.* (1982), 36 O.R. (2d) 669 (Ont. H.C.).

90 *Considine v. Camp Hill Hosp.* (1982), 133 D.L.R. (3d) 11 (N.S.T.D.). Note the evidence of an expert witness at p. 24: "In any teaching setting, there is a higher incidence of perforation during transurethral prostatectomy because the residents are less experienced."

91 No English cases have been reported either. Speller, *Law of Doctor and Patient* 82 (1973).

92 Nathan *supra* n. 24. *See also* Sherman *supra* n. 39 at 229.

93 *Gibbons v. Harris,* [1924] 1 D.L.R. 923 (Alta. C.A.). A chiropractor is the same as a medical doctor or osteopath for the general principles of law. *Penner v. Theobald* (1962), 40 W.W.R. 216 (Man. C.A.).

B. Degree of risk involved[94]

As the degree of risk involved in a certain treatment or procedure increases, so rises the standard of care expected of the doctor. The principle was expressed succinctly as follows:[95]

> The degree of care required by the law is care commensurate with the potential danger . . .

However, the doctor must have known, or ought to have known, of the risk at the material time, which is the time at which the procedure or treatment took place.[96] The doctor's actions of yesterday are not judged in light of what no one knew until today. An illustrative and famous English case is *Roe v. Min. of Health*,[97] in which two men became paralyzed after the administration of spinal anaesthetic. The Nupercaine® used was stored in glass ampoules in a phenol solution, which percolated into the Nupercaine® via invisible cracks in the ampoules. This risk of contamination was unknown in 1947, the time of the accident, but by 1951 warnings were in a leading textbook. When the case was heard in 1953, it was held that the standard of medical knowledge in 1947 was the test, and the anaesthetists were found to have met that standard. In a Canadian case, *McLean v. Weir*,[98] a patient became paralyzed from the inadvertent escape of neurotoxic contrast medium through the blood stream of the castocervical trunk of the spinal cord during an angiogram. This risk, while recognized at the time of the trial in February 1977, was not known in October of 1973 when the angiogram was done. Ironically, the risk was easily avoided by advancing the catheter beyond the opening of the castocervical trunk. The Court of Appeal upheld the decision of Mr. Justice Gould who found the radiologist was not liable because he had met the standard by using the medical knowledge available at the time of the test.

However, a doctor who is found to have had knowledge of a risk and does not meet the higher standard established as a result will not face a sympathetic court.

In a case where a patient who was "suffering from epilepsy with post-epileptic automation" and a "tendency to irresponsible moving about . . . well known to all concerned"[99] jumped from his fourth floor window, it

---

94 See Appendix *infra* where treatment and procedures which were the subject of litigation are identified.

95 *Badger v. Surkan* (1970), 16 D.L.R. (3d) 146 at 153; affirmed [1973] 1 W.W.R. 302 (Sask. C.A.).

96 *Mang v. Moscovitz* (1982), 37 A.R. 221 at 237, 245, 268 (Alta. Q.B.); *see also Ferguson v. Hamilton Civic Hosp.* (1983), 23 C.C.L.T. 254 at 296 (Ont. H.C.).

97 [1954] 2 Q.B. 66 (C.A.).

98 (1977), 3 C.C.L.T. 87; affirmed [1980] 4 W.W.R. 330 (B.C.C.A.); *see also Thompson v. Creaghan* (1982), 42 N.B.R. (2d) 359 (N.B.Q.B.), where the failure to diagnose a type of cancer was not negligent given the knowledge available at the time.

99 *University Hosp. Bd. v. Lepine*, [1966] S.C.R. 561 at 570 *per* Farthing J. at trial.

was found that the defendant neurologist was the one most fully aware of the danger of the patient's injuring himself. The court held that in failing to take special precautions for the patient's supervision the defendant did not meet the high standard of care expected of him.[100]

In terms of the standard of care expected when there is knowledge of a risk, potential risks can be distinguished on the basis of the degree to which their presence will raise the standard of care. At one end, representing those risks whose presence will most dramatically effect an increase in the standard of care, are procedures of an experimental nature; at the other end are risks associated with more common procedures, which generally have less effect on the standard of care.

The highest standard of care is expected of the doctor using a new or experimental procedure or treatment.[101] It is no coincidence that it is in these circumstances that the patient is entitled to a full explanation of all risks.[102] There are not enough cases of experimental medical treatment to allow for specificity with respect to this high standard or how it may be met. However, in a case[103] involving cancer chemotherapy that was described by the judge as novel if not experimental treatment, it was stated that the extreme toxicity of the drug being used, Adriamycin®, "heightened" the standard of care expected of the doctor administering it. Although the patient suffered injury by extravasion, a known adverse effect of the drug for which precautions were to be taken, the family physician was held to have met that heightened standard of care.

A high standard of care is expected where drugs are in use, especially where the potential injury is substantial.[104] In a case where massive doses of neomycin were administered and the defendant surgeon failed to follow the manufacturer's recommended tests for hearing loss, the surgeon was held to be negligent in causing the patient's permanent deafness.[105] A dermatologist was similarly held liable for failing to monitor a patient's use of a drug known as chlorquine (Aralen®), and for failing to detect changes in her condition until permanent injury had occurred.[106]

---

100 *University Hosp. Bd. v. Lepine* (1965), 53 W.W.R. 513 (Alta. C.A.). Note that the Supreme Court of Canada reversed the finding of joint liability of the doctor and the hospital on the basis that the patient's action in jumping from the window was not foreseeable.

101 *Cryderman v. Ringrose supra* n. 33 at 109. As to the difficulties of categorizing a procedure *see supra* Chapters 3, 5.

102 *Halushka v. University of Sask.* (1965), 53 D.L.R. (2d) 436 (Sask. C.A.). *See supra* Chapter 3.

103 *Neufeld v. McQuitty* (1979), 18 A.R. 271 at 272, 276 (Alta. T.D.).

104 *Crichton v. Hastings supra* n. 18. *Foote v. Royal Columbian Hosp.*, [1982] B.C.D. Civ. 2632-05 (B.C.S.C.). For a discussion on tort liability for drugs *see* Linden, *Tort Liability for Defective Drugs* (1977), 1 L. Med. Q. 169; Lenczner, *Who is liable? The Investigator? The Medical Doctor? The Health Protection Branch?* (1977), 1 L. Med. Q. 174.

105 *Male v. Hopmans* (1966), 54 D.L.R. (2d) 592; varied 64 D.L.R. (2d) 105 (Ont. C.A.).

106 *Crossman v. Stewart* (1977), 5 C.C.L.T. 45 (B.C.S.C.). Note that the patient was held to be two-thirds at fault for obtaining the drug without a prescription for part of the time. *See infra* Chapter 5.

Surgery[107] and anaesthesiology[108] may give rise to identifiable risks which will raise the standard of care. In a case where the anaesthetist did not completely shut off the oxygen flow, the patient was seriously burned in an explosion set off by a static spark.[109] The court said:[110]

> When, as here, the anaesthetist was handling a dangerous substance . . . and he knew of the hazard . . . the degree of care required from him was proportionately high and he was bound to take special precautions to prevent injury to his patient. The very high degree of care which is to be exercised by persons who handle dangerous substances is well established and has been authoritatively laid down in the . . . cases . . .

In another case, the patient suffered serious and permanent injury during open heart surgery when the anaesthetist failed to see to the proper closing of a stopcock and air passed from the manometer through the transducer to the patient's venous system.[111] The court found negligence on the basis of the doctor's knowledge of the risk, coupled with his failure to close the stopcock properly or to detect his error quickly. Both the anaesthetist and the resident were held liable.

Many surgical procedures carry with them potentially serious risks which, fortunately, rarely materialize. This was illustrated in an action against an orthopaedic surgeon[112] who, during a disc operation, lacerated and bruised the aorta and the vena cava causing the patient's death. All surgeons recognized the need for special care in this surgery because of the danger of such injury. While the judge at trial and the majority of the Court of Appeal found the doctor not negligent, the Chief Justice of the latter court wrote a strong dissenting judgment. The trial judge, Solomon J., had said:[113]

> Despite the great risk of damage to the aorta artery during disc surgery, such damage rarely happens because of the care taken by orthopedic surgeons. According to statistics only one aorta is damaged in seven thousand disc operations and only 50 per cent of such damage to aorta results in death.

To which the dissenting Chief Justice replied:[114]

> Every surgeon, and more particularly every orthopedic surgeon, is fully aware that in this kind of operation there is a risk of damage to the aorta. How does he avoid that risk? The answer is, by taking due care. If in 7,000 operations of this kind, 6,999 are performed without damage to the aorta one may safely conclude that the surgeons attained this happy

---

107 Two courts have stated that a higher standard of care is required in cosmetic surgery. See *LaFleur v. Cornelis* (1979), 28 N.B.R. (2d) 569 at 573; *MacDonald v. Ross* (1983), 24 C.C.L.T. 242 at 247. For a comment see Bergquist, *Legal Liability of Cosmetic Surgeons* (1983), 21 A.L.R. 533.
108 See *Leadbetter v. Brand* (1980), 37 N.S.R. (2d) 581 at 594-96 (N.S.T.D.) where an anaesthetist sought to identify risks by issuing guidelines to referring doctors and instruction sheets for referred patients.
109 *Crits v. Sylvester*, [1956] S.C.R. 991.
110 *Crits v. Sylvester supra* n. 1 at 511.
111 *Aynsley v. Toronto Gen. Hosp. supra* n. 82.
112 *Chubey v. Ahsan*, [1976] 3 W.W.R. 367 (Man. C.A.).
113 [1975] 1 W.W.R. 120 at 124 (Man. Q.B.).
114 *Supra* n. 112 at 370.

result by the exercise of due care. What can successfully be done in 6,999 cases ought to have been also done in the 7,000th. That it was not done in the 7,000th case must be ascribed to lack of due care. Solomon J. called it misadventure. I call it negligence. I would accordingly hold the doctor liable.

A possible conclusion from this case is that the maintenance of a consistently high standard of care by a specialty may shield the doctor on a single occasion of substandard practice.

Occasional risks present only in a few patients are the least likely to affect the standard of care required. However, the standard of care will be raised in these situations where the doctor has, or ought to have, knowledge of the particular risk. An example is the risk of gangrene in fracture cases:[115]

When in a particular case the danger of gangrene occurring is greater than in the case of an ordinary simple fracture, such calls for the exercise of greater vigilance.

This need for greater vigilance was affirmed by the evidence in *Dean v. York County Hosp. Corp.*,[116] but was absent in the diagnosis and treatment of a patient who suffered a compound fracture during a soccer game. Because the orthopaedic surgeon did not carry out a proper examination and treatment of the wound associated with the fracture, the patient developed gas gangrene and required an amputation. The doctor was held liable.

The risk of infection is present in all surgery but because of the nature of the procedure, or the patient's condition or complaints the doctor may be required to meet a higher standard of care.[117] In *Rietz v. Bruser*[118] the patient had Paget's disease and after surgery contracted an infection which led to the development of Volkmann's ischemic contracture leaving the patient with a "mis-shapen and grotesque" hand. Mr. Justice Hewak held the orthopaedic surgeon liable and said:[119]

It is no excuse to say that the cause of the contracture was precipitated by infection and that infection is a hazard of surgery . . . While one cannot guarantee that post-operative infection will not occur, it is not unreasonable to assume that medical specialists trained in their particular fields should be quick to recognize the development of complications following surgery, such as infection, at the earliest possible moment and to treat them accordingly. More than usual vigilance is expected of them when they are treating a condition that is unique or unusual. To answer by saying that if a doctor were to spend his time re-examining and re-exploring surgical wounds he would not have time for anything else is not an answer that satisfies the duty of care expected of those charged with the

---

115 *Supra* n. 95.

116 (1979), 3 L. Med. Q. 231 (Ont. H.C.).

117 *Wine v. Kernohan, Carreno-Segura* (1978), 2 L. Med. Q. 129 (Ont. H.C.). Cases where the standard of care was met are: *Hajgato v. London Health Assn.* (1982), 36 O.R. (2d) 669 (Ont. H.C.); *Nichols v. Gray,* [1980] B.C.D. Civ. 2632-03 (B.C.S.C.).

118 [1979] 1 W.W.R. 31 (Man. Q.B.). For a case where the judge alluded to possible negligence by an orthopaedic surgeon in treating an infection but where counsel led no evidence, *see Roy v. Goulet* (1977), 19 N.B.R. (2d) 187 at 190 (N.B.Q.B.).

119 *Id.* at 49.

responsibility of looking after the health and well-being of the community. *The fault lies not with the risk or development of infection but with the failure to recognize that it is present as quickly as possible and to take steps to treat it. [emphasis supplied]*

In *Moffatt v. Witelson*[120] it was an ophthalmologist who failed to consider the possibility of infection in the eye of a five-year-old who had a piece of glass puncture his cornea. In finding the doctor liable for the loss of the eye Mr. Justice Galligan said:[121]

> It is common knowledge among ophthalmologists that any infection of the eye can have drastic consequences for the eye. The hazard of infection of the anterior chamber is so great in cases of perforation of the cornea, that in my opinion a high degree of care is called for on the part of an ophthalmologist who is called upon to treat an injury which perforates the cornea into the anterior chamber.

Therefore, to summarize, the risk reasonably perceived defines the standard required.[122]

C. Resources

All the statements[123] of the standard of care contemplate that the court consider the circumstances in which the allegedly negligent treatment occurred. For the purposes of this discussion, circumstances are dealt with under two separate headings: i) facilities, and ii) equipment. The discussion under "facilities" concerns itself with the physical environment in which the treatment is administered, such as a roadside, private home, or hospital. The section on "equipment" deals not only with the actual devices and instruments available, but also methods and technology. Included is an analysis of the effect of an urban as opposed to a rural locality on the standard of care.

The categories of facilities, equipment and locality are obviously not mutually exclusive and some of that which is applicable to any one of them may be applicable to the others as well.

Facilities. In Alberta, Saskatchewan, Nova Scotia and Newfoundland, a doctor or nurse who voluntarily and gratuitously provides emergency treatment where there are inadequate facilities is protected by legislation which reads as follows:[124]

> 2. If, in respect of a person who is ill, injured or unconscious as the result of an accident or other emergency.

---

120 (1980), 111 D.L.R. (3d) 712 (Ont. H.C.).
121 *Id.* at 715.
122 *Palsgraf v. Long Island Ry Co.* (1928), 248 N.Y. 339 *per* Cardozo J. Although he was speaking about negligence in general, his words apply to medical negligence.
123 *See supra.*
124 Emergency Medical Aid Act, R.S.A. 1980, c. E-9 [am. R.S.A. 1980, c. H-5.1, s. 34] Emergency Medical Aid Act, 1971 (Nfld.), No. 15; Emergency Medical Aid Act, R.S.S. 1978, c. E-8; Medical Act, 1969 (N.S.), c. 15, s. 38. Note that the persons protected vary from Alberta (where doctors, dentists, nurses and lay persons are protected) to Nova Scotia (where only the doctor is protected). For a thorough discussion of Good Samaritan statutes in the U.S. see Louisell and Williams, *supra* n. 44 at 21-2.

(a) a physician, registered health occupation member or registered nurse voluntarily and without expectation of compensation or reward renders emergency medical services or first aid assistance and the services or assistance are not rendered at a hospital or other place having adequate medical facilities and equipment, or

(b) a person other than a person mentioned in clause (a) voluntarily renders emergency first aid assistance and that assistance is rendered at the immediate scene of the accident or emergency,

the physician, registered health occupation member, registered nurse or other person is not liable for damages for injuries to or the death of that person alleged to have been caused by an act or omission on his part in rendering the medical services or first aid assistance, unless it is established that the injuries or death were caused by gross negligence on his part.

The scenario of the professional as a Good Samaritan rendering assistance at the site of a motor vehicle accident was undoubtedly in the minds of the well-intentioned legislators. No Canadian cases involving the statutes have been reported[125] and therefore any remarks regarding its legal effect are speculative to a degree.[126]

Whether the situation could be described as an "accident or other emergency" or the facilities as "inadequate" would probably be decided according to the judgment of a reasonable doctor in the same circumstances. The statute is not intended to prevent compensation, and therefore if the doctor were to subsequently receive payment for his services he would not necessarily lose the protection of the legislation as a result. His evidence that he was not providing care with compensation in mind would probably be sufficient.[127]

A person injured in these circumstances (or if he has died, his estate) who wished to sue the doctor would have to prove gross negligence. A satisfactory determination of what constitutes gross negligence has thus far eluded the courts. The law reports contain frequent judicial attempts to define it in the other two contexts in which it appears in Canadian law: gross negligence must be proven to hold a host driver liable to a gratuitous passenger, and to hold a municipality liable for damage resulting from the accumulation of ice or snow on a sidewalk.[128] The Supreme Court of Canada has said that gross negligence

125 See Mapel and Weigel, *Good Samaritan Laws — Who Needs Them?: The Current State of Good Samaritan Protection In the United States* (1983), Specialty Law Digest: Health Care 5 at 28 where it is noted that in the U.S. Good Samaritan laws have been found applicable in only five cases.

126 For a survey of the opinion of Ontario doctors, see Gray and Sharpe, *Doctors, Samaritans and the Accident Victim* (1973), 11 Osgoode Hall L.J. 1. The surveys showed that 90 per cent of Ontario doctors would stop to assist whereas 50 per cent of U.S. doctors would not. See Sharpe and Sawyer, *Doctors and the Law* 55-71 (1978). Note that in Quebec as in some European countries there is an obligation to assist in an emergency. For an excellent discussion see Rodgers-Magnet, *The Right to Emergency Medical Assistance in The Province of Quebec* (1980), 40 R. du B. 373.

127 Louisell and Williams, *supra* n. 44 at 21-24.

128 Linden, *supra* n. 38 at 153-55.

means "very great negligence."[129] Stated another way, this means that a doctor will be held liable for only marked departures from the standard of care which, in realistic terms, has the effect of lowering the standard required in these situations.

The importance of the statute ought not to be over-emphasized. While it has the potential of applying in a variety of situations, there are difficulties both in predicting its effect and with the concept of gross negligence. No Canadian doctor and very few American doctors have been sued in such situations and therefore such legislation appears to have been an over-reaction to a non-existent problem[130] and is in any event the traditional benevolence shown by the law under the normal rules of negligence to those who take affirmative action would more than adequately shield the doctor in these situations.[131] Finally, the statutes only exist in four provinces.

Medical negligence law has shown itself to be sensitive to the difficulties of the doctor in inadequate facilities. Early on a cold December morning a general practitioner in Manitoba[132] was forced to examine a man in a truck because the patient was extremely intoxicated and would not move. Because of the absence of adequate facilities he failed to diagnose extensive damage to the chest, ribs and lungs. The court held that he had met the appropriate standard of care. Mr. Justice Berger came to the same conclusion in *Feller v. Roffman*[133] when a doctor at the hospital at 100 Mile House chose to put the patient's badly-crushed leg in a full immobilizing cast rather than to bi-valve it in order to move the patient to a centre with adequate facilities for treatment. The patient later lost his leg and sued, but the learned justice held that the medical decision was sound under the circumstances. In an Ontario case[134] the doctor failed to meet the required standard of care, not because the hospital's equipment was limited and did not permit lateral X-ray of the patient's spine, but because with this limitation and the paralysis of the patient's left leg the doctor failed to consult a specialist.

---

129 *Studer v. Cowper*. [1950] S.C.R. 450.

130 Mapel and Weigel, *Good Samaritan Laws — Who Needs Them?: The Current State of Good Samaritan Protection in The United States* (1983), Specialty Law Digest: Health Care 5 at 7-8. Markus, *Good Samaritan Laws: An American Lawyer's Point of View* (1975), 10 Rev. Jur. Themis 29 at 31; Monaghan, *Emergency Services and Good Samaritans* (1975), 10 Rev. Jr. Themis 21; McIsaac, *Negligence Actions Against Medical Doctors* (1976), 24 Chitty's L.J. 201.

131 Henderson and Fisk, *The Legal Position of a Doctor in Treating Accident Victims* (1969), 7 Chitty's L.J. 224. *See also* Mapel and Weigel, *Good Samaritan Laws — Who Needs Them?: The Current State of Good Samaritan Protection in The United States* (1983), Specialty Law Digest: Health Care 5 at 6.

132 *Rodych v. Krasey*, [1971] 4 W.W.R. 358 (Man. Q.B.); *see also Hampton v. Macadam* (1912), 22 W.L.R. 31 (Sask. D.C.).

133 [1978] B.C.D. 34698-74 (B.C.S.C.); *see also Benoit v. Muir* [1982] B.C.D. Civ. 2632-06 (B.C.S.C.) where a doctor delayed surgery over Sunday because the hospital staff was not available. The patient was unable to prove this delay caused his injuries.

134 *Thomas v. Port Colborne Gen. Hosp.* (1982), 12 A.C.W.S. (2d) 535 (Ont. H.C.).

In another case[135] where the facilities were more than adequate, the standard was not raised above that expected of the reasonable general practitioner. The patient was a prisoner who suffered a "blow-out fracture of the orbit of the eye" in a recreational hockey match. The trial judge said:[136]

> On consideration of the whole of the evidence, no inference can be made that Dr. Webb did or omitted to do anything that an ordinary reasonably skilled practitioner would have done under the circumstances. In fact, there is no evidence that any general practitioner, possessing the normal equipment that would be available even at Joyceville Institution, which equipment is far superior to that which a general practitioner would normally have, and being given the information or complaints at the various material times that the plaintiff gave to Dr. Webb, would have diagnosed the injury caused to the plaintiff.

Thus, the courts will assess the adequacy of the facilities available to a doctor and adjust the standard of care downward if they are inadequate, but there is no authority that the availability of superior facilities has the opposite effect. A general practitioner might have privileges at a hospital equipped for sophisticated ophthalmological examinations but it would be unjust to expect him as a consequence to meet a higher standard of care when treating problems of the eye.[137]

When there is a choice of facilities the doctor's selection must be guided by the best medical interests of the patient. The consequences of a self-serving choice by a dentist arose in a Saskatchewan case.[138] The patient was a healthy 28-year-old who required the extraction of a number of teeth. The dentist had an arrangement with an anaesthetist who did out-patient anaesthesiology in a nearby office, and told the patient to appear on a certain day at the anaesthetist's office. No history was taken, nor was a physical examination carried out. The patient died of asphixia while under general anaesthesia when he inhaled his own blood during the dental extraction.

The evidence showed that the patient was given no choice between having the extraction performed in the office or in a hospital, where proper preliminary examinations would have been required and where an emergency such as arose could have been handled. Both the anaesthetist and the dentist were found negligent on a number of grounds, including the arbitrary choice by the dentist of the most convenient facilities for himself without regard for the interests of the patient.[139] As to the anaesthetist the trial judge said:[140]

---

135 *Bell v. R.* (1973), 44 D.L.R. (3d) 549 at 550 (Fed. T.D.).
136 *Id.* at 553.
137 He might, however, be under a duty to refer the patient to a specialist who could use the better facilities: *see infra. See also McCormick v. Marcotte supra* n. 33.
138 *Kangas v. Parker, supra* n. 67.
139 *See also Gorback v. Ting*, [1974] 5 W.W.R. 606 (Man. Q.B.). *But see Leadbetter v. Brand* (1980), 37 N.S.R. (2d) 581 at 602 (N.S.T.D.), where Hallett J. distinguished *Gorback* and said there must be evidence of a need to advise the patient of the alternate type of anaesthetic. Note also that the Court of Appeal in *Kangas v. Parker*, [1978] 5 W.W.R. 667 at 668 (Sask. C.A.), while affirming the trial decision, did so on a more narrow ground.
140 *Id.* at 50.

> I find . . . that the defendant Asquith's conduct had fallen far below the high standard of
> care required of an anaesthetist. It seems that the quality of work had been sacrificed for the
> quantity of patients that could be processed assembly-line style . . . It is not required of a
> specialist that he warrant that his treatment will be successful. He is bound to exercise only
> that degree of care and skill which could reasonably be expected of a normal prudent
> practitioner of the same experience and standing. The . . . conduct in this case varied so
> drastically from the methods always used and followed by the other anaesthetists . . .
> before embarking on an operation, that it constitutes to my mind glaring negligence.

On the more mundane level of the facilities, the evidence also showed
that the anaesthetist had no telephone list of doctors who could be called upon
to assist in an emergency, and precious seconds were lost in the attempt to
locate a telephone number.

As was stated earlier,[141] the doctor is entitled to rely on others to assist
him with the treatment of a patient. Whether they are colleagues, nurses, or
other health care personnel, the doctor is entitled to assume that each is
competent and will meet the standard of care required in carrying out his
customary professional duties.[142]

Innovations in equipment. In this section we are concerned not only with
"tools"[143] (implements and devices) but also with "techniques" (methods
and procedures). The issue involved is the effect had on the standard of care
when a new tool or technique comes into use by some members of the
profession, but not by all.

In this situation the law must balance the desirability of promoting
advances in medical technology against the need to caution against resorting
too readily to novel and untested treatment. This was recognized by a court
years ago in these words:[144]

> I think a reckless disregard of a new discovery, and an adhesion to a once approved but
> exploded or abandoned practice resulting in injury to a patient would give a cause of action.
> But, on the other hand, no medical man can be bound to resort to any practice or remedy
> that has not had the test of experience to recommend it, and a physician or surgeon
> resorting to such new practice or remedy with injurious consequence following, would be
> more liable to an action than one who with like result followed the beaten track. Without
> experiment there would be no progress in medical or any other science.

Thus the doctor need not employ the very latest tools or techniques to
meet the standard of care, but neither can he ignore them once they have
found their way into common use.[145] The cases to be discussed show that,
during the transition period, a doctor electing the older method will have his
conduct carefully scrutinized by the courts.

---

141 *See infra* s. 2(a) of this Chapter.

142 *See supra.*

143 This includes drug therapy. *See Parsons. v. Schmok* (1975), 58 D.L.R. (3d) 622 (B.C.S.C.).

144 *McQuay v. Eastwood* (1886), 12 O.R. 402 at 408 (C.A.). For a case where a doctor was
   unsuccessfully sued for his failure to prescribe drug therapy of questionable value *see*
   Parsons v. Schmok id.

145 For a further discussion of the defences available to a doctor who is following the common
   practice *see infra* Chapter 5.

Tremendous advances have occurred in medical technology. In these times of N.M.R. imagery (Nuclear Magnetic Resonance) it is hard to believe that just over 100 years ago doctors were practising blood-letting.[146] Yet many inventions now taken for granted were innovations a short time ago. A doctor was sued in 1932 for failing to x-ray a patient's shoulder after she had suffered a fall.[147] The court held that the doctor met the standard of care by taking the usual tests even though they did not show the dislocation, which an x-ray would have. The Court of Appeal said:[148]

> . . . there is no suggestion of any unskilfulness or want of care on his part except that of his failure to advise an x-ray. The two eminent specialists called for the defendant at the trial approved the defendant's diagnosis and stated that x-ray ought not to be advised in cases where the surgeon is convinced by the use of the usual tests that that course was unnecessary. *It has not surely come to this that if the cause of the trouble is not apparent to the eye of the surgeon or physician he must advise an x-ray* or take the consequences to his reputation and to his pocket for not having done so. Is the x-ray to be the only arbitrator in such a case and are years of study and experience to be cast aside as negligible? [emphasis supplied]

Fifty-six years later, it is hard to imagine a doctor failing to take an x-ray under the same circumstances and relying instead solely on study and experience.[149]

As indicated by the quote, expert evidence from other doctors as to equipment in common use is relied on by the court when determining the standard of care. However, where in the opinion of the court, the tools or techniques used indicate that the standard is too low, the court has the discretion to hold that a higher standard involving the use of superior tools or techniques is required.

This substitution of a lay judicial opinion for an expert medical one is not common, but may occur in situations where the ordinary person is competent to judge, for example, where the taking of precautions is the issue. Such a situation arose in *Chasney v. Anderson*[150] where a surgeon removing a child's adenoids did not avail himself of either of two techniques for assuring that sponges were not overlooked. The evidence was that in some hospitals these

---

146 *See Kelly v. Dow* (1860), 9 N.B.R. 435 (C.A.) where the issue centred around whether the doctor had met his standard of care in bleeding the patient's arm.

147 *Moore v. Large supra* n. 27.

148 *Id.* at 182-183.

149 *See Parkin v. Kobrinsky* (1963), 46 W.W.R. 193 (Man. C.A.); *Hôpital Notre Dame de l'Esperance v. Laurent,* [1978] 1 S.C.R. 605; *Price v. Milawski* (1977), 1 L. Med. Q. 303 at 308 (Ont. C.A.).

150 *Supra* n. 22. Nathan, *supra* n. 24 at 26. *See also Holt v. Nesbitt,* [1951] 4 D.L.R. 478 (Ont. C.A.); affirmed [1953] 1 D.L.R. 671 (S.C.C.); *Bergen v. Sturgeon Gen. Hosp.,* unreported, Feb. 6, 1984, No. 8003-0306 (Alta. Q.B.). *See also Belore v. Mississauga Hosp.,* [1979] 3 A.C.W.S. 695 (Ont. Co. Ct.), where the issue was the use of a mouthgag by a dentist.

techniques were used, but not in all. The Supreme Court of Canada agreed with the Court of Appeal of Manitoba where the Chief Justice had said:[151]

> The practice of medicine and surgery is a progressive science. Experience had shown in the past the danger of leaving foreign substances in the cavities after an operation . . . It is not sufficient for the surgeon to say: "I never adopted the use of either of such precautions in operations of this nature". By doing so he took an unnecessary risk, as both were available for his use on that occasion and he assumed full responsibility for the lack of use of same, and I would hold that he was negligent in so doing.

The decision shows that the standard of care is set by the court; expert testimony as to what the average doctor does is relevant but not conclusive. Where there are precautionary measures available, albeit not by common practice, a court *may* raise the standard of care accordingly.

The situation of precautionary measures and lay opinion aside, generally the doctor is not expected to use the very latest equipment[152] as shown by a dramatic English case.[153] A patient was told that he had inoperable cancer, and with the belief that he had not long to live he severed all ties with England and embarked for the United States where he was diagnosed as having chronic cystitis. Surgery revealed a condition of benign prostrate hypertrophy but no cancer. He sued the English doctor on the basis that the doctor had not met the standard by failing to verify the diagnosis by a cystoscopic examination. However, the House of Lords held that there was no liability saying that, while the type of cystoscope required was in common use in the United States, it was rare in England at the time and the standard of care did not require the doctor, who did not possess one, to use it.

Where the use of an older tool or technique is not negligence *per se,* the availability of newer methods may raise the standard of care required when using the older method. In a case[154] where a doctor performed a mastoid operation using a surgical loupe and a chisel, the patient suffered facial paralysis and underwent a second operation by a different doctor who used more modern tools, a microscope and a dental drill. The Supreme Court of Canada found the first doctor negligent, not for the use of the older method, but for exercising less skill than that of which he was capable. He knew that better vision could have been had with a microscope than a surgical loupe, and thus ought to have exercised more care when checking for bone chips. Where a plastic surgeon doing a rhinoplasty chose a technique abandoned by colleagues because of the very risk that materialized, the court held him

---

151 *Id.* at 75; *Elder v. King,* [1957] Que. Q.B. 87 (C.A.).

152 This was a true statement even in 1930. *See Antoniuk v. Smith,* [1930] 2 W.W.R. 721 at 726 (Alta. C.A.). Note that a doctor is expected to use equipment which is accepted, available and appropriate. *See, for example, Legault-Bellemare v. Madore,* [1975] C.S. 1249 (Que. S.C.); *Demoura v. Mississauga Hosp.* (1979), 3 L. Med. Q. 215 (Ont. H.C.).

153 *Whiteford v. Hunter,* [1950] W.N. 553, 94 S. J. 758 (H.L.).

154 *Eady v. Tenderenda supra* n. 58 at 26.

negligent, not for using this technique, but for failing to take special measures to preclude that risk from occurring.[155] While the doctor in *Doiron v. Orr*[156] chose an uncommon procedure for sterilization, the reversible Aldridge procedure, he was found to have met the standard of care, even though it was unsuccessful.

So far the discussion has been with respect to tools or techniques which enjoy some use but are not yet universally employed. The effect on the standard of care by the use of either an *avant-garde* or obsolete method is more certain.

A doctor who uses an obsolete method does not meet the standard of care. In 1970 a doctor applied a metal plate to a patient's broken leg when a specialist had advised skin traction followed by the insertion of an intramedullary nail. The Supreme Court of Canada held that the doctor had not met the standard of care by using a method which had fallen into disfavour.[157] In a Quebec case, *Cataford v. Moreau*,[158] Chief Justice Deschenes held that a surgeon doing a sterilization "who confesses that his operating 'technique' is not consistent with the teaching in any manual of surgery" with the consequence that his patient became pregnant was negligent "beyond the shadow of doubt."[159] Yet some courts seem reluctant to characterize a technique as obsolete even where there is strong expert evidence to that effect. In *Strachan v. Simpson*,[160] although the only two experts who testified said that the technique employed by the neurosurgeon was "outmoded and dangerous"[161] and not one either would have performed, the trial judge preferring the testimony of the defendant held that the evidence did not support the allegation of negligence.[162] In a Nova Scotia case, *MacKinnon v. Ignacio, Lamond and MacKeough*,[163] a 70-year-old doctor who had been administering anaesthetic for 40 years admitted a lack of knowledge of technological advances which the court found "difficult to excuse," as well as a failure to use an available monitor which the court said "may very well have been negligent."[164] While it appears that the court recognized that the doctor had not met the standard of care of an anaesthetist, it did not find liability because his inadequacies were "not a contributing factor"[165] in the 36-year-old patient's death from a cardiac arrest during thyroid surgery. In each of these cases the

---

155 *LaFleur v. Cornelis* (1979), 28 N.B.R. (2d) 569 (N.B.Q.B.). For a comment *see* Berquist *Legal Liability of Cosmetic Surgeons* (1983), 21 A.L.R. 533.
156 (1978), 86 D.L.R. (3d) 719 (Ont. H.C.).
157 *McCormick v. Marcotte supra* n. 33 at 18.
158 (1978), 114 D.L.R. (3d) 585 (Que. S.C.).
159 *Id.* at 594.
160 (1979), 10 C.C.L.T. 145 (B.C.S.C.).
161 *Id.* at 168.
162 *Id.* at 172-73.
163 (1978), 29 N.S.R. (2d) 656 (N.S.S.C.).
164 *Id.* at 689.
165 *Id.*

frank testimony of the defendant doctor about his preferred, albeit contentious, method was critical to the ultimate decision.

A doctor who chooses to treat with the latest equipment or the newest techniques must meet a higher standard of care. A series of Alberta cases have established this principle.[166] In two cases involving the same obstetrician-gynaecologist, the silver nitrate sterilization technique in issue had been invented and pioneered by him. In upholding the trial decisions in both cases the Alberta Court of Appeal emphasized that a higher standard of care is required where a technique is innovative or experimental. In the *Cryderman* case, at trial, Stevenson Dist. Ct. J. opined that it was neither possible nor desirable to lay down precise formulations of a standard of care, but he held that a "high degree of care" is required. A particular factor relevant to the learned justice was that the doctor was the inventor and the sole researcher of the technique. In the *Zimmer* case McDonald J. said that the experimental nature of the procedure required that the patient receive careful and attentive after care. In both cases the doctor was held not to have met the requisite standard of care and was negligent.[167] Similarly, an Ontario doctor who failed to follow the instructions accompanying a relatively new type of catheter, or to seek guidance was found to be negligent.[168]

Naturally, the doctor ought to avail himself of any available assistance from his colleagues when employing new tools or techniques, and of course ought not to deviate from the approved practice of handling an innovation. An anaesthetist's inexperience and failure to follow the inventor's suggestions when attempting transtracheal ventilation were the bases for a finding of negligence against him.[169]

In summary, the standard of care is higher both for the doctor who uses a very new tool or technique, and also for the doctor who continues to use an older one after his more progressive colleagues have moved to new approaches.[170]

Locality rule. The geographic location of the doctor's practice may have some bearing on the facilities, equipment and staff available to him when treating the patient. Whether the locality ought to affect the standard of care expected is an issue which has been dealt with in various ways by the courts.

---

166 *Zimmer v. Ringrose* (1978), 89 D.L.R. (3d) 646; affirmed 16 C.C.L.T. 51 (Alta. C.A.); leave to appeal dismissed 28 A.R. 92 (S.C.C.); *Cryderman v. Ringrose*, [1977] 3 W.W.R. 109; affirmed [1978] 3 W.W.R. 481 (Alta. C.A.); *see Baills v. Boulanger*, [1924] 4 D.L.R. 1083 at 1100 (Alta. C.A.), where the court held that as the properties of a quartz lamp were not fully understood, it was incumbent of the doctor to use the greatest care possible in its use. *See also Misericordia Hosp. v. Bustillo*, [1983] Alta. D. 2632-01 (Alta. C.A.).
167 Note that there was a third case involving Dr. Ringrose: *Colp v. Ringrose*, unreported, Oct. 6, 1976, No 84474 (Alta. T.D.), wherein no evidence of negligence was found.
168 *Murphy v. St. Catharines Gen. Hosp. supra* n. 77.
169 *Holmes v. Bd. of Hosp. Trustees of London supra* n. 20.
170 Nathan, *supra* n. 24 at 26 and 28.

The early history of Canada and the United States saw vast differences in facilities, equipment and assistants between the rural and the urban practitioner.[171] The situation was aggravated by prohibitive distances between the place of treatment and large centres, and by the often serious nature of disease and injury in those times. Recognition of these differences was taken in the United States in *Tefft v. Wilcox*,[172] the first enunciation of the locality rule, which is commonly stated as follows:[173]

> A physician . . . by taking charge of a case, impliedly represents that he possesses, and the law places upon him the duty of possessing, that reasonable degree of learning and skill that is ordinarily possessed by physicians and surgeons in the locality where he practices . . .

The effect of the locality rule was to compensate for the rural practitioner's disadvantages by lowering the standard of care expected of him; the standard became such that the measure was not the "same locality" but a "similar locality."[174]

Canadian courts also made the adjustment to the standard of care, beginning with *Zirkler v. Robinson*:[175]

> It surely cannot be that the skill of a physician, attending a patient in a private home with few conveniences, and no assistants, is to be measured by the same standard as the city surgeon, provided with an operating room, assistants, nurses, and all the aids of a modern hospital.

For a time the rule in Canada evolved similarly to that in the United States, and later Canadian decisions indicate the use of the American phrase "same or similar locality."

The locality rule enjoyed acceptance in Canada up to 1960,[176] but the jurisprudence was not consistent, and it was suggested in an early case[177] that the standard was not to be automatically lowered for the rural practitioner, but rather an "allowance" ought to be made "for particular circumstances of position."[178] The reasoning which was eventually accepted in Canada was stated in *Town v. Archer*:[179]

> It has been held in some American cases that the locality in which a medical man practises is to be taken into account, and that a man practising in a small village or rural

---

171 Waltz, *The Rise and Gradual Fall of the Locality Rule in Medical Malpractice Litigation* (1968), 18 De Paul L.R. 408 at 410.

172 (1870), 6 Kan. 46; for other early statements of the rule *see Smothers v. Hanks* (1872), 34 Iowa 286, 11 Am. Rep. 141 (Iowa S.C.); *Hathorn v. Richmond* (1876), 48 Vt. 557.

173 *Pike v. Honsinger* (1898), 155 N.Y. 201 at 209, 49 N.E. 760 at 762 (N.Y.C.A.).

174 Mann (1975), 28 Vand. L. Rev. 441 at 442; Waltz, *supra* n. 171 at 411.

175 (1897), 30 N.S.R. 61 at 70 (C.A.); *see also Hodgins v. Banting* (1906), 12 O.L.R. 117 (H.C.). The case of *Town v. Archer* wherein the locality rule was soundly rejected was referred to as authority for removing the case from the jury. The comments of Falconbridge C.J. against the rule (*infra* n. 179) seem to have been ignored.

176 *Wilson v. Swanson supra* n. 41 at 124 *per* Abbott J.; *Challand v. Bell supra* n. 48; Meredith, *supra* n. 10 at 63.

177 *Turriff v. King* (1913), 9 D.L.R. 676 at 678 (Sask. S.C.) *per* Brown J.

178 *Beven on Negligence* 1156 and 1161 (3d ed. 1908) quoted in *Turriff v. King id.*

179 (1902), 4 O.L.R. 383 at 388 (Ont. K.B.).

district is not to be expected to exercise the high degree of skill of one having the opportunities afforded by a large city; and that he is bound to exercise the average degree of skill possessed by the profession in such localities generally. I should hesitate to lay down the law in that way: all the men practising in a given locality might be equally ignorant and behind the times, and regard must be had to the present advanced state of the profession and to the easy means of communication with, and access to, the large centres of education and science.

While reference to the locality rule in Canadian medical neligence suits was not common after 1960,[180] the concept receives just enough sustained attention to survive.

In *McCormick v. Marcotte*,[181] where a general practitioner was held liable for the permanent partial incapacity suffered by his patient after the general practitioner used an obsolete technique in an orthopaedic operation, the Supreme Court of Canada said:[182]

> The medical man must process and use, that reasonable degree of learning and skill ordinarily possessed by practitioners *in similar communities in similar cases*. [emphasis supplied]

This was approved in *Rodych v. Krasey*[183] by Matas J., who also mentioned and approved *Challand v. Bell*[184] and *Wilson v. Swanson*.[185] His judgment seems to be founded on an application of the locality rule, although he backed off somewhat from the narrowness of the rule:[186]

> In the case at bar I find that the plaintiffs have not discharged the onus upon them to show that [the defendant] was negligent under the *particular circumstances* obtaining at the time . . . [emphasis supplied]

Lieberman J. of the Trial Division of the Supreme Court of Alberta, in a thorough and careful judgment delivered in *Tiesmaki v. Wilson*,[187] quoted[188] the locality rule as stated in *Wilson v. Swanson*,[189] and *Meredith*,[190] and based his decision on its application to the case before him:[191]

> On the facts . . . I find that Dr. Wilson . . . acted in his . . . professional capacity within the standards laid down in the cases I have cited. Specifically I find ''that [he] possessed and used that reasonable degree of learning and skill ordinarily possessed by practitioners in similar communities in similar cases'': *Wilson v. Swanson*.

---

180 *See, for example, Male v. Hopmans supra* n. 105; *Pederson v. Dumouchel* (1967), 72 Wash. (2d) 73 (Wash. S.C.); *Douglas v. Bussabarger* (1968), 73 Wash. (2d) 476; *Brune v. Belinkoff* (1968), 235 N.E. (2d) 793 (Mass. S.C.). *See also Waltz, supra* n. 171 at 413; (1969), 44 Wash. L. Rev. 505; Frankel, *Varying Standards of Care in Medicine* (1970), 19 Clev. St. L.R. 43; McCoid, *supra* n. 38.

181 [1972] S.C.R. 18.

182 *Id*. 21.

183 *Supra* n. 132.

184 *Supra* n. 48.

185 [1956] S.C.R. 804, 5 D.L.R. (2d) 113.

186 *Rodych v. Krasey supra* n. 132 at 371.

187 *Supra* n. 46.

188 *Id*. at 44.

189 *Supra* n. 185.

190 *Supra* n. 10.

191 [1974] 4 W.W.R. 19 at 48.

The decision, including the application of the locality rule, was affirmed by the Appellate Division.[192] In 1982 the "similar communities in similar cases" reference was reincarnated in another Alberta judgment[193] with reference for support to *Tiesmaki v. Wilson*[194] (and therein to *Wilson v. Swanson*).[195] *Neufeld v. McQuitty*[196] and *Mang v. Moscovitz*[197] also applied the locality rule. In each case the court related the standard of care to common practice at the time in the City of Calgary.

In 1980 the life line of the locality rule, "the similar communities" factor appeared in the Ontario case of *Davidson v. Connaught Laboratories*.[198] The reference was made to "local practice around the Lindsay area"[199] in a case where the issue was negligence for failure to disclose the risks of anti-rabies vaccine. And thus, the locality rule refuses to die.[200]

The advantages and disadvantages of the rule are worthy of some examination. While the rule protects the rural physician, probably a general practitioner working under adverse conditions, this seems to be the only argument for its retention. On the other hand, the evils that result from rigid application of the locality rule have been paraded in many articles and cases from the United States.[201] The number of witnesses available to either litigant is limited by the need for the witness to be from or familiar with practice "in the same or similar community." Physicians from the same community might be biased in favour of the defendant and the standard he represents. Courts have been bogged down in debates about whether Miami is a community similar to West Palm Beach![202] Furthermore, by applying the rule and thus lowering the standard of care, the courts may be allowing inferior health care to be considered adequate. Few physicians would be prepared to recognize geographic location as more important than education and training when measuring competence.

The rule was created by the judiciary for the limited purpose of protecting some doctors at a certain time in our history, but times have changed. Now with national standards of competence set by professional examinations and the development of continuing medical education there seems less need to

---

192 [1975] 6 W.W.R. 639 (Alta. C.A.).
193 *McBride v. Langton* (1982), 22 Alta. L.R. (2d) 174 (Alta. Q.B.). See also *Layden v. Cope*, [1984] A.W.L.D. 3210 (Q.B.).
194 [1975] 6 W.W.R. 639 at 650 (Alta. C.A.).
195 [1956] S.C.R. 804 at 817 (S.C.C.).
196 (1979), 18 A.R. 271 at 276 (Alta. T.D.).
197 (1982), 37 A.R. 221 at 268 (Alta. Q.B.).
198 (1980), 14 C.C.L.T. 251 at 266 (Ont. H.C.); *see* Irvine, *Annotation* at pp. 253-55.
199 *Id.* at 270.
200 Note that it has even been applied to the standard of care required of a parent toward his child. *Houle v. Calgary* (1983), 24 C.C.L.T. 275 (Alta. Q.B.). For a comment, *see* Klar at 278.
201 Waltz, *supra* n. 171 at 420.
202 *Cook v. Lichtblau* (1962), 144 So. (2d) 312 at 316 (Fla. App.).

lower the standard on the basis of locality alone. If the doctor can show that because of his geographic location adequate facilities or equipment or staff were not available, then the standard of care he must meet ought to be altered accordingly, but it ought not to be automatically lowered. A reasonable approach was set out by an American court:[203]

> The proper standard is whether the physician, if a general practitioner, has exercised the degree of care and skill of the average qualified practitioner, taking into account the advances in the profession. In applying this standard it is permissible to consider the medical resources available to the physician as *one* circumstance in determining the skill and care required. Under this standard some allowance is thus made for the type of community in which the physician carries out his practice . . .
>
> One holding himself out as a specialist should be held to the standard of care and skill of the average member of the profession practising the speciality, taking into account the advances in the profession. and, as in the case of the general practitioner, it is permissible to consider the medical resources available to him.

Hopefully the Canadian courts will follow this approach and thereby permanently bury the locality rule.

The effects of some of the factors in the circumstances surrounding the treatment have been explored. Such matters will have a bearing in each case on the standard of care expected of the practitioner. The doctor is expected only to act reasonably in the practice of his profession, not to insure his patient's health:[204]

> . . . the standard of care which the law requires is not insurance against accidental slips. It is such a degree of care as a normally skilful member of the profession may reasonably be expected to exercise in the actual circumstances of the case in question. It is not every slip or mistake which imports negligence . . .

(c) Injury

(i) An essential

The plaintiff cannot succeed in a negligence action unless he proves that he has suffered a material injury[205] also called a "loss" or "damage." Proof of the other essentials of the negligence action will be of no avail unless he also satisfies the court that he has suffered a loss which was caused by the defendant's actions.[206] The requirement of damage is so basic that cases of careless conduct without resultant harm are rarely brought to court. A patient who has received care or treatment by a doctor that seems below standard but who has suffered no loss may have a basis upon which to report the doctor to

---

203 *Brune v. Belinkoff supra* n. 180 at 798. Note that the rule seems to be a North American phenomenon. Nathan, *supra* n. 24 at 22; *Van Wyck v. Lewis supra* n. 11 at 444; *See also* Sharpe and Sawyer, *Doctors and the Law* 16 (1978). *See also* Vandervort, *Legal Aspects of Medical Treatment of Penitentiary Inmates* (1977), 3 Queen's L.J. 368 at 392.

204 *Mahon v. Osborne*, [1939] 2 K.B. 14 at 31 (C.A.).

205 Linden, *supra* n. 38 at 86.

206 Fleming, *supra* n. 62 at 99.

the professional association, but would be ill-advised to waste time and money on a law suit unless the action could be brought as a battery for which no injury need be proven.[207]

In a Manitoba case[208] the plaintiff who had been wounded in the leg by a bullet consented to recommended surgery to remove fragments of shell. The surgeon could not locate any foreign bodies and the plaintiff continued to suffer and sued, alleging that the seven- to eight-inch incision had caused injury. However, the evidence was that the course of the bullet had been followed and, in any case, the wound healed and the incision caused no injury. The court held that the plaintiff had not established any damage or loss and that any disability was entirely due to the gunshot wound. The result might have been different had the doctor not followed the bullet wound or had infection from the incision resulted.

A strange case[209] involved a plaintiff injured in an accident at his place of employment and attended to by the defendant doctor, who requested that he return for follow-up examinations, which the patient did until he was hospitalized in another city for a different problem. The next time he saw the doctor he was seeking a paper for the purpose of Workmen's Compensation. However, the doctor refused to give him any papers for the Board because he had missed the last visit, and the plaintiff sued for negligence in the original treatment and for the refusal to provide the paper needed. The Court of Appeal dismissed the case, saying that there was no negligence in the treatment and no damage was suffered by the plaintiff from the refusal of the doctor to comply with the patient's request for documentation, as the Board was able to get the required information from other sources. Seeking the assistance of the professional association might have been the patient's appropriate remedy in this situation.

An intern under the supervision of a surgeon negligently removed part of a child's uvula in the course of a tonsillectomy. The expert evidence was that the child would suffer no disability as a consequence and the action was dismissed.[210] In a more recent case[211] when an intern pierced the patient's bladder at the commencement of a tubal ligation, the supervising gynaecologist intervened and made the necessary repairs in 45 minutes. The same intern had earlier failed to intubate the patient but an anaesthetist took over. The trial judge found that "these unfortunate occurrences in no way contributed to the injuries sustained by Amy Mang."[212]

---

207 Although his damages might still be nominal: *see supra* Chapter 3.
208 *Browne v. Lerner* (1940), 48 Man. R. 126 (K.B.).
209 *Pellerin v. Stevenson supra* n. 29.
210 *McNamara v. Smith*, [1934] 2 D.L.R. 417 (Ont. C.A.).
211 *Mang v. Moscovitz* (1982), 37 A.R. 221 (Alta. Q.B.).
212 *Id.* at 235. The patient became a quadriplegic after suffering a "diffuse, multifocal and/or metabolic cerebral insult intraoperatively," *Id.* at 238.

In an English case, a dentist failed to diagnose a jaw fracture which occurred as he was extracting a tooth. The expert evidence indicated that the dentist had met the standard of care and that such fractures could occur without negligence. As to the allegation that it was negligence not to diagnose the fracture, the judge said that there was no proof that any damage resulted from the failure to diagnose because even if it had been, no treatment would have been given.[213]

While it is fatal to a plaintiff's claim in negligence to be unable to prove injury, proof of injury alone is not enough either. In an action against a chiropractor[214] the court acknowledged that the plaintiff had ''suffered cruelly'' from the defendant's manipulations, yet said:[215]

> The plaintiff, however, knew that the defendant merely assumed to treat human ailments in accordance with the system taught in the school of chiropractic and the burden is on him to show by competent evidence, not merely that the treatment given by the defendant was injurious, or ineffective, but that requisite care and skill was not exercised by the defendant in administering it. This he has not done and the action must be dismissed.

The plaintiff had failed to prove that the chiropractor had breached the standard of care.

Therefore negligence cannot be assumed only because an injury has been suffered, but without proof of injury there can never be liability for negligence. The spectre of a patient proving an injury but failing in his attempt to gain compensation because some other aspect of the negligence action is unproven has caused two well-known jurists to make eloquent pleas for correction by legislation.[216]

(ii) Compensation for injury

Assuming that the requirements for a finding of negligence have been proven,[217] the judge, or jury if there is one, has the task of assessing the *quantum* of damages, that is, attaching a dollar value to the plaintiff's claim. The fundamental purpose of negligence law is the compensation of the victim, and the aim is to restore the plaintiff as nearly as possible to his position prior to the negligent act. As explained by a leading Canadian writer:[218]

---

213 *Fish v. Kapur*, [1948] 2 All E.R. 176 (K.B.).

214 *Rutledge v. Fisher*, [1940] 3 W.W.R. 494 (B.C. Co. Ct.); *see also Armstrong v. Bruce supra* n. 12.

215 *Rutledge v. Fisher id* at 499.

216 *Davidson v. Connaught Laboratories* (1980), 14 C.C.L.T. 251 (Ont. H.C.) *per* Linden J.; *Ferguson v. Hamilton Civic Hosp.* (1983), 23 C.C.L.T. 254 (Ont. H.C.) *per* Krever J. *See also Procureur General De La Province De Quebec v. Lapierre*, unreported Oct. 26, 1983 No. 500-09-000935-791 (Que. C.A.).

217 *See supra.*

218 Charles, *Justice in Personal Injury Awards: The Continuing Search for Guidelines* in *Studies in Canadian Tort Law* 37 at 39 (2d ed. Klar 1977); this chapter is an excellent discussion of the principles and practices in damage assessment. Charles, *A New Handbook on the Assessment of Damages in Personal Injury Cases from the Supreme Court* (1978), 3

Since perfect compensation in the sense of physical reconstruction of the victim to his pre-accident condition is generally impossible, the initial premise upon which damage awards are based is that damages should be computed so that the dollars awarded will be adequate compensation for the loss which was suffered by the injured party. To the extent that money damages can make the victim whole again, the award of compensation is considered to be the fairest solution to both plaintiff and defendant.

The principles of quantification will not be discussed in detail because they are no different from those applied in general negligence law, which are adequately dealt with elsewhere.[219] A number of cases are worth noting, however, because of the nature of the injuries involved.

In a case of a six-day-old baby who was left with a deformed penis after a circumcision,[220] the assessment of general damages was extremely difficult because of the age of the child and the unknown emotional effect of the injury on the child, but they were set at $10,000. In two cases involving pain and suffering and unsatisfactory results from negligent cosmetic surgery the awards were: $6,000 general damages[221] for a "nose job" where the deformity was minimal and $8,000 general damages for disfigurement of breasts.[222]

In another case,[223] a polio victim underwent an operation to improve the use of his right leg by the fusion of certain bones. In error, the operation was performed on the left leg. The trial judge found that the permanent deprivation of movement in the formerly good leg was "not as great as might at first be supposed by a layman,"[224] noted that the plaintiff was "the sort of young fellow who will shrug off his physical disabilities"[225] and awarded $8,000 general damages. In a tragic case[226] a surgeon removed a patient's only kidney believing it to be a cyst. The patient was awarded $100,000 general damages and her father who donated one of his kidneys in an unsuccessful transplant was awarded $5,000 general damages.

In an Ontario case,[227] a healthy and active woman entered hospital as an outpatient for a microlaryngoscopy. As a result of the anaesthetist's negligence in performing transtracheal ventilation, she was rendered a quadriplegic,

---

C.C.L.T. 344; *see also* Hawley, *Assessment of Damages for Permanent Incapacitating Injuries* (1975), 13 Alta. L. Rev. 430.

219 Goldsmith, *Damages for Personal Injury and Death in Canada;* Cooper-Stephenson and Saunders, *Personal Injury Damages In Canada* (1981); Bale, *Encouraging the Hearse Horse Not to Snicker: A Tort Fund Providing Variable Periodic Payments For Pecuniary Loss* in *Issues in Tort Law* 189 (Steel, Rodgers-Magnet ed. 1982); Foster, *Structured Settlements* (1982), 20 A.L.R. 434.

220 *Gray v. La Fleche*, [1950] 1 D.L.R. 337 (Man. K.B.).

221 *LaFleur v. Cornelis* (1979), 28 N.B.R. (2d) 569 (N.B.Q.B.).

222 *White v. Turner* (1981), 15 C.C.L.T. 81 (Ont H.C.); affirmed 20 C.C.L.T. xxii (Ont. C.A.).

223 *Staple v. Winnipeg* (1956), 18 W.W.R. 625 (Man. Q.B.).

224 *Id.* at 631.

225 *Id.* at 632.

226 *Urbanski v. Patel* (1978), 84 D.L.R. (3d) 650 (Man. Q.B.); *See* Robertson, *A New Application of The Rescue Principle* (1980), 96 L.Q.R. 19.

227 *Holmes v. Bd. of Hosp. Trustees of London supra* n. 20.

and damages were awarded against three doctors in a total sum in excess of $700,000. This award is consistent with those set for plaintiffs with similar injuries for motor vehicle and sports accidents.[228]

There is one type of claim for compensation that is most difficult because it raises issues of social policy as well as law and arises from the emotionally charged sterilization procedure. In Canada the typical facts are that a sterilization is not effective and the woman becomes pregnant, facing an abortion or an unplanned baby, and probably another sterilization procedure.

In two cases[229] where the women underwent abortions general damages of $5,000 were awarded to each patient.

In the three Canadian cases[230] where the women delivered healthy babies, claims were made by parents for wrongful life and by the children for wrongful birth. All of the wrongful birth claims were dismissed[231] as being "grotesque,"[232] "without foundation" and "not . . . for this child damage, and still less damage compensable in money"[233] and "against public policy."[234]

In two of the three cases no liability was found, but the courts assessed damages at $1[235] and $1,000.[236] In the third case, *Cataford v. Moreau*,[237] liability was found and an interesting assessment of damages took place. Chief Justice Deschenes awarded general damages of $2,000 to the wife for inconvenience, anxiety and suffering and $400 to the husband for loss of consortium. While he did acknowledge the claim of the parents for the cost of raising this eleventh child and did, relying on expert evidence, do a calculation, the parents received no moneys. When the cost of raising the child ($8,500 invested to generate $1,000 per year) was matched against the allowances such a child would be entitled to ($7,557), the balance (under $1,000) was held to be cancelled by the moral and financial benefits the parents could

---

228 See *Andrews v. Grand & Toy* (1978), 3 C.C.L.T. 225 (S.C.C.); *Arnold v. Teno* (1978), 3 C.C.L.T. 272 (S.C.C.); *Thornton v. Prince George Bd. of S. Trustees* (1978), 3 C.C.L.T. 257 (S.C.C.). For an analysis see Charles, *Justice in Personal Injury Awards supra* n. 218.

229 *Cryderman v. Ringrose*, [1977] 3 W.W.R. 109 (Alta. D.C.); affirmed [1978] 3 W.W.R. 481 (Alta. C.A.); *Zimmer v. Ringrose* (1978), 89 D.L.R. (3d) 646 (Alta. T.D.); affirmed 16 C.C.L.T. 51 (Alta. C.A.); leave to appeal dismissed 28 A.R. 92 (S.C.C.).

230 *Colp v. Ringrose*, unreported No. 84474, October 6, 1976 (Alta. S.C.); *Doiron v. Orr* (1978), 86 D.L.R. (3d) 719 (Ont. H.C.); *Cataford v. Moreau* (1978), 114 D.L.R. (3d) 585 (Que. S.C.).

231 Wrongful birth claims have not been successful in other jurisdictions. For England see *Udale v. Bloomsbury Area Health Authority*, [1983] 2 All E.R. 522 (Q.B.). For the U.S., see Thompson and Sanbar, *Wrongful Conception or Wrongful Pregnancy, Who Pays For the Alleged Blessed Event and How Much?* (1983), 11 Legal Aspects Med. Practice 1.

232 *Doiron v. Orr supra* n. 230 at 723.

233 *Cataford v. Moreau supra* n. 230 at 596.

234 *Colp v. Ringrose supra* n. 230 at 3.

235 *Id.*

236 *Doiron v. Orr supra* n. 230.

237 (1978), 114 D.L.R. (3d) 585 (Que. S.C.).

expect from the child. The Chief Justice had, as mentioned, rejected the child's claim for damages for wrongful life.

Traditional assessment guidelines may seem ill-suited to these cases, but the goal remains the same: to award reasonable compensation.[238]

(d) Causation

A plaintiff who proves duty, breach of the standard of care and injury will still be unsuccessful in bringing his action unless he proves the causal link between the breach of the standard of care and his injury. The causal link is tested in two ways: the defendant's conduct must be both the actual cause, or cause-in-fact and the legal cause, or proximate cause of the injury.

(i) Cause-in-fact

This is a determination of the factual, or technical, scientific cause of the plaintiff's injury. The complexity of the human body and the uncertainties which still surround its nature,[239] together with the advanced state of medical technology[240] exacerbate the overwhelming task that the plaintiff has in proving that the defendant's conduct was the factual cause of his injury. A rule of evidence referred to as *res ipsa loquitur* to be discussed in a later chapter[241] is sometimes of great help to plaintiffs, but it is not always available. Likewise, a new test conceived in an English case, *McGhee v. Nat. Coal Bd.*[242] may be of assistance, but to date has received little attention in Canada. Even defendants, who it is assumed have the most knowledge and the best evidence, sometimes have difficulty in proving how or when damage occurred.[243] The subject of the quest is further obscured by the conviction of many plaintiffs that any change in bodily condition following medical treatment has been "caused" by that treatment.[244]

---

238 For excellent discussions of the issues *see:* Kouri, *Non-Therapeutic Sterilization — Malpractice, and the Issues of "Wrongful Birth and Wrongful Life" In Quebec Law* (1979), 57 Can. Bar Rev. 89; Rodgers-Magnet, *Annotation — The Action For Wrongful Life* (1979), 7 C.C.L.T. 242; Robertson, *Civil Liability Arising from "Wrongful Birth" Following an Unsuccessful Sterilization Operation* (1977), 4 Am. J. Law & Medicine 131; Bickenback, *Damages for Wrongful Conception: Doiron v. Orr* (1980), 18 U.W.O.L. Rev. 493.

239 *See, for example, Murphy v. Gen. Hosp. Corp.* (1980), 68 A.P.R. 355 (Nfld. T.D.); *Mang v. Moscovitz* (1982), 37 A.R. 221 (Alta. Q.B.); *Dunn v. Young* (1977), 86 D.L.R. (3d) 411 (Ont. Co. Ct.).

240 *See, for example, Neufeld v. McQuitty* (1979), 18 A.R. 271 (Alta. T.D.); *Schierz v. Dodds,* [1981] C.S. 589 (Que. C.S.).

241 *See infra* Chapter 6.

242 [1972] 3 All E.R. 1008 (H.L.). For a discussion of the *McGhee* test, *see infra.*

243 *See Radclyffe v. Rennie,* [1965] S.C.R. 703 where each defendant was trying to prove who left the gauze in the plaintiff; *see also Mang v. Moscovitz* (1982), 37 A.R. 221 (Alta. Q.B.).

244 *See Girard v. Royal Columbian Hosp.* (1976), 66 D.L.R. (3d) 676 at 680 (B.C.S.C.); *Hankins v. Papillon* (1980), 14 C.C.L.T. 199 (Que. S.C.); *Considine v. Camp Hill Hosp.* (1982), 133 D.L.R. (3d) 11 (N.S.T.D.).

A legal test for cause-in-fact often used in general negligence law is sometimes helpful and has seen some use in medical negligence cases. Although it is not always identified[245] as such, it is in the *sine qua non,* or ''but-for'' test[246] and involves an inquiry as to whether the injury would not have occurred ''but for'' the defendant's conduct.

A case illustrative of the difficulties involved is one in which the plaintiff was suspected of having sarcoidosis involving the larynx,[247] and underwent a scaline node biopsy. The biopsy proved negative, but following the biopsy the plaintiff suffered laryngeal complications. Her husky voice and difficulty in swallowing were found to be due to a paralyzed vocal cord occasioned by injury to a nerve. Many explanations were advanced as to the cause-in-fact of the injury including a tumor, tuberculosis and sarcoidosis, but in any event the doctor was exonerated by the court because the nerve involved could not have been reached during the biopsy.

The difficulty for a judge in settling on the cause-in-fact is evident, and because of the uncertainty in some cases, judges do not always agree. In a case where interns interpreted x-rays and failed to diagnose a dislocated fracture of the neck, the majority of the Supreme Court of Canada ruled that but for this negligence, the plaintiff would not have died.[248] However, a dissenting justice[249] felt that there was no evidence which showed that the paralytic ileus (a paralysis of a portion of the small intestine), which caused the death, was the result of the failure to diagnosis the fracture; there was evidence that paralytic ileus could result from a number of causes.

Occasionally it happens that a court, despite much effort, is unable to determine the cause-in-fact. In one case, a court sat for 27 days and heard a great deal of technical medical evidence but was unable to determine the cause of death, and therefore dismissed the case, because the plaintiff was unable to prove it.[250]

Strong and consistent expert evidence is of crucial importance to a court engaged in this inquiry. Where such evidence is available, the court's task is much eased. For example, in a British Columbia case, a patient had an operation for a diseased artery under spinal anaesthetic administered by the

---

245 *Penner v. Theobald supra* n. 93 at 231; *Smith v. Auckland Hosp. Bd.,* [1965] N.Z.L.R. 191 at 199 (N.Z.C.A.).

246 Linden, *supra* n. 38 at 90; For an excellent critique of the test *see* Weinrib, *A Step Forward In Factual Causation* (1975), 38 Mo. L. Rev. 518.

247 *Finlay v. Auld,* [1975] 1 S.C.R. 338; *see also Bickford v. Stiles* (1981), 128 D.L.R. (3d) 516 (N.B.Q.B.) and *Maynard v. West Midlands Reg. Health Authority,* unreported May 5, 1983 (H.L.).

248 *Fraser v. Vancouver Gen. Hosp. supra* n. 84.

249 *Id.* at 70 *per* Locke J.

250 *Wilson v. Stark supra* n. 51; *see also Cavan v. Wilcox* (1974), 2 N.R. 618 (S.C.C.), an action against a nurse.

defendant.[251] Following the surgery the patient suffered permanent partial paralysis of both legs and brought action. However, tests performed after the operation convinced all the expert witnesses that the spinal cord damage was not caused by the anaesthetist's work, but rather was more likely a consequence of the pre-existing condition of the plaintiff's arteries.

Nevertheless, the determination of the cause-in-fact is as essential as it is difficult because it is preliminary to the determination of whether the defendant's conduct was also the proximate cause of injury alleged; without proof of cause-in-fact, the plaintiff will lose his case.[252]

Where justice and social policy support the compensation of the victim, but the patient is unable to prove by the "but-for" test that it was the defendant doctor's actions that caused his injury, a new body of law supports the patient's right to recover damages. The seminal case[253] was not a medical one but did involve the difficulty of proving cause in respect of disease. The plaintiff was a workman who was exposed to abrasive brick dust and because his employer provided no adequate washing facilities, had to bicycle home caked with sweat and grime. He contracted dermatitis and sued his employer. The trial court applied the "but-for" test and held that although the employer had failed to meet the standard of care, the workman had failed to prove that this failure was the cause of his dermatitis. The House of Lords unanimously reversed this decision and found for the workman formulating a "new" test which like quicksilver is easy to describe but exceedingly difficult to capture or contain.[254] The House of Lords had said that where a plaintiff proves that the defendant's breach of the standard of care caused, *or materially contributed to* his injury the plaintiff's action should succeed, even if there were other contributing factors for which the defendant was not responsible.

Although the diversity in the unanimous judgments make the case an academic's dream, the most oft-quoted judgment is that of Lord Wilberforce who said:[255]

> But the question remains whether a pursuer must necessarily fail if, after he has shown a breach of duty, involving an increase of risk of disease, he cannot positively prove that this

---

251 *Girard v. Royal Columbian Hosp. supra* n. 244; *see also Hutchinson v. Robert,* [1935] O.W.N. 314 (Ont. C.A.), where the defendant's experts testified that the defendant was prudent in leaving a fragment of an instrument in the wound. In any case, the injury complained of, sinus trouble, was not caused by the doctor.

252 *MacKinnon v. Ignacio, Lamond and MacKeough* (1978), 29 N.S.R. (2d) 656 (N.S.T.D.); *Quiroz v. Austrup* (1982), 17 A.C.W.S. (2d) 245.

253 *McGhee v. Nat. Coal Bd.,* [1972] 3 All E.R. 1008 (H.L.).

254 For an excellent discussion *see* Robertson, *Overcoming The Causation Hurdle In Informed Consent: The Principle in McGhee v. N.C.B.* (1983), 21 U.W. Ont. L.R. (to be set); Weinrib, *A Step Forward In Factual Causation* (1975), 30 Mo. L. Rev. 519 at 523; Edwards, Hopkins, White, *Annual Survey of Tort Law* (1982), 14 Ottawa L. Rev. 152 at 196.

255 *Supra* n. 253 at 1012.

increase of risk caused or materially contributed to the disease while his employers cannot positively prove the contrary. In this intermediate case there is an appearance of logic in the view that the pursuer, on whom the onus lies, should fail — a logic which dictated the judgments below. The question is whether we should be satisfied in factual situations like the present, with this logical approach. In my opinion, there are further considerations of importance. First, it is a sound principle that where a person has, by breach of duty of care, created a risk, and injury occurs within the area of that risk, the loss should be borne by him unless he shows that it had some other cause. Secondly, from the evidential point of view, one may ask, why should a man who is able to show that his employer should have taken certain precautions, because without them there is a risk, or an added risk, of injury or disease, and who in fact sustains exactly that injury or disease, have to assume the burden of proving more: namely, that it was the addition to the risk, caused by the breach of duty, which caused or materially contributed to the injury? In many cases of which the present is typical, this is impossible to prove, just because honest medical opinion cannot segregate the causes of an illness between compound causes. And if one asks which of the parties, the workman or the employers should suffer from this inherent evidential difficulty, the answer as a matter in policy or justice should be that it is the creator of the risk who, ex hypothesi, must be taken to have foreseen the possibility of damage, who should bear its consequences.

Making a material contribution to the risk an adequate connection with the cause raises many questions. When will the *McGhee* "material contribution" test apply? What is its effect? Is there a valid basis for this apparent extension, or dilution of the formerly sacrosanct cause-in-fact analysis?

A number of Canadian courts have applied the *McGhee* test in cases involving doctors and hospitals.[256] In *Powell v. Guttman*[257] an orthopaedic surgeon who failed to monitor the patient's condition following the placing of pins in her hip was held to have materially increased the risk of the very fracture that occurred when a second orthopaedic surgeon fractured the patient's femur during surgery. Mr. Justice O'Sullivan, speaking for the Court of Appeal of Manitoba, said after reviewing the *McGhee* case:[258]

> . . . I think the law in Canada is that where a tortfeasor creates or materially contributes to a significant risk of injury occurring and injury does occur which is squarely within the risk thus created or materially increased, then unless the risk is spent, the tortfeasor is liable for injury which follows from the risk, even though there are other subsequent causes which also cause or materially contribute to that injury.

A year later, in a British Columbia case[259] involving orthopaedic work, a doctor who used an unusual procedure for setting a fractured foot and failed to read relevant manufacturer's instructions about the cast used, was found liable

---

256 Note that the *McGhee* test was applied and a hospital found liable in the English case *Clark v. MacLennan*, [1983] 1 All E.R. 416 (Q.B.). *Note also* that the *McGhee* test was applied in the non-medical negligence case *Nowsco Well Service Ltd. v. Can. Propane Gas & Oil Ltd.* (1981), 122 D.L.R. (3d) 228 (Sask. C.A.) and in the dissenting judgment in *Delaney v. Cascade River Holidays* (1983), 24 C.C.L.T. 6 (B.C.C.A.), leave to appeal to S.C.C. granted Feb. 25, 1983; *see also Re Workers' Compensation App. Board v. Penney* (1980), 112 D.L.R. (3d) 95 (N.S.C.A.).

257 (1978), 89 D.L.R. (3d) 180 (Man. C.A.).

258 *Id.* at 192.

259 *Townsend v. Lai* (1979), 2 A.C.W.S. 144 (B.C.S.C.).

when the patient required corrective surgery. The trial judge cited the *McGhee* case in support of finding that the doctor did not meet the standard of care and that this was a "major" cause-in-fact of the injury.

The *McGhee* test was applied in two other cases from British Columbia involving obstetrical accidents.[260] In *Meyer v. Gordon*[261] a hospital was held liable for the failure of nursing staff to examine and monitor the progress of an expectant mother which "materially increased the risk of injury to the child and materially increased the risk of fetal distress and the resulting hypoxia."[262] In *Wipfli v. Britten*[263] a family doctor failed to ascertain that the patient was carrying twins with the result that one baby suffered irreversible cerebral damage. Although there were a number of possible causes for the injury and the trial judge accepted expert evidence that it was not possible to determine the precise cause, he applied the *McGhee* test and held that the failure of the family physician to diagnose the twins was a breach of the standard of care and "materially increased the risk of injury."

The *McGhee* case has not gone unnoticed in Quebec, for it was applied in *Schierz v. Dodds*[264] to allow a patient who suffered a stroke while on oral contraceptives to succeed against the doctor who prescribed them for her when he should have known that she suffered from phlebitis. Mr. Justice Malouf said:[265]

> As stated by Lord Kilbrandon in the *McGhee* case, the victim need only satisfy the Court of a probability, she is not obliged to demonstrate an irrefragable chain of causation which, in the present state of medical knowledge, the victim could probably never do.

While the questions raised earlier are certainly not clearly answered by the cases[266] some guidance to the parameters of the *McGhee* test is possible.

a) When might the *McGhee* "material contribution" test apply?

There has to be a breach of the standard of care required of the defendant.[267] This breach must create a risk of injury to the plaintiff, which risk does in fact

---

260 Note that it was considered but deemed inapplicable on the facts in *Foote v. Royal Columbian Hosp.*, [1982] B.C.D. Civ. 2632-05 (B.C.S.C.); affirmed 19 A.C.W.S. (2d) 304 (B.C.C.A.).

261 (1981), 17 C.C.L.T. 1 (B.C.S.C.).

262 *Id.* at 41-42.

263 (1982), 22 C.C.L.T. 104 (B.C.S.C.). Note that the action against an obstetrician was dismissed.

264 [1981] C.S. 589 (Que. S.C.).

265 *Id.* at 602.

266 *See* Solomon, Feldthusen & Mills, *Cases and Materials On the Law of Torts* (1982), 398 where the authors comment that while Canadian courts have referred to *McGhee*, "it is often difficult to interpret what use they are making of the case."

267 *Foote v. Royal Columbian Hosp.*, *supra* n. 260. The failure to prove this was held by the Chief Justice to preclude the application of *McGhee*. Note that this is sometimes referred to in the cases using the terminology of duty of care. For a discussion of the difference between duty of care and standard of care, *see supra*.

materialize.[268] The plaintiff must have attempted to prove the cause-in-fact of his injuries but have been unable to fulfill the "but-for" test. The plaintiff has to establish that the defendant's substandard conduct *materially increased* the risk of the injury that occurred.

b) What is the effect of the *McGhee* test?

There is a dearth of judicial comment and analysis on the effect of the *McGhee* test. This might lead one to the conclusion that if the plaintiff proves a breach of the standard of care, and the injury coming within the risk thus created, then liability should automatically follow.[269] It is more consistent with established evidentiary principles to conclude that the consequence is that the plaintiff has made out a *prima facie* case and the onus then shifts to the defendant.[270] Indeed, this was the result in the *McGhee* case itself.[271]

It appears that the defendant should then attempt to prove that he was not a cause-in-fact of the injury and that he did not materially increase the risk of the injury. In the *McGhee* case[272] the employer defendant was held to have failed to show that the employee's dermatitis was not due to conditions at work. The court in *Schierz v. Dodds*[273] said that the doctor defendant must bear the loss "unless he shows that the injury resulted from some other cause,"[274] while in *Nowsco Well Services Ltd. v. Can. Gas & Oil Ltd.*,[275] after noting that there was no testimony from the respondents (defendants), Mr. Justice Bayda held them liable and said:[276]

> In the last analysis I find that the factual situation of the present case justifies a shift in onus. That is, it justifies a holding that proof of the breach of duty in question is *prima facie* proof that the fire was caused by the escape of propane gas. The respondents were free to show that the fire was not caused by any breach of duty on their part. They did not attempt to do so, but contented themselves with only disproving the appellant's [plaintiff's] theory. They must bear the consequences.

The effect of the application of the *McGhee* test, an onus shift, is to be contrasted with the effect of the application of the doctrine of *res ipsa liquitur*

---

268 Note that in *Nowsco Well Service Ltd. v. Can. Propane Gas & Oil Ltd.* (1981), 122 D.L.R. (3d) 228 (Sask. C.A.) the adjective "unreasonable" is used to describe the nature of the risk. *Quaere* whether this is a confusion of the cause-in-fact and proximate cause issues. *See* Robertson, *supra* n. 254 who states that this requirement of unreasonableness is "incorrect" as it confuses the standard of care and cause-in-fact issues.

269 *See, for example, Meyer v. Gordon* (1981), 17 C.C.L.T. 1 (B.C.S.C.). *See also Powell v. Guttman* (1978), 89 D.L.R. (3d) 180 (Man. C.A.) where the operation of *novus actus interveniens* was affected.

270 This is the effect stated in *Nowsco Well Services Ltd. v. Can. Propane Gas & Oil Ltd.* (1981), 122 D.L.R. (3d) 228 at 246-48 (Sask. C.A.); *see also Schierz v. Dodds*, [1981] C.S. 589 at 603 (Que. S.C.); *Foote v. Royal Columbian Hosp.*, *supra* n. 260. For an excellent analysis *see* Robertson, *supra* n. 254.

271 *See* Linden, *Canadian Tort Law* 96-97 (1982); Robertson, *supra* n. 254; *see also Clark v. MacLennan*, [1983] 1 All E.R. 416 (Q.B.).

272 *Supra* n. 253.

273 *Supra* n. 264.

274 *Id.* at 602.

275 *Supra* n. 270.

276 *Id.* at 248.

where the defendant need only offer an explanation as consistent with no negligence as with negligence.[277]

c) What is the basis for the *McGhee* test?

A review of the judgments in the aforementioned cases provides this short answer to the question: common sense, public policy and justice.

Lord Reid said in the *McGhee* case:[278]

> But is has often been said that the legal concept of causation is not based on logic or philosophy. It is based on the practical way in which the ordinary man's mind works in the every-day affairs of life. From a broad and practical viewpoint I can see no substantial difference between saying that what the respondents did materially increased the risk of injury to the appellant and saying that what the respondents did made a material contribution to his injury.

Lord Salmon, too, subscribed to common sense as a valid approach to analyzing cause-in-fact. Quoting himself in another case, he said:[279]

> The nature of causation had been discussed by many eminent philosophers and also by a number of learned judges in the past. I consider, however, that what or who has caused a certain event to occur is essentially a practical question of fact which can best be answered by ordinary common sense rather than abstract metaphysical theory.

Mr. Justice Bayda, speaking for the majority of the Manitoba Court of Appeal, concurred with the common sense approach, but added:[280]

> Briefly put, if causation is overwhelmingly difficult to prove or impossible to prove then it *is a matter of public policy or justice* that it is the creator of the risk who should be put to the trouble of hurdling the difficulty or bearing the consequences.
>
> There is precedent in the Canadian law for departing from the normal onus rule respecting causation where for practical reasons justice requires that to be done. The most notable example is *Cook v. Lewis*, [1952] 1 D.L.R. 1, [1951] S.C.R. 830 . . .
>
> I am cognizant that the factual situation in *Cook v. Lewis* is not analogous to that in the present case. I cite the case merely to emphasize that *the law is not so rigid as to fail to accommodate a shift in onus where for practical reasons, justice requires such a shift.* [emphasis supplied]

In conclusion, the *McGhee* test has been transplanted into Canadian jurisprudence. Its latency belies its strength for it is in medical negligence cases that very often proof of cause-in-fact is overwhelmingly difficult or impossible. Using the *McGhee* test, once the patient has proven a breach of the standard of care and that the injury suffered is within the risk created by such a breach and that the substandard conduct materially contributed to this

---

277 For a discussion of *res ipsa loquitur see* Chapter 6. Note that the effect in England of this doctrine is an onus shift. *Quaere* whether in Canada it would be desirable to have the effects of the *McGhee* test and *res ipsa loquitur* consistent.

278 *Supra* n. 253 at 1011. Note that the "material contribution" reference seems to refer to the substantial factor test which has long been a part of tort law. *See* Fleming, *The Law of Torts* 173 (1983).

279 *Supra* n. 253 at 1017 quoting *Alphacell v. Woodward*, [1972] 2 All E.R. 475 at 489-90 (H.L.).

280 *Supra*, n. 270 (*Nowsco*) at 246-48.

risk, he has established a *prima facie* case of negligence.[281] The onus then shifts to the defendant doctor or hospital who must, in addition to disproving the patient's theory, disprove the breach of the standard of care, the injury, or the causal link between the two. It remains for each court to decide whether common sense, social policy, or justice should require the particular defendant to bear the loss in each case.[282] The *McGhee* test has the potential to re-shape causation jurisprudence.

(ii) Proximate cause

Determining cause-in-fact is a more or less scientific inquiry into the cause-effect relationship which brought about the injury. Proximate cause, on the other hand, is an entirely different inquiry which really relates in no way to "true" cause, although the courts often use the language of causation. Rather, the notion of proximate cause or "remoteness" is a liability limiting device invented by the courts. It is an accepted tenet of general negligence law that a defendant ought not necessarily to be liable for all damage that his conduct causes, but only for that which was "foreseeable" to a reasonable person in the defendant's position.[283] Any damage occurring which falls outside of that which is reasonably foreseeable is said to be "too remote" and the defendant will not be held liable for it. For example, assume that the cause-in-fact of a patient's death is complications arising from paralysis of the small intestine (paralytic ileus) arising out of an undiagnosed neck fracture.[284] While scientifically the cause of the patient's death may be the failure to diagnose and then treat the neck fracture, this may not be the proximate cause. It could be held that it was not foreseeable that a failure to diagnose a neck fracture would result in the death of the patient by paralytic ileus; in other words, this ailment is too remote from the failure to diagnose to justify holding the doctor liable.[285]

---

281 As to the implications of *McGhee* with regard to negligent disclosure see the excellent discussion in Robertson, *supra* n. 254; *see also* Chapter 3 *infra*.

282 Two well-known Canadian judges have expressed concern about present jurisprudence which precludes the compensation of the patient: *Davidson v. Connaught Laboratories* (1980), 14 C.C.L.T. 251 (Ont. H.C.) *per* Linden J. and *Ferguson v. Hamilton Civic Hosp.* (1983), 23 C.C.L.T. 254 (Ont. H.C.) *per* Krever J.

283 *Overseas Tankship (U.K.) v. Morts Dock & Enrg. Co. (The Wagon Mound)*, [1961] A.C. 388 (P.C.). For a thorough discussion of the various tests used to delineate proximate cause *see* Linden, *supra* n. 38 at 342-54; Cf. the majority decision of Madam Justice Wilson and the dissenting judgment of Mr. Justice Zuber in *Zamparo v. Brisson* (1981), 16 C.C.L.T. 66 (Ont. C.A.). *See also Worth v. Royal Jubilee Hosp.* (1980), 4 L. Med. Q. 59 (B.C.C.A).

284 The facts are those of *Fraser v. Vancouver Gen. Hosp. supra* n. 84.

285 *See* dissent of Locke J. *id.* at 57; *see also Elverson v. Doctors Hosp.* (1974), 4 O.R. (2d) 748 (Ont. C.A.), where it was held that the back injury suffered by the patient's husband who assisted a nurse in lifting a bed was not reasonably foreseeable and *Worth v. Royal Jubilee Hosp.* (1980), 4 L. Med. Q. 59 (B.C.C.A.), where it was held that it was not reasonably foreseeable that a psychiatric patient would become a paraplegic by attempting to escape.

It is clear that the Supreme Court of Canada regards the reasonable foreseeability test as the appropriate one for determining proximate cause in medical negligence cases. In the words of the court in *Cardin v. Montreal*:[286]

Certainly, *doctors should not be held responsible for unforeseeable accidents* which may occur in the normal course of the exercise of their profession. Cases necessarily occur in which, in spite of exercising the greatest caution, accidents supervene and for which nobody can be held responsible. The doctor is not a guarantor of the operation which he performs or the attention he gives. If he displays normal knowledge, if he gives the medical care which a competent doctor would give under identical conditions, if he prepares his patient before operation according to the rules of the art, it is difficult to sue him in damages, if by chance an accident occurs. Perfection is a standard required by law no more for a doctor than for other professional men, lawyers, engineers, architects, etc. Accidents, imponderables, what is foreseeable and what is not, must necessarily be taken into account. [emphasis supplied]

And from *University Hosp. Bd. v. Lepine*:[287]

The question of whether there was or was not negligence in a given situation has been dealt with in many judgments and by writers at great length. One principle emerges upon which there is universal agreement, namely, that *whether or not an act or omission is negligent must be judged not by its consequences alone but also by considering whether a reasonable person should have anticipated that what happened might be a natural result of that act or omission.* As was said by Lord Thankerton in *Glasgow Corporation v. Muir* [[1943] A.C. 448 at 454-55],

''The court must be careful to place itself in the position of the person charged with the duty and to consider what he or she should have reasonably anticipated as a natural and probable consequence of neglect, and not to give undue weight to the fact that a distressing accident has happened . . .'' [emphasis supplied]

Apart from setting out the general principle, these extracts also constitute a directive from the highest court in Canada that the remoteness principle must be applied with reason and justice.

A review of the decisions shows that while medical negligence law is usually consistent with general negligence law with respect to the finding of proximate cause, this is not always so.

A. Pre-treatment conditions

Medical care is frequently administered to a person who has (i) a peculiar weakness or susceptibility, (ii) a pre-existing disease, or (iii) a traumatic condition brought about by injury.[288] Each situation will be discussed in turn.

Thin-skull rule. In general negligence law, to some extent at least, the

---

For cases where death was not too remote an injury *see DeMoura v. Mississauga Hosp.* (1979), 3 L. Med. Q. 215 (Ont. H.C.) and *Leonard v. Knott,* [1980] 1 W.W.R. 673 (B.C.C.A.).

286 *Supra* n. 36 at 494.
287 *Supra* n. 99 at 579-80.
288 *See* Rozovsky, *supra* n. 24 at 59.

defendant takes his victim as he finds him. This has been described as the thin-skull rule,[289] and stated as follows:[290]

> . . . one who is guilty of negligence to another must put up with idiosyncracies of his victim that increase the likelihood or extent of damage to him: it is no answer to a claim for a fractured skull that its owner had an unusually fragile one.

Furthermore:

> If the negligence of the defendant *renders* the skull of the plaintiff thin, making him more susceptible to additional injury or sickness, the defendant is responsible for the further complications.[291]

The thin-skull victim might not recover damages under a strict application of the foreseeability test because peculiar weakness or susceptibility is often not foreseeable, but there is authority that he is not precluded from recovery either.[292] There are policy reasons for the creation and nurturing of this exception to the foreseeability test, which include the difficulty of determining with certainty what is foreseeable, the protection of vulnerable persons, the deterrence of substandard conduct, and the wider distribution of loss due to tortious activity.

The critical questions when determining the causation issue are: 1) Was the doctor's conduct a cause-in-fact of the injury and, if so, was it a proximate cause? 2) If the answer to the first part of the question is yes and to the second part is no, then might the patient still recover as a thin-skull person? Has the negligence of the doctor rendered the patient a thin-skulled person?

Although many of the fact situations in medical negligence cases would seem to have been appropriate for the application of the thin-skull rule, there is only one case in which it has been expressly applied. In *Powell v. Guttman*[293] Dr. Guttman, an orthopaedic surgeon, was found to be negligent in his management of the patient's care after surgery, during which time the patient developed avascular necrosis and the pins placed in her hip during the surgery changed position. The trial judge held that the failure to monitor these developments and to suggest remedial surgery was negligence for which Dr. Guttman had to compensate the patient. The Court of Appeal extended Dr. Guttman's liability to include the fractured femur suffered by the patient during the subsequent surgery by another orthopaedic surgeon to salvage the hip.

---

289 *Dulieu v. White & Sons*, [1901] 2 K.B. 669 (C.A.). For an excellent discussion of the thin-skull problem and the case law *see* Linden, *supra* n. 38 at 59-68.

290 *Owens v. Liverpool Corp.*, [1939] 1 K.B. 394 at 400 (C.A.).

291 Linden, *supra* n. 38 at 363. Quoted with approval in *Powell v. Guttman* (1978), 89 D.L.R. (3d) 180 at 190 (Man. C.A.).

292 *Smith v. Leech Brain & Co.*, [1962] 2 Q.B. 405 (Q.B.D.).

293 (1978), 89 D.L.R. (3d) 180 (Man. C.A.). *See also Craig v. Soeurs de Charite de la Providence*, [1940] 2 W.W.R. 80; affirmed [1940] 3 W.W.R. 336 (Sask. C.A.), where the patient's damages for a hot water bottle burn were not lessened because as a diabetic he suffered more. In modern times, it could be implied that the defendant hospital took him as he was.

Mr. Justice O'Sullivan, speaking for the Court, came to this result after stating that the law in Canada was as stated by Professor Linden (now Linden J.) in the quotation above. The learned justice then went on to base liability on a combination of the "rendering thin-skulled rule" and the *McGhee* test for cause-in-fact. He said:[294]

> However, I think the law in Canada is that where a tortfeasor *creates* or materially contributes to a significant risk of injury occurring and injury does occur which is squarely within the risk thus *created* or materially increased, then unless the risk is spent, the tortfeasor is liable for injury which follows from the risk, even though there are other subsequent causes which also cause or materially contribute to that injury. [emphasis supplied]

The patient's femur was foreseeably now susceptible to the fracture because of Dr. Guttman's negligence.

Other cases that might have seen reference to the thin-skull rule have included cases where the patients have had a pre-existing circulatory or blood problem[295] and a susceptibility to toxic or allergic reactions to drugs.[296] The doctor's actions have included giving an anaesthetic[297] or injection,[298] and failing to diagnose[299] or prescribe drug thereapy.[300] Notwithstanding that in all cases the patients suffered injury, in none of them were they awarded compensation. In all of the cases the courts seemed to rule that the doctors' actions were not the cause-in-fact, and with that decision the case for the plaintiff was over.

The result may be just in view of the fact that unlike the motor vehicle operator, who will rarely injure a thin-skull person, the doctor treats many patients who are peculiarly vulnerable, and thence his potential exposure to liability is much greater. On the other hand, the doctor's training and constant experience with such persons place him in a position where he is more able to

---

294 *Id.* at 192.
295 *Girard v. Royal Columbian Hosp. supra* n. 244; *Parsons v. Schmok supra* n. 143; *Serre v. de Tilly* (1975), 58 D.L.R. (3d) 362 (Ont. H.C.); *Thompson v. Toorenburgh* (1973), 50 D.L.R. (3d) 717 (B.C.); affirmed without written reasons [1973] S.C.R. at vii; *Van Hartman v. Kirk*, [1961] V.R. 544 (Vic. S.C.); *MacKinnon v. Ignacio, Lamond and MacKeough* (1978), 28 N.S.R. (2d) 656 (N.S.T.D.); *Leadbetter v. Brand* (1980), 37 N.S.R. (2d) 581 (N.S.T.D.).
296 *Robinson v. Post Office*, [1974] 2 All E.R. 737 (C.A.); *Winteringham v. Rae* (1965), 55 D.L.R. (2d) 108 (Ont. H.C.).
297 *Girard v. Royal Columbian Hosp. supra* n. 244; *MacKinnon v. Ignacio, Lamond and MacKeough* (1978), 29 N.S.R. (2d) 656 (N.S.T.D.); *Leadbetter v. Brand* (1980), 37 N.S.R. (2d) 581 (N.S.T.D.).
298 *Robinson v. Post Office supra* n. 296; *Winteringham v. Rae supra* n. 296.
299 *Serre v. de Tilly supra* n. 295. *See also Yepremian v. Scarborough Gen. Hosp.* (1978), 20 O.R. (2d) 510 (Ont. H.C.); affirmed 110 D.L.R. (3d) 513 (Ont. C.A.); *(No. 2)* (1981), 31 O.R. (2d) 384 (Ont. H.C.), where although the courts construed the risk within very narrow limits *i.e.,* of cardiac arrest, it would seem that holding the risk to be all the consequences of undiagnosed and untreated juvenile diabetes (including electrolyte imbalances which *led to* cardiac arrest) would have meant that Drs. Golbach and Chin should have been liable for "rendering the patient thin-skulled." *See also*, Picard *Comment* (1980), 14 C.C.L.T. 81.
300 *Parsons v. Schmok supra* n. 143.

foresee their peculiar condition. However, the practice of medicine is high in social utility, and the courts are inclined not to increase the potential liability (by, for example, applying the thin-skull rule) of persons engaged in such enterprises.[301]

Two cases are worth noting because in each case it appears that the doctor's conduct could have been characterized as below the standard of care and the patient was certainly a thin-skull person.

In an English case[302] the doctor administered an injection of anti-tetanus serum to a patient who had had such treatment before. The experts agreed that encephalitis was one of the risks, albeit rare, of administering the serum to such a patient. While the doctor was aware that the patient had been similarly treated in the past, he did not follow the proper test dose procedure, and the patient contracted encephalitis. Clearly "but for" the administration of the serum with a test dose, the patient would not have suffered the brain damage that he did, but the court held that the doctor's negligence was not the cause of the injury. The patient required the treatment because of a wound suffered at work, and the defendant employer was held liable both for the wound and the brain damage. Had the issue of the doctor's negligence for administering the serum at all been resolved in favour of the patient, the doctor would have been liable for the extreme injuries suffered by this thin-skull patient.

A Canadian case, no less complicated,[303] involved a patient with a history of arterial disease who was operated on for a "left femoral popliteal vein by-pass graft" under a spinal anaesthetic administered by the defendant. The expert evidence indicated that the introduction by the defendant of an analgesic could send an artery into spasm and, as the patient suffered from a pre-existing plaque (fatty tissue) problem, the result would be a reduced blood supply, causing partial paralysis, which was what happened. It appears that the action of the doctor was the cause-in-fact and even if the injury was not foreseeable, given that the patient was a thin-skull person, he could have recovered under general negligence principles. However, the thin-skull rule does not apply unless a breach of the standard of care is found, and none was found in the procedure (although there was evidence that the surgeon had booked a general anaesthetic and the patient had prohibited a spinal, yet a spinal was given).

It is arguable that a type of thin-skull case occurs when an injured plaintiff commits suicide and one authority has argued that a negligent

---

301 Linden *supra* n. 38 at 102.
302 *Robinson v. Post Office supra* n. 296.
303 *Girard v. Royal Columbian Hosp. supra* n. 244; *see also Thompson v. Toorenburgh supra* n. 295 where a patient previously diagnosed as having a mitral stenosis was treated with "harmful procedures" after an accident but these were not found to have caused her death. *See infra.*

defendant should be required to compensate for it.[304] However, in medical negligence cases the reasonable foreseeability test has been applied in such cases without any reference to the thin-skull rule.[305]

The dearth of judicial comment on the thin-skull rule in the medical negligence case may be due to any one or a combination of the following factors: the cases that have arisen did not fulfill the requirements, policy reasons precluded its application to doctors and hospitals, or the determination of cause-in-fact and proximate cause from complex medical evidence in some cases was nearly impossible.

Disease. Many patients who seek medical care have a disease evidenced by symptoms.[306] If the condition worsens with the administration of medical care or the lack of it, the patient may sue and the court must decide whether the doctor's conduct was the cause-in-fact of the injury and, if so, whether it was the proximate cause.[307] Liability will not be imposed for a breach of the standard of care and the resultant injury unless the answer to both inquiries is affirmative. Unfortunately it is usually impossible to ascertain from the judgments in which no liability is found which question was answered in the negative.

In an early case it was decided that "septicemia had set in without any fault of the defendant"[308] who had attended her in childbirth. In another early case[309] a doctor who misdiagnosed a kidney condition was said not to have met the requisite standard of care. But while he was held liable for damages for the extra treatment and pain undergone by the plaintiff he was held not responsible for the damage to her kidney which took place prior to his being called in on the case. An early case[310] from Ontario involved a child who was suffering from diphtheria, but through a conflict of a doctor and a medical health officer received no medical care for several days. When the health officer eventually visited her she seemed to be recuperating but died shortly thereafter of "paralysis of the heart." The court held that negligence of the officer was not proved to be the cause of the injury.

The foreseeability test as we know it had not been enunciated at the time of these early cases, but it would seem that the damage in each was thought to

---

304 Linden, *supra* n. 38 at 64.
305 Recovery was barred in *University Hosp. Bd. v. Lepine supra* n. 99; *Stadel v. Albertson,* [1954] 2 D.L.R. 328 (Sask. C.A.), but allowed in *Villimure v. Turcot,* [1973] S.C.R. 716.
306 Compare with the thin-skull cases, *supra,* where there may be no symptoms.
307 *See, for example, Hankins v. Papillon* (1980), 14 C.C.L.T. 198 at 205-206 (Que. S.C.).
308 *McQuay v. Eastwood* (1886), 12 O.R. 402 (C.A.). A modern fact situation is seen in *Mudrie v. McDonald* (1975), unreported (B.C.S.C.) Hutcheon J., where the patient alleged negligence in the removal of an I.U.D. in that she suffered afterwards from an inflammatory disease of the pelvis. The court held that there was no negligence and questioned whether the disease was present at the time of the removal.
309 *Turriff v. King supra* n. 177 at 676.
310 *Simpson v. Local Bd. of Health of Belleville* (1917), 40 O.L.R. 406 (C.A.).

be too remote from the doctor's actions to justify liability. This issue has arisen in a number of cases. In *Finlay v. Auld*[311] the Supreme Court of Canada held that a pre-existing disease, sarcoidosis, was the sole cause-in-fact of the plaintiff's injuries. The other case is a little different in that the action was based in part on the failure to treat.[312] The patient related to the doctor by telephone what seemed like innocuous symptoms, but it later developed that the condition was serious. The court held that there was no causal link established between the failure to treat and the injury suffered because a reasonable person in the doctor's position would not have foreseen the consequences.

In an Ontario case[313] the finding of the trial judge, accepted by the Court of Appeal, was that while two doctors who attended on a patient suffering from juvenile diabetes were negligent, they were "insulated from liability" by the negligence of a specialist who saw the patient later because his negligence was not foreseeable.

Trauma. Many of those who seek medical care have suffered trauma from an accident or some other cause. If the doctor is sued after rendering treatment, the court must determine whether the doctor's action was a contributing cause-in-fact of the injury complained of and, if so, whether his action was also a proximate cause. As stated previously,[314] there will be no liability unless both criteria are satisfied,[315] and again, the courts rarely state the basis of a holding that there has been no causal link.

In an early Nova Scotia case[316] a patient who had been run over by a coke trolley alleged that the doctor had severed a nerve in his leg. The trial judge held that the nerve was severed in the accident, and thus the doctor's actions were not the cause-in-fact of the nerve damage. In a more recent case[317] a patient seriously injured in a car accident tried to prove that he was capable of some body movement upon admission to hospital, but became paraplegic through medical negligence. The Court of Appeal agreed with the trial judge who found that the damage to his spinal cord was "complete and irreversible" prior to medical treatment.

---

311 *Supra* n. 247. *See Poulin v. Health Sciences Centre* (1982), 18 Man. R. (2d) 274 (Man. Q.B.), where the court said, *obiter,* that had the doctor been negligent it would have held the pre-existing arthritis to be the cause of the patient's damage.
312 *Cavan v. Wilcox* (1973), 44 D.L.R. (3d) 42 (N.B.C.A.); reversed (no appeal on this point) 2 N.R. 618 (S.C.C.); *Dale v. Munthali supra* n. 66.
313 *Yepremian v. Scarborough Gen. Hosp.* (1980), 110 D.L.R. (3d) 513 at 520-21, 546-47 (Ont. C.A.); *see also* Picard, *Comment* (1980), 14 C.C.L.T. 81.
314 *Cardin v. Montreal supra* n. 36 and *University Hosp. Bd. v. Lepine supra* n. 99 at 579-80.
315 *See generally* Linden, *supra* n. 38. See also *Lachambre v. Perreaulti Commission des Accidents du Travail de Quebec, Intervenante* (1983), 22 A.C.W.S. (2d) 94 (Que. C.A.).
316 *Zirkler v. Robinson supra* n. 175. A new trial was directed, since the trial judge found liability on an issue not put forward by the pleadings, namely, the failure to suture the nerve.
317 *Nash v. Olson,* [1982] B.C.D. Civ. 3392-01 (B.C.S.C.), appeal dismissed unreported March 1, 1984 No. CA820396 (B.C.C.A.).

The victim of what became a murder attended at the emergency department of an English hospital complaining of vomiting and malaise.[318] Receiving no treatment, he returned to his place of work and died of arsenic poisoning within six hours. In his widow's action against the doctor and the hospital, it was held that the failure to admit and treat the plaintiff was a breach of the standard of care, but that this negligence was not the cause of death because the required treatment could not have been administered in time even if the deceased had been admitted. Again, the negligence was not the cause-in-fact of the injury.

In *Gordon v. Davidson*[319] the medical evidence was divided on the cause of the necrosis of the patient's dorsal muscles with resulting loss of power to the toes, mid-foot and ankle. One view was that it was attributable to a snowmobile accident and the 1½ hours the victim spent in the snow, but the other was that it was the failure of the doctor to recognize the onset of the condition. In any case, the trial judge held that the doctor had met the standard of care and was not liable.

Another case involving failure to diagnose and improper treatment[320] concerned a patient who had previously been diagnosed as having "a moderately severe mitral stenosis, a narrowing of the opening of the valve which allows blood to come back from the lung to the left side of the heart." She was treated in an emergency department for apparently minor injuries sustained in a motor vehicle accident and released. In fact, the collision precipitated acute pulmonary edema, and she was re-admitted two hours later. For two hours until her death she was given incorrect and actually harmful treatment, but the court concluded:[321]

> The harmful procedures may have hastened the patient's death, but, if they did (upon which I express no opinion), they did not cause it. Death was the result of acute pulmonary edema and the edema was brought on by the collision. Mrs. Thompson would almost certainly have recovered if proper treatment had been applied speedily; the doctors failed to apply that treatment and so failed to save her life, but they did not cause her death.

At first this may appear to be a finding of no cause-in-fact, but it seems clear that the negligence was the cause-in-fact, and therefore the case is better regarded as a no-proximate-cause decision.

In a very unusual case[322] the accidental removal by a doctor of a woman's only kidney was held to be the cause-in-fact and the proximate cause of her father's loss of the kidney he chose to donate. The doctor admitted his liability to the daughter and was held by the court to be liable to the father because "given the disaster which befell [the daughter] it was entirely

---

318 *Barnett v. Chelsea & Kensington Hosp.*, [1968] 2 W.L.R. 422 (Q.B.).

319 (1980), 4 L. Med. Q. 131 (Ont. H.C.).

320 *Thompson v. Toorenburgh supra* n. 295.

321 *Id.* at 721.

322 *Urbanski v. Patel* (1978), 84 D.L.R. (3d) 650 (Man. Q.B.). Unfortunately the father's transplanted kidney was rejected by the daughter's body.

foreseeable that one of her family would be invited, and would agree, to donate a kidney for transplant . . . ''[323]

Thus the reasonable foreseeability test of proximate cause is flexible enough to allow compensation in a novel situation.[324]

B. Combined cause

There are some cases where the conclusion of the court is that there was more than one cause of the patient's injury.[325] This combined negligence may be of doctors[326] or of a hospital or its employees, such as a nurse or member of the house staff and a doctor[327] or even of a health care professional and a manufacturer.[328] Legislation in each province requires that in such cases the court determine the degree in which each person is negligent.[329] Then each is jointly and severally liable to the plaintiff and each is liable to make contribution and indemnify the other in the degree he is found at fault.[330]

For example, in *Meyer v. Gordon*[331] the hospital was found to be 75 per cent at fault for the negligence of nurse-employees and a doctor 25 per cent responsible for causing the patient's injuries. While the effect of the legislation is that either could be called upon by the patient to pay the total of her assessed damages, with that party left to seek the appropriate reimbursement from his fellow defendant, it is more likely that each party would pay his proportion of the damages to the plaintiff.

Where it is not possible to determine the degree of negligence between the defendants, they are deemed by legislation to be equally at fault.[332]

---

323 *Id.* at 671.

324 Note that the father was characterized as a "rescuer." For a critique of the case, *see* Robertson, *A New Application of the Rescue Principle* (1980), 96 L.Q.R. 19.

325 *See supra* discussion of cause-in-fact.

326 *Price v. Milawski* (1977), 82 D.L.R. (3d) 130 (Ont. C.A.); *Kangas v. Parker*, [1978] 5 W.W.R. 667 (Sask. C.A.), involving an anaesthetist and a dentist; *Sunne v. Shaw*, [1981] C.S. 609 (Que. S.C.), involving a dentist and a plastic surgeon. *See also Considine v. Camp Hill Hosp.* (1982), 133 D.L.R. (3d) 11 at 20 (N.S.T.D.), where the evidence was not clear as to which surgeon made the accidental "cut".

327 *Meyer v. Gordon* (1981), 17 C.C.L.T. 1 (B.C.S.C.); *Misericordia Hosp. v. Bustillo*, [1983] Alta. D. 2632-01 (Alta. C.A.), where the apportionment at trial of 87 1/2 per cent to the hospital and 12 1/2 per cent to the doctor was varied to 60 per cent and 40 per cent respectively; *Osburn v. Mohindra* (1980), 29 N.B.R. (2d) 340 (N.B.Q.B.); *Cosgrove v. Gaudreau* (1981), 33 N.B.R. (2d) 523 (N.B.Q.B.).

328 *Dunsmore v. Deshield* (1977), 80 D.L.R. (3d) 386 (Sask. Q.B.).

329 *See, for example,* Contributory Negligence Act, R.S.A. 1980, c. C-23; Negligence Act, R.S.O. 1980, c. 315.

330 Note *Dunsmore v. Deshield* (1977), 80 D.L.R. (3d) 386 at 390 (Sask. Q.B.), where the two defendants were held jointly and severally liable and then one defendant was ordered to indemnify the other for the entire judgment plus costs. For a discussion of indemnification *see* Klar, *Developments In Tort Law: The 1981-82 Term* (1983), 5 Sup. Ct. L.R. 273 at 287.

331 *Supra* n. 327.

332 *See supra* n. 329; *Price v. Milawski supra* n. 326; *Kangas v. Parker supra* n. 326; *Sunne v. Shaw supra* n. 326. Note that in the U.S. case of *Sindell v. Abbott Laboratories* (1980), 607

Injuries from a non-medical accident and from a doctor's negligence may combine to cause the patient's ultimate loss. When this happens, the courts attempt to delineate the consequences of the two causes and hold the doctor liable only for the loss caused by his negligence. This is so whether the negligent treatment precedes or follows the accident, so a surgeon was held liable only for severing a nerve and not for the reflex sympathetic syndrome resulting from the plaintiff's accidents,[333] and a general practitioner was held liable only for the difference between moderate and minimal muscle loss of a leg where it was found that the accident would have caused the plaintiff the lesser injury.[334] Placing a dollar value on the doctor's portion of such losses is very difficult.

The court's attempts to attribute cause to the proper source are well illustrated by the cases in which the patient has complained of disease or trauma following non-negligent medical care. Injury which followed proper treatment of a dislocation was attributed to the patient rather than the doctor,[335] as was the occurrence of a pelvic disease following the non-negligent removal of an intrauterine contraceptive device.[336] Similarly, a second disc extrusion was held to be the cause of the patient's need for a second operation, rather than the first operation.[337]

Two possibilites exist when the patient is the victim of a tortfeasor, for example, a negligent motor vehicle operator. If the medical treatment administered is not negligent, but does cause further injury, the original tortfeasor is liable for the entire loss, since medical treatment is a foreseeable consequence of injuring another.[338] However, if the medical treatment is negligent, the plaintiff must sue both the original tortfeasor and the doctor.[339] This situation is referred to as one of *novus actus interveniens*; that is, it is said that the chain of causation between the original tortfeasor's conduct and the plaintiff's

---

P. (2d) 924 (Cal. S.C.), the court found liability against a number of drug manufacturers in proportion to their share of the market. For a comment, *see* Irvine, *Annotation* (1980), 14 C.C.L.T. 252; Downey and Gulley, *Theories of Recovery for DES Damage* (1983), 4 J. Legal Med. 167.

333 *McKeachie v. Alvarez supra* n. 62.

334 *Park v. Stevenson Memorial Hosp.* (1974), unreported (Ont. H.C.) Holland J.

335 *Stamper v. Rhindress* (1906), 41 N.S.R. 45 (C.A.).

336 *Mudrie v. McDonald supra* n. 308.

337 *Lepp v. Hopp supra* n. 64.

338 *Papp v. LeClerc* (1977), 77 D.L.R. (3d) 536 (Ont. C.A.); *Mercer v. Gray*, [1941] O.R. 127 (C.A.); *Winteringham v. Rae supra* n. 296; *Watson v. Grant* (1970), 72 W.W.R. 665 (B.C.S.C.); *Thompson v. Toorenburgh* (1972), 29 D.L.R. (3d) 608; affirmed 50 D.L.R. (3d) 717 (B.C.C.A.); *Robinson v. Post Office supra* n. 296; *Robinson v. Englot*, [1949] 2 W.W.R. 1137 (Man. K.B.).

339 If the victim sues only the original tortfeasor he may third party another such as a doctor or dentist; *see Katzman v. Yaeck; Silverman, Third Party* (1982), 136 D.L.R. (3d) 536 (Ont. C.A.). For a case involving a doctor as the first tortfeasor *see Price v. Milawski supra* n. 149.

injury has been broken by the intervening act of a third party, in this case the doctor. In the United States, the original tortfeasor is held liable for the total loss in such situations,[340] and the plaintiff is not placed in the undesirable position of having to sue more than once. A similar move in Canadian law would find support in the remarks of an Ontario trial court[341] where it was said than an original tortfeasor may be responsible for the subsequent negligence of a doctor or hospital unless it is "outside the range of normal experience." This seems to imply that some negligent medical treatment is foreseeable, and some is not, and since such a determination would be extremely difficult, if not impossible, the present Canadian approach where each tortfeasor bears the burden of the loss he has caused seems preferable.[342]

As can be seen from this discussion, the causal link between the defendant's breach of the standard of care and the plaintiff's injury may be a complex series of permutations and combinations of events. Prudent parties to litigation endeavour to prove or disprove as suits their case and as the legal standard of proof requires. The task of the judge in such cases is not enviable. Along with justice and reason, judgments should reflect common sense and the values of society as Mr. Justice Clement of the Alberta Court of Appeal stated:[343]

> The common law has always recognized that causation is a concept that in the end result must be limited in its reach by a pragmatic consideration of consequences: the chain of cause and effect can be followed only to the point where the consequences of an act will be fairly accepted as attributable to that act in the context of social and economic conditions then prevailing and the reasonable expectations of members of the society in the conduct of each other.

3.   DUTIES AND ATTENDANT STANDARDS OF CARE

The most common components of the doctor's duty of care to his patient are the duty to attend, diagnose, refer, treat and instruct. It is impossible to state in the abstract what course of action will be negligent and therefore the scope of the standard of care involved in the discharge of each of these duties will be analyzed with reference to the case law.

(a)   The Duty to Attend

As has been discussed,[344] while a doctor is under no legal duty to treat a patient, once he undertakes to do so, certain legal consequences follow.

---

340 *Thompson v. Fox* (1937), 192 A. 107 (Pa. S.C.).
341 *Kolesar v. Jeffries* (1974), 9 O.R. (2d) 41; varied 12 O.R. (2d) 142; affirmed on other grounds (*sub nom, Joseph Brant Memorial Hosp. v. Koziol*) 2 C.C.L.T. 170 (S.C.C.) with no ruling on this point. *See also* Fleming, *supra* n. 62 at 197-98.
342 *See* Picard, *Informed Consent Takes Shape* (1983), 24 C.C.L.T. 250 at 251. For a contrary opinion *see* Linden, *supra* n. 38 at 393.
343 *Abbot v. Kasza*, [1976] 4 W.W.R. 20 at 28 (Alta. C.A.). *See also* Linden, *supra* n. 38 at 354-58.
344 *See supra* Chapter 1 and s. 2(a) of this Chapter.

Assuming that the doctor-patient relationship has been formed, what is the scope of the duty to attend a patient?

The doctor will be held to have failed to meet his duty to attend only if it leads to injury or damage to the patient. He may be infamous among his colleagues for his lack of diligence in attending on his patients in hospital, or among his patients for his failure to keep office appointments or return calls, yet there will be no liability if this unprofessional and substandard conduct falls short of causing foreseeable injury to the patient.

If it appears that a patient has been injured, reference will be had to the relevant standard of care in the circumstances. The court will consider the urgency of the request, the nature of the condition described, the alternatives available and the other commitments the doctor may have. Each case will depend upon its own circumstances.[345]

A patient being treated by his doctor for pneumonia was given an injection in the arm which became bruised, swollen, cold to touch and very painful. Early the following morning the patient's wife telephoned[346] the doctor, who suggested warm compresses and said that he would see the patient the next day. Gangrene set in and the patient required amputation of his fingers and thumb, and sued both the doctor and nurse who administered the shot. It was found that the bicillin injected had "found its way into the circumflex artery," but the nurse was not held negligent. The Court of Appeal[347] also said that the doctor was not negligent in failing to attend on his patient after receiving the information that the arm was bruised and painful, because from the condition described there appeared no urgency and an examination had been set for a reasonable time after the call.[348]

Another decision[349] has raised the possibility that such a call would require the doctor at least to make inquiries where the information given was scanty. Since the doctor is in the best position to know what symptoms would be a cause for concern, it seems appropriate to expect him to ask questions where the information received is scanty or vague. If he is in any doubt, the cautious and, it would seem, fairly standard practice is to have the patient attend at a hospital emergency department forthwith or at his office if appropriate.

A child who was ill with fever and stomach pains was taken to the same hospital emergency department on two consecutive days and examined but not admitted on both occasions. She was finally admitted at another hospital and an operation was performed. However, she became a quadriplegic.[350] The

---

345 *Smith v. Rae* (1919), 46 O.L.R. 518 (C.A.); Nathan, *supra* n. 24 at 42.

346 A common method of requesting attendance; Meredith, *supra* n. 10 at 70.

347 *Cavan v. Wilcox supra* n. 312; affirmed regarding the nurse; regarding the doctor, no appeal from the dismissal in the Appellate Division.

348 *See also, Bissell v. Vancouver Gen. Hosp.*, [1979] 2 A.C.W.S. 433 (B.C.S.C.).

349 *Dale v. Munthali supra* n. 66.

350 *Mumford v. Children's Hosp. of Winnipeg*, [1977] 1 W.W.R. 666 (Man. C.A.).

case was heard on an application to extend the limitation period, which was denied, and so the matter never came to trial. If it had done so, one issue would have been the duty of the first doctor to attend by admitting the child.

In an English case[351] the doctor on duty in emergency was found to have been negligent by failing to examine or admit a patient with symptoms of what turned out to be arsenic poisoning, but because no causal link between that negligence and the patient's death was made out no liability was found.

When a patient presents himself or is brought to emergency the request for care should be presumed to be urgent in spite of the fact that emergency departments are sometimes misused by some patients. It should be remembered that it takes little for the doctor-patient relationship, the basis of legal duty, to be created.[352]

An early Saskatchewan case[353] illustrates that if alternate medical care is available a doctor is justified in assuming that a patient who says that he will pursue it, will do so. A doctor was returning from a professional visit to a remote area when the patient's husband called him because the patient was in early labour. Shortly after his arrival she was delivered of a three to four months' fetus. The doctor did the best he could with the equipment he had, but a portion of the placenta remained in the uterus. The court accepted his testimony that the patient said she would come into the hospital for further treatment and held that he was entitled to rely on her commitment to attend to her own health by consulting her family doctor. In fact, he had out of interest inquired of her family doctor and at the hospital regarding her condition, and she was not successful in her suit against the doctor for negligent treatment.

A doctor's other responsibilities are relevant to the question of when he must attend on his patient.[354] A doctor who was notified by a husband of an expectant mother about 7:30 p.m. that the patient was in labour, advised him that because of other patients he could not attend before 8:30 p.m. The husband acquiesced, saying that the attending nurse believed that the child would arrive at about 11:00 or 12:00 p.m. As it happened the child was born dead by 8:20. Holding that the doctor was not negligent, the court said:[355]

> I do not think that the plaintiff is right in the contention that when a doctor undertakes to attend a case of this description he thereby undertakes to drop all other matters in hand to attend the patient instantly upon receiving a notification. *The doctor must, having regard to all circumstances, act reasonably.* Here the first message received did not indicate any urgency. It was a request for him to call some time during the evening, and the message

---

351 *Barnett v. Chelsea & Kensington Hosp. supra* n. 318. For a discussion of other English cases, *see* Jackson & Powell, *Professional Negligence* (1982), 227-28.

352 *See supra* Chapter 1. For a discussion of the creation of a relationship arising from a statute *see Simpson v. Local Bd. of Health of Belleville supra* n. 310.

353 *Hampton v. Macadam supra* n. 132.

354 *Smith v. Rae supra* n. 345; Nathan, *supra* n. 24 at 42.

355 *Smith v. Rae id.* at 522.

received from the husband did not then indicate any extreme urgency. The doctor had other patients who had some claim upon his time and attention. Had he been given to understand that the plaintiff's situation was critical, undoubtedly he should, and I think he would, have dropped everything and gone to her assistance; but in view of the information that he had, I do not think it would possibly be said that he acted negligently or unreasonably. [emphasis supplied]

A plastic surgeon who was "out of town" during part of his patient's convalescence was said to have been perhaps unwise but definitely not negligent. Mr. Justice Linden said:[356]

Although it is certainly disconcerting for a patient to learn that her doctor will not be personally available during her entire convalescence, this is not negligence as long as adequate alternative arrangements are made, as was done here. Doctors are human, too, and they are entitled to attend conferences and take vacations, as long as appropriate steps are taken to see that a competent substitute is available to their patients during their absence.

An extreme case of failure to attend a patient in hospital is *Vail v. MacDonald*[357] where, after a closed reduction of a fracture, a general surgeon showed no concern regarding the patient's condition in spite of being alerted to it by the nursing staff. He neither consulted another doctor, prescribed medication, nor took any other steps to remedy the apparent circulatory problem until it was too late. His attendance on the patient was described by the Court of Appeal as "casual",[358] and by the Supreme Court of Canada as "neglect".[359] "Incredible" was the conclusion of a Nova Scotia court[360] when a urologist did not attend on his patient at all prior to performing major surgery on him. Hospital record-keeping practices and monitoring committees have an important role in setting standards in regard to the doctor's attendance upon and care of hospitalized patients.

These cases have shown that no rigid principles can be set down about the duty to attend. Some important factors have been identified and examples of conduct related, but the most that can be said is that the doctor must act reasonably, having regard to all circumstances.[361]

---

356 *White v. Turner* (1981), 15 C.C.L.T. 81 at 105 (Ont. H.C.); appeal dismissed 20 C.C.L.T. xxii (Ont. C.A.). For a case where alternative arrangements were "just about non-existent," *see Videto v. Kennedy* (1980), 107 D.L.R. (3d) 612 at 616 (Ont. H.C.); affirmed on this issue 17 C.C.L.T. 307 (Ont. C.A.).
357 *Supra* n. 52.
358 (1973), 41 D.L.R. (3d) 321 at 348.
359 *Supra* n. 52 at 531.
360 *Considine v. Camp Hill Hosp.* (1982), 133 D.L.R. (3d) 11 at 39 (N.S.T.D.). Note, however, that the plaintiff's action was dismissed as the causation issue was not proven.
361 *Smith v. Rae supra* n. 345.

(b) The Duty to Diagnose

Once the doctor has taken a person as a patient, he is under a duty to make a diagnosis[362] and to advise the patient of it.[363] If he cannot come to a diagnosis he has a duty to refer the patient to others who can.[364] The duty is not as onerous as it might seem; a doctor is not bound at his peril to make no mistake, although he is expected to exercise reasonable care, skill and judgment in coming to a diagnosis. If he does so he will not be held liable[365] if mistaken. Thus a mistaken diagnosis is not necessarily a negligent one because the doctor may have met the standard of care required of him when making it. The best judicial statement of this appears in an English authority:[366]

> . . . no human being is infallible; and in the present state of science even the most eminent specialist may be at fault in detecting the true nature of a diseased condition. A practitioner can only be held liable in this respect if his diagnosis is so palpably wrong as to prove negligence, that is to say, if his mistake is of such a nature as to imply an absence of reasonable skill and care on his part, regard being had to the ordinary level of skill in the profession.

A number of cases have commented on the care, skill and judgment to be exercised by a doctor when formulating his diagnosis.[367] In one case[368] a patient suffering from severe headache, nausea, dizziness, numbness and photophobia was diagnosed in 15 minutes by a doctor employed in an emergency ward[369] as having "migrainous headaches plus nervous overtone." In fact he was in the early stages of a subarachnoid hemorrhage, and some days later a recurrence caused his death. The court found liability for a misdiagnosis.[370]

> In my opinion the cases have established that an erroneous diagnosis does not alone determine the physician's liability. But if the physician, as an aid to diagnosis, does not *avail himself of the scientific means and facilities* open to him for the collection of the best

---

362 Defined as "the determination of the nature of a case or disease" — *Dorland's Illustrated Medical Dictionary*, W. B. Saunders, Philadelphia, 25th ed. (1974).

363 *Reibl v. Hughes* (1980), 14 C.C.L.T. 1 (S.C.C.); *Barr v. Hughes* (1982), 14 A.C.W.S. (2d) 112 (B.C.S.C.).

364 *See infra.*

365 *Gibbons v. Harris supra* n. 93; *Penner v. Theobald supra* n. 93; *Dale v. Munthali supra* n. 66.

366 Nathan, *supra* n. 24 at 57 referring to *Mitchell v. Dixon,* [1914] A.D. 519 (S. Africa C.A.).

367 For a discussion of some interesting English cases, *see* Jackson & Powell, *Professional Negligence* (1982), 228-30.

368 *Wade v. Nayernouri* (1978), 2 L. Med. Q. 67 (Ont. H.C.).

369 It is worth noting that many of the actions for misdiagnosis are against doctors involved in out-patient or emergency care.

370 *Supra* n. 368 at 16. *See also Piche v. Ing,* unreported (1983), 22 A.C.W.S. (2d) 297 (Ont. H.C.) where an ophthalmologist was liable for a failure to diagnose a detached retina in an examination that took "a couple of minutes". *See also Bergen v. Sturgeon Gen. Hospital* unreported Feb. 6, 1984 No. 8003-03036 (Alta. Q.B.).

factual data upon which to arrive at his diagnosis, does not accurately obtain the patient's *history*, does not avail himself in this particular case of the need for *referral* to a neurologist, does not perform the stiff neck tests and the lumbar punctive *test*, the net result is not an error in judgement but constitutes negligence. [emphasis supplied]

Thus, a thorough history, appropriate tests and possibly consultations are clearly basic to a proper diagnosis, but a reasonable doctor should also heed a patient's complaints during treatment for they may be harbingers of change in his condition.[371]

While it may be possible to identify some of the steps to be taken in exercising reasonable care and skill, determining whether a misdiagnosis is the result of breach of the standard or only an error of judgment is not easy. This difficulty flows from the important role played by medical judgment. As one court put it:[372]

Diagnosis is, above all, an exercise of the physician's judgement based on his training, experience and, perhaps, intuition.

In that case the medical judgment of an orthopaedic surgeon was that a laceration and a fracture suffered by a soccer player were unrelated and so he used a closed reduction of the fracture. In fact, the patient had suffered a compound fracture requiring an open reduction. The court held that the doctor had chosen to make his judgment before exploring the wound and its relationship to the fracture. He was liable to the patient who lost his leg because of a gas gangrene infection. In another case[373] involving a judgment call a gynaecologist did a tubal ligation on a patient who afterwards suffered abdominal distension which eventually was diagnosed by a second doctor to be caused by a damaged ureter. The evidence was that although the doctor had missed the correct diagnosis, he had exercised reasonable care, skill and judgment in both the surgery and the post-surgical treatment and was not negligent. Perhaps all that a court can do is analyze whether the available "scientific means and facilities" were used with the intelligence, concern and judgment expected of a reasonably competent doctor.

Probably the best known case of liability for misdiagnosis is that of *Vancouver Gen. Hosp. v. Fraser*[374] where two interns in the emergency department examined an accident victim, misinterpreted his x-rays and sent the patient home, missing the diagnosis of a dislocated fracture of the neck. Upon analysis, it seems that their skill at reading x-rays and their judgments in ignoring the patient's complaints were inadequate because of inexperience.

---

371 *Osburn v. Mohindra* (1980), 29 N.B.R. (2d) 340 at 347 (N.B.Q.B.); *Hajgato v. London Health Assn.* (1982), 36 O.R. (2d) 669 at 674-76 (Ont. H.C.); *Rietze v. Bruser*, [1979] 1 W.W.R. 31 at 41 (Man. Q.B.); *Layden v. Cope*, [1984] A.W.L.D. 321 (Q.B.).

372 *Dean v. York County Hosp. Corp.* (1979), 3 L. Med. Q. 231 at 238 (Ont. H.C.); *see also Gordon v. Davidson* (1980), 4 L. Med. Q. 131 at 144 (Ont. H.C.).

373 *Hobson v. Munkley* (1976), 1 C.C.L.T. 163 (Ont. H.C.).

374 *Fraser v. Vancouver Gen. Hosp. supra* n. 84 and *Hôpital Notre Dame de l'Esperance v. Laurent*, [1978] 1 S.C.R. 605.

The answer, and the court so held, would have been to refer the case to the specialist on call for assistance in diagnosis.

A doctor missed a "text book" diagnosis in an early Saskatchewan case.[375] The symptoms, the experts said, were clearly of "an abscess in the lumbar region" (an abscess of the kidney from a stone in it), but the doctor diagnosed "rheumatism of the sciatic nerve or neuritis", and was held liable for failing to meet his standard of care in diagnosis. The patient suffered under this misdiagnosis for over a month, and the judge remarked:[376]

> When a medical man finds that his treatment, after fair trial, does not assist the patient, one wonders that he is not willing to nobly admit defeat and advise the calling in of someone who may be more expert. Such a course would not, it seems to me, be at all humiliating, and in any event no man with a proper appreciation of the value of human life should hesitate for a moment to adopt it.

Clearly, discharging the duty to diagnose sometimes means admitting defeat and seeking assistance.

However, of the reported cases, far more tell of doctors exonerated than held liable. Perhaps the best known Canadian case is the often quoted *Wilson v. Swanson*[377] where a surgeon made a diagnosis of cancer prior to an operation and during surgery received a pathologist's report that confirmed the probability. On the basis of this diagnosis, he proceeded to do radical surgery. The diagnosis was wrong, and the plaintiff brought action alleging that further tests ought to have been done. The Supreme Court of Canada[378] disagreed, because the tests suggested would not have been any surer a guide to the exercise of judgment than those upon which the surgeon relied. In an English case[379] with similar facts it was held not to be negligence to misdiagnose cancer although the use of a diagnostic tool rare in England would have enabled a more certain diagnosis.

A patient suffering from pain, weakness, menstrual abnormality and a mass in the uterus submitted to an exploratory operation performed by her family doctor and a gynaecologist.[380] They had misdiagnosed her condition

---

375 *Turriff v. King supra* n. 177. *See also Bergen v. Sturgeon Gen. Hosp*, unreported Feb. 6, 1984, No. 8003-03036 (Alta. Q.B.), where three doctors seeing a patient over a period of $4^1/_2$ days in a modern urban hospital failed to diagnose appendicitis. *But see Osburn v. Mohindra* (1980), 29 N.B.R. (2d) 340 at 346 (N.B.Q.B.), where liability was found for a failure to diagnose a dislocated lunate in the wrist which medical textbooks described as "commonly overlooked."

376 *Id.* at 678.

377 [1956] S.C.R. 804. See also *Lefebvre v. Osborne* (1983), 22 A.C.W.S. (2d) 350 (Ont. H.C.). *But see Down v. Royal Jubilee Hosp.* (1981), 24 B.C.L.R. 296 (B.C.S.C.), where a doctor admitted negligence in diagnosing cancer of the breast which led to a mastectomy.

378 The Court of Appeal (1956), 2 D.L.R. (2d) 193 had agreed with the plaintiff.

379 *Whiteford v. Hunter supra* n. 153; *see supra* s. 2(b)(ii)c. of this chapter. *See also Pudney v. Union-Castle Mail S.S. Co.*, [1953] 1 Lloyd's Rep. 73 (Q.B.).

380 *Finlay v. Hess* (1973), 44 D.L.R. (3d) 507 (Ont. H.C.); *see Bickford v. Stiles* (1981), 128 D.L.R. (3d) 516 (N.B.Q.B.), where exploratory surgery was done in an endeavour to eliminate a diagnosis such as cancer or tuberculosis; *see also Strachan v. Simpson* (1979), 10 C.C.L.T. 145 (B.C.S.C.); *Reibl v. Hughes* (1980), 14 C.C.L.T. 1 (S.C.C.).

(she was pregnant and later had a normal child). She brought action, but the court relied on expert evidence that her symptoms could have indicated an ectopic pregnancy, a fibroid tumour or ovarian cancer, and pointed out that an error in diagnosis does not mean an error in medical judgment.

Another case[381] did not end so happily for the patient whose symptoms were tiredness, dizziness, frequent urination accompanied by burning and difficulty in breathing and walking. She died of a "hemorrhage in the lower brain stem and upper cervical cord from an unknown cause." The court held that the doctor's diagnosis of hysteria was consistent with her symptoms at the time of the examination. The fact that another doctor might have made a different finding or that a blood test would have indicated a possible platelet defect did not fix the doctor with negligence.

A doctor engaged to look after workers at a camp in 1927 diagnosed skin eruptions as the after-effects of influenza or as erythema.[382] Later, a health officer diagnosed them as mild cases of smallpox with an unusual rash, but expert evidence indicated that without the appearance of a typical lesion, smallpox is difficult to diagnose, and the court held the doctor not liable. A doctor in 1960 diagnosed a child's condition as an acute upper respiratory infection.[383] Her condition deteriorated and she suffered a convulsion followed by cessation of breathing and serious brain damage. Experts examining the symptoms in retrospect could not agree on the diagnosis or cause of the child's injury. Two agreed it was probably encephalitis with a degree of epiglottitis, while another thought it was due to epiglottitis alone. All agreed that epiglottitis, then a rare disease, would not have been known in 1960 to a general practitioner, and the defendant's diagnosis and follow-up care was held to have met the standard expected of him.

By 1973 epiglottitis was described as a well-known disease of a "treacherous nature" requiring the diagnosis of even "a high risk of suspicion" of its possible presence.[384] A surgeon working in an emergency department failed to diagnose the condition in a patient who died of it. He was found liable. His explanation for his substandard care was overwork (100 patients in a busy period) and the common nature of the complaint of a sore throat. But this was not considered persuasive in the face of his admission that although he was not busy at the time, he had examined the patient in just over two minutes using only a tongue depressor and a flashlight when a laryngeal mirror was available and the patient had complained of difficulty in breathing and swallowing.

---

381 *Serre v. de Tilly supra* n. 295.

382 *Hamilton v. Phoenix Lbr. Co.*, [1931] 1 W.W.R. 43 (Alta. C.A.).

383 *Tiesmaki v. Wilson supra* n. 46.

384 *Demoura v. Mississauga Hosp.* (1979), 3 L. Med. Q. 215 at 218 (Ont. S.C.): *see also Moffatt v. Witelson* (1980), 111 D.L.R. (3d) 712 (Ont. H.C.), where an ophthalmologist was held liable for failing to diagnose "one of the greatest dangers" of the patient's injury, namely an infection.

A general practitioner escaped liability in 1964 for failing to diagnose carbon monoxide poisoning.[385] His diagnosis was influenza, which was prevalent at the time, and the court held that in all the circumstances, the doctor could not have been expected to detect an odourless, deadly gas, in spite of the fact that a specialist and the chief coroner were definitely of the opinion that the doctor should have considered carbon monoxide poisoning. Another general practitioner also testified saying that he had rarely seen such cases. A doctor who[386] failed to diagnose mastoiditis was chastised by the court which said that he was not prudent in stating so confidently that there was no mastoid trouble when he was unable to make a diagnosis. He was, however, held to have met the requisite standard of care. It was also suggested that he might have admitted defeat and called in a specialist although that time there was found to be no duty to do so.[387]

In a case from Nova Scotia[388] a general practitioner after a ten minute examination of an obese, diabetic patient complaining of chest and stomach pain and nausea diagnosed gastritis but the patient died from a myocardial infarction within one hour of leaving the doctor's office. Although the doctor did not check the patient's pulse, heart, or blood pressure she was found not liable. The judge said that the diagnosis of gastritis was correct and the failure to diagnose the heart disease was not negligence.

In an Ontario case, a doctor's diagnosis of gastroenteritis where the patient had meningitis was held not negligent at trial,[389] in spite of his failure to test for what the experts testified were two classic symptoms: headache and stiff neck. The trial court found that these were either absent or not reported to him and found his diagnosis to be proper, but held him liable for his failure to hospitalize a very sick man. The Court of Appeal[390] concurred in the result but interpreted the trial judge as meaning that it was negligent to arrive at a diagnosis without the "further testing and probing" possible in a hospital. The evidence indicated that when the doctor saw the patient, there were symptoms more severe than those associated with a viral infection. The doctor had also been alerted to the fact that the patient had no spleen which, according to the evidence, is a condition rendering a patient more vulnerable to the disease. Yet the doctor neither carried out the simple tests nor inquired about headache. Furthermore, his scanty notes included only the patient's name, health care number and the incorrect diagnosis.

---

385 *Ostash v. Sonnenberg supra* n. 49.

386 *Jarvis v. Int. Nickel Co. supra* n. 68.

387 There is now a duty to refer. *See infra.*

388 *Ehler v. Smith* (1978), 29 N.S.R. (2d) 309 (N.S.T.D.); *see also Athansious v. Guzman,* unreported Oct. 4, 1977 No. 37190/75 (B.C.S.C.).

389 *Dale v. Munthali* (1977), 16 O.R. (2d) 532 (Ont. H.C.). *See also Sadler v. Henry,* [1954] 1 Brit. Med. J. 1331; *Vachon v. Moffett* (1911), 40 S.C. 166 (Que.).

390 *Dale v. Munthali* (1978), 21 O.R. (2d) 554 at 557 (Ont. C.A.).

A doctor's role in diagnosis cannot be just a passive one. Within reason, if simple tests are indicated they should be carried out and if certain symptoms could be critical they should be canvassed.

A Manitoba judge, in holding an orthopaedic surgeon liable when a patient developed a serious complication after surgery, said:[391]

> It is not sufficient, in my view, for a medical practitioner to say, "Of the two or three probable diagnoses I have chosen diagnosis A over diagnosis B or C." It must be expected that the practitioner would choose diagnosis A over B or C because *all* of the facts available to that practitioner and *all* of the methods available to check the accuracy of those facts and that diagnosis have been exercised, with the result that diagnosis A remains as the most *probable* of all. For example, if there were symptoms of persistent pain and puffiness associated with a limb encased in a cast and if that cast was split in an attempt to eliminate the cast as the source and cause of pain and puffiness, then if the symptoms of pain and puffiness still persisted an alternative procedure or check would be indicated to determine an alternate cause.

Even specialists, who have to meet a higher standard, may not be liable for a failure to diagnose.[392] An orthopaedic surgeon who diagnosed a "slipped disc" and operated was satisfied that the operation was successful and that the patient would be relieved of his prior symptoms. Recovery was not as expected, however, and a second operation was performed by a neurosurgeon who discovered "a large chunk of extruded disc material" in the area. The patient sued the orthopaedic surgeon for failure to diagnose, locate and remove this material in the first operation. The evidence left some doubt as to whether the extrusion found in the second operation was present during the first but the trial judge held that even if it was, the doctor as a specialist had met his standard of care in the diagnosis and surgery. Regarding the diagnosis, he had examined the patient, tested extensively and arrived at a reasonable diagnosis. As an Ontario court said in holding that another orthopaedic surgeon had met the required standard of care:[393]

> No human being is infallible and in the present state of science even the most eminent specialist may err in detecting the true nature of these conditions.

The tests that a doctor is expected to carry out are only those in common practice.[394] A doctor in 1932 was held not liable for missing the diagnosis of a dislocated shoulder. All of the normal tests were consistent with his diagnosis of sprain but an unusual congential defect in the patient led to the incorrect diagnosis. An x-ray would have exposed the problem but was not in common use and was expensive for the patient, and the doctor's failure to use it was not negligence.

---

391 *Rietze v. Bruser*, [1979] 1 W.W.R. 31 at 47 (Man. Q.B.); *see also Legault-Bellemare v. Madore*, [1975] C.S. 1249 (Que. S.C.).

392 *Lepp v. Hopp supra* n. 64.

393 *Hajgato v. London Health Assn.* (1982), 36 O.R. (2d) 669 (Ont. H.C.).

394 *Moore v. Large supra* n. 27.

Where there is no justification for a test it should not be done. Two specialists involved in doing a "package" health program of executives were liable when a patient died as a result of an allergic reaction to the contrast medium used in a pyelogram done as a "routine test" without any clinical indications for it.[395]

In summary, the duty to diagnose requires a doctor to take a full history, use appropriate tests and consult or refer if necessary. He must take reasonable care to detect signs and symptoms and formulate a diagnosis using good judgment. He cannot act only on what he is told; nor ignore what he is told. Sophisticated tests and continuing knowledge of disease must be employed when appropriate. His skill and judgment must be in step with that of his colleagues but need not be in advance of theirs, and if he meets this standard of care in the circumstances he will not be held liable to a patient injured by his misdiagnosis.

(c) The Duty to Refer

Recognizing that no person is infallible nor master of all knowledge and skill, the Supreme Court of Canada has said there is a duty upon a doctor in some circumstances to refer a patient to another doctor.[396] The term "refer" may mean either that the doctor confer with a colleague and then carry on treatment himself, or that the patient is passed completely into the care of another doctor.[397]

There is no absolute test to ascertain when a doctor should refer or consult, but the cases suggest that it is indicated when:[398]

i) the doctor is unable to diagnose the patient's condition;[399]

ii) the patient is not responding to the treatment being given;[400]

iii) the patient needs treatment which the doctor is not competent to give;[401]

---

395 *Leonard v. Knott,* [1980] 1 W.W.R. 673 (B.C.C.A.).

396 *Vail v. MacDonald supra* n. 52; *Ares v. Venner,* [1970] S.C.R. 608. Earlier authority to the contrary, namely, *Jarvis v. Int. Nickel Co. supra* n. 68 is overruled. *See also* Nathan, *supra* n. 24 at 46; Sherman, *supra* n. 39; Fiscina, *Duty to Consult* (1983), 11 Legal Aspects of Med. Practice 6.

397 *Beninger v. Walton,* [1979] B.C.D. Civ. 2632-02 (B.C.S.C.).

398 *Chipps v. Peters supra* n. 76.

399 *See supra* n. 396.

400 *Osburn v. Mohindra* (1980), 29 N.B.R. (2d) 340 (N.B.Q.B.); *Turriff v. King supra* n. 177; *Layden v. Cope,* [1984] A.W.L.D. 321 (Q.B.).

401 *Bell v. R. supra* n. 135; *Kunitz v. Merei,* [1969] 2 O.R. 572 (H.C.). *See also* Canadian Medical Protective Association, *Annual Report 1976* at 13 where it is stated: "Do only the work for which you are trained; refer work you cannot or should not do to someone who can." Magnet, *Withholding Treatment From Defective Newborns: Legal Aspects* (1982), 42 R. du B. 187 at 256.

iv) the doctor has a duty to guard against his own inexperience (e.g. the student doctor); or[402]

v) the doctor cannot continue to treat a patient (e.g. while on vacation).[403]

A critical factor in the duty to refer is the timing. How soon must the counsel of a colleague be sought? In a large hospital or an urban setting this step may be simply and expeditiously taken. Indeed, in a large teaching hospital it will be common. However, a rural general practitioner may have to balance many factors such as his ability, available equipment and facilities, the patient's prognosis, the distances involved and the effect of a move on the patient before sending the patient to another doctor.[404] Nonetheless, advice and the opportunity to collaborate with a colleague can be achieved quickly by telephone. The cases indicate that the courts realize that it is easy to be wise after the fact and so long as the referral is made within a reasonable time no liability has followed. In a case where the patient had polyps removed by an otolaryngologist, there was extensive bleeding and 24 hours later her eye was swollen, bruised and bulging. The next day it was worse and the patient complained of loss of sight so the doctor referred her to an ophthalmologist but he could not see her for six hours. One expert testified he would have acted on the symptoms more promptly but the otolaryngologist was held not liable for the permanent loss of vision in the eye.[405] On the other hand, a surgeon who failed to confer for 20 days while his patient showed clear signs of circulatory impairment was held liable for a failure to refer[406] as were general practitioners who failed to refer after serious symptoms had persisted for two days.[407]

Overlaps between the limits of professional competence cause difficulties for the courts who must depend on expert evidence to set the boundaries.[408] In a case[409] where a general surgeon removed a patient's uterus and did "repair work to improve her bladder condition and stop the protrusion of her organs," the patient argued that she should have been referred to a gynaecologist.

402 *Fraser v. Vancouver Gen. Hosp. supra* n. 84; *Daoust v. R.,* [1969] D.R.S. 594 (Ex. C.C.).

403 *Wilson v. Stark supra* n. 51; *White v. Turner* (1981), 15 C.C.L.T. 81 at 105 (Ont. H.C.); affirmed 20 C.C.L.T. xxii (Ont. C.A.); *Re Lesk,* [1947] 3 D.L.R. 326 (B.C.S.C.); *Bergstrom v. G.,* [1967] C.S. 513 (Que. S.C.).

404 *Harquail v. Sedgwick* (1982), 14 A.C.W.S. (2d) 47 (Ont. H.C.); *see Zimmer v. Ringrose* (1981), 16 C.C.L.T. 51 at 63 (Alta. C.A.), where the court said a reasonable doctor would have referred his patient to a city hospital for an abortion, not to the United States.

405 *Kunitz v. Merei supra* n. 401; *see also Bell v. R. supra* n. 135.

406 *Vail v. MacDonald supra* n. 52.

407 *Thomas v. Port Colborne* (1982), 12 A.C.W.S. (2d) 535 (Ont. H.C.), with respect to paralysis of leg; *Eaglebach v. Walters,* unreported 19 June 1974 No. 22494/71 (B.C.S.C.), with respect to head injuries.

408 *See, for example, Gordon v. Davidson* (1980), 4 L. Med. Q. 131 at 141 (Ont. S.C.).

409 *Chipps v. Peters supra* n. 76.

The trial judge and the Court of Appeal were not in accord, however, because of the equivocal nature of the expert evidence as indicated by these words:[410]

> While it is true that a surgical procedure such as that undertaken here would not have been carried out by a general surgeon in the major teaching hospitals in Toronto and London, but would have been performed by a specialist in gynaecology, nevertheless the evidence did not go so far as to establish that the surgery was beyond the sphere of the competence of a general surgeon. Indeed there was evidence to the contrary. Dr. Morgan, who is a specialist of the highest qualification, and whose extensive responsibilities include the training of general surgeons insofar as procedures in gynaecological matters are concerned, established that there is a role for the general surgeon in this field, and that surgery such as that in question is performed by general surgeons.

The standards set by the courts in regard to competence and division between specialties can only be as clear or certain as the medical profession itself is on the matter.

Although arrangements for a patient's care during a doctor's absence, for example, during vacation, have often been made casually, the persistence of patients and courtesy of colleagues has rarely resulted in liability being found in Canada on the basis of abandonment,[411] which is a failure to refer at its most extreme.

(d) The Duty to Treat

(i) Quality of care

A doctor who has undertaken the attendance and diagnosis of a patient, perhaps with consultation, has a duty to treat *the patient*. The best medical care is as individualized as the human beings it involves; indeed, it is the essence of medical care that the care a patient receives be unique to him. Adversarial relationships between doctor and patient often stem from the patient's complaint that the doctor did not deal with *him,* that he was just another "gall bladder" or "neurotic." Reactions of some doctors to these complaints include the notions that a doctor should not get personally involved with his patient, that the less said to the patient the better, or that the doctor would spend all his time talking instead of operating. These doctors miss the point. The essence of a professional relationship, especially the doctor-patient relationship, is care and communication. The absence of this rapport is always found somewhere in the facts of a case that is litigated, which the Canadian Medical Protective Association regularly points out to the membership in the Annual Reports.[412]

---

410 *Id.* at 8.
411 *Re Lesk supra* n. 403; *Wilson v. Stark supra* n. 51. *But see Bergstrom v. G. supra* n. 403. *See also* Canadian Medical Protective Association *Annual Report 1975* at 15 for a case where liability was admitted.
412 *See, for example,* Canadian Medical Protective Association, *supra* n. 401 at 11.

It is not feasible to discuss under this heading every case in which it has been alleged that a doctor was negligent in his treatment of a patient. Covered here are only the most litigious areas and troublesome cases. The section discusses surgical and anaesthetic mishaps, problems with drugs and injections, and complications from casts.

(ii) Surgery

Many lawsuits have been commenced as a consequence of surgical mishaps and as the basic principle of all negligence law has been applied in them it is, perhaps, worth repeating. Any doctor who undertakes the surgical treatment of a patient must, in doing so, meet the standard of care of a reasonable medical person considering all of the circumstances.

The cases indicate that surgical problems coming before the courts fall into four categories: 1) surgery more extensive than necessary; 2) damage to other tissue or organs; 3) objects left inside the body; and 4) substandard care following surgery. Anaesthesiological mishaps are also common but are dealt with separately.

In the mistaken belief than an ulcer patient was suffering from cancer, a doctor removed "large portions of the plaintiff's stomach, pancreas and the entire spleen."[413] The doctor was exonerated because he had met the standard of care in his reliance on a pathologist's report and his pre surgical diagnosis was reasonable. But the surgeons who operated on the wrong leg of a polio victim,[414] fused the wrong cervical vertebrae,[415] removed the patient's only kidney,[416] and performed an unnecessary mastectomy[417] could not be said to have acted as reasonable surgeons in the circumstances and were held liable. Likewise, a dentist had to compensate his patient for mistakenly extracting a tooth[418] which he had intended to leave to support a denture.

Accidental injury during surgery has often been a subject of litigation. While removing an infected cyst, a surgeon damaged the patient's spinal accessory nerve and in the light of expert evidence was held liable,[419] as was a surgeon who damaged a facial nerve while performing surgery on a patient's ear,[420] and a surgeon who severed a nerve when operating on a patient's

---

413 *Wilson v. Swanson supra* n. 377. *See supra* s. 2.(b) of this chapter.
414 *Staple v. Winnipeg supra* n. 223.
415 *David v. T.T.C.* (1976), 77 D.L.R. (3d) 717 (Ont. H.C.).
416 *Urbanski v. Patel* (1978), 84 D.L.R. (3d) 650 (Man. Q.B.); for a case comment, *see* Robertson, *A New Application of the Rescue Principle* (1980), 96 L.Q.R. 19.
417 *Down v. Royal Jubilee Hosp.* (1980), 24 B.C.L.R. 296 (B.C.S.C.). *But see Guertin v. Kester* (1981), 20 C.C.L.T. 225 (B.C.S.C.), where removing too much skin from the patient during a blepharoplasty was not negligence.
418 *Murano v. Gray* (1982), 19 Alta. L.R. (2d) 393 (Alta. Q.B.).
419 *Fizer v. Keys,* [1974] 2 W.W.R. 14 (Alta. S.C.).
420 *Zamparo v. Brisson* (1981), 16 C.C.L.T. 66 (Ont. C.A.).

wrist.[421] The evidence of negligence was irrefutable in another case where a second operation showed the wall of the patient's bladder to have been "tied into" a hernia repair done by the first surgeon who had accidently cut and then sutured it.[422].

That even a "simple and common" procedure may hold risks for the doctor and patient was borne out where the surgeon removing polyps from the patient's nose caused a retrobulbar hemorrhage.[423] The action was dismissed because the otolaryngologist had met the standard of care to be expected of him. A surgeon who damaged a patient's ureter while doing a tubal ligation was held not liable because there was no evidence to support the allegation.[424] In a number of cases perforation of the bowel during sterilization surgery has been held not to be negligence.[425] Also, the perforation of the prostate capsule during a transurethral resection of the prostate was not substandard surgery according to a Nova Scotia court.[426] An action was also dismissed against a surgeon carrying out an inherently more dangerous procedure which caused the death of the patient; in removing a disc, the orthopaedic surgeon lacerated the aorta and the vena cava.[427] Another orthopaedic surgeon escaped liability for fracturing a patient's femur during surgery.[428]

The story of objects lost and found during surgery is an old one. One authority[429] has said "the danger of swabs being overlooked at the end of an abdominal operation is a very real and grave one and in consequence extraordinary precautions are commonly taken in an attempt to reduce this risk as far as possible." Most of the reported cases occurred during the period from 1920 to 1950.[430] The precautions employed included the use of sponges with tapes attached, sponge counting systems and vesting the surgeon with a residual duty to ensure that nothing was left behind. In two Canadian cases a doctor[431]

---

421 *McKeachie v. Alvarez supra* n. 62. *But see Konkolus v. Royal Alexandra Hosp.* (1982), 21 Alta. L.R. (2d) 359 (Alta. Q.B.), where with contradictory expert evidence the court found there was no liability; *see also Jodouin v. Mitra* (1978), 2 L. Med. Q. 72 (Ont. H.C.).

422 *Melvin v. Graham,* [1973] D.R.S. 659 (Ont. H.C.).

423 *Kunitz v. Merei supra* n. 401; *see also Patterson v. Yves de la Bastide* (1983), 22 A.C.W.S. (2d) 244 (Ont. H.C.). *See also* Canadian Medical Protective Association, *supra* n. 401 at 14.

424 *Hobson v. Munkley supra* n. 373.

425 *Videto v. Kennedy* (1981), 17 C.C.L.T. 307 (Ont. C.A.); *McBride v. Langton* (1982), 22 Alta. L.R. (2d) 174 (Alta. Q.B.); *Gouin-Perrault v. Villeneuve* (1982), 23 C.C.L.T. 72 (Que. S.C.); *Mang v. Moscovitz* (1982), 37 A.R. 221 (Alta. Q.B.) (bladder cut).

426 *Considine v. Camp Hill Hosp.* (1982), 133 D.L.R. (3d) 11 (N.S.T.D.).

427 *Chubey v. Ahsan supra* n. 112; *see also Kapur v. Marshall* (1978), 4 C.C.L.T. 204 (Ont.).

428 *Powell v. Guttman* (1978), 89 D.L.R. (3d) 180 (Man. C.A.). Note, however, that the expert evidence was divided and there was an issue about the doctor's truthfulness.

429 Nathan, *supra* n. 24 at 78.

430 *See Jewison v. Hassard supra* n. 10; *Waldon v. Archer* (1921), 20 O.W.N. 77 (H.C.); *Van Wyck v. Lewis supra* n. 11; *James v. Dunlop,* [1931] 1 Brit. Med. J. 730. A thorough discussion of the "swab" cases appears in Nathan, *supra* n. 24 at 77-86.

431 *Anderson v. Chasney supra* n. 22.

and a dentist[432] were held to be negligent when their patients died by suffocation on a sponge left behind after a tonsillectomy and asphyxia from a gauze swab left after dental extractions. While modern surgical practice and the system of assigning a nurse to count sponges has reduced the risk of sponges and other foreign material being left in the body, it still occurs on occasion.[433] In fact, a case occured in 1978 when a surgical sponge or lap pad was left in the abdomen of an 83-year-old patient.[434] Although the hospital and doctor had agreed before the trial to accept any responsibility equally, the trial judge made it clear that the doctor bears the ultimate responsibility. Mr. Justice Miller said:[435]

> There is evidence . . . that Dr. Gaudreau followed a normal and general practice of relying on a nurse's count to satisfy himself that all the sponges had been removed. In my opinion this oversimplifies the duty of the doctor to his patient. It is my view that *a person has the right to expect that a medical doctor — a specialist in surgery, will perform a surgical procedure without leaving a foreign body within the patient.* [emphasis supplied]

When surgical instruments are left behind in the patient's body, liability does not necessarily follow. In a case from New Zealand[436] in which a pair of forceps was discovered in the patient's abdomen after surgery, expert evidence indicated that they probably slipped in because it was the surgeon's habit to place instruments on the patient's chest, but that this practice was "usual and proper." Similarly, in two early Canadian cases where a tube was left in an incision[437] and a portion of a broken forceps was left behind[438] there was no liability. In the first case it was the nurse who was held negligent and in the second no injury was proven to have been caused by the foreign body. However, surgeons were held liable in two later cases. In a New Brunswick case[439] seven months after a Caesarian operation "an Allis forceps $5^3/_4$ to $5^7/_8$ inches long and two inches broad at the handles," was removed from over the right kidney of the patient, and the surgeon was held to have breached the standard of care expected of him. In an Alberta case,[440] a surgeon used his own instruments in performing a Caesarian section, and five years later the patient required surgery to retrieve the doctor's Kelly forceps (about six inches long) which had been left in her abdomen. The surgeon was held negligent.

Allegations of negligent care after surgery have increased markedly. The facts in cases where liability was found tell of the failure to monitor the

---

432 *Holt v. Nesbitt*, [1953] 1 D.L.R. 671 (S.C.C.).

433 *Karderas v. Clow supra* n. 9; *see also Radclyffe v. Rennie supra* n. 243 where the issue was whether gauze found in the patient's body in 1961 had been left in 1944 or 1959 on the occasions of previous surgery.

434 *Cosgrove v. Gaudreau* (1981), 33 N.B.R. (2d) 523 (N.B.Q.B.).

435 *Id.* at 527.

436 *MacDonald v. Pottinger*, [1953] N.Z.L.R. 196 (S.C.).

437 *Thomson v. Barry*, [1932] 1 D.L.R. 805; reversed [1932] 2 D.L.R. 814 (Ont. C.A.).

438 *Hutchinson v. Robert supra* n. 251.

439 *Taylor v. Gray* (1937), 11 M.P.R. 588 (N.B.C.A.).

440 *Gloning v. Miller* (1953), 10 W.W.R. 414 (Alta. S.C.).

patient's condition[441] and to anticipate serious but common complications[442] such as gangrene.[443] Obviously a surgeon cannot take the position that his duty to the patient ends with the last suture.

An Ontario judge[444] labelled the arrangements for the post-operative care of a patient by an obstetrician-gynaecologist to be "just about non-existent" and "casual" if not "callous."[445] The patient was discharged on a Friday immediately following a laparoscopic sterilization during which her bowel was accidently perforated. All attempts to contact the doctor over a weekend were thwarted by his having no answering or paging service and his office and the hospital being unable or unwilling to assist. By Monday the patient was seriously ill in an advanced stage of peritonitis and required two further operations.

By contrast, in the cases where the patient's claim of substandard after care did not succeed the facts indicate that arrangements were made for the patient to have access to post-operative medical advice.[446] In cases where complications occurred the doctors were successful in proving that a follow-up on the patient did occur and medical assessments and judgments were made.[447]

(iii) Anaesthesiology

Anaesthetic mishaps can both occur very quickly and result in serious injury to the patient. The Canadian Medical Protective Association has advised its membership:[448]

> The complexities of modern anaesthesia nowadays demand not only the undivided attention of the doctor administering the anaesthetic but also that the anaesthetist have the knowledge, skill and experience to recognize and deal promptly with complications which may arise insidiously or suddenly and unexpectedly.

As well it has counselled against the occasional practice of anaesthesiology:[449]

---

441 *Zimmer v. Ringrose* (1981), 16 C.C.L.T. 51 (Alta. C.A.); *see also O'Connell v. Munro* (1983), 22 A.C.W.S. (2d) 349 (Ont. H.C.).

442 *Powell v. Guttman*, [1978] 5 W.W.R. 228 (Man. C.A.); *Osburn v. Mohindra* (1980), 29 N.B.R. (2d) 340 (N.B.Q.B.).

443 *Thomas v. Scarborough Gen. Hosp.*, [1978] 2 A.C.W.S. 143 (Ont. Co. Ct.).

444 *Videto v. Kennedy* (1980), 107 D.L.R. (3d) 612 (Ont. H.C.); affirmed as to negligent after care 17 C.C.L.T. 307 (Ont. C.A.).

445 *Supra* (1980), 107 D.L.R. (3d) 612 at 616-17.

446 *White v. Turner* (1981), 15 C.C.L.T. 81 (Ont. H.C.); appeal dismissed 20 C.C.L.T. xxii (Ont. C.A.); *see also Tacknyk v. Lake of the Woods Clinic* (1982), 17 A.C.W.S. (2d) 154 (Ont. C.A.) where there was a doctor available even in the patient's "inaccessible area".

447 *Reibl v. Hughes* (1980), 14 C.C.L.T. 1 (S.C.C.); *Ferguson v. Hamilton Civic Hosp.* (1983), 23 C.C.L.T. 254 (Ont. H.C.); *Hajgato v. London Health Assn.* (1982), 36 O.R. (2d) 669 (Ont. H.C.); *Rawlings v. Lindsay* (1982), 20 C.C.L.T. 301 (B.C.S.C.).

448 Canadian Medical Protective Associaton, *supra* n. 401 at 12; see *Kangas v. Parker*, [1976] 5 W.W.R. 25 at 52 (Sask. Q.B.) *per* Sirois J. "For every anaesthetic, one must be ready at all times for the worst that may occur;" affirmed [1978] 5 W.W.R. 667 (Sask. C.A.).

449 *Supra* n. 401 at 14.

It is still widely accepted in Canada that doctors need not necessarily possess specialist certification in order to practise anaesthesia safely and completely. This notwithstanding, nowadays it must be appreciated that anaesthetic work is not for the occasional anaesthetist who may be lacking in detailed knowledge of the pharmacology of patent and dangerous anaesthetic agents and who may have only infrequent opportunities for the necessary experience in their use. From a medico-legal standpoint such deficiencies can be unacceptable.

The cases bear out the warnings.[450] The Supreme Court of Canada has heard cases against anaesthetists and found them to be liable. In one case[451] an explosion resulted from the doctor's negligence in leaving the oxygen flowing into an ether can while the Magill tube (a small tube introduced into the trachea) was not connected to it. A spark of static electricity set the oxygen-ether mixture aflame. The Court of Appeal[452] found a breach of the high standard of care expected because of the handling of dangerous agents. In the second case[453] an anaesthetist administered a caudal anaesthetic comprised of Xylocaine added to adrenalin. Serious inflammation of the spinal cord resulted in permanent paraplegia. The expert evidence was that paralysis would not normally follow the proper administration of a caudal anaesthetic and the defendant's hypothesis that the patient had a sensitivity to the drugs used was rejected. The result for the patient was as insidious here as it was sudden in the first case.

The complexities of modern anaesthesia are underscored in two other cases. During the preliminaries to an "open heart" operation, a stopcock was not completely turned off allowing air into the venous system of the patient who was thereby seriously injured. The court commented on the great danger to the patient if air passed through the line and on the failure to utilize the means and methods known and available to eliminate the danger. Both the anaesthetists required on this sophisticated procedure were held liable.[454] In an Ontario case[455] a patient became a quadriplegic when an anaesthetist using a new method of artificial ventilation, "transtracheal ventilation," deviated from the practice laid down by its inventor with the result that the patient suffered from massive tissue emphysema. Negligence was found and the damages awarded at trial were over $700,000.

---

450 However, a 70-year-old doctor with no special training in anaesthesia, who admitted he had not kept up with modern technology and did not use a cardiac monitor for reasons "not entirely satisfactory" to the trial judge was insulated from liability by the court that held these factors were not contributing factors to the patient's cardiac arrest and death. *MacKinnon v. Ignacio* (1978), 29 N.S.R. (2d) 656 (N.S.T.D.).

451 *Crits v. Sylvester supra* n. 1; *see also Paton v. Parker* (1942), 65 C.L.R. 187 (Aust. H.C.).

452 *Crits v. Sylvester id.*

453 *Martel v. Hotel-Dieu St-Vallier* (1969), 14 D.L.R. (3d) 445 (S.C.C.); *see also Walker v. Bedard*, [1945] O.W.N. 120 (H.C.) where the patient died from the effect of Nupercaine, a spinal anaesthetic, and *Villeneuve v. Sisters of St. Joseph*, [1975] 1 S.C.R. 285 where a child lost his right hand from a misplaced pre-operative anaesthetic. *See also Roe v. Min. of Health supra* n. 97; *Jones v. Manchester Corp.*, [1952] 2 All E.R. 125 (C.A.).

454 *Aynsley v. Toronto Gen. Hosp.*, [1969] 2 O.R. 829 (Ont. H.C.); affirmed [1972] S.C.R. 435.

Tragedy occurred[456] when a patient misled an anaesthetist about his fluid intake prior to surgery for ingrown toenails. Difficulties were encountered in anaesthetizing the patient because he had laryngeal spasms and regurgitated into the lungs. Death ensued after a cardiac arrest, but the anaesthetist was not held liable; he had no duty to interrogate the patient. In a case[457] where an anaesthetist did question the patient about whether she took medication for high blood pressure, nerves or her heart, he was entitled to rely on her negative response. The court said that by his examination and questioning of the patient he had more than met the standard of care required. Modern courts have accepted at least one mishap[458] during anaesthesia as not being evidence of the substandard skill of an anaesthetist. The needle carrying anaesthetic sodium pentothal can slip out of a vein so that the drug leaks into the surrounding tissue. Injury to the patient is usually minor but there has been no liability even where the damage has been profound.[459]

The standard of care expected of any doctor is affected by the risks involved. Clearly, in anaesthesiology the risks are high and it follows that the standard of care is high. Furthermore, the extensive injury often suffered by the patient means that the compensation required is large. Anaesthesia is an area of high risk: for the patient of injury, for the doctor of liability.[460]

(iv) Drugs and injections

The use of a drug always involves risk. It may be the possibility, albeit remote, of an allergic reaction by the patient,[461] or it may be the choice of the wrong drug or carelessness in its administration. The future might even see actions for a failure to treat with drugs.[462]

The standard of care is elevated by the greater risks in this area, but liability is not automatic. The requirements for the finding of negligence

---

455 *Holmes v. Bd. of Hosp. Trustees of London supra* n. 20. Note that two other doctors were held liable for their negligence in contributing to the injuries suffered.

456 *Webster v. Armstrong,* [1974] 2 W.W.R. 709 (B.C.S.C.).

457 *Leadbetter v. Brand* (1980), 37 N.S.R. (2d) 581 (N.S.T.D.).

458 *Allan v. New Mount Sinai Hosp.* (1980), 11 C.C.L.T. 299 (Ont. H.C.), trial finding on this issue not appealed 19 C.C.L.T. 76 (Ont. C.A.); *Lloy v. Milner* (1981), 15 Man. R. (2d) 187 (Man. Q.B.).

459 *Id.*

460 *See Gorback v. Ting,* [1974] 5 W.W.R. 606 (Man. Q.B.), where the injury was a chipped tooth, no liability; *Kangas v. Parker supra* n. 67, where the injury was death, liability. *Girard v. Royal Columbian Hosp. supra* n. 244; *see also* Canadian Medical Protective Association, *supra* n. 401 at 12 and 16. Note that another high risk area, the recovery room, is discussed in Chapter 9.

461 Note that cases of adverse reaction may be litigated as negligent disclosure, *see Davidson v. Connaught Laboratories* (1980), 14 C.C.L.T. 251 (Ont. H.C.); *Ferguson v. Hamilton Civic Hosp.* (1983), 23 C.C.L.T. 254 (Ont. H.C.).

462 *See Parsons v. Schmok supra* n. 143, where the plaintiff unsuccessfully alleged that anti-hypertensive drug therapy could have averted his stroke. *See also Vail v. MacDonald supra* n. 52.

must, as always, be proven by the plaintiff,[463] and because of the complexities of pharmacology and physiology it may be difficult to prove the causal link between the drug and the injury,[464] even with the assistance of the evidentiary doctrine of *res ipsa loquitur*.

Cases dealing with an adverse reaction to a drug are illustrative of this difficulty. A doctor was held not liable when the victim of a dog bite suffered a toxic reaction to an anti-tetanus shot.[465] The expert evidence was that the reaction was extremely rare and the doctor had met his standard of care in administering the injection which, while it was the cause-in-fact of the serum neuritis, was not held to be the proximate cause. The owner of the dog was held liable, though, as the patient was found to be a thin-skull person and thus an exception to the foreseeability rule.[466] The same hurdle, that of a reaction so rare as not to be reasonably foreseeable, precluded recovery by a patient who was hypersensitive to Nupercaine[467] and one who went beyond the desired state of drowsiness to unconsciousness from treatment with Thorazine.[468] In a modern Ontario case, *Davidson v. Connaught Laboratories*,[469] a doctor was held to have met the standard of care required in prescribing and administering anti-rabies vaccine because of the seriousness of rabies measured against the rare incidence of neuritis and paralysis as a reaction to the vaccine. Of interest in this case is the claim made against the drug company for a failure to warn of the side effects of neuritis and myelitis.[470] Mr. Justice Linden found the warning contained in the boxes of vaccine[471] to be inadequate and unreasonable but concluded on the evidence that this had no effect on the medical judgment and, thus, there was no causal link to the injury.

If tests are available or suggested in conjunction with drug therapy the standard of care may require that they be carried out. It was important in the anti-tetanus cases whether preliminary tests were done,[472] and a doctor who failed to follow the manufacturer's suggestion that hearing tests be conducted

---

463 For a case where a patient was successful *see Reynard v. Carr* (1983), 50 B.C.L.R. 166 (B.C.S.C.).

464 *Webster v. Armstrong supra* n. 456.

465 *Winteringham v. Rae* and *Robinson v. Post Office supra* n. 296.

466 *See supra.*

467 *Walker v. Bedard supra* n. 453; *see also Martel v. Hotel-Dieu supra* n. 453, where the hypersensitivity argument was rejected.

468 *Buchanan v. Fort Churchill Gen. Hosp.*, [1969] D.R.S. 586 (Man. Q.B.).

469 (1980), 14 C.C.L.T. 251 (Ont. S.C.).

470 For an excellent discussion *see* MacIntosh, *Liability and Compensation Aspects of Immunization Injury: A Call For Reform* (1980), 4 O.H.L.J. 584; *see also* (1977), 3 L. Med. Q. 162-87. Note that contract law is relevant to the relationships of doctor-patient-drug manufacturer. *See* Chapter 2. *See also Buchan v. Ortho Pharmaceutical* unreported, April 19, 1984 (No. unavailable) (Ont. S.C.).

471 As to information brochures accompanying drugs, *see* Cook, *The Package Insert and Its Legal Implications* (1980), 4 L. Med. Q. 258.

472 *Supra* n. 296.

during the course of the treatment with massive doses of neomycin was liable to the patient who suffered a permanent hearing loss.[473] Similarly, a patient who was allergic to penicillin was successful in a suit against a doctor who neither inquired nor checked her records prior to giving her an injection of procaine penicillin.[474] In another case[475] the patient was treated with chloroquine for a skin disorder by her doctor who referred her to an ophthalmologist after reading that it could cause permanent loss of vision. However, the doctor did not read carefully enough the ophthalmologist's report which indicated corneal changes. The judge said that "the standard of care, having regard to the inherent dangers involved in the use of the drug, must, of necessity, be very high," and held the doctor negligent.[476] Those words ring especially true for the case where a "new" drug is being used. The court then looks for evidence of considered medical judgment[477] reflected in planning for the particular patient's care and safety.[478] A general practitioner[479] administering the drug Adriamycin® to a patient suffering from cancer was held to have met this standard whereas an operating ophthalmologist[480] who looked at the labelled bottle containing a new drug but failed to see that it was not the proper one was held to have made "a very serious oversight" and was liable.

An error in the administration of a drug, be it the wrong drug, the wrong dosage, or a misplaced injection, often results in liability. Mistakes as to drug or dosage are often patent while the misplaced injection may be more difficult to prove especially in terms of causation.[481]

Liability has been found in a number of wrong drug cases. In a very old one in Quebec the doctor wrote "bi-sulphate of morphine" instead of "bi-sulphate

---

473 *Male v. Hopmans supra* n. 105.

474 *Chin Keow v. Gov. of Malaysia,* [1967] 1 W.L.R. 813 (P.C.).

475 *Crossman v. Stewart supra* n. 106.

476 *Id.* at 56. Note that the patient was held two-thirds to blame because she had been obtaining drugs from a salesman after her prescription ran out. *See also Molnar v. Conway* unreported June 22, 1978, No. S.C. 114193 (Alta. T.D.), where the patient, by deceit, was obtaining additional quantities of the stimulant drug Ritalin®. His action against the doctor who first prescribed it was dismissed.

477 *See Meyer v. Gordon* (1981), 17 C.C.L.T. 1 (B.C.S.C.), where the court noted that the doctor had exercised "very little judgement" in prescribing Demerol® (*not* a "new" drug but a potent one) by telephone with inadequate information about the patient; *see also Leonard v. Knott,* [1980] 1 W.W.R. 673 (B.C.C.A.), where a dangerous physiological test was ordered for a healthy patient.

478 *See Foote v. Royal Columbian Hosp.,* [1982] B.C.D. Civ. 2632-05 (B.C.S.C.); affirmed 19 A.C.W.S. (2d) 304 (B.C.C.A.), where a doctor who changed the medication of an epileptic, but did not alert hospital staff to the increased risks to her of a *grand mal* seizure, was found liable.

479 *Neufeld v. McQuitty* (1979), 18 A.R. 271 (Alta. T.D.); *see also Moore v. Shaugnessy Hosp.* (1982), 15 A.C.W.S. (2d) 389 (B.C.S.C.).

480 *Misericordia Hosp. v. Bustillo,* [1983] Alta. D. 2632-01 (Alta. C.A.).

481 *See supra* "anaesthetists" for a decision of the misplaced injection during anaesthesia.

of quinine'' in a prescription for a child, who died from it.[482] In a modern case,[483] a doctor doing a minor operation on a thumb intended to inject Novocaine but in error injected adrenalin. The patient died. In a remarkably similar fact situation five years earlier[484] which also resulted in the patient's death a doctor setting a thumb asked for Novocaine® but was given adrenalin by the nurse. It was found that the doctor could rely on the nurse and was not negligent, but the nurses and hence the hospital were held accountable. Considering the extreme consequences to a patient it is preferable to require a doctor also to check the label under such circumstances.[485]

Liability has followed the administration of an excessive dose or the wrong drug in a number of English cases as well.[486]

Where an injection is misplaced or a needle broken negligence has sometimes been found. When vaccinating a young girl a doctor chose an inner rather than an outer aspect of the arm and when she suffered ''multiple takes'' of the vaccine and a secondary infection, she sued but was unsuccessful.[487] The expert evidence was that the area chosen was acceptable, that the standard of care had been met, and in any event the vaccination was not the proximate cause of the infant's suffering. By contrast an anaesthetist in another case[488] was held liable where a young boy was restrained while he attempted to inject pentothal into a vein but instead injected it into an artery, which caused the child's eventual loss of his right hand. In another case the patient did prove that he lost fingers and a thumb as a result of bicillin getting into an artery and that a nurse had given him an injection of bicillin, but the Supreme Court of Canada[489] said the nurse had discharged the evidentiary burden resting on her by showing that the misfortune suffered by the patient

---

482 *Jeanotte v. Couillard* (1894), 3 R.J. 461 (Que. Q.B.). The pharmacist had substituted sulphate of morphine but it was held bi-sulphate of morphine would have had the same effect. He was held one-sixth at fault and the doctor five-sixths at fault. *See also Filipewich v. University Hosp. Bd.* unreported July 1973 No. 432 (Sask. Q.B.). A child died when given mercaptomerin instead of mercaptopurine. The action against the hospital as employer of the pharmacist and a doctor was settled before trial.

483 *Pollard v. Chipperfield* (1952), 7 W.W.R. 596 (Sask. C.A.).

484 *Bugden v. Harbour View Hosp. supra* n. 14.

485 *Misericordia Hosp. v. Bustillo*, [1983] Alta. D. 2632-01 (Alta. C.A.). Nathan, *supra* n. 24 at 60. This would be consistent with the residual duty to check the operating area for foreign material left. *See supra.*

486 *Strangeways-Lesmere v. Clayton*, [1936] 1 All E.R. 484 (K.B.D.); *Collins v. Hertfordshire County Council*, [1947] 1 All E.R. 633 (K.B.D.), *Jones v. Manchester Corp.*, [1952] 2 All E.R. 125 (C.A.). *See* Nathan, *supra* n. 24 at 58-59.

487 *Gent v. Wilson*, [1956] O.R. 257 (C.A.).

488 *Villeneuve v. Sisters of St. Joseph supra* n. 453; *see Armstrong v. McClealand* (1930), 38 O.W.N. 297, where no liability followed the transfusion of blood into an artery when the attempt had been to put it inside a vein: *see also Caldeira v. Gray*, [1936] 1 All E.R. 540 (P.C.).

489 *Cavan v. Wilcox* (1974), 2 N.R. 618 (S.C.C.); *see also Hughston v. Jost*, [1943] 1 D.L.R. 402 (Ont. H.C.).

could have occurred without negligence on her part. The Court of Appeal[490] had held her liable, saying her story that she must have followed a particular technique but did not specifically remember this case was not sufficiently convincing. It seems clear that the injection was the cause-in-fact of the injury but the courts differed on whether it ought to have been regarded as the proximate cause.

Similarly, when the injury to the patient occurs from a broken needle the issue of foreseeability of risk of harm has been the decisive factor. In a Quebec case[491] that went to the Supreme Court of Canada a young boy resisted an injection but the doctor insisted on proceeding over the protests of the mother. Upon the prick of the needle the boy moved his arm and a portion of the needle broke underneath the skin necessitating three operations and causing temporary paralysis and permanent scars. The court said the cause of the injury was the injection which the doctor chose to administer in spite of the risk. On the other hand, in another Quebec case[492] a needle broke in a dental patient's jaw, and the court held that the dentist met the standard of care by using the same type of needle others used. Obviously the court felt that in this instance a needle breaking was not foreseeable. The use of disposable needles has removed the risk of fracture from use. However, the cases show that the risk of fracture from movement remains, especially where children are involved. Should a doctor experience such an accident he has a duty to inform the patient of what has occurred.[493]

The administration of drugs exposes the doctor to potential liability and the injured patient to possible difficulties in proving causation. The cases involving wrong drugs or dosages and broken needles in children are relatively easy for the patient to prove and, accordingly, it is likely that the doctor will be found liable. However, the cases involving adverse reactions to drugs are especially difficult to prove and the doctor can meet his standard of care by following approved practice and testing the patient for allergies or known side effects. Because there is a sense of frustration in both the medical and legal professions about accountability for drug induced injuries, litigation will likely increase. Doctors are finding it more and more difficult to keep up to date[494] and pharmacists are expanding their role as monitors and advisors in

---

490 *Cavan v. Wilcox supra* n. 312.
491 *Cardin v. Montreal supra* n. 36.
492 *Bouillon v. Poire* (1937), 63 Que. K.B. 1 (C.A.); *see also Gerber v. Pines* (1934), 79 Sol. Jo. 13 (K.B.); *Hunter v. Hanley,* [1955] S.L.T. 213 (1st Div.); *Mitchell v. Dixon supra* n. 366. Nathan, *supra* n. 24 at 57.
493 *Hutchinson v. Robert,* [1935] O.W.N. 172 at 176; reversed [1935] O.W.N. 314 (C.A.) with no reference to this point.
494 For a comment *see* Junewicz, *Physicians Liability For Failure to Anticipate and Control Reactions and Interactions Precipitated By Prescribed or Administered Drugs* (1980), 2 Specialty Law Digest: Health Care 3.

drug therapy.[495] Lawyers and judges are expressing concern that victims are not being compensated.[496] Meanwhile both professions appear to the public to be unable to resolve allegations of drug misuse in neo-natal units[497] and prisons[498] and uncertain about the risk-benefit analysis of mass immunizations.[499]

If present Canadian law is found inadequate to resolve these issues, reform could be sought through legislation,[500] a move to strict liability in tort law,[501] or by the use of contract as a basis for liability.[502] It seems likely that the responsibilities of manufacturers, pharmacists and patients will receive closer scrutiny.

(v) Casts

Complications following treatment with casts have received a great deal of attention in Canadian courts. The Supreme Court of Canada has heard three major cases and found the doctors liable.[503] Of these three cases two involved circulatory impairment and one an infection following insertion of an intramedullary nail.[504] There are surprising similarities among the three cases. All involved a closed reduction of a fracture with symptoms following that made it clear all was not well. In each, the evidence was that the patient's deteriorating condition was ignored and the doctors' follow-up treatment was described variously as "inept,"[505] "neglectful"[506] or "concerned more with maintaining the good fracture reduction . . . than with the maintenance of good circulation."[507] A failure to consult or refer was found in each case and a failure to bi-valve the cast or prescribe anti-coagulants was found in two.[508] Two patients suffered amputations and the third serious permanent damage.

---

495 For an excellent discussion *see* Haunholter, *Negligence and The Pharmacist* (1978), 2 L. Med. Q. 2.
496 *Davidson v. Connaught Laboratories* (1980), 14 C.C.L.T. 251 at 281 (Ont. H.C.) and especially, the arguments and judgment regarding costs reported only at (1981), 5 L. Med. Q. 143; McIntosh, *Liability and Compensation Aspects of Immunization Injury: A Call For Reform* (1980), 4 O.H.L.J. 585.
497 Magnet, *Withholding Treatment From Defective Newborns: Legal Aspects* (1982), 42 R. du B. 187 at 264.
498 *See, for example,* Hughes, *Inmates Detail Bug Juice Therapy,* Edmonton Journal, Fri. Sept. 16, 1983..
499 *See* McIntosh *supra* n. 496.
500 *See Davidson v. Connaught Laboratories supra* n. 496.
501 *See* McIntosh *supra* n. 496; *see also* McClellan, *Strict Liability For Drug Induced Injuries: An Excursion Through the Maze of Products Liability, Negligence and Absolute Liability* (1979), 4 Specialty Law Digest: Health Care 5.
502 *See Chapter 2.*
503 *Ares v. Venner supra* n. 52; *McCormick v. Marcotte supra* n. 33; *Vail v. MacDonald supra* n. 52.
504 *McCormick v. Marcotte supra* n. 33.
505 *id.* at 22.
506 *Vail v. MacDonald supra* n. 52 at 531.
507 *Ares v. Venner supra* n. 52 at 615.
508 *Ares v. Venner* and *Vail v. MacDonald* both *supra* n. 52.

Unheeded circulatory problems can lead to loss of limbs, and the seriousness of this risk has moved the courts[509] to impose a common standard of care on all doctors whose treatment of a patient raises this risk. It should be recognized that this formulation of the standard of care is a departure from the norm which bases the standard of care primarily on the qualifications of the doctor. It also indicates the magnitude of the risk for patients as perceived by the courts.[510]

Other cases worth noting also have these apparently common features to varying degrees. In a Saskatchewan case[511] a patient suffered fractures of both legs, and after casts were applied he complained of pain and nurses' notes indicated the feet were cold and numb and the toes were cyanotic. After 36 hours the casts were univalved (cut down one side) and the next day bivalved, but it was too late; both legs had to be amputated. The doctor was held negligent in the follow-up treatment. In another case[512] a woman was put in a cast for a "chronic draining sinus" and sent home. Motivated by pain she tried to contact the doctor but, it being a holiday weekend, four days passed before her calls were returned. The doctor removed the cast two days after that, but she was suffering from gangrene and her leg was amputated. The court found the doctor was negligent by failing to make proper arrangements for checking the patient during the weekend, and by failing to see her earlier.

While recent cases have involved the recurrence of the same post-operative complications of circulatory impairment[513] and infection[514] the consequences for the defendant doctors have been very different and they have not had to compensate the patient. An exception was the case of *Dean v. York County Hosp.*[515] where an orthopaedic surgeon, by not probing the wound near the patient's displaced fracture of the tibia and fibula of his leg, diagnosed a simple fracture when it was a compound one. He was held liable for the gangrene that made an amputation necessary.

In a Manitoba case[516] a patient broke her ankle in a fall and the intern who x-rayed it found a simple transverse fracture with no displacement. He

---

509 *See* O'Byrne J. at Alta. T.D. in *Ares v. Venner;* affirmed in [1970] S.C.R. 608 at 614 and in *Vail v. MacDonald supra* n. 52 at 534.

510 But see the more recent case, *Gordon v. Davidson* (1980), 4 L. Med. Q. 131 at 136, 144 (Ont. S.C.), where the standard of care was set by the doctor's qualifications as a general surgeon and he was exonerated on the basis of his medical judgment.

511 *Badger v. Surkan*, [1973] 1 W.W.R. 302 (Sask. C.A.); *see also Park v. Stevenson Memorial Hosp. supra* n. 334.

512 *Bergstrom v. G. supra* n. 27.

513 *Gordon v. Davidson* (1979), 4 L. Med. Q. 131 (Ont. H.C.).

514 *Hajgato v. London Health Assn.* (1982), 36 O.R. (2d) 669 (Ont. H.C.); *Roy v. Goulet* (1977), 19 N.B.R. (2d) 187 (N.B.Q.B.).

515 (1979), 3 L. Med. Q. 231 (Ont. H.C.). *See also Leachman v. MacLachlan,* unreported Feb. 23, 1984, No. C813325 (B.C.S.C.).

516 *Parkin v. Kobrinsky supra* n. 149. *See also Moore v. Large supra* n. 27, where it was held not negligent to fail to take x-rays. The standard of care changed in the 33 years between these cases. *See also Price v. Milawski supra* n. 149.

taped on a plastic slab and the defendant doctor put on a walking cast the next day but took no further x-rays. Expert evidence was that a second x-ray should have been taken to ascertain if any displacement occurred in the interim. After 18 days of ''excruciating pain'' an x-ray was taken which showed a displacement of at least one half an inch, which led to the patient having a deformed ankle. It was held that the doctor had failed to meet the standard of care by not taking x-rays prior to and after applying the cast. It was a failure to follow the patient's progress, or lack of it, that resulted in liability for an orthopaedic surgeon when the pins he placed in her hip changed position and she developed avascular necrosis making her vulnerable to a fracture during later surgery.[517] A breakdown in procedure whereby a radiologist's report was not sent to the treating doctor resulted in a hospital being held liable to the patient, both for the radiologist and for the doctor who misdiagnosed a dislocated lunate in the wrist.[518]

A review of the more recent cases under this heading leaves one with the strong feeling of *deja-vu*.

(e)   The Duty to Instruct the Patient[519]

It may be necessary for the doctor to delegate certain duties of the medical treatment to the patient or his family. Most doctors depend on the patient to report some symptoms or details of the progress of treatment, and in these circumstances, the patient has a duty to act reasonably in his own welfare.[520] His failure to do so may prejudice any claim he may have against the doctor.

The question is whether it is reasonable in the circumstances for the doctor to shift responsibility to the patient. There is no doubt that it is so where the duties are those a reasonable person could be expected to carry out, such as taking drugs as prescribed,[521] refraining from eating or drinking for a limited time,[522] or returning for treatment as requested[523] or as required.[524] In

---

517 *Powell v. Guttman* (1978), 89 D.L.R. (3d) 180 (Man. C.A.); *see also Townsend v. Lai*, [1979] B.C.D. Civ. 2632-03 (B.C.S.C.).

518 *Osburn v. Mohindra* (1980), 29 N.B.R. (2d) 340 (N.B.Q.B.); *see also Price v. Milawski* (1977), 1 L. Med. Q. 303 (Ont. C.A.), where the absence of proper x-rays resulted in an incorrect diagnosis.

519 For a discussion of the communication required by law between a doctor and his patient, *see supra* Chapter 3.

520 *See infra* Chapter 5.

521 *Crossman v. Stewart* (1977), 5 C.C.L.T. 45 (B.C.S.C.).

522 *Webster v. Armstrong supra* n. 456; *Barsy v. Govt. of Man.* (1966), 57 W.W.R. 169 (Man. Q.B.).

523 *Ostrowski v. Lotto* (1972), 31 D.L.R. (3d) 715 (S.C.C.); *More v. Large supra* n. 27; *Chapman v. Rix*, The Times, Dec. 22, 1960.

524 *Murrin v. Janes*, [1949] 4 D.L.R. 403 (Nfld. S.C.).

1912 there was a case[525] where the medical evidence was in conflict as to whether it was reasonable for the doctor to rely on an infant patient's mother to notify him of a displacement of a fracture. The patient was a young child of a poor family living a considerable distance away on very poor roads. But there was a telephone in the town, which the patient's parent could use to contact the doctor. The leg was well bandaged in splints, and the mother was thoroughly instructed, so the doctor left the patient to the mother's care. There were further visits by the doctor, but also evidence that the mother interfered with the weights on the apparatus in order to relieve the child's pain. Eventually, due to misunion, an operation was necessary, but again because of the mother's failure to obey the doctor's instructions the child was left with a deformed leg. It was held that the doctor was reasonable in this reliance on the mother.

When the doctor delegates to the patient the performance of some part of the treatment, there is a duty on the doctor to explain clearly what is expected of him and to warn him as may be required by the circumstances. As was said in an early case:[526]

> . . . where, in the nature of the case the doctor cannot perform the service himself, he is bound to give such instructions as will enable an ordinary person to follow his directions; and, if he failed to do so and injury resulted to the patient therefrom, he would be guilty of actionable negligence.

In another early case, quoted with approval by Meredith[527] a judge warned:[528]

> The failure on the part of a medical man to give a patient proper instructions as to the care and use of an injured limb is negligence for which the medical man is liable for injury resulting therefrom.

In a Newfoundland case[529] a patient lost a great volume of blood after a dental extraction. When he finally sought medical assistance he was near collapse, but the dentist was not held liable for the failure to warn him of the limits of normal blood loss. The trial judge said, "any adult of sound mind must be expected to know and appreciate the effect of too much loss of blood." Regarding the warning a doctor should give about symptoms, he said:[530]

> Now, I am prepared to believe that in some kinds of cases, particularly in this domain of medicine and surgery, the failure by a doctor or surgeon to warn a patient as to the meaning

---

525 *Rickley v. Stratton* (1912), 3 O.W.N. 1341 (Ont. H.C.); *see also Town v. Archer* (1902), 4 O.L.R. 383 (K.B.), where the patient herself relaxed the bandages with similar consequences.
526 *McQuay v. Eastwood supra* n. 144 at 410.
527 Meredith *supra* n. 10 at 88.
528 *Town v. Archer supra* n. 525 at 389. For modern cases bearing out this warning, *see Powell v. Guttman* (1978), 89 D.L.R. (3d) 180 at 186 (Man. C.A.); *Osburn v. Mohindra* (1980), 29 N.B.R. (2d) 340 at 346 (N.B.Q.B.).
529 *Murrin v. Janes supra* n. 524. *Tacknyk v. Lake of the Woods Clinic* (1982), 17 A.C.W.S. (2d) 154 (Ont. C.A.).
530 *Id.* at 405.

of certain symptoms, the significance of which might not be apparent to a layman, might properly expose the practitioner to a charge of negligence. The physician cannot always be in constant attendance upon his patient, who may have to be left to his own devices; and *if the former knows of some specific danger and the possibility of its occurring, it may well be part of his duty to his patient to advise him of the proper action in such emergency.* As an example that occurs to me, a bandage or plaster cast may stop the circulation of the blood; if this occurs the patient may think it perfectly normal and do nothing about it, while if given the proper instructions beforehand he could at once inform the doctor or hospital. [emphasis supplied]

Thus, if the symptoms to be watched for are of a readily observable kind, or commonly known such as in the previous case, there may be little or no duty for the practitioner to warn the patient, since a reasonable person in the position of the patient would become concerned with such an event.[531] If, on the other hand, the warning signs that may occur are not pronounced, appear unrelated to the illness being treated, or may be unfamiliar to the patient, there may be a heavier burden on the practitioner to warn his patient.[532] For example, a doctor was held liable when he failed to warn a patient following knee surgery that the drug he prescribed for her was an anti-coagulent which had the dangerous possible side effect of causing hemorrhage.[533]

Similarly, a practitoner must warn a patient of the possible results that may be occasioned by a change in treatment. In a British Columbia case[534] the patient had diabetes and had taken insulin for 11 years. He went to the doctor to see if he could receive a special diet which would enable him to reduce and possibly to eliminate the dosage of insulin. The doctor put him on a special diet and reduced the insulin substantially. A diabetes specialist, called for the patient at the trial, said that this was a risky procedure because the results are difficult to predict. Within a week the patient was ill in a condition of pre-coma, and went to hospital where his condition improved. At the trial there was a dispute as to the instructions the doctor had given the patient. The doctor blamed the patient for not following instructions. The trial judge found that the only warning given was that the patient might expect a reaction and might be away from work for several days. The court found that the doctor had not met the standard of care in carrying out his duty to instruct the patient because the treatment was dangerous and the doctor did not monitor the patient as carefully as he should have.[535]

---

531 *Moffatt v. Witelson* (1980), 111 D.L.R. (3d) 712 at 719 (Ont. H.C.); *Bissell v. Vancouver Gen. Hosp.*, [1979] 2 A.C.W.S. 433 (B.C.S.C.).

532 *Videto v. Kennedy* (1980), 107 D.L.R. (3d) 612 at 617 (Ont. H.C.); affirmed on this issue 17 C.C.L.T. 307 at 313 (Ont. C.A.).

533 *Crichton v. Hastings supra* n. 18.

534 *Marshall v. Rogers*, [1943] 2 W.W.R. 545 (B.C.C.A.); see also *Foote v. Royal Columbian Hosp.*, [1982] B.C.D. Civ. 2632-05 (B.C.S.C.); affirmed 19 A.C.W.S. (2d) 304 (B.C.C.A.).

535 *Id.* at 555.

> There might be cases in which certain duties might be properly delegated by an attending physician to others . . . but in a case such as this, where admittedly a dangerous remedy was being tried, it would seem to me that the appellant was negligent in delegating to the patient himself the duty of deciding what his real condition was from time to time from what might be called only his subjective symptoms without having daily tests made.

Had the doctor in this case given adequate or reasonable instructions and warnings which the patient had not followed, then the patient might have lost his case or been held contributorily negligent.[536]

4.   CONCLUSION

The principles of negligence law have been discussed in some detail and with reference to the cases that have come before our courts, in the hope that they will thus be more easily understood. Of all areas of private law, negligence is the most flexible and sensitive to necessary change. Because it is continually developing and being applied to novel purposes, there tends to be some inconsistency in terminology and analysis.[537] This troubles many in both the legal and medical professions, but it should be remembered that this is only a symptom of its adaptability, which in turn justifies an optimistic expectation of the continued utility of tort law for adjudicating disputes between doctors and patients and, more importantly, for contributing to positive changes in the doctor-patient relationship.

A doctor must care for his patients according to the duties and standards discussed in this chapter; but he is neither guarantor nor insurer of good results:[538]

> It is so easy to be wise after the event and to condemn as negligence that which was only a misadventure. We ought always to be on our guard against it, especially in cases against hospitals and doctors. Medical science has conferred great benefits on mankind, but these benefits are attended by considerable risks. Every surgical operation is attended by risks. We cannot take the benefits without taking the risks. Every advance in technique is also attended by risks. Doctors, like the rest of us, have to learn by experience; and experience often teaches in a hard way . . .

---

536 *Crossman v. Stewart supra* n. 521.

537 For an example of this with regard to duty *see* Smith, *supra* n. 3.

538 *Roe v. Min. of Health supra* n. 97 at 83 *per* Denning L.J. *See also Clark v. MacLennan,* [1983] 1 All E.R. 416 at 433 (Q.B.) where the judge said: "I hope [the doctor] will take comfort in the thought that even Apollo, the god of healing, and the father of Aesculapius, had his moments of weakness."

5

Defences to an Action
in Negligence

The preceding chapter studied the negligence action primarily from the point of view of the plaintiff describing what the plaintiff in a negligence action against a doctor or hospital[1] must prove. This chapter deals with the action from the defendant's point of view, and describes the various defences available to a doctor or hospital in a negligence action.

The defences can be roughly divided into two groups, informally labelled for the purpose of this discussion as "passive" and "active" defences. A plaintiff in a negligence action must succeed in proving all the elements discussed in Chapter Four; his failure to do so will result in his losing the case. The term "passive defence" means a defence which relies upon the plaintiff's failure to prove one of the elements of his case. This can occur in two ways.

First, a plaintiff who fails to show the existence of a duty,[2] breach of the standard of care, injury or causation may face at the end of his case the defendant's application for a "non-suit" which is a request that the action be stopped then and there because the plaintiff has failed to make out a *prima facie* case, that is, a case in which all the required elements appear to be supported by some evidence. If the defendant's application is successful, the action will be dismissed and no defence will be required.[3] This rarely occurs, however, because cases of such little substance are rarely taken to trial.

---

1 The position of the hospital is discussed in more detail *infra* Chapter 9.
2 This is very rare in medical negligence cases.
3 *Dean v. York County Hosp. Corp.* (1979), 3 L. Med. Q. 231 (Ont. S.C.).

Second, which is the more usual instance, the defendant may attack the essentials of the plaintiff's claim by the introduction of evidence of his own and by the discrediting of the plaintiff's evidence through cross-examination and other adversarial techniques.[4] The passive defences need not be discussed any further; they are easily implied from an understanding of the elements of the negligence action, discussed in Chapter Four.

Frequently, however, a defendant will find it necessary to take advantage of what we have for convenience called the "active" defences. These are the subject of this chapter and involve proof by the doctor that:

(a) he followed the approved practice and was therefore not negligent;

(b) he was at most guilty of an error of judgment from which no liability flows;

(c) the patient was wholly or partially the author of his own misfortune; or

(d) the action is technically barred from a hearing on its merits because the limitation period has lapsed.

A very real problem affecting the analysis of cases for these defences is that the judge frequently canvasses both of the defences of approved practice and error of judgment, but may not make the basis for his judgment clear.[5]

1.   APPROVED PRACTICE[6]

This defence is responsive to the allegation that the defendant has breached the standard of care. It is an attempt by the defendant to prove that the practice or procedure he followed was generally approved and employed by his colleagues at the time in issue and therefore ought not to be regarded as negligence. In medical cases the defence is very old[7] but is still surrounded by considerable uncertainty. Reference to what other members of a profession or business do by custom is not uncommon in negligence actions generally, but such evidence is sometimes relied upon to a greater degree in medical negligence cases.[8]

The treatment which is in issue is compared to the approved practice at the time and in the circumstances in which the treatment occurred,[9] and therefore what was approved practice yesterday may be obsolete today. The doctor who fails to keep pace with advances in medical science may discover that his tried and true but outdated tools or techniques are found wanting.[10] On

---

4 Described *infra* Chapter 7.

5 *See, for example, Lloy v. Milner* (1981), 15 Man. R. (2d) 187 (Q.B.).

6 Also in use are the terms "custom" and "common practice."

7 In *Jackson v. Hyde* (1869), 28 U.C.Q.B. 294 (Ont. C.A.), a new trial was granted.

8 Linden, *Canadian Tort Law* 164 (1982).

9 *Whiteford v. Hunter,* [1950] W.N. 553 (H.L.).

10 *McCormick v. Marcotte,* [1972] S.C.R. 18; *St-Hilaire v. S.,* [1966] C.S. 249 (Que. S.C.).

the other hand, a doctor who acts according to what was approved practice at the time of the alleged negligence will not be viewed in the light of what has developed in the interim between the time of treatment and the time of trial. In a British Columbia case[11] in which the patient was rendered a quadriplegic during the taking of a subclavian angiogram, the defendant radiologist's defence of approved practice was successful. While the cause of the quadriplegia, costocervical leakage into the spinal cord, was recognized in the medical literature at the time of trial, it was an unknown hazard at the time of treatment, and therefore, while failure to take precautions against it today would be negligence, it was not so in 1973.[12]

The defendant bears the onus of proving that his conduct conformed to the approved practice at the time and the role of experts can be crucial in helping him to establish the defence. A patient who required an amputation because of undiagnosed gas gangrene[13] called a surgeon who testified that the proper practice in compound fracture cases was to debride the wound and, if circulatory problems arose, to split the cast. The evidence of the defendant's experts, one of which was an orthopaedic surgeon, was that they would have done just what the defendant did, and the action was dismissed.

The courts do not always follow the experts, however. The Supreme Court of Canada found a psychiatrist liable for the suicide of his patient in the face of testimony from all the experts called that they would have done exactly as the defendant had done.[14] A defendant will also have difficulty proving his case if the practice on which he is relying is limited to, for example, one hospital, if his defence is supported only by the evidence of a non-expert, or if no supporting witness is called at all.[15]

In some recent cases there has been a dearth of evidence as to the approved practice. There are a number of possible reasons for this, including: no approved practice to be established, appropriate witnesses being unavailable, or counsel not taking the necessary steps to have the expert evidence before the court. Courts have resolved the resulting weakness in the evidence in a number of ways such as looking for evidence to corroborate that of either the defendant or the doctor who performed remedial surgery on the patient,[16]

---

11 *McLean v. Weir* (1977), 3 C.C.L.T. 87 (B.C.S.C.); affirmed [1980] 4 W.W.R. 330 (B.C.C.A.); *see also Roe v. Min. of Health*, [1954] 2 Q.B. 66 (C.A.).

12 *McLean v. Weir id.* at 100; *see also Tiesmaki v. Wilson*, [1974] 4 W.W.R. 19; affirmed [1975] 6 W.W.R. 639 (Alta. C.A.); compared to *Demoura v. Mississauga Hosp.* (1979), 3 L. Med. Q. 215 (Ont. S.C.).

13 *Challand v. Bell* (1959), 18 D.L.R. (2d) 150 (Alta. S.C.); *see also Bennett v. C.* (1908), 7 W.L.R. 740 (Man. S.C.).

14 *Villemure v. Turcot*, [1973] S.C.R. 716; reversing [1970] C.A. 538 (Que.).

15 *Anderson v. Chasney*, [1949] 4 D.L.R. 71 at 82; affirmed [1950] 4 D.L.R. 223 (S.C.C.).

16 *Dendaas (Tylor) v. Yackel* (1980), 12 C.C.L.T. 147 at 159 (B.C.S.C.); *see also Cosgrove v. Gaudreau* (1981), 33 N.B.R. (2d) 523 at 527 (Q.B.).

relying primarily upon the opinion of one expert witness,[17] resolving that the medical decision in issue involved judgment alone,[18] or deciding the case on another issue such as cause-in-fact.[19]

Sometimes there is no universal practice.[20] If the common practice is divided but the defendant is among the majority, his position is substantially the same as if no split existed.[21] When he is among the minority, there is authority that the question is whether the practice is followed by "at least a respectable minority of competent practitioners in the same field."[22] This approach seems reasonable as it encourages the adoption of new beneficial medical procedures,[23] yet guards against the use of untested techniques.

Evidence that the defendant's conduct either conformed to or departed from approved practice is clearly significant.[24] In a case[25] where a plastic surgeon was found liable, the expert evidence was that the operation normally took two to four hours and a check of the amount of tissue removed before closing was standard practice. The defendant not only did not take this step, but did not seem to be aware that it was normally done by others. Also, he did the mammoplasty in approximately $1\frac{1}{2}$ hours, a time described by all witnesses as "very fast."

While a departure from the approved practice is a strong indication of failure to meet a reasonable standard of care (although not conclusive)[26] the effect of the defendant's conformity with approved practice is not clear. It may be either a conclusive defence or simply another factor for the court to consider. There is presently no strong statement in Canadian jurisprudence as to which of these is the proper view.[27]

---

17 *Wipfli v. Britten* (1983), 22 C.C.L.T. 104 at 118 (B.C.S.C.).
18 *Gordon v. Davidson* (1980), 4 L. Med. Q. 131 at 136, 144 (Ont. S.C.).
19 *Thompson v. Creaghan* (1982), 42 N.B.R. (2d) 359 at 362-63, 363 (Q.B.).
20 *Karderas v. Clow* (1973), 32 D.L.R. (3d) 303 (Ont. H.C.). For a discussion of English law to the same effect *see* Jackson and Powell, *Professional Negligence* 216 (1982).
21 *Bouillon v. Poire* (1937), 63 Que. K.B. 1 (C.A.). *See also Hunter v. Hanley*, [1955] S.L.T. 213 (1st Div.). Both cases deal with dentists and broken needles; *see also Kobescak v. Chan*, [1981] B.C.D. Civ. 1173-01 (B.C.S.C.).
22 Meredith, *Malpractice Liability of Doctors and Hospitals* 64 (1956), citing two U.S. cases as authority. *See also Bolam v. Friern Hosp.*, [1957] 2 All E.R. 118 (Q.B.).
23 *See LaFleur v. Cornelis* (1979), 28 N.B.R. (2d) 569 at 574 (S.C.). In this case the defendant followed the method used by only 25 per cent of plastic surgeons. He was found negligent in failing to protect the patient's nose, a known risk of this method and the reason others had abandoned it. For a case comment *see* Bergquist, *Case Comment* (1983), 21 A.L.R. 533.
24 *Gent v. Wilson*, [1956] O.R. 257 (C.A.).
25 *White v. Turner* (1981), 15 C.C.L.T. 81 (Ont. H.C.); affirmed 20 C.C.L.T. xxii (Ont. C.A.). *See also Savoie v. Bouchard* (1982), 23 C.C.L.T. 83 (N.B.S.C.); affirmed unreported Sept. 19, 1983 No. 8/83/CA (N.B.C.A.), where the approved practice of doctors and nurses in the operating room was at issue.
26 Fleming, *The Law of Torts* 114 (6th ed. 1983); *see Adderley v. Bremner* (1967), 67 D.L.R. (2d) 274 (Ont. H.C.).
27 Weiler, *Groping Towards A Canadian Tort Law: The Role of the Supreme Court of Canada* (1971), 21 U.T.L.J. 267.

The cases fall into three categories: those that seem to hold that compliance with the approved practice is conclusive of no negligence, those that say it is only *prima facie* evidence of no negligence, and those which are open to either interpretation or are simply unclear.

The seminal case for those cases which hold that compliance with approved practice is a complete defence is *McDaniel v. Vancouver Gen. Hosp.*[28] The patient, who went into hospital with diphtheria was placed in a ward near seven smallpox patients, contracted smallpox, along with eight others. The trial judge and the Court of Appeal found the hospital to be negligent by putting her there where the same nurses were attending all patients, even though the expert evidence was that the defendant's practice was a general one in Canada and the United States. On a direct appeal to the Privy Council in England, the earlier decisions were reversed. Lord Alness said:[29]

> A defendant charged with negligence can clear his feet if he shows that he has acted in accord with general and approved practice.

The case, and these words, have been cited with approval in later Canadian and even English[30] cases, but close scrutiny of the case shows that it has grave flaws. First, Lord Alness cited no authority for the above quoted statement of the law. Second, he uttered earlier the startling proposition that the plaintiff in the case had the onus of proving negligence beyond a reasonable doubt. This was a clear error, as that burden of proof exists only in criminal cases. Third, it appears that the defendant's evidence went virtually unchallenged. The patient called only her family doctor while the defendant had a battery of six experts who affirmed as the general practice the course of action which the defendant had followed. A court faced with cogent uncontradicted evidence has little choice but to follow it and, in such circumstances, even a court which regarded the proof of approved practice as only a factor would likely find for the defendant.

A dearth of evidence by the plaintiff marks many cases following the *McDaniel* rationale. Uncontradicted expert evidence that the patient was treated according to approved practice led to a finding of no liability for a British Columbia hospital[31] when a patient suffering from multiple sclerosis fell out of a bed without side rails. In a similar fact situation an elderly lady awaiting a cataract operation was injured in a fall from a hospital bed, but the hospital was held not liable.[32] The defendant's evidence that guard rails were

---

28 [1934] 4 D.L.R. 593; reversing [1934] 1 D.L.R. 557 (P.C.).
29 *Id.* at 597.
30 *Marshall v. Lindsey County Council*, [1935] 1 K.B. 516; affirmed [1937] A.C. 97 (H.L.).
31 *McKay v. Royal Inland Hosp.* (1964), 48 D.L.R. (2d) 665 (B.C.S.C.); *see also Cahoon v. Edmonton Hosp. Bd.* (1957), 23 W.W.R. 131 (Alta. S.C.).
32 *Florence v. Les Soeurs de Misericorde* (1962), 39 W.W.R. 201 (Man. C.A.).

not required was not rebutted. Finally, in a case[33] where the defendant clearly established that he had followed approved practice in treating a psychiatric patient who committed suicide, the plaintiff had no contrary evidence, and the doctor and hospital were not held negligent.[34] There is a lesson here for counsel in future cases, in connection with the plaintiff's privilege to adduce rebuttal evidence after a doctor has introduced evidence of approved practice:[35]

> The plaintiff had adequate opportunity and was virtually invited to call medical evidence in rebuttal. For the plaintiff the most advantageous of all times in this trial for medical evidence was in rebuttal, after all the defence's experts had been heard. No rebuttal medical evidence was offered. Instead the court was invited, urged, to speculate against the unanimous evidence of exceptionally well qualified experts to bring in a finding contrary to their opinions.

Thus, from *McDaniel v. Vancouver Gen. Hosp.* has come the view that the effect of the approved practice defence is to establish a conclusive defence for the doctor. However, *McDaniel* itself has much to raise doubt as to its authority, and the cases purporting to follow it can be explained as cases of uncontradicted expert evidence, where the plaintiff simply failed to discharge his onus of proving negligence by a preponderance of evidence.

On the other hand, there is a respectable body of law supporting the proposition that compliance with approved practice is only *prima facie* evidence of no negligence. The authorities include more recent cases and a Supreme Court of Canada decision.[36]

In *Anderson v. Chasney,*[37] a case heard by the Supreme Court of Canada, a surgeon who performed a tonsilloadenoidectomy on a child was told by the anaesthetist, after the operation, that all the sponges had not been removed. The surgeon checked and found no sponges, but the child later died by suffocating on one. The defendant testified that it was not his practice to use sponges with strings nor to have a nurse count sponges, and there was evidence that in not doing so he followed the practice in his hospital. Both methods however, were available to him and were used by some surgeons in other hospitals. The Supreme Court of Canada approved the conclusion of the Manitoba Court of Appeal[38] which was that the expert evidence as to approved practice is not conclusive, especially where the conduct being questioned is not technical but relates to taking precautions. The courts decided that, as far as non-technical matters are concerned, an ordinary person is competent to determine what is a safe practice, and held the defendant negligent.

---

33 *Stadel v. Albertson*, [1954] 2 D.L.R. 328 (Sask. C.A.); *see also Karderas v. Clow supra* n. 20.
34 All of these cases cited and applied *McDaniel v. Vancouver Gen. Hosp. supra* n. 28.
35 *McLean v. Weir supra* n. 11 at 101.
36 *See also* Meredith, *supra* n. 22 at 64.
37 *Supra* n. 15; *see also Leadbetter v. Brand* (1980), 37 N.S.R. (2d) 581 at 604 (S.C.).
38 [1949] 4 D.L.R. 71.

In *Crits v. Sylvester,*[39] another tonsillectomy case, the patient became cyanotic during the operation and the anaesthetist took emergency measures to correct the situation. After doing so he left a valve slightly open and some oxygen escaped which exploded, causing injury to the patient. The main issue was whether the anaesthetist was negligent by leaving the oxygen valve partly open, and the doctor's primary defence was that he had followed approved practice. This the Court of Appeal[40] doubted, and added:[41]

> Even it it had been established that what was done by the anaesthetist was in accordance with "standard practice", *such evidence is not necessarily to be taken as conclusive on an issue of negligence,* particularly where the so-called standard practice related to something which was not essentially conduct requiring special medical skill and training either for its performance or a proper understanding of it. This was the view of the Court of Appeal of Manitoba in *Anderson v. Chasney* . . . If it was standard practice, it was not safe practice and should not have been followed. [emphasis supplied]

The anaesthetist's appeal to the Supreme Court of Canada[42] was dismissed. Regarding the main basis for liability the court said that there was no evidence that what the defendant did was within the approved practice. However, on another ground of alleged negligence, the doctor had complied with the approved practice, and the court said:[43]

> But the anaesthetist's conduct in this respect had been approved by other medical witnesses, and it would be dangerous for a Court to attempt in such a matter to proscribe a step approved by the general experience of technicians and not shown to be clearly unnecessary or unduly hazardous.

Thus, while the Supreme Court of Canada indicated that it would be dangerous to reject approved practice, it did not say that the court had no such power;[44] in fact, it implied that a court was to exercise the power if the practice was "clearly unnecessary or unduly hazardous."

These two cases placed restrictions on the court's discretion to hold a defendant liable in the face of approved practice by limiting it to non-technical or precautionary matters. They have been followed in a number of recent cases.

In a case from New Brunswick[45] a sponge was left in the patient's abdomen. Mr. Justice Miller recognized that the approved practice was to rely on the nurse's count, but said that "oversimplifies the duty of the doctor" and held the doctor liable because "a person has the right to expect that a medical doctor . . . will perform a surgical procedure without leaving a foreign body

---

39 [1955] 3 D.L.R. 181 (Ont. H.C.).
40 (1956), 1 D.L.R. (2d) 502 (Ont. C.A.).
41 *Id.* at 514.
42 [1956] S.C.R. 991.
43 *Id.* at 992.
44 *See also Johnston v. Wellesley Hosp.* (1970), 17 D.L.R. (3d) 139 at 148 (Ont. H.C.).
45 *Cosgrove v. Goudreau* (1981), 33 N.B.R. (2d) 523 (Q.B.).

within the patient."[46] A doctor was found to have follwed the approved practice in a Nova Scotia case,[47] but the judge opined that this practice of not consulting the patient's family doctor before the administration of an anaesthetic, although not negligence, should be changed, "if practical."

In another case[48] where it was held that there was no departure from approved practice and no liability, the learned trial judge made some *obiter* comments about the role of the court and the effect of conformity with approved practice. Mr. Justice Callaghan said:[49]

> I do not accept, however, that the Court has no active role in determining the outcome in such matters. I accept that the evidence of approved practice is most helpful and persuasive and I fully recognize an absence of expertise in medical matters on the part of the Court. In my view, however, *a court has a right to strike down substandard approved practice when common sense dictates such a result*. No profession is above the law and the courts on behalf of the public have a critical role to play in monitoring and precipitating changes where required in professional standards. The courts, however, must recognize the limitations of their expertise, and must give full credit to the opinions of professional experts, especially when . . . there is no disagreement among the experts who testified. [emphasis supplied]

There have also been a number of cases where the directives of the Supreme Court of Canada on approved practice seem to have been ignored. Two of these cases are from the Manitoba Court of Appeal. In the earlier one[50] a chiropractor by his manipulations caused serious injury to a patient who was suffering from an extruded vertebral disc. The defendant called expert evidence that in doing so he had been following approved practice. But his own testimony was found to be "conclusive as to the unwisdom of the practice followed,"[51] and he was found liable by both courts. The Court of Appeal affirmed *Anderson v. Chasney*[52] and said:[53]

> Moreover, while it is true that in the great majority of alleged malpractice cases a charge of negligence can be met by evidence to the effect that what was done was in accordance with general and approved practice, nevertheless *it is the courts and not the particular profession concerned which decide whether negligence is established in a particular case*. [emphasis supplied]

In a later case[54] an orthopaedic surgeon was found to have followed approved practice in surgery and in post-operative treatment but the patient died. The Court of Appeal affirmed the trial judge who had said:[55]

---

46 *Id*. at 527.
47 *Leadbetter v. Brand* (1980), 37 N.S.R. (2d) 581 (S.C.).
48 *Hajgato v. London Health Assn*. (1982), 36 O.R. (2d) 669 (H.C.).
49 *Id*. at 692-93; *see also Belore v. Mississauga Hosp*. unreported November 1979 No. 1644/77 (Ont. Co. Ct.), where the judge found the use of a mouthgag by an oral surgeon to be within approved practice and not dangerous.
50 *Penner v. Theobald* (1962), 38 W.W.R. 397; affirmed 40 W.W.R. 216 (Man. C.A.).
51 (1962), 40 W.W.R. 216 at 229.
52 *Supra* n. 15.
53 (1962), 40 W.W.R. 216 at 228-29.
54 *Chubey v. Ahsan*, [1975] 1 W.W.R. 120; affirmed [1976] 3 W.W.R. 367 (Man. C.A.).
55 [1975] 1 W.W.R. 120 at 129.

It is very easy, after the happening of the event of misadventure, to condemn Dr. Ahsan for being negligent because he left the patient in the recovery room in the charge of regular hospital staff before she actually woke up, and proceeded to attend to his other duties in another hospital. In truth, however, this same procedure followed by Dr. Ahsan is practised by most of the orthopaedic surgeons in this area and their patients suffer no ill effects. I would like to point out however that *even had Dr. Ahsan followed accepted practice of the profession, he could not escape liability if such practice did not meet the legal requirement of care for the patient.* [emphasis supplied]

The Supreme Court of Canada in *Villemure v. Turcot*[56] held a psychiatrist and a hospital liable for the death of a patient known to be suicidal who fell from a hospital window.[57] This was done in the face of the unanimous expert evidence that the defendants had followed approved practice in caring for the patient. Two Justices who dissented said the court must be guided by the approved practice. Unfortunately, the majority did not take this opportunity to clarify the law, but simply adopted the reasons of a dissenting Justice of the Court of Appeal of Quebec who had in turn adopted the trial judge's reasons. At trial, two experts said that they would have done exactly what the defendant doctor had done, to which the trial judge replied that had they done so they, too, would have been negligent.

In view of this decision of the Supreme Court of Canada it is difficult to accept the *dicta* of a British Columbia Supreme Court[58] which referred to *McDaniel* but did not consider *Villemure*. The trial judge said:[59]

The court has no status whatsoever to come to a medical conclusion contrary to unanimous medical evidence before it even if it wanted to, which is not the situation in this case. If the medical evidence is equivocal, the court may elect which of the theories advanced it accepts. If only two medical theories are advanced, the court may elect between the two or reject them both; it cannot adopt a third theory of its own, no matter how plausible such might be to the court.

To summarize, a fair synopsis of the present law as to the effect of the approved practice defence is as follows: The defence of approved practice raises a *prima facie* case that the standard of care has been met. When the defendant is a hospital which has followed an approved practice the defence is stronger and may even be conclusive.[60] Whatever the effect, the court has the power to find compliance with approved practice to be negligence. A court is more likely to exercise this power in regard to non-technical matters, or safety precautions where the layman can appreciate the risks to a patient. Where defendants have been exonerated because of compliance with approved practice, those practices have been found to meet the standard of care or have not been

---

56 [1973] S.C.R. 716.
57 Note the case of *University Hosp. Bd. v. Lepine*, [1966] S.C.R. 561, was distinguished as being one where there was no warning of the patient's suicidal tendencies.
58 *McLean v. Weir supra* n. 11.
59 *Id.* at 101; note that the Court of Appeal in dismissing the appeal did not discuss this portion of the trial judgment.
60 *Worth v. Royal Jubilee Hosp.* (1980), 4 L. Med. Q. 59 at 60 (B.C.C.A.).

shown to be substandard by expert evidence presented by the plaintiff. Compliance with approved practice may be negligence, but failure to comply is not necessarily negligence.[61]

Lack of clarity in the law and in some decisions makes it difficult to fit some of the cases into these conclusions. Two important cases serve as good examples. Professor Weiler[62] has characterized *Wilson v. Swanson*[63] as a case where the defence of approved practice was conclusive. Yet the defendant, who had the onus of proving the defence, called no evidence at all, and relied on the plaintiff's failure to establish a *prima facie* case of negligence. Indeed, there is no patent discussion of the defence at any level but in the result it would seem that the decision was that the defendant had followed approved practice; at least he was held to have met the standard of care. In another Supreme Court of Canada case, *Ostrowski v. Lotto*,[64] the evidence was balanced and the doctor was found to be negligent at trial, although he "may well have been consistent with accepted standards,"[65] but not negligent in the higher courts. Approved practice was referred to directly by the Court of Appeal[66] who, ignoring Canadian jurisprudence, chose to adopt law from an English case which held that compliance with approved practice is conclusive of no negligence. The Supreme Court of Canada adopted the Court of Appeal's reasons. Both cases seem to follow the *McDaniel* rationale, but their authority seems weak, given the apparent insufficiency of defence evidence in *Wilson* and the failure to deal with Canadian jurisprudence in *Ostrowski*.

Professor Weiler[67] has called for a reconciliation of the divergent decisions. Unfortunately, the Supreme Court of Canada has not yet had the opportunity to do so. In his decision on informed consent in *Reibl v. Hughes*[68] Mr. Justice Laskin did indicate an unwillingness to allow the medical profession to determine the standard required for the disclosure of risks of medical treatment; however, he also noted that the issue of informed consent was a different one from that of negligent treatment. But for this caveat one might be tempted to predict that Mr. Justice Laskin's rejection of the professional standard in informed consent would mean a rejection of the conclusive defence effect of approved practice as stated in the *McDaniel* case.

If the defence is conclusive, the outcome is determined solely by the expert evidence; the judge plays only a minor role in the decision.[69] However,

---

61 *Hunter v. Hanley supra* n. 21. *See* Linden, *The Negligent Doctor* (1973), 11 Osgoode Hall L.J. 31 at 34.
62 *Supra* n. 27 at 335.
63 [1956] 5 D.L.R. (2d) 113 (S.C.C.).
64 (1972), 31 D.L.R. (3d) 715.
65 These are the words of the trial judge (1968), 2 D.L.R. (3d) 440 at 455 (Ont. H.C.).
66 (1970), 15 D.L.R. (3d) 402 at 412 adopting *Bolam v. Friern Hosp. supra* n. 22.
67 *Supra* n. 27.
68 (1980), 14 C.C.L.T. 1 at 17 (S.C.C.); *White v. Turner* (1981), 15 C.C.L.T. 81 at 100 (Ont. H.C.); affirmed 20 C.C.L.T. xxii (Ont. C.A.).
69 *See* Somerville, *Legal Investigation of A Medical Investigation* (1981), A.L.R. 171 at 190.

if the effect of compliance with approved practice is only to raise a *prima facie* case of no negligence, as is the case with respect to other professions,[70] then the judge maintains an active role in determining the outcome, which seems to be consistent with the often expressed view that it is the court which sets the standard, not the profession.[71]

Reflection on the policy for giving any effect at all to evidence of approved practice would be helpful to the resolution of the issue.[72] A judge has no expertise in medical matters. He is taught by the experts who give evidence and must by listening and asking questions learn enough to review the defendant's exercise of his professional skill and judgment. The process is no different when the defendant is an engineer, lawyer, or any other professional. The approved practice is likely what the professional learned and developed competence in doing.[73] It is what his colleagues expect him to do and may be all he knows how to do. When a court strikes it down as inadequate or substandard, the profession may feel that it has suffered a severe blow.[74] On the other hand, no person or profession is to be above the law. Neither engineer nor artisan is free to set the standard of care the public requires,[75] nor should the medical profession. Inertia is a disease that knows no professional borders. The courts on behalf of the public have a critical role to play in reviewing, monitoring and precipitating change in professional standards. Of course, there must be a balancing of professional and public interests; holding compliance with approved practice to be negligence may be the only route to move some members of a profession to a new, better course,[76] yet may also impede medical progress.[77] The courts are the appropriate organ for the adjustment of this balance, and should not abdicate their responsibility to adjudicate upon the negligence in any profession.

2. ERROR OF JUDGMENT

A doctor is not liable for an honest error of judgment provided he acts

---

70 *Dziwenka v. R.*, [1971] 1 W.W.R. 195 at 205 (Alta. C.A.).

71 *Supra* Chapter 4.

72 Linden, *supra* n. 8 at 166; Magnet, *Withholding Treatment From Defective Newborns: Legal Aspects* (1982), 42 R. du B. 187 at 208.

73 Morris, *Custom and Negligence* (1942), 42 Colum. L. Rev. 1147 at 1148.

74 *See Helling v. Carey* (1974), 519 P. (2d) 981 (Wash. S.C.), where an ophthalmologist was found negligent in failing to administer a simple test to diagnose glaucoma, despite the fact that in failing to do so he had complied with the approved practice. For a comment *see* Mann (1975), 28 Vand. L. Rev. 441. Note Wiley, *The Impact of Judicial Decision on Professional Conduct: An Empirical Study* (1982), 55 S. Calif. L.R. 345 who concludes (at 383) that in the *Helling* case the expert evidence of the approved practice was inaccurate and misleading. *See also* Pearson, *The Role of Custom in Medical Malpractice Cases* (1976), 51 Ind. L.J. 528.

75 *Hajgato v. London Health Assn.* (1982), 36 O.R. (2d) 669 at 693 (H.C.); *Penner v. Theobald* (1962), 35 D.L.R. (2d) 700 at 712 (Man. C.A.).

76 *Anderson v. Chasney supra* n. 15; *Villemure v. Turcot supra* n. 56.

77 *Cryderman v. Ringrose*, [1977] 3 W.W.R. 109; affirmed [1978] 3 W.W.R. 481 (Alta. C.A.).

after a careful examination in what he believes to be the patient's best interests.[78] A doctor can give no guarantee of success, nor insure a cure, so a diagnosis may be inaccurate or treatment may be improper and an injured patient may go uncompensated.[79] Negligence cannot be assumed simply on the basis of the consequences of medical treatment to a patient.[80] The conduct of a doctor is not to be measured by the result, for the practice of medicine is an art as well as a science; a great deal of medical treatment depends on the exercise of judgment. But it is not enough for the doctor to show that he exercised his judgment. He must prove that in doing so he met the standard of care required of him.[81]

Error of judgment is a defence in which the doctor admits he made an error, but denies that he is negligent because he possessed and exercised the skill, knowledge and judgment of the average of his special group when considering the patient's case.[82] There are many Canadian cases in which the defence has been accepted and it is accordingly well defined.

The case most often referred to in defining error of judgment is *Wilson v. Swanson*[83] where the surgeon in the course of an operation had to decide whether to proceed with more radical surgery if the conditions he found indicated a malignant growth rather than a benign one. He made an error of judgment in deciding it was malignant and removed a large portion of the stomach, pancreas and spleen. The court said:[84]

> An error in judgment has long been distinguished from an act of unskilfulness or carelessness or due to lack of knowledge. Although universally accepted procedures must be observed, they furnish little or no assistance in resolving such a predicament as faced the surgeon here. In such a situation a decision must be made without delay based on limited known and unknown factors; and *the honest and intelligent exercise of judgment has long been recognized as satisfying the professional obligation.* [emphasis supplied]

This court and others in Canada have adopted a statement of the law from an American case:[85]

---

78 Meredith, *supra* n. 22 at 63; Linden, *supra* n. 61 at 39.

79 *See* the *obiter* comments of Krever J. in *Ferguson v. Hamilton Civic Hosp.* (1983), 23 C.C.L.T. 254 at 313 (Ont. H.C.).

80 *White v. Turner* (1981), 15 C.C.L.T. 81 at 92 (Ont. H.C.); appeal dismissed 20 C.C.L.T. xxii (Ont. C.A.); *Whitehouse v. Jordan,* [1981] 1 All E.R. 267 (H.L.).

81 Note the English case of *Whitehouse v. Jordan,* [1981] 1 All E.R. 267 at 276, 281, 284 (H.L.). Although the House of Lords dismissed the patient's appeal from the Court of Appeal, a number of law lords, in reacting to the conclusions and concerns of Denning M.R., stated that there could be liability for some (though not ''mere'') errors of judgment. It is submitted that this is confusing. The term ''error of judgment'' should be a term of art reserved for the defence.

82 *Challand v. Bell supra* n. 13 at 154.

83 *Supra* n. 63.

84 *Id.* at 120.

85 *Rann v. Twitchell* (1909), 82 Vt. 79 at 84, 71 A. 1045 at 1046 (Vt. S.C.).

He is not to be judged by the result, nor is he to be held liable for an error of judgment. His negligence is to be determined by reference to the pertinent facts existing at the time of his examination and treatment, of which he knew, or in the exercise of due care, should have known. It may consist in a failure to apply the proper remedy upon a correct determination of existing physical conditions, or it may precede that and result from a failure properly to inform himself of these conditions. If the latter, then it must appear that he had a reasonable opportunity for examination and that the true physical conditions were so apparent that they could have been ascertained by the exercise of the required degree of care and skill. For, if a determination of these physical facts resolves itself into a question of judgment merely, he cannot be held liable for his error.

Johnston v. Wellesley Hosp.[86] is an example of harmful treatment being held to be only an error of judgment. The patient suffered from acne and the doctor, a dermatologist, decided to treat it with a mixture of frozen carbon dioxide and acetone set on the face for 15 seconds. The time turned out to be too long and the patient suffered permanent scarring. The court held this to be "an error in judgment, but no more."[87]

Failure to correctly diagnose the patient's condition has also been held to be an error of judgment in a number of cases.[88] In 1953 a rural general practitioner missed a diagnosis of gas gangrene which required the amputation of part of the patient's arm[89] and in 1960 a small-town general practitioner failed to diagnose a rare throat condition affecting respiration.[90] In 1962 in Saskatchewan a general practitioner misdiagnosed as appendicular colic an acute attack of appendicitis.[91] In 1964 in Alberta a general practitioner diagnosed a family to be suffering from influenza when in fact it was carbon monoxide poisoning and three children died[92] and in 1976 a family practitioner in Nova Scotia[93] diagnosed gastritis but not a concurrent ischemic heart disease from which the patient died within the hour. Specialists have also been successful in the defence of an error of judgment. An Ontario cardiovascular and thoracic surgeon[94] closed a pulmonary artery with circular ligatures that were tied too loosely and slipped, allowing blood into the pleural cavity causing death of the patient. In British Columbia a resident in anaesthesiology[95] commenced the resuscitation of a baby by positive pressure respiration, a procedure expert witnesses said was inappropriate, but within seconds changed to the correct procedure. An Ontario orthopaedic surgeon[96] failed to diagnose an infection in circumstances described by the trial judge as "extraordinary"

---

86 (1970), 17 D.L.R. (3d) 139 (Ont. H.C.).
87 *Id.* at 152.
88 *See supra* Chapter 4.
89 *Challand v. Bell supra* n. 13.
90 *Tiesmaki v. Wilson*, [1975] 6 W.W.R. 639 (Alta. C.A.).
91 *Wilson v. Stark* (1967), 61 W.W.R. 705 (Sask. C.A.).
92 *Ostash v. Sonnenberg* (1968), 63 W.W.R. 257 (Alta. C.A.).
93 *Ehler v. Smith* (1978), 29 N.S.R. (2d) 309 (S.C.).
94 *O'Reilly v. Spratt* (1982), 19 A.C.W.S. (2d) 137 (Ont. H.C.).
95 *Meyer v. Gordon* (1981), 17 C.C.L.T. 1 (B.C.S.C.).
96 *Hajgato v. London Health Assn.* (1982), 36 O.R. (2d) 669 (H.C.).

but was held to have made only an error of judgment. Mr. Justice Callaghan concluded:[97]

> No human being is infallible and in the present state of science even the most eminent specialist may err in detecting the true nature of these conditions.

Finally, in an unusual case it was held that a hospital was not liable because a nurse failed to call an orderly to assist in raising a bed. The failure was merely an error in judgment and thus the hospital was not liable for injuries suffered by the patient's husband when he assisted in lifting the bed.[98]

By contrast, it was not an error in judgment to fail "to carry out a reasonable, adequate and proper post-operative observation of [a patient's] legs to watch for signs of circulatory impairment."[99] In discussing the authorities on the defence the trial judge set out the following explanation of the law:[100]

> The law, as exemplified by the above and other authorities, in my opinion, clearly protects a doctor from liability to his patient for damages in cases where with respect to medical technical matters, the doctor honestly and intelligently applied his mind to the problem presenting itself and arrived at a conclusion or judgment upon which he acted, which conclusion or judgment subsequently proved to be wrong. He made an honest but wrong decision as to what course to take in prevailing circumstances.

Similarly, the defence of error of judgment pleaded by a doctor who operated to remove a cyst was not successful. The doctor was found to be negligent and the court said:[101]

> In the face of the medical evidence of the dangers inherent in removing an infected cyst in that particular area because of the close proximity of the spinal accessory nerve, it seems to me that more than a mere error in judgment was involved; that the doctor should have been aware of these dangers and deferred surgery until the infection had been treated.

Thus, the defence does not avail the doctor who ignores the medical evidence of danger to which he ought to be alert. A Manitoba court[102] held that the complication of surgery called Volkmann's ischemic contracture was just the condition that an orthopaedic surgeon should have anticipated in a patient with Paget's disease. Obviously a mistake such as removing 25 per cent more

---

97 *Id.* at 686-87.

98 *Elverson v. Doctors Hosp.* (1974), 4 O.R. (2d) 748 (Ont. C.A.); *see also Foote v. Royal Columbian Hosp.* (1982), 38 B.C.L.R. 222, (B.C.S.C.); affirmed 19 A.C.W.S. (2d) 304 (B.C.C.A.), where it was held that a failure by the nursing staff to chart an accident was an error of judgment.

99 *Badger v. Surkan* (1970), 16 D.L.R. (3d) 146 at 162; affirmed [1973] 1 W.W.R. 302 (Sask. C.A.); *see also Dean v. York County Hosp. Corp.* (1979), 3 L. Med. Q. 231 at 238 (Ont. S.C.), where the failure to see a wound as evidence of a compound fracture was not an error of judgment.

100 *Id.* at 162.

101 *Fizer v. Keys,* [1974] 2 W.W.R. 14 at 25 (Alta. S.C.).

102 *Rietze v. Bruser,* [1979] 1 W.W.R. 31 (Man. Q.B.); *see also Osburn v. Mohindra* (1980), 29 N.B.R. (2d) 340 (S.C.), where a patient's complaint of pain was ignored.

tissue from one breast resulting in a "severe distortion" of the patient is more than an error of judgment by a plastic surgeon doing a mastectomy.[103]

Unlike the defence of approved practice, the effect of the defence of error of judgment is certain — there is no liability. But it is more difficult to predict when this defence has been established, and the credibility and sincerity of the doctor as well as the strength of his expert evidence are obviously important.[104] As Meredith[105] pointed out, the strength of this defence is often overlooked by plaintiffs.

3.   CONTRIBUTORY NEGLIGENCE OF THE PATIENT

A patient has certain duties toward the doctor and to himself. In carrying out these duties he is expected to meet the standard of care of a reasonable patient. If he does not and the breach of this standard is the factual and proximate cause of his injuries he is contributorily negligent,[106] and his compensation will be reduced accordingly.[107] Of course, if his injury is due exclusively to his own negligence his action will be dismissed.[108]

The effect of such a finding at one time precluded any recovery by the patient in Canada, but all provinces now have legislation directing a court to apportion damages in proportion to the degree of fault found against the respective parties.[109] The legislation also provides that if it is not practicable to determine respective degrees of fault or negligence, the parties are deemed to be equally at fault. Thus, the defence of contributory negligence is no

---

103 *MacDonald v. Ross* (1983), 24 C.C.L.T. 242 at 248 (N.S.S.C.).

104 *Leonard v. Knott*, [1980] 1 W.W.R. 673 at 696 (B.C.C.A.).

105 Meredith, *supra* n. 22 at 63.

106 For a discussion of these *see supra* Chapter 4.

107 Linden, *supra* n. 8 at 463. Note that the duty of every plaintiff to mitigate his damages refers to conduct *after* the accident. Fleming, *Law of Torts* 226 (1982). *See Savoie v. Bouchard* (1982), 23 C.C.L.T. 83 (N.B.Q.B.); affirmed unreported Sept. 19, 1983 No. 8/83/CA (N.B.C.A.). *Poulin v. Health Sciences Centre* (1982), 18 Man. R (2d) 274 (Q.B.); *see also Strickland v. St. John's* (1983), 41 Nfld. & P.E.I.R. 219 (Nfld. D.C.).

108 Meredith, *supra* n. 22 at 88. Note that the defence of *volenti non fit injuria* seems inappropriate in a medical negligence case. *See Linden supra* n. 8 at 501. *See also Savoie v. Bouchard* (1982), 23 C.C.L.T. 83 (N.B.Q.B.). For instances of the defence in the U.S. *see* Louisell and Williams, *Medical Malpractice*, Matthew Bender, New York (1983), at 238. In England, *see Emeh v. Kensington*, The Times, 21 December 1982.

109 Contributory Negligence Act, R.S.A. 1980, c. C-23 and Tort-Feasors Act, R.S.A. 1980, c. T-6; Negligence Act, R.S.B.C. 1979, c. 298; Tortfeasors and Contributory Negligence Act, R.S.M. 1970, c. T90; Contributory Negligence Act, R.S.N.B. 1973, c. C-19, and Tortfeasors Act, R.S.N.B. 1973, c. T-8; Contributory Negligence Act, R.S.N. 1970, c. 61; Contributory Negligence Act, R.S.N.S. 1967, c. 54 and Tortfeasors Act, R.S.N.S. 1967, c. 307; Negligence Act, R.S.O. 1980, c. 315; Contributory Negligence Act, 1978 (P.E.I.), c. 3; Contributory Negligence Act, R.S.S. 1978, c. C-31. Note that in Quebec the notion of *partage de responsabilité* has long been admitted: *Hôpital Notre-Dame de l'Espérance v. Laurent*, [1978] 1 S.C.R. 605. *See* Kouri, *The Patient's Duty to Co-operate* (1972), 3 R.D.U.S. 43 at 57.

longer a complete one in Canada or in England.[110] As with all defences, the onus of proving it is on the defendant doctor or hospital.[111]

A simple example of how apportionment legislation works follows. Assume a doctor is found to be negligent in his treatment of the patient, who is found to be contributorily negligent for failing to follow the doctor's instructions. If the judge assessed the patient's damages at $10,000 and apportioned liability as 60 per cent to the doctor and 40 per cent to the plaintiff, the result would be that the patient would recover $6,000.

While contributory negligence has been discussed in a handful of Canadian cases, there are only two from British Columbia and one from Quebec where it seems to have been applied.[112] Theoretically the law and practice in a medical negligence case should be the same as in any other negligence case and the decision to find contributory negligence has been "quite frequent"[113] in the ordinary negligence action. One explanation for its rare application in medical negligence cases might be that the seemingly unequal position of the parties, in that the plaintiff patient may have been ill, submissive, or incapable of acting in his own best interests, has led the courts to set the standard of care that patients must meet for their own care at an unreasonably low level. As patients strive for a more equal role in their medical care and for taking aggressive steps in their own treatment, it is predictable and just that there will be more patients found to be contributorily negligent with a consequential reduction in the compensation that they will receive.[114]

In the older British Columbia case[115] a patient was held to be two-thirds to blame for the blindness she suffered and her doctor, a dermatologist, one-third to blame. (Thus she would get $26,666 of the $80,000 assessed as damages.) She had consulted the dermatologist for a facial skin disorder and he prescribed a drug known as chloroquine or Aralen® which she took for approximately six months under prescription. Because she was a medical

---

110 For an English case discussing the defence, see *Emeh v. Kensington*, The Times, 21 December 1982. For a discussion of the application of contributory negligence in the U.S., see Louisell and Williams, *Medical Malpractice*, Matthew Bender, New York (1983), at 246.

111 *Town v. Archer* (1902), 4 O.L.R. 383 (K.B.).

112 Note that in *Osburn v. Mohindra* (1980), 29 N.B.R. (2d) 340 (Q.B.), the defendants, a doctor and the hospital, were held liable in proportions of 75 per cent and 25 per cent *of 75 per cent* respectively. The reason for the plaintiff's recovery being reduced by 25 per cent was not discussed.

113 Klar, *Contributory Negligence and Contribution Between Tortfeasors* in Studies in Canadian Tort Law 146 (2d ed. Klar 1977).

114 Note that it has been suggested that it may not be wise from a tactical point of view to plead this defence but, instead, to take the position that the patient was the sole cause of his own injuries. Louisell and Williams, *supra* n. 110 at 249-50.

115 *Crossman v. Stewart* (1977), 5 C.C.L.T. 45 (B.C.S.C.); *see also Molnar v. Conway* unreported 22 June 1978 No. 114193 (Alta. S.C.).

receptionist she was able to obtain the drug from a drug salesman at one-half the price and without a prescription and for seven months she took the drug on this basis. At that time the dermatologist who had been alerted to the possible serious side effects of the drug to vision had all patients whom he had treated with it see an ophthalmologist. Unfortunately, he did not read carefully enough the resulting report on the plaintiff because it would have alerted him to the patient's unorthodox practice. Thereafter for two more years the patient obtained the drug from the salesman and when this man retired she went back to the defendant and was prescribed the drug for at least a further eight months. The trial judge found that at no time was the patient warned of the danger of the prolonged use of the drug but also that the defendant did not have actual knowledge of her continuous use of it either. The evidence indicated that her eyes would not have been damaged had her consumption been limited to the prescriptions.

The patient's negligence was found to lie in obtaining prescription drugs from an unorthodox source, using them on a prolonged basis, and not consulting her doctor. She had failed to meet the standard expected of a reasonable patient and was the major cause of her own injury. The doctor's negligence was based on his failure to carefully peruse the ophthalmologist's report and his failure to discern from "corneal changes" in that report the probability of recent consumption of the drug. This was obviously a clear case for the application of the contributory negligence rules. In fact, it is even arguable that, like the dental patient who nearly bled to death before obtaining medical assistance,[116] this patient was the sole cause of her injury. The standard of care expected of the reasonable patient is tied to the degree of knowledge with respect to medical matters possessed by the layman. Just as the reasonable person is taken to know that loss of a large volume of blood will seriously endanger his health, he ought also to be attributed with the knowledge that obtaining and consuming prescription drugs without medical supervision is risky. However, the fact remains that the plaintiff in this case was given no warning as to the danger of this particular drug and, in fact, after what she would believe was a satisfactory ophthalmological examination, may have had reason to believe that the drug was safe.

In the Quebec case,[117] the evidence of the doctor and patient was in substantial conflict, but the higher courts were not prepared to disturb the trial judge's holding that the patient was contributorily negligent. The doctor was held negligent for failing to diagnose a fracture of the head of the femur, but the patient did not get further medical treatment for over three months and her claim was reduced by one quarter. Unlike the patient in the British Columbia

---

116 *Murrin v. Janes*, [1949] 4 D.L.R .403 (Nfld. S.C.).
117 *Hôspital Notre-Dame de l'Espérance v. Laurent*, [1978] 1 S.C.R. 605; affirming [1974] C.A. 543 (Que.).

case, who was active in her own treatment, this patient was passive: she failed to seek treatment. The difference in conduct is reflected in the amount by which each patient's compensation was reduced.

There is an unusual case from British Columbia[118] where the employer of the doctors, a hockey club, was successful in reducing its liability by 20 per cent because of the contributory negligence of a hockey player who failed to seek further medical care from the team doctors or consult his own doctor when serious symptoms persisted.

The defence was pursued without success in three other Canadian cases. In *Foote v. Royal Columbian Hosp.*[119] a doctor was found liable for failing to alert hospital staff to the risk that an epileptic patient whose medication he had changed might have a seizure at any time. During an unsupervised bath the 15-year-old did have a seizure and suffered injuries. The doctor alleged that she should be found contributorily negligent. The trial judge disagreed but said, *obiter,* that he had been convinced that the patient had understood instructions not to bath unsupervised, he would have held her contributorily negligent to the extent of 50 per cent. A man playing touch football broke a lens in his glasses and injured his eye. The optometrist and lens manufacturer whom he sued pleaded contributory negligence, but the trial judge held that this had not been proven by the defendants.[120] In *Bernier v. Sisters of Service*[121] the patient was admitted to hospital for an appendectomy. While recovering from the anaesthetic she received second and third degree burns to her feet from hot water bottles placed in her bed. The hospital was found liable for the negligence of the nurses who did not test the temperature and placed them without orders. It was argued that the patient was contributorily negligent in failing to call for help, in failing to disclose an earlier bout of frostbite to her feet and in leaving the hospital early against medical advice. All were rejected by the trial judge. He was of the opinion that the injury occurred to the patient while she was still anaesthetized and that it was not unreasonable to fail to disclose having frozen her feet upon entering hospital for an appendectomy. Furthermore, her leaving hospital had not aggravated her injuries. All in all this patient had acted as a reasonable patient. It is possible to see, however, that a patient who fails to disclose a material fact to a hospital or doctor might be found contributorily negligent,[122] as might a

---

118 *Robitaille v. Vancouver Hockey Club Ltd.* (1979), 19 B.C.L.R. 158 (S.C.); varied as to exemplary damages [1981] 3 W.W.R. 481 (C.A.). For a comment *see* Balbi, *Liability of Sports Physicians* (1984), A.L.R.
119 (1982), 38 B.C.L.R. 222 (S.C.); affirmed 19 A.C.W.S. (2d) 304 (C.A.).
120 *Dunsmore v. Deshield* (1977), 80 D.L.R. (3d) 386 (Sask. Q.B.).
121 [1948] 1 W.W.R. 113 (Alta. S.C.). Note that the plea of last-clear-chance or ultimate negligence by the defendant against the plaintiff was denied as well; for a comment *see* Howell, *Case Comment* (1978-79), 43 Sask. L. Rev. 149.
122 *Kouri, supra* n. 109 at 50; *Nykiforuk v. Lockwood,* [1941] 1 W.W.R. 327 (Sask. D.C.); *Guimond v. Laberge* (1956), 4 D.L.R. (2d) 559 (Ont. C.A.); *Leadbetter v. Brand* (1980), 37 N.S.R. (2d) 581 (S.C.); *Ehler v. Smith* (1978), 29 N.S.R. (2d) 309 (S.C.); *see also* Chapter 3.

patient who leaves hospital without notice or against medical advice and as a consequence suffers greater injuries.[123]

Other conduct by a patient that might bring a finding of contributory negligence[124] would include failure to return for treatment,[125] to seek treatment,[126] to co-operate during treatment,[127] or to follow instructions.[128] However, to date, in support there are primarily only *obiter* comments in case law from both inside and outside Canada. It remains to be seen whether the new vitality of the patient's role in his own health care will result in the law requiring a higher standard of him.

The issue of contributory negligence must be differentiated from that of joint and several liability. Just as with contributory negligence, all provinces in Canada have legislation[129] providing for apportionment where an innocent party suffers an injury through the negligence of two or more persons.[130] An example would be where the patient is injured through the joint negligence of a hospital and a doctor. For procedurally advantageous reasons,[131] the patient would likely sue both of them, and if both were found to be negligent the court would have to apportion the fault between them. However, the patient, if he had a joint and several judgment against them, would be entitled to recover the full amount of his damages from either defendant. Between themselves the doctor and the hospital would each be liable to make a contribution and to indemnify each other to the degree to which each was found negligent. There have been a number of cases where the plaintiff sued only one defendant and that party brought proceedings as third party proceedings against others whom he alleged would or should have to contribute for compensation due to a patient.[132] This is an extremely complicated area in

---

123 Meredith, *supra* n. 22 at 156; *Worth v. Royal Jubilee Hosp.* (1980), 4 L. Med. Q. 59 (B.C.C.A.).

124 Kouri, *supra* n. 109.

125 *See Moore v. Large* (1932), 46 B.C.R. 179 at 183 (C.A.); *Hôpital Notre-Dame de l'Espérance v. Laurent supra* n. 109.

126 *Robitaille v. Vancouver Hockey Club Ltd.* (1979), 19 B.C.L.R. 158 (S.C.); varied as to exemplary damages [1981] 3 W.W.R. 481 (C.A.). *See Hampton v. Macadam* (1912), 22 W.L.R. 31 at 35 (Sask.). *See also McDaniel v. Vancouver Gen. Hosp. supra* n. 28.

127 *Antoniuk v. Smith,* [1930] 2 W.W.R. 721 at 734 (Alta. C.A.).

128 *Marshall v. Rodgers,* [1943] 2 W.W.R. 545 at 554 (B.C.C.A.), where failure to be vaccinated for smallpox was advanced but not seriously pressed.

129 *See supra* n. 109 and Quebec Civil Code, 1971, c. 84, s. 1, Art. 1106; *see also* Chapter 4.

130 *See Parmley v. Parmley,* [1945] S.C.R. 635 where a doctor and dentist were held equally liable, each to bear one-half of the patient's loss. *See also Jeannotte v. Couillard* (1894), 3 Q.B. 461 (Que.).

131 *For example,* the opportunity to examine for discovery and discover documents. *See Duxbury v. Calgary,* [1940] 1 W.W.R. 174 (Alta. C.A.).

132 *Churchill v. Young* (1981), 35 Nfld. & P.E.I.R. 412 (Nfld. C.A.); *Campbell v. Bartlett* (1979), 2 Sask. R. 139 (C.A.); *MacKenzie v. Vance* (1977), 2 C.C.L.T. 63 (N.S.C.A.); *Johnson v. Vancouver Gen. Hosp.,* [1973] 1 W.W.R. 361; affirmed [1974] 1 W.W.R. 239 (B.C.C.A.); *Kane v. Haman,* [1971] 1 O.R. 294 (S.C.); *see also* Griffiths, *Claims for Contribution or Indemnity As Between Hospitals, Doctors and Others,* [1963] L.S.U.C. Spec. Lec. 237.

which judges, lawyers and academics are all complaining and requesting law reform.[133]

4.   EXPIRY OF LIMITATION PERIOD

This has proven to be an effective defence for doctors and hospitals for it has stopped a number of actions.[134] It is a procedural rather than a substantive defence and has its basis in statutes although the principles of statutory interpretation are found in the case law. The defendant for whom it is successful has not been tried and exonerated; rather, he has not been tried. Limitation periods exist for most legal actions and refer to the time within which the action must be commenced, after which it will be said to be time-barred and will not be heard by a court except on that issue.

Excellent practical reasons exist for establishing time limits within which suits must be brought: memories fade, records are lost, witnesses may die or become impossible to locate. This is the so-called stale evidence rationale. Furthermore, justice requires that there comes a time when potential liability for negligence ought no longer to hover over one's head. But much dissatisfaction exists with the present law because meritorious claims may be sterilized

---

133 For an excellent discussion *see* Klar, *supra* n. 113. The classical work is Williams, *Joint Torts and Contributory Negligence*, Stevens & Sons, London, 1951.

134 It has barred actions in the following cases: *Fishman v. Waters* (1983), 22 A.C.W.S. (2d) 382 (Man. C.A.); *McBain v. Laurentian* (1982), 19 A.C.W.S. (2d) 70 (Ont. H.C.); *Viktorin v. Koffler Stores Ltd.* (1982), 12 A.C.W.S. (2d) 534 (Ont. H.C.); *Cascone v. Rodney* (1981), 131 D.L.R. (3d) 593 (Ont. H.C.); *Letiec v. Rowe* (1981), 130 D.L.R. (3d) 379 (Nfld. C.A.); *Lapoint-Routhier v. Hôpital Général* (1980), 1 A.C.W.S. (2d) (Que. C.A.); *Whiston v. Deane* (1979), 95 D.L.R. (3d) 184 (B.C.S.C.); *Strachan v. Simpson* (1979), 10 C.C.L.T. 146 (B.C.S.C.); *Workman v. Greer* (1978), 90 D.L.R. (3d) 676 (Man. C.A.); *Goff v. Barker* (1978), 92 D.L.R. (3d) 125 (Ont. H.C.); *Legault-Bellemare v. Madore*, [1975] C.S. 1249 (Que. S.C.); *Mumford v. Children's Hosp. of Winnipeg*, [1977] 1 W.W.R. 666 (Man. C.A.), application for leave to appeal dismissed 25 N.R. 530 (S.C.C.); *Price v. Milawski* (1977), 1 L. Med. Q. 303 (Ont. C.A.); *Murphy v. Mathieson* (1976), unreported (Alta. Dist.Ct.), Belzil J.; *Karderas v. Clow supra* n. 20; *Johnson v. Vancouver Gen. Hosp. supra* n. 132; *Carrier v. McCowan* (1971), 24 D.L.R. (3d) 105 (Alta. S.C.); *McKay v. Winnipeg Gen. Hosp.*, [1971] 1 W.W.R. 65 (Man. Q.B.); *Philippon v. Legate*, [1970] 1 O.R. 392 (C.A.); *Radclyffe v. Rennie*, [1965] S.C.R. 703; *McArthur v. Sask. Cancer Comm.* (1958), 27 W.W.R. 152 (Sask. Q.B.); *Burk v. S.* (1951), 4 W.W.R. 520 (B.C.S.C.); *Winn v. Alexander*, [1940] O.W.N. 238 (H.C.); *Boase v. Paul*, [1931] 4 D.L.R. 435 (Ont. S.C.); *Pierce v. Strathroy Hosp.* (1924), 27 O.W.N. 180 (H.C.); *Tremeer v. Black*, [1924] 2 W.W.R. 97 (Sask. C.A.); *Town v. Archer supra* n. 111; *Miller v. Ryerson* (1892), 22 O.R. 369 (C.A.). It has been an issue in the following cases: *McKenzie v. Vance supra* n. 132; *Cusson v. Robidoux*, [1977] 1 S.C.R. 650; *Denton v. Jones* (1976), 14 O.R. (2d) 382 (H.C.); *Spencer v. Indian Head Union Hosp.*, [1974] 48 D.L.R. (3d) 449 (Sask. C.A.); *Kushner v. Wellesley Hosp.*, [1971] 2 O.R. 732 (C.A.); *Johnston v. Wellesley Hosp.* (1970), 17 D.L.R. (3d) 139 (Ont. H.C.); *Gloning v. Miller* (1953), 10 W.W.R. 414 (Alta. S.C.); *Dixie v. Royal Columbian Hosp.*, [1941] 1 W.W.R. 389 (B.C.C.A.); *McIntosh v. Homewood Sanitarium*, [1940] O.W.N. 118 (H.C.); *Offord v. Ottawa Civic Hosp. Trustees*, [1938] O.W.N. 274 (H.C.); *Hochman v. Willinsky*, [1933] O.W.N. 79 (H.C.); *Harkies v. Lord Dufferin Hosp.*, [1931] 2 D.L.R. 440 (Ont. S.C.); *Prescott v. McArthur* (1928), 62 O.L.R. 385 (H.C.).

prematurely. Legislative reform has been called for and has taken place in some provinces.[135] Within the near future the time periods in other provinces will no doubt be changed which, together with the fact that there are significant differences in the law between provinces in terms of length of time, exceptions, and even the statute in which the times are set out, complicate a thorough discussion of the topic. Fortunately, there are two excellent and current sources on the present law: Williams, *Limitation of Actions in Canada*[136] and MacLaren, *Of Doctors, Hospitals and Limitations — "The Patient's Dilemma"*.[137] Thus, only general observations will be made about the defence.

The limitation period varies for different types of action, for generally it is the basis for the claim and not the type of defendant that marks the suit. So an action brought against a doctor in contract for assault and battery must be brought within the normal limitation rules for those claims.[138] In the former it is usually six years from breach of the contract,[139] while in the latter it is normally two years from the commission of the tort.[140] Lawyers, architects and engineers are by tradition sued in contract[141] and therefore are vulnerable for a six-year period for any breach in professional duty to a client. A hospital may be sued in contract or in tort,[142] but a doctor or other health care professional is to date most often sued in negligence.[143]

Doctors, hospitals and now certain other health professionals are favoured by a shorter limitation period in most Canadian provinces. An action must be brought against a doctor[144] within one year from the termination of services in Alberta,[145] Saskatchewan[146] and Prince Edward Island[147] and within two years of the termination of services in Manitoba,[148] Newfoundland,[149] Nova Scotia,[150]

---

135 Limitation Act, R.S.B.C. 1979, c. 236; Health Disciplines Act, R.S.O. 1980, c. 196; Medical Act, S.N.B. 1981, c. 87, s. 67; Limitation of Actions Act, R.S.N.S. 1967, c. 168 [am. 1982, c. 33, ss. 1, 2].
136 (1980).
137 (1973), 11 Osgoode Hall L.J. 85.
138 Note there is some authority for the proposition that all actions against a doctor fall within the "malpractice" definition; *see, for example, Strachan v. Simpson* (1979), 10 C.C.L.T. 14 (B.C.S.C.); as to hospitals *see Letiec v. Rowe* (1981), 130 D.L.R. (3d) 379 (Nfld. C.A.).
139 Williams, *supra* n. 136 at 51.
140 *Id.* at 61.
141 *See Schwebel v. Telekes*, [1967] 1 O.R. 541 (C.A.).
142 Rozovsky, *Canadian Hospital Law* 16 (1979).
143 *See supra* Chapter 2.
144 *See Johnston v. Regina Gen. Hosp. Bd. of Gov.*, [1982] 1 W.W.R. 15 (Sask. Q.B.), where the limitation defence was not available to a doctor who shielded behind a colleague who had, in error, been sued.
145 Limitation of Actions Act, R.S.A. 1980, c. L-15, s. 55.
146 Medical Profession Act, S.S. 1980-81, c. M-10.1, s. 72.
147 Medical Act, R.S.P.E.I. 1974, c. M-8, s. 31.
148 Medical Act, S.M. 1980-81, c. 11, s. 61. For a case interpreting Manitoba statutes *see Workman v. Greer* (1978), 90 D.L.R. (3d) 676 (Man. C.A.).
149 Medical Act, S.N. 1974, No. 119, s. 25 [am. 1975, No. 13, s. 2].
150 Limitations of Actions Act, R.S.N.S. 1967, c. 168, s. 2 [am. 1982, c. 33, s. 1]. Note that the discretion given the court to extend the time cannot be exercised after four years from the limitation deadline.

the Northwest Territories[151] and the Yukon.[152] In Ontario,[153] the time is one year and in British Columbia[154] two years, but in those provinces time runs from the date the plaintiff has knowledge of the facts relevant to an action. New Brunswick[155] gives the plaintiff the option of two years from the termination of services or one year from knowing the facts.[156] This preferential treatment originated in Ontario in the late nineteenth century, when the Ontario legislature amended[157] the Medical Act[158] by setting a shorter period of one year (the norm was six years at that time) and by setting the termination of services as the time from which the period was to be calculated. The special rule with respect to doctors spread to all the other Canadian jurisdictions and similar protection was established for hospitals and other health care professionals, but the phenomenon was limited to Canada.[159] In an early assessment of the growth of the law an Ontario judge said:[160]

> It is not an Act respecting limitations of actions, but one passed mainly for the benefit of the medical profession; nor is the provision in question an amendment of the provisions of any such statute, but simply a provision for the special protection of the registered members of that profession.

There is no evidence why the termination of services was chosen as a commencement date but it is probable that it was thought to provide some certainty.[161] By comparison, time begins to run in ordinary negligence actions from the time of the occurrence of the damage. However, under the special rule for doctors a patient must know of his injury and sue within one year from the termination of services. Thus when the cause of action is ''hidden,'' as when an object is left in the body and remains inert, adverse consequences of negligent treatment are slow in developing, or a negligent diagnosis is made which delays treatment, the patient may be unaware of the damage he has suffered.[162] Moreover, there is a certain perversity for both parties when the termination of services is the critical date. The doctor-patient relationship is

---

151 Limitation of Actions Ordinance, R.O.N.W.T. 1974, c. L-6, s. 3(1)(d).
152 Limitation of Actions Ordinance, R.O.Y.T. 1971, c. L-7, s. 3(1)(d).
153 Health Disciplines Act, R.S.O. 1980, c. 196, s. 17.
154 Limitation Act, R.S.B.C. 1979, c. 236, s. 3(1), 6(3). Note that no action can be taken after six years from the time when the right arose (s. 8 [am. 1982, c. 19, s. 1]).
155 Medical Act, S.N.B. 1981, c. 87, s. 67.
156 Note that in Quebec a patient may have three years from the date the ''prejudice'' appeared. Civil Code, R.S.Q. 1977, c. C-25, art. 2260a.
157 Act to Amend the Medical Act, 1887 (Ont.), c. 24, s. 2.
158 R.S.O. 1877, c. 142. The isolation of this from other limitation law precluded flexibility. *See* McLaren, *supra* n. 137 at 90.
159 McLaren, *supra* n. 137 at 87-89.
160 *Miller v. Ryerson supra* n. 134 at 373.
161 *See Tremeer v. Black supra* n. 134 at 100.
162 *Id.; Miller v. Ryerson supra* n. 134 at 373; *see Whiston v. Deane* (1979), 95 D.L.R. (3d) 184 (B.C.S.C.), and *Workman v. Greer* (1978), 90 D.L.R. (3d) 676 (Man. C.A.), where the claims of patients who became pregnant after sterilization operations were held to be time-barred.

strained when a doctor is "caught" by continuing to treat his patient and similarly a patient may not receive the best care.[163]

Specifically, the time may be affected by the scope given to the word "service." An Alberta decision[164] has broadened the scope for recovery by holding that the subsequent treatment need not be a necessary or normal extension of the treatment in respect of which negligence is alleged. A doctor left his forceps in a patient who continued to consult him as a family doctor. Indeed, he removed the forceps. Had the patient not continued to consult the doctor she would have been beyond the time period. Clearly, however,[165]

> [b]y any contemporary standards of sound social policy the equivocal situation of the patient in these cases is entirely unsatisfactory and calls out for remedy.

The author of this quote recommends that there be: (1) no disparity between limitation periods for different torts; (2) a common starting point in all negligence actions, *viz.* the occurrence of damage; (3) the coalescence of all limitation periods into one statute; and (4) a belated discovery rule.[166]

The last recommendation deals with the hidden cause of action and recognizes that even a reasonable patient may not discover the damage until the limitation period has passed. A number of attempts have been made to decide what conditions and contingencies ought to be placed on a patient if he is to be allowed to pursue a doctor under such a rule, perhaps years after the event.[167]

Law reform which extends the limitation period is of concern to doctors and hospitals.[168] The balancing of the interests of the patient with that concern can be expected to result in further modifications of limitation statutes.

---

163 *See, for example, Bethune v. L.J.F.* (1982), 138 D.L.R. (3d) 106 at 109 (Ont. H.C.).

164 *Gloning v. Miller supra* n. 134; *see also McKenzie v. Vance* (1977), 2 C.C.L.T. 63 (N.S.C.A.), where the limitation period was extended against a doctor whose later "services" were the filling out of Workers' Compensation Board forms. *But see Town v. Archer supra* n. 111, where the patient only returned to complain and was time-barred; *see also Cook v. Abbott* (1980), 11 C.C.L.T. 217 (N.S.S.C.), where the taking of prescribed drugs was deemed a continuation of professional services. An appeal was allowed on the basis that this issue should not have been decided prior to trial. *Abbott v. Cook* (1980), 13 C.C.L.T. 264 (N.S.C.A.).

165 McLaren, *supra* n. 137 at 93.

166 *Id.* at 97-98.

167 *See* Limitation Act, R.S.B.C. 1979, c. 236, s. 8 [am. 1982, c. 19, s. 1], which sets a six-year limit. Manitoba's solution is in the Limitation of Actions Act, R.S.M. 1970, c. L150, following the English Limitation Act, 1963, c. 47. For a critique *see* McLaren, *supra* n. 137 at 95-97. For a case interpreting the sections, *see Workman v. Greer* (1978), 90 D.L.R. (2d) 676 (Man. C.A.). *See* Health Disciplines Act, R.S.O. 1980, c. 196, s. 17 and a comment in Sharpe, *Periods of Limitation and Medical Malpractice A New Act For Ontario* (1975), 23 Chitty's L.J. 145. *Dobson v. Wellington Tavern (Windsor) Ltd.* (1983), 139 D.L.R. (3d) 255 (Ont. C.A.) points out the conflicts in Ontario's legislation. For a case dealing with the statutory provision for a hidden cause of action in England, *see Hills v. Potter*, The Times, 23 May 1983 (Q.B.).

168 Sharpe and Sawyer, *Doctors and the Law* 158-60 (1978); Marshall, *The Physician and Canadian Law* 65 (1979); Geekie, *The Crisis in Malpractice: Will it Spread to Canada?* (1975), 113 Can. Med. Assoc. J. 327.

6

Proof Of Negligence

1.   INTRODUCTION

In all civil actions the plaintiff has the onus of proving the elements of the action brought. Accordingly, in a medical negligence action against a doctor or hospital[1] it is the patient who must prove the essentials of negligence.[2] If the action brought was based on one of the intentional torts[3] such as battery or false imprisonment or was in the nature of a contract action,[4] then the onus of proving the essentials of these actions would similarly rest on the patient.

Whatever the nature of the action, the essentials are proven by means of evidence introduced by parties to the action. Evidence includes the sworn testimony of witnesses or the parties to the action,[5] documentary evidence and

---

1 Note that the word "hospital" is used to cover the employees, such as nurses, for whom the hospital will be responsible. *See* Chapter 9.

2 *See supra* Chapter 4, (3). For an excellent discussion of the burden of proof in Quebec *see* Mecs, *Medical Liability and the Burden of Proof, An Analysis of Recent Quebec Jurisprudence* (1970), 16 McGill L.J. 163.

3 *Supra* Chapter 2.

4 Sopinka and Lederman. *The Law of Evidence in Civil Cases* 403-406 (1974). *Supra* Chapter 2.

5 Including that from examinations for discovery.

exhibits.[6] Generally any evidence which is relevant to the case will be admissible, that is, it will be heard by the court. However, our legal system, in the course of its evolution, has developed a complex body of rules that determines which evidence is admissible and which is inadmissible. This body of rules also governs the question of how much weight the court ought to attach to various kinds of admissible evidence. Only a few of the rules, those most important to the medical negligence action, will be discussed in this chapter.

The law of evidence is under study by both federal and provincial law reformers[7] and it is expected that the law will be clarified and, hopefully, simplified.

2.   EVIDENCE

(a) Witnesses

The patient attempts to make at least a *prima facie* case of medical negligence through the sworn testimony of himself and his witnesses. Usually his own testimony will be used to prove the duty owed to him and the injury suffered[8] and may help to establish the breach of the standard of care and the causal link between the alleged negligence and the injury.[9] However, establishing these latter two matters will also require the testimony of experts, who will be doctors from the same specialty as the defendant if possible. The court must be satisfied that the expert called is by training, practice and experience particularly knowledgable in the area in issue, and the party calling such a witness must so qualify him.[10]

The proof of breach of standard of care and causation by the means of expert testimony is the most difficult part of the patient's case.[11] Even if there

---

6 These are articles such as forceps, sponges, needles and are introduced into evidence during the testimony of witnesses.

7 *See Report on Evidence* (1982). This is the report of the Federal/Provincial Task Force on Uniform Rules of Evidence. A bill is before the House of Commons: Bill S-33, "An Act to give effect for Canada, to the Uniform Evidence Act adopted by the Uniform Law Conference of Canada".

8 *See Richardson v. Nugent* (1918), 40 D.L.R. 700 (N.B.C.A.), where a new trial was ordered because the patient was allowed to exhibit an open wound to the jury. *See also Gray v. LaFleche*, [1950] 1 D.L.R. 337 (Man. K.B.), where a trial judge refused to allow the injuries of a child who had suffered a deformed penis from a circumcision to be shown to the jury. *But see MacDonald v. Ross* (1983), 24 C.C.L.T. 242 (N.S.S.C.), where a judge, two lawyers and the defendant viewed the breasts of the plaintiff.

9 Note that the plaintiff's evidence may not be accepted by the court. *See Ferguson v. Hamilton Civic Hosp.* (1983), 23 C.C.L.T. 254 at 263 (Ont. H.C.); *see also Poulin v. Health Sciences Centre* (1982), 18 Man. R. (2d) 274 at 275 (Q.B.).

10 *See infra* Chapter 7 for a description of how this is done.

11 Haines, *The Conduct of a Malpractice Action*, [1963] L.S.U.C. Spec. Lec. 273 at 289.

is no difficulty in obtaining the necessary experts[12] both counsel and the court must come to grips with complex medical terminology and information. Furthermore, the defendant, too, will make use of expert evidence to prove that he met the standard or to disprove causation.[13]

Unfortunately, in the modern adversarial context an expert witness is too often seen as, and believes himself to be, a weapon for one side of the action.[14] His true role is simply to assist the impartial court in determining the facts. Nevertheless, the quality of the expert evidence is critical to the proof or disproof of negligence;[15] in many cases in which the plaintiff has been unsuccessful it is clear that his expert evidence was weak.[16]

Although a court has the discretion ultimately to accept or reject expert evidence,[17] it is not likely to reject it unless the issue is non-technical or involves the taking of precautions, or unless the experts' opinions are divided.[18]

A basic rule of evidence is that a witness can testify only to that which he has actually perceived through his own senses. Information from other sources is referred to as hearsay evidence and is not admissible unless it falls into one of the generally recognized exceptions to the hearsay rule. For example,[19] a doctor who examined a patient when he was admitted to hospital is asked to describe the patient's injuries. The evidence is admissible. But if the doctor proceeded to state the opinion given by the radiologist on an x-ray examination of the patient, that would be hearsay and subject to objection. The example points out the main reason for the rule, which is that the best evidence regarding the x-ray would come from the radiologist who should be called and who could then be cross-examined. Two exceptions to the hearsay rule of importance to doctors are that 1) a patient's statement as to his physical

---

12 *See infra* regarding the difficulty of obtaining witnesses.

13 Note that in most jurisdictions the number of expert witnesses is restricted with leave to apply for more in appropriate cases. *See Leonard v. Knott*, [1978] 5 W.W.R. 511 at 515 (B.C.S.C.), where the trial judge stated that he based his decision on evidence by ten doctors. Varied on appeal to find a second doctor also liable, [1980] 1 W.W.R. 673 (B.C.C.A.).

14 *See Strachan v. Simpson* (1979), 10 C.C.L.T. 145 at 169 (B.C.S.C.); *Moffatt v. Witelson* (1980), 111 D.L.R. (3d) 712 (Ont. H.C.).

15 Samuels, *Expert Forensic Evidence* (1974), 14 Med. Sci. L. 17.

16 *See, for example, Wilson v. Swanson*, [1956] S.C.R. 804; *McDaniel v. Vancouver Gen. Hosp.*, [1934] 4 D.L.R. 593 (P.C.); *Hajgato v. London Health Assn.* (1982), 36 O.R. (2d) 669 (H.C.); *Jodouin v. Mitra* (1978), 2 L. Med. Q. 72 (Ont. S.C.).

17 *Anderson v. Chasney*, [1950] 4 D.L.R. 223 (S.C.C.); *Crits v. Sylvester*, [1956] S.C.R. 991; *Price v. Milawski* (1977), 1 L. Med. Q. 303 (Ont. C.A.); Meredith, *Malpractice Liability of Doctors and Hospitals* (1957). *See also* Chapter 5.

18 *Villemure v. Turcot*, [1973] S.C.R. 716; *McLean v. Weir* (1977), 3 C.C.L.T. 87 at 101 (B.C.S.C.); affirmed [1980] 4 W.W.R. 330 (B.C.C.A.); *Kangas v. Parker*, [1978] 5 W.W.R. 667 at 669 (Sask. C.A.); *Hajgato v. London Health Assn.* (1982), 36 O.R. (2d) 669 at 693. Note the ruling that when "the testimony of two believable witnesses comes into conflict, the Court should look for the balance of truth in the corroborative evidence where such exists . . ." (*Dendaas (Tylor) v. Yackel* (1980), 12 C.C.L.T. 147 at 159 (B.C.S.C.)).

19 Meredith, *supra* n. 17 at 47.

or mental sensation or feeling is admissible evidence of the existence of that state (but not the patient's story of how and by whom the symptoms were caused)[20] and 2) a patient's declaration in anticipation of death made *in extremis*[21] may be admissible in a homicide case.

Witnesses qualified by the courts as experts can testify beyond simply what they perceived with their own senses. Besides providing basic information to the court for its comprehension of the scientific or technical issues, the expert is allowed to state his opinion and conclusions.[22]

(b) Documents

Apart from the oral evidence of witnesses the plaintiff or defendant may rely on documentary evidence, such as the hospital record, reports of test results, or the doctor's office records to assist him in the action.[23] A party wishing to procure or produce any of these, or other, documents has at his disposal the process of discovery of documents. Thus a doctor or hospital is bound to disclose any documents made with regard to the patient's care and treatment. However, documents brought into existence to assist a defendant or his legal advisors are privileged[24] as to their contents unless legislation states otherwise.[25] In addition, legislation in most provinces provides the mechanism by which a patient can obtain a copy of his hospital record,[26] and there is also legislation in most provinces allowing hospital records into court as evidence provided they are made in the usual and ordinary course of hospital business and at the time of the act or event recorded, or within a reasonable time afterwards.[27] The admissibility of hospital records in court has been confirmed in the case law.[28]

Admission of a hospital record as an exception to the hearsay rule, whether by virtue of statute or case law, raises the issue as to the weight to be

---

20 *Id.* at 48; Sopinka and Lederman, *supra* n. 4 at 112.

21 Meredith, *supra* n. 17 at 47.

22 *Id.* at 309; *see also Taylor v. Gray* (1937), 11 M.P.R. 588 at 598-99 (N.B.C.A.).

23 *See, for example, Mang v. Moscovitz* (1982), 37 A.R. 221 at 229 (Q.B.). Note that inadequate or improperly completed documents may create difficulties for doctors and hospitals. *See Meyer v. Gordon* (1981), 17 C.C.L.T. 1 (B.C.S.C.); *see also Wipfli v. Britten* (1982), 22 C.C.L.T. 104 at 115 (B.C.S.C.), where a handwriting expert testified.

24 *Crits v. Sylvester*, [1955] O.W.N. 243 (H.C.). See Chapter 10.

25 Evidence Act, R.S.B.C. 1979, c. 116; Manitoba Evidence Act, R.S.M. 1970, c. E150, s. 50 [am. 1971, c. 70, ss. 2, 3; 1976, c. 69, s. 18]; Evidence Act, R.S.O. 1980, c. 145, s. 52; Saskatchewan Evidence Act, R.S.S. 1978, c. S-16, ss. 30-32.

26 *See, for example,* Hospitals Act, R.S.A. 1980, c. H-11, s. 40(5). See Chapter 10.

27 Evidence Act, R.S.B.C. 1979, c. 116, ss. 46-48; Manitoba Evidence Act, R.S.M. 1970, c. E150, s. 58; Evidence Act, R.S.N.B. 1973, c. E-11, s. 49; Evidence Act, R.S.N.S. 1967, c. 94, s. 22; Evidence Act, R.S.O. 1980, c. 145, s. 35; Saskatchewan Evidence Act, R.S.S. 1978, c. S-16, ss. 30-32; Canada Evidence Act, R.S.C. 1970, c. E-10, s. 30(1).

28 *Kolesar v. Jeffries* (1977), 2 C.C.L.T. 170 (S.C.C.); *Zamparo v. Brisson* (1981), 16 C.C.L.T. 66 (Ont. C.A.).

given to it. In a very important case, *Ares v. Venner*[29] the Supreme Court of Canada said:

> Hospital records, including nurses' notes, made contemporaneously by someone having a personal knowledge of the matters then being recorded and under a duty to make the entry or records should be received in evidence as *prima facie* proof of the facts stated therein.

Thus we see judicial reform of the law by the creation of an exception to the hearsay rule in regard to hospital records. The effect of the decision is that what is stated on the record becomes evidence for the party putting it in. To challenge it opposing counsel has to call as his witness the person who made an entry, who can then be cross-examined by the party who put the hospital record into evidence. This is a peculiar reversal of the usual procedure. Normally, a witness who has information is called by the party attempting to prove that fact and then cross-examined by the party challenging the fact. A further criticism of the decision is that it admits not just objective record-keeping such as vital signs, but also subjective observations about the patient, which should be subject to cross-examination.[30] While the law of evidence needs reform, decisions such as *Ares* only serve to contribute to the confusion.[31]

(c) Admissions

In addition to documents and the testimony of witnesses the patient may rely on admissions made by the doctor or hospital. These may occur in the pleadings or, as is more frequent, during examination for discovery or during cross-examination at trial.[32] Such evidence is very significant, because it is presumed that no one would admit something against his own interest if it were not true. Furthermore, there is no doubt that the doctor in the medical negligence action is the best authority on what he did, how he did it, and why he did it.[33] He more than anyone else likely knows whether or not his conduct was substandard.

However, while admissions of sufficient import to decide the case one way or the other are regular fare in Hollywood trials, they rarely occur in real life. Fatal admissions are only obtained through thorough preparation, skilled advocacy and fortuitous circumstances.

---

29 (1970), 14 D.L.R. (3d) 4 at 16 (S.C.C.).

30 *Thompson v. Toorenburgh* (1973), 50 D.L.R. (3d) 717 (B.C.C.A.). For an excellent example of how critical subjective assessments by nurses may be to the outline of an action, *see Park v. Stevenson Memorial Hosp.*, Ont. H.C., Holland J., 1974 (unreported).

31 A critique of the case is found in Sopinka and Lederman, *supra* n. 4 at 78-80. Note that it appears to have been overlooked in *Schweizer v. Central Hosp.* (1974), 6 O.R. (2d) 606 (H.C.). *See also*, Elman, *The Broadening Implications of Ares v. Venner* (1979), 9 C.C.L.T. 14.

32 *See, for example, DeMoura v. Mississauga Hosp.* (1979), 3 L. Med. Q. 215 at 220-22 (Ont. S.C.).

33 Waltz and Inbau, *Medical Jurisprudence* 70 (1971); *See also Kolesar v. Jeffries supra* n. 28.

(d) Conclusion

When all the plaintiff's evidence has been put before the court, the critical question of whether he has established a *prima facie* case must be considered. To satisfy this test the plaintiff must have adduced some evidence which is more consistent than not with negligence on the part of the defendant;[34] the facts must raise an inference of negligence. Once the *prima facie* case has been established, the defendant must then meet the inference of negligence by proving any defences he has available[35] in a fashion similar to that in which the plaintiff has attempted to prove his case: the sworn testimony of himself and his expert witnesses, relevant documents, and admissions by the plaintiff.

In contrast to criminal cases, in which the matter must be proven beyond a reasonable doubt, the standard of proof required in a negligence case, as in all civil actions, is that the plaintiff must prove his case on a balance of probabilities.[36] Thus at the end of the trial the judge or jury[37] must weigh all of the evidence adduced by both sides and decide whether the plaintiff has proven on a balance of probabilities that the defendant was negligent.[38]

3.   DIFFICULTIES OF PROOF

(a) Direct and Circumstantial Evidence

A patient who wishes to establish his case before the court must, as we have seen, prove the essentials of his action whatever they may be before he can succeed. In order to prove the essentials of his action he will try to establish the existence of certain facts. Any fact sought to be established in support of an essential of an action is referred to as a "material" fact. Direct evidence is testimony or a document which itself establishes a material fact, and circumstantial evidence is evidence which shows the existence of circumstances from which the court may infer a material fact.[39] Thus, bits of evidence which of themselves would be of little probative value may when combined justify the court's inference of a material fact.[40] To illustrate,[41] if a

---

34 Nathan, *Medical Negligence* 105 (1957). For a case where the plaintiff failed to discharge the onus of proof, *see Gordon v. Davidson* (1980), 4 L. Med. Q. 131 at 146 (Ont. S.C.).

35 *See supra* Chapter 5.

36 *Parkin v. Kobrinsky* (1963), 46 W.W.R. 193 (Man. C.A.). In *McDaniel v. Vancouver Gen. Hosp. supra* n. 16 at 594, an erroneous statement was made that the onus of proof was the criminal one.

37 *See infra.*

38 Nathan, *supra* n. 34 at 108. Note the civil onus of proof in *Holmes v. London Bd. of Hosp. Trustees* (1977), 17 O.R. (2d) 626 (H.C.); *see also Martel v. Hotel-Dieu St-Vallier; Vigneault v. Martel* (1969), 14 D.L.R. (3d) 445 at 448 (S.C.C.).

39 Sopinka and Lederman, *supra* n. 4 at 31.

40 *Grant v. Australian Knitting Mills Ltd.,* [1936] A.C. 85 (P.C.)

41 Nathan, *supra* n. 34 at 167.

patient alleged that he had contracted an infection from the administration of an anaesthetic, direct evidence may not be available to prove whether the infection resulted from the solution, the instruments, or the individuals. However, evidence that the solution was properly constituted and handled, and that the individuals exercised proper sterile techniques would lead to the inference that the cause of the infection was a failure to disinfect the instruments.

Direct evidence is, of course, the best evidence and the case will be stronger if such evidence is available to show precisely how the accident occurred. However, the difficulty in most medical negligence cases is that the full circumstances of the accident are not known to the patient and therefore evidence of this calibre is not often available.[42] Even if the circumstances are known, their significance may be unnoticed by the patient who lacks and perhaps cannot obtain the necessary expertise.

It seems, however, that Canadian courts are reluctant to infer negligence on the basis of circumstantial evidence in medical negligence cases. One reason is probably a concern that patients with little or no direct evidence would sue too easily in the hope that a court would accept circumstantial evidence, thus crowding the courts and placing a difficult burden on the judiciary. Another explanation was offered in *Girard v. Royal Columbian Hosp.*:[43]

> The human body is not a container filled with a material whose performance can be predictably charted and analysed. It cannot be equated with a box of chewing tobacco or a soft drink. Thus, *while permissible inferences may be drawn as to the normal behaviour of these types of commodities the same kind of reasoning does not necessarily apply to a human being.* Because of this medical science has not yet reached the stage where the law ought to presume that a patient must come out of an operation as well as or better than he went into it. [emphasis supplied]

These arguments invite comment. The mere fact that a court should decide to allow the proof of material fact, in a proper case, from cogent circumstantial evidence would not likely open the floodgates of litigation. Circumstantial evidence is given weight in other civil actions[44] and there is no indication that the practice has sparked an abundance of litigation. Futhermore, the judiciary is in an ideal position to control the extent to which circumstantial evidence would be relied upon and a firm stance by the courts in equivocal cases would serve to discourage frivolous suits.

The *Girard* case suggests that the complexity of the human body militates against the use of circumstantial evidence in medical negligence cases. However, the argument passes over the fact that medical science has succeeded to a considerable extent in identifying deviations from normal physio-

---

42 *See, for example, Radclyffe v. Rennie*, [1965] S.C.R. 703.
43 (1976), 66 D.L.R. (3d) 676 at 691 (B.C.S.C.).
44 Sopinka and Lederman *supra* n. 4 at 33 and 526.

logical behaviour to the point where the risks of various complications arising out of certain procedures can often be expressed in terms of a percentage.[45] The reasoning suggested by this case would have the patient meet his onus in every case by direct evidence alone because the crux of the medical negligence action is always damage to a human body. It is hoped that the courts will take a more moderate view and apply these rules of evidence to medical negligence suits in the same fashion as they are applied in other actions. Otherwise, the effect is to place on patients a higher burden of proof.[46]

Having said this, a plaintiff in certain medical negligence cases may be able to take advantage of one rule of circumstantial evidence developed for his benefit: *res ipsa loquitur*.

(b) Res Ipsa Loquitur

(i) Prerequisites

There has been judicial recognition in negligence cases of the hardship on the plaintiff who is attempting to prove negligence when he knows only that an accident has happened and that he was injured. In many instances the details of the accident are known only to the defendant, but sometimes the mere fact that an accident happened will itself give rise to a presumption of negligence on the part of the defendant because the event is such that it would be unlikely to occur unless there had been negligence.[47] The accident "speaks of negligence;" hence the term used for this circumstance: *res ipsa loquitur,* "the thing speaks for itself."

Variously described as a rule, principle, doctrine and maxim, *res ipsa loquitur* is applied in Canada as part of the law of circumstantial evidence[48] and has been called "one of the great mysteries of tort law."[49]

As with much of the law, the essentials of *res ipsa loquitur* are easy to state, but its application is complicated.[50] The doctrine will only apply when:

---

45 *See, for example, Considine v. Camp Hill Hosp.* (1982), 133 D.L.R. (3d) 11 (N.S.S.C.); *Rawlings v. Lindsay* (1982), 20 C.C.L.T. 301 (B.C.S.C.); *Hajgato v. London Health Assn.* (1982), 36 O.R. (2d) 669 (H.C.); *McBride v. Langton* (1982), 22 Alta. L.R. (2d) 174 (Q.B.).

46 Where a patient has difficulty getting witnesses, the burden is increased further. *See McLean v. Weir* (1977), 3 C.C.L.T. 87 at 95 (B.C.S.C.), where Gould J. acknowledges the difficulty of the plaintiff's position; affirmed [1980] 4 W.W.R. 330 (B.C.C.A.).

47 *Byrne v. Boadle* (1863), 2 H. & C. 722, 159 E.R. 299 (Ex.). Note that the "clumsy language" used in the case has "confounded our courts ever since." *See* Linden, *Canadian Tort Law* 248-49 (1982).

48 Sopinka and Lederman, *supra* n. 4 at 399.

49 Linden, *Canadian Tort Law* 221 (1982). See 245-91 of this book for an excellent review of the law. This is true despite the fact that it is subjected to analysis by authorities in both the law of torts and evidence. *See* Sopinka and Lederman, *supra* n. 4 at 398.

50 Wright, *Res Ipsa Loquitur* in *Studies in Canadian Tort Law* 41 (1st ed. Linden 1968); Fridman, *The Myth of Res Ipsa Loquitur* (1954), 10 U.T.L.J. 223; Paton, *Res Ipsa Loquitur* (1936), 14 Can. Bar Rev. 480; Schiff, *Res Ipsa Loquitur Nutshell* (1976), 26 U.T.L.J. 451.

1) there is no evidence as to how or why the accident occurred;[51]

2) the accident is such that it would not occur without negligence; and

3) the defendant is proven to have been in control of or linked to the situation either personally or vicariously[52].

The possible effects of the doctrine on the onus of proof vary and are best understood by an analysis of the case law on point.

(ii) Application

There are compelling policy reasons for utilizing the doctrine in the medical negligence case. The plaintiff who often knows nothing about the accident, indeed who may have been anaesthetized or very ill,[53] bears a heavy burden yet may have difficulties getting information and witnesses.[54] The defendant, on the other hand, who knows or ought to know often has easy access to the facts.[55]

The courts saw difficulties in trying to distinguish between medical accidents which could not occur without negligence and those which could[56] and for some time it was uncertain whether *res ipsa loquitur* applied in medical negligence cases.[57] However, it is clear since 1953 and *Holt v. Nesbitt*[58] that the courts are to avail themselves of expert evidence as to what is normal and what is not[59] and that justice demands the application of the doctrine in this context:[60]

---

51 Most authorities prefer to state (2) and (3) as requirements and (1) as a prerequisite. In medical negligence cases the order in which they are here set out provides the best understanding.

52 By "vicariously" is meant by virtue of having responsibility for or right to control the wrongdoers, as a hospital for its employees. Fleming, *Law of Torts* 291-92 (6th ed. 1983).

53 *See, for example, Eady v. Tenderenda* [1975], 2 S.C.R. 599; in *Dunn v. Young* (1977), 86 D.L.R. (3d) 411 (Ont. Co. Ct.), the three-year-old patient was injured while anaesthetized for dental surgery.

54 *See infra.*

55 *See McLean v. Weir,* [1977] 3 C.C.L.T. 87 at 95 (B.C.S.C.) where the patient was said to be under a "formidable disadvantage" as a layman suing an expert; affirmed [1980] 4 W.W.R. 330 (B.C.C.A.).

56 *Clark v. Wansbrough,* [1940] O.W.N. 67 at 72 (H.C.); *Hughston v. Jost,* [1943] O.W.N. 3 (H.C.).

57 It was said not to apply in Ontario. *See Hughston v. Jost id.* at 6. There are early cases which recognized it might apply: *Hodgins v. Banting* (1906), 12 O.L.R. 117 (H.C.); *McTaggart v. Powers,* [1926] 3 W.W.R. 513 (Man. C.A.); *Sisters of St. Joseph of the Diocese of London v. Fleming,* [1938] S.C.R. 172; *McFadyen v. Harvie,* [1941] 2 D.L.R. 663; affirmed [1942] S.C.R. 390; *Meyer v. Lefebvre,* [1942] 1 W.W.R. 485 (Alta. A.D.); *Cox v. Saskatoon,* [1942] 1 W.W.R. 717 (Sask. C.A.); *Bernier v. Sisters of Service,* [1948] 1 W.W.R. 113 (Alta. T.D.). And cases where it was applied: *Harkies v. Lord Dufferin Hosp.,* [1931] 2 D.L.R. 440 (Ont. H.C.); *Taylor v. Gray supra* n. 22; *Abel v. Cooke,* [1938] 1 W.W.R. 49 (Alta. A.D.).

58 [1953] 1 S.C.R. 143. Also *Crits v. Sylvester supra* n. 17.

59 *Interlake Tissue Mills Co. v. Salmond,* [1949] 1 D.L.R. 207 (Ont. C.A.); *Hobson v. Munkley* (1976), 1 C.C.L.T. 163 (Ont. H.C.).

60 *Holt v. Nesbitt,* [1951] O.R. 601 at 605-606; affirmed [1953] 1 S.C.R. 143.

It would give to doctors, dentists, and member of other professions an unfair and unwarranted protection in actions where their conduct in the exercise of their profession is called into question. It would permit them to refuse to give an explanation in a court of justice of a happening which has caused injury to a person, even though the occurrence was of such a kind and description that a reasonable man would naturally infer from it that it was caused by some negligence or misconduct. It would place them in a position in the courts that in a case such as the present one the defendant could unfairly and unjustly say: "I alone am responsible for all that happened in the course of the operation. I know all the facts from which it can be decided whether or not I used due care. I can explain the happening, but I refuse to do so." To permit a defendant to take such a position in a court of law would be, in my opinion, a denial of justice to a person who knows nothing of the matter that caused his injury and seeks to recover for the loss suffered by reason of it from the person who possesses full knowledge of the facts.

Nevertheless the courts continue to be cautious in their application of the doctrine in medical negligence cases.[61] To the old fears of lack of expertise, inability to appreciate the difference between the non-negligent accident and the negligent accident and reluctance to find that there is no evidence as to how the accident occurred[62] is now added the modern one of increasing the liability of doctors and hospitals to the point of precipitating a "malpractice crisis."[63] Whether these fears are justified in Canada is not yet clear.

Each of the prerequisites to *res ipsa loquitur* will now be examined with reference to the cases since *Holt v. Nesbitt.*

A. The cause must be unknown

By "cause" is meant the cause-in-fact of the injury, including the facts leading up to the injury itself. When the facts of the accident which caused the patient's injuries are known, the doctrine is inapplicable as, for example, when a patient suffered burns and scarring from a carbon dioxide slush treatment for acne.[64] When the plaintiff knows only part of the story he ought

---

61 Tallin, *Liability of Professional Men for Negligence and Malpractice* (1960), 3 Can. Bar J. 230 at 240. The English courts are also cautious, *see* Mason and McCall Smith, *Law and Medical Ethics* 139 (1983); Samuels, *Medical Negligence Today — An Appraisal* (1983), 23 Med. Sci. Law 31 at 32. U.S. jurisprudence reveals the same progress: *see* Hole, *Medical Malpractice in New York* (1976), 27 Syracuse L.R. 657 at 678.

62 Laidlaw, *The Burden of Proof in Malpractice Actions,* [1963] L.S.U.C. Spec. Lec. 219 at 222. See *Kolesar v. Jeffries* (1976), 12 O.R. 142; affirmed 2 C.C.L.T. 170 (S.C.C.).

63 Teplitsky and Weisstub, *Torts-Negligence Standards and the Physician* (1978), 56 Can. Bar Rev. 121. *See also McBride v. Langton* (1982), 22 Alta. L.R. (2d) 174, where Purvis J. expresses the concern that a broad application of the doctrine could "result in the lowering of the standard of medical care."

64 *Johnston v. Wellesley Hosp.* (1970), 17 D.L.R. (3d) 139 (Ont. H.C.); *see also Kolesar v. Jeffries* (1974), 59 D.L.R. (3d) 367; varied 12 O.R. (2d) 142, affirmed 2 C.C.L.T. 170 (S.C.C.) *supra* n. 26; *Kangas v. Parker,* [1976] 5 W.W.R. 25 (Sask. Q.B.); affirmed [1978] 5 W.W.R. 667 (Sask. C.A.).

to plead and prove what facts he does know and plead *res ipsa loquitur* when he can go no further.[65]

However, if there is evidence of the cause of the accident, the patient cannot ignore it and expect to use the doctrine as a substitute for proving his case.[66] Furthermore, should the true cause of the accident become known during the trial, the doctrine loses its utility and the case proceeds as an ordinary negligence case.[67]

While there is general agreement on this prerequisite,[68] the courts must face the fact that there will occasionally be cases where the cause is impossible to pin down, and it may have to be ruled a mystery.[69]

B. The accident must speak of negligence

This determination causes the courts the most difficulty. Any person knows that certain events, such as bags of sugar falling on people,[70] an oil furnace exploding,[71] or an airplane crashing,[72] bespeak negligence. But few know whether an artery cut during disc surgery[73] or a ureter cut during gynaecological surgery[74] does.

Of course, not every medical accident speaks of negligence. Accidents can and do happen without negligence.[75] The problem is how a judge, a medical layman, is to know the non-negligent accident from the negligent one. The best evidence would be the testimony of experts that the accident that caused damage would not normally occur without negligence on the part of the defendant, and if it is possible to obtain this evidence the patient ought certainly to do so.[76] However, to require such evidence in every case would

---

65 It may be fatal to fail to plead it: *Greschuk v. Kolodychuk* (1959), 27 W.W.R. 157 (Alta. A.D.); *MacDonald v. Ross* (1983), 24 C.C.L.T. 242 at 247 (N.S.S.C.). *But see David Spencer Ltd. v. Field,* [1939] S.C.R. 36.

66 *McLean v. Weir supra* n. 55.

67 Nathan, *supra* n. 34 at 109.

68 *But see* Somerville, *Legal Investigation of a Medical Investigation* (1981), 19 Alta. L.R. 171 at 172, where the author argues that the doctrine ought to apply in some cases where the cause of the damage is known. *See also* the peculiar statement in *Sisters of St. Joseph of the Diocese of London v. Fleming supra* n. 57 at 177: "It is unfortunate that the maxim *res ipsa loquitur,* which serves satisfactorily when applied to certain cases *in which the cause of action is known,* has become a much over-worked instrument in our courts . . ." [emphasis supplied].

69 *Hobson v. Munkley supra* n. 59; *See also Kolesar v. Jeffries supra* n. 64; *see also Cavan v. Wilcox* (1974), 2 N.R. 618 at 626 (S.C.C.).

70 *Scott v. London & St. Katherine Docks Co.* (1865), 3 H. & C. 596, 159 E.R. 665 (Ex. Ch.).

71 *Kirk v. McLaughlin Coal & Supplies Ltd.* (1967), 66 D.L.R. (2d) 321 (Ont. C.A.).

72 *Malone v. Trans-Can. Airlines; Moss v. Trans-Can. Airlines,* [1942] O.R. 453 (C.A.).

73 *Kapur v. Marshall* (1978), 4 C.C.L.T. 204 (Ont. H.C.).

74 *Hobson v. Munkley supra* n. 59.

75 *Crits v. Sylvester supra* n. 17; *McTaggart v. Powers supra* n. 57.

76 *McLean v. Weir supra* n. 55.

be to misinterpret the doctrine and apply it more strictly to medical negligence cases than to ordinary negligence cases,[77] for there are some occurrences that, even to a layman, speak of negligence without the confirmation of expert evidence. As was stated in an English case where the patient proved that the doctor had left a swab in her body:[78]

> The surgeon is in command of the operation. It is for him to decide what instruments, swabs and the like are to be used, and it is he who uses them. The patient, or, if he dies, his representatives, can know nothing about this matter. There can be no possible question but that neither swabs nor instruments are ordinarily left in the patient's body, and no one would venture to say it is proper, though in particular circumstances it may be excusable, so to leave them. If, therefore, a swab is left in the patient's body, it seems to me clear that the surgeon is called upon for an explanation. That is, he is called upon to show, not necessarily why he missed it, but that he exercised due care to prevent its being left there.

Lord Nathan has stated in reflecting upon that case:[79]

> All that is necessary is that the occurrence is more consistent with there having been negligence than with there having been none; and the mere fact that the occurrence may have happened without negligence does not exclude the operation of the maxim if the more probable explanation is that there was negligence.

Therefore, while some events may speak directly to the layman of negligence, others may require the interpretation of an expert. If the former, the court can apply the doctrine on its own; if the latter, the plaintiff must provide the conduit in the form of an expert witness.

Unfortunately Canadian judges have not distinctly stated their position on this issue, but a reading of the cases indicates that they are applying the doctrine. Accidents which have been held to speak of negligence have involved broken needles,[80] misplaced injections causing paralysis[81] and circulatory complications,[82] burns,[83] sponges[84] and forceps[85] left behind, anaesthesiological mishaps,[86] and surgery causing vocal impairment,[87] facial paralysis[88] and Volkmann's contracture (deformity of the hand and arm)[89] as well as the failure to detect and treat an infection before a crippling injury

---

77 Fleming, *Law of Torts* 290 (6th ed. 1983).
78 *Mahon v. Osborne*, [1939] 1 All E.R. 535 at 561 (C.A.). For a Canadian case similar in facts and result, *see Cosgrove v. Gaudreau* (1981), 33 N.B.R. (2d) 523 (Q.B.).
79 *Supra* n. 34 at 116.
80 *Cardin v. Montreal* (1961), 29 D.L.R. 492 (S.C.C.).
81 *Martel v. Hotel-Dieu St-Vallier; Vigneault v. Martel supra* n. 38.
82 *Cavan v. Wilcox supra* n. 69.
83 *Abel v. Cooke supra* n. 57; *Harkies v. Lord Dufferin Hosp. supra* n. 57; *Sisters of St. Joseph of the Diocese of London v. Fleming supra* n. 57.
84 *Karderas v. Clow* (1973), 32 D.L.R. (3d) 303 (Ont. H.C.); *Holt v. Nesbitt supra* n. 58; *Cosgrove v. Gaudreau supra* n. 78.
85 *Taylor v. Gray supra* n. 22.
86 *Holmes v. London Bd. of Hosp. Trustees supra* n. 38.
87 *Finlay v. Auld*, [1975] S.C.R. 338.
88 *Eady v. Tenderenda supra* n. 53.
89 *Rietze v. Bruser*, [1979] 1 W.W.R. 31 (Man. Q.B.).

resulted[90] and to properly conduct an audiogram resulting in a patient's hearing being impaired.[91]

Accidents which have been held not to speak of negligence have involved arterial surgery causing paralysis,[92] ureter[93] and bowel[94] damage during tubal ligation, disc surgery causing arterial damage and death,[95] dental surgery causing a broken jaw,[96] injury to the lip[97] and cardiac arrest,[98] plastic surgery causing deformities in the eyelid,[99] thyroid surgery resulting in a cardiac arrest,[100] prostate surgery during which a hole was cut in the prostate capsule,[101] a fracture[102] during, and an infection[103] following surgery and quadriplegia after an arteriography (dye-injection x-ray).[104]

The courts must be aware of the basic difficulty that while the critical question is whether such an accident would normally occur without negligence, it may be an impossible one for an expert to answer, especially if such an accident has never occurred before. This and the difficulty of cataloguing *res ipsa loquitur* situations call out for flexibility and the use of common sense,[105] as put succinctly by Fleming:[106]

> The maxim contains nothing new; it is based on common sense, since it is a matter of ordinary observation and experience in life that sometimes a thing tells its own story.

C. The negligence must be the defendant's

There is a requirement that the plaintiff link the accident with the defendant.[107] Older authorities spoke of proving that the defendant was "in

---

90 *Hajgato v. London Health Assn.* (1983), 36 O.R. (2d) 669 (H.C.).
91 *Bartlett v. Children's Hosp.* (1983), 40 Nfld. & P.E.I.R. 88 (Nfld. S.C.).
92 *Girard v. Royal Columbian Hosp. supra* n. 43.
93 *Hobson v. Munkley supra* n. 59.
94 *Videto v. Kennedy* (1981), 17 C.C.L.T. 307 (Ont. C.A.).
95 *Kapur v. Marshall supra* n. 73.
96 *Fish v. Kapur*, [1948] 2 All E.R. 176; *Fletcher v. Bench* reported in [1973] 4 Brit. Med. J. 117 at 118.
97 *Dunn v. Young* (1977), 86 D.L.R. (3d) 411 (Ont. Co. Ct.)..
98 *Leadbetter v. Brand* (1980), 37 N.S.R. (2d) 581 (S.C.).
99 *Guertin v. Kester* (1981), 20 C.C.L.T. 225 (B.C.S.C.). *See also Patterson v. Yves de la Bastide* (1983), 22 A.C.W.S. (2d) 244 (Ont. H.C.).
100 *MacKinnon v. Ignacio, Lamond and MacKeough* (1978), 29 N.S.R. (2d) 656 (S.C.).
101 *Considine v. Camp Hill Hosp.* (1982), 133 D.L.R. (3d) 11 (N.S.S.C.).
102 *Powell v. Guttman*, [1978] 5 W.W.R. 228 (Man. C.A.).
103 *Hajgato v. London Health Assn.* (1982), 36 O.R. (2d) 669 (H.C.).
104 *Ferguson v. Hamilton Civic Hosp.* (1983), 23 C.C.L.T. 254 (Ont. S.C.).
105 Wright, *supra* n. 50 at 48 and 61. In 1906, for example, it was held that deformities were a very common result of fractures, even with the most skilled treatment of modern surgery; hence *res ipsa loquitur* should not apply; *see Hodgins v. Banting supra* n. 57. Today, deformities might well speak of negligence. *See Rietze v. Bruser*, [1979] 1 W.W.R. 31 (Man. Q.B.).
106 *Supra* n. 77 at 289.
107 Fleming, *supra* n. 77 at 291.

control'' of the situation and even excluded the operation of the doctrine when there was more than one defendant involved.[108]

Modern courts have exhibited more flexibility in construing this requirement, finding, for example, that control is present where the activity under scrutiny "was the exclusive province of the defendant and that no other agency intervened.''[109] Fleming, a noted torts authority, goes further:[110]

> Yet it surely would be at once more accurate and less confusing to abandon all references to "control" and postulate simply that the apparent cause of the accident must be such that the defendant would most probably be responsible for any negligence connected therewith.

The Alberta Court of Appeal has made it clear that it is possible for more than one defendant to be "in control" of a situation so that *res ipsa loquitur* could be used by a plaintiff alleging that two defendants are linked to the accident.[111]

Regarding the position where there might be vicarious liability for one or more of the defendants Mr. Justice Clement reviewed the case law and said:[112]

> From such cases I draw only the conclusion that where there is vicarious liability on tortfeasors it is not necessary to the operation of the maxim [*res ipsa loquitur*] that the evidence should identify a particular one of the tortfeasors as the person at fault.

This more liberal approach has profound implications for negligence suits against doctors and hospitals. No longer can the operation of the doctrine be said to be precluded because the accident occurred while a patient was in hospital under the care of more than one person. It is important to note that because a hospital is vicariously liable for nurses and house staff, it is not necessary to identify any particular employee as the person at fault in order to make the hospital accountable.[113]

Canadian courts have indicated a readiness to espouse the new approach. In *Cosgrove v. Gaudreau*[114] where a sponge was left in a patient the defendants were a doctor and operating room nurses employed by the hospital. Miller J. said it was clear that the defendant doctor and scrub nurse were "in control of the situation and the sponges.''[115] He applied the doctrine and because their explanations were unsatisfactory, the doctor and the hospital

---

108 *McFadyen v. Harvie*, [1942] S.C.R. 390. *Morris v. Winsbury-White*, [1937] 4 All E.R. 494 (K.B.). There is a more recent county court judgment to the same effect; *see Dunn v. Young* (1977), 86 D.L.R. (3d) 411 (Ont. Co. Ct.).

109 *Kirk v. McLaughlin Coal & Supplies Ltd.*, [1968] 1 O.R. 311 (C.A.).

110 *Supra* n. 77 at 292.

111 *MacLachlan & Mitchell Homes Ltd. v. Frank's Rental Sales* (1979), 10 C.C.L.T. 306 (Alta. C.A.). Followed in *Goldsworthy v. Catalina Agencies Ltd.* (1983), 142 D.L.R. (3d) 281 (Nfld. S.C.); *see Roe v. Min. of Health*, [1954] 2 Q.B. 66 at 82 (C.A.).

112 *Id.* at 322.

113 Fleming, *supra* n. 77 at 291-92. *See also* Powell and Jackson, *Professional Negligence* 220 (1982).

114 (1981), 33 N.B.R. (2d) 523 (Q.B.).

115 *Id.* at 529.

were held liable. In another case[116] Callaghan J. found no difficulty in applying the doctrine where the defendants were an orthopaedic surgeon and two house staff doctors employed by the hospital. All were sued by a patient who suffered injury to a joint from an untreated infection. However, the defendants met the burden of explanation that the doctrine cast on them and there was no liability. Likewise Krever J.[117] was prepared to consider *res ipsa loquitur* where the defendants were a neurosurgeon, two house staff doctors and a nurse employed by the hospital. But the learned justice found that as an injury to the spinal cord during or following a bilateral carotid arteriography may occur without negligence, the doctrine was not appropriate.

The words of Mr. Justice Clement of the Alberta Court of Appeal provide some guidance:[118]

> For myself I do not have difficulty in the application of the maxim [*res ipsa loquitur*] if it is kept in mind that in the case of "several" tortfeasors the hypothetical fault of each is independent of that which may be inferred against the others, and so raises a separate cause of action not linked to the others as in the case of joint tortfeasors. This leads inevitably, in my view, *to the separate consideration of the evidence relating to each alleged tortfeasor* to determine first, whether it supports an inference of negligence within the maxim and, if so, whether that alleged tortfeasor has met it acceptably. On this approach, *if on a reasonable view of the evidence the application of the maxim is warranted against two or more alleged tortfeasors, one or more may repel the inference of negligence raised against him or them and so be absolved.* If neither or none can, *I do not see any strain on justice to hold both culpable,* presumably in such proportions as may be determined under The Contributory Negligence Act . . . [emphasis supplied]

Thus, while the patient must make the best case he can against each doctor and hospital and meet the requirements of the doctrine of *res ipsa loquitur* with respect to each, the defendants' association in the accident which caused the patient's injury does not *per se* absolve them. *Res ipsa loquitur* is now more readily available to the patient.

When the doctrine was more restrictive attempts to assist the patient led to innovative jurisprudence.[119] In an American case, *Ybarra v. Spangard*,[120] a patient who suffered a shoulder injury during appendix surgery sued the entire surgical team. He was nonsuited at trial but on appeal the case was sent back for a new trial and *res ipsa loquitur* was held to be applicable. In Ontario a court[121] attempted to extend the case of *Cook v. Lewis*[122] holding that because

---

116 *Hajgato v. London Health Assn.* (1982), 36 O.R. (2d) 669 (H.C.).

117 *Ferguson v. Hamilton Civic Hosp.* (1983), 23 C.C.L.T. 254 (Ont. H.C.).

118 *MacLachlan & Mitchell Homes Ltd. v. Frank's Rental Sales supra* n. 111 at 324. Note that Lord Denning was of the same mind 25 years before; *see Roe v. Min. of Health supra* n. 111.

119 *See* Wright, *supra* n. 50 at 50-54.

120 (1944), 154 P. (2d) 687 (Cal. S.C.). Wright has criticized this decision *supra* n. 50 at 54.

121 *Kolesar v. Jeffries* (1976), 12 O.R. (2d) 142; affirmed 2 C.C.L.T. 170 (S.C.C.).

122 [1951] S.C.R. 830. This case held that when a person has been injured by one of two persons in circumstances where both have acted carelessly, and the effect is to make it impossible for the plaintiff to show which one's negligence caused the injuries, then both should be held liable unless they can exculpate themselves.

a nurse's negligence precluded a determination of the patient's cause of death it was up to her and her employer, the hospital, to prove cause of death unrelated to their negligence. But the Supreme Court of Canada[123] overruled the decision and reiterated that the negligence must be "brought down" to one or other of the defendants by the plaintiff. The court did leave for the future the possibility that the *Cook v. Lewis* rule could be invoked to help a patient in the right case which, it appears, would have to have very special circumstances. It would be a case where the patient could implicate both defendants in the negligence but be unable to show the cause as flowing from the actions of one or the other of them.[124] Just such a case[125] occurred in California where the plaintiffs were women whose mothers had taken a drug to prevent miscarriages and the defendants were a number of manufacturers of the drug shown to cause cancer in daughters of those who took it. There was no evidence to make the certain connection between a manufacturer and a mother. The Supreme Court of California held that the burden of proof shifted to the defendants to prove that their culpability should not be in proportion to each manufacturer's share of the market at the material time. The flexibility introduced into the *res ipsa loquitur* doctrine described earlier seems a modest step by comparison to such a decision.[126]

The patient is greatly assisted in his search for the appropriate defendant by pre-trial inquiries, especially the examination for discovery. The opportunity afforded to question the doctor or officers or employees of the hospital is sufficient reason for naming all possible negligent actors as defendants and discontinuing afterwards against those who have no place in the action. The practice is not a happy one for the fostering of a better relationship between the professions, but it is a necessary one.

(iii) Effect

Assuming that the prerequisites for the application of the doctrine have been met, the next issue is its effect on the onus of proof in a medical negligence case.

On this point the case law is fairly consistent: the doctrine allows the plaintiff to establish a *prima facie* case of negligence against the defendant.[127] The defendant, to counter this, must offer an explanation of the incident as

---

123 *Kolesar v. Jeffries supra* n. 28 and Klar, *Annotation.*
124 Klar, *id. See Roe v. Min. of Health,* [1954] 2 Q.B. 66 at 82 (C.A.).
125 *Sindell v. Abbott Laboratories* (1980), 607 P. (2d) 924, 163 Cal. Rep. 132 (Cal. S.C.).
126 Note that in a comment Professor Irvine has queried whether this decision is "really so radical and outlandish a further step, that it might not be taken here [in Canada], in the foreseeable future." *See* Irvine, *Annotation* (1980), 14 C.C.L.T. 252 at 255.
127 For an excellent statement *see Holmes v. London Bd. of Hosp. Trustees supra* n. 38.

consistent with no negligence as with negligence.[128] The Supreme Court of Canada has cautioned strongly that the effect of the doctrine ought to be kept at a reasonable level:[129]

> It appears to me that in medical cases where differences of expert opinion are not unusual and the sequence of events often appears to have brought about a result which has never occurred in exactly the same way before to the knowledge of the most experienced doctors, great caution should be exercised to ensure that the rule embodied in the maxim *res ipsa loquitur* is not construed so as to place too heavy a burden on the defendant. Each such case must of necessity be determined according to its own particular facts and it seems to me that the rule should never be applied in such cases by treating the facts of one case as controlling the result in another, however similar those facts may be.

The doctrine has been only rarely held to have the effect of placing on the defendant an onus of disproof of negligence in medical cases,[130] although it frequently happens that a defendant will do so, even in cases in which the doctrine is not strictly applicable.[131] This is so because such a defence is virtually unassailable.

If the defendant offers a satisfactory explanation, then the basic burden of proof remains with the plaintiff who, without more evidence, will not succeed in proving his case on a balance of probabilities.[132] However, it would be an imprudent defendant who offered no explanation, because the effect at a minimum would strengthen the inference of negligence[133] and could possibly result in a finding that the plaintiff had successfully proven his case,[134] or at least preclude a nonsuit.[135]

The defendant's explanation need not prove exactly what happened so long as the theory advanced is supported by reasonable testimony. Accordingly, where a defendant testified and called ''ample medical evidence to support the finding that the injection was given without any fault''[136] the explanation was found adequate. Similarly, it was held that the defendant had successfully discharged his burden of rebutting the inference where he and his medical witnesses testified that it would have been impossible for him in the circum-

---

128 *Finlay v. Auld supra* n. 87 at 343; *Ferguson v. Hamilton Civic Hosp.* (1983), 23 C.C.L.T. 254 at 304 (Ont. H.C.).

129 *Cavan v. Wilcox*, [1975] 2 S.C.R. 663 at 674.

130 *But see Cardin v. Montreal* (1961), 29 D.L.R. (2d) 492 at 495; *McKay v. Royal Inland Hosp.* (1964), 48 D.L.R. (2d) 665 at 670 (B.C.S.C.); *Bartlett v. Children's Hosp. Corp.* (1983), 40 Nfld. & P.E.I.R. 88 at 105 (Nfld. S.C.).

131 *See, for example, McLean v. Weir supra* n. 55 and Picard, *Annotation*.

132 *Cavan v. Wilcox supra* n. 69 at 628.

133 *Mahon v. Osborne supra* n. 78. For a comment *see* Wright, *supra* n. 50 at 53.

134 *Karderas v. Clow supra* n. 84 at 312; *Taylor v. Gray* (1937), 11 M.P.R. 588 at 606. see *supra* n. 22.

135 *McKay v. Gilchrist* (1962), 35 D.L.R. (2d) 568 (Sask. C.A.).

136 *Cavan v. Wilcox supra* n. 69 at 628. It is interesting that the Court of Appeal held the explanation inadequate based on its assessment of the defendant nurse who had no recollection of the procedure she had used.

stances to have caused the damage which formed the basis of the complaint.[137] Where the testimony of doctors was that their failure to diagnose and treat an infection arose as a result of a unique combination of circumstances, the court accepted this explanation as discharging the burden upon them.[138]

On the other hand, a pure hypothesis by the defendant (found to be an unreliable witness) with no support from other witnesses was held not to be an adequate explanation,[139] nor was an explanation which revealed a failure to take precautions on the part of the defendant.[140] Likewise, the excuse that a test had caused no hearing loss "on literally thousands of occasions"[141] was held to be an insufficient answer as was evidence of the cause of a patient's injury when the issue was a failure to diagnose and treat the condition.[142]

The extremes of the adequacy and inadequacy of explanations are not difficult to see from the cases, but the middle area remains muddy, and at least one judge has recognized the need for clarification.[143] Factors that ought to be relevant include whether the defendant testifies, whether any evidence is available to substantiate the explanation, the time at which the theory or explanation was first advanced, and the credibility of the theory.[144] The doctrine of *res ipsa loquitur* is simply a means of assisting the court in having all the relevant evidence brought before it. Properly applied it need not be feared by the doctor or hospital, nor should it be seen by the patient as a means of resuscitating a dead action.

(c) Obtaining Witnesses

A plaintiff in an action against a doctor or hospital often has difficulty in obtaining expert witnesses to testify on his behalf.[145] In the United States, where much is written about the problem, the difficulty has been attributed to a so-called "conspiracy of silence"[146] among members of the medical profession. This view, however, oversimplifies the causes of the phenomenon, which are more numerous and complex than some writers would have us believe.[147]

---

137 *Finlay v. Auld supra* n. 87. *See also Mang v. Moscovitz* (1982), 37 A.R. 221 (Alta. Q.B.).
138 *Hajgato v. London Health Assn.* (1982), 36 O.R. (2d) 669 (H.C.).
139 *Martel v. Hotel-Dieu St-Vallier; Vigneault v. Martel supra* n. 38.
140 *Crits v. Sylvester supra* n. 17; *See also Cosgrove v. Gaudreau* (1981), 33 N.B.R. (2d) 523 (Q.B.); *Lefebvre v. Osborne* (1983), 22 A.C.W.S. (2d) 350 (Ont. H.C.).
141 *Bartlett v. Children's Hosp.* (1983), 40 Nfld. & P.E.I.R. 88 (Nfld. S.C.).
142 *Rietze v. Bruser*, [1979] 1 W.W.R. 31 (Man. Q.B.).
143 *Kolesar v. Jeffries* (1974), 59 D.L.R. (3d) 367 (Ont. H.C.) *per* Haines J.
144 *Holmes v. London Bd. of Hosp. Trustees supra* n. 38.
145 For cases where a patient called no expert evidence and actions were dismissed *see Hajgato v. London Health Assn.* (1982), 36 O.R. (2d) 669 (H.C.); *Considine v. Camp Hill Hosp.* (1982), 133 D.L.R. (3d) 11 (N.S.S.C.); *Jodouin v. Mitra* (1978), 2 L. Med. Q. 72 (Ont. S.C.).
146 Belli, *Ready for the Plaintiff* (1957), 30 Temp. L.Q. 408.
147 *See Leadbetter v. Brand* (1980), 37 N.S.R. (2d) 581 (S.C.) at 607 where Hallett J. says he "disagree[s] with the general statement that the medical profession will not testify against another member."

It is important to remember at the outset that the plaintiff in a medical negligence action is not in a unique position. Obtaining witnesses is a difficulty which arises in all kinds of litigation. While the presence of witnesses, especially expert witnesses, is critical to the just determination of any dispute,[148] there are factors present in all lawsuits which tend to discourage persons from volunteering to testify. First, there is a trend today to keep to one's self and resist involvement in social problems or the affairs of others. Second, the legal process requires time for being interviewed, preparing reports, reviewing notes and records and waiting in court to testify. To many, especially professionals, time is money and this sizeable demand on time is resented. Third, the experience of giving testimony in the witness box can be less than enjoyable. The expert will have to expose his credentials and may be questioned about them, which he may feel is demeaning or even destructive to his professional status. Cross-examination is generally unpleasant for the witness who may find his judgment or credibility called into question, and may feel he is not being permitted to give a complete answer.

In addition to these factors, there are others in the action between a patient and his doctor. First, there is no doubt that there is a feeling of brotherhood among the members of any profession, and indeed, in view of the education, employment environment and, to a degree, the background of the individuals involved it would be surprising if there was not. Second, the sorts of cases which go to trial are precisely those about which doctors are reluctant to testify. Cases in which the negligence is clear and there is no defence do not go to trial because the patient will be compensated by a settlement with a protective association or malpractice insurer. Similarly, cases in which there appears to be no negligence or where there is an unassailable defence do not go to trial because the patient's hopes of success are overshadowed by the cost of bringing the action.[149] Generally it is only those cases in which the negligence alleged or the defence put forward or both are tenuous which go to trial[150] and these often involve matters of judgment,[151] decisions made under pressure[152] or procedures taken which seemed reasonable at the time.[153] Doctors hearing of such cases may think, "there but for the Grace of God go I" and naturally resist standing in judgment of their colleagues.

---

148 Haines, *The Medical Profession and the Adversary Process* (1973), 11 Osgoode Hall L.J. 41. The importance of the medical witness to the court was stressed by Scott in Canadian Medical Protective Association, *Annual Report 1975* at 23.

149 The Canadian Medical Protective Association refuses to settle claims unless liability is clear. They will not settle for "nuisance value." An easy settlement policy has been cited as one of the reasons for the U.S. malpractice crisis. *See* Haines, *supra* n. 148 at 44.

150 *See* Haines, *id.* at 42 where he states that the majority of cases going to trial involve "a terribly grey area where the law may see negligence but medicine sees merely an unexpected occurrence in a very inexact art."

151 *Ostrowski v. Lotto* (1972), 31 D.L.R. (3d) 715 (S.C.C.).

152 *Wilson v. Swanson supra* n. 16.

153 *Anderson v. Chasney supra* n. 17.

The issue also tends to become clouded by aspects of the legal process and in particular its application to the medical negligence suit, which irritates both patients and doctors. The power of the writ of subpoena, which is an order in the name of the sovereign compelling a witness to appear in court or face a fine or possible imprisonment, is resented by many witnesses.[154] Also, the legal action by a patient against his doctor may have strong emotional overtones arising out of the basic nature of the doctor-patient relationship. Furthermore, to the patient's misunderstandings of the legal process is added the mystery of medicine and the patient may feel that the legal and medical professionals involved are closer to each other than he is to either of them.

Certainly there is evidence of a reluctance of doctors and health care professionals in Canada to testify,[155] but as has been shown, the "conspiracy of silence"[156] explanation is incomplete; there are many reasons for the aversion to appear as a witness.

In recognition of this, steps have been taken with the goal in mind of bringing doctors and lawyers together for the benefit of themselves and patients.[157] These include the creation of medical-legal societies, joint professional committees, inter-professional codes,[158] undertakings by national and provincial medical associations to provide witnesses where necessary,[159] and resolutions by doctors and their medical protective associations to testify when requested. Nevertheless, the reluctance to testify will always be with us to a degree, and the lawyer must cope with it in a manner constructive to his client's case and within the best ethical practice of both professions.[160]

---

154 In British Columbia, Manitoba, Ontario and Saskatchewan, a doctor may give evidence in writing (or by way of medical report) instead of appearing in court. *See supra* n. 25. *See* Elliot, *Medical Evidence* (1968), 16 Chitty's L.J. 343; Lightbody, *Doctor in the Courtroom?* (1973), 31 Advocate 269; Smookler, *The Law* (1973), Medical Post, Oct. 14. *See also* Meredith, *supra* n. 17 at 36.

155 *See, for example, McKeachie v. Alvarez* (1970), 17 D.L.R. (3d) 87 at 93 (B.C.S.C.); *but see Girard v. Royal Columbian Hosp.* (1976), 66 D.L.R. (3d) 676 at 693 (B.C.S.C.). *See also* Haines, *Courts and Doctors* (1952), 30 Can. Bar Rev. 483; Province of Ontario, Attorney-General's Committee on Medical Evidence in Court in Civil Cases, *Report* (1965). An empirical study in Ontario showed Ontario doctors to be reticent: Gray and Sharpe, Osgoode Hall Medical Legal Questionnaire, 1971; *see* (1973), 11 Osgoode Hall L.J. 1.

156 One author has labelled it "the infernal silence that besets the medical profession;" Grange, *The Silent Doctor v. The Duty to Speak* (1973), 11 Osgoode Hall L.J. 81.

157 See Louisell and Williams, *Medical Malpractice*, Matthew Bender, New York (1982), at 9-11.

158 *See, for example,* Medico-Legal Society of Toronto, *Inter-Professional Code* (1977). There is now a liasion committee of the Canadian Bar Association and the Canadian Medical Association.

159 *See, for example,* Canadian Medical Association, *Code of Ethics; see also* Marshall, *Medical Evidence in Malpractice Actions* (1970), 18 Chitty's L.J. 6 at 9 and 11.

160 For the perspective of a Canadian doctor-lawyer *see* Marshall, *The Physician and Canadian Law* 8 (1979).

The preparation of a medical negligence suit against a doctor or hospital is an arduous and difficult task, and the following are some practical suggestions to assist with the problem.[161]

Once the lawyer has all the facts, some time ought to be spent with medical dictionaries and texts in an attempt to get a grip on the medical aspects of the case. Engaging the services of qualified medical professionals for assistance ought to be considered.[162] This expert assistance will often be obtainable in exchange for an undertaking that the expert will not be called to testify. The experts should not be relied upon to develop the case for the plaintiff, but should be asked to evaluate theories as to what may have happened, postulated by the lawyer after thorough research.[163]

Experts who are willing to testify should, of course, be treated with the appropriate degree of professionalism. The following is a list of matters which ought to be performed to make the experience of the expert as pleasant as possible.

(1) Make specific arrangements as to required reports, accompanied by the patient's consent and the fee.

(2) Give maximum notice of the time of trial.

(3) Brief the expert before trial as to procedure, the necessity of qualifying him, the questions to be asked of him and the likely areas of cross-examination.

(4) Settle beforehand the amount of the witness fee.

(5) Make arrangements to take the evidence of your expert with as little delay as possible.

(6) After the trial, pay the witness promptly and send along a letter of appreciation and information as to the disposition of the case.

In short, be courteous. It is to be remembered that a lost case can as easily be the result of poor advocacy as poor evidence, and the lawyer who blames only the latter may be deceiving himself.

(d) The Jury

In any legal action there are to be decided questions of both law and fact. The judge always rules on questions of law, and when he sits without a jury he

---

161 For an excellent outline and explanation of many more points than can be set out here *see* Stewart, *The Preparation and Presentation of Medical Proof*, [1955] L.S.U.C. Spec. Lec. 155. *See also* Haines, *supra* n. 11.

162 *See* Haines, *supra* n. 11.

163 Kramer, in *The Negligent Doctor*, Crown Publications, New York, 1968, outlines his method: "I have a theory about medical experts, particularly in malpractice cases, that has proved its worth through my years of experience. The best hope of getting one [to testify for the plaintiff] — always a difficult matter — is to do the necessary medical research in advance and ferret out the authorities and data that fortify your claim. It is one thing to ask a doctor for his opinion as to whether or not there was careless or negligent practice, but it is quite another to spell out in detail the acts of negligence, support with literature and then ask him if he is in accord. When you have done the latter, the expert is usually more receptive."

also determines the questions of fact. If a jury is present, it will decide questions of fact and be directed on the law by the judge. If the judge believes that the plaintiff's evidence is insufficient, he has the discretion to "withdraw the case from the jury" and dismiss the action.[164] However, if the case goes to jury, it is the task of the jurors to assess the credibility of the witnesses, and where there is a conflict in testimony to decide which version is to be accepted.[165]

Neither the trial judge nor a court of appeal should substitute its own opinion on those matters for that of the jury. The test is not whether the verdict appears to the judge or appeal court to be correct, but whether the jury as reasonable persons could have reached such a decision. Thus, the decision of a properly instructed jury carrying out its assignment is often impossible to upset.[166]

The use of juries in medical negligence cases has not been common in Canada.[167] The procedure is cumbersome, expensive, time consuming and leaves to inexperienced persons the difficult job of assessing damages.[168] There is also a concern that juries tend to unfairly favour the plaintiff.[169] However, the basis for rejecting applications for jury trials has been a fear that laymen would not understand the complex evidence that may be involved in a law suit against a health care professional or a hospital.[170]

Recently there have been some strong opinions, sometimes *obiter,* that a jury trial should not be denied to a patient on such a basis because jury members of today are "of greater sophistication,"[171] and have proven their abilities at inquests and in difficult criminal cases.[172]. Furthermore, medical experts have shown themselves able to discuss complex medical issues in

---

164 *Fields v. Rutherford* (1878), 29 U.C.C.P. 113 (C.A).

165 *McNulty v. Morris* (1901), 2 O.L.R. 656 at 658 (Div. Ct.).

166 *Eady v. Tenderenda* (1974), 3 N.R. 26 (S.C.C.) upholding a jury verdict; *Zablotny v. Levine,* [1981] B.C.D. Civ. 2632-01 (B.C.S.C.); *see also Child v. Vancouver General Hosp.,* [1970] S.C.R. 477; *but see McQuay v. Eastwood* (1886), 12 O.R. 402 (C.A.) where a jury verdict was reversed; *see also Hankai v. York County Hosp.* (1981), 9 A.C.W.S.(2d) 354 (Ont. C.A.), where a new trial was ordered for assessment of damages when a jury awarded general damages of $35,000 and punitive damages of $25,000 for battery.

167 *See Morrow v. Royal Victoria Hosp.* (1971), 23 D.L.R. (3d) 441 at 450; reversed on other grounds 42 D.L.R. (3d) 233 (S.C.C.); *see also* Sopinka and Ledermen, *supra* n. 4 at 6.

168 *See Hankai v. York County Hosp. supra* n. 166.

169 *Jackson v. Hyde* (1869), 28 U.C.Q.B. 294; *Key v. Thomson* (1868), 12 N.B.R. 295 at 306 (S.C.).

170 *See, for example, Marshall v. Curry,* [1933] 3 D.L.R. 198 (N.S.S.C.); *Durkin v. Les Soeurs de Charité,* [1940] 1 W.W.R. 558 (Man. C.A.); *York v. Lapp* (1967), 65 D.L.R. (2d) 351 (B.C.S.C.); *Wenger v. Marien* (1977), 78 D.L.R. (3d) 201 (Alta. S.C.); *Mang v. Moscovitz* (1980), 28 A.R. 148 (Q.B.); *Damien v. O'Mulvenny* (1981), 34 O.R. (2d) 448 (H.C.); *Whealy v. Torbar* (1982), 40 O.R. (2d) 378 (H.C.).

171 *Placido v. Shore* (1982), 15 A.C.W.S. (2d) 537 (Ont. H.C.).

172 *DeMoura v. Mississauga Hosp.* (1979), 3 L. Med. Q. 215 at 224 (Ont. S.C.); *Fast v. Lane,* [1979] B.C.D. Civ. 36-53-13 (B.C.S.C.).

layman's terms.[173] There is also the opinion that health care professionals and hospitals should not be given preferential treatment by being insulated from juries.[174]

Old presumptions and practices[175] with respect to juries are being critically scrutinized. But the right and interest of the patient[176] in a jury trial must be balanced with the right and concern of a health care professional or a hospital for a just determination of the issues. Each application for a jury must be carefully considered by the judge hearing it.

---

173 *Falez v. Boothroyd* (1980), 22 B.C.L.R. 41 at 43 (S.C.); *Dunn v. Henderson*, [1980] B.C.D. Civ. 3653-02 (B.C.S.C.).

174 *DeMoura v. Mississauga Hosp. supra* n. 172; *Soldwisch v. Toronto General Hosp.* (1982), 139 D.L.R. (3d) 642 at 645 (Ont. H.C.).

175 *Soldwisch v. Toronto General Hosp.*, unreported October 12, 1983 No. 962/82 (Ont. Div. Ct.) examined old law and decided that a judge in Ontario has a discretion to allow trial by jury. For an article predicting this result *see* Jack, *Jury Notices In Medical Malpractice Cases — Judicial Reconsideration of Older Authorities* (1977-78), 1 Advoc. Q. 387.

176 There are those who call for the return of the civil jury because they believe that the patient's interests are not being adequately protected by the present tort system. Teplitsky and Weisstub, *Torts-Negligence Standards and the Physician* (1978), 56 Can. Bar Rev. 121.

7

The Doctor in Court

1.   INTRODUCTION

Differences in the education and experience of doctors and lawyers have sometimes led to misunderstandings between the professions. The doctor's education emphasizes the assimilation of complex factual knowledge and objective scientific inquiry; the lawyer's emphasizes the acquisition of a special type of reasoning power and the development of adversarial and debating techniques. Doctors see themselves as co-operating in the common objective of preserving or restoring a patient's health, whereas the practice of law in both the courtroom and the office depends upon debate and challenge to resolve disputes. It has therefore been suggested that the legal process and particularly the adversary system is alien to doctors.[1]

These generalizations, even if only partially true, demonstrate that there is a risk that each profession may feel it will never understand the other. However, the basic commitment of both doctors and lawyers is to serve

---

1 For an excellent discussion *see* Louisell and Williams, *Medical Malpractice*, Matthew Bender, New York (1982), at 5-11. *See also* Haines, *The Medical Profession and the Adversary Process* (1973), 11 Osgoode Hall L.J. 41; Griffiths, *Some Comments on Forensic Medicine* (1966), 9 C.B.J. 306.

those who seek help; this ought to be seen by members of both professions as a common objective. The challenge of maintaining understanding and good-will between the professions can be met with ease if the intelligence and insight possessed by the members of both professions is directed toward an appreciation of the world in which each functions.

To this point in the book, the doctor's role in court has been seen primarily as a defendant or as an expert witness in a medical negligence suit, and these roles will be discussed in more detail presently. However, a doctor could be summoned by a court of law to act in any of a number of capacities.[2] In civil cases, his knowledge of a patient's medical condition or prognosis is frequently required by the court[3] as an aid to assessing damages or benefits, determining testamentary capacity, granting divorce, custody and adoption, or determining standard of care, approved practice and error of judgment. In criminal cases, his evidence may be required to establish injuries, the cause of death, or the mental or physical state of the accused.[4] In all cases, his role is to assist the court in arriving at a just decision.[5]

A unique role for the medical expert which has rarely been utilized in Canada is that of independent court expert.[6] Rules of procedure[7] in many jurisdictions provide that a court expert may be appointed to assist the court in determining some facts in issue upon the application of a party or on the court's own motion. While the process has its roots deep in the common law, its use in tort cases is viewed with suspicion by modern lawyers and judges because of fears that too much weight might be attached to the findings of

---

2 The importance of a doctor's evidence has been recognized for a very long time. *See, for example, Slater v. Baker* (1767), 2 Wils. 359, 95 E.R. 860 (C.P.).

3 For the difficulty faced by a court without such evidence *see Robinson v. Englot,* [1949] 2 W.W.R. 1137 at 1142 (Man. K.B.). Statutes in some jurisdictions provide for the admission of medical reports which have been signed by a legally qualified practitioner. *See* Evidence Act, R.S.B.C. 1979, c. 116, ss. 12, 13; Manitoba Evidence Act, R.S.M. 1970, c. E150, s. 50 [am. 1971, c. 70, ss. 2, 3; 1976, c. 69, s. 18]; Evidence Act, R.S.O. 1980, c. 145, s. 52; Saskatchewan Evidence Act, R.S.S. 1978, c. S-16, ss. 30-32. *See Harris v. Lazarenko,* [1982] Sask. D. 3340-01. *See also Report of the Federal/Provincial Task Force on Uniform Rules of Evidence* 95-101 (1982).

4 An excellent text is Schiffer, *Psychiatry Behind Bars* (1982). There are many excellent articles dealing with psychiatric evidence. *See, for example,* Goldberg and Zisman, *The Admissibility of Psychiatric Evidence on the Issues of Identity and Credibility* (1976), 33 C.R.N.S. 1; Manning and Mewet, *Psychiatric Evidence* (1976), 18 Crim. L.Q. 325; Silverman, *Psychiatric Evidence in Criminal Law* (1972), 14 Crim. L.Q. 145.

5 The Canadian Medical Association, Code of Ethics (1982), sets this out as a responsibility to society.

6 *See* Sopinka and Lederman, *The Law of Evidence in Civil Cases* 331-35 (1974); Jacobs, *The Court Expert — Rule 218* (1975), 13 Alta. L. Rev. 475.

7 *See, for example,* Supreme Court Rules, Alta. Reg. 390/68 (1968) [am. Rules 218, 235].

such an expert.[8] But as one judge has said:[9] "It is rather quaint that we should expect our judges to be expert in everything." This is especially true in regard to medical evidence where the experts may not be in accord, or where the judge may have grave doubts about the evidence of the experts.[10] There are two reported cases where a medical court expert has been properly used,[11] both from Quebec. In *Bergstrom v. G.*,[12] the trial judge had before him the testimonies of "two schools of doctors, to wit: the orthopedic surgeons and the vascular specialists." He suggested that an expert be appointed, to which the parties agreed, and the doctor so appointed, after reviewing the testimony and the exhibits, gave his views on the treatment given to the patient, and the court agreed with his opinion. In *Boivin v. Remillard*,[13] where the medical evidence was in conflict, a psychiatrist was appointed by the judge to examine a man to decide whether he was fit to manage his affairs, and the resulting opinion was accepted.

The Federal/Provincial Task Force on the Uniform Rules of Evidence[14] has recommended that a judge be given the power on application of any party or on his own motion to appoint an independent expert who must give his opinion in writing and be available to testify and be cross-examined.

2.   AS WITNESS

(a) Interviews

A doctor who is to be called as a witness must be interviewed personally by the lawyer, probably on more than one occasion.[15] The most benefit is obtained from this contact after each has reviewed all available and relevant notes, documents and records. The interview is of value to both participants. The lawyer has the opportunity to explore the doctor's evidence and opinions, which will assist him in preparing for cross-examination. This is also the time

---

8 *See, for example,* Lord Denning's comments in *Re Saxton,* [1962] 3 All E.R. 92 (C.A.), on an equivalent rule; *see also* Samuels, *Expert Forensic Evidence* (1974), 14 Med. Sci. Law 17. This is especially true in a medical negligence suit: *Hay v. Bain,* [1924] 1 D.L.R. 165 (Alta. S.C.).

9 Haines, *supra,* n. 1. Basten, *The Court Expert in Civil Trials — A Comparative Appraisal* (1977), 40 Med. L. Rev. 174.

10 *See, for example, Villemure v. Turcot,* [1973] S.C.R. 716.

11 *See also Featherstone v. Grunsven,* [1972] 1 O.R. 490 (C.A.), where prior to trial the judge appointed an independent medical expert to examine a plaintiff in a personal injuries case. He used the opinion but did not reveal it to counsel. On appeal a new trial was ordered.

12 [1967] C.S. 513 (Que.).

13 [1969] C.S. 203 (Que.).

14 *Report on Evidence* 104-110 (1982).

15 If acting for a patient suing in a medical negligence suit, *see* Haines, *The Conduct of Malpractice Action,* [1963] L.S.U.C. Spec. Lec. 273.

to establish the limits of the doctor's evidence and opinions, and to go over with him the questions to be asked in examination-in-chief. The doctor ought at this time to be made aware of what will happen in the courtroom, and of other aspects of the case or the legal process. His qualifications should be reviewed and some time should be spent on the subject of cross-examination: the rationale, the scope and the pitfalls.

(b) Qualifications

When the doctor is first called to testify, he must be qualified as an expert witness.[16] The lawyer will ask the doctor to outline his training, degrees, publications, experience, and possibly his steps in keeping abreast of medicine or increasing his expertise by taking courses, reading journals, participating in conferences and so on. In many cases, the lawyer for the opposite side will simply state that he accepts the qualifications, which means that this recital need not take place unless the lawyer calling the witness wishes to have the qualifications made obvious to the court and put on the record of the trial. After the doctor outlines his qualifications, the lawyer for the opposing side may cross-examine him on them but this rarely occurs in Canada. Doctors subjected to a review of their qualifications or possibly to cross-examination on them may resent what they see as a questioning of their competence.[17] However, because a court relies so heavily upon the evidence of experts in medical negligence cases, it must be certain that the witness is qualified as an expert in the relevant area.

(c) Giving Evidence

(i) Nature of the evidence

A doctor who has treated a patient may give evidence not only to his observations, diagnosis and treatment but, because he is an expert, can go further:[18]

> Most witnesses are called to prove ordinary facts, like the facts of an accident which they observed, or the conduct of others which they have seen. But a duly qualified doctor is usually an expert witness, and employs his skill and knowledge to express a medical opinion and draw conclusions from symptoms he has observed from facts that have been proven. The law permits him to do this because the tribunal, judge, or jury, is not in itself qualified to draw such conclusions and therefore relies on a specialist to tell it what the proper deduction is.

---

16 *See generally*, Sopinka and Lederman, *supra* n. 6 at 309-313.
17 *See for example, Chubey v. Ahsan*, [1975] 1 W.W.R 120 at 121; affirmed [1976] 3 W.W.R. 367 (Man. C.A.); *Mang v. Moscovitz* (1982), 37 A.R. 221 (Q.B.).
18 Viscount Simon, *The Doctor in the Witness Box*, [1953] 2 Brit. Med. J. 4826; approved in Meredith, *Malpractice Liability of Doctors and Hospitals* 80 (1956).

A modern authority states it this way:[19]

> An expert is usually called for two reasons. He provides basic information to the court necessary for its understanding of the scientific or technical issues involved in the case. In addition, because the court alone is incapable of drawing the necessary inferences from the technical facts presented, an expert is allowed to state his opinion and conclusions.

However, an expert can give opinion evidence only on matters within his field of expertise. In every case, the court has the final discretion to accept or reject expert evidence[20] and can draw inferences from the failure to call such evidence.[21]

(ii) Examination-in-chief

If a medical-legal report has been prepared and there have been pre-trial conferences between the doctor and lawyer, the examination-in-chief of the doctor should contain no surprises for the doctor or the lawyer who calls him. While testifying the doctor is free to refer to his own notes to refresh his memory,[22] including his medical-legal report, and may also refer to texts, periodicals, or other authorities, if he bases his opinion on them.[23] Two types of questions are of interest: leading and hypothetical.

Leading questions[24] are those which suggest the answer and are not permissible in examination-in-chief unless used only to introduce evidence not in issue. For example, the lawyer when beginning his examination-in-chief may say, "Doctor, did the plaintiff consult you in your professional capacity?" On the other hand, leading questions are permissible on cross-examination[25] and thus a doctor must listen carefully to the question and be sure he understands it before replying.

If a doctor called as an expert has no personal knowledge of facts which are in dispute, he can still be asked his opinion through the use of a hypotheti-

---

19 Sopinka and Lederman, *supra* n. 6 at 309.
20 *Ostrowski v. Lotto* (1972), 31 D.L.R. (3d) 715 at 721 (S.C.C.); *Chubey v. Ahsan supra* n. 17 at [1975] 1 W.W.R. 128; *Badger v. Surkan*, [1973] 1 W.W.R. 302 at 313 (Sask. C.A.); *see also* Meredith, *supra* n. 18 at 35 and 64; Shaw, *The Law and the Expert Witness* (1976), 69 Proceedings of the Royal Society of Medicine 1.
21 *Ostrowski v. Lotto* (1970), 15 D.L.R. (3d) 402 at 409 (Ont. C.A.); affirmed (1972), 31 D.L.R. (3d) 715 (S.C.C.).
22 Meredith, *supra* n. 18 at 45. See the critical comments of Linden J. about a doctor who failed to do so in *White v. Turner* (1981), 15 C.C.L.T. 81 (Ont. H.C.); affirmed 20 C.C.L.T. xxii (Ont. C.A.). Note that the trial may take place many years after the event. *See Allan v. New Mount Sinai Hosp.* (1980), 11 C.C.L.T. 299 (Ont. H.C.); reversed 19 C.C.L.T. 77 (Ont. C.A.), where over seven years elapsed.
23 *R. v. Anderson* (1914), 16 D.L.R. 203 at 219-20 (Alta. S.C.); *Reference re Sections 222, 224, 224A of The Criminal Code* (1971), 3 C.C.C. (2d) 243 at 254 (N.B.C.A.); Sopinka and Lederman, *supra* n. 6 at 326-28.
24 *See* Sopinka and Lederman, *id.* at 481-85; Meredith, *supra* n. 18 at 45.
25 Sopinka and Lederman, *supra* n. 6 at 498.

cal question.[26] The hypothetical fact situation is actually formulated from facts proven at trial and must be put to the expert in a clear, uncontradictory manner. He is asked to assume that certain facts exist and asked for his opinion on a specific issue such as what the diagnosis might be. These questions may be long and complicated and the doctor should be very certain that he understands what facts he is being asked to assume before he gives his opinion.[27]

(iii) Cross-examination

Cross-examination is the part of testifying that doctors seem to fear most.[28] It is the heart of the adversary system and the doctor knows that the goal is to elicit replies that weaken or destroy the evidence given in examination-in-chief, that support the cross-examining lawyer's case, or even that discredit the doctor as a witness.[29]

Caution should be exercised by the lawyer who, by cross-examination, may seem only to make the other side's case stronger.[30] Experienced lawyers realize the risk of "taking on" an expert, and anecdotes about the question that should never have been asked abound. It goes without saying that the lawyer should know the medical evidence as thoroughly as possible, but to have his own medical expert in court is helpful, and his presence may prevent exaggeration by witnesses called by the other side. Many excellent books are available to assist the lawyer in developing the art of advocacy,[31] but some advice to medical witnesses[32] might be of assistance to the medical reader.

---

26 *Id.* at 314-15.

27 For examples of the use of the hypothetical question, *see Ehler v. Smith* (1978), 29 N.S.R. (2d) 309 (S.C.); *Leadbetter v. Brand* (1980), 37 N.S.R. (2d) 581 (S.C.).

28 Gibson, *Courts and Doctors* (1952), 30 Can. Bar Rev. 498 at 499. For an example of unfair treatment of an expert witness, *see* Brownlie, *Expert Evidence in the Light of Preece v. H.M. Advocate* (1982), 22 Med. Sci. Law 237.

29 Sopinka and Lederman, *supra* n. 6 at 496-521; Meredith, *supra* n. 18 at 48-49. For cases where cross-examination was effective, *see Wipfli v. Britten* (1982), 22 C.C.L.T 104 at 111 (B.C.S.C.); *DeMoura v. Mississauga Hosp.* (1979), 3 L. Med. Q. 215 at 222 (Ont. S.C.); *Dean v. York County Hosp. Corp.* (1979), 3 L. Med. Q. 231 (Ont. S.C.).

30 *Gordon v. Davidson* (1980), 4 L. Med. Q. 131 at 146 (Ont. S.C.). Stewart, *The Preparation and Presentation of Medical Proof,* [1955] L.S.U.C. Spec. Lec. 155 at 171.

31 *See, for example,* Cecil, *Brief to Counsel,* Michael Joseph, London, (1972); Harris, *Harris's Hints on Advocacy,* Stevens, London, (1926); Harris, *Illustrations in Advocacy,* Stevens and Haynes, London, (1915); Keeton, *Trial Tactics and Methods,* Prentice-Hall, New York, (1954); Parry, *Seven Lamps of Advocacy,* Books for Libraries Press, New York, (1968); Stryker, *The Art of Advocacy,* Simon and Schuster, New York, (1954); Wrottesley, *The Examination of Witnesses in Court,* Sweet and Maxwell, London, (1961).

32 For excellent practical guides to lawyers *see* Stewart, *supra* n. 30; McIsaac, *The Presentation of Medical Evidence* (1968), 11 C.B.J. 363. If acting for the patient *see* Haines, *supra* n. 15. For an equally helpful series of "tips" for the doctor, *see* Scott, *Report of General Counsel for the Year 1975* in Canadian Medical Protective Association, *Annual Report 1976* 23-29.

(1) Listen to the question and be sure you understand it before answering. Questions and answers are the foundations of a law suit.

(2) Answer the question fully. If you are cut off or feel you are being restricted, ask to be permitted to finish your answer.[33]

(3) Do not hesitate to say you do not know the answer or to refuse to answer a question outside the scope of your expertise.

(4) Do not get angry; be firm but polite.

(5) You are not an advocate for the side that called you. Your duty is to assist the court. You are not expected to be an expert on the legal implications of your evidence.

(6) Address yourself to the judge when answering. Seek his assistance if you feel you are being unfairly treated by a lawyer examining you.

(7) Use simple language. Where medical terms are useful or unavoidable explain them clearly.[34]

Many of these points are common sense; they go far in assuring fair treatment of a doctor in court.

(d) The Medical-Legal Report

This document is in most cases the most important one to both doctor and lawyer.[35] It is prepared by the doctor for the information of a lawyer about a patient he has treated or has seen for purposes of evaluating the patient's condition. It assists the lawyer in assessing the patient's case and possible compensation and sets out the evidence that the doctor can substantiate when called as a witness. Furthermore, it may under certain rules of practice[36] be reviewed by lawyers on the other side and by other doctors. Since it is prepared for a lawyer in contemplation of litigation it is privileged, that is, exempt from production at trial unless legislation in the jurisdiction provides otherwise.[37] Whether the patient is one of the doctor's own or one he is seeing on an assessment basis only, he ought to obtain a written consent to release information. This, together with the fee for the report,[38] should be forwarded by the lawyer when the report is requested.

There are no rigid requirements for the organization of the report, but many lawyers when requesting a report do suggest a format of topics they

---

33 An interesting suggestion offered by one author is for the witness to pause, then make a note. The lawyer who called the doctor can on a re-examination allow him to add to his earlier reply. *See* Stewart, *supra* n. 30 at 167-68.

34 This point has been emphasized by doctors, *see* Gibson, *supra* n. 28 at 502, as well as lawyers; *see* Meredith, *supra* n. 18 at 46; Steward, *id.*

35 *See* Gibson, *supra* n. 28 at 499.

36 *See, for example,* Supreme Court Rules, Alta. Reg. 390/68 (1968) [am. R. 217].

37 *Supra* n. 3.

38 The cost of medical-legal reports may be allowed as damages; *see Hôpital Notre Dame de l'Espérance v. Laurent,* [1978] 1 S.C.R. 605.

wish to be covered.[39] As a general rule the following points should be covered by a medical-legal report dealing with personal injuries to a patient.[40] First, the report should set out preliminary data including the patient's name, age, address, marital status, occupation, the time, date and nature of the alleged injury and the time of examination. Second, there ought to be as clear a description as possible of the accident and the resultant injury, including a list of all the patient's complaints, including pain. Third, the state of the patient's health prior to the injury and information regarding any previous illness or injury should be set out. Fourth, as far as possible, tests should be carried out in regard to all complaints. There may also have been tests carried out before that are important and arrangements should be made to obtain their results. An experienced doctor has outlined his thoughts on this topic.[41]

> Complete physical examination of a patient would take hours or days and is not expected of the examiner. A doctor who is reasonably competent will select the outstanding features of the case and try to concentrate on them. Indeed a complete examination would only lead to confusion; it is the duty of the examiner to select what is relevant and omit the non-essentials. Make the examination of the relevant features as thorough, precise and detailed as possible. If shortening of a limb is present, measure the amount; if there is wasting, note the circumference of the two limbs at corresponding levels. Every doctor should carry a tape-measure. Never omit examination of the central nervous system. A patient seen recently, who complained only of pain in the back, turned out to be an early case of multiple sclerosis. Always carry a safety-pin. Apart from its plebeian virtues as a potential friend in need, it enables you to mark out areas corresponding to sharp and blunt stimuli which may unmask a purely subjective psychic loss of sensation or a hysterical paralysis. Needless to say, never hesitate to have radiographic examination. That introduces you to a realm of surprises.

Also, a report on diagnosis and treatment should appear where appropriate. It will not be so when the doctor is doing only an assessment of a patient. However, where the doctor has treated the patient for the injuries in issue this portion of the report is important. Besides the obvious report of the diagnosis and the treatment recommended, it might be appropriate to indicate whether the suggested treatment has been followed and if not, why not, and the probable consequences.

Finally, all of the above information must be "collated and correlated"[42] by the doctor with a view to explaining and then evaluating the patient's complaints. The lawyer will be interested in the period and degree of temporary incapacity, the degree of permanent disability and the prognosis, includ-

---

39 For an example of a model report *see* Edwards, *Medical Reports and the Ontario Evidence Act* (1971), 5 Gazette 186; *see also* Sharpe and Sawyer, *Doctors And The Law* 123-33 (1978); Marshall, *The Physicians and Canadian Law* 10-12 (1979); Livingston, *Are Current Medical-Legal Reports Adequate?* (1978), 2 L. Med. Q. 263.

40 This is essentially the format recommended by Meredith, *supra* n. 18 at 39-43; *see also* Gibson, *supra* n. 28.

41 Gibson, *supra* n. 28 at 500.

42 *Id.* at 501.

ing any deformities or possible or probable changes or complications, and opinions of the doctor, for example, that the patient is malingering or suffering from a litigation neurosis. This information is better revealed first in a medical-legal report than at trial.[43] An accurate, objective report with reasonable conclusions supported by his findings is a most important asset to the doctor in his testimony,[44] the lawyer in pleading his case, and the patient in obtaining fair compensation.

3.   AS DEFENDANT

(a) Advice and Co-operation

The doctor who believes he may have been negligent or knows he has made a "mistake" should not discuss this with the patient until he has reviewed it with someone else.[45] A colleague, the Canadian Medical Protective Association, or a lawyer, may each or all be appropriate advisors depending upon the circumstances. A doctor has the same right to advice regarding his legal position as any other citizen.

It is human nature to ignore unpleasantries, but unfortunately a defendant cannot afford to ignore a law suit. A doctor who is threatened with a suit, or is served with a statement of claim must act promptly. The usual advice to a defendant is to seek the advice of a lawyer, but doctors who are members of the Canadian Medical Protective Association should note that it advises against consulting a lawyer without instructions from the Association.[46] If a lawyer is retained, the doctor should supply him with all relevant information including notes and records.[47] The lawyer cannot handle the defence effectively unless he knows all of the facts both favourable and unfavourable.

An important step in the defence is the selection and interviewing of expert witnesses who might be called by the defence. Obviously, it is the lawyer who knows the evidence necessary for a successful defence and the type of witnesses who will be most effective. However, the doctor can be of great assistance here, and the choice ought to be made by the lawyer in

---

43 Meredith, *supra* n. 18 at 41-43; Gibson, *id.*

44 *See supra.*

45 *See, for example, McKeachie v. Alvarez* (1970), 17 D.L.R. (3d) 87 at 96 (B.C.S.C.), where the doctor admitted to the patient a few days after surgery that he had cut the radial nerve; *see also Walker v. Bedard*, [1945] O.W.N. 120 (H.C.); *MacKinnon v. Ignacio, Lamond and MacKeough* (1978), 29 N.S.R. (2d) 656 at 676 (S.C.).

46 *See* Canadian Medical Protective Association *Annual Report 1977* at 2; *Annual Report 1978* at 23-31. Note the author's closing words in an excellent English book: "One cannot be judge in one's own case; liability should therefore never be admitted:" Taylor, *The Doctor and Negligence* 146 (1971).

47 Good notes and records are critical to a good defence; *see infra* Chapter 10; *Dale v. Munthali* (1977), 16 O.R. (2d) 532 (H.C.).

consultation with the doctor. Many lawyers like to have the experts study the case and submit a written opinion prior to the drafting of the statement of defence.[48] The experts called to testify are usually doctors from the same specialty as the defendant.[49] The notion that professional brethren provide the evidence upon which a judicial determination of a colleague is made is repugnant to some who say the medical profession is thereby setting its own standards[50] and that it breeds a reluctance of one doctor to testify against another.[51] But, as has been discussed,[52] the court has the ultimate discretion in dealing with the evidence. Furthermore, the same practice is followed in negligence actions against members of any other profession or skilled group.

(b) Giving Evidence

The doctor defendant's evidence at trial will be primarily factual rather than opinion.[53] He can expect to be asked what he did, and why he did it, and what he did not do, and why he did not do it. The doctor's failure to testify can be extremely deleterious to his defence;[54] the judge, in the interests of justice, likes to hear the defendant's story and to have the opportunity to assess his credibility and, generally, to "size him up."[55] The decision whether to testify or not must be made in consultation between the doctor and his lawyer. While the doctor may have a natural reluctance to take the stand it may be prudent that he do so.

The doctor must work with his lawyer in preparing for his examination-in-chief and cross-examination, and the suggestions made earlier to assist the expert witness are appropriate to the doctor as defendant.[56]

---

48 Meredith, *supra* n. 18 at 54.
49 *See Wilson v. Swanson* (1956), 5 D.L.R. (2d) 113 at 126 (S.C.C.), where the evidence of a doctor who was not was held to be inadequate.
50 King, *In Search of a Standard of Care for the Medical Profession: The Accepted Practice Formula* (1975), 28 Vand. L. Rev. 1213.
51 Curran, *Professional Negligence — Some General Comments* (1959), 12 Vand. L. Rev. 535.
52 *See* authorities listed *supra* n. 20.
53 Meredith, *supra* n. 18 at 55. Note that a doctor can properly be asked his expert opinion at his examination for discovery. *See Nicholson v . McCulloch* (1972), 26 D.L.R. (3d) 384; affirming 21 D.L.R. (3d) 126 (Alta. C.A.); *Shickele v. Rousseau* (1966), 55 W.W.R. 568 (B.C.C.A.); *Czuy v. Mitchell,* [1976] 6 W.W.R. 676 (Alta. C.A.); *Hilder v. East Gen. Hosp.,* [1971] 3 O.R. 777 (H.C.).
54 *See Holmes v. Bd. of Hosp. Trustees of London* (1978), 5 C.C.L.T. 1 (Ont. H.C.). Note that where a doctor dies before the trial the action is continued against his executors *see Gordon v. Davidson* (1980), 4 L. Med. Q. 131 (Ont. S.C.); *Wipfli v. Britten* (1982), 22 C.C.L.T. 104 (B.C.S.C.); *Ferguson v. Hamilton Civic Hosp.* (1983), 23 C.C.L.T. 254 (Ont. H.C.).
55 *See* comments on this point in *Chubey v. Ahsan supra* n. 17; *Powell v. Guttman,* [1978] 5 W.W.R. 228 at 232 (Man. C.A.); *DeMoura v. Mississauga Hosp.* (1979), 3 L. Med. Q. 215 at 223 (Ont. S.C.); *Leadbetter v. Brand* (1980), 37 N.S.R. (2d) 581 at 600 (S.C.).
56 *See supra.*

Being sued is a painful experience for anyone and in the case of a doctor sued for medical negligence, it can be both personally and professionally debilitating. A better understanding of the law and a recognition that others have had the same experience can be of some help.

(c) Costs

A party in whose favour a law suit is resolved is normally awarded ''costs'' of the action but the judge has a discretion whether or not to make the award.[57] Costs are a sum calculated according to tables found in the Rules of Court of each jurisdiction which generally the ''loser'' must pay to the ''winner,'' but it does not include the lawyer's fee to his client.

There are a number of cases where a judge has not awarded costs to a successful doctor or hospital because he felt that the patient was reasonable in pursuing his legal remedies.[58] In some cases, the patient was hampered in his attempts to prove his case by the refusal of a hospital to provide medical records or the very poor record-keeping of a doctor.[59] The rationale was well put in an Ontario case:[60]

> Although, for the reasons I have given, I dismiss the plaintiff's action, I do not do so with costs. This case is, in my view, one of exceptional circumstances justifying the plaintiff's decision to bring the action. It would not be fair to apply the deterrent of an award of costs to the successful defendant in these circumstances. I am not entitled to provide that the defendant pay the plaintiff the costs of the action, but I do have a discretion, which it is proper for me to exercise now, to provide that there shall be no award of costs.

A judge also has a discretion to order an unsuccessful defendant to pay the costs of a successful one. It has been suggested that in order to get the whole story a patient may have to sue, for example, both a doctor and a hospital.[61] If the patient should lose against the hospital but win against the doctor, the judge has a discretion to order the doctor to pay to the patient the

---

57 *Kangas v. Parker*, [1977] 1 W.W.R. 28 (Sask. Q.B.); *Davidson v. Connaught Laboratories* (1981), 5 L. Med. Q. 143 (Ont. H.C.).

58 Perhaps the most interesting discussion on this issue took place in the exchange between Mr. Lenczner, acting for the defendant doctors, and Mr. Justice Linden in *Davidson v. Connaught Laboratories* reported only at (1981), 5 L. Med. Q. 143. *Considine v. Camp Hill Hosp.* (1982), 133 D.L.R. (3d) 11 (N.S.S.C.); *Poulin v. Health Sciences Centre* (1982), 18 Man. R. (2d) 274 (Q.B.); *Wipfli v. Britten* (1982), 22 C.C.L.T. 104 (B.C.S.C.); *Letiec v. Rowe* (1981), 130 D.L.R. (3d) 379 (Nfld. C.A.); *Strachan v. Simpson* (1979), 10 C.C.L.T. 145 (B.C.S.C.); *Doiron v. Orr* (1978), 86 D.L.R. (3d) 719 (Ont. H.C.); *Dunn v. Young* (1977), 86 D.L.R. (3d) 411 (Ont. Co. Ct.); *Legault-Bellemare v. Madore*, [1975] C.S. 1249 (Que. S.C.).

59 *Murphy v. Gen. Hosp. Corp.* (1980), 25 Nfld. & P.E.I.R. 355 (Nfld. S.C.); *Hajgato v. London Health Assn.* (1982), 36 O.R. (2d) 669 (H.C.); *Powell v. Guttman*, [1978] 5 W.W.R. 228 (Man. C.A.).

60 *Hobson v. Munkley* (1976), 1 C.C.L.T. 163 at 179 (Ont. H.C.).

61 *See supra* Chapter 6.

costs he must pay to the hosptial. This will be done only when the patient was reasonable in suing both.[62]

Hopefully, the information and suggestions in this chapter will assist the doctor in adjusting to the courtroom on those occasions when he must appear and will facilitate better communication between the professions.

---

62 This is called a "Bullock order;" *Bullock v. London Gen. Omnibus Co.*, [1907] 1 K.B. 264 (C.A.). Cases where such an order was granted are: *Moffatt v. Witelson* (1980), 111 D.L.R. (3d) 712 (Ont. H.C.); *Rietze v. Bruser*, [1979] 1 W.W.R. 55 (Man. Q.B.); *Strachan v. Simpson* (1979), 10 C.C.L.T. 145 (B.C.S.C.); *Badger v. Surkan*, [1973] 1 W.W.R. 302 (Sask. C.A.).

8

The Doctor's Liability for the Acts of Others

1. GENERAL PRINCIPLES OF VICARIOUS LIABILITY

Thus far, we have discussed the personal liability of the doctor, but there is another basis upon which he may be liable to a patient who is injured: under some circumstances the law will hold one person responsible for the torts of another. This is referred to as vicarious liability or liability based on *respondeat superior* (let the principal answer).[1] Liability for the torts of another will only be imposed on a person when he and the tortfeasor are in a relationship which justifies the result, such as employer-employee. The relationships which might lead to a doctor being held vicariously liable are few compared to those involving a hospital. The hospital serves the patient only through its many employees and the concept of vicarious liability is fundamental to the legal position of such an institution. For this reason, vicarious liability as it relates to the hospital will be discussed in a separate chapter.[2]

---

1 Fleming, *The Law of Torts* 338 (6th ed. 1983); Fridman, *The Law of Agency* 233 (4th ed. 1976). In Quebec, Civil Code, 1971, c. 84, s. 3 [am. 1977, c. 72, s. 7], art. 1054. *See La Responsabilitié Civile de l'Infirmière* (1972), 3 R.D.U.S. 1; Crépeau, *La Responsabilité Médicale et Hospitaliere dans La Jurisprudence Québécoise Récente* (1960), 20 R. du B. 433.

2 *See infra* Chapter 9.

There are clear policy reasons for holding one person[3] accountable for the misconduct of another, and an appreciation of these assists in understanding the decisions that follow. The main justification is that the person who engages others to work for him so that his economic interests are advanced should be the one liable for losses which result from the enterprise. Also, he will likely be better able to pay or insure for such accidents. Theoretically, he will see the benefits in accident prevention programs and better employer-employee (or, as they are called in law, master-servant) relationships.[4] Furthermore, the choice of whether to hire or dismiss an employee is that of the employer.

The effect of holding parties vicariously liable is to render them joint tortfeasors.[5] This means that both parties are liable but the servant's liability is personal or direct, whereas the master's is indirect. In practice the patient will likely sue both parties,[6] but the damages are usually collected from the employer[7] who has the right to be indemnified by the employee.[8] However, indemnity is rarely sought by the employer and, furthermore, his contract of insurance for the risk of vicarious liability may preclude it.[9] This seems just in view of the policy reasons for vicarious liability.

Vicarious liability flows from the employer-employee relationship which must be contrasted with the relationship of principal and independent contractor from which vicarious liability does not flow.[10] When an employer engages someone to accomplish a certain result but the work is to be done independently of the employer's supervision, though for his benefit, the relationship is of principal-independent contractor. An employee is said to have a contract of *service* whereas the independent contractor is bound by a contract for *services*.[11] The traditional test as to whether a given individual is more properly regarded as an employee or as an independent contractor was the "control" test. The employee is "subject to the command of the master [employer] as to the manner in which he shall do his work,"[12] whereas an

---

3 Note that the corporate entity of the hospital is referred to in law as a "person," and so this term is now used to cover both the doctor and the hospital.

4 Fleming, *supra* n. 1 at 339.

5 *See supra* Chapter 5.

6 *See* Fleming, *supra* n. 1 at 230. Each can then be examined for discovery, which can be important where the employer knows little about the accident and it is wished to use the answer at trial.

7 Fleming, *supra* n. 1 at 340.

8 For it is an implied term of the contract. *See Lister v. Romford Ice & Cold Storage Co.*, [1957] A.C. 555 (H.L.); Fleming, *supra* n. 1 at 238-39. *But see Morris v. Ford Motor Co.*, [1973] 1 Q.B. 792 (C.A.).

9 Griffiths, *Claims for Contribution or Indemnity As Between Hospitals, Doctors & Others*, [1963] L.S.U.C. Spec. Lec. 237; *see also* Fleming, *Developments in the English Law of Medical Liability* (1959), 12 Vand. L. Rev. 633 at 640.

10 Meredith, *Malpractice Liability of Doctors & Hospitals* 122-23 (1957).

11 Fleming, *supra* n. 1 at 342.

12 *Yewens v. Noakes* (1880), 6 Q.B.D. 530 at 532 (C.A.) quoted by Fleming, *supra* n. 1 at 342.

independent contractor "undertakes to produce a given result but is not, in the actual execution of the work, under the order or control of the person for whom he does it."[13] But employer-employee relationships have changed dramatically over the years and alternate tests have been canvassed.[14] Many are not helpful but one may be of some utility in this context, namely, the organization test.[15] The person's work is viewed in the light of whether it is an integral part of the organization, because he is employed as part of it, in which case he would make the employer vicariously liable or whether his work, although done for the organization, is not integrated into it but is only accessory to it, in which case he is an independent contractor for whom, as a general rule, the employer is not vicariously liable. This test may be more useful than the control test to analyze the status of the new health care professionals and paramedics and as will be seen[16] is more consistent with the modern cases on the vicarious liabilty of hospitals.

The employer's vicarious liability for an employee extends only to work done "in the course of the employment." While this restriction does set some limit to the liability of the employer it is a very flexible one. For example, liability would still follow an unauthorized mode of performing an authorized task and even a prohibition by an employer may not protect him.[17] But liability does not attach to the employer if the employee engages in an independent task of his own.[18] When the employee acts outside of the scope of his employment he is said to be on a "frolic of his own" and the employer is not vicariously liable. While a great volume of perplexing general case law does exist, examples from medical cases are not available to clarify many of these issues. Suppose, however, a nurse employed by a doctor or hospital invited a friend to come to her place of work to have her ears pierced, a procedure outside the scope of her employment. If negligence could be proven against the nurse her employer would have a strong argument that, as she was acting outside of the scope of her employment, she ought to be solely liable to compensate the injured person.

Thus, in order to arrive at a decision about vicarious liability we see the necessity firstly of characterizing the relationship as that of employer-employee or employer-independent contractor[19] by utilizing the traditional control test

---

13 *Queensland Stations v. Fed. Commr. of Taxation* (1945), 70 C.L.R. 539 at 545 (Aust. H.C.), quoted by Fleming, *supra* n. 1 at 342.

14 *Cassidy v. Min. of Health*, [1951] 1 All E.R. 574 (C.A.); *Kennedy v. C.N.A. Assur. Co.* (1978), 6 C.C.L.T. 201 (Ont. H.C.); affirmed 116 D.L.R. 384 (Ont. C.A.); *see* Picard, *The Liability of Hospitals in Common Law Canada* (1981), 26 McGill L.J. 997.

15 *Roe v. Min. of Health*, [1954] 2 Q.B. 66 (C.A.); *see* Fleming, *supra* n. 1 at 344.

16 *See infra* Chapter 9.

17 *Guar. Trust Co. v. Mall Medical Group* (1969), 4 D.L.R. (3d) 1 (S.C.C.); for a more detailed discussion *see* Fleming, *supra* n. 1 at 348-56.

18 *Bugge v. Brown* (1919), 26 C.L.R. 110 at 132 (Aust. H.C.).

19 For a discussion of the categories of agent *see* Fridman, *supra* n. 1.

or the more modern organization test, and secondly, of considering whether he was acting within the course of his employment. Cases in which a doctor has been held vicariously liable will serve to illustrate the application of the rules.

2. RELATIONSHIPS WITH OTHERS AND VICARIOUS LIABILITY

It is possible to confuse the doctor's personal liability with his vicarious liability in some situations. The doctor-patient relationship gives rise to many duties which cannot be delegated.[20] For while the doctor is entitled to rely on hospital staff to carry out their duties properly[21] he cannot delegate his duties to them.[22] Furthermore, he will be held personally liable if he is aware, or ought to be aware, that a person is discharging his duty in a careless or negligent manner but takes no action to safeguard the patient.[23] Thus, the doctor's vicarious liability is founded not on his personal negligence but on that of his employee which is imputed to him.

(a) Office Staff

A doctor is vicariously liable for torts committed during the course of employment of a receptionist, secretary, office manager, or other office personnel whom he employs.[24] In this regard he is in the same position as any employer with the exception that some patients might assume that a person working in a doctor's office has some medical expertise, especially if in uniform. Such an employee who dispensed medical advice (or medication) could put the doctor in a very vulnerable position[25] provided the patient was reasonable in his reliance on the employee and was injured as a consequence.[26] Authorizing employees to act beyond those tasks for which they are trained is a practice fraught with risks for both patient and doctor.[27]

---

20 *Crichton v. Hastings*, [1972] 3 O.R. 859 (C.A.); *see* Canadian Medical Protective Association, *Annual Report 1974* at 23; *see supra* Chapter 4.

21 *Villeneuve v. Sisters of St. Joseph*, [1975] S.C.R. 285; *Laidlaw v. Lions Gate Hosp.* (1969), 70 W.W.R. 727 (B.C.S.C.); *Karderas v. Clow* (1973), 32 D.L.R. (3d) 303 (Ont. H.C.). *See infra* Chapter 9.

22 *Cosgrove v. Gaudreau* (1981), 33 N.B.R. (2d) 523 (N.B.Q.B.); *Holmes v. Bd. of Hosp. Trustees of London* (1978), 5 C.C.L.T. 1 (Ont. H.C.); Rozovsky, *Canadian Hospital Law* 63 (1979).

23 *Jones v. Manchester Corp.*, [1952] 2 All E.R. 125 (C.A.); *see also McQuay v. Eastwood* (1886), 12 O.R. 402 (C.A.); *Perionowsky v. Freeman* (1866), 4 F. & F. 977, 176 E.R. 873 (Q.B.).

24 *Hancke v. Hooper* (1835), 7 C. & P. 81, 173 E.R. 37 (Nisi Prius).

25 *See Smith v. Auckland Hosp. Bd.*, [1965] N.Z.L.R. 191 at 198 (C.A.); *see also* Canadian Medical Protective Association, *supra* n. 20 at 25; *McQuay v. Eastwood supra* n. 23 where a so-called nurse was not a nurse at all.

26 Note that liability could be based on the case of *Hedley Byrne & Co. v. Heller & Partners*, [1963] 2 All E.R. 575 (H.L.).

27 In a U.S. case an office nurse put a fracture in traction: *see Olsen v. McAtee* (1947), 181 Ore. 503, 182 P. (2d) 979 (S.C.).

(b) Nurses

Many doctors engage nurses as employees in their offices and clinics. It is clear that a doctor is vicariously liable for torts committed within the scope of employment of a nurse whom he employs. An interesting case[28] arose in Alberta when a patient who suffered from epilepsy but had ceased taking her medication attended at her doctor's office saying that she felt she was about to have a seizure. A nurse employed there placed her on an examination table and left her for one minute in order to get her file. In the nurse's absence the patient had a seizure and fell from the table, breaking her arm. The court held the nurse to be negligent by leaving the patient in a position in which she could suffer harm. She had failed to meet the minimum standard of care to be expected from the professional attendant in a medical clinic. The defendant, a partnership of general practitioners, was held vicariously liable.

In an earlier case from Alberta[29] a nurse employed by a doctor was instructed by him to use an x-ray machine to treat a patient suffering from a skin problem. The trial judge found the nurse negligent by failing to warn the patient of the dangers of the treatment, from which the patient suffered an electric shock and burns. The doctor was found to be not personally negligent in his prescription of the treatment, use of the machine or selection and instruction of the nurse, but was found vicariously liable for the nurse's negligence. On appeal[30] the nurse was found to be not negligent and thus the action was dismissed.

These cases illustrate that a nurse-employee will be expected to meet the standard of the reasonable nurse in the circumstances and a failure to do so will render the doctor-employer vicariously liable.

A doctor is not liable for the torts of nurses employed by a hospital and is entitled to rely on the nurses to carry out their duties properly.[31] A nurse has a duty to execute the doctor's orders and if she does so properly[32] yet the patient is injured it may be that the doctor will be held liable because he was personally negligent in giving such an order. In this situation even if she were

---

28 *Dowey v. Rothwell & Assoc.*, [1974] 5 W.W.R. 311 (Alta. S.C.). The appeal to the Appellate Division was dismissed on the basis that the court would not disturb the findings of fact of the trial judge.

29 *Antoniuk v. Smith*, [1930] 2 W.W.R. 721 (Alta. C.A.).

30 *Id.* at 729.

31 *Villeneuve v. Sisters of St. Joseph supra* n. 21; *Misericordia Hosp. v. Bustillo*, [1983] Alta. D. 2632-01 (Alta. C.,A.); *Laidlaw v. Lions Gate Hosp. supra* n. 21; *McFadyen v. Harvie*, [1942] 4 D.L.R. 647 (S.C.C.); *Armstrong v. Bruce* (1904), 4 O.W.R. 327 (Ont. H.C.); *R. v. Giardine* (1939), 71 C.C.C. 295 (Ont. Co. Ct.); *see also Morris v. Winsbury-White*, [1937] 4 All E.R. 494 (K.B.); *Ingram v. Fitzgerald*, [1936] N.Z.L.R. 905 (C.A.).

32 *Lavere v. Smith's Falls Pub. Hosp.* (1915), 35 O.L.R. 98 (C.A.).

negligent, it would be the hospital that was vicariously liable rather than the doctor.[33]

Because of an *obiter* remark in an English case[34] it was thought at one time that a nurse in the operating room might become the employee of the surgeon on the basis that she was a "borrowed servant."[35] There are no reported cases[36] where a hospital has been relieved of its usual vicarious liability on this basis, and thus in the medical context it appears that the "borrowed servant" rule is not applicable.[37]

(c) Other Health Care Professionals

Each relationship into which the doctor enters as an employer must be analyzed to ascertain whether the other party is an employee or an independent contractor, since the doctor is generally not liable vicariously for the independent contractor. The issue has risen in importance because of the emergence of paramedical personnel,[38] the metamorphosis in some older professsions such as nursing,[39] and the multi-discipline approach to treatment.[40] The "nurse" employed by a doctor might not be an employee but a nurse practitioner[41] who by the tests outlined ought more properly to be regarded as an independent contractor. Because so many of these developments are very recent there is no case law to provide precedents, and even if there were they would be of questionable value, since all such situations will have to be analyzed separately on the basis of their own facts.

There are few cases which seem to indicate the limits. In a case[42] that went to the Supreme Court of Canada, a doctor who was part of a medical clinic employed a remedial gymnast[43] to whom he gave written instructions regarding exercises for the patient. During exercises administered by the gymnast the patient's knee cap was fractured. The Supreme Court of Canada restored the trial judgment in finding that it was pressure applied by the

---

33 *See* discussion *infra* Chapter 9, 3(b).
34 *Hillyer v. Governors of St. Bartholomew's Hosp.*, [1909] 2 K.B. 820 (C.A.). Quoted with approval in *Bugden v. Harbour View Hosp.*, [1947] 2 D.L.R. 338 (N.S.S.C.), although the concept was not applied in the case.
35 *Mersey Docks & Harbour Bd. v. Coggins & Griffith*, [1946] 2 All E.R. 345 (H.L.).
36 Rozovsky, *supra* n. 22 at 23.
37 Meredith, *supra* n. 10 at 132. *See infra* Chapter 9, 3(b).
38 Ballenger, *The Physician's Assistant, Legal Considerations* (1971), 45 Hospitals, No. 11, 58.
39 *See* Good and Kerr, *Contemporary Issues in Canadian Law for Nurses* (1973).
40 *See Haines v. Bellissimo* (1977), 1 L. Med. Q. 292 (Ont. S.C.); *see also Kennedy v. C.N.A. Assur. supra* n. 14.
41 Boudreau, *Report of the Committee on Nurse Practitioners*, Dept. Nat. Health and Welfare, Ottawa, 1972. *See Hall v. Lees*, [1904] 2 K.B. 602 (C.A.), for an excellent analysis of the relationship of nurses to an association wherein they were found not to be employees.
42 *Guar. Trust Co. v. Mall Medical Group supra* n. 17.
43 He is referred to *id.* at 2 as a physiotherapist by Judson J. (dissenting) but was not qualified as such: *see* Hall J. *id.* at 6.

employee rather than movement by the patient that caused the injury. It is important to note that in applying this pressure the employee was carrying out the authorized treatment, exercises, but in an unauthorized manner, using pressure. Indeed, the written instructions specifically stated that no pressure was to be used. In the result the employer, the medical clinic, was held vicariously liable for the negligence of the remedial gymnast.

In an older case[44] from Ontario, a doctor was vicariously liable for the negligence of an employee whose job it was to operate the x-ray machine and who had left a cone off the machine, which then caused burns to the patient. By either test the remedial gymnast and the x-ray machine operator were engaged by contract of service and were therefore employees.

In an old Ontario case[45] the association of a doctor and a pharmacist was analyzed. The practice was that the doctor would write a prescription which the pharmacist would then fill, but the doctor paid the pharmacist and the patient paid only the doctor. The doctor prescribed hydrochloric acid and, in error, the pharmacist's clerk dispensed hydrocyanic acid from which the patient suffered injury. It was found that the doctor was not negligent personally or vicariously, but that the pharmacist was vicariously liable for the error of his clerk. The doctor and pharmacist were held to be separate professionals not even in an employer-independent contractor relationship. This was also the decision in a case[46] where a pharmacist dispensed formaldehyde instead of the prescribed paraldehyde. It remains to be seen where liability will rest for the torts of other health care professionals.[47]

(d) Other Doctors

A doctor is not vicariously liable for the torts of other doctors[48] because he normally does not employ them either as employees or even as independent contractors.[49] In a case in which the surgeon had to assist the anaesthetist by

---

44 *Hochman v. Willinsky,* [1933] O.W.N. 79 (H.C.).

45 *Stretton v. Holmes* (1889), 19 O.R. 286 (Q.B.); *see also Jeannotte v. Couillard* (1894), 3 Q.B. 461 (Que.).

46 *Williams v. Jones* (1977), 79 D.L.R. (3d) 670 (B.C.S.C.).

47 *See Haines v. Bellissimo supra* n. 40, where a psychologist who was on the staff of a medical centre was sued along with a psychiatrist when their patient committed suicide. Since the psychologist was held to be not negligent, the issue of the psychiatrist's vicarious liability did not have to be canvassed.

48 This includes dentists. *See Parmley v. Parmley,* [1945] S.C.R. 635; *Kangas v. Parker,* [1976] 5 W.W.R. 25 (Sask. Q.B.); affirmed [1978] 5 W.W.R. 667 (Sask. C.A.). But *see Kennedy v. C.N.A. Assur. supra* n. 14, where the plaintiff, who was both a dentist and a medical doctor, was held to be an employee of a dental partnership. Linden J. applied the organization test.

49 *Jewison v. Hassard* (1916), 10 W.W.R. 1088 (Man. C.A.); *see Park v. Stevenson Memorial Hosp.* (1974), unreported (Ont. H.C.) Holland J., where a doctor who assigned the care of his patient to his doctor-wife for one day was held not vicariously liable for her negligence.

inserting the needle the court held[50] that each doctor had his separate function and was responsible for the manner in which he discharged it. This same view has been taken of a surgeon and his assistant[51] and of an anaesthetist and his assistant.[52] Within the hospital setting such assistants may be interns or other house staff who are employees of the hospital and for whom it will be vicariously liable.[53] There is an Ontario case[54] where a surgeon was sued when an intern assisting him with a tonsillectomy accidentally removed the patient's uvula. No liability followed because it was found the patient suffered no injury thereby. However, the trial and appeal courts seemed to have assumed that it was the surgeon who would have been liable. In a more recent Nova Scotia case[55] there was also no liability found but the trial judge said, *obiter*, that had he found a resident negligent he would have held the surgeon equally responsible. It is not clear in either case whether such liability would have been based on personal negligence in the surgeon delegating a duty he himself owed to the patient or on vicarious liability. Only the former basis would be consistent with the bulk of the case law.

It is difficult to imagine a doctor binding another to a contract of service[56] where the employee-doctor would be told not only what to do but how to do it by the employer-doctor. Thus it seems that a case of vicarious liability of one doctor for another[57] would be very rare.

3.   PARTNERSHIPS

A doctor who practices in a partnership is jointly and severally liable for the torts committed by other partners during the course of the partnership.[58]

---

50 *Walker v. Bedard*, [1945] O.W.N. 120 (H.C.).

51 *Karderas v. Clow supra* n. 21; *McFadyen v. Harvie supra* n. 31; *see also Macdonald v. Pottinger*, [1935] N.Z.L.R. 196 (S.C.).

52 *Toronto Gen. Hosp. Trustees v. Matthews*, [1972] S.C.R. 45.

53 Rozovsky, *supra* n. 22 at 18.

54 *McNamara v. Smith*, [1934] 2 D.L.R. 417 (Ont. C.A.).

55 *Considine v. Camp Hill Hosp.* (1982), 133 D.L.R. (3d) 11 (N.S.S.C.); *see also Lloy v. Milner* (1981), 15 Man. R. (2d) 187 (Man. Q.B.), where the court noted that an anaesthetist "accepted responsibility" for the resident.

56 The substitute doctor engaged as a *locum tenens* by a doctor who is absent might, under the right circumstances, fall into this category.

57 A doctor has, however, been held to have engaged another doctor as an independent contractor when he had a contract with a company to furnish medical services to its employees and arranged for another doctor to attend at a work camp for his purpose: *see Hamilton v. Phoenix Lbr. Co.*, [1931] 1 W.W.R. 43 (Alta. C.A.). For cases where it was argued without success that a doctor was an employee *see Staple v. Winnipeg* (1956), 18 W.W.R. 625; affirmed 19 W.W.R. 672 (Man. C.A.); *Jarvis v. Int. Nickel Co.*, [1929] 2 D.L.R. 842 (Ont. H.C.); *Thompson v. Columbia Coast Mission* (1914), 20 B.C.R. 115 (C.A.). *See also Daoust v. R.*, [1969] D.R.S. 594 (Ex. C. C.), where the Crown was held liable for the negligence of a doctor employed at a penitentiary.

58 Partnership Act, R.S.A. 1980, c. P-2, ss. 12 and 14; Partnership Act, R.S.B.C. 1979, c. 312, ss. 12 and 14; Partnership Act, R.S.M. 1970, c. P30, ss. 13 and 15; Partnership Act,

Thus one doctor found to be negligent exposes all his partners to liability.[59] Furthermore the partnership will be vicariously[60] liable for a negligent employee of the partnership or of one partner. Not all group practices are partnerships,[61] and a doctor is wise to seek legal advice on the advantages and disadvantages. If a partnership is desired, a formal agreement ought to be drafted by a competent solicitor.

The general principles of vicarious liability and the law of partnership apply to the doctor and the hospital with the result that either can be liable for the acts of the other. However, each individual relationship must be analyzed separately, and recent changes in some traditional relationships make such scrutiny more critical today than ever before.

R.S.N.B. 1973, c. P-4, ss. 11 and 13; Partnership Act, R.S.N. 1970, c. 287, ss. 11 and 13; Partnership Act, R.S.N.S. 1967, c. 224, ss. 12 and 14; Partnerships Act, R.S.O. 1980, c. 370, ss. 11 and 13; Partnership Act, R.S.P.E.I. 1974, c. P-2, ss. 12 and 14; Partnership Act, R.S.S. 1978, c. P-3, ss. 12 and 14.

59 *Town v. Archer* (1902), 4 O.L.R. 383 (K.B.); *McKeachie v. Alvarez* (1970), 17 D.L.R. (3d) 87 (B.C.S.C.); *Badger v. Surkan*, [1973] 1 W.W.R. 302 (Sask. C.A.); *see also Milot v. Tataryn, Reid & Iwaniuk*, [1983] A.W.L.D. 752.

60 *Guar. Trust Co. v. Mall Medical Group supra* n. 17; *Dowey v. Rothwell supra* n. 28; *Kennedy v. C.N.A. Assur. supra* n. 14.

61 *See MacKinnon v. Ignacio, Lamond and McKeough* (1978), 29 N.S.R. (2d) 656 (S.C.), where it was held, *obiter*, that an operating team would not have been a partnership.

9

The Hospital

1. LIABILITY IN GENERAL

Throughout the preceding chapters reference has been made to the legal position of the hospital[1] for in law this institution is a "person" (albeit an artificial one) which has responsibilities to a patient both directly as a corporate entity and indirectly through the acts of its employees. All that has gone before, apart from Chapter One and the doctor's duties set out in Chapter Four, are applicable to the hospital. It can be sued by a patient for negligence, breach of contract, assault and battery, false imprisonment and defamation, and it can raise any of the defences outlined,[2] including approved practice, error of judgment, contributory negligence, or consent.[3] The conduct of a

---

1 Throughout this book the term "hospital" has been used as meaning any institution operated for the care and treatment of those requiring medical or surgical attention. *See* Jacob, *Speller's Law Relating to Hospitals and Kindred Institutions* 1 (6th ed. 1978); *see also* Hospitals Act, R.S.A. 1980, c. H-11, s. 1(1).

2 *See supra* Chapters 3 and 5.

3 *See supra* Chapter 3. Although consent to most medical treatment given by the hospital can be implied, it has fallen to the hospital to obtain the express consent for the doctor's touching of the patient. (Much difficulty might be avoided by the hospital by requiring the doctor to obtain and place on the patient's hospital record consent to the treatment for which he is responsible.)

civil action[4] and the law and practice in regard to proof[5] are essentially no different for the hospital as a defendant than for the doctor.[6]

It is necessary, however, to examine the duties owed by the hospital to the patient for they do differ from those owed by the doctor,[7] and to review those relationships which today will result in the hospital being held vicariously liable.

2.   DIRECT LIABILITY

The hospital, in former times a place where the impoverished ill were deposited for medical attendance, has evolved to an institution where the doctor can treat his patient with the assistance of highly skilled and well-organized medical and non-medical personnel with sophisticated equipment in modern facilities.[8] Just as the function of the hospital has expanded, so has its responsibility to the patient. These responsibilities may be characterized as non-delegable duties[9] owed to the patient and a failure to discharge them properly may result in an action against the hospital for breach of contract or negligence. Indeed, in many cases both actions are alleged from the same set of facts. For example, in a case[10] where a psychiatric patient injured a non-psychiatric one, the hospital was sued for breach of contract to provide care and protection and alternatively for negligence in permitting a mentally ill patient with a propensity for violence to be at large in the hospital without control or supervision. The Chief Justice of Canada noted that the issue was whether a certain statute had the effect of relieving the hospital of liability for its own breach of duty[11] "whether arising out of contract or in tort."

Another common allegation is breach of contract in failing to provide proper personnel together with negligence as a consequence of the conduct of

---

4 *See supra* Chapter 7.

5 *See supra* Chapter 6.

6 Note Professor Crepeau has pointed out the need for anyone who is interested in the law relating to hospitals in Quebec to read, *for example,* Crepeau, *La responsabilité civile de l'establissement hospitalier en droit civil canadien* (1981), 26 McGill L.J. 673.

7 Note that doctor-patient duties may be important to a hospital where the doctor is an employee of the hospital.

8 For a discussion of problems of the modern hospital and patient, *see* Picard, *The Liability of Hospitals in Common Law Canada* (1981), 26 McGill L.J. 997. *See also* Dickens, *The Right to Natural Death* (1981), 26 McGill L.J. 847 at 856-57. *See also* Freedman, *A Prolegomenon To the Allocation of Responsibility In Hierarchical Organizations: The Hospital Context* (1980), 4 L. Med. Q. 35.

9 Note that the implication of a non-delegable duty is that the hospital remains responsible for it even though an independent contractor (for whom an employer is normally not liable) is engaged to carry it out. *See* Picard, *The Liability of Hospitals in Common Law Canada* (1981), 26 McGill L.J. 997 at 1008-1012.

10 *Lawson v. Wellesley Hosp.* (1977), 15 N.R. 271 (S.C.C.).

11 *Id.* at 274.

an employee for whom the hospital is vicariously liable.[12] This too is a mixed tort and contract action, but the alleged negligence of the hospital is not direct but vicarious.

(a) Breach of Contract

In the past, a hospital's direct liability to the patient was usually founded on the contract between it and the patient. The requirements[13] for a contract were not difficult to find and the issue between the patient and the hospital was most often whether a certain service was a term of the contract.[14] Only rarely was the contract express,[15] it being more common for the patient to enter the hospital with no discussion of the terms, which were therefore implied.[16]

Thus if the patient was alleging breach of contract against the hospital, the court looked for a written contract or express terms, or failing these, for implied terms. Factors relevant to finding an implied term include legislation,[17] hospital by-laws[18] and even public expectations[19] as well as the conduct of the parties themselves. Obviously some terms, such as those to provide and organize certain nursing, ward and technical personnel, equipment, and facilities are easily implied[20] while others, such as those to provide medical care and define its scope are not.[21] Apart from the problem of ascertaining terms in certain contracts, some of the other difficulties outlined in Chapter Two may exist in regard to the contract action, not the least of which is the unequal position of the two parties. Whatever the reasons, the courts have been most reluctant to subject the hospital-patient relationship to a thorough, conclusive contractual analysis.[22] Thus, while it is not uncommon for a patient to plead breach of contract or for a court to note the provision of a certain service as a term of the contract, most cases against hospitals have proceeded on the basis of negligence.[23]

---

12 *Aynsley v. Toronto Gen. Hosp.*, [1972] S.C.R. 435; *see also Elverson v. Doctors Hosp.* (1974), 49 D.L.R. (3d) 196; affirmed 65 D.L.R. (3d) 382n (S.C.C.).
13 *See supra* Chapter 2.
14 *Abel v. Cooke*, [1938] 1 W.W.R. 49 (Alta. C.A.).
15 *Lavere v. Smith's Falls Pub. Hosp.* (1915), 26 D.L.R. 346 (Ont. C.A.).
16 *Nyberg v. Provost*, [1927] S.C.R. 226.
17 *Lawson v. Wellesley Hosp. supra* n. 10.
18 *Fraser v. Vancouver Gen. Hosp.*, [1952] 2 S.C.R. 36.
19 *Aynsley v. Toronto Gen. Hosp. supra* n. 12.
20 *See* Rozovsky, *Canadian Hospital Law* 17 (1979).
21 *See Hôpital Notre Dame de l'Espérance v. Laurent* (1978), 3 C.C.L.T. 109 (S.C.C.).
22 Magnet, *Liability of a Hospital for the Negligent Acts of Professionals* (1978), 3 C.C.L.T. 135.
23 Keith, *Claims Arising out of the Relationship Between Hospital and Patient*, [1963] L.S.U.C. Spec. Lec. 203. For an excellent discussion of the two possible actions, *see* Fridman, *Hospital Liability For Professional Negligence* (1980), 4 L. Med. Q. 80.

A recent New Brunswick case may herald a change. In *Osburn v. Mohindra*,[24] Mr. Justice Stratton found a hospital liable to a patient in contract. The learned justice found the terms of the contract by looking at "all the circumstances of the entrance of the patient into the hospital, of what is sought by him and the nature of what is done to and for him."[25] Important facts were that the patient was admitted to the emergency department maintained by the hospital and staffed by family practitioners. The patient, who went on the suggestion of his vacationing doctor's nurse, was following a common practice of seeking medical care at hospital emergency wards. The court held that there were two breaches of contract by the hospital. The first was a failure to have an organized "system of work"[26] such that an attending doctor would receive a copy of a radiologist's report. The second was a failure to provide non-negligent medical treatment. While the existence of the latter duty is not settled,[27] the former has been recognized for many years as a non-delegable responsibility of a hospital.[28]

The focus on hospital user fees in some provinces and the restriction or cut-back in services which seems inevitable in most may make a contractual analysis a most realistic basis for ascertaining what hospitals are able to provide and what patients have the right to expect from their relationship.[29]

(b) Negligence

Negligence as a basis for liability has been thoroughly analyzed in Chapters Four and Five. As in the case with the doctor, the duty of the hospital arises upon the formation of the hospital-patient relationship and therefore the issue in negligence cases brought against hospitals is generally the scope of a duty rather than its existence.[30] Just as in any negligence action, the patient must prove the duty owed to him, the breach of the requisite standard of care and his injury. He must also show that the hospital's conduct was the cause-in-fact and proximate cause of his injury.[31]

The duties owed by a particular hospital to a specific patient must be

---

24 (1980), 29 N.B.R. (2d) 340 (Q.B.); *see also Yepremian v. Scarborough Gen. Hosp.* (1980), 110 D.L.R. (3d) 513 at 565 (Ont. C.A.).

25 *Id.* at 351-52 quoting *Vancouver Gen. Hosp. v. Fraser*, [1952] 2 S.C.R. 36 at 45 (S.C.C.).

26 *Id.* at 353.

27 *Infra.*

28 *Infra.*

29 *See* Melicke and Storch, *Perspective on Canadian Health and Social Services Policy: History and Emerging Trends* (1980).

30 *See Cassidy v. Min. of Health*, [1951] 1 All E.R. 574 at 585 (C.A.); *Worth v. Royal Jubilee Hosp.* (1980), 4 L. Med. Q. 59 at 68 (B.C.C.A.).

31 *See Child v. Vancouver Gen. Hosp.*, [1970] S.C.R. 477, where this issue is discussed in regard to the hospital's vicarious liability for the negligence of a nurse.

ascertained in each case but it is possible to set out and discuss some of the most common ones.[32]

It must be remembered that those responsibilities characterized as duties in a negligence action would be labelled terms of the contract in a contract action.[33] The standard of care and skill which the hospital must meet is the same in either case.[34]

(c) Responsibilities

(i) Personnel

A. Selection

Historically, the hospital's first duty to the patient was to select competent staff because it held itself out as being a place where patients would be attended by skilled persons. This responsibility was very narrowly interpreted for many years so that the hospital had only to ascertain that the professional employees such as nurses were qualified and competent; otherwise it had no responsibility for their negligence as professionals.[35] The responsibility has been broadened in Canada[36] so that a hospital may be vicariously liable for employees even if they are professionals.[37]

Even where the person giving medical care is not an employee, as is the case with most doctors, the hospital has a non-delegable duty to review and monitor qualifications and competence.[38] A hospital would be liable if it knew or ought to have known that a doctor lacked the skill, knowledge or judgment to carry out the medical treatment it had granted him privileges to provide.[39] Although the hospital's responsibilities in this regard must be carried out by committees, the hospital itself is liable if they are done negligently because the duty is non-delegable.[40] Thus the earliest and still basic and non-delegable

32 *See, for example,* Nathan, *Medicial Negligence* 94-104 (1957).

33 *See* Rozovsky, *supra* n. 20 at 17 and 65-66; Meredith, *Malpractice Liability of Doctors and Hospitals* 120-21 (1957).

34 *Worth v. Royal Jubilee Hosp.* (1980), 4 L. Med. Q. 59 at 67; *Bernier v. Sisters of Service,* [1948] 1 W.W.R. 113 (Alta. S.C.).

35 *See, for example, Abel v. Cooke supra* n. 14. For an analysis of the change *see infra* s. 3.

36 *Sisters of St. Joseph of the Diocese of London v. Fleming,* [1938] S.C.R. 172.

37 For a discussion *see infra.*

38 *Yepremian v. Scarborough Gen. Hosp.* (1980), 110 D.L.R. (3d) 513 at 532 (Ont. C.A.); *see Valderama v. Swan* (1978), 23 N.B.R. (2d) 165 (Q.B.); *Canadian Health Facilities Law Guide* 2264 (1983); Magnet, *Corporate Negligence As a Basis For Hospital Liability* (1978), 6 C.C.L.T. 121 at 127; *see also Thompson v. Creehan* (1982), 42 N.B.R. (2d) 359 at 366-67 (Q.B.).

39 Stradiott, *Malpractice Actions Against Hospitals* in *Medical and Hospital Liability* 33 at 43 (Can. Bar Assoc., Ont. 1979).

40 *See, for example,* Hospitals Act, R.S.A. 1980, c. H-11, ss. 29, 32. For an extreme example of inaction in terminating the privileges of a mentally and emotionally ill physician *see* the

duty[41] of the hospital is to ensure that those who treat patients are qualified and competent.

B. Instruction and supervision

Related to the duty of selection of personnel is the duty to ensure that each person is working within his competence. In an Ontario case[42] a hospital was held liable for the injury suffered by a patient when an intern in giving an intravenous injection severed the catheter leaving over nine inches of it in the patient's vein. The court said that the hospital had a duty to the patient to provide instruction, direction, and supervision to its staff in the use of an Intracath unit, and not having met this standard of care, was negligent. Similarly, an English case[43] held a hospital negligent in leaving the administration of a dangerous anaesthetic to an inexperienced doctor without adequate supervision. A hospital in Newfoundland[44] was held liable for the negligence of an audiologist, a technician trained and employed by the hospital. The judge was critical of the failure to provide a properly organized and supervised training program.

Assuring adequate instruction and supervision of hospital staff is an enormous responsibility for a hospital, necessitating job descriptions, training programs, testing and screening procedures, evaluations, and systems for supervision. The description and assessment of these is beyond the scope of this book, but clearly a hospital must have such programs, including special provision for the instruction and supervision of student professionals and employees-in-training.

(ii) Organization

A hospital has the responsibility for establishing such systems as are required for the co-ordination of personnel, facilities and equipment so that the patient receives reasonable care.[45] In actions for negligence based on

---

U.S. case, *Corleto v. Shore Memorial Hosp.* (1975), 350 A. (2d) 534 (N.J.S.C.). For comments *see* Stroedel, *Thy Brother's Keeper* (1982), 12 Legal Aspects Med. Prac. 1; Miller, *Medical Malpractice — Hospital May Be Held Liable For Permitting Incompetent Independent Physician To Operate* (1976), 8 Rutgers — Camden L.J. 177.

41 *Kolesar v. Jeffries* (1974), 59 D.L.R. (3d) 367 at 376; affirmed 2 C.C.L.T. 170 (S.C.C.).

42 *Murphy v. St. Catharines Gen. Hosp.* (1963), 41 D.L.R. (2d) 697 (Ont. H.C.).

43 *Jones v. Manchester Corp.*, [1952] 2 All E.R. 125 (C.A.).

44 *Bartlett v. Children's Hosp. Corp.* (1983), 40 Nfld. & P.E.I.R. 88 (Nfld. S.C.).

45 Note that a hospital may be liable to a doctor where systems are not followed. The doctor (plaintiff) and the hospital (defendant) were found equally at fault where the approved practice for removing syringes during surgery was not followed by the plaintiff or the nurse, resulting in the doctor contracting a virus from a "needle stick." *Savoie v. Bouchard* (1982), 23 C.C.L.T. 83 affirmed, unreported Sept. 19, 1983 No. 8/83/CA (N.B.C.A.). *See also Bergen v. Sturgeon Gen. Hosp.*, unreported Feb. 6, 1984 No. 8003-03036 (Alta. Q.B.), where negligence was found when a hospital failed to enforce its own system for keeping patient records.

failures in this area, the defence of approved practice has been significant.[46] Certain specific areas of the hospital and of patient care can be identified as having given rise to problems, and will now be discussed.

A. The emergency department

Emergency departments of large hospitals, apart from their important role as true emergency centres to substitute for the house-call, may also function as consultation centres where a patient whose symptoms may not indicate a serious condition can be seen and diagnosed by his doctor or by house staff who report to the doctor. It is not possible to generalize with any certainty about the duty owed by a hospital to a patient to provide him with care in an emergency department. While in some circumstances no duty may exist,[47] there are factors which are important to weigh in these cases. Public expectations that medical care can be obtained at any emergency department, the government funding of hospitals and the possible creation of a patient-hospital relationship by virtue of the hospital taking even a minor step toward the patient's care all tend to favour the existence of a duty.[48] Once present, of course, the hospital must meet a standard of reasonable care by providing competent personnel, adequate facilities and equipment and systems for the operation of the emergency department.

Although in most cases the hospital's liability arises from the negligence of an employee and is thus vicarious, in a New Brunswick case[49] a hospital was held directly liable. The system of work to assure that the x-ray report of a radiologist would be sent to the doctor who attended to the patient in the emergency department was inadequate, which meant that a misdiagnosis of a fracture was not detected for some time.

A few other cases are worth noting on these points. In an English case[50] the plaintiff was one of three night-watchmen who became ill after drinking tea and then presented themselves at the emergency department of a hospital. A nurse interviewed him briefly, telephoned the doctor on call, and relayed the doctor's message that the patient should go home to bed and call his own doctor. The man died of poisoning within hours. The court, noting that there was no other case to give it guidance, addressed the issue of whether there

---

46 *See supra* Chapter 5.

47 There may be a statutory duty; *see* Public Hospitals Act, R.S.O. 1980, c. 410, s. 7.

48 *See* the comments of Blair J.A. (dissenting) in *Yepremian v. Scarborough Gen. Hosp.* (1980), 110 D.L.R. (3d) 513 at 545-80 (Ont. C.A.). Note that after being successful in the Court of Appeal and before a hearing in the Supreme Court of Canada the hospital settled the action: *Yepremian v. Scarborough Gen. Hosp.* (1981), 31 O.R. (2d) 384 (H.C.): *see also Hôpital Notre Dame de L'Espérance v. Laurent,* [1974] C.A. 543, which found the hospital liable; reversed [1978] 1 S.C.R. 605. For a comment *see* Magnet *supra* n. 22.

49 *Osburn v. Mohindra* (1980), 29 N.B.R. (2d) 340 (Q.B.).

50 *Barnett v. Chelsea & Kensington Hosp.,* [1969] 1 Q.B. 428.

was a duty on those who provide and run an emergency department "when a person presents himself at that department complaining of illness or injury and before he is treated and received into the hospital wards."[51] The judge noted that the department was open, that the night-watchman entered without hindrance, complained to the nurse who passed this on to a doctor, and advice was given by the doctor. He said:[52]

> In my judgment, there was here such a close and direct relationship between the hospital and the watchmen that there was imposed upon the hospital a duty of care which they owed to the watchmen.

As discussed in this case, the standard of care to be met depends upon the facts of the case. Here, the hospital was found negligent by failing to examine, admit and treat the patient but there was no liability because had they done so no treatment could have been provided in time to save the man's life: the hospital's actions were not the cause-in-fact of the patient's death. In the absence of any Canadian authority, this case would be persuasive here for the founding of a duty in similar circumstances.

In a Canadian case,[53] a mother brought her sick child to a hospital on two consecutive days and although the child was examined, she was not admitted on either occasion and, it appears, was suffering from acute appendicitis. Eventually she was admitted to another hospital and underwent surgery but became a spastic quadriplegic. The action was barred by a limitation period but a hospital report indicated that a closer observation and monitoring of systems should have been carried out.

In a case from British Columbia,[54] the treatment received by an accident victim in an emergency department was held to be harmful. The patient was suffering from undiagnosed acute pulmonary edema and the procedures used to treat her were incorrect and may have hastened her death. It was held, however, that the motor vehicle accident had caused the pulmonary edema and the actions of the hospital were not a *novus actus interveniens*,[55] notwithstanding that it was indicated by the evidence that the patient would have recovered if proper treatment had been given in the emergency department.

The cases show that a duty of care to the patient is not difficult to find, and the hospital, like the doctor, will not be found liable where it has met the standard of care or where it cannot be proven that it was the cause of the patient's injuries.[56]

---

51 *Id.* at 436.
52 *Id.*
53 *Mumford v. Children's Hosp. of Winnipeg*, [1977] 1 W.W.R. 666 (Man. C.A.).
54 *Thompson v. Toorenburgh* (1973), 50 D.L.R. (3d) 717 (B.C.C.A.).
55 *See supra* Chapter 5.
56 *See, for example, DeMoura v. Mississauga Hosp.* (1979), 3 L. Med. Q. 215 (Ont. S.C.); *Murphy v. Gen. Hosp. Corp.* (1980), 25 Nfld. & P.E.I.R. 355 (Nfld. S.C.).

The problem of obtaining proper consents to treatment is a very real one for emergency departments. Although a hospital may have an extremely efficient system for having the consent form signed, the consent must fulfill the legal requirements outlined earlier.[57]

B. The recovery room

Whereas the emergency department by its very nature may seem to be an area of high potential liability for a hospital, the recovery room may in fact hold more risks. The importance of constant monitoring and observation of the patient in a post-anaesthetic state requires the hospital to organize personnel and facilities accordingly.[58] Moreover, the injuries to the patient caused by a failure to meet the high standard of care required are usually extreme.

Two cases have been reported in Canada in recent times. In the first case[59] a nurse left to monitor five patients[60] while the other nurse went for coffee also had to deal with an immediate order to obtain and inject a narcotic drug, and a personal telephone call. During the time these events were taking place the patient was left unobserved and developed breathing difficulties which caused brain damage, and was rendered permanently and totally disabled. The trial judge stated that a high standard of care was expected of both the hospital and nurses because the recovery room, as the most important room in the hospital, was the one where the patient required the greatest protection from known and ever-present risks. While he was critical of the "lackadaisical attitude" regarding coffee breaks and the failure of the hospital to correct and control the situation, he held the hospital to have met the necessary standard of care by providing two registered nurses for the room who were supposed to take coffee breaks before any patients arrived. However, the first nurse was held negligent for leaving the room, and the second nurse for agreeing to this situation, failing to care properly for the patient, and failing to get relief help. Because the nurses were employees and were acting within the scope of their employment the hospital was held vicariously liable.

The result was the same in the second case[61] where a young boy suffered a respiratory arrest followed by a cardiac arrest and eventually died. In reference to allegations made against the hospital regarding scheduling and organization, the trial judge questioned whether these would be matters of direct or vicarious liability. In the result the hospital was found vicariously

---

57 *See supra* Chapter 3.

58 *Bernier v. Sisters of Service supra* n. 34. A hospital was held liable where, after surgery, a patient was left unattended on the ward for ten hours. *Traynor v. Vancott* (1979), 3 L. Med. Q. 69 (Ont. H.C.).

59 *Laidlaw v. Lions Gate Hosp.* (1969), 70 W.W.R. 727 (B.C.S.C.).

60 The recommended ratio was one nurse to three patients.

61 *Krujelis v. Esdale*, [1972] 2 W.W.R. 495 (B.C.S.C.).

liable for the negligence of the five assigned recovery room nurses who failed to observe the patient for 20 to 28 minutes and three of whom went for coffee at the busiest time of the day. The evidence of each of these cases indicates that the proper systems were established by the hospital, but that they were not adequately monitored. While the courts found it easier to require the hospital to compensate the patient on the basis of vicarious liability, both cases point out a breakdown in organization which, it is suggested, was as much the duty of the hospital to monitor as it was the duty of any individual employee to follow.[62]

C. Handling of drugs

The hospital has a duty to set up systems for the efficient and safe handling of drugs.[63] As in the case of the recovery room, the hospital's liability for drug related problems has usually been vicarious rather than direct,[64] but injury to a patient through human error in obtaining or administering a drug may point out the need for a review of the hospital's system for handling drugs.[65]

D. Communication of infection

The hospital has a duty to protect patients from infection[66] and a duty not to discharge a patient whom it knows or ought to know is infectious.[67] The responsibility for assuring that aseptic procedures are followed is also basic to the hospital.[68]

E. Patient surveillance

The hospital may in some cases have a duty to establish procedures to prevent the patient from injuring himself. In a number of cases a patient has leapt from a hospital window and later sued the hospital alleging that there

---

62 *See also Meyer v. Gordon* (1981), 17 C.C.L.T. 1 (B.C.S.C.), where nurses left an expectant mother unattended for the last half hour prior to birth.

63 Meredith, *supra* n. 33 at 121.

64 *Misericordia Hosp. v. Bustillo*, [1983] Alta. D. 2632-01 (Alta. C.A.).

65 *Bugden v. Harbour View Hosp.*, [1947] 2 D.L.R. 338 (N.S.S.C.)

66 *McDaniel v. Vancouver Gen. Hosp.*, [1934] 4 D.L.R. 593, (P.C.); *see supra* Chapter 5 for a discussion of this case; *see also Lindsey County Council v. Marshall,* [1936] 2 All E.R. 1076 (H.L.). Note that infection is responsible for more deaths than any other iatrogenic illness. *Science Digest* 27 (April 1982). Provincial standards for infection control in Alberta hospitals have been compiled: (1983), 22 *Hospital Alta.* 1.

67 *Hajgato v. London Health Assn.* (1982), 36 O.R. (2d) 669 at 682 (Ont. H.C.). *Evans v. Liverpool Corp.*, [1906] 1 K.B. 160; *see also* Nathan, *supra* n. 32 at 103.

68 *Voller v. Portsmouth Corp.* (1947), 203 L.T.J. 264 (K.B.); *see also* Meredith, *supra* n. 33 at 122. For a discussion of the responsibility of a hospital to a doctor *see Savoie v. Bouchard* (1982), 23 C.C.L.T. 83; affirmed unreported Sept. 19, 1983 No. 8/83/CA (N.B.C.A.).

was a duty to provide surveillance and safeguards. In the sole case[69] in which liability was found against the hospital, the patient was a psychiatric patient with suicidal tendencies who fell to his death from a hospital window. He had been transferred to a semi-private room from the psychiatric ward and, according to the evidence, was recognized as being a "patient to be watched." The majority of the Supreme Court of Canada wrote no judgment in this important case but adopted that of the dissenting member of the Court of Appeal. The hospital's liability seems to have been both direct and vicarious and it is unfortunte that the Supreme Court of Canada did not take this opportunity to clarify some of the issues in this important area.

In another case[70] that went to the Supreme Court of Canada, the court held that the neurological patient's sudden leap through the window was not foreseeable and could only have been avoided by taking extreme precautions such as using a restraining device or putting the patient at ground level. However, the lower courts[71] had held that the hospital was negligent by failing to provide constant supervision of this patient who was suffering from "epilepsy with post-epileptic automatism" and whose "tendency to irresponsible moving about was well known to all concerned."[72]

In the third case[73] to go to our highest court the plaintiff was a surgical patient who, following abdominal surgery, became confused, disturbed and suffered from vivid hallucinations. The hospital assigned three special nurses to care for the patient on eight-hour shifts, but during one of the nurse's coffee breaks he went through a window. All parties to the action agreed that there was no direct liability upon the hospital because the procedures and treatment it had set up for the patient's care met the standard of care expected. Furthermore, there was no vicarious liability found because the risk of the patient doing what he did was not foreseeable to the nurse.

In three other cases[74] the hospitals were also exonerated on the basis that the patient's self-inflicted injury was not a foreseeable risk. In all cases where no liability was found the court accepted evidence that there was no sign that the patient needed special surveillance or that the patient was a danger to himself.

A British Columbia case[75] presents a marked contrast to all those dis-

---

69 *Villemure v. Turcot*, [1973] S.C.R. 716; for an English case where liability was found, *see Selfe v. Ilford* The Times, Nov. 26, 1970 discussed in Jacob *supra* n. 1 at 246.
70 *University Hosp. Bd. of Lepine*, [1966] S.C.R. 561.
71 (1965), 53 W.W.R. 513; which varied 50 W.W.R. 709 (Alta. C.A.).
72 *University Hosp. Bd. v. Lepine supra* n. 70 at 570 quoting Farthing J. at trial.
73 *Child v. Vancouver Gen. Hosp. supra* n. 31.
74 *Stadel v. Albertson*, [1954] 2 D.L.R. 328 (Sask. C.A.); *Flynn v. Hamilton*, [1950] O.W.N. 224 (C.A.); *Brandeis v. Weldon* (1916), 27 D.L.R. 235 (B.C.C.A.).
75 *Worth v. Royal Jubilee Hosp.* (1980), 4 L. Med. Q. 59 (B.C.C.A.).

cussed because the Court of Appeal accepted a new standard of care described by the trial judge in these terms:[76]

> Taking their evidence, [the defendant's experts] as well as that of other witnesses with professional qualifications and experience in this field of expertise, a *clear picture emerges of a drastic change in the medical approach* to the hospitalization and treatment of mentally confused or disturbed patients over the last three decades. The old "locked asylum" concept was non-therapeutic and, as one witness put it, resulted in most people incarcerated in such institutions rarely getting out again. Today the emphasis is on therapy rather than imprisonment; and most mental insitutions have, in common with EMI, an "open door" policy with respect to all except the most seriously, or permanently, disturbed patients, with the emphasis on cure and return to the community.
>
> *That this system has its risks is clear from the evidence.* Patients escape (or "elope") in numbers which I found astonishing; and suicides are a far from uncommon occurrence, although there is no evidence that the "open door" policy has increased this risk. As Dr. McFarlane put it, *a decision must be made whether to run a prison, or a hospital;* and no hospital, he said, can be made "totally suicide proof". [emphasis supplied]

After the open door policy was applied as an appropriate standard of care the hospital was held not to be directly or vicariously liable when a patient injured herself in an escape attempt. Mr. Justice Craig said the issue was whether it was reasonably foreseeable that *this* patient might jump over the wall on the roof garden in an attempt to escape. Two other aspects of the judgment are worth noting: a subjective test of the patient was accepted and the test used for measuring proximate cause was unusually precise.

While a subjective appraisal of a psychiatric patient would seem patently reasonable, the direction of Canadian jurisprudence has been that it is not necessary to foresee the "precise concatenation of events: it is enough to fix liability if one can foresee in a general way the class or character of injury which occurred."[77] Because escapes were common, and by the new standard of care foreseeable, and because there were "countless ways" escaping patients might be injured, it seems liability would have followed had the accepted test of proximate cause been applied in this case. It remains to be seen whether the "open door policy" standard and its consequences will be accepted by other courts.[78]

Thus, it would seem that the duty to supervise a patient will arise when the hospital knows or ought to know of the risk of self-injury.[79] However, the

---

76 *Id.*

77 *R. v. Coté* (1974), 51 D.L.R. (3d) 244 at 252 (S.C.C.) (*per* Dickson J.) quoted in Linden, *Canadian Tort Law* 345 (1982).

78 *See* Schiffer, *Psychiatry Behind Bars* 154 (1982), where the author *quaeres* how the "open door" policy is to be reconciled with the statutory requirement that an involuntary (and apparently dangerous) patient be supervised and controlled for her own welfare and the protection of others.

79 *See Foote v. Royal Columbian Hosp.* (1983), 19 A.C.W.S. (2d) 304 (B.C.C.A.). The high risk of a patient suffering a seizure while bathing was held not to have been "understood" by nurses.

hospital is not an insurer against all hazards and would not be liable if the event in which the patient is injured was not foreseeable.

A related question was raised by some very interesting litigation involving a psychiatric hospital.[80] A non-psychiatric patient was injured by a psychiatric patient whose propensity for violence was known to the hospital. The issue at all levels was whether a statute[81] purporting to exempt the hospital for a tort of a patient was effective to bar the action against the hospital. The Supreme Court of Canada held that the section had no application to protect the hospital against its own direct negligence and the case would proceed to trial.[82] Under common law a hospital was not vicariously liable for the torts of patients, thus the basis for any liability in such a fact situation would have to be based on direct liability, that is, a failure to meet the standard care in carrying out the duty to provide the organization necessary so that the patient receives reasonable care. Put simply, a hospital may be liable directly for negligence in failing to provide adequate supervision of patients. In future cases the main issue will be what standard of care is reasonable in the circumstances.[83]

(iii) Facilities and equipment[84]

A hospital is under a duty to provide proper facilities and equipment and to maintain them.[85] To meet the standard of care a hospital need not have the latest and best facilities and equipment[86] but it cannot ignore those which have found their way into common use.[87] Furthermore, there is a clear statement in a case against a hospital that locality is not a justification for a lower standard of care in a rural hospital.[88]

There have been a number of cases in which hospitals have been sued for a failure to provide bed rails with the result that a patient has fallen from his bed suffering injuries, but in no case have the courts found liability. In two

---

80 *Lawson v. Wellesley Hosp. supra* n. 10.

81 Mental Health Act, R.S.O. 1970, c. 269, s. 59.

82 The case is not reported as having gone to trial and was, no doubt, settled out of court.

83 For an excellent discussion of the case *see* Brandt, *Liability of Custodial Institutions For Torts of Patient Inmates* (1977), 1 L. Med. Q. 193; *see also* Sharpe, *Hospital Responsibility for Acts of Patients* (1976), 4 Chitty's L.J. 140; Sharpe, *Mental State as Affecting Liability in Tort* (1975), 23 Chitty's L.J. 46.

84 For a detailed discussion of this topic *see supra* Chapter 4.

85 *Cahoon v. Edmonton Hosp. Bd.* (1957), 23 W.W.R. 131 (Alta. S.C.); *Abel v. Cooke supra* n. 14; *see also* Meredith, *supra* n. 33.

86 *See Thomas v. Port Colborne Hosp.* (1982), 12 A.C.W.S. (2d) 535 (Ont. H.C.). *See also* Southwick, *Hospital Liability* (1983), 4 J. of Legal Med. 1 at 20.

87 For example, a suctioning device in an emergency bundle in a case room. *Meyer v. Gordon* (1981), 17 C.C.L.T. 1 at 37 (B.C.S.C.).

88 *Bernier v. Sisters of Service supra* n. 34.

cases it was held that such equipment posed a physical[89] or psychological[90] risk to the patient, and in another,[91] in which a young man fell onto a hot radiator, it was important that unenclosed radiators were in "all older type hospital buildings." The defence of approved practice was also important in another case[92] where the court observed that hospital authorities cannot be influenced by the request of every patient or anxious relative for specific facilities or equipment. The defence of approved practice has proven to be a most effective one throughout the cases dealing with the hospital's direct liability.

In three very similar cases[93] young children suffered serious burns from equipment set up for steam inhalation. In each the hospital was held liable not for the equipment itself, but for a failure to supervise the use of such equipment near infant patients. Hospitals have a responsibility to see that the use of equipment is in competent hands and, if necessary, to provide instruction as to its proper use.[94]

Hospitals do not, however, have a responsibility to "employ overseers to ensure that anaesthetists or surgeons of proved ability who are privately engaged use the appliances which the hospital has at hand."[95] But where a technician trained and employed by the hospital uses a piece of equipment in testing patients it is the responsibility of the hospital to see that the equipment is checked and safe for use and, if necessary, to arrange for repairs.[96]

As an occupier and perhaps owner of premises, a hospital has certain duties to persons on those premises.[97] The topic of occupiers' liability is beyond the scope of this book,[98] but it is worth noting that this field is now covered by legislation in some provinces.[99]

---

89 *Robinson v. Annapolis Gen. Hosp.* (1956), 4 D.L.R. (2d) 421 (N.S.S.C.).

90 *McKay v. Royal Inland Hosp.* (1964), 48 D.L.R. 665 (B.C.S.C.)

91 *Cahoon v. Edmonton Hosp. Bd. supra* n. 85.

92 *Florence v. Les Soeurs de Misericorde* (1962), 39 W.W.R. 201 (Man. C.A.); *see also Hôtel Dieu de Montreal v. Couloume,* [1975] 2 S.C.R. 115, where there was held to be no liability when a patient fell from his bed during an epileptic seizure. *But see Beatty v. Sisters of Misericorde of Alberta,* [1935] 1 W.W.R. 651 (Alta. S.C.), where there was vicarious liability when a sedated patient fell from her bed.

93 *Shaw v. Swift Current Union Hosp. Bd.,* [1950] 1 W.W.R. 736 (Sask. C.A.); *Sinclair v. Victoria Hosp.,* [1943] 1 W.W.R. 30 (Man. C.A.); *Harkies v. Lord Dufferin Hosp.,* [1931] 2 D.L.R. 440 (Ont. H.C.).

94 *Murphy v. St. Catharines Gen. Hosp. supra* n. 42.

95 *Crits v. Sylvester* (1956), 1 D.L.R. (2d) 502 at 504; affirmed [1956] S.C.R. 991; *see also Anderson v. Chasney,* [1949] 4 D.L.R. 71 at 87; affirmed [1950] 4 D.L.R. 223 (S.C.C.). *See also Jendrick v. Greidanus,* [1982] Alta. D. 2632-01 (Q.B.).

96 *Bartlett v. Children's Hosp.* (1983), 40 Nfld. & P.E.I.R. 88 (Nfld. S.C.).

97 *See, for example, Penner v. Bethel Hosp.* (1981), 8 Man. R. (2d) 310 (Q.B.); *Peters v. University Hosp. Bd.* (1981), 12 Sask. R. 332 (Q.B.); *Dagenais v. Children's Hosp.* (1980), 1 A.C.W.S. (2d) 432 (Ont. H.C.).

98 *See* Jacob, *supra* n. 1; *Canadian Health Facilities Law Guide* 1071 (1983).

99 Occupiers' Liability Acts: Alberta, R.S.A. 1980, c. O-3; British Columbia, R.S.B.C. 1979, c. 303; Ontario, R.S.O. 1980, c. 322.

3.   VICARIOUS LIABILITY

The most common basis upon which a hospital must compensate a patient for the damage he has suffered is vicarious liability, described in the preceding chapter.[100] Put briefly, an employer is liable for the torts of an employee committed within the scope of his employment but is generally not liable for those of an independent contractor.

Because vestiges of past jurisprudence continue to influence modern law[101] on this topic it is necessary to review briefly the growth of the hospital's vicarious liability for professionals such as doctors and nurses.[102] The early authorities were English cases, but they influenced our courts for many years.[103]

In 1906 an English[104] court held that a hospital was not vicariously liable for the negligence of a doctor who was an employee because it did not have control over him in his professional activities. Similarly, in a famous English case, *Hillyer v. St. Bartholomew's Hosp.*,[105] the court held that a hospital's responsibilities were to ensure that the persons giving medical care were competent and had proper apparatus and appliances. It would be vicariously liable for negligent acts of professionals while exercising their "ministerial or administrative duties," but not while they were carrying out professional duties, the reason for the distinction being the perceived absence of control of the employer over those professional activities. It is worth noting that it was also held that in any case at the critical time the nurses were under the control of the operating surgeon. This *obiter* comment lives on, seemingly full of potential never realized.[106]

Thus, a hospital was for many years not liable for doctor-employees or for any negligence nurse-employees committed in carrying out their professional duties. Its main responsibility was to select personnel carefully. Eventually, however, in 1942 in *Gold v. Essex County Council*,[107] this strange split in responsibility was discarded as being "unworkable and contrary to common sense." The negligence involved was that of a radiology technician but the

---

100 *See supra* Chapter 8.
101 *See* discussion of "borrowed servant".
102 *See* Fleming, *Developments in the English Law of Medical Liability* (1959), Vand. L. Rev. 633. As for Canada *see* Linden, *Changing Patterns of Hospital Liability in Canada* (1966-67), 5 A.L.R. 212.
103 See Rozovsky, *The Hospital's Responsibility for Quality of Care Under English Common Law* (1976), 4 Chitty's L.J. 132.
104 *Evans v. Liverpool Corp. supra* n. 67.
105 [1909] 2 K.B. 820 (C.A.).
106 *See* Rozovsky, *supra* n. 20 at 23. *See also* Southwick, *Hospital Liability* (1983), 4 J. of Legal Med. 1 at 14-16.
107 [1942] 2 K.B. 293 (C.A.); *see also Logan v. Waitaki Hosp. Bd.*, [1935] N.Z.L.R. 385 (S.C.).

position was held to be the same as that of the nurse. Whatever confusion remained was removed in *Cassidy v. Min. of Health*[108] where the hospital was held liable for the negligence of a house surgeon employed as part of the permanent staff. The *Hillyer* decision was reviewed and restricted to its facts. Denning L.J. said:[109]

> Relieved thus of *Hillyer's* case, this court is free to consider the question on principle, and this leads inexorably to the result that, when hospital authorities undertake to treat a patient and themselves select and appoint and employ the professional men and women who are to give the treatment, they are responsible for the negligence of those persons in failing to give proper treatment, no matter whether they are doctors, surgeons, nurses, or anyone else. Once hospital authorities are held responsible for the nurses and radiographers, as they have been in *Gold's* case, I can see no possible reason why they should not also be responsible for the house surgeons and resident medical officers on their permanent staff.

Denning L.J. pointed out that it is employers who choose and can dismiss employees and this power is the reason that they should be held vicariously liable even where they cannot for various reasons control the employee.[110] Furthermore, the old control test had become somewhat of an anachronism and it was apparent that one of the policy reasons for restricting the liability of hospitals, that of protecting the privately supported or charity hospital, was no longer present as state-supported hospitals became more common. Thus the questions became whether the person's work was an integral part of the hospital organization and whether the patient employed him.[111] As will be seen, the last question may have come to be paramount.[112] In the last English case in the chain, *Roe v. Min. of Health*,[113] the English Court of Appeal went a step further by holding that a hospital would be liable for a part-time anaesthetist employed and paid by the hospital as a member of the permanent staff but who also carried on a private practice. The potential of this decision will be discussed later in this chapter.

While Canadian courts did follow the *Hillyer* decision[114] it was not applied consistently and was restricted as early as 1916 by an Ontario court[115] which said it should not be taken as an exposition of the whole law. In an important decision in 1938, *Sisters of St. Joseph of the Diocese of London v. Fleming*,[116] the Supreme Court of Canada said the ministerial-professional

---

108 [1951] 1 All E.R. 574 (C.A.).

109 *Id.* at 586.

110 *See* Rozovsky, *supra* n. 103 at 133, where the author notes that hospitals have this same power of sanction over independent contractor doctors who have been granted privileges.

111 Fleming, *The Law of Torts* 345 (6th ed. 1983); *see also* Goodhart, *Hospitals and Trained Nurses* (1938), 54 L.Q. Rev. 553.

112 *See* discussion of the case of *Yepremian v. Scarborough Gen. Hosp. infra.*

113 [1954] 2 Q.B. 66 (C.A.).

114 *Abel v. Cooke supra* n. 14; *Vuchar v. Toronto Gen. Hosp. Trustees*, [1937] O.R. 71 (C.A.).

115 *Lavere v. Smith's Falls Pub. Hosp. supra* n. 15.

116 [1938] S.C.R. 172.

distinction set out in the *Hillyer* case was entitled to great respect but the court was not bound to follow it; in any event the negligent action of the nurse in the case was held to be ministerial. There are a number of similar cases[117] in which courts delcared themselves unprepared to espouse the *Hillyer* principle, yet found the conduct from which the negligence arose to be ministerial.

Canadian courts rejected the *Hillyer* principle more strongly with the decisions of *Fraser v. Vancouver Gen. Hosp.*[118] in which the hospital was held liable for the negligence of an intern, and *Petite v. MacLeod*[119] in which all of the law was reviewed and it was said by the court, *obiter,* that there was no difference between professional and non-professional acts.

More modern authority has made it clear that there is no bar to a hospital being found liable for doctors, nurses or other professionals.[120] Unfortunately, no precise test exists to determine when liability will follow; a frequent judicial suggestion is that each case must be examined and dealt with on its own facts.[121] There are some basic principles, however, which will now be discussed.

(a) Doctors

Whether a hospital will be vicariously liable for the negligence of a doctor depends upon the relationship among the hospital, the doctor and the patient.

In the great majority of cases,[122] the patient engages and pays the doctor (usually through medicare plans) and has the power to dismiss him. The hospital does not employ the physician nor is he carrying out any of the hospital's duties to the patient. He is granted the privilege of using personnel, facilities and equipment provided by the hospital but this alone does not make him an employee. He is an independent contractor who is directly liable to his patient for his negligence.

But the relationships may give rise to hospital liability. The clearest situation for vicarious liability is for those doctors employed as house staff (residents or interns).[123] In these situations the employer-employee arrange-

---

117 *See, for example, Nyberg v. Provost supra* n. 16; *see also* Linden, *supra* n. 102 at 215.
118 *Supra* n. 18.
119 [1955] 1 D.L.R. 147 (N.S.S.C.). Note that it was found that the doctor was not on the house staff and that the evidence regarding a swab was insufficient, rendering the hospital not liable.
120 *Aynsley v. Toronto Gen. Hosp. supra* n. 12.
121 *See Toronto Gen. Hosp. v. Aynsley* (1969), 7 D.L.R. (3d) 193 at 203 (Ont. C.A.); affirmed *supra* n. 12.
122 *Hôpital Notre Dame de l'Espérance v. Laurent supra* n. 21; *Tiesmaki v. Wilson,* [1974] 4 W.W.R. 19; affirmed [1975] 6 W.W.R. 639 (Alta. C.A.); *Serre v. de Tilly* (1975), 58 D.L.R. (3d) 362 (Ont. H.C.); *Johnston v. Wellesley Hosp.* (1970), 17 D.L.R. (3d) 139 (Ont. H.C.); *Petite v. MacLeod supra* n. 119.
123 *Aynsley v. Toronto Gen. Hosp. supra* n. 12; *Fraser v. Vancouver Gen. Hosp. supra* n. 18; *Karderas v. Clow* (1973), 32 D.L.R. (3d) 303 (Ont. H.C.); *Murphy v. St. Catharines Gen.*

ment is set out in a written contract between the hospital and the doctor.[124] The employer's attempts to control the activities of such house staff are usually evident from manuals and directives issued by the hospital.[125]

An alternate basis for the hospital being held liable for the actions of house staff is that it has a duty to the patient to select only competent, qualified staff.[126] The cases in which the negligence of house staff has made the hospital vicariously liable were discussed earlier.[127]

The possibility of joint liability of the hospital and a doctor was raised in *Considine v. Camp Hill Hosp.*[128] The facts showed that it was a resident who did the pre-operative care and performed the surgery which resulted in injury to the patient. Mr. Justice Clarke concluded *obiter* that had he found the resident negligent, he would have held the urologist who charged the patient's health care plan "equally responsible" because he had "either accepted or must be deemed to have accepted, or both, the risks inherent in his permitting [the resident] to perform all or a part of the surgical procedure."[129] After examining the means of control of the resident by the hospital and supervising doctor the learned justice said:[130]

> . . . I am convinced that liability in some instances is not beyond his [the resident's] reach, while in other instances it may be the responsibility of some other person, agency or corporation.

There are doctors whose relationship to the hospital does not fit into either of the personal doctor-independent contractor or house staff-employee categories, and in these cases the facts must be carefully analyzed.[131] A number of cases outlined in Chapter Four dealt with the negligence of anaesthetists.[132] In some of those cases the hospital was vicariously liable and

---

Hosp. supra n. 42; *Cox v. Saskatoon,* [1942] 1 W.W.R. 717 (Sask. C.A.); *Beatty v. Sisters of Misericorde of Alberta supra* n. 92.

124 Note that there may be an agreement between the hospital and a university relating to educational matters. *See Ferguson v. Hamilton Civic Hosp.* (1983), 23 C.C.L.T. 254 (Ont. S.C.), where Krever J. said *obiter* that even where such an agreement existed and provided that the university pay a resident, the hospital was the resident's employer.

125 For a description of hospital systems within which house staff work *see Hajgato v. London Health Assn.* (1982), 36 O.R. (2d) 669 (Ont. H.C.).

126 *Murphy v. St. Catharines Gen. Hosp. supra* n. 42.

127 *Supra* Chapter 4. For an English case *see Clark v. MacLennan,* [1983] 1 All E.R. 416 (Q.B.).

128 (1982), 133 D.L.R. (3d) 11 (N.S.S.C.); *see also Lloy v. Milner* (1981), 15 Man. R. (2d) 187 (Q.B.) where the court noted that an anaesthetist "accepted responsibility" for the resident. *Quaere* whether the reasoning in these cases is based on the defunct "borrowed servant" rule. *See infra.*

129 *Considine v. Camp Hill Hosp. supra* n. 128 at 30.

130 *Id.* at 29. Note that if a resident or intern is reasonable in acting on a supervising doctor's instructions, albeit that they are negligent, it will be the supervising doctor who is liable. *Junor v. McNichol,* The Times, March 26, 1959 (H.L.). For a discussion of this case *see* Jacob, *supra* n. 1 at 242.

131 *Cassidy v. Min. of Health supra* n. 108.

132 *Supra* Chapter 4.

in some it was not. For example, in *Martel v. Hôtel-Dieu St-Vallier*[133] it was found that the anaesthetist was a salaried employee of the hospital also receiving a portion of the fees for service charged by the hospital. The patient did not choose him, as anaesthesia services were provided by the hospital and assignments were made by the head of anaesthesia. The court said:[134]

> The anaesthetist in this case gave his services as he was obliged to do under his contract of employment with the hospital, as did the other members of the staff: radiologists, laboratory technicians, hospital attendants, nurses, etc. The fact that he was a specialist changes nothing. It would be contrary to the evidence, to consider the hospital as a mandatary which had ordered professional anaesthesia services for the plaintiff. This is not what happened.

In another case, the Quebec Court of Appeal identified similar factors.[135]

> It is established that Dr. Forest was employed by the hospital as chief anaesthetist and despite the efforts made to show that the salary paid him was for services rendered in a special and restricted field I am satisfied that he was held out to plaintiff as the hospital's anaesthetist, that he acted in this capacity and that plaintiff accepted him because of this. In this case the patient contracted with the hospital for all necessary services; of these one was the giving of the anaesthetic. On this premise and since for the purposes of this action I see no essential difference between the position of Dr. Forest and that of any other employee, the hospital must answer for his fault.

In an important English case referred to earlier, *Roe v. Min. of Health,*[136] two anaesthetists provided anaesthetic coverage for a hospital. They were paid from a fund set up for all medical and surgical staff (including visiting and consulting doctors) and could carry on private anaesthetic practices as well. While the trial judge held the hospital's obligation to be limited to providing competent anaesthetists,[137] the Court of Appeal held the hospital to be vicariously liable. One judge considered it to be a matter of law that in all cases a hospital undertakes a duty of care in regard to all care and treatment provided by the staff it has selected, employed, and paid[138] while another preferred to leave it that a hospital's obligations can only be decided by considering the circumstances of each particular case.[139] The latter approach is one favoured by Canadian courts,[140] but the former raises the possibility that the hospital has a direct responsibility to a patient which goes beyond ensuring the competence of medical personnel.[141]

In other Canadian cases hospitals have not been vicariously liable for negligent anaesthetists. The important facts in those cases were that the

---

133 (1969), 14 D.L.R. (3d) 445 (S.C.C.). Note that the doctor was referred to as a "resident anaesthetist" but because he had his specialist certificate, it was indicated that he was not characterized as a resident-house staff-doctor.

134 *Id.* at 451.

135 *Beausoleil v. La Communauté des Soeurs de la Charité* (1964), 53 D.L.R. (2d) 65, [1965] Q.B. 37 at 43 (Que. C.A.).

136 *Supra* n. 113.

137 *Id.* at 69.

138 *Id.* at 82 *per* Lord Denning.

139 *Id.* at 88 *per* Lord Morris.

140 *Aynsley v. Toronto Gen. Hosp. supra* n. 12.

141 *See* Picard, *The Liability of Hospitals in Common Law Canada* (1981), 26 McGill L.J. 997.

doctors were retained by the patients[142] on a direct contractual fee-for-service basis with no remuneration from the hospital.[143]

An Australian case[144] held a hospital liable for the negligence of an outside radiologist to whom, in the absence of its employee-radiologist, it had referred x-rays. The hospital had undertaken to provide the patient with diagnostic x-ray services and was held liable when this was negligently done, albeit by a non-employee.

In summary there are some factors which can be identified as being common in those cases where a hospital has been found liable for a doctor's negligence. The patient has generally not chosen the doctor; he has been provided by the hospital as part of certain services. There may be a public expectation that such a doctor or service will be provided by the hospital.[145] There is an absence of control by the patient, usually stemming from the fact that the patient was not the one who engaged the doctor. Also, the doctor may well be described as being an integral part of the hospital organization rather than an accessory to it. Most obvious, but not necessarily most important, a stipend or salary received from the hospital is often a factor.[146]

Most of the above factors were present in the important decision of Holland J. in the Ontario Supreme Court.[147] The patient was a 19-year-old man whose first symptoms were increased frequency of urination and fluid intake but who within hours was hyperventilating and then semi-comatose. Within 35 hours of being treated by the first of three doctors and being through the emergency department and intensive care unit of a hospital he suffered a cardiac arrest with consequential serious brain damage, the cause of which was found to be the negligence of an internist, Dr. Rosen, to diagnose and then properly treat for diabetes. The diagnosis was eventually made by a nurse and the prescribed medication, sodium bicarbonate and excessive dosages of insulin, caused the patient's potassium level to fall and although potassium was then ordered it was too little and too late. Dr. Rosen was a non-employee, an independent contractor who had hospital privileges and who was the internist on call for emergency. But Dr. Rosen was not sued by the patient Yepremian. Action was brought against the general practitioner who first saw the patient in his office and diagnosed "tonsillitis" and the general practitioner on duty in emergency who diagnosed "hyperventilation,"

---

142 This was the situation with the anaesthetists in *Aynsley v. Toronto Gen. Hosp. supra* n. 12 and in *Crits v. Sylvester*, [1956] S.C.R. 991.
143 *Gorback v. Ting*, [1974] 5 W.W.R. 606 (Man. Q.B.). These factors are also relevant in English cases. Jacob, *supra* n. 1 at 259-60.
144 *Samois v. Repatriation Comm.*, [1960] W.A.R. 219.
145 Rozovsky, *supra* n. 103 at 133.
146 *See Yepremian v. Scarborough Gen. Hosp.* (1980), 110 D.L.R. (3d) 513 at 578 (Ont. C.A.), where Blair J.A. accepted this statment.
147 *Yepremian v. Scarborough Gen. Hosp.* (1978), 20 O.R. (2d) 510 (H.C.).

which is actually a sign, not a diagnosis. The trial judge found that these two doctors were negligent but that their negligence was not the proximate cause of the patient's injuries, for it was not foreseeable that the patient would subsequently receive negligent treatment. Further, their negligence was not found to be a contributing cause-in-fact. The hospital was not vicariously liable because its nurses and laboratory technicians had followed both the doctor's orders and the approved practice. The trial judge did an extensive review of the English and Canadian authorities examined earlier in this chapter and noted provisions in the Public Hospitals Act[148] requiring a hospital to admit a patient and found there the intention that the hospitals be directly responsible for the quality of care provided. He also referred to and quoted from the landmark American case *Darling v. Charleston Community Hosp.*[149] where a hospital was held liable for the negligence of a doctor who was an independent contractor on the basis of a direct corporate liability rather than vicarious liability.

The United States court, quoting Fuld J. in *Bing v. Thunig* in the *Darling* case said:[150]

"The conception that the hospital does not undertake to treat the patient, does not undertake to act through its doctors and nurses, but undertakes instead simply to procure them to act upon their own responsibility, no longer reflects the fact. Present-day hospitals, as their manner of operation plainly demonstrates, do far more than furnish facilities for treatment. They regularly employ on a salary basis a large staff of physicians, nurses and internes, as well as administrative and manual workers, and they charge patients for medical care and treatment, collecting for such services, if necessary, by legal action. Certainly, the person who avails himself of 'hospital facilities' expects that the hospital will attempt to cure him, not that its nurses or other employees will act on their own responsibility."

Holland J. summarized the principles[151] in the case before him and gave judgment:

Except in exceptional circumstances,

1. A hospital is not responsible for negligence of a doctor not employed by the hospital when the doctor was personally retained by the patient;

2. A hospital is liable for the negligence of a doctor employed by the hospital;

3. Where a doctor is not an employee of the hospital and is not personally retained by the patient, all of the circumstances must be considered in order to decide whether or not the hospital is under a non-delegable duty of care which imposes liability on the hospital.

The present case falls into the third category. I think the case must be considered from the point of view of the patient, the hospital and the doctor. In so far as this particular patient was concerned, he was semi-comatose on admission. It was not even his decision to

---

148 R.S.O. 1970, c. 378, ss. 17 [re-en. 1972, c. 90, s. 11], 41.

149 (1965), 211 N.E. (2d) 253 (Ill. C.A.). Note that this case has been widely discussed in the U.S. but not specifically adopted by any other jurisdiction. *See* Curran and Shapiro, *Law, Medicine and Forensic Science* 614 (5th ed. 1977).

150 *Id.* at 257 quoting from another U.S. case *Bing v. Thunig* (1957), 143 N.E. (2d) 3 at 8 (N.Y.C.A.).

151 *Yepremian v. Scarborough Gen. Hosp. supra* n. 147 at 533-35.

go the hospital; it was the decision of his parents. Tony Yepremian was taken to the hospital because he was obviously seriously ill and in need of treatment. The public as a whole, and Tony Yepremian and his parents in particular, looked to the hospital for a complete range of medical attention and treatment. In this case there was no freedom of choice. Tony Yepremian was checked into the emergency department by Dr. Chin and not by a doctor of his choice. Dr. Chin was required to work for certain periods of time in the emergency department. When Tony Yepremian was admitted to the intensive care department of the hospital he was admitted under the care of Dr. Rosen. Tony Yepremian had no choice in the matter. The fact that Dr. Rosen happened to be the internist at the time of admission was the luck of the draw so far as the Yepremians were concerned. They really, I suppose, had no concern other than an expectation that this hospital would provide not only a room, but everything else that is required to make sure, so far as is possible, that the patient's ailments are diagnosed and that proper treatment is carried out, whether this is done by an employed doctor, a general practitioner or a specialist. From the point of view of the hospital, the hospital, by virtue of the provisions of the *Public Hospitals Act* above referred to, and as a matter of common sense, has an obligation to provide service to the public and has the opportunity of controlling the quality of medical service. From the point of view of the doctor, through the surrender of some independence by reason of the control that may be exercised over him by the hospital and by making his services available at certain specified times, he attains, by accepting a staff appointment, the privilege of making use of the hospital facilities for his private patients. I have come to the conclusion that in the circumstances of this case, by accepting this patient the hospital undertook to him a duty of care that could not be delegated. It may be that the hospital has some right of indemnity against the doctor but that is not before me.

For the above reasons I have come to the conclusion that the hospital is responsible in law for the negligence of Dr. Rosen.

Thus the hospital was held liable for the negligence of a doctor who was not an employee but an independent contractor. However, the Ontario Court of Appeal[152] reversed the trial decision because the majority held that there was no duty of care owed by the hospital to the patient in the circumstances. The concerns of Arnup J.A. (Morden J.A. concurred on this point) and MacKinnon A.C.J.O. about creating such a duty were expressed by the Associate Chief Justice as follows:[153]

It was pressed upon us, and I think properly, that the *medical profession and hospitals have ordered their professional lives and practices in a particular way in this Province for many years*. The practice of medicine and the operation of hospitals have been conducted on the understanding and belief that the law established and supported the independence of the medical profession, in the manner in which they practised, free from the control and direction of hospital boards, unless they were servants or employees (as those words are commonly understood) of the hospital. The Courts hitherto have supported this view.

No matter how much our sympathies may be engaged in a particular case, in my view to reverse the long standing experience and law would be to enter into a matter of policy, the consequence of such entry being unexamined and unknown to us, and which requires

---

152 (1980), 110 D.L.R. (3d) 513 (Ont. C.A.). For a comment *see* Picard (1980), 14 C.C.L.T. 81.
153 *Id.* at 553-54. For a comment expressing concerns about hospital liability *see* Magnet, *Corporate Negligence as a Basis for Hospital Liabilty* (1978), 6 C.C.L.T. 121, and *Liability of a Hospital for the Negligent Acts of Professionals* (1977), 3 C.C.L.T. 135.

public debate and consideration. I do not view the issue as a novel one — quite the contrary. It is an issue which, if change were to be effected, would now require the legislative intervention based on a consideration of all the ramifications of such change, particularly its effect on public institutions and on a profession which has cherished its independence. To alter the legal position now by judicial legislation would not, in my view, be appropriate.

> *The present legal situation, even though one might conclude it would be "better" or "fairer" or "more logical" to fix hospitals with responsibilty for the negligence of doctors who are carrying out their medical duties by virtue of having been granted "hospital privileges", does not, of course, prevent injured parties from suing the negligent doctors.* If that had been done in the instant case the Court would not, I am sure, have been faced with the task of seeking to establish a new principle by destroying an old one and declaring a liability relationship based on facts and circumstances that have long existed in this province and which have hitherto been otherwise interpreted. [emphasis supplied]

Mr. Justice Blair dissented and after a most thorough analysis of all the relevant cases and authorities decided that a duty of care could and did exist. He said:[154]

> *The recognition of a direct duty of hospitals to provide non-negligent medical treatment reflects the reality of the relationship between hospitals and the public in contemporary society.* This direct duty arises from profound changes in social structures and public attitudes relating to medical services and the concomitant changes in the function of hospitals in providing them. It is obvious that as a result of these changes *the role of hospitals in the delivery of medical services has expanded.* The public increasingly relies on hospitals to provide medical treatment and, in particular, on emergency services. Hospitals to a growing extent hold out to the public that they provide such treatment and such services. [emphasis supplied]

About the concern that judges should not change the law to reflect a change in society, he said:[155]

> *When confronted with a novel situation, the Court makes a policy decision* whether it decides to expand the area of liability or refuses to do so. It expresses a view, in either case, as to what "ought" or "ought not" to be done. Whatever decision is made in this case will be open to legislative review, but that fact does not, in my respectful opinion, relieve the Court of its obligation to reach a decision on the case presented to it. [emphasis supplied]

Mr. Justice Houlden also dissented and, like Arnup J.A., held that there was a duty of care.[156]

In conclusion, of the six justices who heard this case three were prepared to find a duty on the part of a hospital to provide medical treatment and three were not. However, since the three who were not formed the majority of the Court of Appeal the final judgment meant that the patient lost his action. In spite of this favourable decision, but in the face of an appeal to the Supreme Court of Canada, the hospital voluntarily agreed to pay the patient a guaran-

---

154 *Id.* at 579.
155 *Id.* at 563.
156 *Id.* at 517.

teed minimum of $1,839,095.28.[157] It is possible that the hospital[158] was concerned that the dissenting opinions in the Court of Appeal might have been upheld in the Supreme Court of Canada thereby setting a precedent that would have established a duty to provide medical treatment under similar circumstances.

The result in this case leaves important questions unanswered.[159] First, might the distinction between employees and independent contractors become unimportant in the hospital context? That is, could the hospital's non-delegable duty of care to a patient to ensure that he receives proper treatment from the staff it provides now include even those doctors who are primarily independent contractors but whom the hospital may be seen as "holding out" as competent?[160] The obvious cases are those of anaesthetists, radiologists and doctors on call in emergency.[161]

Second, would the legal basis for such a duty be that it is a true direct responsibility under certain circumstances to provide competent medical treatment or would it be that by the application of the organization test the doctor is deemed to be an employee?[162] If the hospital's liability for doctors does expand, will the procedure for granting privileges and the monitoring of standards have to be re-examined?[163] The trend toward greater accountability of hospitals to the public seems clear.[164] Unfortunately, the *Yepremian* case has left the jurisprudence unsettled.

---

157 *Yepremian v. Scarborough Gen. Hosp.* (1981), 31 O.R. (2d) 384 (Ont. H.C.). Note that this was a structured settlement providing for periodic payments.

158 It is unclear from the judgment *id.* whether the Canadian Medical Protection Association contributed to the settlement. If this occurred it was a voluntary payment. Note that in England the Medical Defense Union, which is similar to the C.M.P.A., has an arrangement with hospitals whereby when a doctor is found liable any payment made to the patient is apportioned between the doctor and hospital as agreed privately between them, or, in default of an agreement, in equal shares. Jacob, *supra* n. 1 at 725 referring to Ministry Circular H.M. (54) 73.

159 For an excellent discussion of some theoretical difficulties *see* Fridman, *Hospital Liability for Professional Negligence* (1980), 4 L. Med. Q. 80. *See also,* Fleming, *supra* n. 111 at 344-45; Nathan, *supra* n. 32 at 132.

160 For a criticism of this approach *see* Magnet, *Ostensible Agency in American Hospital Law — Does Canada Need It?* (1980), 10 C.C.L.T. 187.

161 *See Murphy v. Gen. Hosp.* (1980), 25 Nfld. & P.E.I.R. 355 (Nfld. S.C.), where a doctor in charge of an emergency department was said to be an employee of the hospital.

162 It might make no difference to the patient who would be compensated either way, but it would make a difference to the hospital's and doctor's insurers. *See Kennedy v. C.N.A. Assur. Co.* (1978), 6 C.C.L.T. 201; affirmed 116 D.L.R. (3d) 384 (Ont. C.A.), where by application of either the control or organization test a doctor/dentist was held to be an employee of a dental partnership.

163 *See* Alberta Hospitals Act, R.S.A. 1980, c. H-11, ss. 29, 33.

164 *See* Picard, *The Liability of Hospitals in Common Law Canada* (1981), 26 McGill L.J. 997; Magnet, *Preventing Medical Malpractice In Hospitals: Perspectives From Law and Policy* (1979), 3 L. Med. Q. 197; Samuels, *The Basis of The Legal Liability of the Hospital* (1982), 22 Med. Sci. Law 140.

(b) Nurses

A hospital is vicariously liable for negligence committed within the scope of a nurse's employment.[165] As discussed earlier,[166] this was not always true and for that reason cases decided in the first half of the century must be read with caution.

In virtually all hospital-patient relationships today it is an implied term of the contract that the hospital undertakes not only to select competent nurses but also to nurse the patient. Thus it is arguable that this is an alternate basis for the hospital's direct liability.[167]

Since the *obiter* comment in *Hillyer v. St. Bartholomew's Hosp.*[168] that a hospital would not be liable for the negligence of nurses or doctors in the operating room, a number of courts[169] and other authorities[170] have felt compelled to comment on whether a nurse might be viewed in law as ceasing to be the employee of the hospital and become an employee of a doctor or even the patient. This has been called the borrowed servant rule.[171] While the original premise has been destroyed (hospitals can now be held liable for the negligence of employees in the operating room)[172] the theory has remained that a nurse might in some circumstances become a borrowed servant.[173] To do so, however, a nurse would have to be so far outside her duties as a nurse that it is not surprising that there are no reported Canadian or English cases where a hospital has been relieved of liability on that basis.[174]

In the modern hospital a nurse is in an anomalous position. She is a professional with certain skills, knowledge and judgment,[175] yet she is an

---

165 *Kolesar v. Jeffries supra* n. 41; *see also Petite v MacLeod supra* n. 119; *Sisters of St. Joseph of the Diocese of London v. Fleming,* [1938] S.C.R. 172; *Hôpital Générale v. Perron,* [1979] 3 A.C.W.S. 410 (Que. C.A.).

166 *Supra.*

167 *Bernier v. Sisters of Service supra* n. 34; *see also Lavere v. Smith's Falls Pub. Hosp. supra* n. 15, where the contract was express.

168 *Supra* n. 105.

169 *See, for example, Savoie v. Bouchard* (1982), 23 C.C.L.T. 83 at 108; affirmed unreported Sept. 19, 1983 No. 8/83/CA (N.B.C.A.); *Johnston v. Wellesley Hosp. supra* n. 122; *Vuchar v. Toronto Gen. Hosp. Trustees supra* n. 114.

170 Meredith, *supra* n. 33 at 131; Nathan, *supra* n. 32 at 62; Rozovsky, *supra* n. 20 at 19.

171 *See Mersey Docks & Harbour Bd. v. Coggins & Griffith,* [1946] 2 All E.R. 345 (H.L.).

172 *Aynsley v. Toronto Gen. Hosp. supra* n. 12; *Karderas v. Clow supra* n. 123; *Bugden v. Harbour View Hosp. supra* n. 65.

173 Meredith, *supra* n. 33 at 131. When the borrowed servant was assisting a surgeon, the latter's liability was based on "the captain of the ship" doctrine.

174 Rozovsky, *supra* n. 20 at 23. Note that there have been some cases in the U.S. but the courts there have restricted both the borrowed servant and the captain of the ship doctrines. *See* Southwick, *Hospital Liability* (1983), 1 J. of Leg. Med. 1 at 14-17.

175 Note, however, that the Chief Justice of B.C. has stated: ". . . I wish to observe that nurses are not computers, and knowledge of all information known to the hospital and immediate recall of all such information cannot be attributed to them:" *Foote v. Royal Columbian Hosp.* unreported July 5, 1982 No. 811062; affirmed 19 A.C.W.S. (2d) 304 (B.C.C.A.).

employee of the hospital[176] and, although she is an indispensable part of the health care team, she has a duty to carry out the doctor's orders and he can rely on her to do so.[177] If she falls below the standard of the reasonable nurse, she will be negligent and the hospital will be vicariously liable.

Nurses and hospitals have become increasingly concerned about liability where the nurse is required by a doctor to carry out an order which she believes is inappropriate.[178] On the one side is the long-standing rule that it is the doctor alone who is in charge of medical treatment while on the other is the nurse's professional training, experience and, perhaps, closer daily contact with the patient. While there are no Canadian cases on point, a House of Lords decision[179] indicates that a professional acting on orders from a doctor will be liable for negligence only where the order should have been recognized by a reasonable professional as being manifestly wrong.[180]

Because the consequences of a nurse following a negligent order is that the hospital would be vicariously liable, some mechanism should be set up to allow for the serious concerns of nurses and house staff about doctors' orders to be brought to the attention of those doctors and the hospital administration. Such a procedure is consistent with the hospital's goals of providing the best possible care for the patient and with improved risk management.[181]

A hospital is not liable for the negligence of a private or special nurse engaged and paid by the patient and carrying out the patient's duties.[182] It is liable, of course, if it employs the nurse, as where a patient requires special care.[183] However, a hospital could be exposed to liability from the relationship between the hospital patient and special nurse in some circumstaces.[184] If

---

176 As such she may have a duty to accommodate a doctor's variations of normal procedures. See *MacKinnon v. Ignacio, Lamond and MacKeough* (1978), 29 N.S.R. (2d) 656 (S.C.); *Savoie v. Bouchard* (1982), 23 C.C.L.T. 83 (N.B.Q.B.); affirmed unreported Sept. 19, 1983 No. 8/83/CA (N.B.C.A.). But there are duties, such as being certain that no foreign body is left in the patient, for which the doctor is ultimately accountable. *Cosgrove v. Gaudreau* (1981), 33 N.B.R. (2d) 523 (Q.B.).

177 *Serre v. de Tilly supra* n. 122; *Laidlaw v. Lions Gate Hosp. supra* n. 59 at 738; *Lavere v. Smith's Falls Pub. Hosp. supra* n. 15. *Misericordia Hosp. v. Bustillo*, [1983] Alta. D. 2632-01 (Alta. C.A.).

178 *For example*, the case of the infant Candace Taschuk who was given an overdose of morphine by a nurse following a doctor's order (University Hospital, Edmonton, Alberta, October 1982).

179 *Junor v. McNicol* The Times, March 25, 1959 (H.L.). *See also* Rozovsky, *supra* n. 20 at 23.

180 Note that in that case the professional was a resident but the principle can be applied to a nurse. *See* O'Sullivan, *Law For Nurses And Allied Health Professionals In Australia* 121 (1983).

181 *See* Magnet, *Preventing Medical Malpractice In Hospitals: Perspectives From Law and Policy* (1979), 3 L. Med. Q. 197 at 200. *See also* Norman, *Nurses and Malpractice* (1983), 11 Leg. Aspects Med. Prac. 1, where it is suggested that hospitals should have protocols and manuals to cover difficult interfaces between nurses and doctors.

182 *Tiesmaki v. Wilson supra* n. 122; *see also* Meredith, *supra* n. 33 at 136.

183 *Child v. Vancouver Gen. Hosp. supra* n. 31; *Logan v. Colchester*, [1928] 1 D.L.R. 1129 (N.S.S.C.).

184 *See* Rozovsky, *supra* n. 20 at 24.

the hospital selected or recommended a nurse the patient could argue a duty of care was created. Further, if a hospital knew or ought to have known that a special nurse was acting in a careless or negligent manner toward the patient it is arguable that failure to advise the patient would be a breach of the standard of care owed to him. Finally, if a special nurse was allowed to carry out duties which were normally part of the hospital's undertaking the hospital might be liable. There have been so few Canadian cases that it is impossible to predict the outcome of these theoretical situations with certainty.

A hospital is liable for negligence committed within the scope of a student nurse's employment. In a Saskatchewan case[185] an infant being weighed by a student nurse rolled off the scale onto a hot radiator and the hospital was held vicariously liable. The result was the same in an Ontario case where an infant in the charge of a student nurse was scalded by steam from an inhalation apparatus.[186] As mentioned with regard to nurses and house staff the basis for liability in such cases may also be a breach of the hospital's responsibility to select and instruct personnel. The hospital has an obvious interest in instructing and supervising students.[187]

Certain areas can be identified as giving rise to negligence actions against nurses, for which a hospital will be held liable. There are quite a large number of older cases where patients have suffered burns from hot water bottles, steam inhalators and even x-ray machines.[188] The negligence of nurses in the recovery room has led to extensive liability of hospitals in two remarkably similar modern cases.[189] Liability has followed the administration of the wrong drug[190] or an injection in the wrong location.[191] Allegations related to the failure to report signs of circulatory impairment[192] or to observe patients who injure themselves[193] have not generally been successful.

---

185 *Farrell v. Regina*, [1949] 1 W.W.R. 429 (Sask. K.B.).
186 *Harkies v. Lord Dufferin Hosp. supra* n. 93.
187 For excellent practical suggestions *see* Rozovsky, *supra* n. 20 at 25. *See also* Jacob, *supra* n. 1 at 251.
188 *Sisters of St. Joseph of the Diocese of London v. Fleming supra* n. 165; *Nyberg v. Provost supra* n. 16; *Bernier v. Sisters of Service supra* n. 34; *Sinclair v. Victoria Hosp. supra* n. 93; *Craig v. Soeurs de Charité de la Providence*, [1940] 2 W.W.R. 80; affirmed [1940] 3 W.W.R. 336 (Sask. C.A.); *Abel v. Cooke supra* n. 14; *Davis v. Colchester*, [1933] 4 D.L.R. 68 (N.S.S.C.); *Shaw v. Swift Current Union Hosp. supra* n. 93; *Eek v. Bd. of High River Mun. Hosp.*, [1926] 1 W.W.R. 36 (Alta. S.C.); *Lavere v. Smith's Falls Pub. Hosp. supra* n. 15.
189 *Supra* s. 2(c)(ii)B.
190 *Bugden v. Harbour View Hosp. supra* n. 65; *Barker v. Lockhart*, [1940] 3 D.L.R. 427 (N.B.C.A.); *Walker v. Sydney City Hosp.* (1983), 19 A.C.W.S. (2d) 57 (N.S.S.C.); *Misericordia Hosp. v. Bustillo*, [1983] Alta. D. 2632-01 (Alta. C.A.); *see also supra* Chapter 4.
191 *Fiege v. Cornwall Gen. Hosp.* (1980), 4 L. Med. Q. 124 (Ont. S.C.). *Huber v. Burnaby Gen. Hosp.*, [1973] D.R.S. 653 (B.C.S.C.); *Laughlin v. Royal Columbian Hosp.*, [1971] D.R.S. 694 (B.C.C.A.); *see also Cavan v. Wilcox* (1974), 2 N.R. 618, 50 D.L.R. (3d) 687; reversing 44 D.L.R. (3d) 42 (S.C.C.).
192 *See, for example, Vail v. MacDonald* (1976), 66 D.L.R. (3d) 530 (S.C.C.).
193 *See supra*.

An extreme case of negligent nursing appears in the case of *Joseph Brant Memorial Hosp. v. Koziol*. The patient had had back surgery and was placed in a Stryker frame. Some 17 hours after being placed on the ward he died of "pulmonary edema and haemorrhage secondary . . . to the aspiration of gastric juice. His bladder was grossly distended."[194] His death was held to have been caused by negligent nursing care in that he was not roused to cough and breathe deeply, or to perform simple body movements. he was given large quantities of fluid and his blood pressure, respiration, pulse and temperature were not taken nor recorded properly. The medical record was not properly kept. In general, care was found to be below the standard expected of a professional nurse and the hospital was vicariously liable.

In a more recent case, *Meyer v. Gordon*,[195] a newborn suffered brain damage as a consequence of negligent nursing. Because of a breakdown in systems at Grace Hospital, three nurses failed to take adequate care of an expectant mother.[196] The nurses did not: take a history, monitor and record her progress, examine her as required before giving her medication and, in spite of her husband's pleas, left her unattended and unobserved in a supine position until he alerted them to the baby's birth. There was evidence that the medical record which was totally inadequate had been altered. Mr. Justice Legg characterized the nursing as a ". . . long duration of . . . inadequate and at times non-existent care . . ."[197] He found the hospital 75 per cent liable.

(c) Other Employees

The hospital is liable for the negligence of all of its employees within the scope of their employment. Cases brought before the courts have involved pharmacists,[198] physiotherapists,[199] x-ray[200] and laboratory technicians,[201] an audiologist,[202] a ward aide[203] and an orderly.[204]

---

194 (1977), 2 C.C.L.T. 170 (S.C.C.).
195 (1981), 17 C.C.L.T. 1 (B.C.S.C.). *See also Bergen v. Sturgeon Gen. Hosp.* unreported Feb. 6, 1984, No. 80003-03036 (Alta. Q.B.), where nursing care of a patient suffering from undiagnosed appendicitis was substandard.
196 Two testified that she was not their patient and the third (whose patient she may have been) went off to lunch.
197 *Supra* n. 195 at 60. Note that the patient's doctor was held 25 per cent liable.
198 *Misericordia Hosp. v. Bustillo*, [1983] Alta. D. 2632-01 (Alta. C.A.); *Filipewich v. University Hosp.* unreported July, 1973 (settled) (Sask. Q.B.). For an excellent discussion of the liability of pharmacists *see* Haunholter, *Negligence And The Pharmacist* (1978), 2 L. Med. Q. 2; *see also* King, *Liability For Negligence of Pharmacists* (1959), 12 Vand. L.R. 695; Strauss, *The Pharmacist and The Law* (1980).
199 *McKay v. Royal Inland Hosp.* (1964), 48 D.L.R. (2d) 665 (B.C.S.C.).
200 *Murphy v. Gen. Hosp.* (1980), 25 Nfld. & P.E.I.R. 355 (Nfld. T.D.); *Pepin v. Hôpital du Haut Richelieu* (1983), 24 C.C.L.T 259 (Que. C.A.); *Abel v. Cooke supra* n. 14.
201 *Neufville v. Sobers* (1983), 18 A.C.W.S. (2d) 407 (Ont. H.C.).
202 *Bartlett v. Children's Hosp.* (1983), 40 Nfld. & P.E.I.R. 88 (Nfld. S.C.).
203 *Wyndham v. Toronto Gen. Hosp.*, [1938] O.W.N. 55 (Ont. H.C.).
204 *Brennan v. Director of Mental Health* unreported Feb. 18, 1977 No. 83414 (Alta. S.C.).

(d) Volunteers

There are no reported Canadian cases where a volunteer has injured a patient and put the position of the hospital in issue. However, the hospital could be held either directly or vicariously liable within the principles outlined in this chapter and thus care and planning is required when allowing volunteers into the hospital.[205]

In summary, the responsibilities of the hospital to the patient have expanded greatly in breadth and depth in this century.[206] Hospitals have become much more than the hotel-employment agency they once were but with their greater size and sophistication has come an impersonal approach often aggravated by poor public relations. Public attitudes to hospitals have changed partially, the consequence no doubt of the removal of barriers to liability but largely due to the apparent means of hospitals, through government funding, to compensate. Public expectations that hospitals will provide total care and make all arrangements are influencing courts in determining the responsibilities of hospitals. If the hospital is to bear more responsibility for the doctor, present systems and organization may have to be reviewed. It is clear that the doctor-hospital relationship had never been more important and it must be improved.[207]

In this search for roles, relationships and responsibilities a basic principle should be kept in sight: compensation will only be required to be paid to patients who have suffered a legal wrong and consequential injury.

---

205 *See* Rozovsky, *supra* n. 20 at 27-29 for suggestions.
206 *See* Fleming, *supra* n. 102 at 638; *see also* Picard, *The Liability of Hospitals in Common Law Canada* (1981), 26 McGill L.J. 997; Fridman, *Hospital Liability For Professional Negligence* (1980), 4 L. Med. Q. 80.
207 This statement was accepted by Blair J.A. in *Yepremian v. Scarborough Gen. Hosp.* (1980), 110 D.L.R. (3d) 513 at 578-79 who said it "accurately reflects the current state of the law and public attitudes towards it . . ."

10

Medical Records

1.   IMPORTANCE

During the course of a medical negligence trial, a great amount of evidence is adduced by each side, but this evidence rarely assumes the importance borne by the doctor's or hospital's record of the patient. This chapter concerns itself with the importance of accurate and complete medical records, their contents, and their availability to a patient before and at trial.[1]

(a) As An Adjunct to Medical Care

In today's complex health care delivery system, the patient's medical record is assuming increasing importance. Quite apart from the legal significance of the medical record, it can profoundly influence the quality of care received by the patient. This was emphasized in a case when the trial judge quoted the Canadian Council on Hospital Accreditation as follows:[2]

---

1 Note that the terms "health record" and "patient record" are also used. For a discussion of confidentiality *see supra* Chapter 1.
2 *Kolesar v. Jeffries* (1974), 59 D.L.R. (3d) 367 at 373; varied 12 O.R. (2d) 142; affirmed 2 C.C.L.T. 170 (S.C.C.).

Medical records are an important tool in the practice of medicine. They serve as a basis for planning patient care; they provide a means of communication between the attending physician and other physicians and with nurses and other professional groups contributing to the patient's care; they furnish documentary evidence of the course of the patient's illness, treatment and response to treatment. Very importantly in the accredited hospital, they serve as the basic document for the medical staff's review, study and evaluation of the medical care rendered to the patient. For these reasons the C.C.H.A. considers the quality of medical records not only *an important indication of the quality of patient care* given in a hospital, but a valuable tool to maintain quality care and promote staff education. [emphasis supplied]

Along with its primary purpose of facilitating a high standard of medical care[3] for a patient, a medical record may be used in teaching, research, or for purposes of an audit or an accreditation review.[4] Exemplary record keeping is as important to the health care system as it is to the patient.[5]

(b) As Legal Documents

In the context of the medical negligence action, the patient's record fulfills two important functions. First, of course, as evidence brought into court at trial, the medical record can provide either a major weapon to a plaintiff [6] or a formidable defence to a defendant.[7] Second, because trials often take place years after the event, the medical record can be vital in refreshing the memory of the parties involved,[8] especially doctors and nurses whose recollection of a particular patient is hampered by the treatment of hundreds of patients every year. The point was underscored in an extreme case[9] in which the trial was delayed for thirteen years:[10]

. . . it is difficult, and in most cases impossible, for witnesses today to recall with complete accuracy the details of events that took place over 13 years ago. Happily in this case the memories of many of the witnesses with respect to significant facts have been refreshed by notes made either contemporaneously with the happening of the events or shortly after their occurrence.

---

3 Hospitals Act, R.S.A. 1980, c. H-11, s. 40 [am. 1980 (Supp.), c. H-51, s. 36; 1983, c. N-14.5, s. 128; c. R-10.1, s. 55]. *See Osburn v. Mohindra* (1980), 29 N.B.R. (2d) 340 (Q.B.), where a serious conflict in diagnosis apparent in the medical record went unnoticed for almost one month.

4 Rozovsky, *Canadian Hospital Law* 87 (1979). For an excellent analysis and discussion *see* Rozovsky, L.E. and F.A. *The Canadian Law of Patient Records* (1984).

5 The Canadian College of Health Record Administrators (Canadian Health Record Association) is a national organization representing over 2500 administrators and technicians with the purpose of establishing standards in the field of health record science. 187 King St. E., Oshawa, Ont.

6 *See Dean v. York County Hosp.* (1979), 3 L. Med. Q. 231 at 234, 239 (Ont. S.C.); *Meyer v. Gordon* (1981), 17 C.C.L.T. 1 at 15, 57 (B.C.S.C.).

7 *MacKinnon v. Ignacio, Lamond and McKeough* (1978), 29 N.S.R. (2d) 656 at 687 (S.C.).

8 Marshall. *The Physician and Canadian Law* 5 (1979).

9 *Tiesmaki v. Wilson*, [1974] 4 W.W.R. 19; affirmed [1975] 6 W.W.R. 639 (Alta. C.A.).

10 *Id.* at 21.

Delays of this magnitude are relatively rare, but memories can fail in much shorter periods. Furthermore, a doctor's estate can be sued after his death[11] and in such cases the only direct evidence available from the deceased doctor will be that found in his patient records. Also, if limitation period reform incorporates a belated discovery rule,[12] the reliance on records will be even greater.

At trial, the uses to which medical records are put are to reconstruct the events,[13] opinions,[14] and knowledge[15] of the parties and others[16] at the relevant time, and to resolve conflicts in testimony.[17] Discovering the factual side of what occurred during the patient's treatment or stay in hospital is one of the more important aspects of a trial, and courts sometimes have difficulty in reconstructing events from conflicting testimony where there is no objective record of what happened.[18]

The desirability of maintaining good records is apparent once their significance in a court of law is appreciated. Because of their critical importance in litigation, "every word, every nuance, every inference can become an issue and therefore it is important that records be kept accurately and objectively."[19] To the requirements of accuracy and objectivity may be added contemporaneity and completeness.

Courts dislike poorly kept records. Apart from the difficulties in establishing the facts that arise as a result, there is created a generally poor

---

11 *See, for example, Parkin v. Kobrinsky* (1963), 46 W.W.R. 193 (Man. C.A.); *Gordon v. Davidson* (1980), 4 L. Med. Q. 131 (Ont. S.C.); *Wipfli v. Britten* (1982), 22 C.C.L.T. 104 (B.C.S.C.); *Ferguson v. Hamilton Civic Hosp.* (1983), 23 C.C.L.T. 254 (Ont. H.C.).

12 *See supra* Chapter 5.

13 *See University Hosp. Bd. v. Lepine* (1965), 50 W.W.R. 709 at 713-18; affirmed on hospital's liability, reversed on doctor's liability 53 W.W.R. 513; which was reversed [1966] S.C.R. 561; *Wilson v. Stark* (1967), 61 W.W.R. 705 (Sask. Q.B.); *Badger v. Surkan,* [1973] 1 W.W.R. 302 (Sask. C.A.); *Park v. Stevenson Memorial Hosp.* (1974), unreported (Ont. H.C.) Holland J.; *Vail v. MacDonald* (1976), 66 D.L.R. (3d) 530 (S.C.C.); *Tiesmaki v. Wilson,* [1975] 6 W.W.R. 639 (Alta. C.A.); *Holmes v. Bd. of Hosp. Trustees of London* (1977), 17 O.R. (2d) 626 (H.C.); *Rietze v. Bruser,* [1979] 1 W.W.R. 31 at 33, 37 (Man. Q.B.).

14 *Schweizer v. Central Hosp.* (1974), 6 O.R. (2d) 606 (H.C.); *Holmes v. Bd. of Hosp. Trustees of London supra* n. 13; *Gordon v. Davidson* (1980), 4 L. Med. Q 131 at 139 (Ont. S.C.). *But see Meyer v. Gordon* (1981), 17 C.C.L.T. 1 (B.C.S.C.).

15 *University Hosp. Bd. v. Lepine supra* n. 13, 53 W.W.R. 513 at 522 (Alta. C.A.); *White v. Turner* (1981), 15 C.C.L.T. 81 at 89 (Ont. H.C.); affirmed 20 C.C.L.T. xxii.

16 *Badger v. Surkan supra* n. 13; *Worth v. Royal Jubilee Hosp.* (1980), 4 L. Med. Q. 59 at 65 (B.C.C.A.).

17 *See, for example, Badger v. Surkan id.; Tiesmaki v. Wilson supra* n. 13; *Meyer v. Gordon supra* n. 14.

18 *Rickley v. Stratton* (1912), 3 O.W.N. 1341 (H.C.); *Kolesar v. Jeffries supra* n. 2; *Gagnon v. Stortini* (1974), 4 O.R. (2d) 270 (Dist. Ct.); *Dale v. Munthali* (1977), 16 O.R. (2d) 532 (H.C.); *Meyer v. Gordon supra* n. 14.

19 Korcok, *When the Lawyer is Called in Your Best Friend is a Good Set of Records* (1977). 116 Can. Med. Assn. J. 687.

impression of the care received: the corollary of the "empirically valid assumption that good records are in themselves an index — though not a warranty — of good medical care."[20] This was illustrated in *Kolesar v. Jeffries*,[21] in which the trial judge stated that the nursing records of the defendant hospital were not "worthy of the term" and described the procedure used in making up the records as "remarkable." In *Meyer v. Gordon*,[22] the hospital record contained alterations and additions which caused the trial judge to "view with suspicion the accuracy of many of the observations . . . recorded."[23] The result was that the defendant doctor's defence was ineffectual because experts called by him had to base their opinions on this unreliable record of the patient's treatment.[24]

When reconstructing fact situations at trial, a court is naturally most interested in and tends to give the most weight to the more objective evidence before it. Accordingly, where a conflict arises between oral testimony of a party and an entry on the medical record, the courts tend to favour the latter, particularly if it was made before any legal proceedings were contemplated:[25]

> Attention must be called to the particular importance of the documentary evidence . . . while almost all the evidence of the plaintiffs, and some of that of the defendants, was a matter of recollection only, the operative reports were documents prepared with scientific and professional detachment immediately after the performance of the operation and at a time when there was no thought of any possiblity of legal action being taken.

Similarly, where a conflict exists between written records, the entries made closest in time to the event in question will generally be preferred.[26]

When the records made by the doctor or hospital are scanty, inaccurate or incomplete, the consequences to the doctor or hospital are not good, for the court will generally favour the testimony of the plaintiff. This was explained in *Dale v. Munthali*:[27]

> It is unfortunate that [the defendant] did not make careful notes. This was a routine house call to him and he did not hear of the death until notified . . . some months later . . . [The plaintiff's] memory of the events leading up to her husband's death would, of course, be sharpened by the impact of his death. In retrospect this was not just a routine house call to her and I think she would tend to remember every detail of what occurred.

---

20 Matte, *Legal Implications of the Patient's Record* in Wecht, ed. *Legal Medicine Annual: 1971* 345 at 360.

21 *Supra* n. 2.

22 (1981), 17 C.C.L.T. 1 (B.C.S.C.).

23 *Id.* at 15.

24 *But see Hajgato v. London Health Assn.* (1982), 36 O.R. (2d) 669 (Ont. H.C.), where the defendant doctor's denial that he had altered the hospital record was accepted and he was exonerated.

25 *Radclyffe v. Rennie* (1964), 43 D.L.R. (2d) 360 at 375-76; affirmed [1965] S.C.R. 703; *see also Kolesar v. Jeffries supra* n. 2 in 59 D.L.R. 367 at 374 where the trial judge observed that "One is always suspicious of records made after the event . . ."

26 *Tiesmaki v. Wilson supra* n. 2.

27 *Supra* n. 18 at 536; *see also Gagnon v. Stortini supra* n. 18; *LaFleur v. Cornelis* (1979), 28 N.B.R. (2d) 569 at 575 (Q.B.).

The doctor's only hope in such a situation is that the plaintiff will turn out to be an unreliable witness so that the doctor's oral evidence will be preferred to that of the plaintiff.[28]

Omissions from the medical record are interpreted against the doctor or hospital. In a case in which no entries were made for seven hours on the chart of a patient who was recovering from anaesthesia, the trial judge said that the absence of entries on the chart permitted the inference "that nothing was charted because nothing was done."[29] Similarly, where no doctor's progress notes were made for three consecutive days the inference was made that[30]

> . . . there was no great concern on the part of [the patient's] attending physicians although as it became clear later this was a time when treatment might have . . . made a significant difference . . .

The clear lesson from the cases is that records should be kept on *all* patients,[31] and that the records ought to be accurate, objective, as contemporaneous with the event recorded as possible, and complete. It is now appropriate to consider what is contained in a "complete" medical record.

2.   CONTENTS

The contents of the medical record will be based largely on the requirements of the individual doctor or hospital. Nevertheless, there are some items which should appear in every record, and in the case of hospitals, there are mandatory requirements is some provinces. The concerns surrounding the contents of medical records are somewhat different for doctors than they are for hospitals; therefore, each will be discussed separately.

(a)   Hospital Records

(i) Statutory requirements

Regulations under hospital legislation in most provinces set out with some degree of specificity the items which must be included in every patient's

---

28 *Rickley v. Stratton supra* n. 18.
29 *Kolesar v. Jeffries supra* n. 2 in 59 D.L.R. at 373-74. *But see Ferguson v. Hamilton Civic Hosp.* (1983), 23 C.C.L.T. 254 at 290 (Ont. H.C.), where Krever J. held that "it would be extending that principle too far to apply it to routine inspections of the patient by the nurses." *See also Hajgato v. London Health Assn. supra* n. 24.
30 *Holmes v. Bd. of Hosp. Trustees of London supra* n. 13 at 648.
31 *See, for example, Gagnon v. Stortini supra* n. 18 where the dentist kept records only of his "regular patients," and not those who came in on a "casual or emergency" basis. *See Bergen v. Sturgeon Gen. Hosp.* unreported Feb. 6, 1984 No. 8003-03036 (Alta. Q.B.) where hospital records were thrown out by a nursing assistant when clearing a patient's room.

record.[32] The items required by these jurisdictions can be classified into four types of information, and even where not statutorily required would seem to be the sensible contents of a medical record. First, identification information and legal documents such as consent forms. Second, information relating to the diagnosis. This will include histories, physical examination report, provisional diagnosis, reports of diagnostic tests and procedures, pathology reports, consultations, and final diagnosis. Third, information concerning treatment, including orders for treatment, surgical and treatment reports, reports of drugs administered, progress notes, and nurses' notes. Fourth, discharge information. This will include a discharge summary and follow-up care report, or death certificate or autopsy report or both, if applicable. In short, the hospital record ought to contain sufficient information "to justify the diagnosis and warrant the treatment given"[33] and to provide as complete a picture as possible of what happened to the patient from admission to discharge.[34]

(ii) Incident reports

When unusual events or mishaps occur, most hospitals, like any other employer,[35] require that the employees involved write a report on the incident for the hospital's records.[36] While these incident reports could concern any sort of accident, they often involve patients, and being written by persons without legal knowledge often contain speculation, opinion and even accusations which can be most advantageous to the patient's case.[37] For this reason, most hospital administrators realize the desirability of keeping such reports confidential and out of the hands of the patient's solicitors. It is appropriate at this point to consider the policy reasons involved in making accident reports unavailable.

Use of the incident report as a communication to the hospital's lawyer is only part of its value. It provides the hospital with a means of investigating accidents and mishaps with a view to preventing their recurrence.[38] It has

---

32 *See, for example,* Alta. Reg. 146/71, s. 12(2); B.C. Reg. 289/73, s. 13(1); R.R.M. 1971, Reg. P130-R1, s. 4(1); N.B. Reg. 66/47, s. 19(1); N.S. Reg. 16/79, s. 16; R.R.O. 1980, Reg. 865, s. 38; R.R.P.E.I. 1981, c. H-11, s. 37; R.R.Q., c. S-5, r. 1, s. 84; R.R.S. 1979, Reg. 331, s. 12.

33 Alta. Reg. 146/71, s. 12(2)(b).

34 For many helpful suggestions *see* Rozovsky, *supra* n. 4 at 89-92.

35 *See, for example, Sowa v. Alta. Power Ltd.,* [1982] 3 W.W.R. 660 (Alta. Q.B.), where the "incident" was a power failure.

36 Note that there may be limitations such as those expressed in *Savoie v. Bouchard* (1982), 23 C.C.L.T. 83 at 93; affirmed unreported Sept. 19, 1983 No. 8/83/CA (N.B.C.A.), where the evidence was that no incident report was made with respect to any accident involving a doctor.

37 *See Meyer v. Gordon* (1981), 17 C.C.L.T. 1 (B.C.S.C.), where the trial judge compared the incident report with the medical record to the discredit of the nurse who prepared both.

38 For an excellent discussion *see* Rozovsky, *The Canadian Law of Patient Records supra* n. 4 at 106-15. Orlikoff, *Malpractice Prevention and Liability Control for Hospitals* 34-41 (Am. Hosp. Assoc. 1981).

been suggested that making incident reports available to patients or their lawyers might tend to discourage the practice of incident reporting which in turn would not only hamper the hospital's solicitor in investigating facts for the conduct of a defence[39] but also bring about a decline in hospital standards by removing an important tool for improvement.[40] Another argument for keeping incident reports secret would be that a plaintiff can get the information he desires by examining the employee involved in an examination for discovery, and in some cases he will not be prejudiced because he will be able to rely on the doctrine of *res ipsa loquitur*.

However, the hospital need fear no interference in the formulation of its defence or in the improvement of procedure if its employees are trained to fill out incident reports in a factual and objective manner. And the fact remains that the inability to obtain the information in an incident report can seriously prejudice a patient's case. An examination for discovery of the employee involved, an expensive and time-consuming procedure, is made more so if it is wished to use the employee's answers as evidence at trial because the answers can be so used only if the employee is made a party to the action. This not only adds to the cost and complexity of the litigation but may penalize the plaintiff in costs against the employee. Finally, it is certainly not every case in which *res ipsa loquitur* applies and if one of the conditions for its application[41] cannot be met, the plaintiff may be unable to prove part of his case.

Policy considerations aside, under the law as it now stands the hospital cannot be assured that the incident report will not be subject to subpoena, but precautions can be taken which will increase the likelihood of it remaining confidential.

As will be discussed in a later section, legislation in most provinces allows a patient or someone authorized by him to inspect or obtain a copy of his hospital record. Therefore, unless required to do so by legislation,[42] the prudent hospital will ensure that no copies of an incident report appear in the patient's hospital record.[43] Apart from legislation specifically requiring the disclosure of hospital records, all provinces have rules relating to the discov-

---

39 *Crits v. Sylvester*, [1955] O.R. 332 at 333 (Ont. H.C.).

40 Horty, *Why Incident Reports Must be Kept Confidential* (Nov. 1968) Modern Hospital 62.

41 *See supra* Chapter 6.

42 Incident reports are required to be included in the patient's hospital record in Quebec. *See* R.R.Q., s. S-5, r. 1, s. 84(n). Quebec is also among those provinces which allow the disclosure of the hospital record to a patient; *see Levinson v. Royal Victoria Hosp.* unreported November 18, 1982 No. (unavailable) (Que. C.A.).

43 *But see Fiege v. Cornwall Gen. Hosp.* (1980), 4 L. Med. Q. 124 at 129-30, where the trial judge required counsel to explain why the incident report was not in the medical record and produced with it; *see also Laplante v. Matsqui-Sumas-Abbotsford Gen. Hosp.* (1980), 23 B.C.L.R. 1 at 4 (B.C.S.C.).

ery of documents requiring a party to a lawsuit to produce all documents "which are or which have been in [the party's] possession or power relating to all matters or questions in the cause or matter"[44] unless the documents are privileged. The challenge for the hospital then is to see that the incident report will be regarded by the court as a privileged document, the basis for which, in the case of the incident report, being that it is a communication between solicitor and client.[45]

In an English case, *Patch v. United Bristol Hosp. Bd.*,[46] there arose the question of whether incident reports, written at the time of the event and before any intimation that the plaintiff intended to make a claim, were privileged. It was argued that the reports could not be said to have come into existence for the purpose of enabling the hospital's solicitors to advise with respect to impending litigation, and therefore ought not to be privileged, but the court held that:[47]

> . . . when something goes wrong in medical or surgical treatment which reasonably gives rise to anticipation of litigation, any statement which is then made by persons concerned with the patient in anticipation of the kind of claim which may be made is quite clearly privileged.

Incident reports are usually prepared to serve the dual goals of allowing the hospital to monitor standards and systems and to ready itself for any possible litigation. Since there is authority that the "dominant" or "substantial" purpose must be the instruction of a solicitor for possible litigation in order for a document such as an incident report to be privileged,[48] the critical question will be: why was this hospital incident report prepared?

It is open to a court to view the whole practice of incident reporting in hospitals as administrative or managerial in purpose, particularly if copies of the report are widely distributed within the hospital, and to hold the report to be not privileged.[49]

---

44 Supreme Court Rules, Alta. Reg. 390/68, s. 186(2).

45 *See supra* Chapter 1.

46 [1959] 1 W.L.R. 955.

47 *Id.* at 956-57. Professor Robertson has suggested that "the authority of *Patch* is now highly doubtful" because of the decision of *Waugh v. Br. Ry. Bd.*, [1980] A.C. 521 (H.L.), wherein it was held that advice on litigation was not the dominant purpose of a report on a railway accident and, thus, there was no privilege. *See* Robertson, *Discovery of Hospital Accident Reports* (1983), 133 New Law J. 1020.

48 *Nova v. Guelph Enrg.*, [1983] 6 W.W.R. 501 (Alta. Q.B.); *Christie (Gondola Pizza) v. Royal Ins. Co. of Can.* (1981), 22 C.P.C. 258 (Man. Q.B.); *Wood v. Barbrick* (1981), 50 N.S.R. (2d) 556; application for leave to appeal dismissed 50 N.S.R. (2d) 210 (C.A.); *Shaw v. Roemer* (1979), 11 C.C.L.T. 35 (N.S.Q.B.); *See also* Sopinka and Lederman, *The Law of Evidence in Civil Cases* 171 (1974); *Canadian Health Facilities Guide* 3116 (1982). *But see Sowa v. Alta. Power*, [1982] 3 W.W.R. 660 (Alta. Q.B.), where the Master seemed able to find two substantial purposes of an industrial accident incident report.

49 Note that there does not seem to be a reported Canadian case directly on point. *See* Horty *supra* n. 40.

All possible steps should be taken to keep the incident report confidential, since privilege will not apply unless the client and the solicitor intended that the communication be kept confidential.[50] The incident report ought to be seen by as few hospital personnel as possible. The fact that the contents of a communication may be known by someone other than the solicitor and the client will not vitiate the claim of privilege if the third party's presence or knowledge is necessary to the consultation.[51] Incident reports should be sent directly from the employee making the report to the hospital administrator. This contributes significantly to the confidential nature of the report as the only persons who will see it are those who must: the person making it, the administrator, and the hospital's solicitor.

Some hospital administrators believe that the incident report can be kept out of court by such means as keeping it in special files in a locked cabinet, having it dictated onto tape, or conducting the whole incident reporting system on an oral basis. None of these methods will be efficacious. The rules relating to discovery of documents are concerned only with whether the party being discovered has the documents in his "possession or power" and keeping them separate will not reduce their vulnerability. Similarly, in most jurisdictions "document" is defined in very wide terms, including "recordings of sound."[52] Finally, an oral incident reporting system, apart from its administrative inefficiency may only result in the administrator being summoned to court to testify in person, there being no written record available.

Until the evidentiary status of the hospital incident report is settled, either by case law or legislation, a cautious course of action for the hospital is to ensure that its employees fill out incident reports as factually and objectively as possible, perhaps by use of a standard form. The administration could then, when warranted, ask the employee for a more complete report (including his opinions and speculation), to be sent directly to the hospital's solicitor, which would almost certainly be privileged.

(b) Office Records

Much of what appears in the doctor's office record of a patient will be dictated by common sense.[53] Identification information, the patient's history, records of all visits, ailments, and injuries, copies of the results of tests performed, diagnoses, and notes on treatment administered, drugs prescribed

---

50 Sopinka and Lederman, *supra* n. 48 at 106; *See Strass v. Goldsack* (1975), 58 D.L.R. (3d) 397 (Alta. C.A.).

51 Rozovsky, *supra* n. 4 at 101; *See Wood v. Barbrick supra* n. 48.

52 *See, for example,* Supreme Court Rules, Alta. Reg. 390/68, s. 186(1); jurisdictions with similar provisions include British Columbia and Nova Scotia. *See* Supreme Court Rules. B.C. Reg. 310/76, O. 31, Rule 12(a); N.S. Rules of the Supreme Court, Rule 1.05(1)(g).

53 *See* Sharpe and Sawyer, *Doctors and the Law* 115 (1978).

or periods of hospitalization should, of course, all be present. The words in the regulations to the Alberta Hospitals Act quoted earlier[54] are probably equally applicable in this context.

The risk to the doctor in the case of his own office records is not so much one of omission but arises from the manner in which certain items are recorded, or from the presence of irrelevant or unprofessional remarks.

With respect to the first matter mentioned, care must be taken when recording items on a patient's record which relate to sensitive items such as drug or alcohol addiction, mental competency or sexual deviation.[55] Such conditions have legal overtones and the doctor must be certain to obtain verification from another party, his previous knowledge of the patient, or an admission of the patient himself.[56]

Similarly, all original entries and pages in a patient's record should remain as first made. Deletions, alterations, or clarifications should be added to the record leaving the original legible and intact.[57] Such changes should be dated, initialled and explained, as entries on a record in various colours of ink can be misinterpreted later as indicating inefficiency or even fabrication.[58]

The second danger to a doctor which could arise from his office record is the inclusion of unprofessional descriptions of colleagues[59] to whom the patient was referred or of the patient himself. Some physicians use less than complimentary phrases or caricatures to "trigger" their memory, but this should be avoided wherever possible; the doctor may be making himself vulnerable to an action in defamation, although the defence of qualified privilege would be available in most cases.[60] In any event, a court looking at the record in the future would not regard with favour flippant remarks on the record.[61]

It is important for the doctor to bear in mind that there is no magic in the form in which notes or observations are made. For legal purposes, tape recordings, movies, and drawings are little different from written records. The practice of dictating medical notes which contain unprofessional remarks increases exposure to a defamation action because the hearing of the tapes by the transcribing typist constitutes publication.[62]

---

54 *See supra* text at n. 33.
55 Ficarra, *Professional Liability v. Doctors of Medicine* in Wecht, ed. *Legal Medicine Annual: 1975* 117 at 126.
56 *Id.*
57 *Id.*
58 *Id.* at 127.
59 *See* the example quoted by Ficarra, *id.* at 125 wherein the doctor referred to a colleague as a "kook."
60 *See supra* Chapter 2.
61 Ficarra *supra* n. 55 at 125-26.
62 Williams, *The Law of Defamation* 61 (1976); *Salmond on Torts* 157 (16th ed. Heuston 1973).

3. OBLIGATION TO PRODUCE

The discussion in this and the following section is concerned primarily with the production and admissibility of hospital and office records in the context of the usual medical negligence action, that is, when the doctor or hospital is the defendant.[63] This section concerns itself with the right of the patient to obtain a copy of his hospital record or his doctor's office record, and the following section deals with the admissibility of the records at trial.

An important point for those holding medical records to remember is that without the patient's consent, no medical record or portion of one ought to be revealed to anyone, including the patient's solicitor, employer or, technically, doctors to whom the patient is referred, although implied consent would be easily found in this case.[64] Statutory exceptions to the consent requirement exist for medical care insurance and workers' compensation purposes[65] as well as for various public health reasons.[66]

(a) Hospital Records

There is no doubt that the actual records, as property, are under the ownership of the hospital, and therefore the patient is not entitled to the records themselves.[67] In most provinces legislation permits the patient to have access to his hospital record.[68] In Alberta,[69] Quebec[70] and Nova Scotia[71] if the hospital refuses the patient can apply to a court for an order requiring

---

63 For other situations, for example, disclosure to third parties, *see supra* Chapter 1.

64 *See Re Gen. Accident Assur. Co. and Sunnybrook Hosp.* (1979), 96 D.L.R. (3d) 335 (Ont. H.C.), where it was held that when a patient commences an action against a hospital he "opens up for inspection" his medical record "to all persons properly interested in the action."

65 *See, for example,* Alberta Hospitals Act, R.S.A. 1980, c. H-11, s. 40 [am. 1980 (Supp.) c. H-5.1, s. 36; 1983, c. N-14.5, s. 128; c. R-10.1, s. 55].

66 *See supra* Chapter 1.

67 *See, for example,* Hospital Act, R.S.B.C. 1979, c. 176, s. 43(1); Hospitals Act, S.N. 1971, No. 81, s. 36(1); Public Hospitals Act, R.S.O. 1980, c. 410, s. 11; Sask. Reg. 331/79, s. 16.

68 N.B. Reg. 66-47, s. 19(3); Hospitals Act, S.N. 1971, No. 81, s. 36(3); R.R.O. 1980, Reg. 865, s. 49(6); R.R.P.E.I. 1981, c. H-11, s. 46(5); R.R.S. 1979, Reg. 331, s. 16(2); R.R.N.W.T. 1980, Reg. 275, s. 75(1). British Columbia and Manitoba do not have legislation. For case law supporting access in B.C. *see Pallos v. Green* (1981), 32 B.C.L.R. 184 (S.C.); *Dayne v. Traversy* (1983), 47 B.C.L.R. 143 (S.C.); *Choboter v. Reimer* unreported Sept. 12, 1983 No. CA001098 (B.C.C.A.); *see also Jones v. Nelson* (1980), 24 B.C.L.R. 57 (S.C.); and *Bachmann v. Sandoz* (1978), 6 B.C.L.R. 57 (S.C.). For a rejection of the right by a Manitoba court, *see Andree v. Misericordia Gen. Hosp.*, [1980] 2 W.W.R. 380 (Man. C.A.).

69 Alberta Hospitals Act, R.S.A. 1980, c. H-11, s. 40 [am. 1980 (Supp.), c. H-5.1, s. 36; 1983, c. N-14.5, s. 128; c. R-10.1, s. 55].

70 Health Services and Social Services Act, L.R.Q. 1977, c. S-5, art. 7. For an excellent analysis, *see* Knoppers, *Confidentiality and Accessibility of Medical Information: A Comparative Analysis* (1982), 12 R.D.U.S. 395.

71 Hospitals Act, R.S.N.S. 1967, c. 249, s. 63 [am. 1977, c. 45, s. 8].

disclosure. There is considerable case law supporting the right to access.[72] Apart from these authorities a hospital as a defendant would be compellable under rules of practice concerning discovery of documents to make the records available.

The policy reasons for making the patient's record available to him are clear: in many cases, without this information an injured patient would have no way of discovering the events which led to his misfortune, and it would be manifestly unfair not to compel the disclosure of the information by those who know.

Mr. Justice Krever in the *Report of the Commission of Inquiry into the Confidentiality of Health Information*[73] canvassed the arguments raised against patient access to medical records: that it is not in the best interests of the patient; that information could be misleading or misinterpreted. He found that few instances of actual harm were provided in support of these concerns.

He found that those advocating access raised the following points: access to such personal information is an incident of human dignity; corrections to the record by a patient ought to be possible; a better understanding of treatment and a feeling of trust would be fostered; access would allow for an informed consent to release of the records to others. Mr. Justice Krever's recommendation was[74] that legislation be enacted to express the general rule that a person has the right to inspect and receive copies of any health information of which he is the subject.

(b) Office Records

The position with respect to a doctor's office records of a patient is less clear. Like the hospital, the doctor is the owner of the records, but the patient may still be entitled to the information contained in them.[75] This is based on a

---

72 In Alberta, *Lindsay v. D.M.*, [1981] 3 W.W.R. 703 (Alta. C.A.); *Tomkow v. Oldale* (1980), 118 D.L.R. (3d) 755 (Alta. Q.B.). In B.C., *see supra* n. 68. In Newfoundland, *see Murphy v. Gen. Hosp.* (1980), 25 Nfld. & P.E.I.R. 355 at 359 (Nfld. S.C.); *see also Mitchell v. Aldrete* (1981), 31 Nfld. & P.E.I.R. 340 (Nfld. C.A.). In Ontario *see Strazdins v. Orthopaedic & Arthritic Hosp. (Toronto)* (1978), 22 O.R. (2d) 47 (H.C.); *Mitchell v. St. Michael's Hosp.* (1980), 29 O.R. (2d) 185 (S.C.). For a comment *see* Morrison, *Production of Hospital Records: Any Time At All?* (1980), 2 A.Q. 193.

73 455-91 (1980). For a report on the practical implications of this report *see* Galloway, *The Review of the Report On Confidentiality of Health Information* Ont. Min. of Health (1981). For a critique of the present legislation and a recommendation for change, see Knoppers *supra* n. 70. For an analysis of the U.S. position *see* Connell, *Medical Records — How Much Patient Access?* (1982), 10 Leg. Aspects of Med. Practice 1.

74 *Id.* at 489. He also recommended that a person have the right to correct the record and the right to appeal a refusal of information.

75 *Id.* at 472. The College of Physicians and Surgeons of Ontario stated in its submission to the Krever Commission:
It seems clear that the physician owns the office records which he prepares, but it is equally clear that the patient has an interest in the information contained in those records.

theory that the information in the record is part of what the patient "purchases" from the doctor. Of course, the opposing argument is that the patient is paying only for services and treatment, not information, and therefore has no access to the information as a matter of right.[76]

The rules regarding discovery of documents have been successfully invoked to compel a defendant doctor to make his records available to the patient's lawyers.[77] No defence of privilege either legal[78] or medical[79] seems available to the doctor even in Quebec, where the doctor-patient privilege is statutorily enshrined.[80] Furthermore, the policy reasons for the disclosure to the patient stated above are equally applicable here. Mr. Justice Krever expressed his concern about restricting patient access to records in these words:[81]

> Knowledge is power. Knowledge about another person, knowledge, that is, that the other person does not have is, surely power over that person. Does the therapeutic relationship truly require that a physician have power over his or her patient?

4. ADMISSIBILITY AT TRIAL

The admissibility of medical records as documentary evidence has already been discussed,[82] but some points bear brief repetition.

Legislation in most provinces permits the admission of hospital records into court as evidence provided that they are made in the usual and ordinary course of hospital business and at the time of the act or event recorded, or within a reasonable time afterwards.[83] Quite apart from any statutory admissibility, there is a great deal of case law indicating that there is little question as to the admissiblity of hospital records as proof of the facts stated therein.[84]

See also Lamothe v. Mokleby (1979), 106 D.L.R. (2d) 233 (Sask. Q.B.). See also Dworkin, Medical Records — Discovery, Confidentiality and Privacy (1979), 42 Mo. L. R. 88 at 90.

76 Jacob, Speller's Law Relating to Hospitals and Kindred Institutions 335 (1978).

77 LaPlante v. Matsqui-Sumas-Abbotsford Gen. Hosp. (1980), 23 B.C.L.R. 1 (S.C.); Morgan v. Fekete (1979), 25 O.R. (2d) 237 (S.C.); appeal dismissed by Hollingsworth J. April 10, 1979 at 237n. See also Reid v. Belzile unreported June 18, 1980 No. 550-05-000421 (Que. S.C.) cited in Knoppers, supra n. 70 at 411.

78 See supra.

79 See supra Chapter 1.

80 See Meredith, Malpractice Liability of Doctors and Hospitals 8 (1956); see also supra Chapter 1.

81 Supra n. 73 at 10. For an expression of concern about patient/prisoner access to medical records see Schiffer, Psychiatry Behind Bars 83-89 (1982). For the perspectives of patient, hospital administrator and others see (1981), 2 H.L. in C. 3-23.

82 See supra Chapter 6.

83 Evidence Act, R.S.B.C. 1979, c. 116, ss. 46, 47, 48; Evidence Act, R.S.M. 1970, c. E150, s. 58; Evidence Act, R.S.N.B. 1973, c. E-11, s. 49; Evidence Act, R.S.N.S. 1967, c. 94, s. 22; Evidence Act, R.S.O. 1980, c. 145, s. 35; Saskatchewan Evidence Act, R.S.S. 1978, c. S-16, ss. 30, 31, 32; Evidence Act, R.S.C. 1970, c. E-10, s. 30(1).

84 Kolesar v. Jeffries supra n. 2; Aynsley v. Toronto Gen. Hosp., [1968] 1 O.R. 425 (H.C.); Adderley v. Bremner, [1968] 1 O.R. 621 (H.C.); authorities listed supra ns. 13, 16-18; but

One aspect of *Ares v. Venner*[85] which raised some controversy was the fact that the records admitted also contained subjective observations, and this contributed to some confusion surrounding the admissibility of opinion evidence.[86] In some jurisdictions, the problem has been solved by legislation permitting a doctor to give evidence by report instead of appearing in court.[87]

see *Schweizer v. Central Hosp. supra* n. 14. *See* Ewart, *Documentary Evidence: The Admissibility At Common Law of Records Made Pursuant to a Business Duty* (1981), 59 C.B.R. 52.

85 [1970] S.C.R. 608.

86 *See Adderley v. Bremner supra* n. 84; *Aynsley v. Toronto Gen. Hosp. supra* n. 84; *Thompson v. Toorenburgh* (1973), 50 D.L.R. (3d) 717 (B.C.C.A.).

87 *Report on Evidence* 95-96 (1982). *See* Elliot, *Medical Evidence* (1968), 16 Chitty's L.J. 343; Lightbody, *Doctor in the Courtroom?* (1973) 31 Advocate 269; Smookler, *The Law* (1973), Medical Post, Oct. 14. *See also* Meredith, *supra* n. 80 at 36.

11

The Future

1. Will there be a "Crisis" in Canada?
2. Is there a Better System for Compensating Patients?
3. Proposals

1. WILL THERE BE A "CRISIS" IN CANADA?

The simple answer is that we do not have the information upon which to base an opinion.[1] The first step in obtaining an answer is to make a commitment to a Canadian perspective on the question. For while the United States has apparently suffered from a "malpractice crisis"[2] for years and there may be "no effective quarantine along the world's longest undefended border,"[3] let us be sure we have the disease before we take the medicine. Rozovsky[4] has said about the fear in Canada:

> The fear of such a crisis already exists in this country on the theory that what happens in the United States eventually takes place in Canada. This fear has led to irresponsible and uninformed public statements, unnecessary and sometimes foolish administrative actions and misguided legislative enactments.

---

1 Note that the situation has not changed since the first edition of this book in 1978.
2 Note that Richard Gerry, the President of the Association of Trial Lawyers of America, has characterized the crisis as a "malpractice insurance premium ripoff" and said in the Association's national publication *Trial*, June 1982 at 6:
"During the artificial medical malpractice "crisis" of the middle 1970s, the insurance companies based tremendous increases in premiums charged to the medical and related professions upon dire predictions for the late 1970s and the 1980s. These high premiums added to escalating health care costs. Today, by use of 20/20 hindsight, we know that their predictions were actuarially unsound and based upon assumptions not supported by fact. The reports of the insurance companies themselves as well as independent authorities indicate that there has been no dramatic increase in the number of malpractice cases or in losses paid by the insurance carriers."
3 Geekie, *The Crisis in Medical Malpractice: Will it Spread to Canada* (1975), 113 Can. Med. Assn. J. 327. *See also* Brooke Barnett, *Medical Malpractice: The American Disease. Is It Infectious?* (1980), 48 Med. Law J. 63.
4 Rozovsky, *Medical Malpractice in Canada* (1977), 1 L. Med. Q. 2. *See also* Fleming, *The Law of Torts* 105 (1983).

Once it is accepted that the first determination must be the state of affairs in *this* country, there must follow assessment of the information that is available and inquiry directed to those organizations which are seeking solutions.

Our situation cannot be analyzed with accuracy without reliable statistical information on the past. Unfortunately, however, the only source of statistics regarding legal actions brought against doctors and hospitals in Canada is the Canadian Medical Protective Association.[5] Canadian hospitals are insured through private companies and no national statistics on claims are available.[6]

Empirical studies are essential. In recent years a number of significant studies have been completed and this marks an exciting commitment to inter-disciplinary research.[7] Credit must also be given to earlier work such as that of the Sunnybrook Health Attitude Survey[8] which showed, among other things, that while 86 per cent of the patients surveyed believed that "doctors do a good job,"[9] most patients were greatly misinformed about health care benefits and costs.[10] The survey done by lawyers Sharpe and Gray[11] showed that over 90 per cent of Ontario doctors would stop to help an injured person whereas two polls of United States physicians found that 50 per cent of those who answered said they would not stop. The reason given for failing to stop was the same in both surveys: fear of a negligence action.[12] It seems clear that such research must expand, so that the significant facts can be found and conclusions can be drawn and tested.[13]

---

5 Note that private insurers are attempting to displace C.M.P.A. and should this occur less information would be available.

6 Rozovsky, *id.* at 3; *see* Kendrick, *Malpractice — The Insurance Problem* in *Canadian Hospital Association Papers and Proceedings of the National Conference on Health and the Law* 66 (1975), where a few figures are available.

7 Robertson, *Informed Consent In Canada: An Empirical Study* (1984), 22 O.H.L.J. (to be set); Christie, Hoffmaster, Bass and McCracken, *How Family Physicians Approach Ethical Problems* (1983), 16 Journal Family Prac. 1133; *Therapeutic Abortion and The Criminal Code: Physician Opinion Survey* (1983), 129 Can. Med. Assn. J. 1; Deschamps and Farley, *L'evalution Des Poursuites en Dommages — interets Contre Les Professionnels De La Sante* in *Le Medeun Du Quebec* October 1981 at 47; Magnet, *Withholding Treatment From Defective Newborns: A Description of Canadian Practices* (1980), 4 L. Med. Q 271; Harris and Tupper, *A Study of Therapeutic Abortion Committees in British Columbia* (1977), 11 U.B.C.L. Rev. 81; Centre de Droit Prive et Compare McGill University, *Interpretation de Certaines Donnees Relatives Aux Accidents Latrogeniques* (1978).

8 Le Riche et al. eds., *People Look at Doctors: The Sunnybrook Health Attitude Survey* (1971).

9 *Id.* at 102.

10 *Id. at 103.*

11 Gray and Sharpe, *Doctors, Samaritans and the Accident Victim* (1973), 11 Osgoode L.J. 1. Another Ontario study is reported in (1970), 3 *Report of the Ontario Committee on the Healing Arts* 71.

12 For the reasonableness of this fear *see supra* Chapter 4.

13 Note the recommendations of the Arthurs Committee in this regard in *Law and Learning* Report to the Social Sciences and Humanities Research Council of Canada (1983).

Groups have formed at both the local and national levels to face the medical-legal challenge, but they require co-ordination. Precious research funds and human resources must be used wisely, as duplication of research and competition in this regard benefits too few in the end. Moreover, groups formed primarily from the professions of law and medicine may tend to be too introspective; the public and patients must be a part of the search for information and solutions. The pressures and influences of special interest groups directed to achieving their goals at any cost must be resisted and balanced perspectives be sought on contentious topics.

There are now excellent publications available to the researcher in Canada. Credit must be given to the Law Reform Commission of Canada, to publishers and to university law reviews for the materials available on medical-legal topics. Canadians interested in learning about the state of the law in Canada can do so easily.[14] But further, legal and health care professionals who are dissatisfied with the law must make their views known in a form that encourages inter-disciplinary comment and, if necessary, law reform.

However, until we have more information any analysis or prediction regarding a "malpractice crisis" in Canada is not as reliable as it could and should be.

Having said this, an opinion is now ventured. At present we have many descriptions of the United States' malpractice crisis and excellent analyses of the factors responsible for its growth.[15] We also have Canadian authorities prepared to contrast and assess those with the situation in our own country.[16] As has been stated, because of a dearth of data all opinions are subjective.[17]

The factors which have been identified can be roughly grouped as arising from the legal process,[18] the insurance programs, the relationships between the professions and public attitudes and expectations. Within the legal process

---

14 An attempt has been made throughout the preceding chapters to refer to relevant Canadian materials. For the excellent publications of the Law Reform Commission of Canada write to 130 Albert Street, Ottawa, Canada K1A 0L6.

15 *See, for example,* Bernzweig, *Malpractice — The Situation in the U.S.* in *Canadian Hospital Association Papers and Proceedings of the National Conference on Health and The Law* 1 (1975); *see* Rozovsky, *supra* n. 4, for a description of the Commission on Medical Malpractice and the Rikecoff Report. *See* Gerry *supra* n. 2.

16 *See, for example,* Rozovsky, *supra* n. 4; Scott, *Malpractice — The Legal Situation* in *Canadian Hospital Association Papers and Proceedings of the National Conference on Health and The Law* 1 (1975); Geekie, *supra* n. 3; *see also* Haines, *The Medical Profession and the Adversary Process* (1973), 11 Osgoode L.J. 40. Sharpe and Sawyer, *Doctors and The Law* 245-61 (1978).

17 A good example is the opinions of the effect on the contingent fee which range from seeing it as a factor in a possible Canadian crisis to seeing it as assisting in maintaining the competence of doctors. *See* Minish, *The Contingent Fee: A Re-examinae* (1979), 10 Man. L.J. 65.

18 Some of the differences in the law itself such as that relating to informed consent, contributory negligence and *res ipsa loquitur* have been discussed.

there are great differences between Canada and the United States, ranging from the style of advocacy and use of the jury to the size of damage awards and the type of contingent fee used.[19] The absence of national health insurance in the United States[20] and the practices of the private insurance companies who cover doctors there are a striking contrast to our scheme of medicare and the Canadian Medical Protective Association.[21] The style of practice and inter-professional relations of doctors and lawyers are different in the United States.[22] No doubt some of the antagonism is the consequence of the crisis but the large numbers of professionals and the more business-like approach has led to a more competitive atmosphere wherein, for example, professional services are advertised and fees are paid directly by the patient.

Though the institutions of the two countries may diverge on these bases, citizens of both countries seem to share a belief that there is a breakdown in the doctor-patient relationship[23] and may also hold an unreasonable expectation of what the health care system can deliver.

Perhaps in our search for the answer to the question of whether there will be a ''malpractice crisis'' in Canada we can set up mechanisms to preclude it. But the cautious conclusion can be reached that we have not had, do not have and need not have a ''crisis'' in Canada.

---

19 It is as yet unclear whether rights set out in the Constitution Act, 1982, Part I: Canadian Charter of Rights and Freedoms will through judicial interpretation approach those enshrined in the Bill of Rights of the United States of America. *See* McDonald, *Legal Rights In the Canadian Charter of Rights and Freedoms* 2 (1982).

20 Canada has been the subject of a study by the U.S.: *see* Andreopoulos, *National Health Insurance: Can We Learn From Canada?* (1975).

21 See the comments of the President of the Association of Trial Lawyers of America *supra* n. 2. *See also* Scott, *Report of General Counsel For The Year 1982* in *C.M.P.A. Annual* Report 25 (1983).

22 Doctors are suing lawyers who have sued them. *See* Kisner, *Malicious Prosecution: An Effective Attack on Spurious Medical Malpractice Claims?* (1976), Case Western Reserve L.R. 653. Tillotson and Sagall, *The Physician Countersuit: ''More Than Having To Say You're Sorry''* (1977), 5 Medico Legal News 4; Higgs, *Physician Countersuits — A Solution To the Malpractice Dilemma?* (1978), 28 Drake L. Rev. 81; Rawson, *Wong v. Tabor: The Latest Word In Physician-Attorney Countersuits* (1983), 17 Valparaiso L. Rev. 755.

23 *Rozovsky, supra* n. 4 at 6.

Table 1

			CMPA Receipts, Actions and Expenditures				
Year	Dues $	No. of writs served	Awards settlements $	Legal costs $	Admin. costs $	Mem- bership	Average of awards, settlements $
1945	5	9	nil	6,216	3,608	3,367	
1950	5	11	11,770 (4 settlements)	7,616	8,214	6,389	2,942.50
1955	20	11	54,864 (3 awards & 9 settlements)	21,056	27,263	8,983	4,572.00
1960	20	16	49,259 (1 award & 5 settlements)	23,755	49,311	12,243	8,209.83
1965	15	49	168,119 (3 awards & 12 settlements)	67,553	93,134	15,940	11,207.93
1970	35	80	223,951 (8 awards & 21 settlements)	238,818	224,486	21,959	7,722.45
1971	35	131	276,292 (10 awards & 22 settlements)	251,924	218,988	23,668	8,634.13
1972	50	152	253,371 (4 awards & 29 settlements)	427,250	312,555	24,945	7,677.91
1973	50	168	325,087 (2 awards & 32 settlements)	441,662	310,685	26,588	9,561.38
1974	50	220	896,858 (9 awards & 58 settlements)	664,116	391,492	29,096	13,385.95
1975	100	229	951,609 (9 awards & 43 settlements)	766,916	487,282	30,022	18,300.17
1976	200	234	2,664,103 (7 awards & 64 settlements)	1,119,657	686,100	31,421	37,522.58
1977	200	269	2,336,962 (6 awards & 64 settlements)	1,143,121	695,382	31,591	33,385.17
1978	250	323	1,211,038 (14 awards & 67 settlements)	1,455,589	792,183	32,175	14,951.09
1979	250	343	5,273,501 (17 awards & 92 settlements)	1,834,392	961,567	33,202	48,380.74
1980	250	452	3,493,392 (8 awards & 121 settlements)	2,495,989	1,170,819	34,375	27,080.56
1981	350	501	5,276,831 (11 awards & 127 settlements)	3,750,616	1,358,632	35,335	38,237.91
1982	500	516	5,958,001 (9 awards & 144 settlements)	4,532,292	1,713,913	37,317	38,941.18

However, Table I containing statistics available in the Canadian Medical Protective Association Annual Reports[24] documents a dramatic increase in moneys paid out to patients and lawyers. Also, the number of cases settled has risen gradually from 22 in 1971 to 144 in 1982. By comparison the number of actions litigated and lost has not been changed much (except in 1979) with the number being ten in 1971 and nine in 1982. In 1982, C.M.P.A. paid damages in 153 cases based on a membership of 37,317. Thus statistically, 1 out of every 244 doctors was successfully sued.

Although the number of suits litigated and lost is low, having averaged nine per year over the last ten years, the increase in suits settled and writs served requires comment. Since C.M.P.A. settles only claims considered to be valid it follows that there has been an increase in the number of cases where patients merited compensation. The number of writs served on members in 1982 increased nearly four-fold from 1971. Patients are suing more frequently. The increase in suits and no doubt in legal fees explains the increase in legal costs.

The increase in moneys paid out as damages is of concern to doctors and the C.M.P.A. In 1982 the average was $38,941 per suit whereas in 1971 it was $8,634. A possible explanation is that in 1978 the Supreme Court of Canada in a trilogy of cases set out certain rules for the assessment of damages which result in large awards to very seriously injured persons.[25] Another important factor is the increase in the consumer price index which affects many of the bases of damage assessment.[26]

In order to carry out its future responsibilities to members, the C.M.P.A. has just instituted a revised fee schedule to reflect the variation in risk of suits and costliness of types of injuries caused by various medical specialties.[27] The highest risk area includes anaesthesia, cardiovascular surgery, family medicine (with anaesthesia and/or obstetrics constituting more than 30 per cent of work), neurosurgery, obstetrics and orthopaedic surgery while the lowest risk group are in administrative, laboratory or physical medicine, or public health. The new proposed annual fee range is $400 to $2,900 and $300 for interns and residents. The classification seems consistent with the risks seen in the case

---

24 The Canadian Medical Protective Association is a mutual defence organization established in 1901 which gives members advice, legal assistance and pays in full court awards, settlements and costs. Over 80 per cent of Canadian doctors are members. *See The Canadian Medical Protective Association and Its Proposed Funding Policy* (1983).

25 *Andrews v. Grand & Toy (Alta.) Ltd.* (1978), 3 C.C.L.T. 225 (S.C.C.); *Thornton v. Bd. School Trustees of Prince George* (1978), 3 C.C.L.T. 257 (S.C.C.); *Arnold v. Teno* (1978), 3 C.C.L.T. 272 (S.C.C.). For a thorough analysis *see* Charles, *The Supreme Court of Canada Handbook on Assessment of Damages in Personal Injury Cases* (1982). For an excellent discussion of the new approach to paying damages, the structured settlement, *see* Foster, *Structured Settlements* (1982), 20 A.L.R. 434.

26 Scott, *Report of General Counsel For The Year 1979* in *C.M.P.A. Annual Report* 22 (1979).

27 *See supra* n. 24.

law outlined in earlier chapters with the exception of the categorization of interns and residents who would, however, also be covered by insurance carried by a hospital employer.

It is to be hoped that Canadian doctors affected by this marked increase in the fees of their co-operative association will recognize it as reasonable and responsible planning by an administration that has served the professional well for over 80 years.[28]

In summary, while more patients are suing not many more are winning in court. C.M.P.A. has had to settle more suits, ostensibly because they were justified claims. Seriously injured patients will now be awarded higher sums by the courts and the cost of legal advice and assistance has risen with the increased activity.[29]

All of the above viewed in the perspective of the accountability of professionals in general, the new approach to damage assessment, and the economic situation in Canada places doctors in no worse legal position than other professionals in Canada.

2. IS THERE A BETTER SYSTEM FOR COMPENSATING PATIENTS?

Much criticism has been levelled against the present system where a patient must initiate and pursue a legal action against a doctor or hospital in order to obtain compensation for personal injuries.[30] Recently a number of respected judges expressed regret that a patient deserving of compensation is precluded from it by the present requirements of tort law. They have suggested that reform is required.[31] The lawsuit against a doctor or hospital is costly, slow, and complex, although it is still seen to serve useful purposes including the setting and maintaining of standards of medical care.[32]

---

28 The C.M.P.A. has been a major factor in precluding a "malpractice crisis" for Canadian doctors.

29 Note that in its *1982 Annual Report* the British counterpart of the C.M.P.A., the Medical Defence Union states at p. 9:

"In the last five years and allowing for the increasing membership, there has been a significant increase in the number of calls on our services. The cost of dealing with each claim has more than doubled in four years and both legal costs (a large element in our budget) and administrative costs have escalated with inflation."

30 For an excellent analysis *see* Taylor, *The Doctor and Negligence* 141-44 (1971). *See also* Sharpe, *Alternatives to the Court Process for Resolving Medical Malpractice Claims* (1981), McGill L.J. 1036 at 1042.

31 *Davidson v. Connaught Laboratories* (1980), 14 C.C.L.T. 251 at 281 (Ont. S.C.) *per* Linden J.; *Ferguson v. Hamilton Civic Hosp.* (1983), 23 C.C.L.T. 254 at 313 (Ont. H.C.) *per* Krever J.; *Le Procureur General v. LaPierre et Merck, Sharp Ltd.* unreported October 26, 1983 No. 500-09-000935-791 (Que. C.A.).

32 Kretzmer, *The Malpractice Suit: It It Needed?* (1973), 11 Osgoode L.J. 55; Pritchard, *Professional Civil Liability and Continuing Competence* in *Studies in Canadian Tort Law*

The no-fault scheme has become the Cinderella sister of the tort action. There is a plethora of opinion[33] on the topic in regard to motor vehicle accidents. No-fault schemes exist in Canada, for example, workers' compensation schemes and portions of automobile insurance plans. New Zealand has in place a plan that includes coverage for medical, surgical, dental or first-aid misadventure.[34] As the literature and the experience referred to point out, no-fault schemes for medical accidents are, too, fraught with difficulties.[35]

Many concerned and knowledgeable Canadians have expressed the view that there should be a study of the alternatives to the lawsuit for providing for the compensation of injured patients.[36] One possibility is a no-fault scheme.[37] Another is a combination of the tort action and a compensation plan.[38] A practical alternative may be a compulsory arbitration process.[39] In the end a reworking of the present system may be the answer.[40] A joint study by the medical and legal professions is required — soon.

3.   PROPOSALS

Meanwhile we must endeavour to improve the civil litigation system so that it is made as fair as it can be to patients, health care professionals and hospitals. Specific recommendations have been made throughout this book, but taking the larger view, the following recommendations seem appropriate:

(i) We must find and develop our own law. Excellent Canadian legislation and case law does exist and could assist in dealing with current and recurrent medical-legal problems, but it appears that it is not always found. The research done by lawyers in preparing cases could be improved. On most topics there is Canadian jurisprudence much more appropriate to our society than that being transplanted from, for example, the United States. Furthermore,

---

377 (1977); *see also* Linden, *The Negligent Doctor* (1973), 11 Osgoode L.J. 31 at 39; Linden, *Reconsidering Tort Law As Ombudsman* in *Issues in Tort Law* 1 at 3 (Steel and Rodgers-Magnet ed. 1983).

33 For a thorough discussion with references to many other research sources, *see* Linden, *Canadian Tort Law* 609-47 (1982).

34 Woodhouse, *Compensation for Personal Injury in New Zealand* in *Report of the Royal Commission* (1967). For excellent commentaries *see* Klar, *New Zealand's Accident Compensation Scheme: A Tort Lawyer's Perspective* in *Issues In Tort Law* 25 at 31 (Steel and Rodgers-Magnet ed. 1983); Ison, *Accident Compensation* 36 (1980).

35 Ehrenzweig, *Compulsory "Hospital-Accident" Insurance: A Needed First Step Toward the Displacement of Liability for Medical Malpractice* (1964), 31 U. Chi. L. Rev. 279. *See* Sharpe *supra* n. 30 at 1041. *See* the comments of Laycraft J. reported in *The Future of Personal Injury Compensation* 22 (Saunders ed. 1978). "This [a no-fault scheme] simply envisages the development of another court; only the name is changed."

36 For a discussion of the studies in the U.S. *see* Louisell and Williams, *Medical Malpractice*, Matthew Bender, New York (1982) at 12-12.9.

37 *See* Haines, *supra* n. 16 at 52. *See* Sharpe *supra* n. 30 at 1041.

38 *See* Kretzmer, *supra* n. 32 at 79.

39 *See* Sharpe *supra* n. 30 at 1037.

40 See the comment of Mr. Justice Laycraft of the Court of Appeal of Alberta *supra* n. 35.

we should resist any further move to develop a sub-category of legal principles unique to medical-legal issues.[41]

We need more and better judgments to settle medical-legal issues and make the law more predictable. In the past the Supreme Court of Canada has heard very few cases in this area and those decisions sometimes failed to clarify important issues.[42]

There are some excellent recommendations for the reform of federal and provincial legislation and for new legislation. But politicians must act more promptly in bringing forward legislation that is needed.

(ii) We must have more data on issues of concern. As discussed, more statistics are required on the liability of health care professionals and hospitals in Canada. The results of studies must be heeded. An excellent recent study with profound implications for law and medicine was done by Professor Robertson.[43] He sent a seven-page questionnaire to 1,000 Canadian surgeons (620 were returned) asking questions about informed consent and medical practice. He concluded, in part, that recent Supreme Court of Canada cases have had little impact on medical practice. The best efforts of the C.M.P.A. and the many reports in the media have not been successful in alerting this group to the new law. In any case the majority expressed views incompatible with the principles outlined by the Supreme Court of Canada.

(iii) We must enter into and foster new relationships and associations. Too much emphasis has been placed on the differences between doctors and lawyers. Given the common goal of providing the best possible lifestyle for each member of our society these differences pale. Numerous examples exist of the two professions working well together and in conjunction with other health care professionals: medical-legal societies in many Canadian cities, national conferences on health law, sessions on medical-legal topics at conventions, the Canadian Bar Association/Canadian Medical Association liaison committee, the participation of noted Canadian authorities in meetings and seminars. New inter-disciplinary groups must be formed in areas of common and special interest: forensic medicine, sports medicine and psychiatry are obvious examples. The publications of each profession should expand their terms of reference and invite more contributions from others.

More must be done to encourage association among those in the health care professions also. The team approach in health care raises the need of each professional to appreciate the parameters of his or her legal responsibility. Lectures and seminars to all health care professions serving in a hospital can

---

41 *See supra* Chapter 3.
42 Weiler, *Groping Towards A Canadian Tort Law: The Role of the Supreme Court of Canada* (1971), 21 U.T.L.J. 267.
43 *Supra* n. 7.

be most effective. The old fear that each professional will be unresponsive in the company of others is not valid.

However, an advancement in the relationships among those mentioned above leaves a void unless the patient is considered. It seems trite to say that the patient is the raison d'être of the health care system, but this fact seems to be forgotten. Associations of citizens or patients should not be feared but fostered. Lawyers, doctors and other health care professionals should be prepared to work with them and to join them.

(iv) We must work to improve the legal process. Steps have been taken to try to expedite litigation to meet the criticism of slowness and to extend legal aid coverage to answer the cry that it is too costly. Hopefully more will be done. Systems to allow patients better access to doctors who will assess their claims and, if necessary, testify, must be tested and strengthened. If the adversary systems is to work properly, patients' lawyers must become more specialized and perhaps share expertise.

More information about the law and the legal process should reach students in medicine and other health care professions. A few faculties and schools make it part of their curricula. Innovative approaches such as moots on health care topics work very well. Many concerns could be alleviated if time were made for the legal education of health care professionals.

(v) We must communicate. When we fail to realize and utilize opportunities to communicate, we create our own problems. A review of Canadian cases against doctors and hospitals illustrates that in most cases there was a breakdown in communication with the patient. This should serve as a warning to lawyers about their relationships with clients, doctors and other health care professionals. Misunderstanding and hostility grow out of ignorance.

Communication might mean the doctor speaking to the patient the night before surgery, or after the risk has materialized, but it could also mean determining with a colleague who will take responsibility for reading the test results of a common patient.

Communication could also mean the lawyer going to the doctor's office to discuss the medical-legal report and to prepare him to be examined on his qualifications.

Communication should mean the doctor and lawyer being prepared to participate in lectures to students and talks to patients' groups.

Communication alone, however, may not be enough without good will and the sense that to be a professional means to serve the needs of society.

Appendices

NOTES ON THE USE OF THE APPENDICES*

Purpose

The ultimate use of these appendices is to assist researchers in locating Canadian cases dealing with the legal liability of doctors, dentists, hospitals and hospital employees. To this end, reported and unreported decisions, primarily from the common law in Canada have been abridged (Appendix II) and indexed in a variety of ways to facilitate access (Appendix I).

Structure

Traditional medical malpractice or negligence actions occupy the bulk of these appendices, constituting the vast majority of cases in which doctors and hospitals are subjected to legal scrutiny. In response to the usual legal approaches to problems of this nature, Appendix I has been divided into three parts which stand independently but are cross-indexed by common variables. Appendix IA lists the wide variety of defendants who have been directly or indirectly involved in medical negligence proceedings. Appendix IB focuses on the various medical, dental or nursing procedures from which malpractice law suits have arisen. Appendix IC isolates the injuries suffered, allegedly as a result of negligent medical care or treatment. Each of these indices is cross-referenced with the variables of the other two, and indicates whether or not liability was found, and the name of the case.

Appendix II consists of abridgments of all of the cases indexed in Appendix I including a citation, exposition of the facts, and holding of the court for each one.

Appendix IA — Defendant Type

"Defendant" for the purposes of this index includes any health care professional whose conduct was directly in issue, whether or not he was actually sued. Where the "defendant" was not a party to the action, this is expressly noted.

Hospitals are also included as defendants, although in most cases the liability of the hospital for the acts of its employees is vicarious rather than direct.

Doctors are grouped together and then subdivided into the various specialties; the category of "surgeon" is further divided. Because of the often vague designation attached to the defendant by the judge, a precise assessment is sometimes impossible. Categories of "general practitioner" and, for the subcategory of surgeon, "general surgeon," serve as "default" categories as well as including defendants specifically designated as such.

Appendix IB — Procedure Complained Of

Medical procedures are divided into six broad categories: Administration of Anaesthetic, Care, Consultation, Diagnosis, Referral and Treatment, with numerous subcategories subsumed under each.

"Care" by a doctor is indexed independently of care in a hospital, although some redundancy arises where the conduct of both the doctor and the hospital staff are at issue. "Care" for the purposes of this appendix primarily includes pre-operative, during and post-operative procedures, and supervision and control of patients.

"Diagnosis" is divided into situations where the proper diagnosis was not made, and diagnostic procedures negligently carried out. Surgical diagnostic procedures are listed under surgical treatment, but non-surgical diagnostic tests are not listed in the "Treatment" category.

Under the "Treatment" heading, "injection" and "medication" constitute distinct categories, the former indicating that the injection itself allegedly caused the injury, the latter including those cases where the nature of the medication was such as allegedly to result in the injury suffered. Surgical treatment is further subdivided according to the medical name (where available) or to the description provided in the judgment.

Appendix IC — Injury Suffered

Injuries are divided into numerous categories, with a certain degree of redundancy and "pointers" built in to aid in locating relevant information.

"Injury" for the purposes of this appendix includes all injuries complained of and not merely the ultimate result. For example, where the administration of an inappropriate medication induces cardiac arrest in the patient, resulting in brain damage, "injury" will include both of these "events."

As with Appendices IA and IB, some discretion has been exercised, and liberty taken with the *verbatim* descriptions contained in judgments, in order to group cases more effectively. However, the abridgments in Appendix II normally reflect the exact descriptions used in the judgment.

"Further treatment required" includes cases in which the only injury complained of was the need to undergo further medical treatment, or in which the judgment expressly mentioned this as an injury. "Pain and suffering" includes those cases where the action is for damages for mental suffering, or where specific reference was made in the judgment.

In Appendix I, a single asterisk (*) in the "Liability" column indicates that the issue of consent was dealt with in addition to that of negligent conduct. A double asterisk (**) indicates that the case turned entirely on a consent issue.

*The author wishes to thank Brent Windwick and Ursula Tauscher of the Health Law Project, University of Alberta for their work in abridging and indexing the material which appears in this section. They were assisted by the work of Leslie McGuffin and Kerrie Logan from the earlier edition.

PROCEDURE	INJURY	LIAB.	CASE NAME
DEFENDANT: CHIROPRACTOR			
Diagnosis: Failure to diagnose appendicitis	*Death*	No	*R. v. Homeberg*
Diagnosis: Failure to diagnose	*Not specified*	Yes	*Morrow v. McGillivray*
Diagnosis: Failure to diagnose tuberculosis of spinal column	*Further Treatment Req'd:* Aggravated condition	Yes	*Gibbons v. Harris*
Treatment	*Pain & Suffering*	No	*Rutledge v. Fisher*
Treatment: Chiropractic	*Further Treatment Req'd:* Unsuccessful treatment	No	*Cawley v. Mercer*
Treatment: Chiropractic	*Further Treatment Req'd:* Unsuccessful treatment *Pain & Suffering*	Yes	*Penner v. Theobald*
Treatment: Chiropractic	*Paralysis:* Paraplegia	No*	*Strachan v. Simpson*
DEFENDANT: DENTIST			
Care: Dentist: During treatment: "hand over mouth"	*Pain & Suffering* *Scarring/deformity:* Face	No	*Lafleche v. Larouche*
Care: Dentist: During treatment: Sponges	*Death:* Asphyxia	Yes	*Nesbitt v. Holt*
Consultation: Failure to consult specialist	*Dental:* Extraction: Unnecessary	Yes	*Parmley v. Parmley*
Treatment: Dental: Crown and bridge	*Further Treatment Req'd:* Corrective dental	No	*Allard v. Boykowich*
Treatment: Dental: Crown and bridge	*Further Treatment Req'd:* Corrective dental	Yes	*Fluevog v. Pottinger*
Treatment: Dental: Extraction	*Cardiovascular/circulatory:* Bleeding	No*	*Murrin v. Janes*
Treatment: Dental: Extraction	*Death:* Asphyxia	Yes	*Nesbitt v. Holt*
Treatment: Dental: Extraction	*Dental:* Damage *Further Treatment Req'd:* Unsuccessful Treatment *Pain & Suffering*	Yes	*Drinnen v. Douglas*
Treatment: Dental: Extraction	*Dental:* Extraction: Additional Teeth	No*	*Guimond v. Laberge*

PROCEDURE	INJURY	LIAB.	CASE NAME
Treatment: Dental: Extraction	*Dental:* Extraction: Additional Teeth	No*	*Boase v. Paul*
Treatment: Dental: Extraction	*Dental:* Extraction: Permanent Tooth	Yes	*Gagnon v. Stortini*
Treatment: Dental: Extraction	*Dental:* Extraction: Unauthorized	No*	*Nykiforuk v. Lockwood*
Treatment: Dental: Extraction	*Dental:* Extraction: Unnecessary	Yes	*Murano v. Gray*
Treatment: Dental: Extraction	*Further Treatment Req'd:* Corrective Surgery	New Trial	*McTaggart v. Powers*
Treatment: Dental: Extraction	*Further Treatment Req'd:* Pain & Suffering	No	*Legault-Belle-mare v. Madore*
Treatment: Dental: Extraction	*Nerve:* Facial: Numbness	No	*Schinz v. Dickinson*
Treatment: Dental: Extraction	*Nerve:* Facial Numbness/hypersensitivity *Pain & Suffering*	**	*Rawlings v. Lindsay*
Treatment: Dental: Extraction	*Pain & Suffering*	No	*Kobescak v. Chan*
Treatment: Dental: Restorative surgery	*Scarring/deformity:* Lip	No	*Dunn v. Young*

DEFENDANT: DOCTOR
I ANAESTHETIST

Administration of Anaesthetic: Chloroform	*Death*	No	*Fleckney v. DeBrisay*
Administration of Anaesthetic: Experimental	*Brain Damage:* Cardiac Arrest	Yes*	*Halushka v. University of Sask.*
Administration of Anaesthetic: General	*Brain Damage*	No	*Hôpital Gen. de la Region de L'Amiante v. Perron*
Administration of Anaesthetic: General	*Brain Damage:* Cardiac Arrest	No	*Leadbetter v. Brand*
Administration of Anaesthetic: General	*Burn Scarring/Deformity*	Yes	*Crits v. Sylvester*
Administration of Anaesthetic: General	*Death:* Asphyxia	Yes*	*Kangas v. Parker*
Administration of Anaesthetic: General	*Death:* Cardiac Arrest	No	*McKay v. Gilchrist*

PROCEDURE	INJURY	LIAB.	CASE NAME
Administration of Anaesthetic: Injection	*Amputation:* Hand	Yes	*Villeneuve v.* *Sisters of* *St. Joseph*
Administration of Anaesthetic: Injection	*Further Treatment Req'd:* Corrective Skin Grafts *Pain & Suffering* *Scarring/Deformity:* Hand	No	*Lloy v.* *Milner*
Administration of Anaesthetic: Injection	*Pain & Suffering* *Assault/Battery*	No* New Trial	*Allan v.* *New Mt. Sinai* *Hosp.*
Administration of Anaesthetic: Injection	*Paralysis:* Legs	No	*Girard v.* *Royal Columbian* *Hosp.*
Administration of Anaesthetic: Injection	*Paralysis:* Paraplegia	Yes	*Martel v.* *Hotel-Dieu* *St. Vallier*
Administration of Anaesthetic: Injection	*Infection:* Abscess	Yes	*Hughston v.* *Jost*
Administration of Anaesthetic: Intubation	*Death:* Cardiac Arrest	No	*Webster v.* *Armstrong*
Administration of Anaesthetic: Intubation	*Dental:* Damage	Yes*	*Gorback v.* *Ting*
Administration of Anaesthetic: Post-anaesthesia recovery	*Brain Damage*	No	*Laidlaw v.* *Lions Gate Hosp.*
Administration of Anaesthetic: Post-anaesthesia recovery	*Death:* Cardiac Arrest	No	*Krujelis v.* *Esdale*
Administration of Anaesthetic: Spinal	*Death*	No	*Walker v.* *Bedard*
Administration of Anaesthetic: Spinal	*Paralysis:* Paraplegia	Yes	*Beausoleil v.* *Soeurs de la* *Charité*
Administration of Anaesthetic: Transtracheal ventilation	*Infection:* Tissue emphysema	Yes*	*Holmes v.* *Bd. of Hosp.* *Trustees of* *London*
Care: Doctor: During Treatment	*Brain Damage:* Cardiac Arrest	Yes	*Aynsley v.* *Toronto Gen.* *Hosp.*
Care: Doctor: During treatment	*Death:* Cardiac Arrest	No	*MacKinnon v.* *Ignacio*

PROCEDURE	INJURY	LIAB.	CASE NAME
II DERMATOLOGIST			

Care: Doctor
  Case management
Diagnosis: Failure to diagnose
  cancer
	Further Treatment Req'd:
	Aggravated Condition
	Pain & Suffering
		Yes	*Barr v.*
			Hughes

Referral: Follow-up care *Treatment:* Medication Prescription	*Senses:* Sight: Loss	Apportioned	*Crossman v.* *Stewart*
Treatment: Dermatological Slush	*Scarring/Deformity:* Face	No*	*Johnston v.* *Wellesley Hosp.*
III EMERGENCY ROOM PHYSICIAN			
Care: Doctor Emergency	*Paralysis:* Quadriplegia	No	*Nash v.* *Olson*
Diagnosis: Failure to diagnose diabetes	*Death:* Cardiac Arrest	No	*Neufville v.* *Sobers*
Diagnosis: Failure to diagnose epiglottitis	*Death:* Epiglottitis	Yes	*Demoura v.* *Mississauga* *Hosp.*
Diagnosis: Failure to diagnose hemorrhage	*Death:* Hemorrhage	Yes	*Wade v.* *Nayernouri*
Treatment: Medication Administration	*Brain Damage*	Settled	*Yepremian v.* *Scarborough Gen.* *Hosp.*
IV GASTROENTEROLOGIST			
Treatment: Medication Administration	*Cardiovascular/circulatory:* Avascular Necrosis	No*	*Moore v.* *Shaughnessy Hosp.*
Treatment: Medication Prescription	*Bone:* Avascular Necrosis Corrective Surgery	Yes	*Reynard v.* *Carr*
V GENERAL PRACTITIONER			
Administration of Anaesthetic: Injection	*Death:* Injection of wrong drug	No	*Bugden v.* *Harbour View* *Hosp.*
Administration of Anaesthetic: Spinal	*Death*	No	*Walker v.* *Bedard*
Care: Assignment of responsibilities	*Death:* Peritonitis *Infection*	Yes	*Wilson v.* *Stark*
Care: Doctor: During operation	*Pain & Suffering*	No	*Pierce v.* *Strathroy Hosp.*
Care: Doctor: During treatment	*Further Treatment Req'd:* Corrective Surgery	Yes	*Gloning v.* *Miller*
Care: Doctor: General	Fall	No	*McKay v.* *Royal Inland* *Hosp.*

PROCEDURE	INJURY	LIAB.	CASE NAME
Care: Doctor: Post-treatment	*Amputation:* Testicle *Infection:* Gangrene	Yes	*Thomas v. Scarborough Gen. Hosp.*
Care: Doctor: Post-treatment	*Bone:* Leg: Displacement *Scarring/deformity:* Leg	No	*Rickley v. Stratton*
Care: Doctor: Post-treatment	*Cardiovascular/circulatory:* Bleeding		*Tacknyk v. Lake of the Woods Clinic*
Care: Doctor: Post-treatment	*Cardiovascular/circulatory:* Bleeding	No	*McCulligh v. McLean*
Care: Doctor: Post-treatment	*Infection:* Peritonitis *Further Treatment Req'd:* Corrective Surgery	Yes*	*Gonda v. Kerbel*
Care: Doctor: Supervision	*Bone:* Hip: Fracture	No	*Robinson v. Annapolis Gen. Hosp.*
Care: Doctor: Supervision	*Brain Damage*	Yes	*Foote v. Royal Columbian Hosp.*
Consultation: Failure to consult dentist	*Dental:* Extraction Unnecessary	Yes*	*Parmley v. Parmley*
Consultation: Failure to consult specialist	*Amputation:* Foot *Infection:* Gangrene	Yes	*Vail v. MacDonald*
Consultation: Failure to consult specialist	*Further Treatment Req'd:* Aggravated Condition *Paralysis:* Leg	No	*Thomas v. Port Colborne Gen. Hosp.*
Consultation: Failure to consult specialist	*Pain & Suffering*	Yes	*Daoust v. R.*
Diagnosis: Failure to diagnose appendicitis	*Infection:* Peritonitis *Death*	No	*Wilson v. Stark*
Diagnosis: Failure to diagnose appendicitis	*Infection:* Peritonitis *Death*	Yes	*Bergen v. Sturgeon Gen. Hosp. et al.*
Diagnosis: Failure to diagnose arteriosclerosis	*Amputation:* Leg	No	*Harquail v. Sedgewick*
Diagnosis: Failure to diagnose diabetes	*Birth Defects*	No	*Quiroz v. Austrup*
Diagnosis: Failure to diagnose diabetes	*Brain Damage*	Settled	*Yepremian v. Scarborough Gen. Hosp.*
Diagnosis: Failure to diagnose diabetes	*Cardiovascular/circulatory:* Endocarditis	No	*Nichols v. Gray*

PROCEDURE	INJURY	LIAB.	CASE NAME
Diagnosis: Failure to diagnose dislocated hip	*Joint:* Hip: Slipped femoral capital epiphysis	No	*Bruinooge v. Collier*
Diagnosis: Failure to diagnose dislocated hip	*Joint:* Hip: Displacement	Yes	*Dangerfield v. David*
Diagnosis: Failure to diagnosis dislocated shoulder (doctor not party)	*Further Treatment Req'd:* Unsuccessful treatment	Yes	*Thompson v. Columbia Coast Mission*
Diagnosis: Failure to diagnose dislocated wrist	*Joint:* Wrist/Hand Impaired movement	Apportioned	*Osburn v. Mohindra*
Diagnosis: Failure to diagnose encephalitis	*Brain Damage*	No	*Tiesmaki v. Wilson*
Diagnosis: Failure to diagnose fractured ankle	*Joint:* Ankle	No	*Price v. Milawski*
Diagnosis: Failure to diagnose fractured arm	*Further Treatment Req'd:* Corrective	Yes	*Armstrong v. Dawson*
Diagnosis: Failure to diagnose fractured finger	*Further Treatment Req'd:* Corrective Surgery *Scarring/Deformity:* Finger	Yes	*Pepin v. Hôpital du Haut Richelieu*
Diagnosis: Failure to diagnose fractured foot	*Pain & Suffering*	Yes	*Daoust v. R.*
Diagnosis: Failure to diagnose fractured hip	*Amputation:* Leg	Yes	*Cusson v. Robidoux*
Diagnosis: Failure to diagnose fractured hip	*Not Specified*	No	*Stamper v. Rhindress*
Diagnosis: Failure to diagnose fractured spine	*Further Treatment Req'd:* Aggravated Condition *Paralysis:* Leg	Yes	*Thomas v. Port Colborne Gen. Hosp.*
Diagnosis: Failure to diagnose hemorrhage	*Death:* Hemorrhage	No	*Serre v. DeTilly*
Diagnosis: Failure to diagnose heart disease	*Death:* Cardiac Arrest	No	*Ehler v. Smith*
Diagnosis: Failure to diagnose infection	*Death*	No	*R. v. Watson*
Diagnosis: Failure to diagnose infection	*Pain & Suffering* *Scarring/deformity:* Groin	Yes	*Wine v. Dawyd*
Diagnosis: Failure to diagnose internal injuries	*Death*	No	*Rodych v. Krasey*
Diagnosis: Failure to diagnose mastoiditis	*Paralysis:* Face *Senses:* Hearing: Impaired Sight: Impaired	No	*Jarvis v. Int. Nickel Co.*

PROCEDURE	INJURY	LIAB.	CASE NAME
Diagnosis: Failure to diagnose meningitis	*Death:* Meningitis	Yes	*Dale v. Munthali*
Diagnosis: Failure to diagnose multiple gestation	*Birth Defects*	Yes	*Wipfli v. Britten*
Diagnosis: Failure to diagnose pelvic inflammatory disease	*Disease:* Pelvic Inflammatory Disease *Removal:* Fallopian tubes	No	*Mudrie v. McDonald*
Diagnosis: Failure to diagnose pleurisy	*Further Treatment Req'd:* Corrective Surgery *Disease:* Pleurisy	No	*Richardson v. Nugent*
Diagnosis: Failure to diagnose poisoning	*Death:* Poisoning: Carbon Monoxide	No	*Ostash v. Sonnenberg*
Diagnosis: Failure to diagnose	*Senses:* Sight: Impairment	No	*Bell v. R.*
Diagnosis: Incorrect diagnosis of cancer	*Removal:* Mastectomy *Pain & Suffering*	Admitted	*Down v. Royal Jubilee Hosp.*
Diagnosis: Incorrect diagnosis of infection	*Amputation:* Leg	Yes	*Layden v. Cope*
Diagnosis: Procedure Biopsy	*Paralysis:* Vocal Chord	No	*Finlay v. Auld*
Diagnosis: Procedure Fluoroscopy	*Burn:* Back	New Trial	*Abel v. Cooke*
Diagnosis: Procedure Fluoroscopy	*Further Treatment Req'd:* Corrective	Yes	*Armstrong v. Dawson*
Diagnosis: Procedure Sigmoidoscopy	*Further Treatment Req'd:* Corrective Surgery *Infection:* Peritonitis	Yes*	*Gonda v. Kerbel*
Diagnosis: Procedure X-ray	*Burn:* Hand	Yes	*Hochman v. Willinsky*
Diagnosis: Procedure X-ray	*Burn:* Hand/Leg	No	*Antoniuk v. Smith*
Diagnosis: Procedure X-ray	*Joint:* Wrist: Fracture	Yes	*Baltzan v. Fidelity Ins.*
Referral: Failure to refer to specialist	*Amputation:* Leg	No	*Harquail v. Sedgewick*
Referral: Failure to refer to specialist	*Amputation:* Leg	Yes	*Layden v. Cope*
Referral: Failure to refer to specialist	*Paralysis:* Face *Senses:* Sight/Hearing Impairment	No	*Jarvis v. Int. Nickel Co.*

PROCEDURE	INJURY	LIAB.	CASE NAME
Referral: Failure to refer to specialist	*Senses:* Sight/Impairment	No	*Bell v. R.*
Referral: Failure to refer to specialist	*Senses:* Sight/Impairment	Admitted	*Eaglebach v. Walters*
Referral: Followup care	*Senses:* Sight/loss *Further Treatment Req'd:* Corrective Surgery	No	*Beninger v. Walton*
Treatment: Diet	*Death:* Malnutrition	Yes	*R. v. Rogers*
Treatment: Experimental quartz lamp	*Amputation:* Foot *Infection:* Gangrene	Yes	*Baills v. Boulanger*
Treatment: General: Hand	*Further Treatment Req'd:* Corrective Surgery	No	*Hearne v. Flood*
Treatment: Heat: Kelly pad	*Burn:* Back	No.	*Lenzen v. South Vancouver Island Hosp.*
Treatment: Injection: Anaesthetic	*Death:* Injection of wrong drug	No	*Bugden v. Harbour View Hosp.*
Treatment: Injection: Medication	*Burn:* Hand *Further Treatment Req'd:* Corrective Surgery	No	*Neufeld v. McQuitty*
Treatment: Injection: Vaccination	*Disease:* Septicaemia	Yes	*Adderley v. Bremner*
Treatment: Injection: Vaccination	*Further Treatment Req'd:* Corrective Surgery *Paralysis:* Arm *Scarring/deformity:* Arm	Yes	*Cardin v. Montreal*
Treatment: Medication: Administration	*Brain Damage*	Settled	*Yepremian v. Scarborough Gen. Hosp.*
Treatment: Medication: Administration	*Paralysis:* Paraplegia	No	*Davidson v. Connaught Lab.*
Treatment: Medication: Administration	Insulin Shock	Yes	*Marshall v. Rogers*
Treatment: Medication: Prescription	*Bone:* Avascular Necrosis Corrective Surgery	Apportioned	*Reynard v. Carr*
Treatment: Medication: Prescription	*Poisoning*	No	*Stretton v. Holmes*
Treatment: Medication: Prescription	*Senses:* Sight: Loss	Apportioned	*Crossman v. Stewart*

PROCEDURE	INJURY	LIAB.	CASE NAME
Treatment: Obstetrical: Caesarian section	*Further Treatment Req'd:* Corrective Surgery	Yes	*Gloning v. Miller*
Treatment: Obstetrical: Delivery	*Birth Defects*	Apportioned	*Meyer v. Gordon*
Treatment: Obstetrical: Delivery	*Further Treatment Req'd:* Corrective Surgery	No	*Hay v. Bain*
Treatment: Obstetrical: Delivery	*Death:* Hemorrhage	No	*Simard v. R.*
Treatment: Obstetrical: Miscarriage	*Further Treatment Req'd:* Corrective Surgery	No	*Hampton v. MacAdam*
Treatment: Obstetrical: Prenatal care	*Disease:* Septicaemia	No	*McQuay v. Eastwood*
Treatment: Obstetrical: Prenatal diagnosis	*Birth Defects*	No	*Quiroz v. Austrup*
Treatment: Obstetrical: Prenatal diagnosis	*Birth Defects*	Yes	*Wipfli v. Britten*
Treatment: Reduction of fracture and immobilization: Ankle	*Joint:* Ankle: Fusion *Nerve:* Foot: Numbness *Scarring/deformity:* Foot	No	*Gordon v. Davidson*
Treatment: Reduction of fracture and immobilization: Arm	*Bone:* Ankle: Displacement	No	*Town v. Archer*
Treatment: Reduction of fracture and immobilization: Arm	*Amputation:* Arm *Infection:* Gas Gangrene	No	*Challand v. Bell*
Treatment: Reduction of fracture and immobilization: Arm	*Paralysis:* Arm	No	*Vanmere v. Farwell*
Treatment: Reduction of fracture and immobilization: Foot	*Amputation:* Foot *Infection:* Gangrene	Yes	*Bergstrom v. G.*
Treatment: Reduction of fracture and immobilization: Foot	*Further Treatment Req'd:* Corrective surgery *Pain & Suffering*	Yes	*Townsend v. Lai*
Treatment: Reduction of fracture and immobilization: Hip	*Joint:* Hip: Displacement	Yes	*Dangerfield v. David*
Treatment: Reduction of fracture and immobilization: Leg	*Amputation:* Leg *Infection:* Gangrene	Yes	*Badger v. Surkan*
Treatment: Reduction of fracture and immobilization: Leg	*Amputation:* Leg	No	*Feller v. Roffman*

PROCEDURE	INJURY	LIAB.	CASE NAME
Treatment: Reduction of fracture and immobilization: Leg	*Amputation:* Leg	No	*Lachambre v. Perreault*
Treatment: Reduction of fracture and immobilization: Leg	*Bone:* Leg Displacement	No	*Hodgins v. Banting*
Treatment: Reduction of fracture and immobilization: Leg	*Bone:* Leg Displacement *Infection:* Abscess	Yes	*McCormick v. Marcotte*
Treatment: Reduction of fracture and immobilization: Leg	*Bone:* Leg: Displacement *Scarring/deformity:* Leg	No	*Rickley v. Stratton*
Treatment: Reduction of fracture and immobilization: Leg	*Further Treatment Req'd:* Corrective surgery *Scarring/deformity:* Leg	Yes	*Park v. Stevenson Memorial Hosp.*
Treatment: Reduction of fracture and immobilization: Toes	*Bone:* Fracture: Toe	No	*Pellerin v. Stevenson*
Treatment: Surgery: Abdominal	*Pain & Suffering*	No	*Pierce v. Strathroy Hosp.*
Treatment: Surgery: Amputation	*Amputation:* Elbow	No	*Jackson v. Hyde*
Treatment: Surgery: Appendectomy	*Death:* Peritonitis *Infection:* Peritonitis	No	*Wilson v. Stark*
Treatment: Surgery: Circumcision	*Organ:* Penis Damage	Yes	*Gilbert v. Campbell*
Treatment: Surgery: Circumcision	*Organ:* Penis Damage	Yes	*Gray v. Lafleche*
Treatment: Surgery: Cyst (removal of)	*Nerve:* Spinal Accessory: Damage *Pain & Suffering*	Yes	*Fizer v. Keys*
Treatment: Dressing: Wound	*Amputation:* Finger *Further Treatment Req'd:* Unsuccessful treatment	No	*Petit v. Hôpital Ste. Jeanne D'Arc*
Treatment: Surgery: Dupuytren's syndrome (correction of)	*Further Treatment Req'd:* Prolonged recovery	No	*Kenny v. Lockwood*
Treatment: Surgery: Draining abscess	*Pain & Suffering* *Scarring/deformity:* Groin	Yes	*Wine v. Dawyd*
Treatment: Surgery: Gall-bladder	*Removal:* Gall-bladder	No	*Davy v. Morrison*

PROCEDURE	INJURY	LIAB.	CASE NAME
Treatment: Surgery: Gynaecological	*Further Treatment Req'd:* Corrective Surgery *Infection:* Vagina *Scarring/deformity:* Groin	No	*Chipps v. Peters*
Treatment: Surgery: Hand	*Scarring/deformity:* Hand	Yes	*Héritiers de Feu Maurice Massé v. Gaudette*
Treatment: Hypertension (correction of)	*Cardiovascular/circulatory:* Stroke *Paralysis:* Hemiplegia	No	*Parsons v. Schmok*
Treatment: Surgery: Laparotomy	*Unnecessary Treatment*	No	*Finlay v. Hess*
Treatment: Surgery: Scalene node biopsy	*Paralysis:* Vocal chord	No	*Finlay v. Auld*
Treatment: Surgery: Thyroid	*Assault/battery*	No	*Booth v. Toronto Gen. Hosp.*
VI INTERNIST *Diagnosis:* Failure to diagnose infection of spine *Diagnosis:* Procedure: Microlaryngoscopy	*Infection:* Spinal Abscess *Paralysis:* Quadriplegia	Yes	*Holmes v. Bd. of Hosp. Trustees of London*
Diagnosis: Procedure: Pyelogram	*Death*	Apportioned	*Leonard v. Knott*
Treatment: Medication: Administration	*Brain Damage*	Settled	*Yepremian v. Scarborough Gen. Hosp.*
Treatment: Reduction of fracture and immobilization: Leg	*Amputation:* Leg	Yes	*Ares v. Venner*
VII NEUROLOGIST *Care:* Doctor: Supervision	*Brain Damage*	Yes	*Foote v. Royal Columbian Hosp.*
Care: Doctor: Supervision	*Unspecified:* Fall	No	*University Hosp. Bd. v. Lepine*
Treatment: Surgery: Laminectomy	*Paralysis:* Paraplegia	No	*Strachan v. Simpson*
VIII OBSTETRICIAN/ GYNAECOLOGIST *Abortion:* Dilation & curettage	*Brain Damage Paralysis*	No	*Mang v. Moscovitz*

PROCEDURE	INJURY	LIAB.	CASE NAME
Care: Doctor: During treatment	*Further Treatment Req'd:* Corrective Surgery *Pain & Suffering*	No	*Karderas v. Clow*
Care: Doctor: Post-treatment	*Further Treatment Req'd:* Corrective Surgery *Infection:* Peritonitis	Yes*	*McBride v. Langton*
Care: Doctor: Post-treatment	*Further Treatment Req'd:* Corrective Surgery *Infection:* Peritonitis *Scarring/deformity:* Abdomen	No	*Videto v. Kennedy*
Care: Doctor: Post-treatment	*Further Treatment Req'd:* Unsuccessful treatment Abortion *Pregnancy:* Unwanted	Yes	*Zimmer v. Ringrose*
Diagnosis: Failure to diagnose appendicitis	*Infection:* Peritonitis *Death*	Yes	*Bergen v. Sturgeon Gen. Hosp.*
Diagnosis: Failure to diagnose diabetes	*Cardiovascular/circulatory:* Corrective Surgery	No	*Nichols v. Gray*
Diagnosis: Failure to diagnose infection	*Further Treatment Req'd:* Corrective Surgery *Infection:* Peritonitis	Yes	*McBride v. Langton*
Diagnosis: Failure to diagnose multiple gestation	*Birth Defects*	Yes	*Wipfli v. Britten*
Treatment: Medication: Prescription	*Cardiovascular/circulatory:* Stroke	Yes	*Schierz v. Dodds*
Treatment: Obstetrical: Prenatal diagnosis	*Birth Defects*	Yes	*Wipfli v. Britten*
Treatment: Sterilization: Aldridge procedure	*Further Treatment Req'd:* Unsuccessful treatment *Pregnancy:* Unwanted	No*	*Doiron v. Orr*
Treatment: Sterilization: Laparoscopy/Laparotomy	*Further Treatment Req'd:* Corrective Surgery *Infection:* Peritonitis *Scarring/deformity:* Abdomen	No**	*Videto v. Kennedy*
Treatment: Sterilization: Laparoscopy/Laparotomy	*Further Treatment Req'd:* Corrective Surgery *Scarring/deformity:* Abdomen	No*	*Gouin-Perreault v. Villeneuve*
Treatment: Sterilization: Laparotomy	*Further Treatment Req'd:* Corrective surgery	No	*Karderas v. Clow*
Treatment: Sterilization: Laparotomy	*Unnecessary Treatment*	No	*Finlay v. Hess*

PROCEDURE	INJURY	LIAB.	CASE NAME
Treatment: Sterilization: Silver nitrate	*Pregnancy:* Unwanted	No*	*Colp v. Ringrose*
Treatment: Sterilization: Silver nitrate	*Further Treatment Req'd:* Unsuccessful treatment Abortion Hysterectomy *Pregnancy:* Unwanted	Yes*	*Cryderman v. Ringrose*
Treatment: Sterilization: Silver nitrate	*Further Treatment Req'd:* Unsuccessful treatment Abortion *Pregnancy:* Unwanted	No*	*Zimmer v. Ringrose*
Treatment: Sterilization: Tubal ligation	*Brain Damage Paralysis*	No*	*Mang v. Moscovitz*
Treatment: Sterilization: Tubal ligation	*Further Treatment Req'd:* Unsuccessful treatment *Pain & Suffering Pregnancy:* Unwanted	Yes*	*Dendaas (Tylor) v. Yackel*
Treatment: Sterilization: Tubal ligation	*Further Treatment Req'd:* Corrective Surgery *Organ:* Ureter: Damage *Pain & Suffering*	No*	*Hobson v. Munkley*
Treatment: Sterilization: Tubal ligation	*Further Treatment Req'd:* Unsuccessful treatment *Pregnancy:* Unwanted	No	*Sanderson v. Lamont*
IX OPHTHALMOLOGIST *Diagnosis:* Failure to diagnose detached retina	*Senses:* Sight: Loss	Yes	*Piche v. Ing*
Diagnosis: Failure to diagnose infection	*Infection:* Eye *Senses:* Sight: Loss	Yes	*Moffat v. Witelson*
Treatment: Medication: Administration	*Senses:* Sight Impairment	Apportioned	*Misericordia Hosp. v. Bustillo*
X OTOLARYNGOLOGIST *Diagnosis:* Failure to diagnose hemorrhage	*Senses:* Sight: Loss	No	*Kunitz v. Merci*
Diagnosis: Failure to diagnose infection Procedure: microlaryngoscopy	*Infection:* Spinal Abscess *Paralysis:* Quadriplegia	Yes	*Holmes v. Bd. of Hosp. Trustees of London*
Treatment: Ear	*Senses:* Hearing: Impairment	No	*Berry v. Pierce*
Treatment: Nosebleed	*Scarring:* Face *Pain & Suffering*	Yes Admitted	*Van Winkle v. Chen*

PROCEDURE	INJURY	LIAB.	CASE NAME
Treatment: Surgery: Mastoidectomy	*Paralysis:* Face	Yes	*Eady v. Tenderenda*
Treatment: Surgery: Sinus	*Senses:* Sight: Diplopia	No	*Patterson v. de la Bastide*
Treatment: Surgery: Stapedectomy	*Paralysis:* Face	No**	*Zamparo v. Brisson*
Treatment: Surgery: Tonsillectomy	*Dental:* Extraction: Unwanted	Yes	*Belore v. Smith*
XI PATHOLOGIST *Diagnosis:* Incorrect diagnosis of cancer	*Organ:* Fallopian Tubes *Pain & Suffering*	No	*Lefebvre v. Osborne*
XII PEDIATRICIAN *Diagnosis:* Failure to diagnose infection	*Brain Damage:* Pneumonia	No	*Bissell v. Vancouver Gen. Hosp.*
Treatment: Injection: Vaccination	*Disease:* Smallpox *Scarring/deformity:* Arm	No	*Gent v. Wilson*
XIII PSYCHIATRIST *Care:* Doctor: Hospitalization	*Death:* Suicide	No	*Haines v. Bellissimo*
Care: Doctor: Supervision/control	*Death:* Fall	Yes	*Villemure v. Turcot*
Care: Doctor: Supervision	*Paralysis:* Paraplegia	No	*Worth v. Royal Jubilee Hosp.*
Treatment: Medication: Prescription	*Further Treatment Req'd:* Drug overdose	No	*Molnar v. Conway*
XIV RADIOLOGIST *Diagnosis:* Procedure: Angiogram	*Paralysis:* Quadriplegia	No*	*McLean v. Weir*
Diagnosis: Procedure: Pyelogram	*Death*	Apportioned	*Leonard v. Knott*
Treatment: Dermatological X-ray	*Burn*	Yes	*McCaffrey v. Hague*
XV SURGEON (COSMETIC) *Treatment:* Surgery: Abdominoplasty	*Scarring/deformity:* Abdomen	No**	*Petty v. MacKay*
Treatment: Surgery: Blepharoplasty	*Scarring/deformity:* Eyelid *Senses:* Sight Diplopia	No*	*Guertin v. Kester*

PROCEDURE	INJURY	LIAB.	CASE NAME
Treatment: Surgery: Dermabrasion	*Scarring/deformity:* Face	No	*Hankins v. Papillon*
Treatment: Surgery: Jaw	*Dental:* Extraction: Additional Teeth, Denture	Yes	*Sunne v. Shaw*
Treatment: Surgery: Jaw	*Further Treatment Req'd: Dental:* Additional Tooth Extracted	Yes	*O'Connell v. Munro*
Treatment: Surgery: Mammoplasty	*Further Treatment Req'd:* Corrective Surgery *Scarring/deformity:* Breasts	Yes*	*MacDonald v. Ross*
Treatment: Surgery: Mammoplasty	*Further Treatment Req'd: Scarring/deformity:* Breasts	Yes*	*White v. Turner*
Treatment: Surgery: Rhinoplasty	*Scarring/deformity:* Nose	Yes	*LeFleur v. Cornelis*
XVI SURGEON (GENERAL) *Administration of Anaesthetic:* General	*Assault/battery*	No*	*Burk v. S.*
Care: Doctor: During treatment	*Further Treatment Req'd:* Corrective surgery	No	*Radclyffe v. Rennie*
Care: Doctor During treatment	*Joint:* Wrist	No	*Knight v. Sisters of St. Anne*
Care: Doctor: During treatment Surgical instrument	*Further Treatment Req'd:* Corrective Surgery *Pain & Suffering*	Yes	*Taylor v. Gray*
Care: Doctor: During treatment Surgical instrument	*Pain & Suffering*	No	*Hutchinson v. Robert*
Care: Doctor: During treatment Sponge count	*Assault/battery Pain & Suffering*	New Trial	*Winn v. Alexander*
Care: Doctor: During treatment Sponge count	*Death:* Suffocation	Yes	*Anderson v. Chasney*
Care: Doctor: During treatment Sponge count	*Further Treatment Req'd:* Corrective Surgery *Pain & Suffering*	Apportioned	*Cosgrove v. Gaudreau*
Care: Doctor: During treatment Sponge count	*Further Treatment Req'd:* Corrective Surgery *Pain & Suffering*	No	*Jewison v. Hassard*
Care: Doctor: During treatment Sponge count	*Further Treatment Req'd:* Corrective Surgery	No	*Petite v. MacLeod*

PROCEDURE	INJURY	LIAB.	CASE NAME
Care: Doctor: During treatment Sponge count	*Further Treatment Req'd:* Corrective Surgery	No	*Waldon v. Archer*
Care: Doctor: Post-treatment	*Further Treatment Req'd:* Corrective Surgery *Infection:* Osteomyelitis *Pain & Suffering*	No	*Law v. Gomel & Price*
Care: Doctor Post-treatment	*Amputation:* Testicle *Infection:* Gangrene	Yes	*Thomas v. Scarborough Gen. Hosp.*
Care: Doctor Post-treatment	*Paralysis:* Quadriplegia	No*	*Ferguson v. Hamilton Civic Hosp.*
Care: Doctor: Supervision	*Death:* Suffocation	New Trial	*Key v. Thomson*
Consultation: Failure to consult specialist	*Amputation:* Foot *Infection:* Gangrene	Yes	*Vail v. MacDonald*
Diagnosis: Failure to diagnose amputation necessary	*Amputation:* Hands, Feet	New Trial	*Key v. Thomson*
Diagnosis: Failure to diagnose appendicitis	*Infection:* Peritonitis *Death*	Yes	*Bergen v. Sturgeon Gen. Hosp.*
Diagnosis: Failure to diagnose cancer	*Disease:* Cancer	No	*Thompson v. Creaghan*
Diagnosis: Failure to diagnose dislocated shoulder	*Further Treatment Req'd:* Aggravated Condition	No	*Moore v. Large*
Diagnosis: Failure to diagnose dislocated shoulder	*Joint:* Shoulder: Impaired Movement	No	*Clark v. Wansbrough*
Diagnosis: Failure to diagnose fractured hip	*Further Treatment Req'd:* Aggravated Condition *Joint:* Hip: Disability *Pain & Suffering*	Apportioned	*Hôpital Notre-Dame de l'Esperance v. Laurent*
Diagnosis: Failure to diagnose infection	*Brain Damage:* Pneumonia	No	*Bissel v. Vancouver Gen. Hosp.*
Diagnosis: Failure to diagnose infection	*Pain & Suffering* *Scarring/deformity:* Groin	Yes	*Wine v. Dawyd*
Diagnosis: Incorrect diagnosis of cancer	*Organ:* Stomach, Spleen, Pancreas *Removal*	No	*Wilson v. Swanson*
Diagnosis: Incorrect diagnosis of cancer	*Organ:* Fallopian Tubes *Pain & Suffering*	No	*Lefebvre v. Osborne*

PROCEDURE	INJURY	LIAB.	CASE NAME
Diagnosis: Procedure: Biopsy	*Paralysis:* Vocal Chord	**	*Bickford v. Stiles*
Treatment: Blood: Bleeding	*Cardiovascular/circulatory:* Punctured Artery	Yes	*Kelly v. Dow*
Treatment: Blood: Transfusion	*Amputation:* Arm *Infection:* Gangrene	No	*Armstrong v. McClealand*
Treatment: Dressing wound	*Nerve:* Leg: Severed *Paralysis:* Leg	New Trial	*Zirkler v. Robertson*
Treatment: Heat: Diathermy	*Burn*	Yes	*Crysler v. Pierce*
Treatment: Heat: Kelly pad	*Burn:* Back: Shoulder	No	*Armstrong v. Bruce*
Treatment: Medication: Administration	*Death*	No	*R. v. Giardine*
Treatment: Medication: Administration	*Senses:* Sight Impairment	Yes	*Casson v. Haig*
Treatment: Obstetrical/ gynaecological: Caesarian section	*Further Treatment Req'd:* Corrective Surgery *Pain & Suffering*	Yes	*Taylor v. Gray*
Treatment: Obstetrical/ gynaecological: Surgery	*Organ:* Kidney: Removal, donation for transplantation	Admitted	*Urbanski v. Patel*
Treatment: Reduction of fracture and immobilization: Ankle	*Amputation:* Foot *Infection:* Gangrene	Yes	*Vail v. MacDonald*
Treatment: Reduction of fracture and immobilization: Ankle	*Bone:* Ankle: Displacement *Further Treatment Req'd:* Corrective Surgery *Joint:* Ankle: Fusion *Pain & Suffering*	Yes	*Parkin v. Kobrinsky*
Treatment: Reduction of fracture and immobilization: Leg	*Cardiovascular/circulatory:* Avascular Necrosis *Further Treatment Req'd:* Corrective Surgery *Joint:* Hip: Displacement *Pain & Suffering* *Scarring/deformity:* Leg	No	*Benoit v. Muir*
Treatment: Reduction of fracture and immobilization: Leg	*Joint:* Hip Rotation	No*	*Poulin v. Health Sciences Centre*
Treatment: Surgery	*Assault/battery*	No	*Turner v. Toronto Gen. Hosp. Trustees*

PROCEDURE	INJURY	LIAB.	CASE NAME
Treatment: Surgery	*Infection:* Hand	No	*Nelligan v. Clement*
Treatment: Surgery:	*Organ:* Digestive: Removal Unnecessary Treatment	No	*Wilson v. Swanson*
Treatment: Surgery	*Further Treatment Req'd:* Corrective Surgery	No	*Radclyffe v. Rennie*
Treatment: Surgery	N/A	**	*MacDuff v. Vrabec*
Treatment: Surgery: Abscess (draining of)	*Pain & Suffering Scarring/deformity:* Groin	Yes	*Wine v. Dawyd*
Treatment: Surgery: Amputation	*Amputation:* Hand *Assault/battery*	Yes*	*Mulloy v. Hop Sang*
Treatment: Surgery: Appendectomy	*Further Treatment Req'd:* Corrective Surgery *Pain & Suffering*	New Trial	*Meyer v. Lefebvre*
Treatment: Surgery: Arm	*Nerve:* Arm/Wrist: Radial nerve palsy	No	*Jendrick v. Greidanus*
Treatment: Surgery: Caesarian section	*Further Treatment Req'd:* Corrective Surgery *Pain & Suffering*	Yes	*Taylor v. Gray*
Treatment: Surgery: Cautery	*Burn:* Cautery	No	*McFadyen v. Harvie*
Treatment: Surgery: Dupuytren's contracture (correction of)	*Further Treatment Req'd:* Prolonged Recovery	No*	*Kenny v. Lockwood*
Treatment: Surgery: Eye	*Senses:* Sight: Double Vision	Yes**	*Calder v. Gilmour*
Treatment: Surgery: Fusion (ankle)	*Joint:* Ankle: Fusion	Admitted	*Staple v. Winnipeg*
Treatment: Surgery: Fusion (spine)	*Assault/battery*	Yes	*Schweizer v. Central Hosp.*
Treatment: Surgery: Gynaecological	*Further Treatment Req'd:* Corrective Surgery *Infection:* Vagina *Scarring/deformity:* Uterus	No	*Chipps v. Peters*
Treatment: Surgery: Gynaecological	*Organ:* Kidney: Removal	Yes	*Urbanski v. Patel*
Treatment: Surgery: Herniorrhaphy	*Organ:* Bladder: Perforation *Further Treatment Req'd*	Yes	*Melvin v. Graham*
Treatment: Surgery: Herniorrhaphy	*Amputation:* Testicle *Assault/Battery*	No	*Marshall v. Currey*

PROCEDURE	INJURY	LIAB.	CASE NAME
Treatment: Surgery: Labyrinthectomy	*Nerve:* Face: Damage	No	*Barcus v. Brown*
Treatment: Surgery: Meatotomy	*Assault/battery*	Yes*	*Hankai v. York County Hosp.*
Treatment: Surgery: Mediastinoscopy	*Paralysis:* Vocal Chord	**	*Bickford v. Stiles*
Treatment: Surgery: Migraine headache (correction of)	*Senses:* Taste/Smell: Loss	Yes*	*Koehler v. Cook*
Treatment: Surgery: Nasal	*Pain & Suffering*	No	*Hutchinson v. Robert*
Treatment: Surgery: Removal of bullet fragments from leg	*Further Treatment Req'd:* Unsuccessful Treatment	No	*Browne v. Lerner*
Treatment: Surgery: Stapedectomy	*Paralysis:* Face	**	*Zamparo v. Brisson*
Treatment: Surgery: Sterilization: hysterectomy	*Organ:* Kidney: Removal *Further Treatment Req'd:* Corrective Surgery	Yes	*Surkan v. Blott*
Treatment: Surgery: Sterilization: hysterectomy	*Organ:* Fallopian Tubes/ovaries: Removal	No	*Bennett v. C.*
Treatment: Surgery: Sterilization: hysterectomy	*Assault/Battery*	Yes*	*Murray v. McMurchy*
Treatment: Surgery: Sterilization: tubal ligation	*Further Treatment Req'd:* Unsuccessful Treatment *Pain & Suffering* *Pregnancy:* Unwanted	Yes*	*Cataford v. Moreau*
Treatment: Surgery: Sterilization: tubal ligation	*Further Treatment Req'd:* Corrective Surgery *Organ:* Ureter: Damage *Pain & Suffering*	No*	*Hobson v. Munkley*
Treatment: Surgery: Thyroid	*Death:* Cardiac Arrest	No*	*MacKinnon v. Ignacio*
Treatment: Surgery: Tonsillectomy	*Senses:* Taste: Loss Speech: Impairment	No	*McNamara v. Smith*
Treatment: Surgery: Ulnar nerve release	*Nerve:* Elbow: Numbness *Pain & Suffering*	No*	*Konkolus v. Royal Alexandra Hosp.*
Treatment: Surgery: Wrist	*Further Treatment Req'd:* Corrective Surgery *Paralysis:* Arm *Nerve:* Wrist: severed	Yes	*McKeachie v. Alvarez*

PROCEDURE	INJURY	LIAB.	CASE NAME
XVII SURGEON (NEUROSURGEON)			
Care: Doctor: Supervision	*Death:* Suicide	No	*Stadel v. Albertson*
Treatment: Surgery: Discoidectomy	*Cardiovascular/circulatory:* Hemorrhage Death	No	*Kapur v. Marshall*
Treatment: Surgery: Endarterectomy	*Cardiovascular/circulatory:* Stroke *Impotence, Paralysis*	**	*Reibl v. Hughes*
Treatment: Surgery: Laminectomy	*Paralysis:* Paraplegia	No*	*Strachan v. Simpson*
XVIII SURGEON (ORAL)			
Treatment: Dental: Extraction	*Dental:* Extraction: Additional Teeth	No*	*Boase v. Paul*
Treatment: Dental: Extraction	*Dental:* Extraction: Unauthorized	No*	*Nykiforuk v. Lockwood*
Treatment: Dental: Extraction	*Dental:* Damage *Further Treatment Req'd:* Unsuccessful Treatment *Pain & Suffering*	Yes	*Drinnen v. Douglas*
Treatment: Dental: Extraction	*Nerve:* Facial: Numbness/hypersensitivity *Pain & Suffering*	**	*Rawlings v. Lindsay*
Treatment: Dental: Extraction	*Nerve:* Facial Numbness	No	*Diack v. Bardsley*
Treatment: Dental: Surgery	*Brain Damage:* Cardiac Arrest	No	*Leadbetter v. Brand*
Treatment: Dental: Surgery	*Death:* Blood Inhalation	Yes*	*Kangas v. Parker*
Treatment: Dental: Surgery	*Dental:* Extraction: Additional Teeth	Yes	*Sunne v. Shaw*
XIX SURGEON (ORTHOPAEDIC)			
Care: Doctor: Post-treatment	*Cardiovascular/circulatory:* Avascular necrosis *Bone:* Hip: Fracture *Further Treatment Req'd:* Corrective surgery	Yes	*Powell v. Guttman*
Care: Doctor: Post-treatment	*Cardiovascular/circulatory:* Volkmann's Ischaemic Contracture *Scarring/deformity:* Arm	Yes	*Reitze v. Bruser (No. 2)*

PROCEDURE	INJURY	LIAB.	CASE NAME
Diagnosis: Failure to diagnose fracture (compound)	*Amputation:* Leg *Infection:* Gangrene	Yes	*Dean v.* *York County* *Hosp.*
Diagnosis: Failure to diagnose fractured ankle	*Joint:* Ankle	Yes	*Price v.* *Milawski*
Diagnosis: Failure to diagnose hemorrhaging	*Death:* Hemorrhage	No	*Chubey v.* *Ahsan*
Diagnosis: Failure to diagnose infection	*Disease:* Arthritis *Joint:* Hip: Fusion	No*	*Hajgato v.* *London Health* *Assn.*
Diagnosis: Failure to diagnose Volkmann's Ischaemic Contracture	*Cardiovascular/circulatory:* Volkmann's Ischaemic Contracture *Scarring/deformity:* Arm	Yes	*Reitze v.* *Bruser (No. 2)*
Treatment: Medication: Administration	*Cardiovascular/circulatory:* Hemorrhage *Further Treatment Req'd:* Corrective Surgery	Yes	*Crichton v.* *Hastings*
Treatment: Medication: Administration	*Organ:* Kidney: Damage *Senses:* Hearing: Loss	Yes*	*Male v.* *Hopmans*
Treatment: Reduction and immobilization (open reduction): Arm	*Further Treatment Req'd:* Corrective Surgery *Infection:* Staphylococcus *Scarring/deformity:* Arm	No	*Roy v.* *Goulet*
Treatment: Reduction and immobilization: Leg	*Amputation:* Leg *Infection:* Gangrene	Yes	*Dean v.* *York County* *Hosp.*
Treatment: Reduction and immobilization: Leg	*Bone:* Leg Hip fusion	Yes	*Leachman v.* *MacLachlan*
Treatment: Reduction and immobilization (open reduction): Leg	*Bone:* Leg: Shortening *Pain & Suffering* *Scarring/deformity:* Leg	Admit.	*Brennan v.* *Fraser*
Treatment: Surgery: Arthroplasty	*Cardiovascular/circulatory:* Avascular Necrosis *Bone:* Hip: Fracture *Further Treatment Req'd:* Corrective Surgery	Yes	*Powell v.* *Guttman*
Treatment: Surgery: Arthrotomy	*Death:* Cardiac Arrest	No	*McKay v.* *Gilchrist*
Treatment: Surgery: Discoidectomy	*Death:* Hemorrhage	No	*Chubey v.* *Ahsan*
Treatment: Surgery: Fusion (spinal)	*Further Treatment Req'd:* Corrective Surgery	Yes	*David v.* *Toronto Transit* *Comm.*

PROCEDURE	INJURY	LIAB.	CASE NAME
Treatment: Surgery: Fusion (spinal)	*Further Treatment Req'd:* Corrective Surgery *Pain & Suffering*	No	*Bucknam v. Kostiuk*
Treatment: Surgery: Hemilaminectomy	*Further Treatment Req'd:* Aggravated Condition Unsuccessful Treatment	**	*Hopp v. Lepp*
Treatment: Surgery: Knee	*Paralysis:* Foot/Leg Foot Drop	Yes	*Bibby v. Hall*
Treatment: Surgery: Osteotomy	*Further Treatment Req'd:* Corrective Surgery *Nerve:* Leg: Numbness *Pain & Suffering*	No*	*Jodoin v. Mitra*
Treatment: Surgery: Osteotomy	*Nerve:* Arm: Stiffness	**	*Kelly v. Hazlett*
Treatment: Surgery: Osteotomy	*Further Treatment Req'd:* Corrective Surgery *Scarring/deformity:* Arm	No	*Ostrowski v. Lotto*
XX SURGEON (VASCULAR/ CARDIOVASCULAR) *Treatment:* Surgery: Angiogram	*Paralysis:* Quadriplegia	No*	*McLean v. Weir*
Treatment: Surgery: Pneumonectomy	*Death*	No	*O'Reilly v. Spratt*
DEFENDANT: HOSPITAL *Administration of Anaesthetic:* General	*Burn* *Scarring/deformity*	Yes	*Crits v. Sylvester*
Administration of Anaesthetic: General	*Death:* Cardiac Arrest		*McKay v. Gilchrist*
Administration of Anaesthetic: Injection	*Amputation:* Hand	No	*Villeneuve v. Sisters of St. Joseph*
Administration of Anaesthetic: Injection	*Death:* Injection of wrong drug	Yes	*Bugden v. Harbour View Hosp.*
Administration of Anaesthetic: Injection	*Paralysis:* Legs	No	*Girard v. Royal Columbian Hosp.*
Administration of Anaesthetic: Injection	*Paralysis:* Paraplegia	Yes	*Martel v. Hotel-dieu St. Vallier*
Administration of Anaesthetic: Intubation	*Death:* Cardiac Arrest	No	*Webster v. Armstrong*

PROCEDURE	INJURY	LIAB.	CASE NAME
Administration of Anaesthetic: Intubation	*Dental:* Damage	No*	*Gorback v. Ting*
Administration of Anaesthetic: Post-anaesthesia recovery	*Brain Damage:* Respiratory Obstruction	Yes	*Laidlaw v. Lions Gate Hosp.*
Administration of Anaesthetic: Post-anaesthesia recovery	*Death:* Cardiac Arrest	Yes	*Krujelis v. Esdale*
Administration of Anaesthetic: Transtracheal ventilation	*Infection:* Spinal Abscess *Paralysis:* Quadriplegia	No*	*Holmes v. Bd. of Hosp. Trustees of London*
Care: Hospital: Discharge	*Brain Damage:* Pneumonia	No	*Bissell v. Vancouver Gen. Hosp.*
Care: Hospital: During treatment	*Assault/battery Pain & Suffering*	No	*Winn v. Alexander*
Care: Hospital: During treatment	*Brain Damage*	Yes	*Hôpital Gen. de la Région de l'Amiante v. Perron*
Care: Hospital: During treatment	*Disease:* Hepatitis B	Apportioned	*Savoie v. Bouchard*
Care: Hospital: During Treatment:	*Further Treatment Req'd:* Corrective Surgery *Pain & Suffering*	Apportioned	*Cosgrove v. Gaudreau*
Care: Hospital: During treatment	*Further Treatment Req'd:* Corrective Surgery *Pain & Suffering*	No	*Petite v. MacLeod*
Care: Hospital: During treatment	*Further Treatment Req'd:* Corrective Surgery *Pain & Suffering*	Yes	*Karderas v. Clow*
Care: Hospital: During treatment	*Joint:* Wrist: Disability	Yes	*Knight v. Sisters of St. Ann*
Care: Hospital: Emergency	*Birth Defects*	Apportioned	*Meyer v. Gordon*
Care: Hospital: Emergency	*Further Treatment Req'd:* Aggravated condition	No	*Elverson v. Doctors Hosp.*
Care: Hospital: General	*Brain Damage*	Settled	*Yepremian v. Scarborough Gen. Hosp.*
Care: Hospital: General	*Burn*	Yes	*Logan v. Colchester*

PROCEDURE	INJURY	LIAB.	CASE NAME
Care: Hospital: General	*Death*	No	*Brandeis v. Weldon*
Care: Hospital: General	*Death*	No	*Rodych v. Krasey*
Care: Hospital: General	*Death*	No	*Butler v. Toronto*
Care: Hospital: General	*Disease:* Smallpox	No	*McDaniel v. Vancouver Gen. Hosp.*
Care: Hospital: General	*Injury:* Fall	No	*McKay v. Royal Inland Hosp.*
Care: Hospital: Pre-treatment	*Bone:* Hip: Fracture	No	*Florence v. Les Soeurs de Misericorde*
Care: Hospital: Post-treatment	*Burn:* Fall	No	*Cahoon v. Edmonton Hosp. Bd.*
Care: Hospital: Post-treatment	*Burn:* Hot water bottle	Yes	*Davis v. Colchester County Hosp.*
Care: Hospital: Post-treatment	*Burn:* Feet Hot water bottle	Yes	*Eek v. High River Mun. Hosp. Bd.*
Care: Hospital: Post-treatment	*Death:* Aspiration of gastric fluids	Yes	*Joseph Brant Memorial Hosp. v. Koziol*
Care: Hospital: Post-treatment	*Disease:* Arthritis *Joint:* Hip: Fusion	No*	*Hajgato v. London Health Assn.*
Care: Hospital: Post-treatment	*Paralysis:* Leg: Foot Drop	Yes	*Laughlin v. Royal Columbian Hosp.*
Care: Hospital: Post-treatment	*Paralysis:* Quadriplegia	No*	*Ferguson v. Hamilton Civic Hosp.*
Care: Hospital: Post-treatment	*Amputation/Removal:* Eye *Senses:* Sight: Impairment	Yes	*Wyndham v. Toronto Gen. Hosp.*
Care: Hospital: Post-treatment	*Amputation:* Foot *Infection:* Gangrene	No	*Vail v. MacDonald*

PROCEDURE	INJURY	LIAB.	CASE NAME
Care: Hospital: Post-treatment	*Amputation:* Testicle *Infection:* Gangrene	No	*Thomas v. Scarborough Gen. Hosp.*
Care: Hospital: Post-treatment	*Brain Damage:* Respiratory obstruction	Yes	*Laidlaw v. Lion's Gate Hosp.*
Care: Hospital: Post-treatment	*Burn:* Feet	Yes	*Bernier v. Sisters of Service*
Care: Hospital: Post-treatment	*Burn:* Heel	Yes	*Lavere v. Smith's Falls Pub. Hosp.*
Care: Hospital: Post-treatment	*Burn:* Leg Hot water bottle	Yes	*Nyberg v. Provost Mun. Hosp.*
Care: Hospital: Post-treatment	*Death:* Cardiac Arrest	Yes	*Krujelis v. Esdale*
Care: Hospital: Post-treatment	*Nerve:* Arm: Neurapraxia	Yes	*Traynor v. Vancott*
Care: Hospital: Post-treatment	*Pain & Suffering Further Treatment Req'd:* Prolonged Condition	Yes	*Beatty v. Sisters of Misericorde*
Care: Hospital: Supervision	*Birth Defects*	Yes	*Meyer v. Gordon*
Care: Clinic: Supervision	*Bone:* Arm: Fracture	Yes	*Dowey v. Rothwell*
Care: Hospital: Supervision/control	*Assault/battery*	Yes	*Lawson v. Wellesley Hosp.*
Care: Hospital: Supervision/control	*Bone:* Hip: Fracture	No	*Hotel-Dieu de Montreal v. Couloume*
Care: Hospital: Supervision/control	*Bone:* Hip: Fracture	No	*Robinson v. Annapolis Gen. Hosp.*
Care: Hospital: Supervision/control	*Brain Damage*	No	*Foote v. Royal Columbian Hosp.*
Care: Hospital: Supervision/control	*Burn:* Radiator *Scarring/Deformity*	Yes	*Farrell v. City of Regina*
Care: Hospital: Supervision/control	*Burn:* Boiling water	Yes	*Sinclair v. Victoria Gen. Hosp.*
Care: Hospital: Supervision/control	*Death:* Fall	Yes	*Villemure v. Turcot*

PROCEDURE	INJURY	LIAB.	CASE NAME
Care: Hospital: Supervision/control	*Death:* Suicide	No	*Stadel v. Albertson*
Care: Hospital: Supervision/control	*Dental:* Damage Loss of Teeth *Wound*	No	*Penner v. Bethel Hosp. Soc.*
Care: Hospital: Supervision/control	Fall	No	*Flynn v. Hamilton*
Care: Hospital: Supervision/control	Fall	No	*Child v. Vancouver Gen. Hosp.*
Care: Hospital: Supervision/control	*Further Treatment Req'd:* Prolonged Condition *Pain & Suffering*	Yes	*Beatty v. Sisters of Misericorde*
Care: Hospital: Supervision/control	*Infection:* Peritonitis Death	Yes	*Bergen v. Sturgeon Gen. Hosp.*
Care: Hospital: Supervision/control	*Paralysis:* Paraplegia	No	*Worth v. Royal Jubilee Hosp.*
Care: Hospital: Supervision/control	*Unspecified:* Fall	No	*University Hosp. Board v. Lepine*
Diagnosis: Failure to diagnose cancer by doctor	*Disease:* Cancer	No	*Thompson v. Creaghan*
Diagnosis: Failure to diagnose compound fracture by doctor	*Amputation:* Leg *Infection:* Gangrene	No	*Dean v. York County Hosp.*
Diagnosis: Failure to diagnose diabetes by doctor	*Brain Damage*	Settled	*Yepremian v. Scarborough Gen. Hosp.*
Diagnosis: Failure to diagnose dislocated shoulder	*Further Treatment Req'd:* Unsuccessful Treatment	Yes	*Thompson v. Columbian Coast Mission*
Diagnosis: Failure to diagnose dislocated wrist by doctor	*Joint:* Wrist: Impairment	Apportioned	*Osburn v. Mohindra*
Diagnosis: Failure to diagnose emphysema by resident	*Disease:* Emphysema	No	*McCarty v. University of B.C.*
Diagnosis: Failure to diagnose encephalitis by doctor	*Brain Damage*	No	*Tiesmaki v. Wilson*

PROCEDURE	INJURY	LIAB.	CASE NAME
Diagnosis: Failure to diagnose fracture dislocation of spine by intern	*Death*	Yes	*Fraser v. Vancouver Gen. Hosp.*
Diagnosis: Failure to diagnose fractured hip by doctor	*Joint:* Hip	No	*Hôpital Notre Dame de l'Esperance v. Laurent*
Diagnosis: Failure to diagnose infection by doctor	*Brain Damage:* Pneumonia	No	*Bissell v. Vancouver Gen. Hosp.*
Diagnosis: Failure to diagnose infection by doctors	*Infection:* Spinal Abscess *Paralysis:* Quadriplegia	No*	*Holmes v. Bd. of Hosp. Trustees of London*
Diagnosis: Failure to diagnose infection by resident	*Disease:* Arthritis *Joint:* Hip: Fusion	No*	*Hajgato v. London Health Assn.*
Diagnosis: Failure to diagnose hemorrhage by doctor	*Death*	No	*Serre v. DeTilly*
Diagnosis: Failure to diagnose hemorrhage by doctor	*Death*	No	*Wade v. Nayernouri*
Diagnosis: Incorrect diagnosis of cancer	*Organ:* Fallopian Tubes *Pain & Suffering*	Yes	*Lefebvre v. Osborne*
Diagnosis: Misdiagnosis of infection by doctor	*Amputation:* Leg	Yes	*Layden v. Cope*
Diagnosis: Procedure: Angiogram	*Paralysis:* Quadriplegia	No*	*Ferguson v. Hamilton Civic Hosp.*
Diagnosis: Procedure: Fluoroscopy	*Burn:* Back	Yes	*Abel v. Cooke*
Diagnosis: Procedure: X-ray	*Further Treatment Req'd:* Corrective Surgery *Scarring/deformity:* Finger	Yes	*Pepin v. Hôpital du Haut Richelieu*
Diagnosis: Procedure: X-ray	*Paralysis:* Arm	No	*Murphy v. General Hosp.*
Referral: Failure to refer to specialist by Intern	*Disease:* Emphysema	No	*McCarty v. University of B.C.*
Treatment: Dermatological: Slush	*Scarring/deformity:* Face	No	*Johnston v. Wellesley Hosp.*

PROCEDURE	INJURY	LIAB.	CASE NAME
Treatment: General: Infection	*Amputation:* Finger *Further Treatment Req'd:* Unsuccessful Treatment	No	*Petit v. Hôpital Ste. Jeanne D'Arc*
Treatment: Heat: Diathermy	*Burn*	Yes	*Fleming v. Sisters of St. Joseph*
Treatment: Heat: cradle	*Burn:* Thigh	No	*Vuchar v. Toronto Gen. Hosp.*
Treatment: Heat: Kelly pad	*Burn:* Back	Yes	*Lenzen v. S. Vancouver Is. Hosp. Soc.*
Treatment: Heat: Steam inhalation	*Burn*	Yes	*Harkies v. Lord Dufferin Hosp.*
Treatment: Injection: Anaesthetic	*Amputation:* Hand	No	*Villeneuve v. Sisters of St. Joseph*
Treatment: Injection: Anaesthetic	*Death:* Injection of Wrong Drug	Yes	*Bugden v. Harbour View Hosp.*
Treatment: Injection: Anaesthetic	*Paralysis:* Legs	No	*Girard v. Royal Columbian Hosp.*
Treatment: Injection: Anaesthetic	*Paralysis:* Paraplegia	Yes	*Martel v. Hotel-Dieu St. Vallier*
Treatment: Injection: Intravenous feeding		Yes	*Murphy v. St. Catharine's Gen. Hosp.*
Treatment: Injection: Medication	*Nerve:* Sciatic: Damage *Pain & Suffering*	Yes	*Fiege v. Cornwall Gen. Hosp.*
Treatment: Injection: Medication	*Nerve:* Sciatic: Damage	Yes	*Huber v. Burnaby Gen. Hosp.*
Treatment: Injection: Medication	*Nerve:* Sciatic: Foot drop *Paralysis:* Leg	Yes	*Laughlin v. Royal Columbian Hosp.*
Treatment: Medication: Administration	*Bone:* Cheekbone/jaw Fracture	No	*Buchanan v. Fort Churchill Gen. Hosp.*

PROCEDURE	INJURY	LIAB.	CASE NAME
Treatment: Medication: Administration	*Brain Damage*	Settled	*Yepremian v. Scarborough Gen. Hosp.*
Treatment: Medication: Administration	*Cardiovascular/circulatory:* Avascular necrosis	No	*Moore v. Shaughnessy Hosp.*
Treatment: Medication: Administration	*Senses:* Sight: Impairment	Yes	*Barker v. Lockhart*
Treatment: Medication: Administration	*Senses:* Sight: Impairment	Apportioned	*Misericordia Hosp. v. Bustillo*
Treatment: Medication: Administration	*Death:* Injection of wrong drug	Yes	*Bugden v. Harbour View Hosp.*
Treatment: Medication: Prescription	*Death*	Settled	*Filipewich v. University Hosp. Bd.*
Treatment: Obstetrical: Delivery	*Birth Defects*	Apportioned	*Meyer v. Gordon*
Treatment: Reduction of Fracture and immobilization: Leg	*Further Treatment Req'd:* Corrective Surgery *Scarring/deformity:* Leg	No	*Park v. Stevenson Memorial Hosp.*
Treatment: Reduction of fracture and immobilization: Leg	*Amputation:* Leg *Infection:* Gangrene	No	*Dean v. York County Hosp.*
Treatment: Surgery: Angiogram	*Paralysis:* Quadriplegia	No*	*Ferguson v. Hamilton*
Treatment: Surgery: Arm	*Nerve:* Arm/Wrist Radial Nerve Palsy	No	*Jendrick v. Greidanus*
Treatment: Surgery: Arthrotomy	*Death:* Cardiac Arrest	No	*McKay v. Gilchrist*
Treatment: Surgery: Fusion (ankle)	*Joint:* Ankle: Fusion	No	*Staple v. Winnipeg*
Treatment: Surgery: Fusion (spinal)	*Assault/battery*	No*	*Schweizer v. Central Hosp.*
Treatment: Surgery: General	*Assault/battery*	No	*Turner v. Toronto Gen. Hosp.*
Treatment: Surgery: Heart bypass	*Brain Damage:* Cardiac Arrest	Yes	*Aynsley v. Toronto Gen. Hosp.*

PROCEDURE	INJURY	LIAB.	CASE NAME
Treatment: Surgery: Laparotomy	*Pain & Suffering*	Yes	*Karderas v. Clow*
Treatment: Surgery: Ophthalmic	*Senses:* Sight: Impairment	Yes	*Walker v. Sydney City Hosp.*
Treatment: Surgery: Thyroid	*Assault/battery*	No	*Booth v. Toronto Gen. Hosp.*
Treatment: Surgery: Transurethral resection	*Organ:* Bladder: Perforation Incontinence/impotence	No*	*Considine v. Camp Hill Hosp.*

DEFENDANT: HOUSE STAFF: INTERN

Diagnosis: Failure to diagnose Fracture dislocation (spinal)	*Death*	Yes	*Fraser v. Vancouver Gen. Hosp.*
Treatment: Blood: Transfusion	*Infection:* Streptococcus	No	*Cox v. Saskatoon*
Treatment: Injection: Intravenous feeding		Yes	*Murphy v. St. Catharines Gen. Hosp.*
Treatment: Surgery: Tubal ligation	*Brain Damage Paralysis*	No*	*Mang v. Moscovitz*

DEFENDANT: HOUSE STAFF: RESIDENT
I IN ANAESTHESIOLOGY

Administration of Anaesthetic General	*Burn Scarring/deformity*	Yes	*Crits v. Sylvester*
Administration of Anaesthetic Injection	*Further Treatment Req'd:* Corrective Surgery *Pain & Suffering Scarring/deformity:* Hand	No	*Lloy v. Milner*
Care: Doctor: During treatment	*Brain Damage:* Cardiac Arrest	No	*Aynsley v. Toronto Gen. Hosp.*

II IN PEDIATRICS

Treatment: Medication: Prescription	*Death*	Settled	*Filipewich v. University Hosp. Bd.*

III IN RADIOLOGY

Diagnosis: Procedure: Angiogram	*Paralysis:* Quadriplegia	No*	*Ferguson v. Hamilton Civic Hosp.*

PROCEDURE	INJURY	LIAB.	CASE NAME
Treatment: Surgery: Transurethral resection	*Organ:* Bladder: Perforation Incontinence/impotence	No*	*Considine v. Camp Hill Hosp.*
I IN SURGERY (ORTHOPAEDIC)			
Care: Doctor: During treatment *Treatment:* Surgery: Laparotomy (not party)	*Further Treatment Req'd:* Corrective Surgery *Pain & Suffering*	Yes	*Karderas v. Clow*
Diagnosis: Failure to diagnose Infection	*Disease:* Arthritis Joint: Hip: Fusion	No*	*Hajgato v. London Health Assn.*
Diagnosis: Failure to diagnose emphysema *Referral:* Failure to refer to specialist	*Disease:* Emphysema	No	*McCarty v. University of B.C.*
Diagnosis: Failure to diagnose Volkmann's Contracture	*Pain & Suffering:* Deformity: Hand	Yes	*Rietze v. Bruser*
Treatment: Emergency	*Birth Defects*	No	*Meyer v. Gordon*
DEFENDANT: NURSE			
Administration of Anaesthetic Injection (not party)	*Amputation:* Hand	No	*Villeneuve v. Sisters of St. Joseph*
Care: Hospital: During treatment (not party)	*Brain Damage*	Yes	*Hôpital Gen. de la Région de L'Amiante v. Perron*
Care: Hospital: During treatment	*Disease:* Hepatitis B	Apportioned	*Savoie v. Bouchard*
Care: Hospital: General	*Further Treatment Req'd:* Aggravated Condition	No	*Elverson v. Doctors Hosp.*
Care: Hospital: General (not party)	*Burn*	Yes	*Logan v. Colchester*
Care: Hospital: General (not party)	*Death*	No	*Brandeis v. Weldon*
Care: Hospital: General	*Death*	No	*Rodych v. Krasey*
Care: Hospital: Post-treatment (not party)	*Amputation:* Foot *Infection:* Gangrene	No	*Vail v. MacDonald*

PROCEDURE	INJURY	LIAB.	CASE NAME
Care: Hospital: Post-treatment (not party)	*Brain Damage*	Yes	*Laidlaw v. Lions Gate Hosp.*
Care: Hospital: Post-treatment (not party)	*Burn:* Feet: Hot Water Bottle	Yes	*Bernier v. Sisters of Service*
Care: Hospital: Post-treatment (not party)	*Burn:* Feet: Hot Water Bottle	Yes	*Eek v. High River Mun. Hosp. Bd.*
Care: Hospital: Post-treatment (not party)	*Burn:* Leg: Hot Water Bottle	Yes	*Nyberg v. Provost Mun. Hosp. Bd.*
Care: Hospital: Post-treatment	*Death:* Aspiration of Gastric Fluid	Yes	*Joseph Brant Memorial Hosp. v. Koziol*
Care: Hospital: Post-treatment	*Death:* Cardiac Arrest	Yes	*Krujelis v. Esdale*
Care: Hospital: Post-treatment (not party)	*Disease:* Arthritis *Joint:* Hip: Fusion	No*	*Hajgato v. London Health Assn.*
Care: Hospital: Post-treatment (not party)	*Further Treatment Req'd:* Prolonged Recovery *Pain & Suffering*	Yes	*Beatty v. Sisters of Misericorde*
Care: Hospital: Post-treatment (not party)	*Nerve:* Arm: Neurapraxia	Yes	*Traynor v. Vancott*
Care: Hospital: Post-treatment (not party)	*Nerve:* Sciatic: Foot Drop *Paralysis:* Leg	Yes	*Laughlin v. Royal Columbian Hosp.*
Care: Hospital: Post-treatment (not party)	*Paralysis:* Quadriplegia	No*	*Ferguson v. Hamilton Civic Hosp.*
Care: Hospital: Sponge count (not party)	*Further Treatment Req'd:* Corrective Surgery *Pain & Suffering*	Apportioned	*Cosgrove v. Gaudreau*
Care: Hospital: Sponge count (not party)	*Further Treatment Req'd:* Corrective Surgery	No	*Petite v. Macleod*
Care: Hospital: Supervision (not party)	*Birth Defects*	Yes	*Meyer v. Gordon*
Care: Doctor's Office: Supervision (not party)	*Bone:* Arm Fracture	Yes	*Dowey v. Rothwell*

PROCEDURE	INJURY	LIAB.	CASE NAME
Care: Hospital: Supervision (not party)	*Bone:* Hip: Fracture	No	*Robinson v. Annapolis Gen. Hosp.*
Care: Hospital: Supervision (not party)	*Brain Damage*	No	*Foote v. Royal Columbian Hosp.*
Care: Hospital: Supervision (not party)	*Burn:* Boiling Water	Yes	*Sinclair v. Victoria Hosp.*
Care: Hospital: Supervision (not party)	*Further Treatment Req'd:* Prolonged Recovery *Pain & Suffering*	Yes	*Beatty v. Sisters of Misericorde*
Care: Hospital: Supervision	Fall	No	*Child v. Vancouver Gen. Hosp.*
Diagnosis: Failure to diagnose appendicitis by doctor	*Infection:* Peritonitis Death	Yes	*Bergen v. Sturgeon Gen. Hosp.*
Diagnosis: Failure to diagnose hemorrhage by doctor (not party)	*Death:* Hemorrhage	No	*Serre v. DeTilly*
Diagnosis: Failure to diagnose internal injuries by doctor	*Death*	No	*Rodych v. Krasey*
Diagnosis: Procedure: X-ray (not party)	*Burn:* Hand/Leg	No	*Antoniuk v. Smith*
Treatment: Heat: Diathermy (not party)	*Burn*	Yes	*Fleming v. Sisters of St. Joseph*
Treatment: Heat: Kelly pad	*Burn:* Back	Yes	*Lenzen v. Southern Vancouver Island Hosp.*
Treatment: Heat: Steam inhalation (not party)	*Burn*	Yes	*Harkies v. Lord Dufferin Hosp.*
Treatment: Injection: Medication	*Nerve:* Sciatic: Damage *Pain & Suffering*	Yes	*Fiege v. Cornwall Gen. Hosp.*
Treatment: Injection: Medication (not party)	*Nerve:* Sciatic: Damage	Yes	*Huber v. Burnaby Gen. Hosp.*

PROCEDURE	INJURY	LIAB.	CASE NAME
Treatment: Injection: Medication (not party)	*Nerve:* Sciatic: Foot Drop *Paralysis:* Leg	Yes	*Laughlin v. Royal Columbian Hosp.*
Treatment: Injection: Vaccination	*Infection:* Gangrene	No	*Cavan v. Wilcox*
Treatment: Medication: Administration	*Death:* Injection of Wrong Drug	Yes	*Bugden v. Harbour View Hosp.*
Treatment: Medication: Administration	*Senses:* Sight: Impairment	Yes	*Barker v. Lockhart*
Treatment: Medication: Administration (not party)	*Senses:* Sight: Impairment	Apportioned	*Misericordia Hosp. v. Bustillo*

DEFENDANT: OPTOMETRIST

Diagnosis: Failure to diagnose Surgery required	*Further Treatment Req'd:* Corrective Surgery	No	*Murphy v. Mathieson*
Treatment: Optometric: Eyeglass dispensing	*Senses:* Sight: Impairment	Yes	*Dunsmore v. Deshield*

DEFENDANT: PHARMACIST

Treatment: Medication: Prescription (dispensing of)	*Amputation/removal:* Stomach *Further Treatment Req'd:* Corrective Surgery *Pain & Suffering*	Yes	*Williams v. Jones*
Treatment: Medication: Prescription (dispensing of)	*Death*	Settled	*Filipewich v. University Hosp. Bd.*
Treatment: Medication: Prescription (dispensing of)	*Poisoning* *Pain & Suffering*	Yes	*Stretton v. Holmes*
Treatment: Medication: Prescription (dispensing of) (not party)	*Senses:* Sight: Impairment	Apportioned	*Misericordia Hosp. v. Bustillo*
Treatment: Medication: Prescription (dispensing of)	*Further Treatment Req'd:* Drug overdose	No	*Molnar v. Conway*

DEFENDANT: PSYCHOLOGIST

Care: Doctor: Hospitalization	*Death:* Suicide	No	*Haines v. Bellissimo*

DEFENDANT: REHABILITATIVE MEDICAL STAFF
I AUDIOLOGIST

Diagnosis: Procedure: Audiogram (not party)	*Senses:* Hearing: Tinnitus	Yes	*Bartlett v. Children's Hosp.*

PROCEDURE	INJURY	LIAB.	CASE NAME
II PHYSIOTHERAPIST			
Care: Hospital:	Fall	No	*McKay v.*
General			*Royal Inland*
			Hosp.
Treatment: Rehabilitative:	*Pain & Suffering*	No	*Grafton v.*
Physiotherapy	*Bone:* Thigh: Fracture		*Bigelow*
III REMEDIAL GYMNAST			
Treatment: Rehabilitative	*Bone:* Kneecap: Fracture	Yes	*Guar. Trust v.*
remedial exercises			*Mall Medical*
			Group
DEFENDANT: STUDENT			
I MEDICAL			
Treatment: Surgery:	*Senses:* Taste: Loss	No	*McNamara v.*
Tonsillectomy (not party)			*Smith*
II NURSING			
Care: Hospital:	*Burn*	Yes	*Farrell v.*
Supervision (not party)	*Scarring/deformity*		*City of Regina*
DEFENDANT: SUPPORT STAFF			
I ORDERLY			
Care: Hospital:	*Paralysis:* Vocal Chord	No	*Brennan v.*
Supervision/control			*Dir. of*
			Mental Health
II WARD AIDE			
Care: Hospital:	*Amputation/removal:* Eye	Yes	*Wyndham v.*
Post-treatment	*Senses:* Sight: Impairment		*Toronto*
			Gen. Hosp.
DEFENDANT: TECHNICIAN			
I LABORATORY			
Diagnosis: Failure to diagnose	*Death:* Cardiac Arrest	Yes	*Neufville v.*
diabetes			*Sobers*
II X-RAY			
Diagnosis: Procedure:	*Burn:* Back	Yes	*Abel v.*
Fluoroscopy (not party)			*Cooke*
Diagnosis: Procedure:	*Burn:* Hand	Yes	*Hochman v.*
X-ray (not party)			*Wilinsky*
Diagnosis: Procedure	*Further Treatment Req'd*	Yes	*Pepin v.*
X-ray (not party)	Corrective Surgery		*Hôpital du Haut*
	Scarring/deformity: Finger		*Richelieu*
DEFENDANT: UROLOGIST			
Treatment: Surgery:	*Incontinence/Impotence*	No*	*Considine v.*
Transurethral resection	*Organ:* Bladder: Perforation		*Camp Hill Hosp.*
	Pain & Suffering		

INJURY	DEFENDANT	LIAB.	CASE NAME
PROCEDURE: ADMINISTRATION OF ANAESTHETIC			
I CHLOROFORM			
Death	Doctor: Anaesthetist	No	Fleckney v. Desbrisay
II EXPERIMENTAL			
Brain Damage: Cardiac Arrest	Doctor: Anaesthetist	Yes*	Halushka v. Univ. of Sask.
III GENERAL			
Assault/battery	Doctor: Surgeon: General	No	Burk v. S.
Brain Damage	Doctor: Anaesthetist	No	Hôpital Générale v. Perron
Brain Damage: Cardiac arrest	Doctor: Anaesthetist	No	Leadbetter v. Brand
Burn Scarring/deformity	Doctor: Anaesthetist	Yes	Crits v. Sylvester
IV INJECTION			
Amputation: Hand	Doctor: Anaesthetist	Yes	Villeneuve v.
	Hospital	No	Sisters of
	Nurse (not party)	No	St. Joseph
Death: Injection of wrong drug	Doctor: General Practitioner	No	Bugden v.
	Hospital	Yes	Harbour View
	Nurse	Yes	Hosp.
Further Treatment Req'd: Skin grafts Pain & Suffering Scarring/deformity: Hand	Doctor: Anaesthetist	No	Lloy v.
	House Staff: Resident	No	Milner
Infection: Abscess	Doctor: Anaesthetist	No	Hughston v. Jost
Nerve: Facial: Numbness	Dentist	No	Schinz v. Dickinson
Pain & Suffering	Doctor: Anaesthetist	No*	Allan v. New Mt. Sinai Hosp.
Paralysis: Legs	Doctor: Anaesthetist	No	Girard v.
	Hospital	No	Royal Columbian Hosp.
Paralysis: Paraplegia	Doctor: Anaesthetist	Yes	Martel v.
	Hospital	Yes	Hôtel-Dieu St. Vallier
V INTUBATION			
Death: Cardiac arrest	Doctor: Anaesthetist	No	Webster v.
	Hospital		Armstrong

INJURY	DEFENDANT	LIAB.	CASE NAME
Dental: Damage	*Doctor:* Anaesthetist	Yes	*Gorback v.*
	Hospital	No	*Ting*
VI POST-ANAESTHESIA RECOVERY			
Brain Damage	*Doctor:* Anaesthetist	No	*Laidlaw v.*
	Hospital	Yes	*Lions Gate Hosp.*
	Nurse (not party)	Yes	
Death: Cardiac arrest	*Doctor:* Anaesthetist	No	*Krujelis v.*
	Hospital	Yes	*Esdale*
	Nurse	Yes	
VII SPINAL			
Death	*Doctor:* Anaesthetist	No	*Walker v.*
	Doctor: General Practitioner	No	*Bedard*
Further Treatment Req'd: Unsuccessful treatment	*Doctor:* Surgeon: General	No	*Browne v.* *Lerner*
Paralysis: Paraplegia	*Doctor:* Anaesthetist	Yes*	*Beausoleil v.*
	Hospital	Yes	*Soeurs de la Charité*
VIII TRANSTRACHEAL VENTILATION			
Paralysis: Quadriplegia **Infection:** Spinal abscess	*Doctor:* Anaesthetist	Yes*	*Holmes v.* *Bd. of Hosp.* *Trustees* *of London*

PROCEDURE: CARE

I(a) DOCTOR: ATTENDING PATIENT (FAILURE)

INJURY	DEFENDANT	LIAB.	CASE NAME
Amputation: Feet	*Doctor:* Surgeon: General	New Trial	*Key v.* *Thomson*
Death: Peritonitis *Infection:* Peritonitis	*Doctor:* General Practitioner	Yes	*Wilson v.* *Stark*

I(b) DOCTOR: ATTENDING PATIENT (VARIOUS)

INJURY	DEFENDANT	LIAB.	CASE NAME
Brain Damage: Cardiac arrest	*Doctor:* Anaesthetist *House Staff:* Resident	Yes Yes	*Aynsley v.* *Toronto* *Gen. Hosp.*
Death: Cardiac arrest	*Doctor:* Anaesthetist *Doctor:* Surgeon: General	No No	*MacKinnon v.* *Ignacio*
Joint: Wrist	*Doctor:* Surgeon: General	No	*Knight v.* *Sisters of* *St. Ann*
Pain & Suffering *Scarring/deformity:* Wrist	*Dentist*	No	*Lafleche v.* *Larouche*
Pain & Suffering	*Doctor:* General Practitioner	No	*Pierce v.* *Strathroy Hosp.*
Senses: Sight Impairment	*Doctor:* Surgeon: General *Hospital* *Pharmacist* (not party)	Apportioned	*Misericordia* *Hosp. v.* *Bustillo*

INJURY	DEFENDANT	LIAB.	CASE NAME
I(c) DOCTOR: CASE MANAGEMENT			
Further Treatment Req'd:	*Doctor:* Dermatologist	Yes	*Barr v.*
Aggravated condition			*Hughes*
Pain & Suffering			
I(d) DOCTOR: DURING TREATMENT (SPONGES)			
Assault/battery	*Doctor:* Surgeon: General	No	*Winn v.*
	Hospital	No	*Alexander*
Death: Asphyxia	*Doctor:* Surgeon: General	Yes	*Anderson v.*
			Chasney
Death: Asphyxia	*Doctor:* Dentist	Yes	*Nesbitt v. Holt*
Further Treatment Req'd:	*Doctor:* Surgeon: General	Appor-	*Cosgrove v.*
Corrective Surgery		tioned	*Gaudreau*
Pain & Suffering			
Further Treatment Req'd:	*Doctor:* Surgeon: General	No	*Jewison v.*
Corrective Surgery			*Hassard*
Pain & Suffering			
Further Treatment Req'd:	*Doctor:* Surgeon: General	No	*Petite v.*
Corrective surgery			*MacLeod*
Further Treatment Req'd:	*Doctor:*	No	*Karderas v.*
Corrective surgery	Obstetrician/Gynaecologist		*Clow*
Pain & Suffering			
Further Treatment Req'd:	*Doctor:* Surgeon: General	No	*Radclyffe v.*
Corrective surgery			*Rennie*
Further Treatment Req'd:	*Doctor:* Surgeon: General	No	*Waldon v.*
Corrective surgery			*Archer*
I(e) DOCTOR: DURING TREATMENT (SURGICAL INSTRUMENTS)			
Further Treatment Req'd:	*Doctor:* General Practitioner	Yes	*Gloning v.*
Corrective surgery			*Miller*
Further Treatment Req'd:	*Doctor:* Surgeon: General	Yes	*Taylor v.*
Corrective surgery			*Gray*
Pain & Suffering			
Scarring: Face	*Doctor:*	Yes	*Van Winkle v.*
Pain & Suffering	Otolaryngologist		*Chen*
I(f) DOCTOR: HOSPITALIZATION			
Death: Suicide	*Doctor:* Psychiatrist	No	*Haines v.*
	Psychologist	No	*Bellissimo*
I(g) DOCTOR: POST TREATMENT			
Amputation/removal: Testicle	*Doctor:* General Practitioner	No	*Thomas v.*
Infection: Gangrene	*Doctor:* Surgeon: General	Yes	*Scarborough*
	Hospital	No	*Gen. Hosp.*
Bone: Jaw: loss of teeth	*Doctor:* Surgeon: Cosmetic	Yes*	*O'Connell v.*
			Munro

INJURY	DEFENDANT	LIAB.	CASE NAME
Bone: Hip: Fracture *Cardiovascular/circulatory:* Avascular necrosis	*Doctor:* Surgeon: Orthopaedic	No	*Powell v.* *Guttman*
Bone: Leg: Displacement *Scarring/deformity:* Leg	*Doctor:* General Practitioner	No	*Rickley v.* *Stratton*
Bone: Wrist: Fracture	*Doctor:* General Practitioner	Yes	*Baltzan v.* *Fidelity Ins.*
Cardiovascular/circulatory: Bleeding	*Doctor:* General Practitioner	No	*Tacknyk v.* *Lake of the* *Woods Clinic*
Cardiovascular/circulatory: Volkman's Ischaemic Contracture	*Doctor:* Surgeon: Orthopaedic	Yes	*Rietze v.* *Bruser (No. 2)*
Further Treatment Req'd: Corrective surgery	*Doctor:* General Practitioner	No*	*Gonda v.* *Kerbel*
Further Treatment Req'd: Corrective surgery	*Doctor:* General Practitioner *Doctor:* Gastroenterologist	Yes Yes	*Reynard v.* *Carr*
Further Treatment Req'd: Corrective surgery	*Doctor:* Surgeon: General	No	*Law v.* *Gomel*
Further Treatment Req'd: Corrective surgery	*Doctor:* Obstetrician/ Gynaecologist	Yes*	*McBride v.* *Langton*
Further Treatment Req'd: Corrective surgery	*Doctor:* Surgeon: Orthopaedic	No	*Powell v.* *Guttman*
Further Treatment Req'd: Corrective surgery	*Doctor:* Obstetrician/ Gynaecologist	No**	*Videto v.* *Kennedy*
Further Treatment Req'd: Unsuccessful treatment	*Doctor:* Obstetrician/ Gynaecologist	Yes*	*Zimmer v.* *Ringrose*
Infection: Osteomyelitis	*Doctor:* Surgeon: General	No	*Law v.* *Gomel*
Infection: Peritonitis	*Doctor:* General Practitioner	Yes*	*Gonda v.* *Kerbel*
Infection: Peritonitis	*Doctor:* Obstetrician/ Gynaecologist	Yes*	*McBride v.* *Langton*
Infection: Peritonitis	*Doctor:* Obstetrician/ Gynaecologist	No**	*Videto v.* *Kennedy*
Pain & Suffering	*Doctor:* Surgeon: General	No	*Law v.* *Gomel*
Paralysis: Quadriplegia	*Doctor:* Neurosurgeon *House Staff:* Resident	No* No*	*Ferguson v.* *Hamilton Civic* *Hosp.*
Pregnancy: Unwanted	*Doctor:* Obstetrician/ Gynaecologist	Yes*	*Zimmer v.* *Ringrose*

INJURY	DEFENDANT	LIAB.	CASE NAME
Scarring/deformity: Abdomen	*Doctor:* Obstetrician/ Gynaecologist	No**	*Videto v. Kennedy*
Scarring/deformity: Leg	*Doctor:* Surgeon: Orthopaedic	No	*Ostrowski v. Lotto*
Surgery: Bleeding	*Doctor*	No	*McCulligh v. McLean*
I(h) DOCTOR: SUPERVISION/CONTROL			
Bone: Arm: Fracture	*Doctor:* General Practitioner	Yes	*Dowey v. Rothwell & Assoc.*
Bone: Hip: Fracture	*Doctor:* General Practitioner	No	*Robinson v. Annapolis Gen. Hosp.*
Brain Damage	*Doctor:* Neurologist	Yes	*Foote v. Royal Columbian Hosp.*
Brain Damage	*Hospital*	Settled	*Yepremian v. Scarborough Gen. Hosp.*
Burn	*Hospital* *Nurse* (not party)	Yes	*Logan v. Colchester*
Death	*Hospital* *Nurse* (not party)	No	*Brandeis v. Weldon*
Death	*Hospital* *Nurse* (not party)	No	*Rodych v. Krasey*
Death: Fall	*Doctor:* Psychiatrist	Yes	*Villemure v. Turcot*
Death: Suicide	*Doctor:* Neurosurgeon	No	*Stadel v. Albertson*
Disease: Smallpox	*Hospital*	No	*McDaniel v. Vancouver Gen. Hosp.*
Disease	*Hospital*	No	*Butler v. Toronto*
Fall	*Hospital* *Physiotherapist*	No	*McKay v. Royal Inland Hosp.*
Paralysis: Paraplegia	*Doctor:* Psychiatrist	No	*Worth v. Royal Jubilee Hosp.*
Unspecified Fall	*Doctor:* Neurologist	No	*University Hosp. Bd. v. Lepine*

INJURY	DEFENDANT	LIAB.	CASE NAME
II(a) IN HOSPITAL (ASSIGNMENT OF RESPONSIBILITIES)			
Death: Peritonitis	*Doctor:* General Practitioner	Yes	*Wilson v.*
Infection: Peritonitis			*Stark*
II(b) IN HOSPITAL (DISCHARGE)			
Brain Damage: Pneumonia	*Doctor:* General Practitioner	No	*Bissell v.* *Vancouver* *Gen. Hosp.*
II(c) IN HOSPITAL (DURING TREATMENT)			
Assault/Battery	*Doctor:* General Practitioner	No	*Winn v.* *Alexander*
Brain Damage	*Hospital* *Nurse* (not party)	Yes	*Hôpital Générale* *v. Perron*
Disease: Hepatitis B	*Hospital* *Nurse*	Appor-tioned	*Savoie v.* *Bouchard*
Further Treatment Req'd: Corrective surgery *Pain & Suffering*	*Hospital* *Nurse*	Appor-tioned	*Cosgrove v.* *Gaudreau*
Further Treatment Req'd: Corrective surgery	*Hospital* *Nurse* (not party)	No	*Petite v.* *MacLeod*
Joint: Wrist	*Hospital*	Yes	*Knight v. Sisters* *of St. Ann*
Further Treatment Req'd: Corrective surgery *Pain & Suffering*	*Hospital* *House Staff:* Resident *Nurse* (not party)	Yes	*Karderas v.* *Clow*
II(d) IN HOSPITAL (EMERGENCY)			
Birth Defects	*Hospital* *House Staff:* Resident *Nurse* (not party)	Appor-tioned	*Meyer v.* *Gordon*
Paralysis: Quadriplegia	*Hospital*	No	*Nash v.* *Olson*
Further Treatment Req'd: Aggravated condition	*Hospital* *Nurse*	No No	*Elverson v.* *Doctors Hosp.*
II(e) IN HOSPITAL (GENERAL)			
Brain Damage	*Hospital*	Settled	*Yepremian v.* *Scarborough* *Gen. Hosp.*
Burn	*Hospital* *Nuse* (not party)	Yes	*Logan v.* *Colchester*
Death	*Hospital* *Nurse* (not party)	No	*Brandeis v.* *Weldon*
II(f) IN HOSPITAL (PRE-TREATMENT)			
Bone: Hip: Fracture	*Hospital*	No	*Florence v.* *Les Soeurs de* *Misericorde*

INJURY	DEFENDANT	LIAB.	CASE NAME
II(g) IN HOSPITAL (POST-TREATMENT)			
Amputation/removal: Eye	*Hospital*	Yes	*Wyndham v.*
	Ward Aide	Yes	*Toronto Gen.*
			Hosp. Trustees
Amputation/removal: Foot	*Hospital*	No	*Vail v.*
	Nurse (not party)		*MacDonald*
Amputation/removal: Testicle	*Hospital*	No	*Thomas v.*
			Scarborough
			Gen. Hosp.
Cardiovascular/circulatory: Bleeding	*Clinic*	No	*Tacknyk v.*
			Lake of the
			Woods Clinic
Brain Damage	*Hospital*	Yes	*Laidlaw v.*
	Nurse (not party)		*Lions Gate Hosp.*
Burn	*Hospital*	No	*Cahoon v.*
			Edmonton
			Hosp. Bd.
Burn	*Hospital*	Yes	*Davis v.*
			Colchester
Burn: Feet	*Hospital*	Yes	*Bernier v.*
	Nurse (not party)		*Sisters of Service*
Burn: Feet	*Hospital*	Yes	*Eek v.*
	Nurse (not party)		*High River*
			Mun. Hosp. Bd.
Burn: Heel	*Hospital*	Yes	*Lavere v.*
	Nurse (not party)		*Smith's Falls*
			Pub. Hosp.
Burn: Leg: Hot water bottle	*Hospital*	Yes	*Nyberg v.*
	Nurse (not party)		*Provost Mun.*
			Hosp. Bd.
Death: Cardiac arrest	*Hospital*	Yes	*Krujelis v.*
	Nurse	Yes	*Esdale*
Death: Aspiration of gastric fluid	*Hospital*	Yes	*Joseph Brant*
	Nurse	Yes	*Memorial Hosp.*
			v. Koziol
Further Treatment Req'd: Prolonged Recovery	*Hospital*	Yes	*Beatty v.*
	Nurse (not party)		*Sisters of*
			Misericorde
Infection: Gangrene	*Hospital*	No	*Thomas v.*
			Scarborough
			Gen. Hosp.

INJURY	DEFENDANT	LIAB.	CASE NAME
Joint: Hip: Fusion	*Hospital*	No*	*Hajgato v.*
	Nurse (not party)		*London Health*
			Assn.
Nerve: Arm: Neurapraxia	*Hospital*	Yes	*Traynor v.*
	Nurse (not party)		*Vancott*
Pain & Suffering	*Hospital*	Yes	*Beatty v.*
	Nurse (not party)		*Sisters of*
			Misericorde
Paralysis: Leg	*Hospital*	Yes	*Laughlin v.*
	Nurse (not party)		*Royal Columbian*
			Hosp.
Paralysis: Quadriplegia	*Hospital*	No*	*Ferguson v.*
	Resident	No*	*Hamilton Civic*
	Nurse (not party)		*Hosp.*
Senses: Sight	*Hospital*	Yes	*Wyndham v.*
impairment	*Ward Aide*	Yes	*Toronto Gen.*
			Hosp. Trustees
II(h) IN HOSPITAL (SUPERVISION/CONTROL)			
Birth Defects	*Hospital*	Appor-	*Meyer v.*
	House Staff: Resident	tioned	*Gordon*
	Nurse (not party)		
Bone: Arm: Fracture	*Clinic*	Yes	*Dowey v.*
	Nurse (not party)		*Rothwell & Assoc.*
Bone: Hip: Fracture	*Hospital*	No	*Hôtel-Dieu v.*
			Couloume
Bone: Hip: Fracture	*Hospital*	No	*Robinson v.*
	Nurse (not party)		*Annapolis*
			Gen. Hosp.
Brain Damage	*Hospital*	No	*Foote v.*
	Nurse (not party)		*Royal Columbian*
			Hosp.
Burn: Boiling Water	*Hospital*	Yes	*Sinclair v.*
	Nurse (not party)		*Victoria Hosp.*
Burn: Radiator	*Hospital*	Yes	*Farrell v.*
	Student (not party)		*Regina*
Death:	*Hospital*	Yes	*Villemure v.*
Fall			*Turcot*
Death:	*Hospital*	No	*Stadel v.*
Suicide			*Albertson*
Death	*Hospital*	No	*Barsey v.*
			Govt. of Man.

INJURY	DEFENDANT	LIAB.	CASE NAME
Dental: Damage	*Hospital*	No	*Penner v. Bethel*
Paralysis: Paraplegia	*Hospital*	No	*Worth v. Royal Jubilee Hosp.*
Paralysis: Vocal Chord	*Hospital* *Orderly*	No No	*Brennan v. Dir. of Mental Health*
Scarring/deformity	*Hospital*	No	*University Hosp. v. Lepine*
Scarring/Deformity: Fall	*Hospital* *Nurse*	No No	*Child v. Vancouver Gen. Hosp.*
Scarring/Deformity: Assault	*Hospital*	Yes	*Lawson v. Wellesley Hosp.*
Scarring/Deformity: Fall	*Hospital*	No	*Flynn v. Hamilton*

PROCEDURE: CONSULTATION
I FAILURE TO CONSULT SPECIALIST

INJURY	DEFENDANT	LIAB.	CASE NAME
Amputation: Foot *Infection:* Gangrene	*Doctor:* General Practitioner	Yes	*Vail v. MacDonald*
Amputation: Leg	*Doctor:* General Practitioner	Yes	*Layden v. Cope*
Further Treatment Req'd: Aggravated Condition *Paralysis:* Leg	*Doctor:* General Practitioner	Yes	*Thomas v. Port Colborne Gen. Hosp.*
Pain & Suffering	*Doctor:* General Practitioner	Yes	*Daoust v. R.*

II FOLLOW UP CARE

INJURY	DEFENDANT	LIAB.	CASE NAME
Senses: Sight: Loss	*Doctor:* Dermatologist	Apportioned	*Crossman v. Stewart*

PROCEDURE: DIAGNOSIS
I(a) FAILURE TO DIAGNOSE (AMPUTATION NECESSARY)

INJURY	DEFENDANT	LIAB.	CASE NAME
Amputation: Feet/hands	*Doctor:* Surgeon: General	New Trial	*Key v. Thomson*

I(b) FAILURE TO DIAGNOSE (APPENDICITIS)

INJURY	DEFENDANT	LIAB.	CASE NAME
Death	*Chiropractor*	No	*R. v. Homeberg*
Death	*Doctor:* Attending Physician *General Surgeon:* Gynaecologist *Hospital:* Nurse	Yes Yes Yes	*Bergen v. Sturgeon Gen. Hosp.*

INJURY	DEFENDANT	LIAB.	CASE NAME
Death: Peritonitis	*Doctor:* General Practitioner	No	*Wilson v.*
Infection: Peritonitis	*Hospital*	No	*Stark*
I(c) FAILURE TO DIAGNOSE (ARTERIOSCELEROSIS)			
Amputation: Leg	*Doctor:* General Practitioner	No	*Harquail v.*
			Sedgewick
I(d) FAILURE TO DIAGNOSE (CANCER)			
Disease: Cancer	*Doctor:* Surgeon: General	No	*Thompson v.*
	Hospital	No	*Creaghan*
Further Treatment Req'd:	*Doctor:* Dermatologist	No	*Barr v.*
Aggravated condition			*Hughes*
Pain & Suffering			
Unnecessary Treatment	*Doctor:* Surgeon: General	No	*Wilson v.*
(Incorrect diagnosis)			*Swanson*
I(e) FAILURE TO DIAGNOSE (DIABETES)			
Birth Defects	*Doctor:* General Practitioner	No	*Quiroz v.*
			Austrup
Brain Damage	*Doctor:* General Practitioner	Settled	*Yepremian v.*
	Doctor: Internist (not party)		*Scarborough*
	Hospital		*Gen. Hosp.*
Cardiovascular/circulatory:	*Doctor: Gen. Practitioner:*	No	*Nichols v.*
Endocarditis	Obstetrician/	No	*Gray*
Further Treatment Req'd:	Gynaecologist		
Open heart surgery			
Death:	*Doctor:* Emerg. Rm. Physician	No	*Neufville*
Cardiac arrest	*Hospital*	Yes	*v. Sobers*
	Technician: Laboratory	Yes	
I(f) FAILURE TO DIAGNOSE (DISLOCATION)			
Further Treatment Req'd:	*Doctor:* Surgeon: General	No	*Moore v.*
Aggravated condition			*Large*
Further Treatment Req'd:	*Doctor:* General Practitioner	Yes	*Thompson v.*
Unsuccessful treatment	(not party)		*Columbia Coast*
			Mission
Joint: Hip: Displacement	*Doctor:* General Practitioner	Yes	*Dangerfield v.*
			David
Joint: Hip: Displacement	*Doctor:* General Practitioner	No	*Bruinooge v.*
			Collier
Joint: Shoulder:	*Doctor:* Surgeon: General	No	*Clark v.*
Impaired movement			*Wansbrough*
Joint: Wrist:	*Doctor:* General Practitioner	Appor-	*Osburn v.*
Impaired movement	*Hospital*	tioned	*Mohindra*
I(g) FAILURE TO DIAGNOSE (EMPHYSEMA)			
Disease: Emphysema	Clinic	No	*McCarty v.*
	House Staff: Resident	No	*University*
			of B.C.

INJURY	DEFENDANT	LIAB.	CASE NAME
I(h) FAILURE TO DIAGNOSE (ENCEPHALITIS)			
Brain Damage	*Doctor:* General Practitioner	No	*Tiesmaki v. Wilson*
I(i) FAILURE TO DIAGNOSE (EPIGLOTTITIS)			
Death: Epiglottitis	*Doctor:* Emerg. Rm. Physician	Yes	*De Moura v. Mississauga Hosp.*
I(j) FAILURE TO DIAGNOSE (FRACTURE: ANKLE)			
Joint: Ankle	*Doctor:* General Practitioner	No	*Price v.*
	Doctor: Surgeon: Orthopaedic	Yes	*Milawski*
I(k) FAILURE TO DIAGNOSE (FRACTURE: ARM)			
Further Treatment Req'd: Corrective	*Doctor:* General Practitioner	Yes	*Armstrong v. Dawson*
I(l) FAILURE TO DIAGNOSE (FRACTURE: COMPOUND)			
Amputation: Leg	*Doctor:* Surgeon: Orthopaedic	Yes	*Dean v.*
Infection: Gangrene	*Hospital*	No	*York County Hosp. Corp.*
I(m) FAILURE TO DIAGNOSE (FRACTURE: FINGER)			
Further Treatment Req'd: Corrective surgery	*Doctor:* General Practitioner	Yes	*Pepin v.*
	Hospital	Yes	*Hôpital du*
Scarring/deformity: Finger	*Technician:* X-ray (not party)		*Haut Richelieu*
I(n) FAILURE TO DIAGNOSE (FRACTURE: FOOT)			
Pain & Suffering	*Doctor:* General Practitioner	Yes	*Daoust v. R.*
I(o) FAILURE TO DIAGNOSE (FRACTURE: HIP)			
Amputation: Leg	*Doctor:* General Practitioner	Yes	*Cusson v. Robidoux*
Further Treatment Req'd: Aggravated condition *Joint:* Hip: Disability	*Doctor:* Surgeon: General *Hospital*	Apportioned	*Hôpital Notre Dame v. Laurent*
Further Treatment Req'd: Unsucessful treatment	*Doctor:* General Practitioner	Yes	*Stamper v. Rhindress*
I(p) FAILURE TO DIAGNOSE (FRACTURE: SPINE)			
Death: Adynamic ileus	*Hospital*	Yes	*Fraser v.*
	House Staff: Intern	Yes	*Vancouver Gen. Hosp.*
Further Treatment Req'd: Aggravated condition *Paralysis*	*Doctor:* General Practitioner	No	*Thomas v. Port Colborne Gen. Hosp.*
I(q) FAILURE TO DIAGNOSE (HEART DISEASE)			
Death: Cardiac arrest	*Doctor:* General Practitioner	No	*Ehler v. Smith*
I(r) FAILURE TO DIAGNOSE (HEMORRHAGE)			
Death: Hemorrhage	*Doctor:* Surgeon: Orthopaedic	No	*Chubey v. Ahsan*

INJURY	DEFENDANT	LIAB.	CASE NAME
Death: Hemorrhage	*Doctor:* General Practitioner *Hospital* *Nurse* (not party)	No No	*Serre v.* *DeTilly*
Death: Hemorrhage	*Doctor:* Emerg. Rm. Physician *Hospital*	Yes No	*Wade v.* *Nayernouri*
Senses: Sight: Loss	*Doctor:* Otolaryngologist	No	*Kunitz v.* *Merei*
Amputation: Leg	*Doctor:* General Practitioner	Yes	*Layden v. Cope*
I(s) FAILURE TO DIAGNOSE (INCORRECT DIAGNOSIS)			
Mastectomy: Unnecessary: Incorrect diagnosis of cancer	*Doctor*	Admit- ted	*Down v.* *Royal Jubilee* *Hosp.*
Organ Removed: Fallopian tubes: Incorrect diagnosis of cancer	*Doctor:* Surgeon: Pathologist *Hospital:* Hospital Laboratory	Admit- ted	*Lefebvre v.* *Osborne*
Organ: Stomach, spleen, pancreas removal	*Doctor:* Surgeon: General	No	*Wilson v.* *Swanson*
I(t) FAILURE TO DIAGNOSE (INFECTION)			
Brain Damage: Pneumonia	*Doctor:* Pediatrician *Doctor:* Surgeon: General	No No	*Bissell v.* *Vancouver* *Gen. Hosp.*
Death	*Doctor:* General Practitioner	No	*R. v. Watson*
Disease: Arthritis	*Doctor:* Surgeon: Orthopaedic *Hospital* *House Staff:* Resident *Nurse* (not party)	No* No	*Hajgato v.* *London Health* *Assn.*
Further Treatment Req'd: Aggravated condition	*Doctor:* General Practitioner	Yes	*Turriff v.* *King*
Further Treatment Req'd: Corrective surgery *Infection:* Osteomyelitis	*Doctor:* Surgeon: General	No	*Law v.* *Gomel*
Further Treatment Req'd: Corrective surgery *Infection:* Peritonitis	*Doctor:* Obstetrician/ Gynaecologist	Yes*	*McBride v.* *Langton*
Joint: Hip: Fusion	*Doctor:* Surgeon: Orthopaedic *Hospital* *House Staff:* Resident *Nurse* (not party)	No* No	*Hajgato v.* *London Health* *Assn.*
Pain & Suffering	*Doctor:* General Practitioner	Yes	*Turriff v.* *King*
Pain & Suffering	*Doctor:* General Practitioner *Doctor:* Surgeon: General	Yes Yes	*Wine v.* *Dawyd*

INJURY	DEFENDANT	LIAB.	CASE NAME
Paralysis: Quadriplegia	*Doctor:* Anaesthetist	Yes	*Holmes v.*
	Doctor: Internist	Yes	*Bd. of Hosp.*
	Doctor: Otolaryngologist	Yes	*Trustees of London*
Scarring/deformity: Groin	*Doctor:* General Practitioner	Yes	*Wine v.*
	Doctor: Surgeon: General	Yes	*Dawyd*
Senses: Sight: Loss	*Doctor:* Opthamologist	Yes	*Moffat v. Witelson*
I(u) FAILURE TO DIAGNOSE (INTERNAL INJURIES)			
Death	*Doctor:* General Practitioner	No	*Rodych v.*
	Hospital	No	*Krasey*
	Nurse (not party)		
I(v) FAILURE TO DIAGNOSE (MASTOIDITIS)			
Paralysis: Face	*Doctor:* General Practitioner	No	*Jarvis v.*
Senses: Sight/hearing Impairment			*Int. Nickel Co.*
I(w) FAILURE TO DIAGNOSE (MENINGITIS)			
Death: Meningitis	*Doctor:* General Practitioner	Yes	*Dale v. Munthali*
I(x) FAILURE TO DIAGNOSE (MITRAL STENOSIS)			
c/c: Mitral stenosis	*Doctor:* General Practitioner	No	*Athanslous v.*
Death			*Guzman*
I(y) FAILURE TO DIAGNOSE (MULTIPLE GESTATION)			
Birth Defects	*Doctor:* General Practitioner	Yes	*Wipfli v.*
	Doctor: Obstetrician/ Gynaecologist	No	*Britten*
I(z) FAILURE TO DIAGNOSE (OPHTHALMIC)			
Senses: Sight Impairment	*Doctor:* General Practitioner	No	*Bell v. R.*
Senses: Sight: Loss	*Doctor:* Ophthalmologist	Yes	*Piche v. Ing*
I(aa) FAILURE TO DIAGNOSE (PLEURISY)			
Further Treatment Req'd: Corrective surgery *Disease:* Pleurisy	*Doctor:* General Practitioner	No	*Richardson v. Nugent*
I(bb) FAILURE TO DIAGNOSE (POISONING)			
Death Carbon monoxide poisoning	*Doctor:* General Practitioner	No	*Ostash v. Sonnenberg*
I(cc) FAILURE TO DIAGNOSE (SURGERY REQUIRED)			
Further Treatment Req'd: Corrective surgery	*Optometrist*	No	*Murphy v. Mathieson*
I(dd) FAILURE TO DIAGNOSE (TUBERCULOSIS)			
Further Treatment Req'd: Aggravated condition	*Chiropractor*	Yes	*Gibbons v. Harris*

INJURY	DEFENDANT	LIAB.	CASE NAME
I(ee) FAILURE TO DIAGNOSE (UNSPECIFIED)			
	Chiropractor	Yes	Morrow v. McGillivray
I(ff) FAILURE TO DIAGNOSE (VOLKMANN'S CONTRACTURE)			
Cardiovascular/circulatory: Volkmann's Ischaemic Contracture Scarring/deformity: Arm	Doctor: Surgeon: Orthopaedic	Yes	Rietze v. Bruser (No. 2)
II(a) PROCEDURE (ANGIOGRAM)			
Paralysis: Quadriplegia	Doctor: Neurosurgeon	No*	Ferguson v.
	Hospital	No	Hamilton
	House Staff: Resident	No*	Civic Hosp.
Paralysis: Quadriplegia	Doctor: Surgeon: Vascular	No	McLean v.
	Doctor: Radiologist	No	Weir
II(b) PROCEDURE (AUDIOGRAM)			
Senses: Hearing Impairment	Hospital	Yes	Bartlett v.
	Rehab. Medicine: Audiologist	Yes	Children's Hosp. Corp.
II(c) PROCEDURE (BIOPSY)			
Paralysis: Vocal Chord	Doctor: Surgeon: General	No**	Bickford v. Stiles
Paralysis: Vocal Chord	Doctor: General Practitioner	No	Finlay v. Auld
II(d) PROCEDURE (FLUOROSCOPY)			
Burn: Back	Doctor: General Practitioner	No	Abel v.
	Hospital	Yes	Cooke
	Technician: X-ray (not party)		
Further Treatment Req'd: Corrective surgery	Doctor: General Practitioner	Yes	Armstrong v. Dawson
II(e) PROCEDURE (PYELOGRAM) Death	Doctor: Internist: Radiologist	Yes	Leonard v. Knott
II(f) PROCEDURE (SIGMOIDOSCOPY)			
Further Treatment Req'd: Corrective surgery Infection: Peritonitis	Doctor: General Practitioner	Yes*	Gonda v. Kerbel
II(g) PROCEDURE (X-RAY)			
Bone: Wrist: Fracture	Doctor: General Practitioner	Yes	Baltzan v. Fidelity Ins. Co.
Burn: Hand	Doctor: General Practitioner	Yes	Hochman v.
	Technician: X-ray (not party)	No	Willinsky
Burn: Hand/leg	Doctor: General Practitioner	No	Antoniuk v.
	Nurse (not party)	No	Smith

INJURY	DEFENDANT	LIAB.	CASE NAME
Further Treatment Req'd:	*Doctor:* General Practitioner	Yes	*Pepin v.*
Corrective surgery	*Hospital*	Yes	*Hôpital du*
Scarring/deformity: Finger	*Technician:* X-ray (not party)		*Haut Richelieu*
Paralysis: Arm	*Hospital*	Yes	*Murphy v.*
			St. Catharines
			Gen. Hosp.

PROCEDURE: REFERRAL
I FAILURE TO REFER TO SPECIALIST

INJURY	DEFENDANT	LIAB.	CASE NAME
Amputation: Leg	*Doctor*	No	*Lachambre v.*
			Perraulti
Amputation: Leg	*Doctor:* General Practitioner	Yes	*Layden v.*
			Cope
Amputation: Leg	*Doctor:* General Practitioner	No	*Harquail v.*
			Sedgewick
Disease: Emphysema	*Clinic*	No	*McCarty v.*
	House Staff: Resident	No	*Univ. of B.C.*
Paralysis: Face	*Doctor:* General Practitioner	No	*Jarvis v.*
Senses: Sight/hearing:			*Int. Nickel Co.*
Impairment			
Senses: Sight	*Doctor:* General Practitioner	Admit-	*Eaglebach v.*
Impairment		ted	*Walters*
Senses: Sight	*Doctor:* General Practitioner	No	*Bell v.*
Impairment			*R.*

II FOLLOW UP CARE

INJURY	DEFENDANT	LIAB.	CASE NAME
Senses: Sight: Loss	*Doctor:* Dermatologist	Appor-	*Crossman v.*
		tioned	*Stewart*
Senses: Sight: Loss	*Doctor:* General Practitioner	No	*Beninger v.*
Further Treatment Req'd:			*Walton*
Corrective surgery			

PROCEDURE: TREATMENT
I ABORTION

INJURY	DEFENDANT	LIAB.	CASE NAME
Brain Damage	*Doctor:* Obstetrician/	No*	*Mang v.*
	Gynaecologist		*Moscovitz*
	House Staff: Intern	No	

II(a) BLOOD (BLEEDING)

INJURY	DEFENDANT	LIAB.	CASE NAME
Cardiovascular/Circulatory:	*Doctor:* Surgeon: General	Yes	*Kelly v.*
Punctured artery			*Dow*
Excessive bleeding when dressing	*Doctor*	No	*McCulligh v.*
removed			*McLean*
Scarring: Face	*Doctor:* Otolaryngologist	Yes	*Van Winkle v.*
Pain & Suffering			*Chen*

INJURY	DEFENDANT	LIAB.	CASE NAME
II(b) BLOOD (TRANSFUSION)			
Amputation: Arm *Infection:* Gangrene	*Doctor:* Surgeon: General	No	*Armstrong v.* *McClealand*
Infection: Streptococcus	*House Staff:* Intern	No	*Cox v.* *Saskatoon*
Treatment: Blood: Transfusion	N/A	No**	*Re D.*
Treatment: Blood: Transfusion	N/A	Yes**	*Forsyth v.* *Children's* *Aid Soc.*
Treatment: Blood: Transfusion	N/A	**	*Pentland v.* *Pentland*
Treatment: Blood: Transfusion	N/A	No**	*R. v. Cyrenne*
Treatment: Blood: Transfusion	N/A	No*	*Wintersgill v.* *Min. of Social* *Services*
III CHIROPRACTIC			
Further Treatment Req'd: Unsuccessful treatment	*Chiropractor*	No	*Cawley v.* *Mercer*
Further Treatment Req'd: Unsuccessful treatment *Pain & Suffering*	*Chiropractor*	Yes	*Penner v.* *Theobald*
Pain & Suffering	*Chiropractor*	No	*Rutledge v.* *Fisher*
Paralysis: Paraplegia	*Chiropractor*	No*	*Strachan v.* *Simpson*
IV DENTAL (CROWN & BRIDGE)			
Death: Asphyxia	*Dentist*	Yes	*Nesbitt v.* *Holt*
Dental: Extraction: Additional teeth	*Dentist:* Dental Surgeon	No*	*Boase v.* *Paul*
Dental: Extraction: Additional teeth	*Dentist*	No*	*Guimond v.* *Laberge*
Dental Extraction: Additional teeth	*Oral Surgeon* *Cosmetic Surgeon*	Yes* Yes	*Sunne v.* *Shaw*
Dental: Extraction: Permanent tooth	*Dentist*	Yes	*Gagnon v.* *Stortini*
Dental: Extraction: Unauthorized	*Dentist:* Dental Surgeon	No*	*Nykiforuk v.* *Lockwood*
Dental: Extraction: Unnecessary	*Dentist*	Yes	*Murano v.* *Gray*
Dental: Extraction: Unnecessary	*Dentist*	No*	*Parmley v.* *Parmley*

INJURY	DEFENDANT	LIAB.	CASE NAME
Dental: Extraction *Cardiovascular/circulatory:* Bleeding	*Dentist*	No*	*Murrin v. Janes*
Dental: "Hand Over Mouth" *Pain & Suffering* *Scarring/deformity:* Face	*Dentist*	No	*Lafleche v. Larouche*
Dental: Restorative surgery *Scarring/deformity:* Lip	*Dentist:* Paedodontist	No	*Dunn v. Young*
Dental: Surgery *Death:* Asphyxia	*Dentist:* Dental Surgeon	Yes	*Kangas v. Parker*
Further Treatment Req'd: Corrective dental	*Dentist:* Prosthodontist	Yes	*Fluevog v. Pottinger*
Further Treatment Req'd: Corrective surgery	*Dentist*	No	*McTaggart v. Powers*
Further Treatment Req'd: Residual root	*Dentist*	No	*Legault-Bellemare v. Madore*
Further Treatment Req'd: Unsuccessful treatment	*Dentist:* Dental Surgeon	Yes	*Drinnen v. Douglas*
Further Treatment Req'd: Unsuccessful treatment	*Dentist*	No	*Allard v. Boykowich*
Nerve: Facial: Numbness	*Dentist*	No*	*Schinz v. Dickinson*
Nerve: Facial: Numbness	*Oral Surgeon*	No*	*Diack v. Bardsley*
Nerve: Facial Numbness/hypersensitivity	*Oral Surgeon*	Yes**	*Rawlings v. Lindsay*
Pain & Suffering	*Dentist*	No	*Kobescak v. Chan*
Pain & Suffering	*Dentist*	Yes	*Murano v. Gray*
V(a) DERMATOLOGICAL (DERMABRASION) *Scarring/deformity:* Face	*Doctor:* Surgeon: Cosmetic	No*	*Hankins v. Papillon*
V(b) DERMATOLOGICAL (SLUSH) *Scarring/deformity:* Face	*Doctor:* Dermatologist *Hospital*	No No	*Johnston v. Wellesley Hosp.*
VI DIET *Death:* Malnutrition	*Doctor:* General Practitioner	Yes	*R. v. Rogers*

INJURY	DEFENDANT	LIAB.	CASE NAME
VII DRESSING WOUND			
Nerve: Leg: Severed	*Doctor:* Surgeon: General	No	*Zirkler v.*
Paralysis: Leg			*Robinson*
VIII EMERGENCY			
Care: Hospital	*Hospital*	No	*Elverson v.*
Emergency	*Nurse*	No	*Doctors Hosp.*
Paralysis: Quadriplegia	*Doctor:* Emerg. Rm. Physician	No	*Nash v.*
			Olson
Treatment:	N/A	**	*Supt. of Family*
Surgery: Shunt			*& Child Services*
			v. Dawson
IX(a) EXPERIMENTAL (ANAESTHETIC)			
Brain Damage	*Doctor:* Anaesthetist	Yes*	*Halushka v.*
			University
			of Sask.
IX(b) EXPERIMENTAL (QUARTZ LAMP)			
Amputation: Foot	*Doctor:* General Practitioner	Yes*	*Baills v.*
Infection: Gangrene			*Boulanger*
IX(c) EXPERIMENTAL (STERILIZATION)			
Further Treatment Req'd:	*Doctor:* Obstetrician/	Yes*	*Cryderman v.*
Unsuccessful treatment	Gynaecologist		*Ringrose*
X(a) HEAT (DIATHERMY)			
Burn	*Hospital*	Yes	*Fleming v.*
	Nurse (not party)		*Sisters of*
			St. Joseph
X(b) HEAT (HEAT CRADLE)			
Burn: Thigh	*Hospital*	No	*Vuchar v.*
	Nurse (not party)		*Toronto Gen.*
			Hosp. Trustees
X(c) HEAT (KELLY PAD)			
Burn: Back	*Doctor:* General Practitioner	No	*Lenzen v.*
	Hospital	Yes	*Southern*
	Nurse	Yes	*Vancouver*
			Island Hosp.
Burn: Back/Shoulder	*Doctor:* Surgeon: General	No	*Armstrong v.*
	Nurse (not party)		*Bruce*
X(d) HEAT (STEAM INHALATION)			
Burn	*Hospital*	Yes	*Harkies v.*
	Nurse (not party)		*Lord Dufferin*
			Hosp.
XI HYPERTENSION (CORRECTION OF)			
Cardiovascular/circulatory: Stroke	*Doctor:* General Practitioner	No	*Parsons v.*
Paralysis: Hemiplegia			*Schmok*

INJURY	DEFENDANT	LIAB.	CASE NAME
XII INFECTION (CORRECTION OF)			
Amputation: Finger	*Doctor:* General Practitioner	No	*Petit v.*
	Hospital	No	*Hôpital Ste.*
			Jeanne D'Arc
XIII(a) INJECTION (ANAESTHETIC)			
Amputation: Hand	*Doctor:* Anaesthetist	Yes	*Villeneuve v.*
	Hospital	No	*Sisters of*
	Nurse (not party)		*St. Joseph*
Death: Injection of	*Doctor:* General Practitioner	No	*Bugden v.*
wrong drug	*Hospital*	Yes	*Harbour View*
	Nurse	Yes	*Hosp.*
Further Treatment Req'd:	*Doctor:* Anaesthetist	No	*Lloy v.*
Corrective skin grafts	*House Staff:* Resident	No	*Milner*
Pain & Suffering			
Pain & Suffering	*Doctor:* Anaesthetist	No*	*Allan v.*
			New Mount
			Sinai Hosp.
Paralysis: Legs	*Doctor:* Anaethetist	No	*Girard v.*
	Hospital	No	*Royal Columbian*
			Hosp.
Paralysis: Paraplegia	*Doctor:* Anaesthetist	Yes	*Martel v.*
	Hospital	Yes	*Hotel-Dieu*
			St. Vallier
XIII(b) INJECTION (INTRAVENOUS FEEDING)			
Treatment: Injection:	*Hospital*	Yes	*Murphy v.*
Intravenous feeding	*House Staff:* Intern		*St. Catharines*
			Gen. Hosp.
XIII(c) INJECTION (MEDICATION)			
Burn: Hand	*Doctor:* General Practitioner	No	*Neufeld v.*
Further Treatment Req'd:			*McQuitty*
Corrective surgery			
Nerve: Sciatic: Damage	*Hospital*	Yes	*Huber v.*
	Nurse (not party)		*Burnaby*
			Gen. Hosp.
Nerve: Sciatic: Damage	*Hospital*	Yes	*Fiege v.*
Pain & Suffering	*Nurse*	Yes	*Cornwall*
			Gen. Hosp.
Nerve: Sciatic: Foot Drop	*Hospital*	Yes	*Laughlin v.*
Paralysis: Leg	*Nurse* (not party)		*Royal Columbian*
			Hosp.
XIII(d) INJECTION (VACCINATION)			
Disease: Septicemia	*Doctor:* General Practitioner	Yes	*Adderley v.*
			Bremner

INJURY	DEFENDANT	LIAB.	CASE NAME
Disease: Smallpox	*Doctor:* Pediatrician	No	*Gent v. Wilson*
Further Treatment Req'd: Corrective surgery	*Doctor:* General Practitioner	Yes	*Cardin v. Montreal*
Infection: Gangrene	*Nurse*	No	*Cavan v. Wilcox*
Paralysis: Arm	*Doctor:* General Practitioner	Yes	*Cardin v. Montreal*
Paralysis: Quadriplegia	*Doctor:* General Practitioner	No	*Davidson v. Connaught*
Scarring/deformity: Arm	*Doctor:* General Practitioner	Yes	*Cardin v. Montreal*
Scarring/deformity: Arm	*Doctor:* Pediatrician	No	*Gent v. Wilson*

XIV(a) MEDICATION (ADMINISTRATION)

INJURY	DEFENDANT	LIAB.	CASE NAME
Bone: Cheekbone/Jaw: Fracture	*Hospital* *Nurse* (not party)	No	*Buchanan v. Fort Churchill Gen. Hosp.*
Brain Damage	*Doctor:* Emerg. Rm. Physician *Doctor:* Internist (not party)	Settled	*Yepremian v. Scarborough Gen. Hosp.*
Cardiovascular/circulatory: Avascular necrosis	*Doctor:* Gastroenterologist *Hospital*	No* No	*Moore v. Shaughnessy*
Cardiovascular/circulatory: Hemorrhage *Further Treatment Req'd:* Corrective surgery	*Doctor:* Surgeon: Orthopaedic	Yes	*Critchton v. Hastings*
Death	*Doctor:* Surgeon: General	No	*R. v. Giardine*
Insulin Shock	*Doctor:* General Practitioner	Yes	*Marshall v. Rogers*
Paralysis: Quadriplegia	*Doctor:* General Practitioner	No*	*Davidson v. Connaught*
Senses: Sight Impairment	*Hospital* *Nurse*	Yes Yes	*Barker v. Lockhart*
Senses: Sight Impairment	*Doctor:* Surgeon: General	Yes	*Casson v. Haig*
Senses: Sight Impairment	*Doctor:* Surgeon: General	Appor- tioned	*Misericordia Hosp. v. Bustillo*

INJURY	DEFENDANT	LIAB.	CASE NAME
XIV(b) MEDICATION (PRESCRIPTION)			
Amputation/removal: Stomach *Further Treatment Req'd:* Corrective	*Pharmacist*	Yes	*Williams v.* *Jones*
Bone Destruction: Avascular necrosis *Further Treatment Req'd:*	*Doctor:* General Practitioner *Doctor:* Gastroenterologist	Yes Yes	*Reynard v.* *Carr*
Cerebral Vascular Accident: Stroke Partial permanent disability	*Doctor:* Gynaecologist	Yes	*Schierz v.* *Dodds*
Death	*Hospital* *House Staff:* Resident *Pharmacist*	Settled	*Filipewich v.* *University* *Hosp. Bd.*
Further Treatment Req'd: Drug overdose	*Doctor:* Psychiatrist *Pharmacist*	No[•] No	*Molnar v.* *Conway*
Poisoning	*Doctor:* General Practitioner *Pharmacist*	No Yes	*Stretton v.* *Holmes*
Senses: Sight Impairment	*Hospital* *Nurse* (not party) *Pharmacist* (not party)	Apportioned	*Misericordia* *Hosp. v.* *Bustillo*
Senses: Sight: Loss	*Doctor:* Dermatologist	Apportioned	*Crossman v.* *Stewart*
XV(a) OBSTETRICS/GYNAECOLOGY (CAESARIAN SECTION)			
Assault/battery	*Doctor:* Surgeon: General	New Trial	*Winn. v.* *Alexander*
Further Treatment Req'd: Corrective surgery	*Doctor:* General Practitioner	Yes	*Gloning v.* *Miller*
Further Treatment Req'd: Corrective surgery	*Doctor:* Surgeon: General	Yes	*Taylor v.* *Gray*
XV(b) OBSTETRICS/GYNAECOLOGY (DELIVERY)			
Birth Defects	*Doctor:* General Practitioner *Hospital* *House Staff:* Resident *Nurse* (not party)	Apportioned	*Meyer v.* *Gordon*
Death: Hemorrhage	*Doctor:* General Practitioner	No	*Simard v.* *R.*
Further Treatment Req'd: Corrective surgery	*Doctor:* General Practitioner	No	*Hay v.* *Bain*
XV(c) OBSTETRICS/GYNAECOLOGY (MISCARRIAGE)			
Further Treatment Req'd: Corrective surgery	*Doctor:* General Practitioner	No	*Hampton v.* *MacAdam*
XV(d) OBSTETRICS/GYNAECOLOGY (PRENATAL CARE/DIAGNOSIS)			
Birth Defects	*Doctor:* General Practitioner	No	*Quiroz v.* *Austrup*

INJURY	DEFENDANT	LIAB.	CASE NAME
Birth Defects	*Doctor:* General Practitioner	Yes	*Wiplfi v.*
	Doctor: Obstetrician/		*Britten*
	Gynaecologist	No	
Disease: Septicemia	*Doctor:* General Practitioner	No	*McQuay v.*
			Eastwood

XV(e) OBSTETRICS/GYNAECOLOGY (STERILIZATION: ALDRIDGE)

Further Treatment Req'd:	*Doctor:* Obstetrician/	No*	*Doiron v.*
Unsuccessful treatment	Gynaecologist		*Orr*

XV(f) OBSTETRICS/GYNAECOLOGY (STERILIZATION: HYSTERECTOMY)

Amputation/removal: Kidney	*Doctor:* Surgeon: General	Yes	*Surkan v.*
Further Treatment Req'd:			*Blott*
Corrective surgery			

XV(g) OBSTETRICS/GYNAECOLOGY (STERILIZATION: LAPAROSCOPY/LAPAROTOMY)

Further Treatment Req'd:	*Doctor:* Obstetrician/	No	*Karderas v.*
Corrective Surgery	Gynaecologist		*Clow*
Further Treatment Req'd:	*Doctor:* Obstetrician/	No	*McBride v.*
Corrective surgery	Gynaecologist		*Langton*
Infection: Peritonitis			
Further Treatment Req'd:	*Doctor:* Obstetrician/	No**	*Videto v.*
Corrective surgery	Gynaecologist		*Kennedy*
Infection: Peritonitis			
Scarring/Deformity: Abdomen	*Doctor:* Obstetrician/	No*	*Gouin-Perrault v.*
Further Treatment Req'd:	Gynaecologist		*Villeneuve*
Corrective surgery			
Scarring/deformity: Abdomen			
Unnecessary treatment	*Doctor:* General Practitioner	No	*Finlay v.*
	Doctor: Obstetrician/	No	*Hess*
	Gynaecologist		

XV(h) OBSTETRICS/GYNAECOLOGY (STERILIZATION: SILVER NITRATE)

Further Treatment Req'd:	*Doctor:* Obstetrician/	Yes*	*Cryderman v.*
Unsuccessful treatment	Gynaecologist		*Ringrose*
Pregnancy: Unwanted			
Further Treatment Req'd:	*Doctor:* Obstetrician/	Yes*	*Zimmer v.*
Unsuccessful treatment	Gynaecologist		*Ringrose*
Pregnancy: Unwanted			
Pregnancy: Unwanted	*Doctor:* Obstetrician/	No*	*Colp v.*
	Gynaecologist		*Ringrose*

XV(i) OBSTETRICS/GYNAECOLOGY (STERILIZATION: TUBAL LIGATION)

Assault/battery	*Doctor:* Surgeon: General	No	*Winn v.*
	Hospital	No	*Alexander*
Brain Damage	*Doctor:* Obstetrician/	No*	*Mang v.*
	Gynaecologist		*Moscovitz*
	House Staff: Intern	No*	

INJURY	DEFENDANT	LIAB.	CASE NAME
Further Treatment Req'd: Unsuccessful treatment *Pregnancy:* Unwanted	*Doctor:* Specialist	No*	*Sanderson v. Lamont*
Organ: Ureter: Damage	*Doctor:* Obstetrician/ Gynaecologist	No*	*Hobson v. Munkley*
Pain & Suffering	*Doctor:* Obstetrician/ Gynaecologist	Yes*	*Dendaas v. Yackel*
Pain & Suffering	*Doctor:* Surgeon: General	Yes*	*Cataford v. Moreau*
Paralysis	*Doctor:* Obstetrician/ Gynaecologist *House Staff:* Intern	No* No	*Mang v. Moscovitz*
Pregnancy: Unwanted	*Doctor:* Obstetrician/ Gynaecologist	Yes*	*Dendaas v. Yackel*
Pregnancy: Unwanted	*Doctor:* Surgeon: General	Yes	*Cataford v. Moreau*
Treatment: Surgery: Sterilization	N/A	No**	*Re Eve*
Assault/Battery	*Doctor:* Surgeon: General	Yes*	*Murray v. McMurchy*
XVI OPTOMETRIC *Senses:* Sight Impairment	*Optometrist*	Yes	*Dunsmore v. Deshield*
XVII(a) REDUCTION OF FRACTURE & IMMOBILIZATION (ANKLE) *Amputation:* Foot	*Doctor:* General Practitioner *Nurse* (not party)	Yes No	*Vail v. MacDonald*
Bone: Ankle: Displacement	*Doctor:* General Practitioner	No	*Town v. Archer*
Bone: Ankle: Displacement *Further Treatment Req'd:* Corrective surgery	*Doctor:* Surgeon: General	Yes	*Parkin v. Kobrinsky*
Further Treatment Req'd: Corrective surgery	*Doctor:* General Practitioner	No	*Gordon v. Davidson*
Infection: Gangrene	*Doctor:* General Practitioner *Nurse* (not party)	Yes No	*Vail v. MacDonald*
Joint: Ankle: Fusion	*Doctor:* Surgeon: General	Yes	*Parkin v. Kobrinsky*
Joint: Ankle: Fusion	*Doctor:* General Practitioner	No	*Gordon v. Davidson*
Pain & Suffering	*Doctor:* Surgeon: General	Yes	*Parkin v. Kobrinsky*

INJURY	DEFENDANT	LIAB.	CASE NAME
Scarring/deformity: Foot	*Doctor:* General Practitioner	No	*Gordon v. Davidson*
XVII(b) REDUCTION OF FRACTURE & IMMOBILIZATION (ARM)			
Amputation: Arm *Infection:* Gas gangrene	*Doctor:* General Practitioner	No	*Challand v. Bell*
Further Treatment Req'd: Corrective *Infection:* Staphylococcus *Scarring/deformity:* Arm	*Doctor:* Surgeon: Orthopaedic	No	*Roy v. Goulet*
Paralysis: Arm	*Doctor:* General Practitioner	No	*Van Mere v. Farwell*
XVII(c) REDUCTION OF FRACTURE & IMMOBILIZATION (FOOT)			
Amputation: Leg *Infection:* Gangrene	*Doctor:* General Practitioner	Yes	*Bergstrom v. C.*
Further Treatment Req'd: Corrective surgery *Pain & Suffering*	*Doctor:* General Practitioner	Yes	*Townsend v. Lai*
XVII(d) REDUCTION OF FRACTURE & IMMOBILIZATION (HIP)			
Joint: Hip: Displacement	*Doctor:* General Practitioner	Yes	*Dangerfield v. David*
XVII(e) REDUCTION OF FRACTURE & IMMOBILIZATION (LEG)			
Amputation: Leg	*Doctor:* Internist	Yes	*Ares v. Venner*
Amputation: Leg	*Doctor:* General Practitioner	No	*Feller v. Roffman*
Amputation: Leg	*Doctor:* General Practitioner Hospital	Yes No	*Badger v. Surkan*
Bone: Leg: Displacement	*Doctor:* General Practitioner	No	*Hodgins v. Banting*
Bone: Leg: Displacement	*Doctor:* General Practitioner	Yes	*McCormick v. Marcotte*
Bone: Leg: Displacement	*Doctor:* General Practitioner	No	*Rickley v. Stratton*
Bone: Leg: Shortening	*Doctor:* Surgeon: Orthopaedic	Admitted	*Brennan v. Fraser*
Cardiovascular/circulatory: Avascular necrosis	*Doctor:* Surgeon: General	No	*Benoit v. Muir*
Further Treatment Req'd: Corrective surgery	*Doctor:* General Practitioner	Yes	*Park v. Stevenson Memorial Hosp.*
Infection: Abscess	*Doctor:* General Practitioner	Yes	*McCormick v. Marcotte*

INJURY	DEFENDANT	LIAB.	CASE NAME
Infection: Gangrene	*Doctor:* General Practitioner *Hospital*	Yes No	*Badger v.* *Surkan*
Infection: Gangrene	*Doctor:* Surgeon: Orthopaedic *Hospital*	Yes No	*Dean v.* *York County* *Hosp. Corp.*
Joint: Hip: Drop	*Doctor:* Surgeon: General	No	*Benoit v.* *Muir*
Joint: Hip: Fusion	*Doctor:* Surgeon: Orthopaedic	Yes	*Leachman v.* *MacLachlan*
Joint: Hip: Rotation	*Doctor:* Surgeon: General	No*	*Poulin v.* *Health Sciences* *Centre*
Pain & Suffering	*Doctor:* Surgeon: General	No	*Benoit v.* *Muir*
Pain & Suffering *Scarring/deformity:* Leg	*Doctor:* Surgeon: Orthopaedic	Admit- ted	*Brennan v.* *Fraser*
Scarring/deformity: Leg	*Doctor:* General Practitioner	Yes	*Park v.* *Stevenson* *Memorial Hosp.*
Scarring/deformity: Leg	*Doctor:* General Practitioner	No	*Rickley v.* *Stratton*

XVII(f) REDUCTION OF FRACTURE & IMMOBILIZATION (OPEN FRACTURE)

INJURY	DEFENDANT	LIAB.	CASE NAME
Amputation: Arm *Infection:* Gas gangrene	*Doctor:* General Practitioner	No	*Challand v.* *Bell*
Further Treatment Req'd: 　Corrective surgery *Infection:* Staphylococcus *Scarring/deformity:* Arm	*Doctor:* Surgeon: Orthopaedic	No	*Roy v.* *Goulet*

XVII(g) REDUCTION OF FRACTURE & IMMOBILIZATION (TOES)

INJURY	DEFENDANT	LIAB.	CASE NAME
Bone: Toe: Fracture	*Doctor:* General Practitioner	No	*Pellerin v.* *Stevenson*

XVIII(a) REHABILITATIVE THERAPY (PHYSIOTHERAPY)

INJURY	DEFENDANT	LIAB.	CASE NAME
Bone: Thigh: Fracture *Pain & Suffering*	*Rehab. Med.:* Physiotherapist	No	*Grafton v.* *Bigelow*

XVIII(b) REHABILITATIVE THERAPY (REMEDIAL EXERCISES)

INJURY	DEFENDANT	LIAB.	CASE NAME
Bone: Kneecap: Fracture	*Rehab. Med.:* Remedial Gymnast	Yes	*Guar. Trust v.* *Mall Medical* *Group*

XIX(a) SURGERY (ABDOMINAL)

INJURY	DEFENDANT	LIAB.	CASE NAME
Further Treatment Req'd: 　Corrective surgery *Pain & Suffering*	*Doctor:* Surgeon: General *Hospital* *Nurse*	Appor- tioned	*Cosgrove v.* *Gaudreau*

INJURY	DEFENDANT	LIAB.	CASE NAME
Pain & Suffering	*Doctor:* General Practitioner	No	*Pierce v. Strathroy Hosp.*
XIX(b) SURGERY (ABDOMINOPLASTY)			
Scarring/deformity: Abdomen	*Doctor:* Surgeon: Cosmetic	No*	*Petty v. MacKay*
XIX(c) SURGERY (AMPUTATION)			
Amputation: Elbow	*Doctor:* General Practitioner	No	*Jackson v. Hyde*
Amputation: Hand	*Doctor:* Surgeon: General	Yes	*Mulloy v. Hop Sang*
Amputation: Leg	*Doctor*	No	*Lachambre v. Perraulti*
XIX(d) SURGERY (ANGIOGRAM)			
Paralysis: Quadriplegia	*Doctor:* Surgeon: Neurosurgeon	No*	*Ferguson v.*
	Hospital	No	*Hamilton*
	House Staff: Resident	No	*Civic Hosp.*
Paralysis: Quadriplegia	*Doctor:* Surgeon: Vascular	No*	*McLean v.*
	Doctor: Radiologist	No	*Weir*
XIX(e) SURGERY (APPENDECTOMY)			
Death:	*Doctor:* General Practitioner	No	*Wilson v.*
Infection: Peritonitis	*Hospital*		*Stark*
Further Treatment Req'd: Corrective surgery *Pain & Suffering*	*Doctor:* Surgeon: General	No	*Meyer v. Lefebvre*
XIX(f) SURGERY (ARM)			
Nerve: Arm/wrist Radial nerve palsy	*Doctor:* Surgeon: General	No	*Jendrick v. Greidanus*
XIX(g) SURGERY (ARTHROPLASTY)			
Cardiovascular/circulatory: Avascular necrosis *Bone:* Hip: Fracture	*Doctor:* Surgeon: Orthopaedic	Yes	*Powell v. Guttman*
XIX(h) SURGERY (ARTHROTOMY)			
Death: Cardiac arrest	*Doctor:* Anaesthetist	No	*McKay v.*
	Doctor: Surgeon: Orthopaedic	No	*Gilchrist*
XIX(i) SURGERY (BIOPSY)			
Paralysis: Vocal chord	*Doctor:* Surgeon: General	No**	*Bickford v. Stiles*
Paralysis: Vocal chord	*Doctor:* General Practitioner	No	*Finlay v. Auld*
XIX(j) SURGERY (BLEPHAROPLASTY)			
Further Treatment Req'd: Corrective surgery *Scarring/deformity:* Eyelid *Senses:* Sight: Blurred vision	*Doctor:* Surgeon: Cosmetic	No*	*Guertin v. Kester*

INJURY	DEFENDANT	LIAB.	CASE NAME
XIX(k) SURGERY (CAESARIAN SECTION)			
Further Treatment Req'd: Corrective surgery	*Doctor:* General Practitioner	Yes	*Gloning v. Miller*
Further Treatment Req'd: Corrective surgery	*Doctor:* Surgeon: General	Yes	*Taylor v. Gray*
XIX(l) SURGERY (CAUTERY)			
Burn	*Doctor:* Surgeon: General	No	*McFadyen v. Harvie*
XIX(m) SURGERY (CIRCUMCISION)			
Organ: Penis: Amputation	*Doctor:* General Practitioner	Yes	*Gilbert v. Campbell*
Organ: Penis: Damage	*Doctor:* General Practitioner	Yes	*Gray v. LaFleche*
XIX(n) SURGERY (COSMETIC: ABDOMINOPLASTY)			
Scarring/deformity: Abdomen	*Doctor:* Surgeon: Cosmetic	No*	*Petty v. MacKay*
XIX(o) SURGERY (COSMETIC: BLEPHAROPLASTY)			
Further Treatment Req'd: Corrective surgery *Scarring/deformity:* Eyclid *Senses:* Sight: Diplopia	*Doctor:* Surgeon: Cosmetic	No*	*Guertin v. Kester*
XIX(p) SURGERY (COSMETIC: DERMABRASION)			
Scarring/deformity: Face	*Doctor:* Surgeon: Cosmetic	No*	*Hankins v. Papillon*
XIX(q) SURGERY (COSMETIC: JAW)			
Further Treatment Req'd: Loss of teeth	*Doctor:* Surgeon: Cosmetic	Yes*	*O'Connell v. Munro*
XIX(r) SURGERY (COSMETIC: MAMMOPLASTY)			
Further Treatment Req'd: Corrective surgery *Scarring/deformity:* Breast	*Doctor:* Surgeon: Cosmetic	Yes*	*MacDonald v. Ross*
Further Treatment Req'd: Corrective surgery *Scarring/deformity:* Breast	*Doctor:* Surgeon: Cosmetic	Yes	*White v. Turner*
XIX(s) SURGERY (COSMETIC: RHINOPLASTY)			
Scarring/deformity: Nose	*Doctor:* Surgeon: Cosmetic	Yes*	*LaFleur v. Cornelis*
XIX(t) SURGERY (CYST: REMOVAL OF)			
Nerve: Spinal accessory damage	*Doctor:* General Practitioner	Yes	*Fizer v. Keys*
XIX(u) SURGERY (DERMABRASION)			
Scarring/deformity: Face	*Doctor:* Surgeon: Cosmetic	No*	*Hankins v. Papillon*

INJURY	DEFENDANT	LIAB.	CASE NAME
XIX(v) SURGERY (DISCOIDECTOMY)			
Cardiovascular/circulatory: Hemorrhage *Death*	*Doctor:* Surgeon: Orthopaedic	No	*Chubey v. Ahsan*
Cardiovascular/circulatory: Hemorrhage *Death*	*Doctor:* Neurosurgeon	No	*Kapur v. Marshall*
XIX(w) SURGERY (DRAINING ABSCESS)			
Pain & Suffering	*Doctor:* General Practitioner	Yes	*Wine v.*
Scarring/deformity: Groin	*Doctor:* Surgeon: General	Yes	*Dawyd*
XIX(x) SURGERY (DUPUYTREN'S CONTRACTURE: CORRECTION OF)			
Further Treatment Req'd: Prolonged recovery	*Doctor:* General Practitioner *Doctor:* Surgeon: General	No* No	*Kenny v. Lockwood*
XIX(y) SURGERY (ENDARTERECTOMY)			
Cardiovascular/circulatory: Stroke *Impotence* *Paralysis:* Right side	*Doctor:* Neurosurgeon	Yes**	*Reibl v. Hughes*
XIX(z) SURGERY (FUSION: JOINT)			
Joint: Ankle: Fusion	*Doctor:* Surgeon: General Hospital	Admitted No	*Staple v. Winnipeg*
Joint: Hip: Fusion	*Doctor:* Surgeon: Orthopaedic	Yes	*Leachman v. MacLachlan*
XIX(aa) SURGERY (FUSION: SPINAL)			
Assault/battery	*Doctor:* Surgeon: General Hospital	Yes No	*Schweizer v. Central Hosp.*
Further Treatment Req'd: Corrective surgery	*Doctor:* Surgeon: Orthopaedic	Yes	*David v. Toronto Transit Comm.*
Further Treatment Req'd: Corrective treatment *Pain & Suffering*	*Doctor:* Surgeon: Orthopaedic	No*	*Bucknam v. Kostiuk*
XIX(bb) SURGERY (GALL BLADDER)			
Further Treatment Req'd: Unsuccessful treatment *Organ:* Gall Bladder: Removal	*Doctor:* General Practitioner	No	*Davy v. Morrison*
XIX(cc) SURGERY (GENERAL: REMOVAL OF BULLET FRAGMENTS)			
Assault	*Doctor:* Surgeon: General	No	*Turner v. Toronto Gen. Hosp. Trustees*
Further Treatment Req'd: Unsuccessful treatment	*Doctor:* Surgeon: General	No	*Browne v. Lerner*
Treatment: Surgery	*Doctor:* Surgeon: General	**	*MacDuff v. Vrabec*

INJURY	DEFENDANT	LIAB.	CASE NAME
XIX(dd) SURGERY (GYNAECOLOGICAL)			
Further Treatment Req'd:	*Doctor:* Surgeon: General	No	*Chipps v.*
Corrective surgery	*Doctor:* General Practitioner	No	*Peters*
Infection: Vaginal			
Scarring/deformity: Uterus			
Organ: Fallopian Tubes	*Doctor:* Surgeon	No	*Lefebvre v.*
Incorrect diagnosis	*Doctor:* Pathologist	No	*Osborne*
Pain & Suffering	*Hospital:* Hospital Laboratory	Yes	
Organ: Kidney: Removal	*Doctor:* Surgeon: General	Admitted	*Urbanski v. Patel*
XIX(ee) SURGERY (HAND)			
Scarring/deformity: Hand	*Doctor*	Yes	*Héritiers de Feu Maurice Massé v. Gaudette*
XIX(ff) SURGERY (HEART BY-PASS)			
Brain Damage:	*Doctor:* Anaesthetist	Yes	*Aynsley v.*
Cardiac arrest	*House Staff:* Resident	Yes	*Toronto*
	Hospital	Yes	*Gen. Hosp.*
XIX(gg) SURGERY (HERNIORRHAPHY)			
Amputation: Testicle	*Doctor:* Surgeon: General	No	*Marshall v. Curry*
Further Treatment Req'd:	*Doctor:* Surgeon: General	Yes	*Melvin v.*
Corrective surgery			*Graham*
Organ: Bladder: Perforation			
Further Treatment Req'd:	*Doctor:* Surgeon: General	No	*Petite v.*
Corrective surgery			*MacLeod*
XIX(hh) SURGERY (HYSTERECTOMY)			
Further Treatment Req'd:	*Doctor:* Surgeon: General	No	*Surkan v.*
Corrective surgery			*Blott*
Organ: Kidney: Removal			
Organ: Ovaries/Fallopian Tubes:	*Doctor:* Surgeon: General	No	*Bennett v.*
Removal			*C.*
XIX(ii) SURGERY (KIDNEY)			
Unspecified	*Doctor:* Surgeon: General	No	*Radclyffe v. Rennie*
XIX(jj) SURGERY (KNEE)			
Nerve: Sciatic: Foot Drop	*Doctor:* Surgeon: Orthopaedic	Yes	*Bibby v.*
Paralysis: Foot/leg			*Hall*
XIX(kk) SURGERY (LABYRINTHECTOMY)			
Nerve: Facial: Damage	*Doctor:* Surgeon: General	No	*Barcus v. Brown*

INJURY	DEFENDANT	LIAB.	CASE NAME
XIX(ll) SURGERY (LAMINECTOMY)			
Further Treatment Req'd: Aggravated condition: Unsuccessful treatment	*Doctor:* Surgeon: Orthopaedic	No**	*Hopp v. Lepp*
Paralysis: Quadriplegia	*Doctor:* Neurologist *Doctor:* Neurosurgeon	No* No*	*Strachan v. Simpson*
XIX(mm) SURGERY (LAPAROSCOPY/LAPAROTOMY)			
Further Treatment Req'd: Corrective surgery *Infection:* Peritonitis	*Doctor:* Obstetrician/ Gynaecologist	No*	*McBride v. Langton*
Further Treatment Req'd: Corrective surgery *Infection:* Peritonitis *Scarring/deformity:* Abdomen	*Doctor:* Obstetrician/ Gynaecologist	No**	*Videto v. Kennedy*
Further Treatment Req'd: Corrective surgery *Pain & Suffering*	*Doctor:* Obstetrician/ Gynaecologist *House Staff:* Resident (not party) *Nurse* (not party)	No Yes Yes	*Karderas v. Clow*
Further Treatment Req'd: Corrective surgery *Scarring/deformity:* Abdomen	*Doctor:* Obstetrician/ Gynaecologist	No*	*Gouin-Perrault v. Villeneuve*
Unnecessary Treatment	*Doctor:* General Practitioner *Doctor:* Obstetrician/ Gynaecologist	No No	*Finlay v. Hess*
XIX(nn) SURGERY (MAMMOPLASTY)			
Further Treatment Req'd: Corrective surgery *Scarring/deformity:* Breast	*Doctor:* Surgeon: Cosmetic	Yes*	*MacDonald v. Ross*
Further Treatment Req'd: Corrective surgery *Scarring/deformity:* Breast	*Doctor:* Surgeon: Cosmetic	Yes*	*White v. Turner*
XIX(oo) SURGERY (MASTECTOMY)			
Unnecessary Mastectomy *Pain & Suffering*	*Doctor*	Admitted	*Down v. Royal Jubilee Hosp.*
XIX(pp) SURGERY (MASTOIDECTOMY)			
Paralysis: Face	*Doctor:* Otolaryngologist	Yes	*Eady v. Tenderenda*
XIX(qq) SURGERY (MEATOTOMY)			
Assault/battery	*Doctor:* Surgeon: General	Yes*	*Hankai v. York County Hosp.*

INJURY	DEFENDANT	LIAB.	CASE NAME
XIX(rr) SURGERY (MEDIASTINOSCOPY)			
Paralysis: Vocal Chord	*Doctor:* Surgeon: General	No**	*Bickford v. Stiles*
XIX(ss) SURGERY (MIGRAINE HEADACHE: COMPLAINED OF)			
Further Treatment Req'd: Corrective surgery	*Doctor:* Surgeon: General	No	*Waldon v. Archer*
Senses: Smell/taste (loss of)	*Doctor:* Surgeon: General	Yes*	*Koehler v. Cook*
Unnecessary Treatment	*Doctor:* Surgeon: General	No	*Wilson v. Swanson*
XIX(tt) SURGERY (NASAL)			
Pain & Suffering	*Doctor:* Surgeon: General	No	*Hutchinson v. Robert*
XIX(uu) SURGERY (OPHTHALMIC)			
Senses: Sight: Diplopia	*Doctor:* Otolaryngologist	No	*Patterson v. de la Bastide*
Senses: Sight Diplopia	*Doctor:* Surgeon: General	Yes**	*Calder v. Gilmour*
Senses: Sight: Loss	*Hospital*	Admit-ted	*Walker v. Sidney City Hosp.*
XIX(vv) SURGERY (ORAL)			
Brain Damage	*Doctor:* Anaesthetist *Doctor:* Surgeon: Oral	No No	*Leadbetter v. Brand*
Death: Asphyxia	*Doctor:* Anaesthetist *Doctor:* Surgeon: Oral	Yes Yes	*Kangas v. Parker*
Dental Extraction: Additional teeth	*Oral Surgeon* *Cosmetic Surgeon*	Yes* Yes	*Sunne v. Shaw*
Nerve: Facial: Numbness	*Oral Surgeon*	No*	*Diack v. Bardsley*
Nerve: Facial: Numbness Hypersensitivity *Pain & Suffering*	*Doctor:* Surgeon: Oral	Yes**	*Rawlings v. Lindsay*
Scarring/deformity: Lip	*Dentist:* Paedodontist	No	*Dunn v. Young*
XIX(ww) SURGERY (OSTEOTOMY)			
Further Treatment Req'd: Corrective surgery *Nerve:* Leg: Numbness *Pain & Suffering*	*Doctor:* Surgeon: Orthopaedic	No*	*Jodouin v. Mitra*
Nerve: Arm: Stiffness	*Doctor:* Surgeon: Orthopaedic	Yes**	*Kelly v. Hazlett*

INJURY	DEFENDANT	LIAB.	CASE NAME
Scarring/deformity: Arm	*Doctor:* Surgeon: Orthopaedic	No	*Ostrowski v. Lotto*
XIX(xx) SURGERY (PNEUMONECTOMY)			
Death	*Doctor:* Surgeon: Cardiovascular/ thoracic	No	*O'Reilly v. Spratt*
XIX(yy) SURGERY (RHINOPLASTY)			
Scarring/deformity: Nose	*Doctor:* Surgeon: Cosmetic	Yes*	*Lafleur v. Cornelis*
XIX(zz) SURGERY ("SHUNT")			
Treatment: Surgery: Shunt	N/A	**	*Supt. of Family & Child Services v. Dawson*
XIX(aaa) SURGERY (STAPEDECTOMY)			
Paralysis: Face	*Doctor:* Otolaryngologist	No**	*Zamparo v.*
	Doctor: Surgeon: General	No*	*Brisson*
XIX(bbb) SURGERY (STERILIZATION: HYSTERECTOMY)			
Organ: Kidney: Removal	*Doctor:* Surgeon: General	Yes	*Surkan v. Blott*
Organ: Ovaries/Fallopian Tubes Removal	*Doctor:* Surgeon: General	No	*Bennett v. C.*
XIX(ccc) SURGERY (STERILIZATION: LAPAROSCOPY/LAPAROTOMY)			
Further Treatment Req'd: Corrective surgery *Infection:* Peritonitis	*Doctor:* Obstetrician/ Gynaecologist	Yes*	*McBride v. Langton*
Further Treatment Req'd: Corrective surgery *Pain & Suffering*	*Doctor:* Obstetrician/ Gynaecologist	No	*Karderas v. Clow*
	Hospital	Yes	
	House Staff: Resident (not party) *Nurse* (not party)	Yes	
Further Treatment Req'd: Corrective surgery *Scarring/deformity:* Abdomen	*Doctor:* Obstetrician/ Gynaeologist	No**	*Videto v. Kennedy*
Further Treatment Req'd: Corrective surgery *Scarring/deformity:* Abdomen	*Doctor:* Obstetrician/ Gynaecologist	No*	*Gouin-Perrault v. Villeneuve*
Unnecessary Treatment	*Doctor:* General Practitioner	No	*Finlay v.*
	Doctor: Obstetrician/ Gynaecologist	No	*Hess*
XIX (ddd) SURGERY (STERILIZATION: TUBAL LIGATION)			
Assault/battery	*Doctor:* Surgeon: General	No	*Winn v. Alexander*
Brain Damage Paralysis	*Doctor:* Obstetrician/ Gynaecologist	No*	*Mang v. Moscovitz*
	House Staff: Intern	No*	

INJURY	DEFENDANT	LIAB.	CASE NAME
Further Treatment Req'd: Unsuccessful treatment *Pain & Suffering* *Pregnancy:* Unwanted	*Doctor:* Surgeon: General	Yes	*Cataford v. Moreau*
Further Treatment Req'd: Unsuccessful treatment *Pain & Suffering* *Pregnancy:* Unwanted	*Doctor:* Obstetrician/ Gynaecologist	No*	*Dendaas v. Yackel*
Further Treatment Req'd: Unsuccessful treatment *Pregnancy:* Unwanted	*Doctor:* Specialist	No*	*Sanderson v. Lamont*
Organ: Fallopian Tubes: Removal *Assault/Battery* *Pain & Suffering*	*Doctor:* Surgeon: General	Yes*	*Murray v. McMurchy*
Organ: Ureter: Damage	*Doctor:* Obstetrician/ Gynaecologist	No*	*Hobson v. Munkley*
Treatment: Surgery: Sterilization	N/A	**	*Re Eve*
XIX(eee) SURGERY (THUMB) *Infection:* Hand	*Doctor:* Surgeon: General	No	*Nelligan v. Clement*
XIX(fff) SURGERY (THYROID) *Assault/battery*	*Doctor:* General Practitioner Hospital	No No	*Toronto Gen. Hosp.*
Death: Cardiac arrest	*Doctor:* Anaesthetist *Doctor:* Surgeon: General	No* No	*MacKinnon v. Ignacio*
XIX(ggg) SURGERY (TONSILLECTOMY) *Death:* Asphyxia	*Doctor:* Surgeon: General	Yes	*Anderson v. Chasney*
Dental: Tooth: Removal	*Doctor:* Otolaryngologist	Yes	*Belore v. Mississauga Hosp.*
Senses: Taste: Loss	*Doctor:* Surgeon: General *Student:* Medical (not party)	No	*McNamara v. Smith*
XIX(hhh) SURGERY (TRANSURETHRAL RESECTION) *Incontinence/impotence* *Organ:* Bladder: Perforation *Pain & Suffering*	*Doctor:* Urologist Hospital *House Staff:* Resident	No* No No	*Considine v. Camp Hill Hosp.*
XIX(iii) SURGERY (TUBAL LIGATION) *Assault/battery*	*Doctor:* Surgeon: General	No	*Winn v. Alexander*
Brain Damage *Paralysis*	*Doctor:* Obstetrician/ Gynaecologist *House Staff:* Intern	No* No*	*Mang v. Moscovitz*

INJURY	DEFENDANT	LIAB.	CASE NAME
Further Treatment Req'd: Unsuccessful treatment *Pain & Suffering* *Pregnancy:* Unwanted	*Doctor:* Surgeon: General	Yes	*Cataford v. Moreau*
Further Treatment Req'd: Unsuccessful treatment *Pain & Suffering* *Pregnancy:* Unwanted	*Doctor:* Obstetrician/ Gynaecologist	No*	*Dendaas v. Yackel*
Further Treatment Req'd: Unsuccessful treatment *Pregnancy:* Unwanted	*Doctor:* Specialist	No*	*Sanderson v. Lamont*
Organ: Fallopian tubes: Removal *Assault/battery* *Pain & Suffering*	*Doctor:* Surgeon: General	Yes*	*Murray v. McMurchy*
Organ: Ureter: Damage	*Doctor:* Obstetrician/ Gynaecologist	No*	*Hobson v. Munkley*
Treatment: Surgery: Sterilization	N/A	**	*Re Eve*
XIX(jjj) SURGERY (ULNAR NERVE RELEASE) *Nerve:* Elbow Numbness *Pain & Suffering*	*Doctor:* Surgeon: General	No*	*Konkolus v. Royal Alexandra Bd. of Govs.*
XIX(kkk) SURGERY (WRIST) *Further Treatment Req'd:* Corrective surgery *Nerve:* Wrist: Severed *Paralysis:* Arm	*Doctor:* Surgeon: General	Yes	*McKeachie v. Alvarez*
XIX(lll) SURGERY (X-RAY) *Bone:* Wrist: Fracture	*Doctor:* General Practitioner	Yes	*Baltzan v. Fidelity Ins. Co.*
Burn: Hand/leg	*Doctor:* General Practitioner *Nurse* (not party)	No	*Antoniuk v. Smith*
Burn: Hand	*Doctor:* General Practitioner *Technician:* X-ray (not party)	Yes No	*Hochman v. Willinsky*
Further Treatment Req'd: Corrective surgery *Scarring/deformity:* Finger	*Doctor:* General Practitioner *Hospital* *Technician:* X-ray (not party)	Yes Yes	*Pepin v. Hôpital du Haut Richelieu*
Paralysis: Arm	*Hospital*	Yes	*Murphy v. St. Catharines Gen. Hosp.*

PROCEDURE	DEFENDANT	LIAB.	CASE NAME

INJURY: AMPUTATION/REMOVAL

I ARM

Treatment: Blood: Transfusion	*Doctor:* Surgeon: General	No	*Armstrong v. McClealand*
Treatment: Reduction of Fracture & Immobilization: Open Fracture: Arm	*Doctor:* General Practitioner	No	*Challand v. Bell*

II BREAST

Diagnosis: Incorrect Diagnosis Of Cancer	*Doctor*	Admitted	*Down v. Royal Jubilee Hosp.*

III ELBOW

Treatment: Surgery *Amputation*	*Doctor:* General Practitioner	No	*Jackson v. Hyde*

IV EYE

Care: Hospital: Post-Treatment	*Hospital*	Yes	*Wyndham v.*
	Support Staff: Ward Aide	No	*Toronto Gen. Hosp. Trustees*

V FALLOPIAN TUBES

Diagnosis: Failure to diagnose pelvic inflammatory disease	*Doctor:* General Practitioner	No	*Mudrie v. McDonald*
Diagnosis: Incorrect Diagnosis Of Cancer	*Doctor:* Surgeon	No	*Lefebvre v.*
	Doctor: Pathologist	No	*Osborne*
	Hospital: Hospital Laboratory	Yes	
Treatment: Surgery: Hysterectomy	*Doctor:* Surgeon: General	No	*Bennett v. C.*

VI FINGER

Treatment: Infection (Correction of)	*Doctor:* General Practitioner	No	*Petit v.*
	Hospital	No	*Hôpital Ste. Jeanne D'Arc*

VII FOOT

Care: Doctor: Failure to attend patient *Diagnosis:* Failure to diagnose amputation necessary	*Doctor:* Surgeon: General	No	*Key v. Thomson*
Consultation: Failure to consult specialist *Treatment:* Reduction of Fracture & Immobilization: Ankle	*Doctor:* General Practitioner	Yes	*Vail v.*
	Hospital	No	*Macdonald*
Treatment: Experimental quartz lamp	*Doctor:* General Practitioner	Yes*	*Baills v. Boulanger*

PROCEDURE	DEFENDANT	LIAB.	CASE NAME
VIII GALL BLADDER			
Treatment: Surgery:	*Doctor:* General Practitioner	No	*Davy v.*
Gall Bladder	*Doctor:* Anaesthetist	No	*Morrison*
IX HAND			
Administration of Anaesthetic:	*Doctor:* Anaesthetist	Yes	*Villeneuve v.*
Injection	Hospital	No	*Sisters of*
	Nurse (not party)		*St. Joseph*
Care: Doctor:	*Doctor:* Surgeon: General	No	*Key v.*
Failure to attend patient			*Thomson*
Diagnosis: Failure to Diagnose			
amputation necessary			
Treatment: Surgery	*Doctor:* Surgeon: General	Yes*	*Mulloy v.*
Amputation			*Hop Sang*
X KIDNEY			
Treatment: Surgery:	*Doctor:* Surgeon: General	Admit-	*Urbanski v.*
Gynaecological		ted	*Patel*
Treatment: Surgery:	*Doctor:* Surgeon: General	Yes	*Surkan v.*
Sterilization: Hysterectomy			*Blott*
XI LEG			
Diagnosis: Failure to diagnose	*Doctor:* General Practitioner	No	*Harquail v.*
arteriosclerosis			*Sedgewick*
Diagnosis: Failure to diagnose	*Doctor:* Surgeon: Orthopaedic	Yes	*Dean v.*
compound fracture			*York County*
			Hosp. Corp.
Diagnosis: Failure to diagnose	*Doctor:* General Practitioner	Yes	*Cusson v.*
fractured hip			*Robidoux*
Referral: Failure to refer	*Doctor:* General Practitioner	No	*Harquail v.*
to specialist			*Sedgewick*
Referral: Failure to transfer to	*Doctor*	No	*Lachambre v.*
better-equipped hospital			*Perreaulti*
Treatment: Reduction of fracture &	*Doctor:* General Practitioner	Yes	*Bergstrom v.*
immobilization: Foot			*C.*
Treatment: Reduction of fracture &	*Doctor:* Internist	Yes	*Ares v.*
immobilization: Leg			*Venner*
Treatment: Reduction of fracture &	*Doctor:* General Practitioner	Yes	*Badger v.*
immobilization: Leg	Hospital		*Surkan*
Treatment: Reduction of fracture &	*Doctor:* General Practitioner	No	*Feller v.*
immobilization: Leg			*Roffman*
Treatment: Reduction of fracture &	*Doctor:* Surgeon: Orthopaedic	Yes	*Dean v.*
immobilization: Leg	Hospital		*York County*
			Hosp. Corp.

PROCEDURE	DEFENDANT	LIAB.	CASE NAME
XII OVARY			
Treatment: Surgery: Hysterectomy	*Doctor:* Surgeon: General	No	*Bennett v. C.*
XIII STOMACH			
Treatment: Medication: Prescription	*Pharmacist*	Yes	*Williams v. Jones*
XIV TESTICLE			
Care: Doctor/Hospital: Post-treatment	*Doctor:* General Practitioner *Doctor:* Surgeon: General	No Yes	*Thomas v. Scarborough Gen. Hosp.*
Treatment: Surgery: Herniorrhaphy	*Doctor:* Surgeon: General	No*	*Marshall v. Curry*
INJURY: ASSAULT/BATTERY			
Administration of Anaesthetic: General	*Doctor:* Surgeon: General	No*	*Burk v. S.*
Care: Hospital: During Treatment: Sponges	*Doctor:* Surgeon: General *Hospital*	No No	*Winn v. Alexander*
Treatment: Surgery: Amputation	*Doctor:* Surgeon: General	Yes*	*Mulloy v. Hop Sang*
Treatment: Surgery: Caesarian section	*Doctor:* Surgeon: General *Hospital*	No No	*Winn v. Alexander*
Treatment: Surgery: Fusion (spinal)	*Doctor:* Surgeon: General *Hospital*	Yes* No	*Schweizer v. Central Hosp.*
Treatment: Surgery: Meatotomy	*Doctor:* Surgeon: General	Yes*	*Hankai v. York County Hosp.*
Treatment: Surgery: Thyroid	*Doctor:* General Practitioner *Hospital*	No* No	*Booth v. Toronto Gen. Hosp.*
Treatment: Surgery: Tubal ligation	*Doctor:* Surgeon: General	Yes*	*Murray v. McMurchy*
Treatment: Surgery: Tubal ligation	*Doctor:* Surgeon: General *Hospital*	No No	*Winn v. Alexander*
Treatment: Surgery	*Doctor:* Surgeon: General *Hospital*	No No	*Turner v. Toronto Gen. Hosp. Trustees*
INJURY: BIRTH DEFECTS			
Diagnosis: Failure to diagnose diabetes *Treatment:* Obstetrical: Prenatal diagnosis	*Doctor:* General Practitioner	No	*Quiroz v. Austrup*

PROCEDURE	DEFENDANT	LIAB.	CASE NAME
Diagnosis: Failure to diagnose multiple gestation	*Doctor:* General Practitioner	Yes	*Wipfli v.*
	Doctor: Obstetrician/	No	*Britten*
Treatment: Obstetrical: Prenatal diagnosis	Gynaecologist		

INJURY: BONE
I DISPLACEMENT

Care: Doctor: Post-treatment	*Doctor:* General Practitioner	No	*Rickley v. Stratton*
Treatment: Reduction of fracture & immobilization: Ankle	*Doctor:* Surgeon: General	Yes	*Parkin v. Kobrinsky*
Treatment: Reduction of fracture & immobilization: Ankle	*Doctor:* General Practitioner	No	*Town v. Archer*
Treatment: Reduction of fracture & immobilization: Leg	*Doctor:* General Practitioner	Yes	*McCormick v. Marcotte*
Treatment: Reduction of fracture & immobilization: Leg	*Doctor:* General Practitioner	No	*Rickley v. Stratton*

II FRACTURE

Care: Doctor: Post-treatment	*Doctor:* General Practitioner	Yes	*Baltzan v. Fidelity Ins. Co.*
Care: Doctor: Post-treatment	*Doctor:* Surgeon: Orthopaedic	No	*Powell v. Guttman*
Care: Hospital: Pre-treatment	*Hospital*	No	*Florence v. Les Soeurs de Misericorde*
Care: Doctor: Supervision	*Doctor:* General Practitioner	No	*Robinson v.*
	Hospital	No	*Annapolis*
	Nurse (not party)		*Gen. Hosp.*
Care: Doctor: Supervision	*Hospital:* Clinic	Yes	*Dowey v.*
	Nurse (not party)		*Rothwell & Assoc.*
Care: Hospital: Supervision	*Hospital*	No	*Hôtel-Dieu de Montreal v. Couloume*
Care: Hospital: Supervision	*Doctor:* General Practitioner	No	*Robinson v.*
	Hospital	No	*Annapolis*
	Nurse (not party)		*Gen. Hosp.*
Diagnosis: Procedure: X-ray	*Doctor:* General Practitioner	Yes	*Baltzan v. Fidelity Ins. Co.*

PROCEDURE	DEFENDANT	LIAB.	CASE NAME
Treatment: Medication: Administration	*Hospital* *Nurse* (not party)	No	*Buchanan v. Fort Churchill Gen. Hosp.*
Treatment: Reduction of fracture & immobilization: Toes	*Doctor:* General Practitioner	No	*Grafton v. Bigelow*
Treatment: Rehabilitative physiotherapy	*Rehab. Med.:* Physiotherapist	No	*Grafton v. Bigelow*
Treatment: Rehabilitative remedial exercises	*Rehab. Med.:* Remedial Gymnast	Yes	*Guar. Trust v. Mall Medical Group*
Treatment: Surgery: Arthroplasty	*Doctor:* Surgeon: Orthopaedic	Yes	*Powell v. Guttman*
III LOSS Avascular necrosis: Hip and shoulder replacement	*Doctor:* General Practitioner *Doctor:* Gastroenterologist	Yes Yes	*Reynard v. Carr*
Jaw: Bone loss: Loss of teeth	*Doctor:* Surgeon: Cosmetic	Yes*	*O'Connell v. Munroe*
Jaw: Bone loss: Loss of teeth	*Oral Surgeon* *Doctor:* Surgeon: Cosmetic	Yes*	*Sunne v. Shaw*
IV SHORTENING *Diagnosis:* Failure to diagnose encephalitis	*Doctor:* General Practitioner *Hospital*	No No	*Tiesmaki v. Wilson*
Treatment: Reduction of fracture and immobilization	*Doctor:* Surgeon Orthopaedic	Admitted	*Brennan v. Fraser*
INJURY: BRAIN DAMAGE *Administration of Anaesthetic:* Experimental	*Doctor:* Anaesthetist	Yes*	*Halushka v. University of Sask.*
Administration of Anaesthetic: General	*Doctor:* Anaesthetist *Hospital* *Nurse* (not party)	No Yes Yes	*Hôpital Gén. v. Perron*
Administration of Anaesthetic: General	*Doctor:* Anaesthetist *Doctor:* Oral Surgeon	No	*Leadbetter v. Brand*
Administration of Anaesthetic: Post-anaesthesia recovery	*Doctor:* Anaesthetist *Hospital* *Nurse* (not party)	No Yes	*Laidlaw v. Lions Gate Hosp.*
Care: Doctor: During treatment	*Doctor:* Anaesthetist *Hospital* *House Staff:* Resident	Yes Yes Yes	*Aynsley v. Toronto Gen. Hosp.*
Care: Doctor: Supervision	*Doctor:* Neurologist	Yes	*Foote v. Royal Columbian Hosp.*

PROCEDURE	DEFENDANT	LIAB.	CASE NAME
Care: Hospital: Discharge	*Hospital*	No	*Bissell v. Vancouver Gen. Hosp.*
Care: Hospital: During treatment	*Hospital* *Nurse* (not party)	No Yes	*Hôpital Gen. v. Perron*
Care: Hospital: Emergency	*Hospital* *House Staff:* Resident *Nurse* (not party)	Apportioned	*Meyer v. Gordon*
Care: Hospital: General	*Hospital*	Settled	*Yepremian v. Scarborough Gen. Hosp.*
Care: Hospital: Post-treatment	*Hospital* *Nurse* (not party)	No	*Laidlaw v. Lions Gate Hosp.*
Care: Hospital: Supervision	*Hospital* *Nurse* (not party)	No	*Foote v. Royal Columbian Hosp.*
Diagnosis: Failure to diagnose diabetes	*Doctor:* General Practitioner *Doctor:* Emerg. Rm. Physician *Doctor:* Internist (not party) *Hospital*	Settled	*Yepremian v. Scarborough Gen. Hosp.*
Diagnosis: Failure to diagnose infection	*Doctor:* Pediatrician *Doctor:* Surgeon: General	No No	*Bissell v. Vancouver Gen. Hosp.*
Diagnosis: Failure to diagnose multiple gestation	*Doctor:* General Practitioner *Doctor:* Obstetrician/ Gynaecologist	Yes No	*Wipfli v. Britten*
Treatment: Experimental	*Doctor:* Anaesthetist	Yes*	*Halushka v. University of Sask.*
Treatment: Medication: Administration	*Doctor:* Emerg. Rm. Physician *Doctor:* Internist (not party) *Hospital*	Settled	*Yepremian v. Scarborough Gen. Hosp.*
Treatment: Obstetrical: Abortion	*Doctor:* Obstetrician/ Gynaecologist *House Staff:* Intern	No* No	*Mang v. Moscovitz*
Treatment: Obstetrical: Delivery	*Doctor:* General Practitioner *Hospital* *House Staff:* Resident *Nurse* (not party)	Apportioned	*Meyer v. Gordon*
Treatment: Obstetrical: Prenatal diagnosis	*Doctor:* General Practitioner *Doctor:* Obstetrician/ Gynaecologist	Yes No	*Wipfli v. Britten*

PROCEDURE	DEFENDANT	LIAB.	CASE NAME
Treatment: Surgery: Heart bypass	*Doctor:* Anaesthetist *House Staff:* Resident Hospital	Yes Yes Yes	*Aynsley v.* *Toronto* *Gen. Hosp.*
Treatment: Surgery: Oral	*Doctor:* Anaesthetist *Doctor:* Oral Surgeon	No No	*Leadbetter v.* *Brand*
Treatment: Surgery: Tubal ligation	*Doctor:* Obstetrician/ Gynaecologist *House Staff:* Intern	No* No	*Mang v.* *Moscovitz*

INJURY: BURN

PROCEDURE	DEFENDANT	LIAB.	CASE NAME
Administration of Anaesthetic: General	*Doctor:* Anaesthetist Hospital *House Staff:* Resident	Yes No No	*Crits v.* *Sylvester*
Care: Hospital: General	Hospital *Nurse* (not party)	No	*Logan v.* *Waitaki* *Hosp. Bd.*
Care: Hospital: Post-treatment	Hospital *Nurse* (not party)	Yes	*Bernier v.* *Sisters of* *Service*
Care: Hospital: Post-treatment	Hospital	No	*Cahoon v.* *Edmonton* *Hosp. Bd.*
Care: Hospital: Post-tatment	Hospital	Yes	*Davis v.* *Colchester*
Care: Hospital: Post-treatment	Hospital *Nurse* (not party)	Yes	*Eek v.* *High River* *Mun. Hosp.*
Care: Hospital: Post-treatment	Hospital *Nurse* (not party)	Yes	*Lavere v.* *Smith's Falls* *Pub. Hosp.*
Care: Hospital: Post-treatment	Hospital *Nurse* (not party)	Yes	*Nyberg v.* *Provost Mun.* *Hosp. Bd.*
Care: Hospital: Supervision	Hospital *Student Nurse* (not party)	Yes	*Farrell v.* *Regina*
Care: Hospital: Supervision	Hospital *Nurse* (not party)	Yes	*Sinclair v.* *Victoria Hosp.*
Diagnosis: Procedure: Fluoroscopy	*Doctor:* General Practitioner Hospital *Technician:* X-ray (not party)	No Yes	*Abel v.* *Cooke*
Diagnosis: Procedure: X-ray	*Doctor:* General Practitioner *Nurse* (not party)	No	*Antoniuk v.* *Smith*

PROCEDURE	DEFENDANT	LIAB.	CASE NAME
Diagnosis: Procedure: X-ray	*Doctor:* General Practitioner *Technician:* X-ray (not party)	Yes	*Hochman v. Willinsky*
Treatment: Dermatological: X-ray	*Doctor:* Radiologist	Yes	*McCaffery v. Hague*
Treatment: Heat: Diathermy	*Doctor:* Surgeon: General	Yes	*Crysler v. Pearse*
Treatment: Heat: Diathermy	*Hospital* *Nurse* (not party)	Yes	*Fleming v. Sisters of St. Joseph*
Treatment: Heat: Cradle	*Hospital* *Nurse* (not party)	No	*Vuchar v. Toronto Gen. Hosp. Trustees*
Treatment: Heat: Kelly Pad	*Doctor:* Surgeon: General *Nurse* (not party)	No	*Armstrong v. Bruce*
Treatment: Heat: Kelly Pad	*Doctor:* General Practitioner *Hospital* *Nurse*	No Yes Yes	*Lenzen v. Southern Vancouver Island Hosp.*
Treatment: Heat: Steam Inhalation	*Hospital* *Nurse* (not party)	Yes	*Harkies v. Lord Dufferin Hosp.*
Treatment: Injection: Medication	*Doctor:* General Practitioner	No	*Neufeld v. McQuitty*
Treatment: Surgery: Cautery	*Doctor:* Surgeon: General	No	*McFadyen v. Harvie*

INJURY: CARDIOVASCULAR/CIRCULATORY
I AVASCULAR NECROSIS

Care: Doctor: Post-treatment	*Doctor:* Surgeon: Orthopaedic	Yes	*Powell v. Guttman*
Treatment: Medication: Administration	*Doctor:* Gastroenterologist *Hospital*	No* No	*Moore v. Shaughnessy*
Treatment: Medication: Hip and shoulder replacement	*Doctor:* General Practitioner *Doctor:* Gastroenterologist	Yes Yes	*Reynard v. Carr*
Treatment: Reduction of fracture & immobilization: Leg	*Doctor:* Surgeon: General	No	*Benoit v. Muir*
Treatment: Surgery: Arthroplasty	*Doctor:* Surgeon: Orthopaedic	Yes	*Powell v. Guttman*

II BLEEDING

Care: Doctor/Clinic: Post-treatment	*Doctor:* General Practitioner *Hospital:* Clinic	No No	*Tacknyk v. Lake of the Woods Clinic*

PROCEDURE	DEFENDANT	LIAB.	CASE NAME
Treatment: Dental extraction	*Dentist*	No	*Murrin v. Janes*
Treatment: Nose	*Doctor*	No	*McCulligh v. McLean*
III CARDIAC ARREST *Administration of Anaesthetic:* Experimental	*Doctor:* Anaesthetist	Yes*	*Halushka v. University of Sask.*
Administration of Anaesthetic: General	*Doctor:* Anaesthetist	No	*Leadbetter v. Brand*
Administration of Anaesthetic: General	*Doctor:* Anaesthetist *Doctor:* Surgeon: Orthopaedic	No No	*McKay v. Gilchrist*
Administration of Anaesthetic: Intubation	*Doctor:* Anaesthetist *Hospital*	No No	*Webster v. Armstrong*
Administration of Anaesthetic: Post-anaesthesia recovery	*Doctor:* Anaesthetist *Nurse*	No Yes	*Krujelis v. Esdale*
Care: Doctor: During Treatment	*Doctor:* Anaesthetist *Doctor:* Surgeon: General	No* No	*MacKinnon v. Ignacio*
Care: Hospital: Post-treatment	*Doctor:* Anaesthetist *Hospital*	No Yes	*Krujelis v. Esdale*
Diagnosis: Failure to diagnose diabetes	*Doctor:* Emerg. Rm. Physician *Hospital* *Technician:* Laboratory	No Yes Yes	*Neufville v. Sobers*
Diagnosis: Failure to diagnose diabetes	*Doctor:* Emerg. Rm. Physician *Doctor:* General Practitioner *Doctor:* Internist (not party) *Hospital*	Settled	*Yepremian v. Scarborough Gen. Hosp.*
Diagnosis: Failure to diagnose heart disease	*Doctor:* General Practitioner	No	*Ehler v. Smith*
Treatment: Experimental: Testing anaesthetic	*Doctor:* Anaesthetist	Yes*	*Halushka v. University of Sask.*
Treatment: Medication: Administration	*Doctor:* Emerg. Rm. Physician *Doctor:* General Practitioner *Doctor:* Internist (not party) *Hospital*	Settled	*Yepremian v. Scarborough Gen. Hosp.*
Treatment: Surgery: Arthrotomy	*Doctor:* Anaesthetist *Doctor:* Surgeon: Orthopaedic	No No	*McKay v. Gilchrist*
Treatment: Surgery: Oral	*Doctor:* Anaesthetist *Doctor:* Surgeon: Oral	No No	*Leadbetter v. Brand*
Treatment: Surgery: Thyroid	*Doctor:* Anaesthetist *Doctor:* Surgeon: General	No* No	*MacKinnon v. Ignacio*

PROCEDURE	DEFENDANT	LIAB.	CASE NAME
INJURY: DEATH			
Administration of Anaesthetic: Chloroform	*Doctor:* Anaesthetist	No	*Fleckney v. Desbrisay*
Administration of Anaesthetic: General	*Doctor:* Anaesthetist *Doctor:* Surgeon: Oral	Yes* Yes	*Kangas v. Parker*
Administration of Anaesthetic: General	*Doctor:* Anaesthetist *Doctor:* Surgeon: Orthopaedic	No No	*McKay v. Gilchrist*
Administration of Anaesthetic: Injection	*Doctor:* General Practitioner *Hospital* *Nurse*	No Yes Yes	*Bugden v. Harbour View Hosp.*
Administration of Anaesthetic: Intubation	*Doctor:* Anaesthetist *Hospital*	No No	*Webster v. Armstrong*
Administration of Anaesthetic: Spinal	*Doctor:* Anaesthetist *Doctor:* General Practitioner	No No	*Walker v. Bedard*
Care: Doctor: Assignment of responsibilities	*Doctor:* General Practitioner	No	*Wilson v. Stark*
Care: Doctor: During treatment (sponges)	*Dentist*	Yes	*Nesbitt v. Holt*
Care: Doctor: During treatment	*Doctor:* Anaesthetist *Doctor:* Surgeon: General	No No	*MacKinnon v. Ignacio*
Care: Doctor: During treatment (sponges)	*Doctor:* Surgeon: General	Yes	*Anderson v. Chasney*
Care: Doctor: Hospitalization	*Doctor:* Psychiatrist *Psychologist*	No No	*Haines v. Bellissimo*
Care: Doctor: Supervision/Control	*Doctor:* Psychiatrist *Hospital*	Yes Yes	*Villemure v. Turcot*
Care: Doctor: Supervision/Control	*Doctor:* Neurosurgeon *Hospital*	No No	*Stadel v. Albertson*
Care: Hospital: General	*Doctor:* General Practitioner *Hospital* *Nurse:* (not party)	No No	*Rodych v. Krasey*
Care: Hospital: General	*Hospital* *Nurse* (not party)	No	*Brandeis v. Weldon*
Care: Hospital: Post-treatment	*Hospital* *Nurse*	Yes Yes	*Joseph Brant Memorial Hosp. v Koziol*
Care: Hospital: Supervision/control	*Doctor:* Psychiatrist *Hospital*	Yes Yes	*Villemure v. Turcot*
Care: Hospital: Supervision/control	*Doctor:* Neurosurgeon *Hospital*	No No	*Stadel v. Albertson*

PROCEDURE	DEFENDANT	LIAB.	CASE NAME
Care: Hospital: Supervision/control	*Hospital*	No	*Barsy v. Gov't of Man.*
Diagnosis: Failure to diagnose appendicitis	*Chiropractor*	No	*R. v. Homeberg*
Diagnosis: Failure to diagnose appendicitis	*Doctor:* Attending Physician: General Surgeon: Gynaecologist *Hospital:* Nurse	Yes Yes Yes	*Bergen v. Sturgeon Gen. Hosp.*
Diagnosis: Failure to diagnose appendicitis	*Doctor:* General Practitioner	No	*Wilson v. Stark*
Diagnosis: Failure to diagnose diabetes	*Doctor:* Emerg. Rm. Physician *Hospital* *Technician:* Laboratory	No Yes Yes	*Neufville v. Sobers*
Diagnosis: Failure to diagnose dislocated spine	*Hospital* *House Staff:* Intern	Yes Yes	*Fraser v. Vancouver Gen. Hosp.*
Diagnosis: Failure to diagnose epiglottitis	*Doctor:* Emerg. Rm. Physician	Yes	*De Moura v. Mississauga Hosp.*
Diagnosis: Failure to diagnose hemorrhage	*Doctor:* Emerg. Rm. Physician *Hospital*	Yes No	*Wade v. Nayernouri*
Diagnosis: Failure to diagnose hemorrhage	*Doctor:* General Practitioner *Hospital* *Nurse* (not party)	No No	*Serre v. De Tilly*
Diagnosis: Failure to diagnose hemorrhage	*Doctor:* Surgeon: Orthopaedic	No	*Chubey v. Ahsan*
Diagnosis: Failure to diagnose heart disease	*Doctor:* General Practitioner	No	*Ehler v. Smith*
Diagnosis: Failure to diagnose infection	*Doctor:* General Practitioner	No	*R. v. Watson*
Diagnosis: Failure to diagnose internal injuries	*Doctor:* General Practitioner *Hospital* *Nurse* (Not Party)	No No	*Rodych v. Krasey*
Diagnosis: Failure to diagnose meningitis	*Doctor:* General Practitioner	Yes	*Dale v. Munthali*
Diagnosis: Failure to diagnose mitral stenosis	*Doctor:* General Practitioner	No	*Athansious v. Guzman*
Diagnosis: Failure to diagnose poisoning by carbon monoxide	*Doctor:* Internist	No	*Ostash v. Sonnenberg*
Diagnosis: Procedure: Pyelogram	*Doctor:* Internist *Doctor:* Radiologist	Yes Yes	*Leonard v. Knott*
Treatment: Dental: Extraction	*Dentist*	Yes	*Nesbitt v. Holt*

PROCEDURE	DEFENDANT	LIAB.	CASE NAME
Treatment: Diet	*Doctor:* General Practitioner	Yes	*R. v. Rogers*
Treatment: Medication: Administration	*Doctor:* General Practitioner *Hospital* *Nurse*	No Yes Yes	*Budgen v.* *Harbour View* *Hosp.*
Treatment: Medication: Administration	*Doctor:* Surgeon: General	No	*R. v.* *Giardine*
Treatment: Medication: Prescription	*Hospital* *House Staff:* Resident *Pharmacist*	Settled	*Filipewich v.* *University* *Hosp. Bd.*
Treatment: Obstetrical: Delivery	*Doctor:* General Practitioner	No	*Simard v. R.*
Treatment: Surgery: Appendectomy	*Doctor:* General Practitioner	No	*Wilson v. Stark*
Treatment: Surgery: Arthrotomy	*Doctor:* Anaesthetist *Doctor:* Surgeon: Orthopaedic	No No	*McKay v.* *Gilchrist*
Treatment: Surgery: Discoidectomy	*Doctor:* Neurosurgeon	No	*Kapur v.* *Marshall*
Treatment: Surgery: Oral	*Doctor:* Anaesthetist *Doctor:* Surgeon: Oral	*Yes Yes	*Kangas v.* *Parker*
Treatment: Surgery: Pneumonectomy	*Doctor:* Surgeon: Cardiovascular/ Thoracic	No	*O'Reilly v.* *Spratt*
Treatment: Surgery: Thyroid	*Doctor:* Anaesthetist *Doctor:* Surgeon: General	No* No	*MacKinnon v.* *Ignacio*
Treatment: Surgery: Tonsillectomy	*Doctor:* Surgeon: General	Yes	*Anderson v.* *Chasney*

INJURY: DENTAL
I DAMAGE TO TEETH

PROCEDURE	DEFENDANT	LIAB.	CASE NAME
Administration of Anaesthetic: Intubation	*Doctor:* Anaesthetist *Hospital*	Yes No	*Gorback v.* *Ting*
Care: Hospital: Supervision	*Hospital*	No	*Penner v.* *Bethel*
Treatment: Dental: Crown & bridge	*Dentist:* Prosthodontist	Yes	*Fluevog v.* *Pottinger*
Treatment: Dental: Extraction	*Dentist:* Dental Surgeon	Yes	*Drinnen v.* *Douglas*
Treatment: Surgery: Tonsillectomy	*Doctor:* Otolaryngologist	Yes	*Belore v.* *Mississauga* *Hosp.*

II EXTRACTION (ADDITIONAL TEETH)

PROCEDURE	DEFENDANT	LIAB.	CASE NAME
Treatment: Dental: Extraction	*Dentist*	No*	*Guimond v.* *Laberge*

PROCEDURE	DEFENDANT	LIAB.	CASE NAME
Treatment: Dental: Extraction	*Dentist:* Dental Surgeon	No*	*Boase v. Paul*
Treatment: Loss of bone and teeth	*Oral Surgeon* *Doctor:* Surgeon: Cosmetic	Yes*	*Sunne v. Shaw*
Treatment: Loss of bone and teeth	*Doctor:* Surgeon: Cosmetic	Yes*	*O'Connell v. Munro*
III EXTRACTION (PERMANENT TEETH)			
Treatment: Dental: Extraction	*Dentist*	No	*Gagnon v. Stortini*
IV EXTRACTION (UNAUTHORIZED)			
Treatment: Dental: Extraction	*Dentist:* Dental Surgeon	No*	*Nykiforuk v. Lockwood*
V EXTRACTION (UNNECESSARY)			
Treatment: Dental: Extraction	*Dentist*	Yes	*Murano v. Gray*

INJURY: DISEASE
I ARTHRITIS

Care: Hospital: Post-treatment	*Doctor:* Surgeon: Orthopaedic	No*	*Hajgato v.*
Diagnosis: Failure to diagnose	*House Staff:* Resident	No	*London*
infection	*Hospital:* Nurse *Nurse* (not party)	No	*Health Assn.*

II CANCER

Diagnosis: Failure to diagnose	*Doctor:* Surgeon General	No	*Thompson v.*
cancer	*Hospital*	No	*Creaghan*

III ENCEPHALITIS

Diagnosis: Failure to diagnose	*Doctor:* General Practitioner	No	*Tiesmaki v.*
encephalitis	*Hospital*	No	*Wilson*

IV ENDOCARDITIS

Diagnosis: Failure to diagnose	*Doctor:* General Practitioner	No	*Nichols v.*
diabetes	gynaecologist		*Gray*

V EPIGLOTTITIS

Diagnosis: Failure to diagnose	*Doctor:* Emerg. Rm. Physician	Yes	*DeMoura v.*
epiglottitis			*Mississauga Hosp.*

VI HEPATITIS

Care: Nursing: During treatment	*Hospital*	Appor-	*Savoie v.*
	Nurse	tioned	*Bouchard*

VII MENINGITIS

Diagnosis: Failure to diagnose	*Doctor:* General Practitioner	Yes	*Dale v.*
meningitis			*Munthali*

VIII PELVIC INFLAMMATORY DISEASE

Diagnosis: Failure to diagnose	*Doctor:* General Practitioner	No	*Mudrie v.*
pelvic inflammatory disease			*MacDonald*

PROCEDURE	DEFENDANT	LIAB.	CASE NAME
IX PNEUMONIA			
Diagnosis: Failure to diagnose	*Doctor:* Pediatrician:	No	*Bissell v.*
infection	Doctor: Surgeon: General	No	*Vancouver*
	Hospital	No	*Gen. Hosp.*
X SEPTICAEMIA			
Treatment: Injection:	*Doctor:* General Practitioner	Yes	*Adderley v.*
Vaccination			*Bremner*
XI SMALLPOX			
Care: Hospital: General	*Hospital*	No	*McDaniel v.*
			Vancouver Gen.
			Hosp.
Treatment: Injection:	*Doctor:* Pediatrician	No	*Gent v.*
Vaccination			*Wilson*
INJURY: ENDOCARDITIS			
Diagnosis: Failure to diagnose	*Doctor:* Obstetrician/	No	*Nichols v.*
diabetes	gynaecologist		*Gray*
INJURY: FURTHER TREATMENT REQUIRED			
I AGGRAVATED CONDITION			
Care: Doctor:	*Doctor:* Dermatologist	Yes	*Barr v.*
Case management			*Hughes*
Care: Hospital: Emergency	*Hospital*	No	*Elverson v.*
	Nurse	No	*Doctors Hosp.*
Diagnosis: Failure to diagnose	*Doctor:* General Practitioner	Yes	*Turriff v.*
abscess			*King*
Diagnosis: Failure to diagnose	*Doctor:* Dermatologist	Yes	*Barr v.*
cancer			*Hughes*
Diagnosis: Failure to diagnose	*Doctor:* Surgeon: General	No	*Moore v.*
dislocated shoulder			*Large*
Diagnosis: Failure to diagnose	*Doctor:* Surgeon: General	Appor-	*Hôpital Notre Dame*
fractured hip	*Hospital*	tioned	*de l'Esperance*
			v. Laurent
Diagnosis: Failure to diagnose	*Chiropractor*	Yes	*Gibbons v.*
tuberculosis of spinal column			*Harris*
Treatment: Surgery:	*Doctor:* Surgeon: Orthopaedic	No**	*Hopp v.*
Hemilaminectomy			*Lepp*
II CORRECTIVE TREATMENT			
Administration of Anaesthetic:	*Doctor:* Anaesthetist	No	*Lloy v.*
Injection	*House Staff:* Resident	No	*Milner*
Care: Doctor:	*Doctor:* Obstetrician/	No	*Karderas v.*
During treatment (sponges)	Gynaecologist		*Clow*
	Hospital	Yes	
	House Staff: Resident (not party)	Yes	

PROCEDURE	DEFENDANT	LIAB.	CASE NAME
Care: Doctor: During treatment (sponges)	*Doctor:* Surgeon: General	No	*Jewison v. Hassard*
Care: Doctor: During treatment (sponges)	*Doctor:* Surgeon: General	No	*Waldon v. Archer*
Care: Doctor: During treatment (surgical instruments)	*Doctor:* Surgeon: General	Yes	*Gloning v. Miller*
Care: Doctor: During treatment (surgical instruments)	*Doctor:* Surgeon: General	Yes	*Taylor v. Gray*
Care: Doctor: Post-treatment	*Doctor:* General Practitioner	Yes*	*Gonda v. Kerbel*
Care: Doctor: Post-treatment	*Doctor:* Surgeon: General	No	*Law v. Gomel*
Care: Doctor: Post-treatment	*Doctor:* Obstetrician/ Gynaecologist	Yes*	*McBride v. Langton*
Care: Doctor: Post-treatment	*Doctor:* Surgeon: Orthopaedic	No	*Ostrowski v. Lotto*
Care: Doctor: Post-treatment	*Doctor:* Surgeon: Orthopaedic	Yes	*Powell v. Guttman*
Care: Doctor: Post-treatment (nerve irritation by sacral hook)	*Doctor:* Surgeon: Orthopaedic	No*	*Bucknam v. Kostiuk*
Care: Doctor: Post-treatment	*Doctor:* Obstetrician/ Gynaecologist	No**	*Videto v. Kennedy*
Care: Hospital: During treatment (sponges)	*Doctor:* Surgeon: General *Hospital* *Nurse*	Yes Yes No	*Cosgrove v. Gaudreau*
Care: Hospital: During treatment (sponges)	*Doctor:* Surgeon: General *Nurse* (not party)	No	*Jewison v. Hassard*
Care: Hospital: During treatment (sponges)	*Doctor:* Surgeon: General *Hospital* *Nurse* (not party)	No No	*Petite v. MacLeod*
Care: Hospital: During treatment (sponges)	*Doctor:* Obstetrician/ Gynaecologist *Hospital* *House Staff:* Resident	No Yes	*Karderas v. Clow*
Diagnosis: Failure to diagnose diabetes	*Doctor:* Obstetrician/ Gynaecologist	No	*Nichols v. Gray*
Diagnosis: Failure to diagnose fractured arm	*Doctor:* General Practitioner	Yes	*Armstrong v. Dawson*

PROCEDURE	DEFENDANT	LIAB.	CASE NAME
Diagnosis: Failure to diagnose fractured finger	*Doctor:* General Practitioner *Hospital* *Technician:* X-ray	Yes Yes No	*Pepin v.* *Hôpital du Haut* *Richelieu*
Diagnosis: Failure to diagnose infection	*Doctor:* Obstetrician/ Gynaecologist	Yes*	*McBride v.* *Langton*
Diagnosis: Failure to diagnose infection	*Doctor:* General Practitioner	No	*Richardson v.* *Nugent*
Diagnosis: Failure to diagnose infection	*Doctor:* Surgeon: General	No	*Law v.* *Gomel*
Diagnosis: Failure to diagnose surgery required	*Optometrist*	No	*Murphy v.* *Mathieson*
Diagnosis: Procedure: Fluoroscopy	*Doctor:* General Practitioner	Yes	*Armstrong v.* *Dawson*
Diagnosis: Procedure: Sigmoidoscopy	*Doctor:* General Practitioner	Yes*	*Gonda v.* *Kerbel*
Referral: Follow-up Care	*Doctor:* General Practitioner	No	*Beninger v.* *Walton*
Treatment: Dental: Extraction	*Dentist*	No	*McTaggart v.* *Powers*
Treatment: Dental: Extraction	*Dentist*	No	*Legault-Bellemare* *v. Madore*
Treatment: General: Hand	*Doctor:* General Practitioner	No	*Hearne v.* *Flood*
Treatment: Injection: Medication	*Doctor:* General Practitioner	No	*Neufeld v.* *McQuitty*
Treatment: Injection: Vaccination	*Doctor:* General Practitioner	Yes	*Cardin v.* *Montreal*
Treatment: Medication: Administration	*Doctor:* Surgeon: Orthopaedic	Yes	*Crichton v.* *Hastings*
Treatment: Medication: Prescription	*Pharmacist*	Yes	*Williams v.* *Jones*
Treatment: Obstetrical: Delivery	*Doctor:* General Practitioner	No	*Hay v.* *Bain*
Treatment: Obstetrical: Miscarriage	*Doctor:* General Practitioner	No	*Hampton v.* *Macadam*
Treatment: Reduction of fracture & immobilization: Ankle	*Doctor:* Surgeon: General	Yes	*Parkin v.* *Kobrinsky*
Treatment: Reduction of fracture & immobilization: Ankle	*Doctor:* General Practitioner	No	*Gordon v.* *Davidson*
Treatment: Reduction of fracture & immobilization: Arm	*Doctor:* Surgeon: Orthopaedic	No	*Roy v.* *Goulet*

PROCEDURE	DEFENDANT	LIAB.	CASE NAME
Treatment: Reduction of fracture & immobilization: Foot	*Doctor:* General Practitioner	Yes	*Townsend v. Lai*
Treatment: Reduction of fracture & immobilization: Leg	*Doctor:* General Practitioner *Hospital*	Yes No	*Park v. Stevenson Memorial Hosp.*
Treatment: Reduction of fracture & immobilization: Leg	*Doctor:* Surgeon: General	No	*Benoit v. Muir*
Treatment: Reduction of fracture & immobilization: Leg	*Doctor:* Surgeon: Orthopaedic	Yes	*Leachman v. MacLachlan*
Treatment: Surgery: Abdominal	*Doctor:* Surgeon: General *Hospital* *Nurse*	Yes Yes Yes	*Cosgrove v. Gaudreau*
Treatment: Surgery: Appendectomy	*Doctor:* Surgeon: General	No	*Meyer v. Lefebvre*
Treatment: Surgery: Arthroplasty	*Doctor:* Surgeon: Orthopaedic	Yes	*Powell v. Guttman*
Treatment: Surgery: Blepharoplasty	*Doctor:* Surgeon: Cosmetic	No	*Guertin v. Kester*
Treatment: Surgery: Caesarian Section	*Doctor:* Surgeon: General	Yes	*Taylor v. Gray*
Treatment: Surgery: Fusion	*Doctor:* Surgeon: Orthopaedic	Yes	*David v. Toronto Transit Comm.*
Treatment: Surgery: Gynaecological	*Doctor:* General Practitioner *Doctor:* Surgeon: General	No No	*Chipps v. Peters*
Treatment: Surgery: Herniorrhaphy	*Doctor:* Surgeon: General *Hospital* *Nurse* (not party)	No No	*Petite v. MacLeod*
Treatment: Surgery: Hysterectomy	*Doctor:* Surgeon: General	No	*Surkan v. Blott*
Treatment: Surgery: Laparoscopy	*Doctor:* Obstetrician/ Gynaecologist	Yes*	*McBride v. Langton*
Treatment: Surgery: Laparoscopy/Laparotomy	*Doctor:* Obstetrician/ Gynaecologist	No*	*Gouin-Perrault v. Villeneuve*
Treatment: Surgery: Laparotomy	*Doctor:* Obstetrician/ Gynaecologist *Hospital* *House Staff:* Resident (not party)	No Yes	*Karderas v. Clow*
Treatment: Surgery: Laparotomy	*Doctor:* Obstetrician/ Gynaecologist	No**	*Videto v. Kennedy*
Treatment: Surgery: Mammoplasty	*Doctor:* Surgeon: Cosmetic	Yes*	*MacDonald v. Ross*

PROCEDURE	DEFENDANT	LIAB.	CASE NAME
Treatment: Surgery: Mammoplasty	*Doctor:* Surgeon: Cosmetic	Yes*	*White v. Turner*
Treatment: Surgery: Osteotomy	*Doctor:* Surgeon: Orthopaedic	No*	*Jodouin v. Mitra*
Treatment: Surgery: Osteotomy	*Doctor:* Surgeon: Orthopaedic	No	*Ostrowski v. Lotto*
Treatment: Surgery: Tubal ligation	*Doctor:* Obstetrician/ Gynaecologist	No*	*Hobson v. Munkley*
Treatment: Surgery: Tubal ligation	*Doctor:* Specialist	No*	*Sanderson v. Lamont*
Treatment: Surgery: Wrist	*Doctor:* Surgeon: General	Yes	*McKeachie v. Alvarez*
III PROLONGED RECOVERY *Care:* Hospital: Post-treatment/Supervision	*Hospital* *Nurse* (not party)	Yes	*Beatty v. Sisters of Misericorde*
Treatment: Surgery: Dupuytren's Contracture (correction of)	*Doctor:* General Practitioner *Doctor:* Surgeon: General	No* No	*Kenny v. Lockwood*
IV UNSUCCESSFUL TREATMENT *Diagnosis:* Failure to diagnose dislocated shoulder	*Doctor:* General Practitioner (not party) *Hospital*	Yes No	*Thompson v. Columbia Coast Mission*
Treatment: Chiropractic	*Chiropractor*	No	*Cawley v. Mercer*
Treatment: Chiropractic	*Chiropractor*	Yes	*Penner v. Theobald*
Treatment: Dental: Crown & bridge	*Dentist*	No	*Allard v. Boykowich*
Treatment: Dental: Crown & bridge	*Dentist:* Prosthodontist	Yes	*Fluevog v. Pottinger*
Treatment: Dental: Extraction	*Doctor:* Surgeon: Oral	Yes	*Drinnen v. Douglas*
Treatment: Infection (correction of)	*Doctor:* General Practitioner *Hospital*	No	*Petit v. Hôpital Ste. Jeanne D'Arc*
Treatment: Sterilization: Aldridge Procedure	*Doctor:* Obstetrician/ Gynaecologist	No*	*Doiron v. Orr*
Treatment: Sterilization: Silver nitrate	*Doctor:* Obstetrician/ Gynaecologist	Yes*	*Cryderman v. Ringrose*
Treatment: Sterilization: Silver nitrate	*Doctor:* Obstetrician/ Gynaecologist	Yes*	*Zimmer v. Ringrose*
Treatment: Sterilization: Tubal ligation	*Doctor:* Obstetrician/ Gynaecologist	No*	*Dendaas v. Yackel*
Treatment: Sterilization: Tubal ligation	*Doctor:* Surgeon: General	Yes*	*Cataford v. Moreau*

PROCEDURE	DEFENDANT	LIAB.	CASE NAME
Treatment: Surgery: Gall bladder	*Doctor:* General Practitioner	No	*Davy v. Morrison*
Treatment: Surgery: Hemilaminectomy	*Doctor:* Surgeon: Orthopaedic	No**	*Hopp v. Lepp*
Treatment: Surgery: Removal of bullet fragments	*Doctor:* Surgeon: General	No	*Browne v. Lerner*

INJURY: HEMORRHAGE

PROCEDURE	DEFENDANT	LIAB.	CASE NAME
Diagnosis: Failure to diagnose hemorrhage	*Doctor:* Emerg. Rm. Physician *Hospital*	Yes No	*Wade v. Nayermouri*
Diagnosis: Failure to diagnose hemorrhage	*Doctor:* General Practitioner *Hospital* *Nurse* (not party)	No No	*Serre v. DeTilly*
Diagnosis: Failure to diagnose hemorrhage	*Doctor:* Surgeon: Orthopaedic	No	*Chubey v. Ahsan*
Treatment: Medication: Administration	*Doctor:* Surgeon: Orthopaedic	Yes	*Crichton v. Hastings*
Treatment: Obstetrical: Delivery	*Doctor:* General Practitioner	No	*Simard v. R.*
Treatment: Surgery: Discoidectomy	*Doctor:* Neurosurgeon	No	*Kapur v. Marshall*
Treatment: Surgery: Discoidectomy	*Doctor:* Surgeon: Orthopaedic	No	*Chubey v. Ahsan*

INJURY: INFECTION

I ABSCESS

PROCEDURE	DEFENDANT	LIAB.	CASE NAME
Administration of Anaesthetic: Transtracheal ventilation *Diagnosis:* Failure to diagnose infection Procedure: Microlaryngoscopy	*Doctor:* Anaesthetist *Doctor:* Internist *Doctor:* Otolaryngologist *Hospital*	Yes* Yes Yes No	*Holmes v. Bd. of Hosp. Trustees of London*

II ENDOCARDITIS

PROCEDURE	DEFENDANT	LIAB.	CASE NAME
Diagnosis: Failure to diagnose endocarditis	*Doctor:* Obstetrician/ Gynaecologist	No	*Nichols v. Gray*

III EYE

PROCEDURE	DEFENDANT	LIAB.	CASE NAME
Diagnosis: Failure to diagnose infection	*Doctor:* Ophthalmologist	Yes	*Moffat v. Whitelson*
Diagnosis: Incorrect diagnosis of cataract	*Doctor:* Ophthalmologist	Yes	*Piche v. Ing*

IV GANGRENE

PROCEDURE	DEFENDANT	LIAB.	CASE NAME
Care: Doctor/Hospital: Post-treatment	*Doctor:* General Practitioner *Doctor:* Surgeon: General *Hospital*	No Yes No	*Thomas v. Scarborough*

PROCEDURE	DEFENDANT	LIAB.	CASE NAME
Treatment: Blood: Transfusion	*Doctor:* Surgeon: General	No	*Armstrong v. McClealand*
Treatment: Experimental quartz lamp	*Doctor:* General Practitioner	Yes*	*Baills v. Boulanger*
Treatment: Injection: Vaccination	*Nurse*	No	*Cavan v. Wilcox*
Treatment: Reduction of fracture & immobilization: Foot	*Doctor:* General Practitioner	Yes	*Bergstrom v. C.*
Treatment: Reduction of fracture & immobilization: Leg	*Doctor:* General Practitioner *Hospital*	Yes No	*Badger v. Surkan*
V GAS GANGRENE *Diagnosis:* Failure to diagnose fracture (compound)	*Doctor:* Surgeon: Orthopaedic *Hospital*	Yes No	*Dean v. York County Hosp.*
Treatment: Reduction of fracture & immobilization: Arm	*Doctor:* General Practitioner	No	*Challand v. Bell*
Treatment: Reduction of fracture & immobilization: Leg	*Doctor:* Surgeon: Orthopaedic	Yes	*Dean v. York County Hosp.*
VI HAND *Treatment:* Surgery: Thumb	*Doctor:* Surgeon: General	No	*Nelligan v. Clement*
VII OSTEOMYELITIS *Diagnosis:* Failure to diagnose infection	*Doctor:* Surgeon: General	No	*Law v. Gomel*
VIII PERITONITIS *Care:* Doctor: Assignment of responsibilities	*Doctor:* General Practitioner	No	*Wilson v. Stark*
Care: Doctor: Post-treatment	*Doctor:* General Practitioner	Yes*	*Gonda v. Kerbel*
Care: Doctor: Post-treatment	*Doctor:* Obstetrician/ Gynaecologist	Yes*	*McBride v. Langton*
Care: Doctor: Post-treatment	*Doctor:* Obstetrician/ Gynaecologist	No**	*Videto v. Kennedy*
Diagnosis: Failure to diagnose appendicitis	*Doctor:* General Practitioner	No	*Wilson v. Stark*
Diagnosis: Failure to diagnose infection	*Doctor:* Obstetrician/ Gynaecologist	Yes*	*McBride v. Langton*
Diagnosis: Procedure: Sigmoidoscopy	*Doctor:* General Practitioner	Yes*	*Gonda v. Kerbel*
Treatment: Surgery: Appendectomy	*Doctor:* General Practitioner	No	*Wilson v. Stark*

PROCEDURE	DEFENDANT	LIAB.	CASE NAME
Treatment: Surgery: Laparotomy/Laparoscopy	*Doctor:* Obstetrician/ Gynaecologist	No**	*Videto v. Kennedy*
Treatment: Surgery: Laparotomy/Laparoscopy	*Doctor:* Obstetrician/ Gynaecologist	Yes*	*McBride v. Langton*
IX PLEURISY *Diagnosis:* Failure to diagnose pleurisy	*Doctor:* General Practitioner	No	*Richardson v. Nugent*
X STAPHYLOCOCCUS *Treatment:* Reduction of fracture & immobilization: Arm	*Doctor:* Surgeon: Orthopaedic	No	*Roy v. Goulet*
XI STREPTOCOCCUS *Treatment:* Blood: Transfusion	*House Staff:* Intern	No	*Cox v. Saskatoon*
XII VAGINAL *Treatment:* Surgery: Gynaecological	*Doctor:* General Practitioner *Doctor:* Surgeon: General	No No	*Chipps v. Peters*
INJURY: INSULIN SHOCK *Treatment:* Medication: Administration	*Doctor:* General Practitioner	No	*Marshall v. Rogers*
INJURY: JOINT I DISPLACEMENT (HIP) *Diagnosis:* Failure to diagnose dislocated hip	*Doctor:* General Practitioner	No	*Bruinooge v. Collier*
Diagnosis: Failure to diagnose dislocated hip *Treatment:* Reduction of fracture & immobilization: Hip	*Doctor:* General Practitioner	Yes	*Dangerfield v. David*
II(a) FUSION (ANKLE) *Treatment:* Reduction of fracture & immobilization: Ankle	*Doctor:* Surgeon: General	Yes	*Parkin v. Kobrinsky*
Treatment: Surgery: Fusion	*Doctor:* Surgeon: General Hospital	Yes No	*Staple v. Winnipeg*
II(b) FUSION (HIP) *Diagnosis:* Failure to diagnose infection *Care:* Hospital: Post-treatment	*Doctor:* Surgeon: Orthopaedic *House Staff:* Resident Hospital *Nurse* (Not Party)	No* No No	*Hajgato v. London Health Assn.*
Treatment: Reduction of fracture & immobilization: Leg	*Doctor:* Surgeon: Orthopaedic	Yes	*Leachman v. MacLachlan*
III GENERAL *Medication:* Avascular Necrosis: Hip and shoulder replacement	*Doctor:* General Practitioner *Doctor:* Gastroenterologist	Yes Yes	*Reynard v. Carr*

PROCEDURE	DEFENDANT	LIAB.	CASE NAME
IV(a) IMPAIRED MOVEMENT (ANKLE)			
Diagnosis: Failure to diagnose fractured ankle	*Doctor:* General Practitioner	Yes	*Price v.*
	Doctor: Surgeon: Orthopaedic	Yes	*Milawski*
IV(b) IMPAIRED MOVEMENT (HIP)			
Diagnosis: Failure to diagnose fractured hip	*Doctor:* Surgeon: General	Appor-	*Hôpital Notre*
	Hospital	tioned	*Dame de l'Esperance v. Laurent*
IV(c) IMPAIRED MOVEMENT (SHOULDER)			
Diagnosis: Failure to diagnose dislocated shoulder	*Doctor:* Surgeon: General	No	*Clark v. Wansbrough*
IV(d) IMPAIRED MOVEMENT (WRIST)			
Diagnosis: Failure to diagnose dislocated wrist	*Doctor:* General Practitioner	Appor-	*Osburn v.*
	Hospital	tioned	*Mohindra*
Care: Doctor/Hospital: During treatment	*Doctor:* Surgeon: General	No	*Knight v.*
	Hospital	Yes	*Sisters of St. Ann*
INJURY: MITRAL STENOSIS			
Diagnosis: Failure to diagnose mitral stenosis	*Doctor:* General Practitioner	No	*Athansious v. Guzman*
INJURY: NERVE (See also PARALYSIS)			
I(a) DAMAGE (FACIAL)			
Treatment: Surgery: Labyrinthectomy	*Doctor:* Surgeon: General	No	*Barcus v.*
	Hospital	No	*Brown*
I(b) DAMAGE (SCIATIC)			
Treatment: Injection: Medication	*Hospital*	Yes	*Fiege v.*
	Nurse	Yes	*Cornwall Gen. Hosp.*
Treatment: Injection: Medication	*Hospital*	Yes	*Huber v.*
	Nurse (not party)		*Burnaby Gen. Hosp.*
I(c) DAMAGE (SPINAL ACCESSORY)			
Treatment: Injection: Cyst (removal of)	*Doctor:* General Practitioner	Yes	*Fizer v. Keys*
II HYPERSENSITIVITY (FACIAL)			
Treatment: Dental: Extraction	*Doctor:* Surgeon: Oral	Yes**	*Rawlings v. Lindsay*
III NEURAPRAXIA (ARM)			
Care: Hospital: Post-treatment	*Hospital*	Yes	*Traynor v.*
	Nurse (not party)		*Vancott*
IV(a) NUMBNESS (ELBOW)			
Treatment: Surgery: Ulnar Nerve Release	*Doctor:* Surgeon: General	No*	*Konkolus v. Royal Alexandra Bd. of Govs.*

PROCEDURE	DEFENDANT	LIAB.	CASE NAME
IV(b) NUMBNESS (FACIAL)			
Treatment: Dental: Extraction	*Doctor:* Surgeon: Oral	Yes**	*Rawlings v. Lindsay*
Treatment: Dental: Extraction	*Dentist*	No*	*Schinz v. Dickinson*
Treatment: Dental: Extraction	*Oral Surgeon*	No*	*Diack v. Bardsley*
IV(c) NUMBNESS (FOOT)			
Treatment: Reduction of fracture & immobilization: Ankle	*Doctor:* General Practitioner	No	*Gordon v. Davidson*
IV(d) NUMBNESS (LEG)			
Treatment: Surgery: Osteotomy	*Doctor:* Surgeon: Orthopaedic	No*	*Jodouin v. Mitra*
V SEVERED			
Treatment: Surgical: Wrist	*Doctor:* Surgeon: General	Yes	*McKeachie v. Alvarez*
VI STIFFNESS			
Treatment: Surgical: Osteotomy	*Doctor:* Surgeon: Orthopaedic	Yes**	*Kelly v. Hazlett*
INJURY: ORGAN			
I ADYNAMIC ILEUS			
Diagnosis: Failure to diagnose fracture dislocation of spine	*Hospital*	Yes	*Fraser v.*
	House Staff: Intern	Yes	*Vancouver Gen. Hosp.*
II(a) AMPUTATION/REMOVAL (FALLOPIAN TUBES)			
Diagnosis: Incorrect diagnosis of cancer	*Doctor:* Surgeon	No	*Lefebvre v.*
	Doctor: Pathologist	No	*Osborne*
	Hospital: Hospital laboratory	Yes	
Treatment: Surgery: Hysterectomy	*Doctor:* Surgeon: General	No	*Bennett v. C.*
II(b) AMPUTATION/REMOVAL (GALL BLADDER)			
Treatment: Surgery: Gall bladder	*Doctor:* General Practitioner	No	*Davy v. Morrison*
II(c) AMPUTATION/REMOVAL (KIDNEY)			
Treatment: Surgery: Gynaecological	*Doctor:* Surgeon: General	Yes	*Urbanski v. Patel*
Treatment: Surgery: Hysterectomy	*Doctor:* Surgeon: General	No	*Surkan v. Blott*
II(d) AMPUTATION/REMOVAL (OVARIES)			
Treatment: Surgery: Hysterectomy	*Doctor:* Surgeon: General	No	*Bennett v. C.*
II(e) AMPUTATION/REMOVAL (PENIS)			
Treatment: Surgery: Circumcision	*Doctor:* General Practitioner	Yes	*Gilbert v. Campbell*

PROCEDURE	DEFENDANT	LIAB.	CASE NAME
II(f) AMPUTATION/REMOVAL (TESTICLE)			
Care: Doctor/Hospital:	*Doctor:* General Practitioner	No	*Thomas v.*
Post-treatment	*Doctor:* Surgeon: General	Yes	*Scarborough*
	Hospital	No	*Gen. Hosp.*
Treatment: Surgery:	*Doctor:* Surgeon: General	No*	*Marshall v.*
Herniorrhaphy			*Curry*
III(a) DAMAGE (KIDNEY)			
Treatment: Medication:	*Doctor:* Surgeon: Orthopaedic	Yes*	*Male v.*
Administration			*Hopmans*
III(b) DAMAGE (PENIS)			
Treatment: Surgery:	*Doctor:* General Practitioner	Yes	*Gray v.*
Circumcision			*LaFleche*
III(c) DAMAGE (URETER)			
Treatment: Surgery:	*Doctor:* Obstetrician/	No*	*Hobson v.*
Tubal ligation	Gynaecologist		*Munkley*
IV DONATION (KIDNEY)			
Treatment: Surgery:	*Doctor:* Surgeon: General	Yes	*Urbanski v.*
Gynaecological			*Patel*
V INCONTINENCE/IMPOTENCE			
Administration of Anaesthetic:	*Doctor:* Anaesthetist	No	*Girard v.*
Injection	*Hospital*	No	*Royal Columbian*
			Hosp.
Treatment: Surgery:	*Doctor:* Neurosurgeon	Yes**	*Reibl v.*
Endarterectomy			*Hughes*
Treatment: Surgery:	*Doctor:* Surgeon: Orthopaedic	No**	*Hopp v.*
Hemilaminectomy			*Lepp*
Treatment: Surgery:	*Doctor:* Urologist	No*	*Considine v.*
Transurethral resection	*Hospital*	No	*Camp Hill*
	House Staff: Resident	No	*Hosp.*
VI PERFORATION (BLADDER)			
Diagnosis: Procedure:	*Doctor:* General Practitioner	Yes*	*Gonda v.*
Sigmoidoscopy			*Kerbel*
Treatment: Surgery:	*Doctor:* Surgeon: General	Yes	*Melvin v.*
Herniorrhaphy			*Graham*
Treatment: Surgery:	*Doctor:* Urologist	No*	*Considine v.*
Transurethral resection	*Hospital*	No	*Camp Hill*
	House Staff: Resident	No	*Hosp.*
INJURY: PAIN AND SUFFERING			
Administration of Anaesthetic:	*Doctor:* Anaesthetist	No	*Lloy v.*
Injection	*House Staff:* Resident	No	*Milner*
Care: Doctor:	*Doctor:* Dermatologist	Yes	*Barr v.*
Case management			*Hughes*

PROCEDURE	DEFENDANT	LIAB.	CASE NAME
Care: Doctor/Hospital: During treatment (sponges)	*Doctor:* Obstetrician/ Gynaecologist *Hospital* *House Staff:* Resident (not party)	No Yes	*Karderas v. Clow*
Care: Doctor/Hospital: During treatment (sponges)	*Doctor:* Surgeon: General *Hospital* *Nurse*	Yes Yes Yes	*Cosgrove v. Gaudreau*
Care: Doctor/Hospital: During treatment (sponges)	*Doctor:* Surgeon: General *Nurse*	No No	*Jewison v. Hassard*
Care: Doctor/Hospital: During treatment (sponges)	*Doctor:* Surgeon: General *Hospital* *Nurse* (not party)	No No	*Petite v. MacLeod*
Care: Doctor/Hospital: During treatment (surgical instrument)	*Doctor:* Surgeon: General	Yes	*Taylor v. Gray*
Care: Doctor: During treatment (surgical procedure)	*Doctor:* Otolaryngologist	Admitted	*Van Winkle v. Chen*
Care: Doctor: During treatment	*Doctor:* General Practitioner	No	*Pierce v. Strathroy Hosp.*
Care: Doctor: Supervision/Control	*Dentist*	No	*Lafleche v. Larouche*
Care: Hospital: Supervision/Control	*Hospital* *Nurse* (not party)	Yes	*Beatty v. Sisters of Misericorde*
Consultation: Failure to consult specialist	*Doctor:* General Practitioner	Yes	*Daoust v. R.*
Diagnosis: Failure to diagnose fractured foot	*Doctor:* General Practitioner	Yes	*Daoust v. R.*
Diagnosis: Failure to diagnose fractured hip	*Doctor:* Surgeon: General *Hospital*	Apportioned	*Hôpital Notre Dame de l'Esperance v. Laurent*
Diagnosis: Failure to diagnose infection (abscess)	*Doctor:* General Practitioner	Yes	*Turriff v. King*
Diagnosis: Failure to diagnose infection	*Doctor:* Surgeon: General	No	*Law v. Gomel*
Diagnosis: Incorrect diagnosis of cancer	*Doctor:* Surgeon *Doctor:* Pathologist *Hospital:* Hospital laboratory	No No Yes	*Lefebvre v. Osborne*
Diagnosis: Incorrect diagnosis of cancer	*Doctor*	Admitted	*Down v. Royal Jubilee Hosp.*

PROCEDURE	DEFENDANT	LIAB.	CASE NAME
Diagnosis: Incorrect diagnosis of cancer	*Doctor:* Surgeon: General	No	*Wilson v. Swanson*
Treatment: Chiropractic	*Chiropractor*	Yes	*Penner v. Theobald*
Treatment: Chiropractic	*Chiropractor*	No	*Rutledge v. Fisher*
Treatment: Dental: Extraction	*Dentist*	No	*Kobescak v. Chan*
Treatment: Dental: Extraction	*Dentist*	Yes	*Murano v. Gray*
Treatment: Dental: Extraction	*Oral Surgeon*	Yes	*Drinnen v. Douglas*
Treatment: Dental: Extraction	*Oral Surgeon*	Yes**	*Rawlings v. Lindsay*
Treatment: Injection: Medication	*Hospital* *Nurse*	Yes Yes	*Fiege v. Cornwall Gen. Hosp.*
Treatment: Reduction of fracture & immobilization: Ankle	*Doctor:* Surgeon: General	Yes	*Parkin v. Kobrinsky*
Treatment: Reduction of fracture & immobilization: Foot	*Doctor:* General Practitioner	Yes	*Townsend v. Lai*
Treatment: Reduction of fracture & immobilization: Leg	*Doctor:* Surgeon: General	No	*Benoit v. Muir*
Treatment: Reduction of fracture & immobilization: Leg	*Doctor:* Surgeon: Orthopaedic	Yes	*Brennan v. Fraser*
Treatment: Reduction of fracture & immobilization: Leg	*Doctor:* Surgeon: Orthopaedic	Yes	*Leachman v. MacLachlan*
Treatment: Rehabilitation therapy: Physiotherapy	*Rehab. Med.:* Physiotherapist	No	*Grafton v. Bigelow*
Treatment: Surgery: Abdominal	*Doctor:* General Practitioner	No	*Pierce v. Strathroy Hosp.*
Treatment: Surgery: Abdominal	*Doctor:* Surgeon: General	Yes	*Cosgrove v. Gaudreau*
Treatment: Surgery: Appendectomy	*Doctor:* Surgeon: General	No	*Meyer v. Lefebvre*
Treatment: Surgery: Caesarian section	*Doctor:* Surgeon: General	Yes	*Taylor v. Gray*
Treatment: Surgery: Cyst (removal of)	*Doctor:* General Practitioner	Yes	*Fizer v. Keys*

PROCEDURE	DEFENDANT	LIAB.	CASE NAME
Treatment: Surgery: Draining abscess	*Doctor:* General Practitioner *Doctor:* Surgeon: General	Yes Yes	*Wine v.* *Dawyd*
Treatment: Surgery: Herniorrhaphy	*Doctor:* Surgeon: General *Hospital* *Nurse* (not party)	No No	*Petite v.* *MacLeod*
Treatment: Surgery: Laparotomy	*Doctor:* Obstetrician/ Gynaecologist *Hospital* House Staff: Resident (not party)	No Yes	*Karderas v.* *Clow*
Treatment: Surgery: Nasal	*Doctor:* Surgeon: General	No	*Hutchinson v.* *Robert*
Treatment: Surgery: Osteotomy	*Doctor:* Surgeon: Orthopaedic	No*	*Jodouin v.* *Mitra*
Treatment: Surgery: Spinal fusion	*Doctor:* Surgeon: Orthopaedic	No*	*Bucknam v.* *Kostiuk*
Treatment: Surgery: Tubal ligation	*Doctor:* Obstetrician/ Gynaecologist	Yes*	*Dendaas v.* *Yackel*
Treatment: Surgery: Tubal ligation	*Doctor:* Obstetrician/ Gynaecologist	No*	*Hobson v.* *Munkley*
Treatment: Surgery: Tubal ligation	*Doctor:* Surgeon: General	Yes*	*Cataford v.* *Moreau*
Treatment: Surgery: Ulnar nerve release	*Doctor:* Surgeon: General	No*	*Konkolus v.* *Royal Alexandra* *Bd. of Govs.*

INJURY: PARALYSIS
I ARM

Diagnosis: Procedure X-Ray	*Hospital*	No	*Murphy v.* *Gen. Hosp.*
Treatment: Injection: Vaccination	*Doctor:* General Practitioner	Yes	*Cardin v.* *Montreal*

II FACE

Diagnosis: Failure to diagnose mastoiditis *Referral:* Failure to refer to specialist	*Doctor:* General Practitioner	No	*Jarvis v.* *Int. Nickel Co.*
Treatment: Surgery: Mastoidectomy	*Doctor:* Otolaryngologist	Yes	*Eady v.* *Tenderenda*
Treatment: Surgery: Stapedectomy	*Doctor:* Otolaryngologist *Doctor:* Surgeon: General	No**	*Zamparo v.* *Brisson*

III HEMIPLEGIA

Treatment: Surgery: Endarterectomy	*Doctor:* Neurosurgeon	Yes**	*Reibl v.* *Hughes*

PROCEDURE	DEFENDANT	LIAB.	CASE NAME
IV LEG			
Administration of Anaesthetic: General	*Doctor:* Anaesthetist	No	*Girard v. Royal*
	Hospital	No	*Columbian Hosp.*
Care: Hospital: Post-treatment	*Hospital*	Yes	*Laughlin v. Royal*
	Nurse (not party)		*Columbian Hosp.*
Consultation: Failure to consult specialist	*Doctor:* General Practitioner	Yes	*Thomas v. Port Colborne Gen. Hosp.*
Treatment: Dressing wound	*Doctor:* Surgeon: General	No	*Zirkler v. Robinson*
Treatment: Injection: Knee	*Doctor:* Surgeon: Orthopaedic	Yes	*Bibby v. Hall*
Treatment: Injection: Medication	*Hospital*	Yes	*Laughlin v. Royal*
	Nurse (not party)		*Columbian Hosp.*
V PARAPLEGIA			
Administration of Anaesthetic: Injection	*Doctor:* Anaesthetist	Yes	*Martel v. Hotel-*
	Hospital	Yes	*Dieu St-Vallier*
Administration of Anaesthetic: Spinal	*Doctor:* Anaesthetist	Yes	*Beausoleil v.*
	Hospital	Yes	*Soeurs de la Charité*
Care: Doctor/Hospital: Supervision	*Doctor:* Psychiatrist	No	*Worth v. Royal*
	Hospital	No	*Jubilee Hosp.*
Treatment: Chiropractic: Surgery: Laminectomy	*Chiropractor*	No*	*Strachan v.*
	Doctor: Neurologist	No	*Simpson*
	Doctor: Neurosurgeon	Yes	
VI POLYNEURITIS			
Treatment: Medication: Administration	*Doctor:* General Practitioner	No*	*Davidson v. Connaught Laboratories*
VII QUADRIPLEGIA			
Administration of Anaesthetic: Transtracheal ventilation	*Doctor:* Anaesthetist	Yes*	*Holmes v.*
	Doctor: Internist	Yes	*Bd. of Hosp.*
	Doctor: Otolaryngologist		*Trustees of London*
Care: Doctor/Hospital: Post-treatment	*Doctor:* Neurosurgeon	No*	*Ferguson v.*
	Hospital	No	*Hamilton*
	House Staff: Resident	No	*Civic Hosp.*
	Nurse (not party)		
Diagnosis: Failure to diagnose infection	*Doctor:* Anaesthetist	Yes*	*Holmes v.*
	Doctor: Internist	Yes	*Bd. of Hosp.*
	Doctor: Otolaryngologist		*Trustees of London*

PROCEDURE	DEFENDANT	LIAB.	CASE NAME
Diagnosis: Procedure: Angiogram	*Doctor:* Neurosurgeon *Hospital* *House Staff:* Resident *Nurse* (not party)	No* No No	*Ferguson v.* *Hamilton* *Civic Hosp.*
Diagnosis: Procedure: Angiogram	*Doctor:* Radiologist *Doctor:* Surgeon: Vascular	No* No	*McLean v.* *Weir*
Treatment: Doctor/Hospital: Emergency	*Doctor:* Emerg. Rm. Physician *Hospital*	No No	*Nash v.* *Olson*
VIII VOCAL CHORD *Diagnosis:* Procedure: Biopsy (Mediastinoscopy)	*Doctor:* Surgeon: General	No**	*Bickford v.* *Stiles*
Diagnosis: Procedure: Biopsy (Scalene Node)	*Doctor:* General Practitioner	No	*Finlay v.* *Auld*

INJURY: POISONING

PROCEDURE	DEFENDANT	LIAB.	CASE NAME
Diagnosis: Failure to diagnose poisoning by carbon monoxide	*Doctor:* General Practitioner	No	*Ostash v.* *Sonnenberg*
Treatment: Medication: Prescription	*Doctor:* General Practitioner *Pharmacist*	No Yes	*Stretton v.* *Holmes*

INJURY: PREGNANCY (UNWANTED)

PROCEDURE	DEFENDANT	LIAB.	CASE NAME
Care: Doctor: Post-treatment	*Doctor:* Obstetrician/ Gynaecologist	Yes*	*Zimmer v.* *Ringrose*
Treatment: Sterilization: Aldridge procedure	*Doctor:* Obstetrician/ Gynaecologist	No*	*Doiron v.* *Orr*
Treatment: Sterilization: Silver nitrate	*Doctor:* Obstetrician/ Gynaecologist	No*	*Colp v.* *Ringrose*
Treatment: Sterilization: Silver nitrate	*Doctor:* Obstetrician/ Gynaecologist	Yes*	*Cryderman v.* *Ringrose*
Treatment: Sterilization: Silver nitrate	*Doctor:* Obstetrician/ Gynaecologist	Yes*	*Zimmer v.* *Ringrose*
Treatment: Sterilization: Tubal ligation	*Doctor:* Obstetrician/ Gynaecologist	Yes*	*Dendaas v.* *Yackel*
Treatment: Sterilization: Tubal ligation	*Doctor:* Specialist	No*	*Sanderson v.* *Lamont*
Treatment: Sterilization: Tubal ligation	*Doctor:* Surgeon: General	Yes*	*Cataford v.* *Moreau*

INJURY: PUNCTURED ARTERY

PROCEDURE	DEFENDANT	LIAB.	CASE NAME
Treatment: Blood: Bleeding	*Doctor:* Surgeon: General	Yes	*Kelly v.* *Dow*

PROCEDURE	DEFENDANT	LIAB.	CASE NAME
INJURY: SCARRING/DEFORMITY			
I ABDOMEN			
Care: Doctor: Post-treatment	*Doctor:* Obstetrician/ Gynaecologist	No**	*Videto v. Kennedy*
Diagnosis: Failure to diagnose infection	*Doctor:* General Practitioner *Doctor:* Surgeon: General	Yes Yes	*Wine v. Kernohan*
Treatment: Surgery: Abdominoplasty	*Doctor:* Surgeon: Cosmetic	No**	*Petty v. McKay*
Treatment: Surgery: Draining abscess	*Doctor:* Obstetrician/ Gynaecologist	Yes	*Wine v. Dawyd*
Treatment: Surgery: Laparoscopy/Laparotomy	*Doctor:* Obstetrician/ Gynaecologist	No*	*Gouin-Perrrault v. Villeneuve*
Treatment: Surgery: Laparoscopy/Laparotomy	*Doctor:* Obstetrician/ Gynaecologist	No**	*Videto v. Kennedy*
II ARM			
Care: Doctor: Post-treatment	*Doctor:* Surgeon: Orthopaedic	No	*Ostrowski v. Lotto*
Treatment: Injection: Vaccination	*Doctor:* General Practitioner	Yes	*Cardin v. Montreal*
Treatment: Injection: Vaccination	*Doctor:* Pediatrician	No	*Gent v. Wilson*
Treatment: Reduction of fracture & immobilization: Arm	*Doctor:* Surgeon: Orthopaedic	No	*Roy v. Goulet*
Treatment: Surgery: Osteotomy	*Doctor:* Surgeon: Orthopaedic	No	*Ostrowski v. Lotto*
III BREAST(S)			
Treatment: Surgery: Mammoplasty	*Doctor:* Surgeon: Cosmetic	Yes*	*MacDonald v. Ross*
Treatment: Surgery: Mammoplasty	*Doctor:* Surgeon: Cosmetic	Yes*	*White v. Turner*
IV EYELID			
Treatment: Surgery: Blepharoplasty	*Doctor:* Surgeon: Cosmetic	No*	*Guertin v. Kester*
V FACE			
Administration of Anaesthetic: General	*Doctor:* Anaesthetist Hospital	Yes No	*Crits v. Sylvester*
Care: Doctor: During treatment: Control of patient	Dentist	No	*Lafleche v. Larouche*
Care: Doctor: Nosebleed	*Doctor:* Otolaryngologist	Admitted	*Van Winkle v. Chen*
Treatment: Dermatological: Dermabrasion	*Doctor:* Surgeon: Cosmetic	No*	*Hankins v. Papillon*

PROCEDURE	DEFENDANT	LIAB.	CASE NAME
Treatment: Dermatological: Slush	*Doctor:* Dermatologist *Hospital*	No* No	*Johnston v.* *Wellesley Hosp.*
VI FINGER *Diagnosis:* Failure to diagnose fractured finger	*Doctor:* General Practitioner *Hospital* *Technician:* X-ray (not party)	Yes Yes	*Pepin v. Hôpital* *du Haut Richelieu*
VII FOOT *Treatment:* Reduction of fracture & immobilization	*Doctor:* General Practitioner	No	*Gordon v.* *Davidson*
VIII HAND *Administration of Anaesthetic:* Injection	*Doctor:* Anaesthetist *House Staff:* Resident	No No	*Lloy v.* *Milner*
Surgery: Failure to remove hematoma	*Doctor*	Yes	*Héritiers de Feu Maurice Massé v. Gaudette*
IX LEG *Care:* Doctor: Post-treatment *Treatment:* Reduction of fracture & immobilization (leg)	*Doctor:* General Practitioner	No	*Rickley v.* *Stratton*
Care: Doctor: Post-treatment *Treatment:* Reduction of fracture & immobilization (leg)	*Doctor:* Surgeon: General	No	*Benoit v.* *Muir*
Care: Doctor: Post-treatment *Treatment:* Reduction of fracture & immobilization (leg)	*Doctor:* Surgeon: Orthopaedic	Yes	*Brennan v.* *Fraser*
Treatment: Reduction of fracture & immobilization (leg)	*Doctor:* General Practitioner *Hospital*	Yes No	*Park v. Stevenson Memorial Hosp.*
X LIP *Treatment:* Dental: Restorative	*Dentist:* Paedodontist	No	*Dunn v. Young*
XI NOSE *Treatment:* Surgery: Rhinoplasty	*Doctor:* Surgeon: Cosmetic	Yes	*LaFleur v.* *Cornelis*
XII UNSPECIFIED *Care:* Hospital: Supervision	*Hospital* *Student Nurse* (not party)	Yes	*Farrell v.* *Regina*
XIII UTERUS *Treatment:* Surgery: Gynaecological	*Doctor:* General Practitioner *Doctor:* Surgeon: General	No No	*Chipps v.* *Peters*

PROCEDURE	DEFENDANT	LIAB.	CASE NAME
INJURY: SENSES			
I(a) HEARING (IMPAIRMENT)			
Diagnosis: Failure to diagnose mastoiditis *Referral:* Failure to refer to specialist	*Doctor:* General Practitioner	No	*Jarvis v. Int. Nickel Co.*
I(b) HEARING (LOSS)			
Treatment: Medication: Administration	*Doctor:* Surgeon: Orthopaedic	Yes*	*Male v. Hopmans*
I(c) HEARING (PERFORATION OF EARDRUM)			
Treatment: Ear	*Doctor:* Otolaryngologist	No	*Berry v. Pierce*
I(d) HEARING (TINNITUS)			
Diagnosis: Procedure: Audiogram	*Hospital* *Rehab. Med.:* Audiologist	Yes Yes	*Bartlett v. Children's Hosp. Corp.*
II(a) SIGHT (BLURRED VISION)			
Treatment: Surgery: Blepharoplasty	*Doctor:* Surgeon: Cosmetic	No*	*Guertin v. Kester*
II(b) SIGHT (DOUBLE VISION)			
Treatment: Surgery: Ophthalmic	*Doctor:* Surgeon: General	Yes**	*Calder v. Gilmour*
Treatment: Surgery: Sinus	*Doctor:* Otolaryngologist	No	*Patterson v. de la Bastide*
II(c) SIGHT (IMPAIRMENT)			
Care: Doctor: During treatment	*Doctor:* Surgeon: General *Hospital*	Apportioned	*Misericordia Hosp. v. Bustillo*
Care: Hospital: Post-treatment	*Hospital* *Support Staff:* Ward Aide	Yes Yes	*Wyndham v. Toronto Gen. Hosp. Trustees*
Diagnosis: Failure to diagnose eye injury *Referral:* Failure to refer to specialist	*Doctor:* General Practitioner	No	*Bell v. R.*
Diagnosis: Failure to diagnose mastoiditis	*Doctor:* General Practitioner	No	*Jarvis v. Int. Nickel Co.*
Diagnosis: Failure to diagnose retinal detachment	*Doctor:* Ophthalmologist	Yes	*Piche v. Ing*
Referral: Failure to refer to specialist	*Doctor:* General Practitioner	Yes	*Eaglebach v. Walters*
Referral: Failure to refer to specialist	*Doctor:* General Practitioner	No	*Jarvis v. Int. Nickel Co.*
Treatment: Medication: Administration	*Doctor:* Surgeon: General	Yes	*Casson v. Haig*

PROCEDURE	DEFENDANT	LIAB.	CASE NAME
Treatment: Medication: Administration	*Hospital* *Nurse*	Yes Yes	*Barker v.* *Lockhart*
Treatment: Medication: Administration/Prescription	*Doctor:* Ophthalmologist *Hospital* *Nurse* (not party) *Pharmacist* (not party)	Apportioned	*Misericordia* *Hosp. v.* *Bustillo*
II(d) SIGHT (LOSS) *Care:* Surgery: Use of improper solution	*Hospital*	Admitted	*Walker v.* *Sydney* *City Hosp.*
Diagnosis: Failure to diagnose hemorrhage	*Doctor:* Otolaryngologist	No	*Kunitz v.* *Merei*
Diagnosis: Failure to diagnose infection	*Doctor:* Ophthalmologist	Yes	*Moffat v.* *Witelson*
Diagnosis: Failure to diagnose mastoiditis	*Doctor:* General Practitioner	No	*Jarvis v.* *Int. Nickel Co.*
III SMELL *Treatment:* Surgery: Migraine headache (correction of)	*Doctor:* Surgeon: General	Yes*	*Koehler v.* *Cook*
IV TASTE *Treatment:* Surgery: Migraine headache (correction of)	*Doctor:* Surgeon: General	Yes*	*Koehler v.* *Cook*
Treatment: Surgery: Tonsillectomy	*Doctor:* Surgeon: General *Student:* Medical (not party)	No	*McNamara v.* *Smith*
INJURY: STROKE *Medication:* Prescription: Oral contraceptives	*Doctor:* Gynaecologist	Yes*	*Schierz v.* *Dodds*
Treatment: Hypertension (correction of)	*Doctor:* General Practitioner	No	*Parsons v.* *Schmok*
Treatment: Surgery: Endarterectomy	*Doctor:* Neurosurgeon	Yes*	*Reibl v.* *Hughes*
UNNECESSARY TREATMENT (See also ASSAULT/BATTERY) *Diagnosis:* Incorrect: Fallopian tubes	*Doctor:* Surgeon *Doctor:* Pathologist *Hospital:* Hospital laboratory	No No Yes	*Lefebvre v.* *Osborne*
Diagnosis: Incorrect: Mastectomy	*Doctor*	Admitted	*Down v.* *Royal Jubilee* *Hosp.*

PROCEDURE	DEFENDANT	LIAB.	CASE NAME
Treatment: Surgery: Abdominal	*Doctor:* Surgeon: General	No	*Wilson v. Swanson*
Treatment: Surgery: Laparotomy	*Doctor:* General Practitioner *Doctor:* Obstetrician/ Gynaecologist	No No	*Finlay v. Hess*

INJURY: VOLKMANN'S CONTRACTURE

Diagnosis: Failure to diagnose Volkmann's Ischaemic Contracture	*Doctor:* Surgeon: Orthopaedic	Yes	*Rietze v. Bruser (No. 2)*

APPENDIX II
CASE DIGESTS

ABEL v. COOKE [1938] 1 W.W.R. 49 (Alta. C.A.)

The plaintiff suffered burns to his back when the defendant physician and an X-ray technician exposed him to an excessive dose of X-ray during a fluoroscopic examination. It was a hospital rule that doctors were not to participate in the operation of the X-ray machine.

Held:

(1) The injury to the plaintiff was caused either by the carelessness of the technician or a defect in the X-ray machine. In either case, the defendant hospital was liable. It had undertaken to provide patients with X-ray examinations and in performing this service their employee was negligent.
(2) In regard to the physician's liability, a new trial was ordered since the charge to the jury amounted to a misdirection.

ADDERLEY v. BREMNER [1968] 1 O.R. 621 (H.C.)

(1) The defendant physician used the same syringe to innoculate 38 patients and used one needle for every two patients vaccinated. As a consequence, the plaintiff developed septicemia.
(2) The plaintiff sought to admit information contained in hospital records as evidence.

Held:

(1) The physician was negligent in failing to adopt the proper procedure for mass innoculations. The instructions accompanying the vaccine expressly stated that a sterile needle and syringe were to be used for each patient.
(2) Under s. 35a of the Evidence Act, R.S.O. 1960, c. 125:
a. information in medical records which involve events preceding the patient's admission to hospital is not admissible;
b. where hospital records are offered as proof of an opinion or diagnosis, they are not admissible as evidence;

c. information obtained in the examination for discovery is admissible to prove the defendant's acts but not to prove the truth of statements made to him by third persons.

ALLAN v. NEW MOUNT SINAI HOSP. (1980) 28 O.R. (2d) 356, reversed in part 33 O.R. (2d) 603 (C.A.)

The defendant anaesthetist injected the left arm of the plaintiff despite her request not to do so because of a history of problems locating the vein. The needle slipped, leaking anaesthetic interstitially and resulting in pain and suffering from an unexpected adverse reaction by the plaintiff.

Ont. H.C. Held:

(1) The defendant was not liable for negligently administering the anaesthetic, having exercised reasonable skill in placing the needle initially and monitoring the anaesthesia during the operation. Needle slippage occurs frequently without negligence and the adverse reaction was rare and unforeseeable.
(2) The defendant was liable in battery for administering the anaesthetic without the patient's consent. The plaintiff's request amounted to an express prohibition of the use of her left arm, imposing on the defendant a duty to comply with her wishes or to try to persuade her to change her mind.

Ont. C.A. Held:

The issue of liability in battery must be retried, since battery was not pleaded at trial.

General Damages: $10,148

ALLARD v. BOYKOWICH [1948] 1 W.W.R. 860 (Sask. K.B.)

Owing to the condition of the patient's teeth and gums, the defendant dentist recommended that she have her teeth extracted. The dentist also suggested that dentures might improve the patient's defective speech. Her speech was not substantially improved.

Held:

The dentist's statement that speech would be improved was not a warranty or a contract.
Where a dentist is duly qualified and registered, there is a presumption that he is competent and that the treatment prescribed is correct, until the contrary is shown.

ANDERSON v. CHASNEY [1950] 4 D.L.R. 223 (S.C.C.)

The defendant, in performing a tonsillectomy on a child, used sponges without any tape or strings attached and proceeded without the assistance of a nurse to check on the number of sponges. The child died by suffocating on an unremoved sponge.

Held:

The defendant failed to discharge the duty incumbent on him to check and remove all sponges and to take reasonable precautions to that end or to make a thorough search. As the child's death was attributable to this failure the defendant was guilty of negligence.

ANTONIUK v. SMITH [1930] 2 W.W.R. 721 (Alta. C.A.)

Although the plaintiff was warned to lie still during treatment, an involuntary movement of her leg caused her to come in contact with the electric current and she suffered two tiny burns, one on her hand and one on her leg.

Held:

The defendant was not liable in negligence because the plaintiff's injuries were not the result of an absence of warning by the nurse-operator acting on behalf of the defendant.

ARES v. VENNER [1970] S.C.R. 608

The day following the reduction of the fracture and immobilization of his leg by the defendant

internist, the plaintiff experienced a loss of feeling in the foot of his injured leg. The defendant internist split the cast eight inches and proceeded, over the next four days, to split further sections until the whole cast was split. As this produced no improvement the defendant referred the plaintiff to cardiovascular specialists who eventually amputated the leg below the knee.

Held:

(1) The trial judge's finding that the defendant was negligent in failing to bivalve the cast sooner was affirmed.
(2) Hospital records are admissible in evidence as *prima facie* proof of the facts stated therein. This does not preclude a party from challenging their accuracy.

ARMSTRONG v. BRUCE (1904) 4 O.W.R. 327 (H.C.)

The plaintiff suffered burns to his back and shoulders as a result of the "Kelly pad" upon which he was placed during the operation having been filled with boiling water. The plaintiff based his claim against the defendant on the nurse's testimony that in filling it with boiling water, she was merely complying with the defendant's instructions.

Held:

The plaintiff's suit failed because the nurse's testimony was deemed inaccurate and because the defendant was not negligent in assuming that the nurse would perform her duties properly.

ARMSTRONG v. DAWSON [1933] 1 W.W.R. 187 (Sask. C.A.)

The defendant's use of the fluoroscopic method of taking X-rays failed to detect fractures in the plaintiff's arm, later revealed by X-ray films.

Held:

The trial judge's finding that the defendant was careless and negligent in employing the fluoroscopic method was reversed.

ARMSTRONG v. McCLEALAND (1930) 38 O.W.N. 297 (H.C.)

In attempting to increase the size of the opening in a vein near the inside of the elbow in order to give a blood transfusion the defendant nicked an artery. Both defendants decided that the right procedure in the circumstances would be to insert the canula into the artery, albeit an unusual practice. The plaintiff's lower arm became gangrenous and was eventually amputated.

Held:

The decision to transfuse into the artery instead of the vein did not amount to negligence.

ATHANSIOUS v. GUZMAN B.C.S.C. No. 37190/75 November 1977 (unreported)

The defendant physician treated the plaintiff over a number of years, failing to diagnose a degenerative heart condition from which the plaintiff ultimately died.

Held:

The defendant was not liable in negligence for failing to make the correct diagnosis at an earlier time, since the manifested symptoms were not marked and were amenable to various diagnoses other than heart disease.

AYNSLEY v. TORONTO GEN. HOSPITAL [1972] S.C.R. 435 affirming [1969] 2 O.R. 829

The defendant Dr. Matthews, who was privately employed by the plaintiff and Dr. Porteus, who was a senior resident in anaesthesiology employed by the co-defendant hospital to assist Dr. Matthews, failed to notice that, in attempting to record the plaintiff's venous pressure air was escaping into her nervous system. This air embolism caused a cardiac arrest from which the plaintiff suffered permanent brain damage.

Ont. C.A. Held:

Affirmed trial decision:

(1) Dr. Matthews was negligent in failing to

guard against the known danger of air escaping into the plaintiff.

(2) Dr. Porteus was likewise negligent and the hospital was vicariously liable for his negligence because the evidence did not disclose sufficient care and control over Dr. Porteus by Dr. Matthews to take this case out of the general rule that a permanent employer is liable for the negligence of its employee.

S.C.C. Held:

Affirmed (2) above. The liability of a hospital for the negligent acts or omissions of an employee vis-à-vis a patient, depends primarily upon the particular facts of the case, *i.e.* the services which the hospital undertakes to provide and the relationship of the physician and surgeon to the hospital.

BADGER v. SURKAN [1973] 1 W.W.R. 302 (Sask. C.A.)

In spite of the presence of recognized symptoms of circulatory impairment, the defendant general practitioner did not bivalve or remove the casts immediately. The plaintiff's lower legs became gangrenous and were amputated.

Held:

The defendant was negligent. He failed to:
(1) apply the skill and knowledge ordinarily displayed in such a case;
(2) carry out an adequate examination of the plaintiff after the casts were applied;
(3) remove the casts when warning signs appeared.

BAILLS v. BOULANGER [1924] 4 D.L.R. 1083 (Alta. C.A.)

The defendant applied quartz light to a bruise on the plaintiff's shin. The plaintiff developed pain in the toes which was ultimately diagnosed as resulting from senile gangrene. The plaintiff's foot was amputated.

Held:

When a medical doctor uses a method of treatment the properties of which are not fully known or understood, such as the quartz lamp, he has a duty to use very great care and failure in this regard amounts to negligence.

BALTZAN v. FIDELITY INS. CO. [1932] 3 W.W.R. 140, affirmed [1933] 3 W.W.R. 203 (Sask. C.A.)

The plaintiff general practitioner failed to secure an examination table which consequently collapsed and injured the patient. The defendant insurance company refused to undertake the defence of the patient's action on the grounds that it was only liable for, and the plaintiff's action did not constitute, "malpractice, error or mistake."

Sask. K.B. Held:
The plaintiff's neglect to fasten the table was malpractice, an error and a mistake in the practising of his profession. A physician must exercise reasonable care and skill towards his patient in everything he requires of a patient.

Sask. C.A. — Appeal dismissed.

BARCUS v. BROWN (1977) 2 A.R. 89 (T.D.)

During a postauricular complete labyrinthectomy the plaintiff's facial nerve was damaged when struck by the burr which separated from the drill at high velocity.

Held:
A surgeon is not a guarantor. In spite of exercising acceptable measures of caution, care and skill, an accident occurred for which the defendant could not be held responsible.

BARKER v. LOCKHART [1940] 3 D.L.R. 427 (N.B.C.A.)

Without ascertaining the strength of the solution, the defendant head nurse administered an excessively strong solution of silver nitrate to the newborn plaintiff's eyes. The plaintiff suffered loss of one eye and damage to the other eye.

Held:
(1) The defendant head nurse was negligent in applying a silver nitrate solution of unascertained strength.
(2) The defendant hospital was vicariously liable, since the head nurse was acting within the scope of her duties as its servant or agent.

BARR v. HUGHES [1982] B.C.W.L.D. 990 B.C.S.C. Legg J. Vancouver No. C804822 23rd April 1982 (not yet reported)

The defendant dermatologist performed a biopsy of the plaintiff's nasal area, the results of which indicated cancer, but failed to advise the plaintiff or her family doctor of the diagnosis. The problem recurred at an advanced stage, requiring prolonged radiotherapy to correct it.

General damages: $9,500

Held:
The defendant was liable for negligently failing to report the test results. Prompt communication would have allowed the condition to be corrected by a minor procedure, preventing the pain and suffering attending the radiotherapy.

BARSY v. GOVT. OF MAN. (1966) 57 W.W.R. 169 (Man. Q.B.)

Although the deceased was warned not to eat prior to treatment and was not fed breakfast, he nonetheless had sufficient stomach content to vomit when electric shock treatment was administered. The regurgitated food was removed from the pharynx but the usual efforts to restore breathing after treatment were unsuccessful. Death was caused by a blockage of the air passage by the regurgitated food.

Held:
(1) The hospital was not negligent in failing to ask the deceased whether he had eaten before treatment or in not placing the deceased under restraint so as to ensure that he ate nothing before treatment. Statistically it was shown

that the hospital's policy of not policing had not exposed similar patients to serious risk.

(2) By clearing the pharynx and following the usual methods of restoring respiration, the attendant doctor met the standard of care required in the circumstances.

BARTLETT v. CHILDREN'S HOSP. CORP. [1983] 40 Nfld. & P.E.I.R. 88 (Nfld. T.D.)

The employees of the defendant hospital administered an audiogram to the plaintiff, during which he suffered acoustic trauma resulting in a severe and permanent hearing impairment.

Held:

The defendant was liable for negligent treatment of the plaintiff. The rule *res ipsa loquitur* was applicable and the defendant failed to rebut the inference of negligence.

General damages: $55,200

BEATTY v. SISTERS OF MISERICORDE OF ALTA. [1935] 1 W.W.R. 651 (Alta. S.C.)

The alleged negligence was with regard to two occurrences:

(1) Shortly after the first operation, while under the influence of a sedative, the plaintiff was left unattended and she fell out of bed. In falling a catheter was pulled out of place and it was subsequently found that the stitches in the vaginal wall had given way.

(2) After an operation to close a fistula connecting the vagina and the rectum, before the healing was complete, one of the defendant nurses, by attempting to replace a rectal tube, tore the sutures and thus destroyed all beneficial results of the operation.

Held:

(1) Falling out of bed prior to sleeping is a foreseeable risk to a patient under the influence of a sedative; therefore the defendant was negligent in not attending the patient until she slept.

(2) The negligence in the second occurrence consisted of the failure of the defendant to appreciate the risks and obtain qualified assistance for the plaintiff.

(3) Hospitals, whether charitable institutions or otherwise, when sued for damages for negligence of their employees, are in exactly the same position as other persons, and whether or not the plaintiff can succeed depends on the facts of the particular case.

BEAUSOLEIL v. SOEURS DE LA CHARITÈ (1966) 53 D.L.R. (2d) 65 (Que. C.A.)

The defendant anaesthetist failed to consult the plaintiff until just prior to the operation when, under sedation, in the face of his insistence, she consented to a spinal anaesthetic. Following the operation the plaintiff was permanently paralyzed from the waist down.

Held:

(1) The defendant anaesthetist had failed to discharge the burden of proving that the plaintiff gave a full and free consent to a spinal anaesthetic, and that there was an absence of any causal relationship between the giving of the spinal and the plaintiff's paralysis.

(2) The defendant hospital was vicariously liable for the fault of the defendant anaesthetist as he was acting in his capacity as chief anaesthetist when the fault was committed.

BELL v. R. (1973) 44 D.L.R. (3d) 549 (Fed. T.D.)

A prison general practitioner failed to diagnose the nature of an eye injury and did not refer the plaintiff to a specialist until eight days after the injury occurred. The plaintiff suffered permanent impairment of his vision.

Held:

(1) There was no evidence that the general practitioner failed to do anything that an ordinary reasonably skilled practitioner would have done under the circumstances. The injury was rare and difficult to diagnose even for the specialist.

(2) There was no evidence that the eight-day delay significantly increased the degree of disability.

Action dismissed.

BELORE v. SMITH [1979] 3 A.C.W.S. 695 Ont. Co. Ct. Misener J. 23rd May 1977 (unreported)

The defendant otolaryngologist performed a tonsillectomy on the six-year-old plaintiff, employing a Boyle-Davis mouth gag to separate the patient's jaws. During the procedure, the plaintiff suffered the loss of one primary and one permanent tooth, both of which had been loose prior to the operation, as a result of pressure from the mouth gag.

Held:
The defendant was liable for negligent performance of the surgery. Since on a clear balance of probability the reason for the injury was ascertainable, the doctrine of *res ipsa loquitur* was inapplicable. Nevertheless, the defendant fell below the standard of care of a specialist of his training, skill and ability by failing to adopt a commonly used alteration in the position of the gag which would have avoided any risk to the tooth.

General damages: $6,000

BENINGER v. WALTON [1979] B.C.D. Civ. 2632-02 B.C.S.C. Rae J. Vancouver No. C774834 11th April 1979 (unreported)

The defendant doctor referred the plaintiff to an ophthalmologist who made a tentative diagnosis of glaucoma, and supplied the clinic employing the defendant with a written report which was not drawn to the plaintiff's attention. The plaintiff changed specialists and did not pursue treatment conscientiously; his condition ultimately deteriorated, requiring surgery and resulting in blindness in one eye.

Held:
The defendant was not liable for negligence in failing, during subsequent unrelated consulta-

tions, to refer back to the problem for which the referral was made. A general practitioner is not under a duty to ensure that effective treatment is carried out after a referral is promptly made to a competent specialist, since it would reasonably be expected that the specialist would attend to the patient with the patient's co-operation.

BENNETT v. C. (1908) 7 W.L.R. 740 (Man. T.D.)

The plaintiff asserted that her present ill-health was due to the fact that the defendant surgeon had removed her ovaries and fallopian tubes in addition to her womb which had been affected by a tumor.

Held:
(1) Since another tumor can develop in the ovaries and fallopian tubes if they are left, the defendant followed the approved principles of surgery in removing them.
(2) There was no evidence to show that the plaintiff's ill-health was caused by any negligence on the part of the defendant.

BENOIT v. MUIR [1982] B.C.W.L.D. 1726 B.C.S.C. Davies J. Vancouver No. C812926 4th August 1982

The defendant surgeon treated the plaintiff's fractured thigh bone, delaying surgery for one day on account of a staff shortage. The plaintiff developed a circulatory impairment around the fracture site causing severe deformity and pain, and requiring corrective surgery which failed to alleviate a permanent disability.

Held:
The defendant was not liable for negligent treatment of the plaintiff, since the damage suffered was not caused by the delay in performing surgery.

BERGEN v. STURGEON GEN. HOSP. Alta. Q.B. No. 8003-03036 6th February 1984 (unreported)

The patient was admitted to hospital with lower

abdominal pain and was treated for Pelvic Inflammatory Disease without any tests performed to determine if she was suffering from appendicitis. The patient experienced an acute "snap" of pain, but nurses decided not to call a doctor until two hours later. Patient died of septic shock from a ruptured appendix. A nursing aide destroyed the bedside records of the patient.

Held:

(1) Three of the defendant doctors, the attending physician, the general surgeon and the gynaecologist were negligent in failing to diagnose appendicitis.
(2) The hospital was liable in negligence for failing to follow the hospital manual and allowing a nursing assistant to destroy the bedside records.
(3) Two attending nurses were negligent in not calling a doctor immediately when the patient experienced the "snap," something neither had seen before.

General damages: $49,607

BERGSTROM v. G. [1967] C.S. 513 (Que. S.C.)

The defendant applied a plaster cast to the plaintiff's foot to treat a "chronic draining sinus." The following day the plaintiff began to experience pain but was unable to contact either the defendant or his temporary replacement. The defendant examined the plaintiff one week after the application of the cast and discovered that the foot was partially gangrenous. The plaintiff's leg was amputated above the knee.

Held:

(1) Although the treatment by plaster cast aggravated an existing situation, it was an approved treatment for which the defendant was not liable.
(2) The defendant was negligent in not visiting the patient for one week after the application of the cast.
(3) The defendant was responsible for the failure of his assistant to replace him during the weekend.

BERNIER v. SISTERS OF SERVICE [1948] 1 W.W.R. 113 (Alta. S.C.)

Following an appendectomy and while the plaintiff was still anaesthetized, she was placed in a bed with two hot water bottles touching her feet. The bottles had not been ordered by the plaintiff's doctor nor had their temperature been checked. The plaintiff suffered severe burns to both heels.

Held:

The defendants were negligent in so far as they:
(1) failed to test the temperature of the hot water bottles in accord with established practice in other hospitals;
(2) placed the bottles in the bed without the express order of the plaintiff's doctor and contrary to the standard rules of other hospitals requiring that the bed in which an anaesthetized patient is placed be empty of hot water bottles;
(3) allowed the hot water bottles to come in direct contact with the plaintiff's feet;
(4) failed to make periodic checks of the hot water bottles;
(5) did not have a nurse in constant attendance on the plaintiff as she was coming out of the spinal anaesthesia just as is usually done with a patient coming out of general anaesthesia.

BERRY v. PIERCE Man. Q.B. Dewar C.J.Q.B. September 1977 (unreported)

The defendant ear, nose and throat specialist treated the plaintiff, who subsequently complained of a perforation of his eardrum.

Held:

The defendant was not liable in negligence, the evidence pointing to the conclusion that the injury was spontaneously caused after the plaintiff's treatment by the defendant had ended.

BIBBY v. HALL (1980) 4 A.C.W.S. (2d) 404 (Ont. H.C.)

The defendant orthopaedic specialist performed

knee surgery on the plaintiff, subsequent to which the plaintiff suffered partial paralysis of the leg and foot upon which the operation had been carried out.

Held:

The defendant was liable for negligently performing the surgical procedure. General damages of $35,000 were awarded.

BICKFORD v. STILES (1981) 128 D.L.R. (3d) 516 (Q.B.)

The defendant surgeon performed diagnostic throat surgery on the plaintiff without informing her of the risk of vocal chord paralysis, which subsequently materialized and resulted in hoarseness and problems in swallowing.

Held:

The defendant was not liable in negligence for failing adequately to inform the plaintiff. The risk of loss or impairment of voice, although very slight, has serious consequences and therefore on an objective test is material. However, a reasonable person in the plaintiff's circumstances, aware of both the risk of vocal chord paralysis and the risk of not diagnosing a more serious condition such as cancer, would have agreed to the operation.

BISSELL v. VANCOUVER GEN. HOSP. [1979] 2 A.C.W.S. 433 B.C.S.C. McKenzie J. 11th June 1979 (unreported)

The infant son of the plaintiffs was discharged from the defendant hospital suffering from a mild respiratory infection of which the plaintiffs were not told. The condition developed into pneumonia, which was treated at another hospital but resulted in severe irreversible brain damage.

Held:

Neither the defendant hospital nor the defendant doctors at the hospital were liable for negligent care of the infant. Failing to isolate each patient suffering from an infection is not a breach of the standard of care, and the unheeded

concerns of the mother did not give any indication of an emergency. Moreover, the preponderance of evidence indicated that the damage-causing complication developed after the infant was discharged from the hospital, and the initial discharge from the hospital was therefore not negligent.

BOASE v. PAUL [1931] O.R. 625 (C.A.)

Although the plaintiff desired the extraction of only one tooth, the defendant removed all his upper teeth because he reasonably misunderstood the plaintiff's request, given the immediate threat of serious disease presented by the condition of the plaintiff's teeth.

Held:

The plaintiff's action in negligence was barred by the limitation period set out in the Dentistry Act, R.S.O. 1927, c. 198, s. 28.

BOOTH v. TORONTO GEN. HOSP. (1910) 17 O.W.R. 118 (K.B.)

The plaintiff (who was not of the highest intelligence) was 19 years of age when he consented to an operation for the removal of part of his enlarged thyroid gland. His parents were not consulted. The plaintiff brought an action in trespass alleging that the operation had been performed without leave or licence of himself or his parents and that it was "entirely unauthorized and unnecessary."

Held:

The plaintiff's consent to the beneficial operation was valid. Although he was not of the highest intelligence, he was 19 years of age and capable of taking care of himself and doing a man's work.

BRANDEIS v. WELDON (1916) 27 D.L.R. 235 (B.C.C.A)

A nurse discovered that the plaintiff's wife had left the hospital and had taken her belongings with her. Since the patient had appeared normal and sensible when she was last seen, the nurse, believing she had returned home, did not notify the plaintiff of his wife's departure. The patient's body was later found in a creek.

Held:

The hospital's staff had attended the patient in a reasonable and proper manner. Moreover, the plaintiff did not establish that the failure to notify was the cause of the patient's death.

BRENNAN v. DIR. OF MENTAL HEALTH Alta. S.C. No. 83414 18th February 1977 (unreported)

While undergoing institutionalized treatment for manic depression psychosis with acute paranoid schizophrenia, the plaintiff suffered permanent injury to his right vocal chord after being restrained by an orderly. The plaintiff's allegations that the orderly knelt on his throat were denied by the orderly.

Held:

Because of his mental condition the evidence and memory of the plaintiff must be suspect. Since the plaintiff's evidence was the only evidence presented against the orderly, he therefore failed to satisfy the onus of proof and could not recover damages.

BRENNAN v. FRASER; FRASER v. WARD (1982) 38 Nfld. & P.E.I.R. 348 (Nfld. T.D.)

The defendant doctors treated the infant plaintiff's leg fracture, reducing the fracture and employing skeletal traction and when that proved unsuccessful, performing an open reduction. The fractured bone healed but caused a shortening of the plaintiff's leg with attendant pain and disability.

General damages: $15,000

Held:

The defendants admitted liability for negligence in treating the plaintiff. Damages were assessed at $15,000.

BROWNE v. LERNER (1940) 48 Man. R. 126 (K.B.)

On the basis of the defendant's advice, the plaintiff consented to an operation to remove bullet fragments from his leg. The plaintiff requested that the operation be performed under spinal anaesthetic. The defendant, after finding lipping of the vertebrae, received the plaintiff's permission to administer a general anaesthetic. The operation was not successful, i.e., the fragments were not removed and the plaintiff sued for professional malpractice.

Held:

The plaintiff failed to rebut the presumption that the defendant acted competently and administered the correct treatment. The plaintiff failed to establish that he suffered any damage from either the administration of the anaesthetic or the performance of the operation.

BRUINOOGE v. COLLIER [1982] Man. D. 2632-01 Man. Q.B. Deniset J. No. 33/79 11th June 1982 (not yet reported)

The defendant doctor diagnosed and treated the plaintiff's painful knee as a pulled muscle, rather than a more serious displacement of the thigh bone which was subsequently diagnosed by an orthopaedic specialist to whom the plaintiff was referred by another doctor. Prolonged treatment was undertaken without complete success.

Held:

The defendant was not liable for negligent diagnosis of the plaintiff's injury, having exercised reasonable care in making an initial diagnosis which might have been revised had the plaintiff returned with the same symptoms.

BUCHANAN v. FORT CHURCHILL GEN. HOSPITAL (1969) 69 D.R.S. 586 (Man. Q.B.)

Following an injection of thorazine, and while awaiting X-rays, the plaintiff fainted. She suffered a severe blow to the lower jaw and a broken cheek bone.

Held:

The failure of the defendant nurse to foresee the possibility of a fainting spell from thorazine was not negligence.

BUCKNAM v. KOSTIUK (1983) 20 A.C.W.S. (2d) 542 (Ont. S.C.)

The defendant orthopaedic surgeon operated on the plaintiff's back for scoliosis using a long spinal fusion technique. Following the surgery, the plaintiff suffered severe pain for six months before it was discovered to be caused by irritation of nerve endings by a sacral hook inserted in the operation. The defendant also did not advise the plaintiff that an alternate procedure, a simple fusion, was available.

Held:

The defendant was not liable. In post-operative care, there was no evidence that a reasonable orthopaedic surgeon would have identified the cause of the plaintiff's pain any earlier. That the defendant did not advise the plaintiff of the alternate procedure does not make him liable because, in the circumstances, the plaintiff would have followed the doctor's advice to have the long spinal fusion operation.

BUGDEN v. HARBOUR VIEW HOSP. [1947] 2 D.L.R. 338 (N.S.S.C.)

The defendant general practitioner requested defendant Nurse A. to obtain novocaine. Nurse A. asked Nurse B. for novocaine, and Nurse B. mistakenly gave her a bottle containing, as labelled, adrenalin. Both Nurse A. and the general practitioner failed to check the label. The plaintiff's husband died from the injection of adrenalin.

Held:

(1) Nurse A. and Nurse B. were negligent in failing to check that the right drug was being given.
(2) The defendant hospital was vicariously lia-

ble for the negligence of Nurse A. and Nurse B., since they were servants of the hospital, acting in the course of their employment, and had not at the material time passed under the control of the doctor.
(3) The defendant physician was not negligent in failing to look at the label, since in such a routine matter, and in the absence of facts to put him on inquiry, he was entitled to rely on experienced nurses.

BURK v. S. (1952) 4 W.W.R. 520 (B.C.S.C.)

The plaintiff underwent an operation performed by Drs. B. & K., when he had expected Dr. S. to do the surgery. The plaintiff alleged that Dr. K. was negligent in administering the anaesthetic but his action was barred by the termination of the limitation period. The plaintiff sought to amend his statement of claim by bringing his action in assault as he had not given his consent to the doctors who performed the operation.

Held:

(1) The application for amendment was dismissed as an infringement of the protection afforded doctors under s. 82 of the Medical Act, R.S.B.C. 1948, c. 206.
(2) The plaintiff could not have reasonably expected Dr. S. to both perform the surgery and administer the anaesthetic.

BUTLER v. TORONTO (1907) 10 O.W.R. 876 (S.C.)

The plaintiff's child, admitted to hospital for the treatment of diphtheria, died of other diseases contracted while in hospital. The plaintiff alleged that the defendants were negligent in failing to isolate the child from further contagion and that the corporation of the city of Toronto, insofar as it employed the servants of the hospital, was vicariously liable for their negligence.

Held:

Action dismissed.

(1) The officers and servants of the hospital

were not servants of the corporation of Toronto in such a sense as to render the corporation liable for their negligence.

(2) An individual who has suffered an injury can maintain no action for nonfeasance, and the statement of claim charges no misfeasance.

CAHOON v. EDMONTON HOSP. BD. (1957) 23 W.W.R. 131 (Alta. S.C.)

While sleeping, the plaintiff fell off his hospital bed against a hot unenclosed radiator and sustained second degree burns. The plaintiff who was recovering from a chipped fracture of the left kneecap was not under sedation nor did he have any fact in his medical history to warn of the risk of his falling out of bed.

Held:

Open radiators are recognized as the standard and usual heating apparatus in rooms occupied by normal patients. That the plaintiff would fall from his bed could not be reasonably foreseen. Therefore, having regard to the mental and physical condition of the plaintiff, the defendant did not fail in its duty to take reasonable care to see that the accommodation provided for the plaintiff, including the unenclosed radiator type of heating equipment, was reasonably safe.

CALDER v. GILMOUR (1978) 3 A.C.W.S. 57 (Sask. Q.B.)

The defendant performed an operation to correct the plaintiff's "wandering" eye. The plaintiff had asked specifically about the risk of recurring double vision, a risk which subsequently materialized resulting in restricted activities, headaches and reduced sexual activity.

Held:

The defendant was liable for failing to inform the plaintiff adequately of the risks of the procedure: by not warning of the risk of enduring double vision, and by leaving the impression that there was no risk.

CARDIN v. MONTREAL [1961] S.C.R. 655

The plaintiff's son, aged 5½ years, was taken by his mother to the Health Service Clinic of the City of Montreal for a booster vaccination. Following a smallpox vaccination, the child became upset and excited but in spite of his mother's suggestion that they could return another time, the defendant doctor attempted to proceed with an injection. Upon feeling the prick of the needle the child moved his arm causing the needle to break off under his skin. Three operations, resulting in permanent scarring, failed to recover the needle and the child suffered temporary paralysis of the arm.

Held:

(1) In the normal course of an injection a needle does not break off under the skin. Thus the author of this event, the defendant doctor, to exonerate himself from a charge of negligence, must demonstrate that there was an outside cause of the injury. The defendant failed to discharge this burden of proof.

(2) The defendant failed to meet the requisite standard of care in the circumstances by not ensuring that the child's arm was securely immobilized before proceeding with the injection. The doctor and the city were liable.

CASSON v. HAIG (1914) 5 O.W.N. 437 (K.B.)

Rather than injecting cocaine as intended, the defendant introduced into the plaintiff's eye a crystal of some corrosive or caustic substance and thereby caused injury.

Held:

The defendant was liable for this mistake.

CATAFORD v. MOREAU (1978) 7 C.C.L.T. 241 (Que. S.C.)

The defendant surgeon performed a tubal ligation sterilization operation on the plaintiff, who became pregnant four months later and eventually gave birth to her eleventh child in twelve years. A second tubal ligation was performed subsequently by another surgeon.

Held:

(1) The defendant was liable for negligently performing the procedure. As a result, the plaintiff parents were entitled to recover damages flowing from the pregnancy and the subsequent corrective sterilization, and for loss of consortium.

(2) The plaintiff parents were entitled to damages for wrongful life. However, in this case no damages were awarded, since the discrepancy between the annual requirement and the available social assistance support was compensated for by the intangible value of the presence of the child.

(3) The plaintiff infant was not entitled to damages for wrongful birth, particularly since he had not suffered damage or injury, on the basis that the ''gift of life'' is not an actionable event warranting damages.

General damages: $2,400

CAVAN v. WILCOX [1975] 2 S.C.R. 663

The defendant nurse, following the proper practice in giving the injection, aspirated the syringe and on seeing that there was no blood injected the bicillin into the deltoid muscle. The antibiotic entered the circumflex artery and as a result the plaintiff developed gangrene in part of his hand.

Held:

(1) Because nurses in training are not instructed with respect to the existence of the circumflex artery's proximity to the deltoid muscle the defendant was in no way blameworthy by reason of the fact that she was unaware of the existence of this potential danger.

(2) In responding to the *res ipsa loquitur* rule, although the defendant could not prove exactly how the damage occurred, she had produced an explanation consistent with no negligence as with negligence. Consequently, she could not be blamed for the accident which caused the plaintiff's injury.

CHALLAND v. BELL (1959) 18 D.L.R. (2d) 150 (Alta. S.C.)

The defendant, a rural practitioner, deciding upon examination that a debriding of the plaintiff's wound was unnecessary proceeded to set the open fracture. When swelling developed shortly thereafter the defendant partially cut the cast. When circulatory changes were apparent two days later the defendant referred the plaintiff to a specialist who amputated the plaintiff's arm, as it was infected with a very uncommon infection called gas gangrene.

Held:

As a general practitioner in a rural area, the defendant must possess and exercise the skill, knowledge and judgment of the average rural practitioner. Because his decision not to debride, based on his failure to foresee the risk of gas gangrene, was the result of exercising the average standard of a rural practitioner, the defendant was not liable for his error in judgment.

CHILD v. VANCOUVER GEN. HOSP. [1970] S.C.R. 477

Noting that the plaintiff was restless and confused when she first came on duty, the defendant sent for the plaintiff's doctor. By the time he arrived, the plaintiff was calm and the doctor determined that he would in future remain so. The defendant left for a coffee break during which time the plaintiff, in attempting to escape from the hospital through the window, fell to the canopy below and seriously injured himself.

Held:

When the opinion upon which a nurse acts coincides with that of the certified surgeon in charge of the case, her conduct is not negligent.

CHIPPS v. PETERS Ont. C.A. 1976 (unreported)

The defendant general practitioner referred the plaintiff to the defendant general surgeon and later assisted him in the corrective surgery which he performed. Post-operatively, the plaintiff developed an infection of the vagina which scarred the tissue and caused it to draw together. When the plaintiff informed the defendant general surgeon of her inability to have sexual intercourse, he assured her that her vagina would stretch. The plaintiff then sought medical advice elsewhere and later underwent further corrective surgery.

Held:

(1) Where a general surgeon is competent to perform an operation which falls within the area of a certain specialty, he is not negligent in failing to refer a patient to a specialist. In this case the defendant surgeon did perform the operation competently.

(2) The damage which occurred, the shortening of the vagina to the extent that it was not suitable for sexual intercourse, was so remote a risk that the defendants were not negligent in failing to inform the plaintiff about it.

(3) The plaintiff had failed to establish that at the time of her last meeting with the defendant general surgeon he should have prescribed something other than the natural process which he believed she and her husband would follow. Whether the natural process would be sufficiently corrective was a question of medical judgment dependent on the condition of the tissue.

CHUBEY v. AHSAN [1976] 3 W.W.R. 367 (Man. C.A.)

During the course of a discoidectomy, the defendant inadvertently pierced the aorta and the vena cava. However, although blood loss during surgery was high, it was not excessive and all vital signs were within normal range. The defendant failed to discover any signs of internal hemorrhaging in his brief visit to the plaintiff in the post-anaesthesia room. In spite of emergency surgery, the plaintiff died of irreversible shock secondary to hemorrhage.

Held:

(1) The risk of damaging the vessels in this operation is known and the proper standard of care requires that it be guarded against. However, failure to avoid this risk does not, in this case,

indicate a departure from the standard of care reasonably to be expected of a competent orthopaedic surgeon.

(2) The defendant was not negligent in visiting the plaintiff only briefly after surgery and thereby failing to discover that she was hemorrhaging. Nothing happened to put him on notice that damage had been done and it is speculative to say that earlier emergency surgery would have saved the plaintiff's life.

CLARK v. WANSBROUGH [1940] O.W.N. 67 (H.C.)

The defendant surgeon treated the plaintiff for a broken humerus diagnosed from X-rays taken of the area of injury. While the defendant did examine for associated injuries and did reduce the fracture under a fluroscope, which gave him further opportunity for a complete check-up he did not order an X-ray of the shoulder or arm above the fracture site. Although the plaintiff complained when the cast was removed of limitation of movement, the defendant attributed this to something which regularly occurs after immobilization in a cast. After six months, the defendant noted in an accident report that the plaintiff had limited shoulder movement but he failed to diagnose a dislocated shoulder. Another doctor diagnosed from X-rays taken of the whole arm including the shoulder joint a dislocation which must have existed for some months.

Held:

(1) The defendant was not negligent in failing to take X-rays which included the shoulder joint at the time of reduction or at the six-month examination. The principle which determines what area is to be included in the X-ray is based on a question of circumstances *i.e.* the condition of the patient and the character of the injuries. According to expert evidence, the association of a shoulder dislocation with a fracture of the lower humerus is unique.

(2) The defendant was not negligent in failing to diagnose the shoulder dislocation at the time of reduction because the signs and symptoms of shoulder injury were either absent or of such a character that reasonably careful men, using approved methods, might well have missed their significance.

COLP v. RINGROSE unreported 6th October 1976, No. 84474 (Alta. T.D.)

Having been informed about two methods of tubal sterilization, surgical severance of the tubes, and blockage of the tubes by a new procedure called "office tubal ligation", excepting that the council of the College of Physicians and Surgeons had passed a motion that a member of the College may not perform a procedure to effect female sterilization outside of a hospital, the plaintiff chose the office method. When she became pregnant after the procedure had been performed she sued the defendant in assault and in negligence.

Held:

(1) The defendant is not liable for trespass or assault. Although the defendant failed to inform the plaintiff about the council's resolution this does not negate her informed consent. The council did not condemn the silver nitrate procedure nor did it take disciplinary action against the defendant for his breach of the resolution. Furthermore, the degree of information required by a patient to give an informed consent to a therapeutic treatment as was administered in this case was sufficient.

(2) The defendant was not negligent in carrying out the procedure nor did he guarantee or warrant that it would be successful.

CONSIDINE v. CAMP HILL HOSP. (1982) 133 D.L.R. (3d) 11 (N.S.T.D.)

The defendants, a resident in urology and a urologist, performed prostate surgery on the plaintiff, the former having discussed with him the nature of the operation but not the risk of permanent incontinence or impotence and the latter failing to communicate with the plaintiff until some days after the operation. During the operation the plaintiff's bladder was perforated by a surgical instrument rendering him incontinent and impotent.

Held:

The defendants were not liable in negligence for inadequately disclosing the risks of the operation. Although the risks of permanent

incontinence and impotence were not mentioned, and the behaviour of the defendant doctors with respect to obtaining consent amounted to "loose practice," a reasonable person in the position of the plaintiff would have undergone the procedure anyway.

COSGROVE v. GAUDREAU (1981), 33 N.B.R. (2d) 523 (Q.B.)

The defendant surgeon performed an abdominal operation on the plaintiff, relying on an inaccurate sponge count by the scrub nurse and leaving a surgical sponge in the plaintiff's abdominal cavity which caused pain and suffering and required surgery to remove the sponge a year and a half later.

Held:

The defendant surgeon was 50 per cent liable for negligent treatment of the plaintiff, and the defendant hospital was 50 per cent liable for the negligence of its employee scrub nurse. "In the ordinary course of things, a sponge is not left in the abdominal cavity after surgery;" there was no evidence as to how or why the accident happened. The surgeon and the scrub nurse were in control of the situation, and therefore the defendants were liable by operation of the doctrine res ipsa loquitur.

General damages: $8,000

COX v. SASKATOON [1942] 1 W.W.R. 717 (Sask. C.A.)

The plaintiff blood donor developed a streptococcus infection at the point where defendant intern had inserted the blood transfusion needle. The defendant had taken every precaution to prevent infection during the procedure.

Held:

The evidence does not support the application of the maxim res ipsa loquitur, since infection could occur even where the most sterile methods were employed. The bacterium causing the infection could have originated within the plaintiff's body and lodged in the tissues punctured by the needle. Thus, negligence on the part of the defendant was not established.

CRICHTON v. HASTINGS [1972] 3 O.R. 859 (C.A.)

The defendant performed surgery on the plaintiff's knee and then, during his absence, turned over the supervision of her convalescence to another orthopaedic surgeon. The defendant had prescribed dicumerol without warning the plaintiff of the risk of hemorrhaging as a possible side effect, and without arranging for those to whom her care was entrusted to give adequate warning of the importance of immediately reporting the appearance of any such side effects. The plaintiff self-administered the drug after her discharge from hospital and when certain side effects developed, she failed to report them immediately. The plaintiff required a tracheotomy and a second incision to treat the hemorrhaging which occurred at the base of her tongue.

Held:
(1) The defendant was negligent in failing to discharge his duty to warn the plaintiff about the potentially dangerous side effects of dicumerol.
(2) The defendant was negligent in not foreseeing and arranging that if the plaintiff was told to continue with dicumerol after leaving hospital, adequate warning of the possible side effects would be given.

CRITS v. SYLVESTER [1956] S.C.R. 991

In administering an anaesthetic to the infant plaintiff by introducing oxygen from a tank into a can of ether located near the plaintiff's head, and then forcing the mixture of ether and oxygen through a Magill tube into his throat, the defendant responded to the plaintiff's immediate development of cyanosis by altering the system in order to administer pure oxygen. The tubes leading to and from the ether can were connected to an oxygen bag. When the oxygen bag was filled, the oxygen tube was restored to the ether can. When the plaintiff's condition returned to normal, the defendant attempted to reconnect the Magill tube with the ether can in order to restore the flow of anaesthetic and an explosion occurred of the ether and oxygen mixture which had accumulated close to the plaintiff's head. The plaintiff suffered serious injuries.

Held:
(1) The defendant was negligent in allowing the oxygen to flow into the ether can while the Magill tube was not connected to it. If the oxygen had been turned off at the tank there would have been no material delay and the danger of explosion, which is always a risk in surgical operations, would have been substantially reduced.
(2) The defendant was not negligent in placing the ether can close to the patient's head. This practice was approved by other medical witnesses and it would be dangerous for a court to attempt in such a matter to prescribe a step approved by the general experience of technicians and not shown to be clearly unnecessary or unduly hazardous.

CROSSMAN v. STEWART (1977) 5 C.C.L.T. 45 (B.C.S.C.)

Upon discovering that the drug chloroquine could cause permanent blindness, the defendant physician had the plaintiff, for whom he had prescribed the drug, examined by an ophthalmologist. Because the defendant was unaware that the plaintiff had continued to use the drug after the prescription had expired, he failed to interpret the ophthalmologist's report correctly with the result that the plaintiff was never warned of its dangerous side effects. Consequently, the plaintiff continued to use the drug, obtaining it from a drug company salesman and ultimately suffered permanent blindness.

Held:
(1) By failing to observe that the ophthalmologist's report indicated that the plaintiff was taking the drug on her own, the defendant failed to discharge the high duty of care imposed upon him when his treatment involved the use of a potentially hazardous drug.
(2) The plaintiff was two-thirds at fault for the lack of prudence she displayed in continuing to use the drug without a physician's prescription.

CRYDERMAN v. RINGROSE [1977] 3 W.W.R. 109 affirmed [1978] 3 W.W.R. 481 (Alta. C.A.)

The plaintiff agreed to be sterilized by a new and experimental procedure, the risks of which the defendant did not describe. These included unreliability and damage to the uterus. When the plaintiff became clinically pregnant, the defendant treated this condition by carrying out the procedure again and performing a biopsy of the uterine lining. This treatment amounted to an unconsented-to abortion. The plaintiff became pregnant again, and concerned over possible damage to the foetus because of changes in the uterus, she underwent a hysterectomy.

Alta Dist. Ct. Held:
The defendant was negligent in failing to inform the plaintiff of the uncertainties of this procedure. When an experimental procedure is employed the common law requires a high degree of care and also disclosure to the patient of the fact that the treatment is new and risky.

CRYSLER v. PEARSE [1943] O.R. 735 (H.C.)

While undergoing diathermy treatment for the removal of an urethral caruncle, alcohol which had been used by the defendant to sterilize the areas surrounding and including the operation site, became ignited and burned the plaintiff.

Held:
The defendant was unskilful and negligent in that he failed to use any of the proper and reasonable precautions which a surgeon of ordinary skill and prudence would take, or might reasonably be expected to take, to avoid the ignition of alcohol used for sterilizing the operation site.

CUSSON v. ROBIDOUX [1977] 1 S.C.R. 650

The defendant operated on the plaintiff to repair a fracture of the left knee which he sustained in a motor vehicle accident. The defendant failed to diagnose a fracture of the hip which was consequently not operated on until two months later. As a result of this delay, there were complications and the limb was amputated.

Held:
The defendant was liable in negligence for the plaintiff's damages.

D. (DAVIS), Re (1982) 22 Alta. L.R. (2d) 228 (Prov. Ct.)

The parents of a child requiring, according to a medical consensus, a blood transfusion, refused to consent to such treatment on religious grounds. The child was apprehended as a neglected child under provincial child welfare legislation and a transfusion was administered. The parents petitioned, questioning the validity of the process.

Held:
(1) The child was a neglected child within the meaning of the Child Welfare Act. Since the child was seriously ill, an immediate transfusion was necessary and the parents refused to consent.
(2) The applicable statutory provisions were not unconstitutional, the statute in pith and substance being in relation to the provincial jurisdiction over child welfare and public health. As between the state's right to protect the health and welfare of children and the freedom of religion of their parents, the former takes precedence.

DALE v. MUNTHALI (1977) 16 O.R. (2d) 532 affirmed 21 O.R. (2d) 554 (C.A.)

The defendant general practitioner conducted a physical examination of the plaintiff's husband and diagnosed his case as gastroenteritis. The husband was actually suffering from meningitis and died two days later.

Held:
(1) Although the defendant was not negligent in failing to diagnose meningitis, he should have realized that the husband's symptoms were indicative of an illness more serious than

gastroenteritis. Consequently, he should have conducted a more extensive examination and admitted the husband to hospital for further testing.

(2) The standard of care and skill required of a physical is not lowered by reason of his lack of experience.

DANGERFIELD v. DAVID (1910) 17 W.L.R. 249 (Sask. S.C.)

Having diagnosed an irregular dislocation of the hip, the defendant succeeded in reducing it as far as it could go, which was not all the way into the socket. Subsequent to this manipulation, the plaintiff's complaints were clearly symptomatic of an unreduced dislocation, or a redislocation to which the defendant failed to respond. Consequently, the plaintiff's hip was permanently out of joint.

Held:

The defendant was negligent in failing to discharge the duty to immediately reset the hip when he learned that it was still out of joint.

DAOUST v. R. (1969) 69 D.R.S. 594 (Ex. C.C.)

A general practitioner employed by the federal penitentiary in which the plaintiff was imprisoned, failed to diagnosis a fracture of the plaintiff's foot. The fracture was later discovered by another practitioner who recommended surgery. Medical evidence indicated that the effect of the subsequent operation would have been the same even if it had been performed at the time of the first physician's examination.

Held:

(1) The general practitioner's failure to consult a specialist when he knew that he was not an expert in interpreting X-rays constituted an unreasonable lack of care.

(2) Due to the fact that the plaintiff had no choice in selecting a medical practitioner, the Crown was liable for the negligent conduct of its employee.

DAVID v. TORONTO TRANSIT COMM. (1977) 16 O.R. (2d) 248 (H.C.)

The plaintiff suffered a neck injury known as 1-2 cervical instability as the result of a car accident caused by the defendant's negligence. Contrary to the approved treatment which involved the fusion of the first and second cervical vertebrae, the third party defendant, a surgeon, fused the second and third vertebrae by mistake. Another operation was required as a consequence. The defendants asserted that the surgeon's conduct constituted a *novus actus interveniens* which excused them from liability for the increase in damages.

Held:

(1) The plaintiff took reasonable care to employ a competent surgeon.

(2) The surgeon was clearly negligent in fusing the wrong vertebrae and should have examined an X-ray if he had any doubt concerning the vertebrae he was to operate on. His negligence represented a *novus actus interveniens.*

DAVIDSON v. CONNAUGHT LABORATORIES (1980) 14 C.C.L.T. 251 (Ont. H.C.)

The defendant doctors administered an antirabies vaccine to the plaintiff, who returned from a cross-country trip for this purpose on the advice of the defendant family physician and a virologist consulted in another province. The plaintiff suffered a rare allergic reaction to the vaccine and consequent paralysis.

Held:

(1) The defendant doctors were not liable for negligent treatment of the plaintiff. A doctor must meet the standard of reasonable care of other doctors of his type in his community or similar communities, and the defendants did so here. Although the risk of rabies was slight its consequences were so severe that caution was warranted, a conclusion concurred with by the virologist.

(2) The defendant doctors were not liable in battery or negligence for failing to discuss the

side effects of the vaccine, having met the standard of care of a general practitioner in that community, knowing rural people and what they require. The risk of paralysis or death from the vaccine was very slight and would not have dissuaded the plaintiff from undergoing the treatment.

DAVIS v. COLCHESTER COUNTY HOSP. (1933) 7 M.P.R. 66 (N.S.C.A.)

While anaesthetized, the plaintiff was placed in a bed containing a hot water bottle from which she suffered injury from burning.

Held:

The defendants failed to take the necessary care to ensure that the plaintiff was not exposed to any such dangers or risks as would arise from placing a superheated water bottle in her bed without taking due care that the patient should not come in contact with it.

DAVY v. MORRISON [1932] O.R. 1 (C.A.)

The defendant performed surgery on the plaintiff's gall-bladder which the plaintiff had misunderstood was to be carried out by another surgeon. The results were unsuccessful and shortly after the plaintiff underwent further operation for the removal of the gall-bladder.

Held:

If the method pursued is an established practice, evidence that some surgeons do not approve of it is not sufficient to establish malpractice. A surgeon does not guarantee success or perfect results, only that he has and will use a reasonable degree of skill and learning and that he will exercise reasonable care and exert his best judgment to bring about a good result.

DEAN v. YORK COUNTY HOSP. CORP. (1979) 3 L. Med. Q. 231 (Ont. H.C.)

The defendant orthopaedic specialist diagnosed and treated the plaintiff's leg injury as a simple rather than compound fracture. Gas gangrene was introduced through the fracture wound, requiring amputation of the leg.

Held:

The defendant doctor was liable for negligent diagnosis and treatment of the plaintiff's injury. Given the proximity of the wound to the fracture site, he should have, but failed to carry out, a complete and proper exploratory examination, and moreover he sutured the fracture wound, facilitating the infection which ensued.

DEMOURA v. MISSISSAUGA HOSP. (1979) 3 L. Med. Q. 215 (Ont. H.C.)

The defendant, a hospital emergency room physician, mistakenly diagnosed and prescribed treatment for the plaintiff's medical problem as a sore throat, rather than epiglottitis, from which she died shortly thereafter.

Held:

The defendant was liable for negligent diagnosis and treatment of the plaintiff's condition. He failed to diagnose its severity, to take a proper medical history of the plaintiff, to make a proper or adequate examination, to admit her to the defendant hospital, and to diagnose acute epiglottitis when he knew or ought to have known that the condition was being encountered in the vicinity.

DENDAAS (TYLOR) v. YACKEL (1980) 12 C.C.L.T. 147 (B.C.S.C.)

The defendant obstetrician/gynaecologist performed a sterilization by tubal ligation on the plaintiff, having discussed the irreversibility of the procedure but not the possibility of its failure. The plaintiff subsequently became pregnant, underwent an abortion and second sterilization, and suffered from anxiety and depression.

Held:

(1) The defendant was not liable in battery for failing to disclose the risk of future pregnancy. If consent is given to perform a certain operation, here a tubal ligation, the battery action is available only if there is a deliberate deviation from that procedure.

(2) The defendant was not liable for breach of

contract in failing to fulfil his promise to render the plaintiff sterile. In the absence of a "meeting of minds" of the two parties on an essential term of the contract, in this case that the plaintiff would never become pregnant again, there is no enforceable contract.

(3) The defendant was liable in negligence for failing to disclose adequately the risks of the procedure. A reasonable woman who wished primarily to be assured of sterility would, if informed of the risk of future pregnancy resulting from a unsuccessful tubal ligation, have opted for an alternative procedure.

(4) The defendant was liable for negligently performing the procedure. Conflicting evidence as to whether the standard of care was met was resolved by corroboration arising from the fact of pregnancy following the procedure.

DIACK v. BARDSLEY (1983) 25 C.C.L.T. 159 (B.C.S.C.)

The plaintiff patient was referred by his family dentist to the defendant specialist in oral and maxillofacial surgery. Both recommended that the plaintiff have all four wisdom teeth removed. The defendant discussed the procedure which would be carried out under general anaesthesia with the patient, explained the side effects but did not, as a general practice, discuss the possibility of permanent paresthesia. The patient signed a consent form. After the surgery, the patient suffered from right mental nerve paresthesia.

Held:

The risk of paresthesia is a material, special and unusual risk which should be disclosed to the patient and here was not. However, even if informed of that risk, the patient would have undergone the surgery, so no liability was found. No reliance was placed on the consent form.

DOIRON v. ORR (1978) 20 O.R. (2d) 71 (H.C.)

The defendant doctor performed a sterilization operation on the plaintiff, employing a relatively uncommon reversible procedure which was in the result unsuccessful, the plaintiff becoming pregnant again and carrying the pregnancy to term before undergoing a second sterilization operation by another doctor.

Held:

(1) The defendant was not liable for negligently performing the sterilization procedure. He acted reasonably in initially suggesting a sterilization of the husband and, when that was refused, the procedure ultimately employed. In any event no sterilization procedure short of a hysterectomy is 100 per cent successful, a fact of which he apprised the plaintiff.

(2) The defendant was not liable for damages sufficient to raise the baby to the age of 21, such an approach to the upbringing of a child being "just simply grotesque."

(3) The defendant was not liable for failing to secure an informed consent, since an explanation of the procedure was provided in writing and verbally, including an explanation of the inherent danger that it might not work.

DOWEY v. ROTHWELL AND ASSOC. [1974] 5 W.W.R. 311 (Alta. S.C.)

The plaintiff was an epileptic patient of the defendant association. Feeling a seizure to be imminent and as no physician was present, she requested the assistance of the defendant's nurse who then observed her while she lay on an examination table. The defendant's nurse left the plaintiff momentarily unattended, during which time the seizure occurred and she fell from the table and broke her arm.

Held:

On leaving such a patient unattended the defendant's nurse failed to meet the standard of care required of a qualified nurse in the circumstances. Furthermore, the injuries which the plaintiff suffered were a foreseeable result of the nurse's negligence. Consequently, the defendant association was vicariously liable for the plaintiff's injuries.

DOWN v. ROYAL JUBILEE HOSP. (1980) 24 B.C.L.R. 296 appeal of quantum dismissed [1982] B.C.D. Div. 3632-08 (B.C.C.A.)

On a misdiagnosis of cancer, the plaintiff had an unnecessary mastectomy. The defendant doctor admitted liability.

Held:
(B.C.S.C.): Damages of $23,000 awarded for pain and suffering and depression.
(B.C.C.A.): Appeal that damages were too low was dismissed.

DRINNEN v. DOUGLAS [1931] 1 W.W.R. 160 (B.C.S.C.)

In extracting the plaintiff's teeth, the defendant dental surgeon broke off the top part of 17 teeth, leaving the nerve exposed. The plaintiff, in addition to enduring pain and suffering, required the services of another dentist to extract the remainder of the 17 teeth.

Held:
The defendant was careless to a degree amounting to negligence and he was therefore liable for the plaintiff's injuries. The rule applicable to all skilled labourers, and which is invoked in this case, is this: if your position implies skill you must use it. If you have not that skill, you are liable, or if having that skill you nevertheless perform your work negligently, you are liable, for a person holding himself out to do certain work impliedly warrants that he possesses the competence to perform it.

DUNN v. YOUNG (1977) 19 O.R. (2d) 708 (Co. Ct.)

The defendant paedodontist carried out restorative procedures on the infant plaintiff's teeth. During the operation the plaintiff developed swelling of the lower lip which prolonged corrective treatment could not alleviate, leaving a noticeable scar.

Held:
The defendant was not liable for negligence in the care or treatment of the infant plaintiff, having exercised reasonable care and taken all reasonable and normal precautionary measures. Negligence could not be inferred by the application of *res ipsa loquitur*, since the plaintiff was at no time under the sole management and control of the defendant.

DUNSMORE v. DESHIELD (1977) 80 D.L.R. (3d) 386 (Sask. Q.B.)

The defendant optometrist ordered eyeglasses with tempered lenses from the defendant manufacturer upon the request of the plaintiff. The plaintiff subsequently suffered a laceration of the cornea from penetrating splinters of a broken lens, requiring temporary hospitalization and resulting in discomfort and a permanent minor impairment of his sight.

Held:
(1) The defendants were jointly and severally liable for the injury, having breached their duty to ensure that the lens would not break under reasonable conditions. The lenses had in fact neither been tempered nor tested as could reasonably have been done.
(2) The defendant optometrist was entitled to full indemnity by the defendant manufacturer, being entitled to rely on the manufacturer to supply the lenses ordered.

General damages: $7,500

EADY v. TENDERENDA [1975] 2 S.C.R. 599

The defendant adopted the hammer and chisel method of performing the mastiodectomy on the plaintiff using a surgical loupe having a 2½ times magnification, rather than employing the newer technique of microscopic surgery using a dental drill. The plaintiff suffered facial paralysis from the operation which was later seen to be caused by two white bone chips pressed into the nerve.

Held:
The defendant negligently treated the plaintiff insofar as he foresaw the possiblity of complications following the hammer and chisel method of performing a mastiodectomy, but he failed to take due care in ensuring that all bone chips were removed from the operative area.

EAGLEBACH v. WALTERS B.C.S.C. McKay J. No. 22494/71 Van. 19th June 1974 (unreported)

The defendant doctor examined the plaintiff's head injury, but failed to transfer her immediately to a neurosurgeon's care, the delay resulting in the permanent loss of the left side of the plaintiff's vision in both eyes.

Held:

The defendant having admitted liability for negligently omitting to transfer the plaintiff for necessary medical treatment, the plaintiff was entitled to damages.

EEK v. HIGH RIVER MUN. HOSP. BD. [1926] 1 W.W.R. 36 (Alta. S.C.)

The plaintiff sustained severe burns to both feet from hot water bottles placed at his feet in the bed. The plaintiff brought an action against the hospital board on the grounds that it failed to meet its contractual obligations to supply proper and sufficient nursing.

Held:

There was an implied contract between the plaintiff and the defendant corporation under which the defendant was liable for the negligence of its employee.

EHLER v. SMITH (1979) 29 N.S.R. (2d) 309 (T.D.)

The defendant doctor diagnosed and treated the plaintiff's stated symptoms of nausea, heartburn and stomach pain as gastritis, failing to undertake blood pressure or electrocardiogram tests. Soon after leaving the defendant's office, the plaintiff suffered a heart attack and died hours later.

Held:

The defendant was not liable for negligently diagnosing the plaintiff's condition, having met the requisite standard of care of an average general practitioner. An error of judgment must be distinguished from an act of carelessness or lack of knowledge; here the symptoms did not indicate heart disease and were compatible with a diagnosis of gastritis. Moreover, it was unclear whether a taking of the pulse or blood pressure would have altered the diagnosis.

General damages: $5,000

ELVERSON v. DOCTORS HOSP. (1974) 4 O.R. (2d) 748 affirmed 65 D.L.R. (3d) 382n (S.C.C.)

Although he knew that because of his congenital back problems he should avoid lifting, the plaintiff voluntarily assisted two nurses in elevating with blocks the foot of the bed in which his wife lay, in order to prevent her from further hemorrhaging. The plaintiff suffered injuries to his back as a result, and brought this action on the basis that both the defendant nurse and, through her, the hospital, were liable in negligence for failing to summon the assistance of an orderly.

Ont. C.A. Held:
(1) The action of the nurse in failing to seek the necessary assistance was only an error in judgment.
(2) The plaintiff's injury was not reasonably foreseeable in the circumstances.

EVE Re (1980) 115 D.L.R. (3d) 283 supplementary reasons 115 D.L.R. (3d) 283 at 320 (P.E.I.C.A.)

The applicant, the mother of a 24-year-old mentally retarded woman, sought to be appointed her committee under the provincial Mental Health Act, and be authorized to consent to a contraceptive tubal ligation sterilization on her behalf.

Held:
The application was granted. The court possesses an inherent parental jurisdiction over minors and the mentally incompetent, exercisable in exceptional circumstances to protect their welfare and best interests where it is shown that the real, genuine object is to protect the child or incompetent, that there is no

overriding contrary interest, and that there is a likelihood of substantial social, mental, physical or economic injury. In this case the failure to perform a sterilization would entail significant social restrictions on "Eve" sufficient to amount to substantial injury.

Note: Leave to appeal to S.C.C. granted.

FARRELL v. REGINA [1949] 1 W.W.R. 429 (Sask. K.B.)

While the student nurse was weighing the infant plaintiff on a pan scale situated on a table which was against a steam radiator, the infant plaintiff, who was active, rolled off the scale and onto the hot radiator. He sustained second degree burns.

Held:
(1) Having in mind the activity of the child and his proximity to the radiator, the student nurse failed to meet the very high degree of care required of her in the circumstances. She was negligent in not having her hand close enough to him to prevent the incident.
(2) The city of Regina, the owner of the hospital, was responsible for the negligence of its employees.

FELLER v. ROFFMAN B.C.S.C. Berger J. Vancouver No. 34968/74 17th March 1978 (unreported)

The defendant doctor treated the plaintiff's badly crushed leg, applying a full immobilizing cast and recommending that he be moved to another hospital where treatment could be administered more effectively. The plaintiff's leg ultimately required amputation because of a circulatory problem.

Held:
The defendant was not liable in negligence for his treatment of the plaintiff, having used reasonable care and skill throughout. The complication giving rise to the need for amputation was caused by the initial injury and there was no causal connection between the treatment given and the amputation.

FERGUSON v. HAMILTON CIVIC HOSP. (1983) 40 O.R. (2d) 577 (H.C.)

The plaintiff, suffering from blurred vision, underwent angiography (dye injection X-ray) as a diagnostic test for blockage of the carotid artery. The defendant neurosurgeon informed him of the nature and purpose but not the risks of the procedure. The defendant resident radiologist who actually carried out the procedure discussed the risks with the plaintiff immediately before the operation but did not mention the risk of a stroke. Subsequent to the operation the plaintiff suffered irreversible quadriplegia.

Held:
(1) The defendant doctors were not liable in battery for failing adequately to inform the plaintiff of the risks of the procedure. The battery action has been restricted to cases of no consent or treatment beyond the scope of consent or misrepresentation or fraud. Here consent was not fraudulently obtained, since a full disclosure of possible endarterectomy surgery after the angiogram was not a condition precedent to a sufficient explanation of the diagnostic procedure and its risks.
(2) The defendant doctors were not liable in negligence for failing to disclose adequately the risks of the procedure. Although there were breaches of a duty to disclose by the defendant neurosurgeon for failing to discuss alternative procedures and by the defendant resident radiologist for failing to warn specifically of the risk of stroke, and although the plaintiff testified that he would not have consented to the procedure had he known of the risks, a reasonable person in the plaintiff's position, whose livelihood was threatened by vision loss, would have opted for the procedure nonetheless.
(3) The defendants were not liable for negligent post-procedure care. The injury suffered was inevitable and irreversible after the occurence of the "triggering event," and although quadriplegia following an angiogram is not common, there was no medical evidence justifying an inference of negligence. Moreover, other possible explanations for the injury dictated a finding that it could have occurred without negligence.

FIEGE v. CORNWALL GEN. HOSP. (1980)
30 O.R. (2d) 691 (H.C.)

The defendant nurse administered an intramuscular drug injection to the buttocks of the plaintiff patient, who subsequently suffered pain and disability in her buttock and leg.

Held:
(1) The defendant nurse was negligent in improperly administering the injection too close to the sciatic nerve, and the defendant hospital was vicariously liable for the nurse's negligence. Damages were however reduced on the bases that the plaintiff's disability had to an extent preceded the incident, and that the plaintiff's allegations about the severity of her injury were suspect.
(2) The defendant hospital was required to produce an incident report relating to the treatment in question. The document should have formed part of the medical record, and was made in the course of treatment rather than in contemplation of litigation.

FILIPEWICH v. UNIVERSITY HOSP. BD.
Sask. Q.B. Q.B. No. 432 July 1973 (unreported)

The infant son of the plaintiffs was admitted to the defendant hospital for treatment. A medication was mistakenly substituted for the prescribed one and was administered to the patient, causing his death.

Note: The case was settled before trial.

FINLAY v. AULD [1975] S.C.R. 338

Following the scalene node biopsy performed by the defendant in order to confirm a diagnosis of sarcoidosis, the plaintiff suffered a paralyzed vocal chord, occasioned by injury to the left recurrent laryngeal nerve.

Held:
In arguing that:
(i) in performing the operation which he did, it would have been virtually impossible for him to interfere in any way with the recurrent laryngeal nerve; and
(ii) the probable cause of loss of function of the left recurrent laryngeal nerve was the disease of sarcoidosis,
the defendant produced an explanation equally consistent with no negligence as with negligence. Thus the plaintiff failed to discharge the burden of establishing that the defendant was negligent.

FINLAY v. HESS [1973] 3 O.R. 91 (H.C.)

The plaintiff was referred to the defendant gynaecologist by the defendant general practitioner regarding her irregular vaginal bleeding and cramps. Two months later, after a negative pregnancy test and a D & C which revealed a possible fibroid growth, the plaintiff's condition remained unchanged except for the addition of severe lower abdominal pain. The defendants jointly performed a laparotomy which revealed that the plaintiff had a septate uterus with a probable pregnancy. The plaintiff gave birth to a healthy child and brought this action for an unnecessary operation.

Held:
The purpose of the laparotomy was to find out the cause of the plaintiff's symptoms. There was no medical evidence that the defendant gynaecologist should have made any further tests or that such tests, if made, would have been of any assistance. Because of the particular history and symptoms of the plaintiff it was reasonable and proper medical practice to perform a laparotomy.

FIZER v. KEYS [1974] 2 W.W.R. 14 (Alta. S.C.)

In removing, by traction, an infected cyst from the plaintiff's shoulder, the defendant caused damage to the spinal accessory nerve which resulted in the plaintiff suffering a permanent partial disability.

Held:
(1) Since the cyst was grossly infected, the

defendant was negligent in not being aware of the dangers inherent in removing an infected cyst in that area and should have deferred surgery until the infection had been treated.

(2) The defendant was negligent in failing to exercise the diligence, care, knowledge, skill, and caution to which the plaintiff as his patient was entitled.

FLECKNEY v. DESBRISAY [1927] 3 D.L.R. 30 (N.S.C.A.)

A qualified anaesthetist administered chloroform to the plaintiff's daughter prior to the extraction of her teeth by the defendant dentist. The daughter suddenly died while under the influence of the anaesthetic.

Held:

The plaintiff failed to prove that the death of her daughter was caused by the negligent conduct of the anaesthetist, and therefore the defendant dentist could not be found liable.

FLEMING v. SISTERS OF ST. JOSEPH [1938] S.C.R. 172

In giving the diathermic treatment ordered by the plaintiff's doctor, the defendant nurse mistakenly turned on a much more powerful electrical current. The plaintiff suffered a severe burn.

Held:

(1) The defendant nurse was negligent.

(2) The defendant hospital was vicariously liable for the defendant nurse's negligence, since at the time she committed the negligent act, she was acting as the agent or servant of the hospital within the ordinary scope of her employment.

FLORENCE v. LES SOEURS DE MISERICORDE (1962) 39 W.W.R. 201 (Man. C.A.)

In disregard of instructions not to get out of bed without assistance, the 88-year-old deceased got out of bed and fell. She fractured her hip and later died of a subsequent pulmonary embolism. The plaintiff (deceased's estate) alleged that the defendant was negligent in not putting up the siderails on the deceased's bed as requested by the son of the deceased.

Held:

(1) The accident would not necessarily have been prevented by raising the siderails.

(2) The hospital authorities were not in any sense bound by the request of the deceased's son to install guardrails when according to good hospital practice, it was not thought necessary to do so by those responsible for the hospital routine on the day in question. A hospital is not bound to obey every suggestion, wish, or demand made by a patient or a patient's relatives.

FLUEVOG v. POTTINGER B.C.S.C. No. 31805 7th February 1977 (unreported)

Although the defendant was not a certified specialist in prosthodontics he attended upon each of the three plaintiffs for crown and bridge work. The treatment of each plaintiff was characterized by a lengthy time period involving numerous appointments in which work was redone as many as three or four times over, and which left each plaintiff in need of corrective dental work.

Held:

The defendant had failed to meet the standard required of a prosthodontic specialist, a standard to which he may be legally held regardless of his lack of formal certification by reason of his training, studies, and experience, and the fact that he held himself out as having special qualifications in this field. Consequently he was liable for the plaintiffs' injuries.

FLYNN v. HAMILTON [1950] O.W.N. 224 (C.A.)

Although the plaintiff's doctor knew that she was suffering from "pregnancy psychosis," on admitting her to hospital for Caesarean section, he did not clearly specify that the hospital was to treat her as a mental patient.

Because he foresaw only a steady improvement in her condition, the plaintiff's doctor prescribed a progressively decreasing amount of sedation. The plaintiff jumped from her hospital room window and consequently sustained serious injuries.

Held:

The hospital was not vicariously liable for the failure of its servants to take precautions to protect the plaintiff from harming herself. A hospital's duty of care to a semi-private patient under the care of her own physician does not extend to forming a diagnosis or laying down precautions for her safety except in a case of obvious emergency.

FOOTE v. ROYAL COLUMBIAN HOSP. (1982) 38 B.C.L.R. 222 (S.C.)

The defendant doctor prescribed a new therapy regime for the plaintiff, an epileptic, without informing the hospital nursing staff or providing for special supervision of the plaintiff, who had suffered a grand mal seizure shortly before entering the defendant hospital. While taking an unsupervised bath in the hospital, the plaintiff suffered another grand mal seizure and nearly drowned, suffering brain damage as a result.

Held:

(1) The defendant hospital was not liable for the plaintiff's injuries in the absence of negligence by the nursing staff. The nurses were not apprised of the plaintiff's condition, and the plaintiff did not appear to require special attention.

(2) The defendant doctor was liable in negligence for failing to exercise proper care for the physical safety of his patient. A doctor is not required to ensure his patient's safety and well-being; however in this case the defendant should have recognized that the plaintiff was a "high risk" patient, and instructed the hospital staff explicitly to that effect.

FORSYTH v. CHILDREN'S AID SOC. OF KINGSTON [1963] 1 O.R. 49 (H.C.)

The parents of a newborn refused on religious grounds to consent to the administration of a blood transfusion considered medically necessary by the attending paediatrician. An application by the Children's Aid Society for temporary wardship of the baby was heard and approved within hours and a transfusion was administered. The parents appealed the order.

Held:

The order was quashed, albeit with no practical effect. Although concerned solely with the welfare of the child, the respondents acted contrary to statutory provisions in failing to give reasonable notice to the parents or to provide for a proper hearing.

FRASER v. VANCOUVER GEN. HOSP. [1952] 2 S.C.R. 36

In response to the plaintiff's complaints of pain and stiffness in his neck resulting from a car accident, the intern in charge of the emergency ward took an X-ray of the neck. The next intern on duty then carried out a neurological test on the plaintiff and examined the X-rays. Without consulting the radiologist who was on call, he concluded that the tests and X-rays revealed no damage, although he was admittedly no expert in reading X-rays. The intern gave this information to the plaintiff's doctor and on this basis was advised to discharge the plaintiff. The plaintiff was readmitted 24 hours later suffering from pain in his neck and abdominal distension evidencing the early stages of adynamic ileus. The plaintiff died five days later from the effects of his discharge from hospital in the hours following the accident.

Held:

The defendant hospital was vicariously liable for the negligence of the intern which consisted of

(1) his misreading of the X-rays and his failure to consult the radiologist whereby he failed to exhibit the skill and care which the defendant hospital undertook would be exercised in the ward;

(2) his failure to convey a true picture of the plaintiff's condition to his doctor which thereby resulted in the plaintiff's discharge.

GAGNON v. STORTINI (1974) 4 O.R. (2d) 270 (Dist. Ct.)

Having initially indicated to the adult plaintiff that he would extract her daughter's bicuspid in order to make room for the emergence of the permanent cuspid, he subsequently extracted the permanent cuspid.

Held:

In removing the permanent cuspid without sound reason, the defendant failed to exercise proper skill in treating the infant plaintiff.

GENT v. WILSON [1956] O.R. 257 (C.A.)

Although the infant plaintiff had an inflamed right thumb, the defendant nonetheless proceeded to vaccinate her on the inner aspect of her left arm (which was not the site suggested by the manufacturer of the vaccine). He subsequently treated her for a brief bout of tonsillitis, and then for the development of "multiple takes" of the vaccination. When these lesions became impetiginous, the infant plaintiff was hospitalized. The infant plaintiff suffered a disfiguring scar on her inner left arm and the loss of her right thumbnail.

Held:

(1) The defendant was not negligent in his selection of the vaccination site. The selection of a site for vaccination is a matter for the judgment of the physician, and the standard site is a variable one according to whether it can be kept clean and reasonably protected.
(2) In concluding, prior to vaccinating, that the infant plaintiff's thumb was not infected, the defendant did exercise the degree of skill and care which the plaintiffs were entitled to expect of a medical doctor in his position. The source of the secondary infection was more probably the tonsillitis.

GIBBONS v. HARRIS [1924] 1 W.W.R. 674 (Alta. C.A.)

The defendant failed to diagnose that the infant plaintiff was suffering from tuberculosis of the spinal column (Pott's disease). The treatment which he applied aggravated her condition.

Held:

Regardless of the particular school of treatment which a practitioner may adhere to, the ability to diagnose disease is, by legislation, an essential qualification. Therefore, a chiropractor who fails to use reasonable skill in making a diagnosis is liable for the damages resulting from the treatment which he applies.

GILBERT v. CAMPBELL B.C.S.C. No. 27731/73 May 1976 (unreported)

The defendant doctor performed a circumcision of the infant plaintiff, in the process accidentally cutting off the tip of the glans.

Held:

The defendant was liable for negligently performing the procedure. Although the failure to protect the head of the penis was not negligent, in light of the frequency of circumcisions performed without incident the defendant did not meet the requisite standard of care.

GIRARD v. ROYAL COLUMBIAN HOSP. (1976) 66 D.L.R. (3d) 676 (B.C.S.C.)

Under spinal anaesthesia an operation to remove a portion of a diseased artery from the plaintiff's leg was successfully performed. However, the plaintiff suffered permanent partial paralysis of both legs.

Held:

Res ipsa loquitur was not applicable. (Medical science has not yet reached the stage where the law ought to presume that a patient must come out of an operation as well as or better than he went into it.) Furthermore, medical evidence indicated that the kind of injury suffered by the plaintiff could have occurred without negligence on anyone's part.

GLONING v. MILLER (1953) 10 W.W.R. 414 (Alta. S.C.)

Five years after the Caesarean section performed by the defendant, the plaintiff required treatment for a lump in her abdomen which was found to be a Kelly forceps.

Held:

(1) An operating surgeon has a duty to make sure that no instruments remain in the body of the person being operated on. The defendant adduced no evidence as to the precautions that were taken at the time of the operation to ensure that no forceps were left in the abdomen and therefore failed to negative the initial presumption of negligence.

(2) This action was not defeated by the Statute of Limitations because the defendant continued to provide professional services to the plaintiff regarding the matter complained of, i.e., the presence of the forceps.

GONDA v. KERBEL (1983) 24 C.C.L.T. 222 (Ont. H.C.)

The defendant family physician performed an internal examination of the plaintiff's rectum and bowel. The plaintiff subsequently developed a serious infection requiring further major surgery and resulting in post-operative complications and other side effects.

Held:

(1) The defendant doctor was not liable for failing to disclose adequately the risks of the procedure. Although the defendant failed to mention the risk of bowel perforation, the plaintiff had discussed the procedure, including presumably all risks associated with it, with a friend who was a doctor. The risk of bowel perforation was not material because there was no risk of death or paralysis resulting from it, and even had the risks been known the plaintiff would have undergone the operation.

(2) The defendant was liable for negligently performing the operation. The rarity of bowel perforations in the type of procedure performed gave rise to an inference of negligence which was not overcome by the defendant.

(3) The defendant was not liable for negligent post-treatment care of the plaintiff, having endeavoured to do everything a reasonable physician would have done in the same circumstances.

GORBACK v. TING [1974] 5 W.W.R. 606 (Man. Q.B.)

The plaintiff was not given the opportunity of

choosing the type of anaesthetic to be used in an operation for excision of a maxilla cyst behind one of her teeth, nor was she informed of the risks in the method that was used. The plaintiff suffered damage to her teeth as a result of the method used.

Held:

Because the operation could be carried out under either a general or a local anaesthetic, the defendant anaesthetist was negligent in failing to offer the plaintiff the opportunity of choosing the method to be used.

GORDON v. DAVIDSON; GORDON v. TURCOTTE (1979) 4 L. Med. Q. 131 (Ont. H.C.)

The plaintiff, injured in a snowmobile accident, was treated by the defendant doctor who reduced her ankle fracture and applied a cast. The fracture gave rise to a serious circulatory problem, which was diagnosed by another too late to prevent death of the foot muscles, and which entailed extensive corrective surgery, scarring, pain and disability.

Held:

The defendant was not liable for negligent treatment of the fracture, having met the standard of care of an average general surgeon. The legal standard was unaffected by a conflict of opinion amongst expert witnesses about the recommended course of treatment.

GOUIN-PERRAULT v. VILLENEUVE (1982) 23 C.C.L.T. 72 (Que. S.C.)

The defendant doctor performed a laparoscopic sterilization operation on the plaintiff after discussions in which the plaintiff expressed strong concerns about minimizing scarring. During the operation the plaintiff's colon was nicked by a surgical instrument and a more extensive laparotomy procedure was carried out to repair the damage, resulting in bad scarring and other post-operative problems, and requiring corrective cosmetic surgery.

Held:

(1) The defendant was not liable for failing to

disclose adequately the inherent risks of the procedure. Although in the case of a surgical intervention of a contractual nature, such as a voluntary sterilization, a physician must disclose to the patient all major, frequent and grave risks, here on an objective test the plaintiff would have opted for the operation in any event.

(2) The defendant was not liable for negligence in performing the operation. A laceration of the intestinal wall is rare in this type of procedure, but the inference of negligence was rebutted by other factors equally logical and compatible with a conclusion of no negligence.

GRAFTON v. BIGELOW B.C.S.C. 1975 (unreported)

The paraplegic plaintiff fell while transferring from a chair to a wheelchair. Since no injury was apparent after two days, the head nurse informed the defendant physiotherapist that the plaintiff could resume her exercises. Upon doing so, it was discovered that the plaintiff had a fractured femur.

Held:

The defendant was not guilty of negligence in resuming the treatment, since there were no signs or complaints of injury from the recent fall and the head nurse had advised her to proceed with the therapy.

GRAY v. LAFLECHE [1950] 1 W.W.R. 193 (Man. K.B.)

In performing a circumcision operation on the infant plaintiff the defendant doctor partially destroyed the glans penis.

Held:

(1) The defendant doctor negligently caused injury by his failure to exercise the necessary degree of skill in performing the operation.

(2) With few exceptions in cases tried with a jury, a plaintiff claiming damages for bodily injury is not entitled to show to the jury parts of the body not normally exposed to enable the jury to judge its condition.

GUAR. TRUST CO. v. MALL MEDICAL GROUP [1969] S.C.R. 541

Contrary to instructions from the defendant surgeon not to apply pressure or force in treating the plaintiff's newly repaired knee-cap, the defendant gymnast, in order to assist movement, applied pressure and consequently refractured the knee-cap.

Held:

The defendant gymnast, by not following the defendant surgeon's instructions failed to exercise the degree of care that was reasonably necessary in the circumstances. The defendant surgeon and medical group were vicariously liable for his negligence.

GUERTIN v. KESTER (1981) 20 C.C.L.T. 225 (B.C.S.C.)

The defendant plastic surgeon performed an operation to remove excess skin from the plaintiff's eyelids. In the course of the procedure the defendant inadvertently removed too much skin and despite employing a common technique to remedy the error failed to replace it adequately. The plaintiff suffered a variety of problems resulting from the inability to close one eye completely, and requiring further surgery to correct.

Held:

(1) The defendant was not liable for negligently performing the surgery. There was no evidence of substandard care, and the doctrine of res ipsa loquitur was inapplicable because the symptoms complained of could have arisen without negligence.

(2) The defendant was not liable in negligence for failing properly to disclose the risks attending the procedure. The complications giving rise to the action did not in their ordinary manifestations amount to material risks, and the unusually severe consequences in this case were too remote to require disclosure.

GUIMOND v. LABERGE (1956) 4 D.L.R. (2d) 559 (Ont. C.A.)

When the plaintiff returned for the agreed-upon extraction of all of her upper teeth, the defendant (from past discussions) also anticipated a decision as to whether or not the plaintiff would consent to the removal of her lower teeth. Before administering the anaesthetic the defendant asked the plaintiff, "Toutes les dents, Madame Guimond?" and she replied "Oui." The defendant removed all of her teeth and the plaintiff brought an action for wrongful extraction of her lower teeth.

Held:

"It may be that in Mrs. Guimond's mind what she meant was 'all the upper teeth' but that is not what she said, and I do not see how the doctor, in the light of the circumstances, could be expected in any way to read her mind." The defendant followed the plaintiff's instructions when he extracted her lower teeth and was thus not liable for assault.

HAINES v. BELLISSIMO (1977) 18 O.R. (2d) 177 (H.C.)

While being treated for paranoid schizophrenia by the defendants under an out-patient treatment plan, the plaintiff's husband committed suicide. At the time of his suicide, except for his known purchase of a shotgun, the deceased presented a stable clinical picture and the defendants decided not to hospitalize him as a result of this act. The plaintiff alleges that the defendants were negligent in failing to hospitalize the deceased and thereby protect him from the reasonably apprehended danger of suicide.

Held:

(1) In deciding not to hospitalize the deceased following his purchase of the first shotgun, the defendant psychologist acted in accord with the accepted practice of psychology and psychiatry at the time and was therefore not liable for his error in judgment.
(2) The defendant psychologist was not negligent in failing to obtain the assistance of the defendant psychiatrist nor should he have recognized that his therapeutic bond with the deceased had broken down. Expert opinion confirms that it was perfectly reasonable in the circumstances for the defendant psychologist

to conclude that his relationship with the deceased was intact.

HAJGATO v. LONDON HEALTH ASSN. (1982) 36 O.R. (2d) 669 affirmed 23 A.C.W.S. (2d) 54 (C.A.)

The defendants, residents in orthopaedic surgery at the defendant hospital, supervised the plaintiff's recovery from surgery to replace her hip joint. After some months of complaints of pain and sickness by the plaintiff, a severe wound infection was discovered under the cast which resulted in arthritis, fusion of the hip joint and consequent permanent disability.

Held:

(1) The defendants were not liable in negligence for failing to advise the plaintiff of the risk of infection associated with the surgical procedure. The risk of infection was disclosed to the plaintiff, and the one to two per cent risk of destruction of the hip joint from such an infection, when weighed against the plaintiff's apprehension about the procedure, justified a generalization of the risk. Moreover, the procedure, though elective, was of sufficient therapeutic effect that a reasonable person in the plaintiff's position would have opted for surgery even if the risk had been disclosed.
(2) The defendants were not liable for negligent post-operative care of the plaintiff, for failing to diagnose the wound infection in time. Although infection is an inherent danger of any operation, in a modern hospital the failure to treat an infection before crippling injury occurs gives rise to an inference of negligence. However, on the facts of this case there was no breach of the professional standard of care in as much as the sole indicia of an increasingly serious infection were subjective complaints of the plaintiff which were reasonably consistent with her course of treatment.

General damages: $100,000

HALUSHKA v. UNIVERSITY OF SASK. (1965) 52 W.W.R. 608 (Sask. C.A.)

The plaintiff was paid $50 to act as a subject in

a research project and was told that the test was safe.

The researchers were actually testing a new anaesthetic with which they had no previous experience. The anaesthetic caused the plaintiff to suffer a cardiac arrest which affected his mental ability.

Held:

Researchers must completely disclose to their subject all facts, probabilities and opinions which a reasonable man would consider before giving his consent. In research cases, there are no exceptions to full disclosure as there may be in ordinary medical practice.

HAMPTON v. MACADAM (1912) 22 W.L.R. 31 (Sask. Dist. Ct.)

After the plaintiff had had a miscarriage, the defendant physician did not remove the portion of the placenta remaining in the uterus, since he had been called in on emergency and did not have the necessary instruments with him. The plaintiff later underwent another operation to remove the remaining placenta.

Held:

(1) Under the circumstances, the defendant was justified in not performing a further operation to remove the placenta.
(2) The plaintiff's failure to seek medical assistance earlier in view of the threatening miscarriage would have constituted contributory negligence had the defendant been found liable.

HANKAI v. YORK COUNTY HOSP. (1981) 9 A.C.W.S. (2d) 354 Ont. C.A. Howland C.J.O., Brooke and Thorson JJ.A. 29th June 1981 (unreported)

The defendant doctor performed surgery on the plaintiff to remove a miscarried foetus, and during the procedure carried out a meatotomy in conformity with his standard procedure. The plaintiff had consented to the first procedure only.

Ont. H.C. Held:

The defendant was liable for battery for performing the unconsented-to meatotomy.

General damages: $60,000

Ont. C.A. Held:

A new trial was directed for reassessment of damages. The trial judge made several errors in directing the jury, which awarded exemplary in addition to general damages.

HANKINS v. PAPILLON (1980) 14 C.C.L.T. 198 (Que. S.C.)

The defendant plastic surgeon performed dermabrasion surgery to remove hormone-produced spots on the plaintiff's face. While the original spots were removed, other permanent spots appeared after the operation.

Held:

The defendant was not liable for failing to inform the plaintiff of the risks of the procedure. In cases of plastic surgery the relative importance of the patient's subjective concerns as against therapeutic benefits dictates that the doctor be extremely careful to disclose completely all material and special risks and their consequences. However, in this case the plaintiff failed to establish that disclosure was in fact inadequate.

HARKIES v. LORD DUFFERIN HOSP. (1931) 66 O.L.R. 572 (H.C.)

In order to treat a three-year-old suffering from pneumonia, a steam inhalation system was set up whereby the steam from a kettle was carried into his crib through a rubber hose. When the nurse returned from an adjoining room, she discovered that the child had been severely scalded.

Held:

(1) According to the evidence the apparatus was safe if used properly, therefore *res ipsa loquitur* is applicable and an inference may be drawn that the child's injury was due to an absence of proper care on the part of the nurses.
(2) The defendant was vicariously liable for the negligence of its staff.
(3) The Public Authorities Protection Act, R.S.O. 1927, c. 120, s. 11, and the Hospitals and Charitable Institutions Act, R.S.O. 1927, c.

349, s. 18, were not applicable to the facts of the case.

HARQUAIL v. SEDGEWICK (1982) 14 A.C.W.S. (2d) 47 Ont. H.C. Anderson J. 27th April 1982 (not yet reported)

The defendant general practitioner treated the plaintiff for symptoms of constant pain in his leg, but could not accurately diagnose the problem. After several months the defendant referred the plaintiff to a surgeon who amputated the leg due to a hardening of the arteries which had not been diagnosed.

Held:

The defendant was not liable in negligence for failing to make the correct diagnosis or refer the patient to a specialist. In light of the unusual symptoms, a failure to make the diagnosis was not a breach of the standard of care, and the failure to consult was no more than an error of judgment.

HAY v. BAIN [1925] 2 D.L.R. 948 (Alta. C.A.)

During the delivery of her child, the plaintiff suffered a second degree tear in the perineum. The defendant physician asserted that he had repaired the tear but two doctors who attended the plaintiff three weeks later noted a third degree tear. The plaintiff had failed to follow the defendant's instructions concerning her post-delivery care and treatment.

Held:

(1) There was no negligence on the defendant's part. The tear observed by the other two doctors could well have developed from a smaller tear caused by factors independent of the physician's conduct.
(2) Direct evidence is usually regarded as superior to expert evidence.

HEARNE v. FLOOD (1919) 16 O.W.N. 28 (S.C.)

Following treatment by the defendant physician of his injured hand, the plaintiff required a further operation. The plaintiff alleged negligence and want of skill in the defendant's treatment of his injury.

Held:

(1) The defendant possessed the requisite amount of skill and exercised the requisite degree of care.
(2) The plaintiff failed to prove that his condition was a consequence of the defendant's conduct.

HERITIERS DE FEU MAURICE MASSE v. GAUDETTE (1983) 21 A.C.W.S. (2d) 218 (Que. C.A.)

The defendant doctor surgically removed fibrous tissue from the palm of the plaintiff patient who was suffering from Depuytren's contracture but failed to remove a hematoma with the result that the plaintiff suffered skin loss, scarring and contracting of the palm of the hand.

Held:

The trial judge should have compared expert evidence of recommended treatment to treatment given and found the defendant doctor liable because he used bad judgment.

General damages: $9,000

HOBSON v. MUNKLEY (1976) 14 O.R. (2d) 575 (H.C.)

As a result of a tubal ligation performed by the defendant surgeon the plaintiff suffered damage to her left ureter. The plaintiff brought an action against the defendant in negligence in performance of the operation, relying on *res ipsa loquitur*. The defendant was unable to explain how the damage occurred.

Held:

The defendant's admission that he could not explain how the plaintiff's ureter was damaged could not support an inference that the injury was caused by his negligence because, in this case, the mere happening of the injury was not evidence that reasonable care had not been used. It cannot be said, as a matter of common experience, that a ureter is not damaged in the course of the surgical removal of an ovary, Fallopian tube, and connecting endometrial tissue and the placing of a mattress suture to control bleeding, unless the surgeon fails to use reasonable care. In this case there was no evidence that the defendant failed to use reasonable care.

HOCHMAN v. WILLINSKY [1933] O.W.N. 79 (H.C.)

The plaintiff's hand was burned while exposed to an X-ray machine operated by a servant of the defendant physician. On the evidence, it appeared that a cone had been left off the machine and that this was the cause of the plaintiff's burn.

Held:

The defendant physician was vicariously liable for his employee's negligence in operating the machine without the cone.

HODGINS v. BANTING (1906) 12 O.L.R. 117 (H.C.)

After the defendant physician set the plaintiff's fractured leg, the bones failed to mend properly, leaving the plaintiff with a shortened leg and slightly everted foot.

Held:

(1) A physician cannot be deemed to be negligent simply because another practitioner of equal skill would have adopted another course of treatment.
(2) The doctrine of *res ipsa loquitur* did not apply, since even where treatment is administered by an extremely skilful physician, the possibility that the fracture will heal improperly still exists.

HOLMES v. BD. OF HOSP. TRUSTEES OF LONDON (1977) 17 O.R. (2d) 626 (H.C.)

The plaintiff, suffering from hoarseness in her throat, was admitted to the defendant hospital for diagnostic surgery. The defendant anaesthetist administered anaesthetic, employing a newly developed method of artificial ventilation, without informing the plaintiff of the nature or risks of the procedure. As a result of improper placement of the ventilation apparatus, the plaintiff suffered massive tissue emphysema and subsequently developed a spinal infection which was incorrectly diagnosed and which ultimately rendered her quadriplegic.

Held:

(1) The defendant anaesthetist was liable for negligently performing the transtracheal ventilation. The evidence established that the plaintiff's initial injuries were caused by the misplacement of the ventilation apparatus, and the defendant was unable to rebut the presumption of negligence raised thereby by the application of *res ipsa loquitur*. However, he was not in breach of his duty to inform the patient; a doctor is not obliged to inform a patient of the risks of his possible negligence.
(2) The defendant's otolaryngologist and internist were liable in negligence for failing to diagnose correctly the plaintiff's spinal infection in light of information revealed by X-rays which was not collected or examined by the doctors.
(3) The defendant hospital was not liable in negligence for the plaintiff's injuries.

General damages were assessed at $716,108.

HOPITAL GENERALE DE LA REGION DE L'AMIANTE INC. v. PERRON (1979) 3 A.C.W.S. 409 Que C.A. Lagoie, Kaufman and Lamer JJ.A. 6th September 1979

The defendant anaesthetist administered anaesthetic to the plaintiff who suffered a cardiorespiratory arrest in the operating room of the defendant hospital, resulting in severe brain damage and total incapacity.

Held:

(1) The defendant anaesthetist was not liable for damages, having rebutted a presumption of fault by demonstrating adherence to the standard of an ordinary, reasonably competent anaesthetist. Moreover, the anaesthetist was

not liable for the personal fault of the operating room nurses in failing to alert him of the patient's changed condition.

(2) The hospital nursing staff was at fault for failing properly to supervise the plaintiff's condition and the hospital was liable for the acts of the nurses as hospital agents.

General damages: $70,000

HOPITAL NOTRE-DAME DE L'ESPERANCE v. LAURENT [1978] 1 S.C.R. 605 (S.C.C.)

Without taking X-rays the defendant surgeon diagnosed the plaintiff's hip injury as a simple "contusion" and after prescribing medication to relieve the pain, he advised her to contact him in a few days regarding her progress. A week later in consultation by telephone he renewed her prescription. Three months later another surgeon diagnosed from X-rays that the plaintiff's continued suffering was caused by a fracture of the neck of the femur. The delay in treatment increased the length and difficulty of the surgical treatment which the plaintiff then underwent as well as the permanent partial disability which she suffered.

Held:

(1) The defendant surgeon was negligent in making his initial diagnosis without the use of X-rays and in failing to concern himself enough about the plaintiff's condition to appreciate the need to see her again.

(2) The plaintiff was contributorily negligent in failing to seek medical help when, as time went on without the pain disappearing, the need for a more thorough examination became increasingly evident.

HOPP v. LEPP [1980] 2 S.C.R. 192

The defendant orthopaedic surgeon performed disc surgery on the plaintiff. Prior to the operation the defendant told the plaintiff that he was qualified to perform the procedure, without elaborating on his experience or training; that the operation could be as well performed in Lethbridge as in the larger centre of Calgary; and that the procedure was not a serious one.

Subsequent examinations revealed the need for further surgery which was performed but could not reverse permanent injury suffered by the plaintiff.

Held:

The defendant was not liable in battery or negligence for failing to secure an informed consent from the plaintiff. A licensed specialist is not obligated, in the absence of questions by the patient, to discuss specific details of his professional qualifications where it is clear he is not inexperienced. The advantage of having the operation performed in Calgary was predicated upon the existence of risks which in this case were not special or unusual and therefore not necessary to disclose. The procedure was a routine one and questions of its seriousness were subsumed under the issues of professional qualification and locale.

HOTEL-DIEU DE MONTREAL v. COULOUME [1975] 2 S.C.R. 115

The plaintiff was re-hospitalized because he was suffering from the effects of a ruptured cerebral aneurism. While in hospital, he began to have epileptic seizures. On learning that the plaintiff had attempted to leave his bed, his doctor ordered that sides be installed on the plaintiff's bed. Later, when the plaintiff complained of pain in his right thigh it was discovered that his right hip had been fractured and it was concluded that the injury was caused by a fall from his bed during the first of his epileptic seizures.

Held:

The hospital was not liable by application of the rule on presumption of fact because there was no evidence that the author of the fact which caused the damage was an employee of the hospital.

HUBER v. BURNABY, GEN. HOSP. [1973] D.R.S. 653 B.C.S.C. Dryer J. New Westminister No. 8057/72 3rd July 1973 (unreported)

While giving an injection in the area of the plaintiff's right buttock, a nurse employed by the defendant hospital damaged the plaintiff's sciatic nerve.

Held:

The defendant hospital was vicariously liable for the nurse's negligence.

HUGHSTON v. JOST [1943] O.W.N. 3 (H.C.)

The anaesthetic escaped into the tissue surrounding the vein causing the development of an abscess which incapacitated the plaintiff for several months.

Held:

(1) The plaintiff failed to prove that the defendant was negligent, i.e., that he failed to use reasonable care and diligence in the exercise and application of his skill and knowledge to accomplish the purpose for which he was employed.

(2) The principle of res ipsa loquitur was inapplicable in a case of this type wherein to draw a conclusion of negligence would have been merely a matter of conjecture.

HUTCHINSON v. ROBERT [1935] O.W.N. 314 (C.A.)

During nose surgery a fragment of a breaking forceps broke off and remained within the wound. The defendant decided to allow the fragment to self-discharge by becoming encysted. As a result the plaintiff developed sinus trouble.

Held:

The plaintiff failed to prove that there was negligence and that the negligence was the cause of the injury complained of.

JACKSON v. HYDE (1869) 28 U.C.Q.B. 294 (Ont. C.A.)

The plaintiff sued the defendant physician for amputating his arm above the elbow instead of below the elbow.

Held:

In a negligence action, the plaintiff must establish a prima facie case. Where the evidence is as consistent with negligence as with the absence of negligence, the plaintiff has failed to prove his case.

JARVIS v. INT. NICKEL CO. (1929) 63 O.L.R. 564 (H.C.)

While the defendant general practitioner was unable to diagnose the cause of the plaintiff's ear trouble, he explicitly rejected a diagnosis of mastoiditis and he did not refer the plaintiff to a specialist. The plaintiff was operated on for mastoiditis by a specialist shortly thereafter. He suffered from partial facial paralysis including damage to his seeing, hearing, and speaking abilities.

Held:

(1) Although the defendant assumed to state confidently that there was no mastoid trouble when he was unable to say what the real trouble was, the plaintiff failed to establish negligence or lack of average skill in the diagnosis.

(2) The plaintiff did not clearly establish that a correct diagnosis at an earlier date would have prevented the troubles from which he now suffers.

(3) A physician who is unable to diagnose a problem is not under a legal obligation to so inform the patient or to advise the calling in of a specialist.

JENDRICK v. GREIDANUS (1980) 28 A.R. 496 (Q.B.)

The defendant doctors performed surgery on the arm of the plaintiff, who subsequently suffered radial nerve palsy of the arm and wrist ultimately rendering his arm useless.

Held:

(1) On a preliminary application to amend the statement of claim to frame the cause of action in contract, the application was dismissed on the basis that the limitation period had expired.

(2) The defendants were not liable for negligently performing the surgery. The plaintiff must prove on a balance of probabilities that his injury was caused by the allegedly negligent conduct; here he failed to do so in light of evidence that the nerve damage did not become evident until some time after his discharge from the hospital.

JEWISON v. HASSARD (1916) 26 Man. R. 571 (C.A.)

During an operation a sponge was left in the plaintiff's abdomen. Before closing the defendant surgeon had checked the operation site and had asked the nurse if all the sponges were accounted for. The nurse had replied affirmatively.

Held:

It is the duty of the nurse to keep count of the sponges so that the surgeon can direct his full attention to the operation. If the surgeon personally examines the site of the operation to see if anything has been left in the incision he has discharged his duty to perform the surgery with reasonable skill and care.

JODOUIN v. MITRA (1978) 2 L. Med. Q. 72 (Ont. H.C.)

The defendant orthopaedic surgeon performed an Irwin osteotomy on the plaintiff to correct deformities of her leg, having discussed the procedure but without mentioning the risk of nerve damage. As a result of the operation, the plaintiff suffered pain and numbness in the opposite leg, from which a bone graft had been taken, the numbness being aggravated by subsequent corrective surgery performed by another doctor.

Held:

(1) The defendant was not liable for negligently performing the operation, since the nerve injury was not an unusual risk of the procedure properly carried out by a competent orthopaedic surgeon.
(2) The defendant was not liable in negligence

for failing to warn the plaintiff of the risks involved. The risk of nerve damage was not so special as to impose a duty on the doctor to warn a patient of it, and the effect of such damage would not have deterred the plaintiff or a reasonable person from undergoing the surgery.

JOHNSTON v. WELLESLEY HOSP. [1971] 2 O.R. 103 (H.C.)

The 20-year-old plaintiff came to the defendant dermatologist as an outpatient and requested a carbon dioxide slush treatment to remove acne scarring. The patient suffered severe pain during treatment but told the defendant to continue when the defendant asked him if he wished to stop the treatment. The plaintiff was exposed to the slush treatment for too long a period thereby causing new scarring.

Held:

(1) The six-month limitation period imposed by s. 33 of the Public Hospitals Act, R.S.O. 1960, c. 322, does not apply to outpatients.
(2) A valid consent for a medical or surgical procedure can be obtained from an obviously intelligent 20-year-old who is as capable of understanding the possible consequences of the procedure as an adult.
(3) The doctrine of *res ipsa loquitur* does not apply in the present case, since the cause of damage to the plaintiff was known.
(4) Any physician, even a specialist, cannot guarantee the success of his treatment. A specialist is only obliged to exercise that degree of care and skill which could reasonably be expected of a normal, prudent physician in the same field of specialization. Physicians are not responsible for errors in judgment as long as they exercise their judgments intelligently.
(5) A hospital is not responsible for the negligence of a physician on active staff who receives no salary or any other emolument from the hospital. When the supervision and control of hospital employees has been transferred from the hospital to a doctor, during an operation, for example, the hospital is not vicariously liable for the actions of its employees.

JOSEPH BRANT MEMORIAL HOSP. v.
KOZIOL (1977) 2 C.C.L.T. 170 (S.C.C.)

Following an automobile accident, the deceased
underwent surgery and was placed in a Stryker
frame. During the night, the defendant nurse
allowed him to sleep soundly. The patient died
as a result of aspirating gastric fluid.

Held:

(1) The defendant nurse failed to take the proper
care to prevent the patient from regurgitating
fluids into his lungs. She should have roused
him hourly and compelled him to cough and
breathe deeply. Furthermore the nurse's notes
on the patient's records were unsatisfactory.
(2) The doctrine of *res ipsa loquitur* was not
applicable, since the cause of death was known.

KANGAS v. PARKER [1978] 5 W.W.R.
667 (Sask. C.A.)

The defendant dental surgeon extracted several
teeth from the mouth of the plaintiff, who was
under a general anaesthetic administered by
the defendant anaesthetist. During the procedure blood escaped from the plaintiff's mouth
into his lungs, resulting in his death.

Held:

The defendants were jointly liable for negligent treatment of the plaintiff. The operation
was carried out by the two defendants as a
team, operating different devices to maintain
an open air passage, and communicating any
complications to each other. Allowing a considerable amount of blood to escape around the
mouth pack into the lungs, combined with a
failure to recognize this, constituted negligence
which resulted in death.

General damages: $130,000

KAPUR v. MARSHALL (1978) 4 C.C.L.T.
204 (Ont. S.C.)

While performing a necessary discoidectomy
on the plaintiff's husband, the defendant
neurosurgeon pierced the right common iliac
artery causing the hemorrhaging from which
the patient later died. The defendant was using
the standard, recognized, conventional procedure for ensuring that the instruments used in
this operation would not leave the disc space.

Held:

The plaintiff did not establish on a reasonable
balance of probabilities that the defendant failed
to conform to that degree of skill and care
required of him as a neurosurgeon in his performance of the operation. The defendant recognized the risk of harm which occurred and took
precautions to avoid it. That the accident happened in this case was not evidence that reasonable care had not been used and consequently
the principle of *res ipsa loquitur* was inapplicable.

KARDERAS v. CLOW [1973] 1 O.R. 730
(H.C.)

After performing an operation to treat a ruptured Fallopian tube, the defendant surgeon
left the operating room instructing the surgical
resident to close the abdomen. The nurse told
the assistant that the sponge count was correct.
In fact, a laparotomy pad had been left in the
patient.

Held:

(1) A surgeon is not liable in tort or contract for
allowing a competent resident to complete an
abdominal closure in his absence.
(2) A surgeon is not liable for the negligence of
his assistant unless evidence of established custom among surgeons shows that his responsibility extends to the actions of his assistant.
(3) Although it is the nurse's duty to note the
number of sponges used, if the surgeon fails to
exercise reasonable care in removing them, his
reliance upon the nurse does not relieve him
from liability.
(4) The hospital is vicariously liable for medical negligence of a resident.

KELLY v. DOW (1860) 9 N.B.R. 435 (S.C.)

In the process of bleeding the plaintiff, the
defendant surgeon mistakenly punctured the
brachial artery causing the plaintiff's arm to

swell and become painful. To alleviate the swelling the surgeon directed that the arm be poulticed.

Held:

The defendant was negligent in his treatment of the swollen arm, since no skilful surgeon would have used a poultice.

KELLY v. HAZLETT (1976) 15 O.R. (2d) 290 (H.C.)

In spite of his attempts to discourage the plaintiff from undergoing an osteotomy, the defendant assented to the plaintiff's request and performed the operation. Partly as a result of the osteotomy, the plaintiff's right arm developed permanent stiffness. In his attempts to dissuade the plaintiff, the defendant had never mentioned this risk.

Held:

(1) If the plaintiff has been informed of the basic nature and character of the operation to be performed, and has agreed to it, then there has been no unconsented-to invasion of the person of the plaintiff, i.e., battery, regardless of any failure to disclose any collateral risks flowing from the operation.
(2) If failure to disclose collateral risks is the cause of the plaintiff's damage because the plaintiff would not knowingly have assented to the risk, and if such failure is not justified by reasonable medical considerations, there may be a cause of action in negligence. On these grounds the defendant was found negligent.

KENNY v. LOCKWOOD [1932] O.R. 141 (C.A.)

The defendant general practitioner referred the patient to the defendant surgeon, advising the patient to be guided by the surgeon. The patient was suffering from Dupuytrene's contracture. The surgeon told the patient that the operation was not serious and that the recovery period was about three weeks. A problem with the recovery developed owing to some obscure condition which supervened after the operation.

Held:

(1) The general practitioner either had no duty to the patient after the referral to the surgeon or committed no breach of duty if one existed.
(2) The surgeon had a duty to honestly inform the patient of the character, importance and probable consequences of the operation. This duty did not extend to warning the patient of possible dangers of the operation which would likely distress or frighten him.

KEY v. THOMSON (1868) 12 N.B.R. 295 (S.C.)

The defendant surgeon informed the plaintiff that he would not lose his hands and feet which had been frozen. The defendant visited the plaintiff only twice during the next three weeks, although the plaintiff sent for him frequently. A portion of the plaintiff's hands and feet were amputated by another surgeon.

Held:

(1) When the plaintiff presents evidence of other physicians as to the proper treatment of the ailment in question, the defendant physician may rebut this evidence by presenting evidence of similar cases in which the course of treatment adopted in the instant case was successful.
(2) A physician may legitimately make a more favourable prognosis than the facts of the case indicate in order to prevent despondency in his patient.

New trial ordered.

KNIGHT v. SISTERS OF ST. ANN (1967) 64 D.L.R. (2d) 657 (B.C.S.C.)

During the operation, the patient's arm, which had been tucked in under the draw sheet by members of hospital staff, became caught and squeezed in the mechanism of the operating table.

Held:

Surgeons in charge of an operation are not liable for the negligence of hospital staff if

their carelessness was not reasonably foreseeable to the surgeon.
The hospital was solely responsible.

KOBESCAK v. CHAN [1981] B.C.D. Civ. 1173-01 B.C.S.C. Legg J. Vancouver No. C802695 26th June 1981 (unreported)

The defendant dentist performed restorative procedures on the plaintiff, including extractions and the provision of dentures. The unsatisfied plaintiff underwent a succession of subsequent treatments.

Held:
The defendant was not liable for negligence in carrying out the treatment. Although one witness testified that he would have employed a different technique, the defendant followed the standard professional treatment in a satisfactory manner.

KOEHLER v. COOK (1975) 65 D.L.R. (3d) 766 (B.C.S.C.)

Prior to consenting, the plaintiff inquired about the risks involved in an operation to cure her migraine headaches. Although the defendant was aware of complaints of both a temporary and permanent loss of smell following similar operations, he assured the plaintiff that there were no lasting complications of importance. The plaintiff suffered a permanent loss of her olfactory sense.

Held:
The test for informed consent is not whether the prudent person would have accepted the risk but whether the plaintiff would have. In this case a weighing of the various considerations produced the finding that the plaintiff would not have accepted the risk had she been informed of it. Consequently, the defendant was liable in trespass for her damages.

KONKOLUS v. ROYAL ALEXANDRA BD. OF GOVS. (1982) 21 Alta. L.R. (2d) 359 (Q.B.)

The defendant surgeon performed an ulnar nerve release operation on the plaintiff's elbow three

times over a period of five years, in each instance unsuccessfully. Subsequent to the third attempt the plaintiff suffered increased numbness and discomfort in the area of the surgery.

Held:
(1) The defendant doctor was not liable for negligence in performing the operation since a variety of factors were consistent with no negligence and the maxim *res ipsa loquitur* therefore was inapplicable.
(2) The defendant was not liable in negligence for failing adequately to inform the plaintiff of the risks attending the procedure. The operation was a minor procedure, the nature of which was understood by the defendant. The risk which materialized was neither inherent in nor peculiar to this type of operation, nor reasonably foreseeable, nor material so as to require disclosure.

KRUJELIS v. ESDALE [1972] 2 W.W.R. 495 (B.C.S.C.)

Following plastic surgery a five-year-old patient was placed in the recovery room in good condition. The patient suffered a respiratory arrest followed by a cardiac arrest and died two months later. Three of the five nurses were having a coffee break at the time of the arrest.

Held:
(1) By taking a coffee break during a busy period, the defendant nurses were clearly negligent in that they failed to provide the patient with adequate observation following surgery. A patient in the recovery room should be looked at every five minutes.
(2) The hospital was vicariously liable for the negligence of its staff which occurred during the course of their regular duties.

KUNITZ v. MEREI [1969] 2 O.R. 572 (H.C.)

Following an operation to remove polyps from the plaintiff's nasal passages, hemorrhaging occurred behind her eyeball. Upon discovering that her vision had been impaired the defendant otolaryngologist consulted an ophthalmologist. The ophthalmologist, who was not able to see the plaintiff for some six hours, continued the defendant's course of treatment but the plaintiff lost the vision in that eye.

Held:

Although the defendant decided to wait six hours for the ophthalmologist to see the plaintiff, he was not negligent, since there was no evidence that another course of action could have prevented the loss of vision. Given the slight risk of hemorrhaging and the even slighter risk of loss of vision, the defendant acted reasonably.

LACHAMBRE v. PERREAULT COMMISSION DES ACCIDENTS DU TRAVAIL DE QUEBEC, INTERVENANTE (1983), 22 A.C.W.S. (2d) 94 (Que. C.A.)

The plaintiff suffered a multiple fracture of the leg while at work which the defendant doctor treated by putting the leg into a cast and only later transferred the plaintiff to a better-equipped hospital. The leg had to be amputated.

Held:

The defendant is not liable because the patient did not prove the amputation was necessary as a result of the doctor's treatment.

LAFLECHE v. LAROUCHE Ont. Small Claims Ct. No. 8631/78 July 1979 (unreported)

The defendant dentist employed a "hand over mouth" technique in treating the child of the plaintiff, who initially had resisted the treatment of his toothache. The child's face was bruised as a result.

Held:

The defendant was not liable for negligence, given that the technique was professionally acceptable, essential in the circumstances, and consented to by the mother with knowledge that bruising might result.

LaFLEUR v. CORNELIS (1979) 28 N.B.R. (2d) 569 (Q.B.)

The defendant cosmetic surgeon performed a nose reduction procedure on the plaintiff, with-out informing her of a ten per cent risk of scarring. The surgery left a scar on the plaintiff's nose which could not be eliminated despite a second operation.

Held:

(1) The defendant was liable for negligently performing the surgery. A medical doctor who performs surgery on an otherwise healthy body for cosmetic purposes has a very high duty to the patient, because the procedure is not medically necessary and the results plainly visible. In this case the doctrine *res ipsa loquitur* was applicable, since the scarring could not have occurred unless the suturing procedure had been carried out negligently.

(2) The defendant was not liable for failing to warn the plaintiff of the risks attending the procedure. Signed consent documents do not relieve a doctor of the duty to inform the plaintiff of risks inherent in procedures. When treatment is elective, a very high degree of disclosure of risks is required, and normally a failure to do so is negligent. In this case, however, the plaintiff was an intelligent person who would have known the incidental risks, and would have undergone the operation even if the ten per cent risk of scarring had been explained. The consent did not extend to negligence, though.

(3) The defendant was liable for breach of contract. A cosmetic surgeon is in a different position from an ordinary surgeon in that he sells a special service. In this case the defendant made an express agreement to perform the surgery, and an express guarantee of its success, without explaining the risks.

LAIDLAW v. LIONS GATE HOSP. (1969) 70 W.W.R. 727 (B.C.S.C.)

The plaintiff suffered a respiratory obstruction in the post-op recovery room which resulted in severe brain damage. The nurse in the recovery room was attending four or five other patients while the other nurse on duty was at coffee.

Held:

A very high standard of care is required of nurses in the recovery room due to potential dangers in the immediate post-operative period.

(1) Both nurses were negligent, one in leaving the patient unobserved for more than three or four minutes, and the other in taking a coffee break when she knew or ought to have known that post-op patients would be arriving.

(2) An anaesthetist is not negligent if he fails to insert a pharyngeal airway before sending a patient to the recovery room since this practice is not common and would not prevent a respiratory obstruction.

LAUGHLIN v. ROYAL COLUMBIAN HOSP. [1971] D.R.S. 694 (B.C.C.A.)

A nurse employed by the defendant hospital administered an intra-muscular injection to the buttock of the plaintiff, who was convalescing in the hospital after surgery. The plaintiff subsequently suffered paralysis of his lower leg and "foot drop," seriously disabling him.

Held:

The nurse was negligent for administering the injection to the wrong area of the buttock, and the defendant hospital was liable for that negligence.

An appeal by the plaintiff of the damage award was dismissed, the sum of $29,500 being not inordinately low.

LAVERE v. SMITH'S FALLS PUB. HOSP. (1915) 35 O.L.R. 98 (S.C.)

While the plaintiff was still anaesthetized following an operation, she suffered a severe burn on her heel as the result of an overheated brick being placed in her bed. This method of warming a patient's bed was a routine duty performed by the nurses.

Held:

(1) A contract existed between the parties whereby the defendant hospital undertook to nurse the plaintiff. The injury to the plaintiff occurred through the negligence of the hospital's employee in carrying out this contract, thereby rendering the hospital vicariously liable.

(2) The test governing a hospital's liability for the negligence of a nurse is whether they undertook to nurse the plaintiff or whether they undertook only to display reasonable care in providing competent nurses.

(3) Where a nurse is not acting under the orders of a doctor, but is performing routine duties in her capacity as a servant of the hospital, the hospital will be held liable for any injury to a patient arising from the negligence of its nurse.

LAW v. GOMEL B.C.S.C. Macdonald J. No. 20493/72 June 1975 (unreported)

The defendant specialists performed surgery on and oversaw the post-operative recovery of the plaintiff who suffered severe pain and suffering until operated on for a serious infection by another surgeon called in by the defendants.

Held:

The defendants were not liable in negligence for failing to diagnose and treat the infection which ultimately required surgery. The evidence failed to establish a lack of reasonable care and skill, and other doctors found the defendant's case management to be reasonable and correct.

LAWSON v. WELLESLEY HOSP. [1978] 1 S.C.R. 893

The plaintiff, a patient in the defendant hospital, was struck in the face and injured by a psychiatric patient in the hospital.

Held:

A hospital has a duty towards visitors and other patients to supervise and control patients who the hospital knows or ought to know have a propensity to violence by virtue of their mental illness. The Mental Health Act, R.S.O. 1970, c. 559, does not relieve the hospital of liability for misconduct of a patient, even though the patient would escape liability owing to his mental illness.

LAYDEN v. COPE [1984] A.W.L.D. 3210 Alta. Q.B. No. 8301-02829 14th March 1984 (not yet reported)

The patient complained of a painful foot which was diagnosed and treated as gout by the two defendant general practitioners. The patient's condition deteriorated and he was transferred to another hospital where the condition was diagnosed as collulitis by the defendant internist. Because of the delay amputation of the foot was necessary.

Held:

(1) The internist was not negligent in his treatment of the patient.

(2) The two general practitioners were negligent in failing to refer the patient to a specialist when the patient failed to improve.

LEACHMAN v. MACLACHLAN [1984] B.C.W.L.D. 1004 B.C.S.C. No. C813325 23rd February 1984 (not yet reported)

The defendant orthopaedic surgeon used a combination of pins to reduce the plaintiff patient's fractured femur, a technique which was contrary to the manufacturer's recommendations and not used by other orthopaedic surgeons. Complications arose necessitating a second operation and eventually a hip fusion operation was performed 1½ years later, resulting in partial, permanent disability.

Held:

The defendant was negligent in using the combination technique. The pecuniary damages assessed were reduced by 50 per cent because of the possibility that the fracture would not have healed and a hip fusion would have been required even without the defendant's negligence.

LEADBETTER v. BRAND (1980) 107 D.L.R. (3d) 252 (N.S.T.D.)

The defendant dental surgeon performed an operation to extract seven teeth from the mouth of the plaintiff, who was under general anaesthetic administered by the defendant anaesthetist. During the surgery the plaintiff suffered a cardiac arrest which resulted in severe brain damage despite extensive emergency resuscitative treatment.

Held:

The defendant anaesthetist was not liable in negligence for his pre-treatment assessment or treatment of the plaintiff. The doctrine *res ipsa loquitur* did not apply, since it was not established that the injury could not have occurred without negligence. The defendant performed a thorough medical examination, considering the minor nature of the proposed surgery. He was entitled to rely on the information provided to him by the patient, who failed to mention her hypertension despite specific questions posed by the defendant and a nurse, and thereby concealed her susceptibility to cardiac disorder.

LEFEBVRE v. OSBORNE (1983) 22 A.C.W.S. (2d) 350 (Ont. H.C.)

A tissue sample was removed from the plaintiff during a tubal ligation sterilization operation and, due to a mix up in the hospital laboratory, was diagnosed as cancerous. As a result, the plaintiff underwent a further operation to remove her Fallopian tubes.

Held:

There is no evidence of negligence on the part of the surgeon or the pathologists. *Res ipsa loquitur* applied and the hospital was found negligent because it gave no explanation consistent with no negligence.

General damages: $10,000

LEGAULT-BELLEMARE v. MADORE [1975] C.S. 1249 (Que. S.C.)

The defendant dentist extracted one of the plaintiff's wisdom teeth after which she suffered from recurrent infections and protracted treatment until another dentist diagnosed and removed a residual piece of root.

Held:

Because of the plaintiff's continued problems, the defendant should have had appropriate X-rays done and was negligent in not doing so.

However, there was no liability because the plaintiff was barred by the limitations period in the Dental Act.

LENZEN v. SOUTHERN VANCOUVER ISLAND HOSP. SOC. B.C.S.C. 1975 (unreported)

The defendant physician ordered that a K-pad be used to relieve the plaintiff's back pain. After three hours the nurse noted that the patient's back was very red but continued the treatment, since the patient requested it. The plaintiff suffered burns to her back.

Held:

(1) The nurse was negligent in continuing to apply the K-pad when she observed the condition of the patient's back. She ought to have appreciated that further exposure to the heat would aggravate the condition she had already noted.
(2) The hospital was vicariously liable for the nurse's conduct, since her negligence occurred within the scope of her employment.
(3) The defendant physician was not liable for prescribing the use of the heating pad.

LEONARD v. KNOTT [1980] 1 W.W.R. 673 varying [1978] 5 W.W.R. 511 (B.C.C.A.)

The defendant radiologist undertook a kidney and urinary tract examination of the plaintiff, who was referred by the defendant specialist in internal medicine as part of an executive health package. The plaintiff died from a severe reaction to the injected contrast medium used in the radiological procedure.

B.C.S.C. Held:

The defendant internist was liable in negligence for ordering the procedure without clear clinical indications, and failing to take preliminary steps or consult with the plaintiff's family doctor. The precise nature if not the fatal extent of the risk was medically predictable and thus legally foreseeable, which a reasonable doctor would not neglect to act on.

B.C.C.A. Held:

The defendant radiologist was 25 per cent liable in negligence for performing the test even though he knew of the danger and considered it unjustified.   ·
General damages: $150,000

LLOY v. MILNER (1981) 15 Man. R. (2d) 187 (Q.B.)

A hospital resident, under the supervision of the defendant anaesthetist, administered the anaesthetic by injection into the back of the plaintiff's hand. Some anaesthetic escaped into the surrounding tissue resulting in prolonged pain and suffering and requiring skin grafts to repair the damage.

Held:

The resident was not negligent, and the defendant was therefore not liable for the plaintiff's injury. A doctor is not expected to be a guarantor of his work, and cannot be held liable for misadventures. In this case the result could have occurred to the most expert practitioner using the utmost care.
General damages: $3,500

LOGAN v. COLCHESTER (1928) 60 N.S.R. 62 (C.A.)

Because of a shortage of nurses in the defendant hospital, the physician engaged a special nurse to ensure that the plaintiff received adequate care. The plaintiff agreed to pay the extra fee for the nurse's services. Through the negligence of the special nurse, the patient was burned.

Held:

The special nurse was employed by the hospital, not by the plaintiff. A hospital is liable for the negligence of the nurses in its employment, unless the nurse is acting under the direct orders of a physician or surgeon in the operating room.

McBRIDE v. LANGTON (1982) 22 Alta. L.R. (2d) 174 (Q.B.)

The defendant obstetrician/gynaecologist performed laparoscopic sterilization surgery on the plaintiff, having discussed the procedure with the plaintiff but having failed to mention the risk of bowel perforation which did occur during the operation. The plaintiff suffered pain and sickness, prolonged by a subsequent misdiagnosis of pelvic inflammatory disease, ultimately requiring corrective surgery by another doctor.

Held:

(1) The defendant doctor was not liable in negligence for failing to disclose the risk of bowel perforation, since that risk was not material. The mere fact that a risk is serious does not necessarily make it material particularly where, as here, it is remote.

(2) The defendant doctor was liable for negligent post-operative care. No recourse was taken post-operatively to standard tests which were available and would have facilitated earlier diagnosis and more timely and effective treatment.

McCAFFREY v. HAGUE [1949] 2 W.W.R. 539 (Man. K.B.)

In the course of treating the plaintiff's eczema, the defendant physician used an X-ray machine that was not designed for that purpose. As a result of the excessive exposure, the plaintiff suffered severe burns.

Held:

(1) A higher degree of care is required of a physician who claims to be a specialist in a certain field.

(2) The defendant displayed a lack of proper skill and care in exposing the plaintiff to high intensity radiation for an excessive period.

McCARTY v. UNIVERSITY OF B.C. [1982] B.C.W.L.D. 917 B.C.S.C. Toy J. Vancouver No. C810795 15th March 1982 (not yet reported)

The plaintiff sought treatment on a number of occasions from the defendant clinic for symptoms including shortness of breath, which were eventually diagnosed as emphysema by a specialist referred by another doctor.

Held:

The defendant clinic was not liable, and its resident doctors were not negligent for failing to undertake further diagnostic tests or refer the plaintiff. Medical doctors are not required to guarantee success, and in this case the plaintiff did not meet the burden of proving negligence.

McCORMICK v. MARCOTTE [1972] S.C.R. 18

Rather than inserting an intermedullary nail as recommended by a consulted orthopaedic surgeon, and without informing the plaintiff, the defendant employed the obsolete "plate and screw method" because he was not qualified to perform the recommended method. Along with the development of an abscess in the wound, the positioning of the bone was unsatisfactory. The plaintiff suffered permanent partial incapacity.

Held:

The defendant chose an obsolete method of setting the bone, but apart from this, his treatment of the plaintiff was inept and inattentive. The defendant failed to live up to the standard of care expected of a doctor in a well-settled part of the province within easy reach of the largest centres of population.

McCULLIGH v. McLEAN (1983) 17 A.C.W.S. (2d) 246 (Ont. Co. Ct.)

When surgical dressings were removed from his nose, bleeding resulted causing the plaintiff to lose consciousness and fall from his bed.

Held:

Action dismissed. Plaintiff's claim that the physician left him on the bed with blood dripping into a basin was not made out by the evidence.

McDANIEL v. VANCOUVER GEN. HOSP. [1934] 3 W.W.R. 619 (P.C.)

While being treated for diphtheria in the defendant hospital, the infant plaintiff contracted smallpox. Smallpox patients had been placed in the rooms surrounding hers and the nurses who attended her had also attended the smallpox patients.

Held:

The hospital's system of handling communicable diseases did not constitute negligence since it conformed to approved practice in Canada and the United States.

MacDONALD v. ROSS (1983) 24 C.C.L.T. 242 (N.S.T.D.)

The defendant plastic surgeon performed a breast reduction operation on the plaintiff, removing 20 to 25 per cent more tissue from the left breast than from the right, which resulted in significant deformity and a disproportion in the relative sizes of the breasts. Corrective surgery was carried out by another doctor, with further attendant scarring.

Held:

(1) The defendant doctor was liable for negligently performing the operation. Although the purpose of the surgery was primarily therapeutic, there was at least a secondary concern about its cosmetic effect, and in any case an error of such magnitude constituted a breach of the standard of care for even therapeutic procedures.
(2) The defendant doctor was not liable in negligence for failing to appraise the plaintiff of the risk which materialized. The actual result was not reasonably forseeable to the defendant, and outside of the risks inherent in the procedure.

MacDUFF v. VRABEC (1982) 24 C.C.L.T. 239 (B.C.S.C.)

In the course of an action against a surgeon for negligently failing to disclose adequately the risks of the procedure, questions were asked by the defence as to other information about the surgery which the plaintiff received from a friend who was a doctor.

Held:

Evidence of information from sources other than the defendant was admissible and relevant to the issue of informed consent. The duty of disclosure must be met by information made available to the patient either directly by the surgeon himself or through other sources.

McFADYEN v. HARVIE [1941] O.R. 90 affirmed [1942] S.C.R. 390

In preparing to operate on the patient, the assistant surgeon sterilized the operative site with alcohol. After waiting for the alcohol to completely evaporate, the defendant surgeon applied a heated cautery to the site. A momentary flame appeared when the cautery was applied causing the patient to suffer a severe burn.

Ont. C.A. Held:

(1) Neither the defendant nor assistant surgeon were negligent in their conduct and res ipsa loquitur did not apply.
(2) There is no rule of law that the surgeon in charge of an operation bears the responsibility for the negligence of his assistant where that assistant is a qualified surgeon and possesses the necessary skill to perform the work entrusted to him.

S.C.C. — Affirmed

McKAY v. GILCHRIST (1962) 40 W.W.R. 22 (Sask. C.A.)

Due to the negligent driving of the defendant Gilchrist, the plaintiff's husband was involved in a car accident in which he sustained injuries to his knee. While the defendant doctors were performing an arthrotomy to treat these injuries, the patient suffered a cardiac arrest and died.

Held:

(1) The defendant doctors exhibited no negligence in administering the sedative and anaesthesia or in performing the surgery.
(2) Since the patient's death could not be attributed to the operation performed on his knee, no act or omission on the part of the defendant driver could be regarded as the cause of his death.
(3) The doctrine of res ipsa loquitur did not apply as the evidence relating to the patient's death failed to support an inference of negligence.

McKAY v. ROYAL INLAND HOSP. (1964) 48 D.L.R. (2d) 665 (B.C.S.C.)

The plaintiff, a patient suffering from multiple sclerosis, fell out of bed while trying to turn over onto her stomach. The guard rails had been left down because the defendant physician and defendant physiotherapist had decided that they would be detrimental to the patient's morale. The physiotherapist had taught the plaintiff how to turn in bed safely.

Held:

The plaintiff failed to establish negligence on the part of either defendant. Since the physiotherapist had instructed the patient in how to change position in bed, and the patient had previously performed the manoeuvre successfully, the physiotherapist could not have anticipated any danger.

McKEACHIE v. ALVAREZ (1970) 17 D.L.R. (3d) 87 (B.C.S.C.)

While performing an operation on the plaintiff's wrist, the surgeon inadvertently severed the radial nerve thereby causing the formation of a neuroma. The plaintiff suffered severe pain and disability which necessitated a further operation to restore the use of the hand.

Held:

(1) The surgeon was negligent in severing the nerve, since a reasonably skilful surgeon would have known that the nerve was located in the operative area and that particular care was required to avoid cutting it.
(2) An inexperienced or novice surgeon is expected to meet the same standard of competence as those who are reasonably skilled and proficient in the field of surgery.
(3) There were two causes of injury — previous accidents and the surgeon's negligence. The surgeon was therefore liable only for the damage he caused.

MacKINNON v. IGNACIO (1978) 29 N.S.R. (2d) 656 (T.D.)

The defendants, surgeons and an anaesthetist, performed a thyroid operation on the plaintiff's wife, during which the patient suffered a sudden cardiac arrest and died shortly thereafter.

Held:

(1) The defendants were not liable for negligence in carrying out the operation. The administration of anaesthetic, while the subject of some conflict of professional opinion, was acceptable, and the failure to use a cardiac monitor was not a contributing factor in the detection or subsequent unsuccessful treatment of the cardiac arrest.
(2) The defendant surgeon was not liable for failing to secure an informed consent to the operation, having explained the procedure to the plaintiff when she first complained of a thyroid problem, and having provided a consent form which was signed.

McLEAN v. WEIR [1980] 4 W.W.R. 330 (B.C.C.A.)

The defendant vascular surgeon referred the plaintiff, who was suffering from impaired circulation in his arms, to a hospital for an angiogram. The defendant radiologist performed the procedure, which rendered the plaintiff quadriplegic as a result of leakage of radiopaque contrast medium from the catheter into his spinal cord.

Held:

(1) The defendant vascular surgeon was not liable for failing to warn the plaintiff of the risks of angiography. Since he was not going to carry out any procedure on the plaintiff, there was nothing for the plaintiff to consent to.
(2) The defendant radiologist was not liable in battery for failing to warn of the risks of the procedure other than bruising or blood clotting at the incision, in the absence of an actual misdescription or misrepresentation of the nature or effect of the procedure.
(3) The defendant radiologist was not liable in negligence for failing to inform the plaintiff of the risk of paralysis. Since at the time of the incident the specific risk of paralysis was not generally known or known by the defendant, he did not breach his duty of disclosure by failing to mention it as part of an otherwise adequate explanation.

(4) The defendant radiologist was not liable for negligently performing the procedure, having conducted it with a generally accepted, fair and reasonable standard of care and competence. Negligence could not be inferred, since the defendant gave an explanation consistent with no negligence.

McNAMARA v. SMITH [1934] O.R. 249 (C.A.)

A medical student under the defendant's supervision accidentally removed part of the uvula, while performing a tonsillectomy. The plaintiff suffered permanent impairment of health, loss of sense of taste and change of speech tone.

Held:
The trial judge's finding was affirmed, based on expert testimony, that the injuries did not result from the removal of the uvula or from any other negligence occurring in the course of the operation. The plaintiff's action was dismissed because of his failure to prove that the injuries complained of resulted directly from the alleged negligence.

McQUAY v. EASTWOOD (1886) 12 O.R. 402 (C.A.)

The defendant physician instructed the plaintiff's sister in assisting with treatment methods during the plaintiff's confinement. The plaintiff developed septicaemia and sued the defendant for negligence in failing to properly instruct and supervise the home treatment.

Held:
The plaintiff failed to (a) present any evidence of neglect or of want of skill on the part of the defendant, and (b) to establish that her injuries were the result of a want of skill or neglect.

McTAGGART v. POWERS [1926] 3 W.W.R. 513 (Man. C.A.)

Following the extraction of several teeth from an anaesthetized patient, one tooth became lodged in the patient's lung. The tooth had to be surgically removed.

Held:
The evidence failed to establish that the tooth found in the patient's lung was one of those extracted. However, since the dentist could have negligently dislodged a tooth during the operation, thereby allowing it to enter the patient's trachea and lungs, a new trial was ordered.

MALE v. HOPMANS [1967] 2 O.R. 457 (C.A.)

In order to bring a staphylococcus haemolyticus infection of the plaintiff's knee joint under control, the defendant physician administered large doses of neomycin. Although the infection healed, the plaintiff became permanently deaf and suffered some kidney damage as a result of the drug used.

Held:
(1) Given the risk of the infection spreading and the development of osteomyelitis, the defendant was not negligent in treating the plaintiff with neomycin.
(2) The defendant was not required to warn the plaintiff of the dangerous side effects of the drug, since his patient would have experienced great difficulty in making an intelligent decision in view of the complicated and uncertain nature of the alternate modes of treatment.
(3) The defendant was negligent in failing to take the necessary precautions to ensure that the neomycin therapy was not affecting the plaintiff's hearing and renal system. Urinalysis and audiometric tests should have been performed frequently during the course of treatment.

MANG v. MASCOVITZ (1982) 37 A.R. 221 (Q.B.)

The defendant gynaecologist performed an abortion and a sterilization operation on the plaintiff, who emerged from the operating room with serious and ultimately permanent brain damage rendering her helpless and in need of 24 hour medical care for the remainder of her life.

Held:
(1) The defendants were not liable in negligence for failing to warn the plaintiff of the

risk of an air embolism in the course of the abortion, a complication which was established to have caused the injury. The plaintiff had no particular predisposition to such an injury and did not ask a specific question about it, and a prudent doctor in the defendant's position would not regard the risk as material. In any event on a balance of probabilities the plaintiff would not have been dissuaded from the operation by the disclosure of this risk.

(2) The defendants were not liable in negligence in carrying out the abortion and sterilization procedures, in the absence of proof of substandard care.

MARSHALL v. CURRY [1933] 3 D.L.R. 260 (N.S.S.C.)

During a hernia operation to which the plaintiff expressly consented, the defendant, discovering that the left testicle was grossly diseased, removed it in order to treat the hernia and to prevent any danger to the life and health of the plaintiff. The plaintiff brought action in assault and battery.

Held:

(1) Even in the absence of consent, if the conditions discovered during surgery make it imperative in the interests of protecting a patient's life and health for the surgeon to operate further, and if he performs the duty skilfully and with due prudence, no action will lie against him.

(2) The Statute of Limitations barred the plaintiff's claim. Actions of assault and battery must be commenced within one year after the cause of such action arises.

MARSHALL v. ROGERS [1943] 2 W.W.R. 545 (B.C.C.A.)

The defendant general practitioner prescribed a rapid reduction of the plaintiff's insulin dosage without performing daily tests to monitor his reaction. Although the defendant knew that the reduction procedure was dangerous, he relied solely on the patient's interpretation of his own symptoms. The plaintiff later required hospitalization for the treatment of his pre-coma condition.

Held:

Where the course of prescribed treatment is admittedly dangerous, a physician is negligent if he delegates to his patient his own professional duty of assessing the patient's true state of health.

MARTEL v. HOTEL-DIEU ST-VALLIER; VIGNEAULT v. MARTEL (1969) 14 D.L.R. (3d) 445 (S.C.C.)

The defendant anaesthetist asserted that he administered the anaesthetic with no deviation from past practices. The plaintiff suffered permanent paraplegy.

Held:

(1) Where injury is caused by a normally non-injurious procedure, there is a presumption that it was caused by negligence. The defendant failed to rebut this presumption by contending: (a) that the plaintiff was particularly sensitive to the anaesthetic; (b) that he believed, without exactly recalling, that he administered the anaesthetic carefully according to routine practice.

(2) The hospital was vicariously liable because the damage suffered by the plaintiff was caused by the defendant anaesthetist during the course of the execution of the functions for which he was employed by the hospital.

MELVIN v. GRAHAM [1973] D.R.S. 659 (Ont. H.C.)

During a herniotomy, the defendant surgeon negligently cut into the patient's bladder. Although he sutured the cut, hemorrhaging occurred about a week later.

Held:

The defendant was negligent in incising the bladder and in his suturing of the bladder wall. His negligence was heightened by his failure to provide any kind of post-operative care when he knew there might be complications from the surgery.

MEYER v. GORDON (1981) 17 C.C.L.T. 1
(B.C.S.C.)

The plaintiff mother was admitted to the defendant hospital for delivery of her baby, and after preliminary examination by a nurse, was left unattended in the labour room where she began to deliver. The plaintiff father alerted medical personnel who administered resuscitative treatment to the infant plaintiff, but failed to prevent partial asphyxia from meconium aspiration, and resultant cerebral palsy and brain damage.

Held:

(1) The defendant hospital was 75 per cent liable for the negligence of its nursing staff. The patient was not given a thorough examination, and was left unattended in spite of her pain and nausea, in a supine position which was a "marked departure" from standard hospital procedure and a recognized cause of the type of complication which ensued. The absence of attending staff to assist the infant at birth further contributed to the event giving rise to the injury. Taken as a whole, the breaches of duty by the nursing staff at least materially increased the risk of damage which occurred.

(2) The defendant family doctor of the mother was 25 per cent liable in negligence for failing to advise the hospital nurse to carry out a vaginal examination before administering a sedative. By failing, when advised of the mother's condition, to make his own assessment of the progress of labour by this means, the defendant materially increased the risk of the fetal distress going undetected.

(3) The defendant resident was not liable for negligent resuscitative treatment since, given the emergency circumstances, the child was resuscitated within a reasonable space of time, and the departure from the advocated standard was merely an error of judgment.

MEYER v. LEFEBVRE [1942] 1 W.W.R. 485 (Alta. C.A.)

A piece of gauze had been left in the patient following an appendectomy. At trial, the jury had found the surgeon negligent in his failure to conduct an X-ray examination of the operative site following the surgery.

Held:

A new trial was ordered, since the jury had not been presented with any evidence to indicate that an X-ray examination would have revealed the gauze.

MILLER v. UNITY UNION HOSP. BD. [1975] 6 W.W.R. 121 (Sask. C.A.)

The plaintiff sustained severe injuries when she slipped on "water spots" on the hospital hallway floor.

Held:

The failure of the defendant's inspection system to disclose the presence of small spots of liquid on the hallway floor did not constitute a breach of the duty owed to the plaintiff. The defendant did use reasonable care to prevent damage from what was an unusual danger.

MISERICORDIA HOSP. v. BUSTILLO [1983] Alta. D. 2632-01 Alta. C.A. Moir, Haddad & Stevenson JJ.A. Edmonton No. 14505 21st January 1983 (not yet reported)

The defendant surgeon, in the course of performing a cataract operation on the plaintiff, administered a solution which had incorrectly been supplied by the pharmacy department of the defendant hospital. The surgeon noticed an irregularity in the appearance of the solution but used it anyway, resulting in damage to the patient's eyes.

Held:

(1) The defendant doctor was 40 per cent liable for negligently failing to act on his initial suspicions about the solution by looking at the solution bottle when it was shown to him, thereby overlooking a clear opportunity to avoid the earlier negligence of the pharmacy and nurse.

(2) The defendant hospital was 60 per cent liable for the negligence of its pharmacy depart-

ment and the operating room nurse in providing an incorrect solution and in failing to recognize the mistake.

MOFFATT v. WITELSON (1980) 29 O.R. (2d) 7 (H.C.)

The defendant ophthalmologist treated the plaintiff, whose cornea had been perforated by splinters of a shattered eyeglass lens. The plaintiff subsequently contracted a wound infection which, though neutralized, rendered him blind in one eye.

Held:

(1) The defendant ophthalmologist was liable in negligence for failing to recognize the serious danger of infection attending a penetrating wound of the cornea, and to take steps to isolate and control it.

(2) Neither the defendant ophthalmologist nor the defendant optical dispensary were negligent in failing to warn the plaintiff against wearing glasses while engaged in rough play. There is no need in law for a professional person to warn of dangers that would be as apparent to the patient as to the doctor. Although the optical dispensary should have warned the plaintiff that the glasses were not unbreakable, on a balance of probabilities the failure to warn did not contribute to the injury suffered.

MOLNAR v. CONWAY Alta. T.D. Waite J. Calgary No. SC114193 22nd June 1978 (unreported)

The defendant psychiatrist diagnosed the plaintiff's condition as manic depression and prescribed a series of drugs including a stimulant. The plaintiff obtained additional quantities of the stimulant by ''shopping'' at various pharmacies, and suffered an overdose which hospitalized him temporarily.

Held:

The defendant was not liable for negligence, having met the requisite standard of care by prescribing the drugs in accordance with proper treatment of the plaintiff. If a patient obtains additional drugs deceitfully he alone must bear the consequnces.

MOORE v. LARGE (1932) 46 B.C.R. 179 (C.A.)

The defendant surgeon examined the plaintiff's shoulder and found no evidence of dislocation. He did not advise the plaintiff to have an X-ray on account of the expense, but told her to consult him again in a few days. After three months she consulted another physician who, upon taking an X-ray, discovered that the shoulder was dislocated. Due to an unknown abnormality in the plaintiff's bone structure, the dislocation could only be detected by X-rays.

Held:

The defendant surgeon displayed reasonable skill in his examination so that his failure to order an X-ray did not constitute negligence. The plaintiff's failure to consult a physician when she knew or ought to have known that her condition was not improving represented an unreasonable lack of care on her part.

MOORE v. SHAUGHNESSY HOSP. (1982) 15 A.C.W.S. (2d) 389 B.C.S.C. Esson J. 22nd July 1982 (not yet reported)

The defendants, specialists in gastroenterology, diagnosed the plaintiff's acute attack of colitis and prescribed intensive steroid therapy, failing to advise her of risks or alternative surgical treatment. Side effects of the steroid therapy included avascular necrosis which rendered the plaintiff severely disabled.

Held:

(1) The defendants were not liable for negligence in prescribing high-dose steroid therapy, as it was the appropriate treatment for the plaintiff's correctly diagnosed condition.

(2) The defendants were not liable for failing to inform the plaintiff of alternative treatments. Although the plaintiff was not adequately informed of the risks or alternatives, she would probably have consented to the treatment in any case.

MORROW v. McGILLIVRAY [1958] O.W.N. 41 (H.C.)

Held:

A chiropractor owes a duty to his patients to use the reasonable degree of care and skill which could be expected of a normal, prudent practitioner of the same experience and standing. This duty of care includes investigating an alleged complaint to ascertain whether or not it is within a chiropractor's field of treatment. Judgment for plaintiff.

MUDRIE v. McDONALD B.C.S.C. 1975 (unreported)

The defendant physician performed a pelvic examination on the plaintiff and then removed the IUD at the plaintiff's request. Two weeks later a pelvic inflammatory disease was discovered which resulted in the removal of the plaintiff's left fallopian tube.

Held:

The symptoms the plaintiff complained of at time of the pelvic examination would not have alerted a reasonable physician of the presence of the inflammatory condition.

MULLOY v. HOP SANG [1935] 1 W.W.R. 714 (Alta. C.A.)

Following examination under anaesthetic of the defendant's injured hand, the plaintiff proceeded to amputate it disregarding the defendant's express request not to amputate. The plaintiff sued for fees. The defendant counterclaimed for damages.

Held:

Although the operation was necessary and was performed in a highly satisfactory manner, the plaintiff's claim failed because he did not do the work he was hired to do. The defendant's claim succeeded on the basis of trespass to the person (battery) and entitled him to substantial damages.

MURANO v. GRAY (1982) 19 Alta. L.R. 393 (Q.B.)

The defendant dentist, in the process of extracting the plaintiff's teeth, inadvertently extracted one of the four teeth which were to be left to support dentures. The plaintiff claimed damages for loss of profits resulting from a delay in opening his new business.

Held:

The defendant was liable for negligently extracting the tooth. It could not be reinserted and as a result the plaintiff suffered additional pain and suffering and his dentures were probably not as satisfactory as they otherwise would have been. However, damages were not awarded for loss of profits, since the plaintiff's evidence as to his loss lacked credibility.

MURPHY v. GEN. HOSP. CORP. (1980) 25 Nfld. & P.E.I.R. 355 (Nfld. T.D.)

The plaintiff was taken to the emergency department of the defendant hospital for treatment of a dislocation fracture of his shoulder. X-rays were taken, whereupon the plaintiff's arm became paralyzed.

Held:

(1) The defendant hospital was not liable in negligence for the treatment of the plaintiff by hospital employees, having discharged its duty to the plaintiff very well and in a highly professional manner. There was no evidence indicating the cause of the paralysis or a breach of duty by the defendant hospital.

(2) Costs were not awarded against the plaintiff because the defendant failed to produce hospital records for inspection by the plaitiff. A certain degree of confidentiality is essential to the keeping of candid records; however, when a patient's lawyer seeks to see the patient's record, the hospital should comply while imposing reasonable safeguards against unnecessary publicity of the record.

MURPHY v. MATHIESON Alta. Dist. Ct. Belzil J. 1976 (unreported)

The defendant recommended that no treatment was necessary for the infant plaintiff's intermittent extropia. One month later an ophthalmologist performed corrective surgery. The plaintiff sued the defendant optometrist in negligence.

Held:

The plaintiff's action was barred because it was not commenced within the limitation period which begins from the date of the breach, negligent act, or omission, and not from the time when a plaintiff seeks other advice. This was not an injustice against the plaintiff because this was not a case of belated discovery of existing damage, nor was the defendant under a contractual retainer which would render him responsible for treatment until the plaintiff sought other advice.

MURPHY v. ST. CATHARINES GEN. HOSP. [1964] 1 O.R. 239 (H.C.)

In attempting to restore an intravenous injection by the use of a unit called "Intercath", the defendant intern severed and lost nine inches of the catheter in the basilic vein of the plaintiff's left arm. Apart from his own reading of the instructions printed on the packaging, the defendant intern had not received instruction in the use of this relatively new method.

Held:

(1) The pharmaceutical company was not negligent in its design or manufacture of the unit or in failing to give warning of a dangerous article. The circumstances of its use were such as to dispense with the necessity of an express warning. Furthermore, they did publish and distribute to the hospital staff member responsible for purchasing the item, a brochure containing detailed instructions and warnings.

(2) In failing to provide proper advice, direction and supervision to its staff regarding the use of the "Intercath," the hospital failed to meet the requisite standard of care and was therefore liable in negligence.

(3) The defendant intern was negligent in failing to follow the printed instructions, in his choice of an injection site, and in not seeking assistance from a staff member trained in the use of the unit.

MURRAY v. McMURCHY [1949] 1 W.W.R. 989 (B.C.S.C.)

During a Caesarian operation on the plaintiff, the defendant surgeon discovered fibroid tumours in the uterine wall. This fact increased the possible hazards of a second pregnancy; therefore he proceeded to tie the plaintiff's fallopian tubes. The plaintiff brought an action in trespass for damages resulting from this unauthorized procedure.

Held:

If a surgical procedure is necessary at the time for the protection and preservation of the life and health of a patient then a surgeon is entitled to proceed without the consent which is normally required. In this case, since the procedure was performed out of convenience without the plaintiff's consent, it constituted a trespass.

MURRIN v. JANES [1949] 4 D.L.R. 403 (Nfld. S.C.)

The plaintiff experienced excessive bleeding after the defendant dentist removed his teeth. Believing that bleeding was beneficial, the patient waited until he was extremely weak before going to the hospital. The plaintiff claimed damages for loss of earnings.

Held:

The dentist was under no duty to expressly warn the plaintiff of the effect of the loss of an excessive amount of blood, since any normally intelligent adult would be expected to appreciate the effect. The plaintiff's delay in obtaining proper medical attention was the sole cause of his subsequent loss.

NASH v. OLSON [1982] B.C.W.L.D. 208 B.C.S.C. McKay J. Vancouver No. B781010

4th December 1982 (not yet reported) affirmed B.C.C.A. No. CA820396 1st March 1984 (not yet reported)

The defendant emergency room physicians attended to the plaintiff who had been injured in an automobile accident. The plaintiff was rendered quadriplegic and alleged that the defendants failed to administer timely treatment to prevent the damage from occurring.

Held:

The defendants were not liable for negligent treatment of the plaintiff, since the damage was "complete and irreversible" prior to the plaintiff being attended by the doctors, and since in any case the standard of care was met.

NELLIGAN v. CLEMENT (1939) 67 K.B. 328 (Que.)

After operating on the plaintiff's thumb to treat an infection, the surgeon advised that the thumb not be interefered with for six months. Two weeks later another physician sent the plaintiff to the defendant surgeon who operated on the thumb. Following the operation, the infection recurred leaving the plaintiff's hand partially crippled.

Held:

The defendant's intervention was undertaken in accordance with approved practice and the evidence did not establish that the recurrence of infection was the result of any negligence on the part of the defendant.

NESBITT v. HOLT [1953] 1 S.C.R. 143

The defendant dentist placed the plaintiff's husband under a general anaesthetic in order to extract several teeth. During the operation a sponge became lodged in the patient's trachea. Despite the defendant's efforts to revive him by artificial respiration, the patient died of asphyxia.

Held:

By failing to check and see that all the sponges were accounted for, the defendant showed a lack of the ordinary care and prudence which the law demands.

NEUFELD v. MCQUITTY (1979) 18 A.R. 271 (T.D.)

The defendant administered an injection to the hand of the plaintiff as part of a chemotherapy treatment. Some of the extremely toxic drug escaped into the surrounding tissue resulting in a severe skin burn requiring corrective surgery.

Held:

The defendant was not liable for negligence in administering the injection, having carefully followed the standard procedure for injecting the drug, without complaint from the plaintiff or noticeable complication.

NEUFVILLE v. SOBERS (1983) 18 A.C.W.S. (2d) 407 Ont. H.C. Holland J. 3rd March 1983 (not yet reported)

The defendant family doctor made a tentative diagnosis of the plaintiff's condition as diabetes and requested that he undergo laboratory tests. The laboratory failed to advise the doctor of the test results until four days later, whereupon the plaintiff was admitted to the hospital but subseqeuntly died of a cardiac arrest.

Held:

(1) The defendants laboratory and laboratory technician were liable in negligence for failing to communicate the abnormal test results, verbally or in writing, in a timely fashion.
(2) The defendant family doctor was not liable for failing to diagnose the plaintiff's medical problem, assuming reasonably that the laboratory would have promptly communicated abnormal results.
(3) The defendant emergency physicians were not liable for negligent treatment of the plaintiff, having met the applicable standard of care.

NICHOLS v. GRAY [1980] B.C.D. Civ. 2632-03 B.C.S.C. Toy J. Vancouver Nos. C776057 & C791471 2nd June 1980 (unreported)

Shortly after giving birth, the plaintiff was treated by the defendant family doctor for symptoms of a vaginal infection, and was referred to the defendant specialists in obstetrics and gynaecology, who undertook all necessary diagnostic procedures and allowed the plaintiff to return home when her condition improved. Similar symptoms recurred and were diagnosed as a very serious infection requiring open-heart surgery and rendering the plaintiff a semi-invalid.

Held:

(1) The defendant family doctor was not liable in negligence for the injuries suffered by the plaintiff, having transferred the responsibility for the care of his patient to specialists more qualified to do so.

(2) The defendant specialists were not liable in negligence for prematurely discharging the plaintiff from the hospital or failing to give her instructions to follow in the event of recurring symptoms. The treatment process, including the discharge of the plaintiff from the hospital, was carried out in accordance with standard procedures and constituted at most an error of judgment.

NYBERG v. PROVOST MUN. HOSP. BD. [1927] S.C.R. 226

While the plaintiff was still unconscious following an operation, he suffered severe burns to his legs as the result of a nurse placing a hot water bottle in his bed. Another bottle filled from the same source had already been removed from the plaintiff's chest because the nurse had noted that it was leaving a red mark.

Held:

(1) Upon admitting the plaintiff, the defendant hospital entered a contract to nurse the patient.

(2) After noticing that the second water bottle was too hot, the nurse was negligent in failing to check the temperature of the bottle placed in the plaintiff's bed.

(3) Ensuring that hot water bottles were safely placed in a patient's bed represented part of the nurse's routine duty, thereby rendering the hospital vicariously liable for her negligence in performing that duty.

NYKIFORUK v. LOCKWOOD [1941] 1 W.W.R. 327 (Sask. Dist. Ct.)

Assuming that the defendant dentist would recall her dental history, the plaintiff cursorily indicated the upper molar which she wanted removed. The defendant interpreted this ambiguous gesture as an instruction to remove two lower molars and his examination substantiated that they could be the cause of her complaints. The plaintiff brought an action for unauthorized removal of the lower molars.

Held:

It is unquestionable that a dentist should endeavour to get clear instructions as to what is required, but there is also a duty upon the patient to be careful not to mislead the dentist in giving the instructions and not to assume, as the plaintiff did in this case, that a busy professional man is going to remember what transpired two years ago. The plaintiff, alone, is responsible for the mistake.

O'CONNELL v. MUNRO (1983) 22 A.C.W.S. (2d) 349 (Ont. H.C.)

The defendant plastic surgeon performed surgery on the plaintiff to correct upper jaw and teeth protrusion and told her to see him three weeks later. Due to the lack of blood supply, the plaintiff suffered a loss of bone and teeth so that she had to wear upper dentures and required further surgery.

Held:

(1) The defendant was liable for negligent post-operative care because he should have seen the plaintiff one week after discharge from the hospital.

(2) The plaintiff would have undergone the operation even if she had known of the risks, so there was no liability for the defendant's failure to inform her of the special risks.

O'REILLY v. SPRATT (1982) 19 A.C.W.S. (2d) 136 Ont. H.C. Maloney J. 18th November 1982 (not yet reported)

The defendant cardiovascular/thoracic surgeon performed an operation on the mother of the plaintiffs to remove her lung. While the patient was in post-operative intensive care, ligatures which had been applied to close the pulmonary artery slipped, resulting in internal bleeding and ultimately her death.

Held:

The defendant was not liable for the negligent performance of the procedure, having used an accepted procedure and having relied on his experience and skill in making a judgment in very difficult circumstances.

OSBURN v. MOHINDRA (1980) 29 N.B.R. (2d) 340 (Q.B.)

The defendant general practitioner attended the plaintiff in the emergency room of the defendant hospital, diagnosing and treating his wrist injury as multiple fractures, but failing to diagnose an additional dislocation. X-rays of the wrist indicated a dislocation but the radiologist's report was not brought to the treating doctor's attention. The plaintiff suffered prolonged pain and discomfort and, despite diagnosis and corrective treatment by another doctor, sustained permanent disability of the wrist and hand.

Held:

(1) The plaintiff was 25 per cent contributorily negligent for his injury. Of the remaining 75 per cent, the defendant doctor was 75 per cent liable for negligence in diagnosing and treating the plaintiff's injury by failing to recognize danger signals when they appeared, and by failing to carry out a thorough examination where indicated. The X-rays ought to have aroused suspicion in the mind of a normal prudent practitioner of the defendant's standing and experience, and have led him to seek the counsel of, or refer the patient to a specialist. Prompt, adequate treatment would probably have facilitated a quicker and more complete recovery.
(2) The defendant hospital was 25 per cent liable for the failure of its agent, the radiologist,

"to communicate the results and interpretations of the X-ray films" to the defendant. The hospital had a contractual obligation to provide the plaintiff with medical services, including careful organization of its system of work, and the lack of a procedure to transfer information from the radiologist to the attending physician was a breach of that duty.

OSTASH v. SONNENBERG (1968) 63 W.W.R. 257 (Alta. C.A.)

Due to the negligent conversion to natural gas of the heating and hot water systems in their home, the plaintiffs were poisoned by the escape of carbon monoxide fumes. The defendant physician discarded the escape of natural gas as a possible cause of their influenza-like symptoms because he detected no odour and because the incidence of influenza was fairly numerous at that time.

Held:

The defendant's diagnosis was an error in judgment and not an act of unskilfullness or carelessness for which he could be held liable.

OSTROWSKI v. LOTTO [1973] S.C.R. 220

The defendant diagnosed the need for and performed a MacMurray osteotomy on the plaintiff. In assessing her post-operative condition, the defendant foresaw the possibility of non-union. After leaving the hospital, the plaintiff sought other medical advice and non-union was diagnosed. The plaintiff brought an action against the defendant for negligent performance of the operation and post-operative treatment.

Held:

The expert evidence presented by the plaintiff did not conflict with the pre- and post-operative diagnoses made by the defendant. Furthermore, the medical opinion presented as a whole clearly established that there was no want of reasonable care and skill in the performance of the operation. The plaintiff failed to discharge her burden of proving that the defendant was negligent.

PARK v. STEVENSON MEMORIAL HOS-
PITAL (1974) unreported (Ont. H.C.)

The plaintiff suffered a fracture of the tibia
and fibula of the left leg which was reduced
by Dr. J. Derjanecz on Saturday afternoon.
On Monday afternoon Dr. B. Derjanecz failed
to diagnose vascular deficiency from the obvious symptoms recorded in the nurses' notes.
On Tuesday afternoon Dr. J. Derjanecz transferred the plaintiff to the Toronto General Hospital for operative treatment which has left her
with a scarred, shortened and angulated leg
with moderate muscle loss.

Held:
(1) Dr. B. Derjanecz was negligent in failing
to diagnose the circulatory impairment at the
time of her Monday visit. She was liable for
the plaintiff's damages because had active
treatment been started earlier the plaintiff's
muscle loss would have been reduced.
(2) As Dr. B.D. was a qualified medical practitioner to whom the case of the plaintiff had
been assigned, Dr. J. Derjanecz could not be
held vicariously responsible for her negligence,
nor was he negligent in assigning the plaintiff
to the care of his wife in the circumstances that
existed.

PARKIN v. KOBRINSKY (1963) 46 W.W.R.
193 (Man. C.A.)

Without taking an X-ray, the defendant surgeon applied a walking cast to treat a simple
transverse fracture of the plaintiff's ankle. The
plaintiff suffered considerable pain and an X-ray
taken two weeks later showed displacement of
the bones. The defendant performed two unsuccessful operations in an attempt to correct the
problem and ultimately the ankle was fused by
another surgeon.

Held:
(1) The defendant was negligent in failing to
take X-rays before and after applying the cast
in order to ensure that the bones remained in
the proper position for healing.
(2) The defendant's failure to recognize that
the continuation of severe pain indicated the

possibility of a displacement represented a departure from the required standard of skill and
care.
(3) The defendant's negligence was the substantial cause of the plaintiff's injury.

PARSONS v. SCHMOK (1975) 58 D.L.R.
(3d) 622 (B.C.S.C.)

Although the defendant physician had recorded
high blood pressure readings for the plaintiff
during the past two years, he had not prescribed medication to treat his hypertension.
The plaintiff suffered a stroke.

Held:
Upon observing the plaintiff's high blood pressure reading on several occasions, the defendant should have conducted further investigations. However, his failure to treat the plaintiff's
hypertensive condition did not constitute
negligence, since such treatment would not
have averted the subsequent stroke.

PATTERSON v. DE LA BASTIDE (1983) 22
A.C.W.S. (2d) 244 (Ont. H.C.)

The defendant specialist in otolarynology performed four operations on the plaintiff patient
to clear up a chronic running nose. The plaintiff subsequently suffered diplopia and a tugging sensation in her left eye. Further surgery
corrected the tugging sensation but the diplopia remained.

Held:
The defendant was not liable as there was no
evidence that the standard of care was not met
and the doctrine of res ipsa loquitur was not
applicable, since it could not be said that the
fracture of the floor of the orbit which gave
rise to the complications would not occur unless
the surgeon was negligent.

PELLERIN v. STEVENSON (1948) 18 M.P.R.
345 (N.B.C.A.)

The defendant physician treated the plaintiff's
fractured toes and requested that the plaintiff

report to him on specific dates to allow him to check the toes. The plaintiff failed to keep these appointments because he was hospitalized in another city for stomach ulcers. After two months the fracture had mended.

When the plaintiff asked the defendant to send a form to the Workmen's Compensation Board the defendant refused because the plaintiff had failed to report to him as requested. A later X-ray revealed an existing fracture in one of the plaintiff's toes.

Held:

(1) By binding the plaintiff's toes with tape in order to immobilize them, the defendant had conformed to the recognized standard of treatment and was therefore not liable in negligence. There was no evidence that the fracture disclosed by the later X-ray was the same one that the defendant had treated.

(2) The defendant's refusal to send the form to the W.C.B. did not prejudice the plaintiff's claim for compensation. Hence, the plaintiff suffered no damage.

PENNER v. BETHEL HOSP. SOC. (1981) 8 Man. R. (2d) 310 (Q.B.)

The eight-year-old son of the plaintiffs, left by his grandmother unattended in the waiting room of the defendant hospital, climbed on to a coat rack and was injured when it toppled over.

Held:

The defendant hospital was not liable in negligence for inadequate supervision of the child, since the accident was unforeseeable and a finding of liability would make the hospital an insurer.

PENNER v. THEOBALD (1962) 40 W.W.R. 216 (Man. C.A.)

The defendant chiropractor treated the plaintiff's lower back pain by administering a "lumbar roll." Although the defendant suspected that the plaintiff was suffering from an extruded disc and knew that the plaintiff had experienced severe back pain following the "lumbar

roll" he performed that same treatment three more times. The plaintiff had to undergo surgery for an extruded disc.

Held:

(1) A chiropractor must display the same degree of care as could reasonably be expected of the ordinary, careful and competent chiropractor.

(2) A chiropractor's conduct must be judged against the methods and practices normally adopted by the field of health care of which he is a member. His conduct is not measured against that of a medical doctor.

(3) A chiropractor is not liable for an honest mistake in judgment. In view of the possibility that the plaintiff had an extruded disc, the defendant's administration of a "lumbar roll" amounted to a reckless disregard of his own judgment for which he was liable.

PENTLAND v. PENTLAND (1978) 20 O.R. (2d) 27 (H.C.)

The mother and legal guardian of a 17-year-old boy seriously injured in a motorcycle accident and, in the opinion of attending doctors, requiring life-saving blood transfusions, refused to consent to the treatment on religious grounds, her son being incapable of consenting at the time. The applicants, including the respondent's estranged husband, sought a variation of the custody order to allow another party to consent on the child's behalf.

Held:

The order was granted to the grandmother, even though the natural father requested it. Every child has a fundamental right to the best medical care available in his community, and if neglected to the extent that such treatment is wilfully withheld by a parent or guardian, a duty of the court arises to transfer custody of the child to a party who will not deny this fundamental right.

PEPIN v. HOPITAL DU HAUT RICHELIEU (1983) 24 C.C.L.T. 259 (Que. C.A.)

An X-ray technician, employed by the defendant hospital, X-rayed the wrong finger on the plaintiff's hand, resulting in a diagnosis of a sprain rather than a fracture. The fracture was subsequently diagnosed at another hospital and required surgery to correct the deformity which had developed.

Held:

The defendant hospital was liable for the negligence of the X-ray technician, and the diagnosing doctor was negligent for failing to notice the incorrect X-ray during a subsequent visit by the plaintiff. The damage was caused by the acts of the hospital, since a correct diagnosis would likely have precluded the need for corrective surgery.

PETIT v. HOPITAL STE. JEANNE d'ARC (1940) 78 S.C. 564 (Que. S.C.)

The plaintiff's infected finger was treated according to usual and accepted practice. When the infection could not be brought under control, the physicians decided that amputation was necessary.

Held:

(1) A hospital is not responsible for the negligence of the physicians and surgeons who carry on their practice in that hospital.

PETITE v. MACLEOD [1955] 1 D.L.R. 147 (N.S.C.C.)

The plaintiff had undergone three operations at the same site. She alleged that it was during the hernia operation undertaken by the defendant surgeon that a sponge tape was left in the incision. On that occasion, two nurses had counted the sponges used and both had arrived at a correct count.

Held:

The evidence indicated that the sponge could have been left in the plaintiff's abdomen during a prior operation. Therefore, the defendants were not liable.

PETTY v. MACKAY (1979) 10 C.C.L.T. 85 (B.C.S.C.)

The defendant plastic surgeon performed surgery on the plaintiff, an exotic dancer, to remove excess skin from her abdominal area, using a modified technique in accordance with her wishes. The defendant did not inform the plaintiff of a five to ten per cent risk of complications attending the procedure. Complications ensued resulting in deformity, scarring and continued unsightliness.

Held:

The defendant was not liable in negligence for failing to inform the plaintiff of the risk of complications. Notwithstanding the plaintiff's evidence to the contrary, a reasonable prudent person in the plaintiff's position would have gone ahead with the operation even if informed of the five to ten per cent risk.

PICHE v. ING (1983) 22 A.C.W.S. (2d) 297 (Ont. H.C.)

The plaintiff patient went to see the defendant ophthalmologist because of sudden loss of vision in her left eye. The defendant diagnosed a small cataract when the patient actually had a detached retina. Because of delay in surgical intervention, the patient lost vision in her eye to the extent that she became legally blind in that eye.

Held:

The doctor was liable for misdiagnosis. A reasonably competent ophthalmologist would have considered retinal detachment in the circumstances.

PIERCE v. STRATHROY HOSP. (1924) 27 O.W.N. 180 (H.C.)

Six months after an abdominal operation, X-rays revealed that the plaintiff's continuing pain was caused by a drainage tube which had been left in the wound. The defendant physician who had performed the surgery continued to treat the plaintiff for four months after the tube was discovered. The plaintiff commenced this action after one year from the date when, in the matter complained of, the defendant's professional services terminated.

Held:

If the defendant physician had no suspicion that the tube was in the wound, he was grossly ignorant; if he did suspect, he was negligent and should be held liable for negligence. However, the defendant is saved by the Ontario Medical Act which provides that the plaintiff's action must fail as it was not commenced within the one year limitation period.

POULIN v. HEALTH SCIENCES CENTRE (1982) 18 Man. R. (2d) 274 affirmed 22 A.C.W.S. 166 (C.A.)

The defendant doctor treated the plaintiff's leg fractures, applying casts but allowing an overlap of the bones at the fracture site. The plaintiff subsequently developed a hip rotation which rendered her seriously disabled.

Held:

(1) The defendant was not liable for negligent treatment of the fractures. A bone overlap represented the method most conducive to healing of the fracture, the only other reasonable alternative having been refused by the plaintiff. Moreover the disability resulted from the hip rotation which was unrelated to the complications attending the fracture.
(2) The defendant was not liable for negligent counselling, since the plaintiff received a reasonable explanation of the available alternatives.

POWELL v. GUTTMAN (1978) 6 C.C.L.T. 183 (Man. C.A.)

The defendant orthopaedic specialist inserted steel pins into the plaintiff's hip as part of the treatment of her leg fracture. The plaintiff subsequently developed a degenerative bone condition around the pin site, and underwent surgery by the second defendant to replace the

head of the thigh bone, suffering another fracture in the process.

Held:

(1) The defendant orthopaedic specialist was liable for negligent care of the plaintiff's case subsequent to the initial treatment of the fracture, since the degenerative condition which developed was a common complication of the procedure which should have been recognized and treated before it in fact was.
(2) The defendant's liability extended to the fracture suffered during further surgery by another doctor because the defendant's negligence caused the plaintiff's leg to be more susceptible to fracture during the corrective procedure. Where a tortfeasor creates or materially contributes to a significant risk of injury occurring and the injury does not occur, then the tortfeasor is liable for the injury even if there are subsequent factors causing or materially contributing to the injury.
(3) The second defendant surgeon was not liable for negligently performing the corrective surgery. Where, as in this case, the bone is soft a fracture of the type that occurred can occur without negligence, being merely an error of judgment.

PRICE v. MILAWSKI (1977) 18 O.R. (2d) 113 (C.A.)

While playing soccer, the plaintiff fractured his ankle. The defendant physician, working in the emergency department, inadvertently ordered an X-ray of the plaintiff's foot instead of his ankle and consequently concluded that there was no fracture. Experiencing continuing pain, the plaintiff consulted his family doctor who diagnosed his injury as a torn ligament based upon the hospital records, which reported no fracture of the ankle. Because the ankle was still extremely swollen and painful two months later, the plaintiff was examined by the defendant orthopaedic surgeon who also relied on the erroneous hospital records in treating the patient. Another surgeon finally discovered the fracture but the plaintiff was left with some permanent disability as the result of the long delay in receiving appropriate treatment.

Held:

(1) The defendant who saw the plaintiff in emergency was negligent in both ordering the wrong X-ray and in his failure to realize that the X-ray he examined was a view of the plaintiff's foot and not his ankle.

(2) The defendant family doctor conformed to the required standard of skill and care, since a general practitioner could not be expected to examine X-rays and check the accuracy of a radiologist's reports.

(3) The defendant orthopaedic surgeon was liable for his failure to personally refer to the original X-rays and for his failure to take new ones in view of the lack of improvement in the plaintiff's condition.

QUIROZ v. AUSTRUP (1982) 17 A.C.W.S. (2d) 245 Ont. H.C. Montgomery J. 8th December 1982 (not yet reported)

The defendant doctor treated the female plaintiff during her pregnancy and delivery, failing to carry out tests which would have revealed that she was a gestational diabetic. The infant plaintiff was born with birth defects.

Held:

The defendant was not liable for negligent treatment of the female plaintiff. It was not proven that the diagnosis and treatment of gestational diabetes, nor a delivery by Caesarian section, would have prevented the damage which occurred.

RADCLYFFE v. RENNIE [1965] S.C.R. 703

During an operation in 1961, a piece of gauze was discovered near the plaintiff's kidney. The gauze was not radiopaque and could have been left in the plaintiff during an operation performed in 1944 by Dr. Rennie or during a 1959 operation performed by Dr. McBeath.

Held:

The plaintiff failed to prove on a balance of probabilities that the gauze had been inserted during the 1959 operation. The operative site of 1959 was isolated from the place in which

the gauze was discovered by a layer of tissue and an X-ray taken in 1947 indicated the presence of some substance at the point where the gauze was finally located. An action for the 1944 operation would have been statute-barred.

RAWLINGS v. LINDSAY (1982) 20 C.C.L.T. 301 (B.C.S.C.)

The defendant oral surgeon removed the plaintiff's wisdom teeth, advising beforehand of a ten per cent risk of nerve damage causing numbness, but failing to elaborate on the duration of the numbness or other side effects. The plaintiff suffered nerve damage resulting in long-term facial numbness as well as hypersensitivity and considerable pain and discomfort.

Held:

The defendant was liable in negligence for failing to disclose adequately the risks attending the surgery. A medical person must disclose all material, special or unusual risks, that is "those risks to which a reasonable patient would likely attach significance in deciding whether or not to undergo the proposed treatment." A five to ten per cent risk of nerve impairment is not a miniscule risk attended by serious consequences requiring disclosure of all attendant symptoms. A reasonable person in the plaintiff's position would not have undergone the procedure had she been properly apprised of the risks.

R. v. CYRENNE (1981) 62 C.C.C. (2d) 238 (Ont. Dist. Ct.)

The accused, the father and mother of a seriously ill 12-year-old child, refused to consent to a blood transfusion for the child and with the assistance of their minister (the third accused), removed the child from the hospital when they perceived that a transfusion would be administered despite their refusal. The child who had not been formally consulted but had, according to her mother said "No," died days later.

Held:

The accused were not guilty of criminal negligence in the death of their child. Having regard to the information available to them in light of their knowledge, background, training and experience at the time of the decision, on an objective test reasonable parents in the position of the accused would not have denied their child the only hope of avoiding death. However, in this case it was not established beyond a reasonable doubt that the actions of the accused caused the child's death, since a transfusion might have been ineffective or even fatal.

R. v. GIARDINE (1939) 71 C.C.C. 295 (Ont. Co. Ct.)

The defendant surgeon administered diarsonal instead of the drug which he had ordered when he failed to check the label of the ampule containing the drug which a nurse had mistakenly set out for him. The patient died as a result of the injection.

Held:

Because the defendant was justified in assuming that the drug supplied by the nurse was the drug he ordered there is not sufficient evidence of gross negligence, or wanton misconduct or *mens rea* to render him criminally responsible.

R. v. HOMEBERG [1921] 1 W.W.R. 1061 (Alta. C.A.)

The defendant chiropractor treated a 15-year-old girl for spinal problems when she was actually suffering from appendicitis. She died two days later.

Held:

(1) Since the defendant did not undertake to "administer surgical or medical treatment," he was not guilty of manslaughter under s. 246 of the Criminal Code.
(2) The evidence did not establish that the defendant's failure to diagnose appendicitis caused the girl's death.

R. v. ROGERS (1968) 65 W.W.R. 193 (B.C.C.A.)

The defendant physician treated a one-year-old child for exfoliative dermatitis by placing him on a low protein diet. Within two months the child died of gross malnutrition. The defendant was not licensed at the time, since he had been struck off the rolls six years before.

Held:

A doctor is under a duty to possess reasonable medical knowledge and any practitioner possessing such knowledge would have foreseen the ultimate result of the defendant's treatment. Hence, the defendant was criminally negligent in persisting with his treatment in view of the dangerous consequences of which he was taken to have foreseen.

R. v. WATSON [1936] 2 W.W.R. 560 (B.C.C.A.)

The defendant physician failed to diagnose that the patient was suffering from a perinephritic abscess. Although the defendant recommended surgery, the operation was performed too late and the patient died.

Held:

Before a doctor can be found criminally negligent under s. 246 of the Criminal Code, the evidence must establish that he omitted to administer "surgical or medical treatment" known to him or which should have been known to him and that such an omission caused the patient's death. The Crown failed to prove either.

REIBL v. HUGHES [1980] 2 S.C.R. 880

The plaintiff consented to surgery to unblock an artery in his neck in the erroneous belief that this surgery would relieve his persistent headaches. He was not apprised of the risk of mortality or morbidity attending the procedure, nor that the surgery would not cure his headaches. As a result of the operation the plaintiff suffered a massive stroke which paralyzed the right side of his body and rendered him impotent.

Held:

(1) The defendant neurosurgeon was not liable in battery for failing to disclose the risk of

mortality or morbidity. Battery actions is respect of medical treatment should be confined to cases where consent is not given at all, or where the treatment administered exceeds the consent given, or where consent is induced by fraud or misrepresentation.

(2) The defendant was liable in negligence for failing to disclose the material risk of mortality or morbidity attending the procedure. A doctor must answer all questions posed by the patient and without prompting disclose the nature and seriousness of the proposed treatment and any material or special or unusual risks which may arise. The risks of undergoing surgery were not immediate here and in the circumstances a reasonable person, if properly informed, would have declined to undergo the procedure.

REYNARD v. CARR 28th December 1983 No. C772920 (B.C.S.C.) (unreported)

The plaintiff patient was suffering from ulcerative colitis and was referred by his general practitioner to a specialist in gastroenterology. The specialist prescribed a steroid drug, prednisone which the patient took for two years, when he developed a vascular necrosis, a known side effect of the drug. The patient required total hip and shoulder replacements.

Held:

Both the general practitioner and gastroenterologist were liable in negligence. The reasonable, competent doctor should have known about the side effects of the drug and should have informed the patient.

RICHARDSON v. NUGENT (1918) 40 D.L.R. 701 (N.B.C.A.)

The defendant physician thought the plaintiff was suffering from rheumatic fever and treated him accordingly. The plaintiff's condition grew worse prompting the plaintiff to consult another doctor who diagnosed his case as pleurisy and performed an operation to drain off the fluid. At trial, the plaintiff was permitted to show his unhealed incision to the jury.

Held: New trial ordered

(1) In an action for medical malpractice, the plaintiff is not permitted to exhibit to the jury the part of his body involved when such a display serves no other purpose than to arouse the jurors' sympathy.

(2) The defendant's error in diagnosis did not aggravate the plaintiff's condition so as to render the subsequent operation necessary.

RICKLEY v. STRATTON (1912) 3 O.W.N. 1341 (H.C.)

The defendant physician placed the child's broken leg in splints and warned the mother that the leg would not heal properly if the splints were interfered with. The defendant did not visit the child for two weeks but told the parents to call him if anything happened. During the two weeks the bone was displaced, leaving the leg crooked. There was some evidence that the mother tampered with the splint in order to ease the child's pain.

Held:

The defendant was not negligent in failing to see the child for two weeks, since he had instructed the parents to inform him if any displacement occurred.

RIETZE v. BRUSER [1979] 1 W.W.R. 31; [1979] 1 W.W.R. 27; [1979] 1 W.W.R. 55 (Man. Q.B.)

The defendant orthopaedic surgeon performed a bone graft procedure on the plaintiff's arm to strengthen a bone weakened by Paget's disease, and undertook post-operative treatment in response to symptoms of pain and swelling which he concluded to be psychological. After being discharged from the hospital the plaintiff developed a serious circulatory impairment which destroyed muscle tissue in her left arm resulting in deformity and disability.

Held:

(1) The defendant was liable for negligent post-operative treatment of the plaintiff. While free-

dom from post-operative infection cannot be ensured, a reasonable medical specialist should be capable of prompt recognition and timely treatment of such a complication, particularly where as in this case the condition is unique or unusual. Moreover, the defendant was unable to meet the burden arising from the application of *res ipsa loquitur*.

(2) Medical reports dealing with matters other than the plaintiff's medical condition were admissible, since the authors had "personal knowledge of the matters dealt with" in conformity with the Manitoba Evidence Act.

(3) The defendant doctor was liable to pay costs sustained by the successful defendants, the hospital and a resident, it being reasonable and necessary for the plaintiff to sue all three defendants to establish her claim of negligence.

ROBINSON v. ANNAPOLIS GEN. HOSP. (1956) 4 D.L.R. (2d) 421 (N.S.S.C.)

The patient fell and fractured her hip after getting out of bed. She was rather confused and had been put back to bed on several occasions by the nurses. A bell for summoning a nurse was readily available to her in bed.

Held:

(1) The defendant's nurses exercised reasonable skill, care and judgment in supervising the patient and acted according to approved practice. Only constant surveillance could have prevented the plaintiff from getting out of bed and such attention would place an undue burden on the defendant hospital.

(2) The defendant physician could not have anticipated that the plaintiff would attempt to get out of bed, since she made no such attempts during his daily visits to her.

RODYCH v. KRASEY [1971] 4 W.W.R. 358 (Man. Q.B.)

The defendant general practitioner first examined the deceased at night by flashlight because he refused to leave his truck and come into the defendant's house. Although he diagnosed only a minor injury he admitted the deceased to

hospital where he died the following morning of injuries partially masked by his intoxicated condition.

Held:

(1) The defendant general practitioner possessed and used that reasonable degree of learning and skill ordinarily possessed by practitioners in similar communities in similar cases.

(2) The plaintiff's claim against the nurses and the hospital was dismissed.

ROY v. GOULET (1977) 19 N.B.R. (2d) 187 (Q.B.)

The defendant specialist in orthopaedic surgery treated the plaintiff's compound arm fracture, performing an open reduction and applying casts. The plaintiff subsequently developed a serious infection around the fracture site, attended by severe pain and preventing the bone from healing. Deformity and disability ultimately resulted.

Held:

The defendant was not liable for negligence in treating the plaintiff. While the infection likely prevented proper healing of the fractured arm, there was no evidence that a proper course of treatment was not followed, nor that alternative treatments would have been more successful.

RUTLEDGE v. FISHER [1940] 3 W.W.R. 494 (B.C. Co. Ct.)

As a result of the defendant chiropractor's treatment of his neck, the plaintiff experienced intense pain. The defendant did not take an X-ray which would have revealed that the plaintiff was suffering from arthritis.

Held:

(1) As long as a chiropractor exercises the requisite skill and care in treating the patient, he will not be liable, even though his patient suffers excruciating pain.

(2) Although an X-ray would have provided the defendant with valuable information, he was not required to obtain one.

SANDERSON v. LAMONT (1983) 21 A.C.W.S. (2d) 157 (B.C.S.C.)

The defendant specialist performed a tubal ligation sterilization operation on the plaintiff who became pregnant 16 months later resulting in the birth of a fourth child. A second tubal ligation was performed subsequently by another doctor.

Held:

The action was dismissed. On the evidence, the doctor did inform the plaintiff of the risk of failure of the procedure and the plaintiff would have had the operation even if she had known of the risk.

SAVOIE v. BOUCHARD (1983) 23 C.C.L.T. 83; appeal and cross-appeal dismissed with small variation in calculation of damages N.S.C.A. 19th September 1983 (unreported)

The plaintiff surgeon suffered a needle prick of his finger from a syringe left in the operating field during surgery, and as a result contracted hepatitis from his patient, who was known to be a carrier of the disease.

Held:

(1) The defendant scrub nurse was 50 per cent negligent for omitting to remove the sharp instrument, which was in the area of her immediate view, from the operating field. The defendant, or a scrub nurse in her position, had a legal duty to do so as soon as possible, knowing she had given the syringe to the doctor in the first place.
(2) The plaintiff surgeon was 50 per cent contributorily negligent for failing to return the syringe to the scrub nurse after using it, in accordance with professionally approved practice. However, he was not contributorily negligent for failing to seek appropriate and timely medical treatment following the incident. A plaintiff is responsible for taking all reasonable steps to mitigate his loss, but a medical doctor would be expected to make the final decision as to method of treatment, even of himself, and therefore did not act unreason-

ably in failing to follow the recommendation of another doctor.
(3) The defendant hospital was vicariously liable for the negligence of the defendant scrub nurse, since she was carrying out her professional duties as part of support services supplied by the hospital.
(4) The plaintiff surgeon was not vicariously liable for the acts or omissions of the scrub nurse in the operating room, since an injured party cannot be vicariously liable for the negligence of the party who caused the injury.
(5) The doctrine of *res ipsa loquitur* was not applicable, since it was not established that the thing giving rise to the injury (*i.e.* the syringe) was in the sole management or control of the defendant scrub nurse.
(6) The plaintiff surgeon did not assume the risk of injury by operation of the rule *volenti non fit injuria*, in the absence of an express or implied agreement with the defendant scrub nurse exempting her from liability for her negligence.

SCHIERZ v. DODDS [1981] C.S. 489

Shortly after first taking oral contraceptives prescribed by the defendant doctor, the plaintiff experienced pain in her right leg which was diagnosed by another doctor as phlebitis. A year later, at the plaintiff's request, the defendant again prescribed oral contraceptives. Ten months later, the patient, then 20 years old, suffered a stroke resulting in partial permanent disability.

Held:

The defendant was found liable in negligence. In light of the suspected phlebitis episode, the defendant should not have prescribed oral contraceptives for the plaintiff when a preponderance of medical evidence indicated oral contraceptives are contra-indicated in patients with phlebitis. Since the defendant created the risk, to escape liability he must show the injury resulted from another cause. The defendant did not do so. Also, the defendant failed to disclose the risks of oral contraceptive therapy to the plaintiff and could not rely on the enclosed pamphlet.

SCHINZ v. DICKINSON (1983) 20 A.C.W.S. (2d) 456 (B.C.S.C.)

The plaintiff had a number of inflammations of a partially impacted wisdom tooth which her dentist recommended she have extracted and referred her to another dentist, the defendant. Without any discussion of the risks involved, the defendant, after multiple injections of anaesthetic, removed her tooth. The plaintiff was left with permanent lingual nerve damage resulting in a permanent loss of sensation in part of her tongue.

Held:

The defendant is not liable. The damage to the nerve was caused by the administration of anaesthetic; however, there is no evidence of negligence in doing so, nor in the subsequent extraction of the tooth. Because of the extremely low incidence of such damage in such extraction, there is no duty to warn the patient of the risk and would only cause her needless worry.

SCHWEIZER v. CENTRAL HOSP. (1974) 6 O.R. (2d) 606 (H.C.)

The plaintiff who was being treated for both foot and back injuries consented to surgery on his foot. The defendant surgeon mistakenly performed a spinal fusion. The plaintiff sued in intentional trespass.

Held:

The onus was on the defendant to establish a sufficient and effective consent was not met; therefore the defendant was found liable.

SERRE v. DE TILLY (1975) 8 O.R. (2d) 490 (H.C.)

The defendant physicians examined the patient without taking blood tests and diagnosed her condition as "hysteria." The patient died several days later as the result of a hemorrhage in the lower brain stem.

Held:

(1) The patient's symptoms were consistent with the defendants' diagnosis and even if the defendants had diagnosed her condition correctly, there was no indication that they could have prevented her death.
(2) The defendants may have committed an error in judgment in neglecting to take a blood test, but such an error does not create liability.
(3) Unless a physician's diagnosis is clearly incompetent, a nurse is not permitted to interfere with his instructions.

SIMARD v. R. (1963) 43 C.R. 70 (Que. C.A.)

In order to effect the delivery of a premature baby, the defendant chose to proceed by means of forceps. The entire procedure was carried out in a completely normal manner but the baby suffered a cerebral hemorrhage. The defendant was charged under ss. 191 and 192 of the Criminal Code with causing death by criminal negligence.

Held:

The defendant, under the circumstances, proceeded in a normal and reasonable manner and did not commit any criminal negligence.

SINCLAIR v. VICTORIA HOSP. [1943] 1 W.W.R. 30 (Man. C.A.)

While attempting to grab the inhalator beside his crib, the infant plaintiff fell out of his crib thereby spilling the boiling water in the inhalator on top of himself.

Held:

(1) The nurses were negligent in placing the inhalator within the infant's reach, since they should have foreseen that he would interfere with it if he was left unattended.
(2) Since the nurses' negligence occurred during the performance of their regular duties, the hospital was vicariously liable.

STADEL v. ALBERTSON [1954] 2 D.L.R. 328 (Sask. C.A.)

After being rendered unconscious in a fall from a hayrack, the deceased developed symptoms which led to his admission to the psychiatric wing of a hospital. He was then transferred to the care of the defendant neurosurgeon in the surgical ward of the main hospital because two psychiatrists concluded that he was suffering from some organic disorder, e.g., a brain lesion. The deceased committed suicide by jumping from the window of the main hospital. The plaintiff alleges that the defendants were negligent in failing to take sufficient care to guard the deceased against self-inflicted injury.

Held:

(1) There was no evidence on which the defendant neurosurgeon could be found to have been negligent.

(2) The defendant hospital was not negligent in giving the deceased the same care that any patient in his condition would have received and there was no evidence that such a patient was a danger to himself.

(3) There was no evidence which would justify a reasonable jury in concluding that anything the defendants did or omitted to do had any causal connection with the tragedy that followed or that any injury to the deceased might have been foreseen.

STAMPER v. RHINDRESS (1906) 41 N.S.R. 45 (C.A.)

The defendant physicians failed to diagnose a fracture of the plaintiff's hip, despite the fact that they had conducted a thorough examination. The plaintiff consulted another physician who discovered that the hip was fractured and treated it accordingly.

Held:

The defendants' failure to diagnose the fracture cannot be attributed to negligence on their part, since they did everything possible to discover the fracture.

STAPLE v. WINNIPEG (1956) 18 W.W.R. 625 affirmed 19 W.W.R. 672 (Man. C.A.)

During an operation to fuse the ankle joints, the defendant surgeon inadvertently fused the ankle and foot bones of a polio patient's healthy leg. A second defendant surgeon employed by the defendant hospital assisted in the operation but made no decisions.

Held:

(1) The assistant surgeon was not negligent, since he did not direct the operation.

(2) Before a hospital will be made liable for the negligence of an operating surgeon, the relationship of master and servant must exist between the hospital and the surgeon. The defendant hospital exercised no control over the operating surgeon's decisions or actions and cannot, therefore, be vicariously liable for his negligence.

(3) The operating surgeon admitted his negligence.

STRACHAN v. SIMPSON [1979] 5 W.W.R. 315 (B.C.S.C.)

The plaintiff, suffering from a progressive inability to use his legs, underwent treatment by the two defendant chiropractors and, when that proved unsuccessful, by the defendant neurologist and the defendant neurosurgeon, who agreed that exploratory spinal surgery was necessary. The defendant neurosurgeon performed the procedure, having explained it to the plaintiff but having failed to discuss the risk of paraplegia which ultimately occurred.

Held:

(1) The defendant chiropractors could not be sued for negligence because the statutory limitation period had expired. An amended statement of claim against the defendant doctors, including the chiropractors as parties, was legally insupportable. An attempt to sue the chiropractors for assault and battery was barred by statute and was, moreover, an inappropriate cause of action.

(2) The defendant neurosurgeon was not liable for negligently performing the exploratory operation, in light of evidence that irreversible paraplegia was found upon exploration and in the absence of evidence supporting negligence.

(3) The defendant neurologist was not liable for failing to warn the plaintiff of the risks of surgery, since the procedure was to be carried out by the neurosurgeon.

(4) The defendant neurosurgeon was liable in

negligence for failing to warn of the risk of paraplegia attending the procedure. The failure to reveal the risk was not in compliance with professional custom, and the plaintiff, had he known of the risk, would have declined the surgery.

STRETTON v. HOLMES (1889) 19 O.R. 286 (Q.B.)

In preparing the defendant physician's prescription for the plaintiff, the defendant pharmacist's clerk mistakenly added hydrocyanic acid instead of hydrochloric acid. The plaintiff suffered the effects of temporary poisoning.

Held:
(1) Since the physician displayed no negligence in writing up the prescription and was not in any way involved in its preparation or administration he could not be held liable.
(2) The pharmacist was vicariously liable for the negligent act of his employee.

SUNNE v. SHAW [1981] C.S. 609 (Que. S.C.)

The defendant plastic surgeon and the defendant oral surgeon operated on the plaintiff to correct a congenital facial deformity by aligning her teeth. Four years later, because of bone and root loss, eight teeth had to be removed.

Held:
Both defendants were equally liable. The risk of this complication did not have to be disclosed to the plaintiff because it was too remote; however, the defendants should have disclosed that another method of treatment involving fewer risks was available. Thus, both defendants were found liable in negligence and in contract.

SUPT. OF FAMILY & CHILD SERVICE v. D. (R.); RUSSELL, PUB. TRUSTEE FOR B.C. v. SUPT. OF FAMILY & CHILD SERVICE (1983) 42 B.C.L.R. 173 (S.C.)

The applicants, parents of a six-year-old boy with severe irreversible retardation, blindness, partial deafness and various other profound disabilities, refused to consent to remedial "shunt" surgery to relieve pressure on the brain and thereby prolong his life. The provincial government assumed custody of the child as being "deprived of necessary medical attention."

Held:
The child was properly apprehended for the purposes of carrying out the medical treatment refused by the parents. The court's inherent *parens patriae* jurisdiction in this matter was based on a presumption in favour of life. Moreover, there was a real possibility here of the child's life being prolonged with pain and progressive deterioration even if the treatment was not carried out.

SURKAN v. BLOTT [1981] B.C.D. Civ. 2632-04 B.C.C.A. Taggart, Seaton & MacDonald JJ.A. Victoria No. 38/81 16th October 1981 (unreported)

The defendant surgeon, in completing a hysterectomy operation on the plaintiff, misplaced a suture resulting in a constriction of the ureter and requiring further surgery to remove a kidney.

Held:
The defendant was not liable for negligence in performing the surgery. The complication was a well-known hazard of the procedure, capable of occurring without negligenee.

TACKNYK v. LAKE OF THE WOODS CLINIC (1982) 17 A.C.W.S. (2d) 154 Ont. C.A. Morden, Thorson & Cory JJ.A. 25th November 1982 (not yet reported)

The defendant doctor performed a tonsillectomy on the plaintiff and released him from the defendant clinic with instructions to consult a doctor if complications arose. The plaintiff returned home to an area inaccessible to the defendant doctor, where he suffered gross bleeding some days later.

Held:
The defendants were not liable for negligent post-operative care of the plaintiff's case, hav-

ing performed it reasonably in the circumstances. Moreover, there was a doctor available in the plaintiff's community who did everything that could have been done.

TAYLOR v. GRAY [1937] 4 D.L.R. 123 (B.C.C.A.)

During a Caesarian section performed by the defendant surgeon a pair of Allis forceps were left in the plaintiff's abdominal cavity.

Held:

In a case where *res ipsa loquitur* applies, although the defendant is not required to explain the accident, he must show that he was not guilty of negligence which the defendant has failed to do. A count of sponges and instruments should be made prior to closing the incision.

THOMAS v. PORT COLBORNE GEN. HOSP. (1982) 12 A.C.W.S. (2d) 535 Ont. H.C. Holland J. 10th February 1982 (not yet reported)

The defendant family physician treated the plaintiff's paralyzed leg at the defendant hospital, carrying out diagnostic tests but, due to unsophisticated X-ray equipment, failed to discover a spinal fracture dislocation. An accurate diagnosis was made subsequently at another hospital, the delay having increased the plaintiff's disability.

Held:

(1) The defendant was not liable for negligent diagnosis, since the injury was not unusual, the symptoms did not indicate a cervical spinal problem, and complete X-rays to the extent they could be carried out were inconclusive.
(2) The defendant was liable in negligence for failing to consult with a specialist when the paralysis had persisted.

THOMAS v. SCARBOROUGH GEN. HOSP. [1978] 2 A.C.W.S. 143 Ont. Co. Ct. Loukidelis Co. Ct. J. 9th March 1979 (unreported)

The defendant surgeon performed an operation on, and the defendant physician administered

treatment to the plaintiff, a patient in the defendant hospital. The plaintiff suffered a postoperative gangrene infection requiring the amputation of one testicle.

Held:

(1) The defendant hospital was not liable for negligence.
(2) The defendant physician was not liable for negligence.
(3) The defendant surgeon was liable in negligence for failing to instruct the defendant physician to closely supervise the patient's postoperative progress, given the slow and complicated nature of the recovery. Moreover, depending on which theory of the development of gangrene was accepted, the defendant surgeon could also be liable for negligently performing the surgery.

THOMPSON v. COLUMBIA COAST MISSION (1914) 20 B.C.R. 115 (C.A.)

A physician practising out of the defendant hospital negligently misdiagnosed the plaintiff's condition as chronic rheumatism when he had actually suffered a dislocated shoulder. The plaintiff sued the hospital.

Held:

(1) The hospital fulfilled its duty to the plaintiff by making available to him the services of a duly qualified physician.
(2) The hospital cannot be held liable for the negligence of a physician, since his professional activities are not subject to its control.

THOMPSON v. CREAGHAN (1982) 42 N.B.R. (2d) 359 affirmed 46 N.B.R. (2d) 271 (Q.B.)

The defendant surgeon removed a lump from the patient's neck, but did not send the excised material for pathological examination, and when the lumps recurred, diagnosed the problem as dermatological. The plaintiff's condition was diagnosed three months later by another doctor as lymphatic cancer at an advanced stage.

Held:

(1) Neither the defendant doctor nor the defen-

dant hospital was liable for the lack of a pathological examination performed on the surgically excised lump. The failure to send the excised material for tests, while not good medical practice, did not contribute to the failure to diagnose the disease, since the medical evidence indicated that a pathological examination would not have revealed the presence of cancer.

(2) The defendant doctor was not liable for negligence in failing to diagnose cancer when the lumps reappeared. Apart from the lumps, no other symptoms of the disease were present. Moreover, timely diagnosis would not have revealed the disease at a stage where it could have been successfully treated.

THOMSON v. BARRY (1932) 41 O.W.N. 138 (C.A.)

A rubber drainage tube was left in the plaintiff's body after surgery performed by the defendant surgeon.

Held:

(1) No negligence on the part of the defendant was shown. In the absence of evidence that it was the duty of the defendant to advise that an X-ray be taken, it could not be inferred that the defendant was negligent in not so advising.

(2) The fact that a tube was left in the incision was the result of a nurse's negligence.

TIESMAKI v. WILSON [1975] 6 W.W.R. 639 (Alta. C.A.)

The plaintiff was admitted to hospital with an ailment diagnosed by the defendant general practitioner as "acute upper respiratory infection." She was kept under constant surveillance and immediately upon cessation of breathing following a convulsion, the defendant carried out a tracheotomy. The plaintiff suffered permanent brain damage from anoxia following the convulsion. The trial judge concluded that the plaintiff's injuries were caused by encephalitis.

Held:

The plaintiff failed to prove that the various defendants did not meet the standards of care incumbent upon each of them. The test of reasonable care and ordinary skill with respect to the defendant Dr. Wilson was modified to include the ordinary skill of a general practitioner in a town (Banff) at the given time (1960), so that although he failed to diagnose encephalitis, this fact does not establish that the standard of care exercised by him in the circumstances fell below the standard expected of him. Furthermore, such a diagnosis would not have prevented the injuries which the plaintiff had suffered.

TOWN v. ARCHER (1902) 4 O.L.R. 383 (K.B.)

The defendant physician set the plaintiff's broken fibula. The plaintiff disturbed the bandaging thereby causing permanent injury which she now suffers. Although the plaintiff visited the defendant on two occasions after her cast was removed, prior to her second visit, at approximately six months from the date the cast was removed, she consulted another doctor. This action was commenced one year later.

Held:

(1) The plaintiff's action was barred by the Ontario Medical Act, R.S.O. 1897, c. 176, s. 41, because it was not commenced within one year from the date when the defendant's professional services regarding the matter complained of terminated. The two visits after the cast was removed were not a renewal of the doctor-patient relation. The consultation of another surgeon in the absence of, and without notice to or leave of the surgeon in charge is an indication of want of confidence in the latter, and would be treated by him, when he came to know of it, as tantamount to a dismissal of him by the patient.

(2) The defendant was not liable for the plaintiff's present injuries because they were caused by her own conduct and not by his proper diagnosis and treatment of her original injury.

TOWNSEND v. LAI [1979] B.C.D. Civ. 2632-03 B.C.S.C. Murray J. New Westminster No. C771181 4th May 1979 (unreported)

The defendant doctor applied a series of casts to the plaintiff's fractured foot. The fracture did not knit properly, causing pain, requiring a new cast applied by a different doctor, and corrective surgery.

Held:

The defendant was liable for negligently treating the injury. The procedure employed was not the normal one and the defendant applied the cast without reading the manufacturer's instructions for its use. The quantum of damages was $15,649.

TRAYNOR v. VANCOTT (1979) 3 L. Med. Q. 69 (Ont. H.C.)

The plaintiff underwent surgery by the defendant doctor while a patient in the defendant hospital. During post-operative recovery, the plaintiff developed a loss of feeling and control in her left arm caused by prolonged pressure on the radial nerve.

Held:

The defendant hospital was liable for the negligence of its nursing staff. The plaintiff could not have received the injury while receiving regular nursing care, and for a hospital to leave a patient in the plaintiff's condition unattended for ten hours amounted to negligence.

TURNER v. TORONTO GEN. HOSP. TRUSTEES [1934] O.W.N. 629 (H.C.)

The defendant surgeon operated on the plaintiff, a patient in the public ward of the defendant hospital. The plaintiff alleged that the operation was performed without his consent and contrary to his express refusal, and thus constituted an assault.

Held:

(1) The hospital trustees were not liable because their duty extended only to engaging properly qualified medical and surgical practitioners to officiate and operate their hospital, and this duty had been fully performed.
(2) The position of the defendant surgeon was purely a matter of credibility and the plaintiff failed to satisfy the onus of proof as to his allegation that the operation was unauthorized.

TURRIFF v. KING (1913) 3 W.W.R. 862 (Sask. S.C.)

The plaintiff was suffering from, and displayed all the common symptoms of a lumbar abscess, yet the defendant diagnosed her condition as rheumatism of the sciatic nerve or as neuritis. The defendant's prescribed treatment only increased the plaintiff's pain and suffering.

Held:

In failing to make the correct diagnosis, and in persisting with a wholly unsuccessful treatment method, the defendant failed to exercise a competent degree of skill and care.

UNIVERSITY HOSP. BD. v. LEPINE [1966] S.C.R. 561

The plaintiff, while under the care of the defendant neurologist, was placed on the neurologist's ward on the fourth floor of the hospital. In the presence of the doctor and three policemen, and while experiencing a seizure, the plaintiff leapt through the fourth floor window and consequently sustained injuries. The plaintiff sued in negligence.

Held:

The plaintiff's sudden leap through the window was not an event which a reasonable man would have foreseen and have been required to take more precautions than were available in this case. The plaintiff's action was dismissed.

URBANSKI v. PATEL; FIRMAN v. PATEL (1978) 84 D.L.R. (3d) 650 (Man. Q.B.)

The defendant surgeon performed exploratory surgery on the plaintiff, removing what he thought to be an ovarian cyst, which was in fact a kidney. The plaintiff suffered serious disability and inconvenience, requiring dialysis and resulting in two unsuccessful transplantations, on one occasion of a kidney donated by the plaintiff, father of the first plaintiff. The defendant admitted liability to the first plaintiff and her husband for negligently performing the surgery.

Held:

The defendant was liable to the third plaintiff, father of the first plaintiff and donor of a kidney, for damages suffered as a result of the donation. In light of modern medicine, a transplant must be viewed as an expected result of the loss of kidney function; and it is foreseeable that a family member would agree to donate a kidney for that purpose.

VAIL v. MACDONALD [1976] 2 S.C.R. 825

The defendant general practitioner reduced the plaintiff's fractured ankle and immobilized it in a cast. The nurses noted a loss of feeling in the plaintiff's toes the next morning and reported it to the defendant who took no measures to correct the situation for two days. He then performed exploratory surgery but failed to discover the cause of the circulatory impairment. The plaintiff's foot became gangrenous and had to be amputated.

Held:

(1) (a) The defendant's failure to consult a cardiovascular specialist when he found himself unable to discover the origin of the plaintiff's circulation problem, (b) his failure to prescribe anti-coagulants until it was too late, and (c) his generally indifferent manner toward the plaintiff amounted to medical negligence.
(2) Although the hospital nurses may have been negligent in not reporting the initial changes in the plaintiff's condition, their negligence did not contribute to his loss.

VAN MERE v. FARWELL (1886) 12 O.R. 285 (C.A.)

The plaintiff alleged that the defendant physician's treatment of the infant's fractured arm was negligent in that he applied the primary bandage too tightly, with the result that the arm became permanently useless.

Held:

The fact that some physicians would resort to the defendant's course of treatment while others would not does not indicate that the defendant displayed a lack of skill in prescribing the treatment. The defendant's use of the primary bandage did not constitute negligence.

VAN WINKLE v. CHEN B.C.S.C. No. 46/80 16th February 1984 (not yet reported)

The defendant eye, nose and throat specialist used a Foley catheter to stop the patient's nosebleed without using an anaesthetic during the insertion and did not pad the clamp that held it in place. The patient experienced pain on insertion of the catheter and ulceration of the skin underneath the nose, requiring further surgery and resulting in scarring. The defendant admitted liability.

Held:
General damages for pain and suffering assessed at $10,000.

VIDETO v. KENNEDY (1981) 33 O.R. (2d) 497 (C.A.)

The defendant obstetrician/gynaecologist performed a laparoscopic sterilization operation on the plaintiff, having discussed the attendant risk of scarring but not the more extensive scarring consequent upon the more serious version of the same procedure. During the operation the plaintiff suffered a bowel perforation resulting in a near fatal infection and required further major surgery with permanent serious scarring of her abdomen.

Held:
(1) The defendant was not liable in negligence for failing to disclose the risks, particularly of a larger scar, of the more serious laparotomy procedure. The risk of a larger scar from major corrective surgery resulting from a bowel perforation was not material. The plaintiff had been very concerned about the scarring factor, but established neither real nor constructive knowlege by the defendant of the significance of that concern.
(2) The defendant was not liable in negligence for failing to provide adequate post-operative care. (Trial).

VILLEMURE v. TURCOT [1973] S.C.R. 716

The plaintiff's husband fell to his death from a window of the hospital where he had been admitted for psychiatric treatment after being transferred from a ward with barred windows to a semi-private room in response to his request.

Held:

The trial judge's decision that the defendant psychiatrist and the hospital were liable for the death was affirmed. In spite of expert evidence supporting the defendant psychiatrist's decision to accede to the patient's request, the court's decision turned on the fact that the defendant was warned that the patient required strict surveillance, and the fact that in the short time (30 hours) in which he had been admitted to the hospital, an investigation could have been made into his condition in order to more accurately diagnose his true situation.

VILLENEUVE v. SISTERS OF ST. JOSEPH [1975] S.C.R. 285

Although the infant plaintiff was being restrained by two nurses because he was restless and upset, he moved his arm as the syringe was compressed, thereby causing the defendant to insert the needle into the infant's right antecubital fossa. The plaintiff developed circulatory problems in his right hand which eventually required amputation.

Held:

(1) The defendant physician was negligent in proceeding with the injection when he realized that the plaintiff was restless and upset. He was in complete charge of the situation and the total responsibility must rest on him.
(2) The nurses were not negligent because they were not responsible for the defendant's decision to go ahead despite the risks of movement.

VUCHAR v. TORONTO GEN. HOSP. TRUSTEES [1937] O.R. 71 (C.A.)

The plaintiff, admitted to the defendant hospital with a puerperal infection, suffered serious burns to her thighs as a result of excessive exposure to a heat cradle.

Held:

(1) The hospital has a duty to exercise reasonable care to ensure that its patients are treated by competent physicians, surgeons and nurses and that these individuals have access to proper medical equipment.
(2) The hospital is liable where a nurse's negligence occurs in the performance of a routine or administrative duty.
(3) The hospital will not be liable where a nurse is exercising her professional knowledge and skill under the direct instructions of a doctor in the operating room or on the ward. In this case, the nursing supervisor was required to use her own judgment and knowledge as to the amount of heat required, and in doing so, she was not under the direction of the defendant hospital. Hence, the hospital was not liable.

WADE v. NAYERNOURI (1978) 2 L. Med. Q. 67 (Ont. H.C.)

When the defendant physician attended the plaintiff's husband in the emergency ward of the defendant hospital he diagnosed a migraine headache without taking a careful history and without ordering neurological testing which would have indicated a "warning leak." Two weeks later, the plaintiff's husband was admitted to hospital in an unconscious state and a diagnosis of subarachnoid hemorrhaging was made. He died during the waiting period prior to surgical treatment.

Held:

(1) The defendant physician was negligent i.e. he failed to meet the requisite standard of care in failing to do the following: properly employ all usual diagnostic aids in reaching his conclusion, take a proper history from the deceased or his wife, consider the possibility of a subarachnoid hemorrhage, take adequate neurological tests, and referring the case to a neurologist before discharging him.
(2) The action against the defendant hospital was discontinued.

WADE v. SISTERS OF ST. JOSEPH (1976) 2
C.P.C. 37 (Ont. H.C.)

When the defendant physician attended the
plaintiff's husband in the emergency ward of
the defendant hospital he diagnosed a migraine
headache without taking a careful history and
without ordering neurological testing which
would have indicated a "warning leak." Two
weeks later, the plaintiff's husband was admitted to hospital in an unconscious state and a
diagnosis of subarachnoid hemorrhaging was
made. He died during the waiting period prior
to surgical treatment.

Held:
(1) The defendant physician was negligent, i.e.
he failed to meet the requisite standard of care
in failing to do the following: properly employing all usual diagnostic aids in reaching his
conclusion, taking a proper history from the
deceased or his wife, considering the possibility of a subarachnoid hemorrhage, taking adequate neurological tests, and referring the case
to a neurologist before discharging him.
(2) The action against the defendant hospital
was discontinued.

WALDON v. ARCHER (1921) 20 O.W.N. 77
(S.C.)

The defendant surgeon left a sponge in the
plaintiff's abdomen during an operation.

Held:
Because the operation had to be completed in
the shortest possible time in order to save the
plaintiff's life, the defendant's failure to remove
the sponge did not amount to actionable
negligence. Considering the circumstances, he
exercised the proper degree of skill.

WALKER v. BEDARD [1945] O.W.N. 120
(H.C.)

The defendant anaesthetist assisted by the defendant physician administered the injection after
confirming that the patient's history was normal.
All efforts to save the patient from "shock"
failed.

Held:
The plaintiff failed to prove that the defendants
were lacking in skill when they administered
the anaesthetic and that negligence was the
proximate cause of the patient's death.
Furthermore, the deceased's hypersensitivity
to the anaesthetic was not foreseeable.

WALKER v. SYDNEY CITY HOSP. (1983)
19 A.C.W.S. (2d) 56 (N.S.S.C.)

By use of an improper solution during surgery,
the infant plaintiff's eyes were damaged to the
extent that she became legally blind in one eye.
The other was scarred. The defendant admitted
liability.

Held:
Damages were assessed at $47,000 taking into
account loss of enjoyment of her childhood
and increased danger of total loss of sight.

WEBSTER v. ARMSTRONG [1974] 2
W.W.R. 709 (B.C.S.C.)

Although the patient was informed by Dr. R.
that it was important that he not consume
fluids within five hours of surgery, he did not
notify anyone that he had coffee at 2:45, and so
at 6:00 the defendant anaesthesiologist began
administering the general anaesthetic. Due to
laryngeal spasms Dr. A. had difficulties anaesthetizing the patient but he continued in his
attempt to intubate the patient. The patient
ultimately died as a result of aspiration and
cardiac arrest.

Held:
(1) The conduct of the defendants was not such
so as to constitute negligence. Dr. A.'s decision to continue his efforts to intubate the
patient was reasonable in the circumstances,
since he could not bring the patient back to
consciousness until he had succeeded in intu-
bating him.
(2) An anaesthesiologist is not obliged to inquire
personally as to the patient's food and liquid
intake before administering a general anaesthetic.

WHITE v. TURNER (1981) 31 O.R. (2d) 773 (H.C.)

The defendant cosmetic surrgeon performed a breast reduction operation on the plaintiff. The plaintiff subsequently suffered serious scarring, bleeding, pain and discomfort as a result of insufficient tissue having been removed, and ultimately required corrective surgery, resulting in further scarring.

Held:

(1) The defendant was liable for negligently performing the surgery, failing to meet his standard of care by carrying out the procedure too quickly, by removing insufficient tissue and by failing to check his work before closing the incisions.

(2) The defendant was liable in negligence for failing adequately to disclose the risks of the procedure. Where the primary objective of a procedure is cosmetic, possible risks affecting appearance are "material," and risks of serious scarring and corrective surgery to repair a bad result are "special or unusual." A reasonable person in the plaintiff's position would not have undergone the surgery, except in rare circumstances, had she been properly apprised of the risks.

WILLIAMS v. JONES (1977) 79 D.L.R. (3d) 670 (B.C.S.C.)

In filling a prescription for the plaintiff husband, the defendant pharmacist dispensed formaldehyde instead of paraldehyde. Both the husband and wife ingested the medication and had to be hospitalized. The wife underwent surgery for the removal of her stomach.

Held:

(1) The defendant was clearly negligent in dispensing the wrong medication.

(2) Since the defendant knew that the plaintiffs were alcoholics and that paraldehyde had previously been prescribed for the husband's alcoholism, he could have foreseen that the wife would also take some of the drug to remedy her own alcoholic problem.

WILSON v. STARK (1967) 61 W.W.R. 705 (Sask. Q.B.)

The deceased was admitted to the defendant Stark's hospital two days before Stark was to leave for a holiday. The defendant Coneghan had consented to "cover" for him in his absence. Stark diagnosed the deceased's condition as a mild case of gastritis similar to that from which he had previously suffered. Following Stark's absence, and as the deceased's condition worsened, the defendant Coneghan was called, who, accompanied by the defendant Pavelely, diagnosed acute peritonitis brought on by a ruptured appendix. The defendants Coneghan and Paveley, later assisted by the defendant Richardson conducted a four-hour operation in which they failed to find and remove the appendix. The defendant Coneghan prescribed antibiotics and fluids as post-operative treatment measures. The patient died five days later.

Held:

(1) The defendant Stark's intitial diagnosis was an honest and intelligent exercise of his judgment, but he was negligent in not making proper provision for medical attention, i.e., constant observation of his patient in his absence. However, the defendant Stark was not liable because as the cause of death was undetermined, the plaintiff failed to prove on the balance of probabilities that the defendant Stark's negligence caused or contributed in a material way to the death of the deceased.

(2) The defendants Coneghan, Paveley and Richardson were general practitioners, not surgical specialists. Therefore, although the excessive length of the operation could only have had a prejudicial effect, and although a specialist would have had little difficulty in locating a retrocecal appendix, they were not negligent. They were met with a sudden emergency under difficult conditions and, using their best judgment, did what they thought was necessary. Furthermore, although their prescribed post-operative treatment was criticized by experts as insufficient in quantity, this was not conclusively the cause of the patient's death.

WILSON v. SWANSON [1956] S.C.R. 804

In reliance on a biopsy which indicated cancer, the defendant surgeon performed radical surgery removing the plaintiff's spleen and most of his stomach and pancreas. Prior to the operation, the defendant had secured all the available information concerning his patient's condition. After the operation the results of the biopsy were reversed, i.e., it was found to be benign.

Held:

Where a surgeon is compelled to make an immediate decision without the aid of all the pertinent information and results of various tests, he will not be found liable for an erroneous decision as long as he exercises his judgment honestly and intelligently in making that decision.

WINE v. KERNOHAN (1978) 2 L.Med.Q. 129 (Ont. H.C.)

The plaintiff came under the defendant general practitioner's care for treatment of an infection which was rapidly spreading from his rectal to his groin area. The defendant general practitioner failed to diagnose an anaerobic infection and did not order surgical intervention to drain the abscess until four days after the plaintiff was admitted to his care. The defendant surgeon then failed to drain wholly the infected area. As a result of the defendants' treatment, the plaintiff suffered a horrible scarring in addition to severe pain and discomfort, all of which could have been reduced or eliminated by prompt correct treatment.

Held:

(1) The defendant general practitioner was negligent in failing to order surgical treatment sooner.
(2) The defendant surgeon was negligent in failing to incise and clean out the inguinal area.

WINN v. ALEXANDER [1940] O.W.N. 238 (H.C.)

Eight years after her Caesarean delivery, the plaintiff was operated on for a growth in her abdomen. This operation revealed that a surgical sponge had been left in her abdomen after delivery and that, without her consent, her fallopian tubes had been resected. The plaintiff further alleged that the defendant doctor and hospital fraudulently concealed any knowledge of their negligence and that the surgeon had committed the alleged assault.

Held:

In a motion for judgment upon the admissions of fact:
(1) The plaintiff's claim in negligence against the defendant surgeon and hospital was barred by the expiration of the statutory limitation period.
(2) The plaintiff's claim in assault and fraudulent conspiracy against the defendant surgeon was allowed to stand for trial.

WINTERSGILL AND MIN. OF SOCIAL SERVICES, RE (1981) 131 D.L.R. (3d) 184 (U.F.C.)

The parents of a premature newborn refused on religious grounds to consent to the administration of blood transfusions considered medically necessary by the attending neonatologist. As a consequence, an application was made under provincial legislation to commit the child to the care of the government as a child in need of protection.

Held:

The application was granted. Blood transfusions were, and continued to be the only "proper" treatment available in the circumstances, and the fact that the child was at the point of death when the medical decision to transfuse was initially made rendered parental consent unnecessary. Parents must provide that available care which a duly qualified medical practitioner deems essential to the life and health of the child.

WIPFLI v. BRITTEN 22 C.C.L.T. 104 supplementary reasons [1983] 3 W.W.R. 424 (B.C.S.C.)

The defendant family physician attended the plaintiff throughout the term of her pregnancy, without diagnosing multiple gestation. In the aftermath of a Caesarean section operation by the defendant obstetrician to deliver one newborn, a second was discovered in the womb. Emergency resuscitative measures saved his life but failed to prevent irreversible brain damage and severe physical handicaps including cerebral palsy.

Held:

(1) The defendant family physician was liable in negligence for failing to diagnose multiple gestation. While the failure to diagnose twins does not necessarily import negligence, in this case there were sufficient indici and tests available to arouse the defendant's suspicions. His failure to make the correct diagnosis materially increased the risk of injury ultimately suffered by the second newborn.

(2) The defendant obstetrician was not liable in negligence for failing to diagnose twins in the absence of sufficient evidence to that effect.

WORTH v. ROYAL JUBILEE HOSP. (1980) 4 L. Med. Q. 59 (B.C.C.A.)

The plaintiff was voluntarily committed to a psychiatric hospital, having taken an overdose of drugs and been classified as potentially suicidal. While attempting to escape from the hospital, the plaintiff jumped from a 30-foot high wall to the ground, rendering her paraplegic.

Held:

The defendants, doctor and hospital, were not liable for the plaintiff's injuries. The doctor met the standard of care with respect to therapy programs and suicide precautions for the plaintiff. Whether the cause of action be in contract or tort the hospital owed a duty to provide reasonable facilities, which it did. While the escape route taken was an accessible one, the minor risk of injury to suicidal or escaping patients was justified by the therapeutic effect of freedom to move about the institution. It was not foreseeable that the plaintiff would jump from the wall in an attempt to escape.

WYNDHAM v. TORONTO GEN. HOSP. TRUSTEES [1938] O.W.N. 55 (H.C.)

As a result of being fed unreasonably hot soup, the plaintiff burned her mouth and involuntarily jerked her head back. The sudden movement caused a prolapse of the right eye which had just been operated on for the removal of cataracts. The plaintiff's right eye had to be removed.

Held:

The defendant hospital was vicariously liable for the loss of vision suffered by the plaintiff as a consequence of the prolapse.

YEPREMIAN v. SCARBOROUGH GEN. HOSP. (1980) 28 O.R. (2d) 494 (C.A.)

The plaintiff was diagnosed and treated incorrectly for tonsillitis by the defendant family doctor. Upon admission to the defendant hospital in a semi-comatose state the plaintiff was treated by an emergency room physician, who prescribed drugs which worsened his condition; and by an internist who eventually diagnosed diabetes 12 hours later (after a nurse had done so), and failed to administer potassium soon enough or in sufficient quantity to prevent a subsequent cardiac arrest and resultant permanent brain damage.

Held: Ont. C.A.

(1) The defendant hospital was not liable for negligence of the emergency room physician or the internist, who were not personally parties to the action. Although members of the hospital staff, neither were hospital employees, since they received no remuneration and did not exercise independent control over the standard of treatment given; the rule of *respondeat superior* was therefore inapplicable. A hospital does not owe a non-delegable duty of care to its patients, a patient being entitled to expect that the hospital has chosen its medical staff with care, but not that it will assume responsibility for negligent acts of that staff. Any alteration of this view ought to be through legislative,

not judicial intervention.

(2) The defendant family physician was not liable for negligent diagnosis of the plaintiff's symptoms. Although the failure to diagnose diabetes was negligent, the active cause of the damage was improper treatment by the defendant internist which had no causal relationship to the family physician's conduct.

(3) Dissent: The defendant hospital was liable for the negligence of the internist. A hospital can undertake a non-delegable duty of care toward its patients, as a consequence of the profoundly changed relationship between the hospital institution and the public, and the resultant expansion of the role of hospitals in the delivery of medical services. The provision of a wide range of services is an integral and essential part of the operation of a modern hospital, and negligent acts by individuals represent part of the overall care provided by the hospital. The defendant hospital did undertake such a duty to the plaintiff, since his life was placed completely in the hospital's hands, in reliance on its use of resources and personnel. NOTE: Leave to appeal to S.C.C. granted (1980), 120 D.L.R. (3d) 337 (Ont. C.A.); action settled out of court and approved (1981), 120 D.L.R. (3d) 341 (Ont. H.C.).

YULE v. PARMLEY [1945] S.C.R. 635

On the basis of the plaintiff's suggestion that she would like two teeth removed while she was under anaesthetic for a tonsillectomy, the defendant physician arranged for the defendant dentist to carry out the extractions. The plaintiff never communicated directly with the dentist because he failed to interview her prior to her being anaesthetized but he nonetheless proceeded, on the basis of the physician's communiqué, to extract all of her upper teeth and one lower tooth.

Held:

(1) The defendant dentist, in proceeding to extract the teeth on the basis of the physician's vague and general statements did so without the consent of the plaintiff and was therefore guilty of trespass.

(2) The defendant dentist was negligent in pro-

ceeding with the extractions without advising and consulting the plaintiff before she was anaesthetized.

(3) The defendant physician was negligent in using vague, general, and ambiguous terms in communicating with the defendant dentist and in not protecting the plaintiff from the conduct of the defendant dentist.

ZAMPARO v. BRISSON (1981) 32 O.R. (2d) 75 (Ont. C.A.)

The defendant, a surgeon trained as an otolaryngologist, performed elective surgery on the plaintiff to correct her hearing impairment of one ear and remedy her headaches. The plaintiff decided to undergo the operation on the advice of her own doctor, the defendant having declined to recommend or warn against it. Surgery was aborted upon the discovery of a congenital abnormality of the facial nerve, but the nerve was damaged resulting in paralysis of the left side of the plaintiff's face.

Held:

The defendant was not liable in negligence for failing to advise the plaintiff against having surgery. Although a surgeon has a duty to give his patient a relative assessment of the risks and benefits of surgery, in the case of elective procedures the importantly subjective element of the patient's decision militates against a direct recommendation by the doctor. Moreover, in this case medical indications in favour of surgery were quite strong as evidenced by advice from the plaintiff's family doctor, and in any event the risk was too remote to require disclosure.

ZIMMER v. RINGROSE (1981) 16 C.C.L.T. 51 leave to appeal to S.C.C. refused 37 N.R. 289

The defendant doctor performed sterilization of the plaintiff using a newly-developed silver nitrate procedure, having provided her with general information about the procedure but having failed to indicate its relative effectiveness and that it was not generally accepted in the medical community. The plaintiff subsequently became pregnant and underwent an abortion in the United States on the advice of the defendant.

Held:

(1) The defendant was not liable in battery for failing to obtain the plaintiff's legal consent. The disclosure of information by a doctor to a patient does not constitute grounds for a battery action, but rather is one of the duties of care arising from a doctor-patient relationship giving rise in the breach to a negligence action.

(2) The defendant was not liable in negligence for failing to inform the plaintiff adequately about the procedure. A reasonable practitioner would have disclosed the comparative effectiveness of the procedure and whether it was professionally approved. However, a reasonable person in the plaintiff's position would not have refused this procedure even with full knowledge of the risks, since her paramount concern could not have been satisfied by any alternative procedure.

(3) The defendant is liable for negligent post-treatment care of the plaintiff, in failing to conduct regular medical examinations which would have revealed pregnancy at an earlier stage, and failing to provide a reasonable standard of medical and hospital care to the plaintiff when she decided to abort the pregnancy.

ZIRKLER v. ROBINSON (1897) 30 N.S.R. 61 (C.A.)

While treating the plaintiff in the plaintiff's home for a wound in the leg, the defendant failed to suture the ends of the severed popliteal nerve. The plaintiff suffered permanent partial loss of the use of the leg.

Held:

(1) The defendant must be judged by his surroundings at the time. The skill of a physician, attending a patient in a private house with few conveniences and no assistants, is not to be measured by the same standard as the city surgeon, provided with an operating room, assistants, nurses, and all the aids of a modern hospital.

(2) A new trial was ordered because the defendant was called upon to answer a case of which the pleadings gave him no notice.

INDEX